THE POEMS AND FABLES OF
JOHN DRYDEN

JOHN DRYDEN

Born, Aldwinkle All Saints, Northamptonshire 9 August 1631
Died, Gerrard Street, London 1 May 1700

THE POEMS AND
FABLES OF
JOHN DRYDEN

EDITED BY

JAMES KINSLEY

OXFORD UNIVERSITY PRESS
LONDON   OXFORD   NEW YORK
1970

Oxford University Press

LONDON OXFORD NEW YORK

GLASGOW TORONTO MELBOURNE WELLINGTON

CAPE TOWN SALISBURY IBADAN NAIROBI DAR ES SALAAM LUSAKA ADDIS ABABA

BOMBAY CALCUTTA MADRAS KARACHI LAHORE DACCA

KUALA LUMPUR SINGAPORE HONG KONG TOKYO

This new OXFORD STANDARD AUTHORS edition of *The Poems and Fables of John Dryden*, edited by James Kinsley from his four-volume edition for the Oxford English Texts (Clarendon Press, 1958), first published by Oxford University Press, London, 1962.

First issued as an Oxford University Press paperback 1970

PRINTED IN GREAT BRITAIN

PREFACE

THE text of this edition is reprinted from the complete collection of Dryden's poetry published by the Clarendon Press in 1958. It contains all the original poems; poems of which Dryden was part author; prologues, epilogues, and songs from plays in which he collaborated with others; a few pieces ascribed to him on good if inconclusive evidence; and the complete text of *Fables Ancient and Modern*. Much of Dryden's finest verse, in his translations of Virgil, Juvenal and Persius, Ovid, Horace, and other classical poets, has had to be set aside; but it is hoped that this selection will meet the needs of students as far as they can be met in the compass of a single volume without sacrificing readability.

Copy-text chosen for each poem is normally the first edition, collated with all subsequent editions published in Dryden's lifetime and with contemporary transcripts and miscellany reprints. Apparently authoritative variants from these have been admitted, and silently brought into conformity with the style of the copy-text. The text has been prepared mainly from copies in the Bodleian Library, the library of Worcester College, and the editor's collection. The typography of titles is standardized, and for short poems originally printed in italics the type has been reversed. Long 's' and merely typographical devices have been discarded. Errors of spacing and numbering, turned letters, wrong founts, obvious misprints, and irregularities in the use of 'æ' and 'œ' in classical names and quotations have been silently corrected; the distinction between italicized plurals in —'s and possessives in roman —'s has been regularized; proper names in roman type have been italicized in appropriate contexts; and corrections made on errata slips have been silently incorporated.

In the Clarendon Press edition the apparatus recorded significant changes in the accidentals of the copy-text and all substantive variants from other early printings. In this edition the apparatus has been restricted to a record of substantive departures from the copy-text. It does not record rejected readings from unauthorized texts or from reprints, which are of merely historical interest, except in a few places where the rejected source is nearly contemporaneous with the copy-text and is not related to it as immediate ancestor or descendant. The complete record of editions collated for each text is not reprinted here from the Clarendon Press edition; printings and manuscripts are given in the textual head-note to a poem only when variants from them have been admitted to the text or apparatus.

University College of Swansea
April 1961

J. K.

CONTENTS

Upon the death of the Lord *HASTINGS*

MUST Noble *Hastings* Immaturely die,
 (The Honour of his ancient Family?)
Beauty and Learning thus together meet,
To bring a *Winding* for a *Wedding-sheet*?
Must *Vertue* prove *Death*'s Harbinger? Must She,   5
With him expiring, feel Mortality?
Is *Death* (Sin's wages) Grace's now? shall Art
Make us more Learned, onely to depart?
If Merit be Disease, if Vertue Death;
To be Good, Not to be; who'd then bequeath   10
Himself to Discipline? Who'd not esteem
Labour a Crime, Study Self-murther deem?
Our *Noble Youth* now have pretence to be
Dunces securely, Ign'rant healthfully.
Rare Linguist! whose Worth speaks it self, whose Praise, 15
Though not his Own, all Tongues Besides do raise:
Then Whom, Great *Alexander* may seem Less;
Who conquer'd Men, but not their Languages.
In his mouth Nations speak; his Tongue might be
Interpreter to *Greece, France, Italy.*   20
His native Soyl was the Four parts o' th' Earth;
All *Europe* was too narrow for his Birth.
A young Apostle; and (with rev'rence may
I speak'it) inspir'd with gift of Tongues, as They.
Nature gave him, a Childe, what Men in vain   25
Oft strive, by Art though further'd, to obtain.
His Body was an Orb, his sublime Soul
Did move on Vertue's and on Learning's Pole:
Whose Reg'lar Motions better to our view,
Then *Archimedes* Sphere, the Heavens did shew.   30
Graces and Vertues, Languages and Arts,
Beauty and Learning, fill'd up all the parts.
Heav'ns Gifts, which do, like falling Stars, appear
Scatter'd in Others; all, as in their Sphear,
Were fix'd and conglobate in 's Soul; and thence   35
Shone th'row his Body, with sweet Influence;

Letting their Glories so on each Limb fall,
The whole Frame render'd was Celestial.
Come, learned *Ptolomy*, and trial make,
If thou this Hero's Altitude canst take;   40
But that transcends thy skill; thrice happie all,
Could we but prove thus Astronomical.
Liv'd *Tycho* now, struck with this Ray, (which shone
More bright i' th' Morn, then others beam at Noon)
He'd take his *Astrolabe*, and seek out here   45
What new Star 't was did gild our Hemisphere.
Replenish'd then with such rare Gifts as these,
Where was room left for such a Foul Disease?
The Nations sin hath drawn that Veil, which shrouds
Our Day-spring in so sad benighting Clouds.   50
Heaven would no longer trust its Pledge; but thus
Recall'd it; rapt its *Ganymede* from us.
Was there no milder way but the Small Pox,
The very Filth'ness of *Pandora*'s Box?
So many Spots, like *næves*, our *Venus* soil?   55
One Jewel set off with so many a Foil?
Blisters with pride swell'd; which th'row 's flesh did sprout
Like Rose-buds, stuck i' th' Lily-skin about.
Each little Pimple had a Tear in it,
To wail the fault its rising did commit: 60
Who, Rebel-like, with their own Lord at strife,
Thus made an Insurrection 'gainst his Life.
Or were these Gems sent to adorn his Skin,
The Cab'net of a richer Soul within?
No Comet need foretel his Change drew on,   65
Whose Corps might seem a *Constellation*.
O had he di'd of old, how great a strife
Had been, who from his Death should draw their Life?
Who should, by one rich draught, become what ere
Seneca, *Cato*, *Numa*, *Cæsar*, were: 70
Learn'd, Vertuous, Pious, Great; and have by this
An universal *Metempsuchosis*.
Must all these ag'd Sires in one Funeral
Expire? All die in one so young, so small?
Who, had he liv'd his life out, his great Fame   75
Had swoln 'bove any *Greek* or *Romane* Name.

But hasty Winter, with one blast, hath brought
The hopes of Autumn, Summer, Spring, to nought.
Thus fades the Oak i' th' sprig, i' th' blade the Corn;
Thus, without Young, this *Phœnix* dies, new born.   80
Must then old three-legg'd gray-beards with their Gout,
Catarrhs, Rheums, Aches, live three Ages out?
Times Offal, onely fit for th' Hospital,
Or t' hang an Antiquaries room withal;
Must Drunkards, Lechers, spent with Sinning, live   85
With such helps as Broths, Possits, Physick give?
None live, but such as should die? Shall we meet
With none but Ghostly Fathers in the Street?
Grief makes me rail; Sorrow will force its way;
And, Show'rs of Tears, Tempestuous Sighs best lay.   90
The Tongue may fail; but over-flowing Eyes
Will weep out lasting streams of *Elegies*.

But thou, O *Virgin-Widow*, left alone,
Now thy belov'd, heaven-ravisht *Spouse* is gone,
(Whose skilful Sire in vain strove to apply   95
Med'cines, when thy Balm was no Remedy)
With greater then *Platonick* love, O wed
His Soul, though not his Body, to thy Bed:
Let that make thee a Mother; bring thou forth
Th' *Idea's* of his Vertue, Knowledge, Worth;   100
Transcribe th' Original in new Copies; give
Hastings o' th' better part: so shall he live
In 's Nobler Half; and the great Grandsire be
Of an Heroick Divine Progenie:
An Issue, which t' Eternity shall last,   105
Yet but th' Irradiations which he cast.
Erect no *Mausolæums*: for his best
Monument is his Spouses Marble brest.

To his friend the Authour, on his divine Epigrams

THOU hast inspir'd me with thy soul, and I
  Who ne're before could ken of Poetry
Am grown so good proficient, I can lend
A line in commendation of my friend;
Yet 'tis but of the second hand, if ought   5
There be in this, 'tis from thy fancy brought.
Good thief who dar'st Prometheus-like aspire,
And fill thy poems with Celestiall fire:
Enliven'd by these sparks divine, their rayes
Adde a bright lustre to thy crown of bayes.   10
Young Eaglet who thy nest thus soon forsook,
So lofty and divine a course hast took
As all admire, before the down begin
To peep, as yet, upon thy smoother Chin;
And, making heaven thy aim, hast had the grace   15
To look the sunne of righteousnesse ith' face.
What may we hope, if thou go'st on thus fast!
Scriptures at first; Enthusiasmes at last!
Thou hast commenc'd, betimes, a saint: go on,
Mingling Diviner streams with Helicon: 20
That they who view what Epigrams here be
May learn to make like, in just praise of thee.
Reader, I've done, nor longer will withhold
Thy greedy eyes; looking on this pure gold
Thou'lt know adult'rate copper, which, like this,   25
Will onely serve to be a foil to his.

To his friend the Authour. Text from John Hoddesdon's Sion and Parnassus, Or Epigrams
On severall texts of the Old and New Testament, *1650*

TO HONOR DRYDEN

To the faire hands of Madame Honor Dryden these crave admittance.

Madame

If you have received the lines I sent by the reverend Levite, I doubt not
but they have exceedingly wrought vpon you; for beeing so longe in a
Clergy-mans pocket, assuredly they have acquired more Sanctity then
theire Authour meant them. Alasse Madame for ought I know they
may become a Sermon ere they could arrive at you; and believe it 5
haveing you for the text it could scarcely proove bad, if it light vpon
one could handle it indifferently. but I am so miserable a preacher
that though I have so sweet and copious a subject, I still fall short in my
expressions. And in stead of an vse of thanksgiveing I am allways make-
ing one of comfort, that I may one day againe have the happinesse to 10
kisse your faire hand. but that is a Message I would not so willingly do
by letter as by word of mouth. This is a point I must confesse I could
willingly dwell longer on, and in this case what ever I say you may
confidently take for gospell. But I must hasten. And indeed Madame
(Beloved I had almost sayd) hee had need hasten who treats of you; for 15
to speake fully to every part of your excellencyes requires a longer
houre then most persons have allotted them. But in a word your selfe
hath been the best Expositor vpon the text of your own worth, in that
admirable Comment you wrote vpon it, I meane your incomparable
letter. By all thats good (and you Madame are a great part of my Oath) 20
it hath put mee so farre besides my selfe that I have scarce patience to
write prose. and my pen is stealing into verse every time I kisse your
letter. I am sure the poore paper smarts for my Idolatry, which by
wearing it continually neere my brest will at last bee burnt and
Martyrd in those flames of adoration it hath kindled in mee. But I for- 25
gett Madame, what rarityes your letter came fraught with besides
words; You are such a Deity that commands worship by provideing the
Sacrifice: you are pleasd Madame to force mee to write by sending mee
Materialls, and compell mee to my greatest happinesse. Yet though I
highly vallue your Magnificent presents, pardon mee if I must tell the 30
world they are but imperfect Emblemes of your beauty; For the white
and red of waxe and paper are but shaddowes of that vermillion and
Snowe in your lips and forehead. And the Silver of the Inkehorne if it

To Honor Dryden. Text from letter in the William Andrews Clark Memorial Library

presume to vye whitenesse with your purer skinne, must confesse it
selfe blacker then the liquour it containes. What then do I more then 35
retrieve your own guifts? and present you that paper adulterated with
blotts which you gave spotlesse?

> For since t'was mine the white hath lost its hiew
> To show t'was n'ere it selfe but whilst in you;
> The Virgin Waxe hath blusht it selfe to red   40
> Since it with mee hath lost its Maydenhead.
> You (fairest Nymph) are waxe; oh may you bee
> As well in softnesse so as purity;
> Till fate and your ow[n] happy choise reveale
> Whom you so farre shall blesse to make your Seale.   45
>   Fairest Valentine the vnfeigned
>   wishe of yor humble Votary.
>   Jo: Dryden.

Cambridge
May the 23^d
16[53?]

Heroique Stanza's, Consecrated to the Glorious
Memory of his most Serene and Renowned
Highnesse OLIVER Late *LORD PROTECTOR*
of this Common-Wealth, &c.
Written after the Celebration of his Funerall

I

A ND now 'tis time; for their Officious haste,
   Who would before have born him to the sky,
Like *eager Romans* ere all Rites were past
Did let too soon the *sacred Eagle* fly.

Heroique Stanza's. Text from Three Poems Upon the Death of his late Highnesse
Oliver, *1659, collated with the reprint of* c. *1691.*

2

Though our best notes are treason to his fame　　　5
Joyn'd with the loud applause of publique voice;
Since Heav'n, what praise we offer to his name,
Hath render'd too authentick by its choice:

3

Though in his praise no Arts can liberall be,
Since they whose muses have the highest flown　　　10
Add not to his immortall Memorie,
But do an act of friendship to their own:

4

Yet 'tis our duty and our interest too
Such monuments as we can build to raise;
Lest all the World prevent what we should do　　　15
And claime a *Title* in him by their praise.

5

How shall I then begin, or where conclude
To draw a *Fame* so truly *Circular*?
For in a round what order can be shew'd,
Where all the parts so *equall perfect* are?　　　20

6

His *Grandeur* he deriv'd from Heav'n alone,
For he was great e're Fortune made him so;
And Warr's like mists that rise against the Sunne
Made him but greater seem, not greater grow.

7

No borrow'd Bay's his *Temples* did adorne,　　　25
But to our *Crown* he did fresh *Jewells* bring,
Nor was his Vertue poyson'd soon as born
With the too early thoughts of being King.

8

Fortune (that easie Mistresse of the young
But to her auncient servants coy and hard)   30
Him at that age her favorites rank'd among
When she her best-lov'd *Pompey* did discard.

9

He, private, mark'd the faults of others sway,
And set as *Sea-mark's* for himself to shun;
Not like rash *Monarch's* who their youth betray   35
By Acts their Age too late would wish undone.

10

And yet *Dominion* was not his Designe,
We owe that blessing not to him but Heaven,
Which to faire Acts unsought rewards did joyn,
Rewards that lesse to him than us were given.   40

11

Our former Cheifs like sticklers of the Warre
First sought t'inflame the Parties, then to poise;
The quarrell lov'd, but did the cause abhorre,
And did not strike to hurt but make a noise.

12

Warre our consumption was their gainfull trade,   45
We inward bled whilst they prolong'd our pain:
He fought to end our fighting, and assaid
To stanch the blood by breathing of the vein.

13

Swift and resistlesse through the Land he past
Like that bold *Greek* who did the East subdue;
And made to battails such Heroick haste   50
As if on wings of victory he flew.

14

He fought secure of fortune as of fame,
Till by *new maps* the Island might be shown,
Of Conquests which he strew'd where e're he came   55
Thick as the *Galaxy* with starr's is sown.

15

His *Palmes* though under weights they did not stand,
Still thriv'd; no *Winter* could his *Laurells* fade;
Heav'n in his Portraict shew'd a Workman's hand   60
And drew it perfect yet without a shade.

16

Peace was the Prize of all his toyles and care,
Which Warre had banisht and did now restore;
Bolognia's Walls thus mounted in the Ayre
To seat themselves more surely then before.

17

Her safety rescu'd *Ireland* to him owes;   65
And Treacherous *Scotland* to no int'rest true,
Yet blest that fate which did his Armes dispose
Her Land to Civilize as to subdue.

18

Nor was he like those *starr's* which only shine
When to pale *Mariners* they stormes portend,   70
He had his calmer influence; and his Mine
Did Love and Majesty together blend.

19

'Tis true, his Count'nance did imprint an awe,
And naturally all souls to his did bow;
As *Wands of Divination* downward draw   75
And point to Beds where Sov'raign Gold doth grow.

63 Walls 91: wall

20

When past all Offerings to *Feretrian Jove*
He *Mars* depos'd, and Arms to Gowns made yield,
Successefull Councells did him soon approve
As fit for close *Intrigues,* as open field.   80

21

To suppliant *Holland* he vouchsaf'd a peace,
Our once bold Rivall in the *British Main*
Now tamely glad her unjust claime to cease,
And buy our Friendship with her Idoll gaine.

22

Fame of th' asserted Sea through *Europe* blown   85
Made *France* and *Spaine* ambitious of his Love;
Each knew that side must conquer he would own
And for him fiercely as for Empire strove.

23

No sooner was the *French man*'s cause embrac'd
Than the leight *Mounsire* the grave *Don* outwaigh'd,   90
His fortune turn'd the Scale where it was cast,
Though *Indian Mines* were in the other layd.

24

When absent, yet we conquer'd in his right;
For though some meaner Artist's skill were shown
In mingling colours, or in placing light,   95
Yet still the *faire Designment* was his own.

25

For from all tempers he could service draw,
The worth of each with its alloy he knew;
And as the *Confident* of *Nature* saw
How she Complexions did divide and brew.   100

26

Or he their single vertues did survay
By *intuition* in his own large brest,
Where all the rich *Idea's* of them lay,
That were the rule and measure to the rest.

27

When such *Heröique Vertue* Heav'n sets out,   105
The Starrs like *Commons* sullenly obey;
Because it draines them when it comes about,
And therefore is a taxe they seldome pay.

28

From this high-spring our forraign-Conquests flow
Which yet more glorious triumphs do portend,   110
Since their Commencement to his Armes they owe,
If Springs as high as Fountaines may ascend.

29

He made us *Freemen* of the *Continent*
Whom Nature did like Captives treat before,
To nobler prey's the *English Lyon* sent,   115
And taught him first in *Belgian walks* to rore.

30

That old unquestion'd Pirate of the Land
Proud *Rome*, with dread, the fate of *Dunkirk* har'd;
And trembling wish't behind more *Alpes* to stand,
Although an *Alexander* were her guard.   120

31

By his command we boldly crost the Line
And bravely fought where *Southern Starrs* arise,
We trac'd the farre-fetchd Gold unto the mine
And that which brib'd our fathers made our prize.

32

Such was our Prince; yet own'd a soul above   125
The highest Acts it could produce to show:
Thus poor *Mechanique Arts* in publique moove
Whilst the deep Secrets beyond practice goe.

33

Nor dy'd he when his ebbing Fame went lesse,
But when fresh Lawrells courted him to live;   130
He seem'd but to prevent some new successe;
As if above what triumphs Earth could give.

34

His latest Victories still thickest came
As, near the *Center*, *Motion* does increase;
Till he, pres'd down by his own weighty name,   135
Did, like the *Vestall*, under spoyles decease.

35

But first the *Ocean* as a tribute sent
That Gyant *Prince* of all her watery Heard;
And th' *Isle* when her *Protecting Genius* went
Upon his *Obsequies* loud sighs confer'd.   140

36

No Civill broyles have since his death arose,
But *Faction* now by *Habit* does obey:
And *Warrs* have that respect for his repose,
As *Winds* for *Halcyons* when they breed at Sea.

37

His Ashes in a peacefull Urne shall rest,   145
His Name a great example stands to show
How strangely high endeavours may be blest,
Where *Piety* and *valour* joyntly goe.

To my Honored Friend,
Sr ROBERT HOWARD,
On his Excellent Poems

As there is Musick uninform'd by Art
In those wild Notes, which with a merry heart
The Birds in unfrequented shades expresse,
Who better taught at home, yet please us lesse:
So in your Verse, a native sweetnesse dwells,   5
Which shames Composure, and its Art excells.
Singing, no more can your soft numbers grace
Then Paint adds charms unto a beauteous Face.
Yet as when mighty Rivers gently creep,
Their even calmnesse does suppose them deep,   10
Such is your Muse: no Metaphor swell'd high
With dangerous boldnesse lifts her to the sky;
Those mounting Fancies when they fall again,
Shew sand and dirt at bottom do remain.
So firm a strength, and yet withall so sweet,   15
Did never but in *Sampson*'s Riddle meet.
'Tis strange each line so great a weight should bear,
And yet no signe of toil, no sweat appear.
Either your Art hides Art, as Stoicks feign
Then least to feel, when most they suffer pain;   20
And we, dull souls, admire, but cannot see
What hidden springs within the Engine be:
Or 'tis some happinesse that still pursues
Each act and motion of your gracefull muse.
Or is it Fortune's work, that in your head   25
The curious* Net that is for fancies spread,
Let's through its Meshes every meaner thought,
While rich Idea's there are onely caught?
Sure that's not all; this is a piece too fair
To be the child of Chance, and not of Care.   30
No Atoms casually together hurl'd
Could e're produce so beautifull a world.

Rete Mirabile

To my Honored Friend. Text from Poems . . . By the Honorable Sr Robert Howard, *1660*.

Nor dare I such a doctrine here admit,
As would destroy the providence of wit.
'Tis your strong Genius then which does not feel   35
Those weights would make a weaker spirit reel:
To carry weight and run so lightly too
Is what alone your *Pegasus* can do.
Great *Hercules* himself could ne're do more
Than not to feel those Heav'ns and gods he bore.   40
Your easier Odes, which for delight were penn'd,
Yet our instruction make their second end,
We're both enrich'd and pleas'd, like them that woo
At once a Beauty and a Fortune too.

Of Morall Knowledge Poesie was Queen,   45
And still she might, had wanton wits not been;
Who like ill Guardians liv'd themselves at large,
And not content with that, debauch'd their charge:
Like some brave Captain, your successfull Pen
Restores the Exil'd to her Crown again;   50
And gives us hope, that having seen the days
When nothing flourish'd but Fanatique Bays,
All will at length in this opinion rest,
"A sober Prince's Government is best."

This is not all; your Art the way has found   55
To make improvement of the richest ground,
That soil which those immortall Lawrells bore,
That once the sacred *Maro*'s temples wore.
Elisa's griefs, are so exprest by you,
They are too eloquent to have been true.   60
Had she so spoke, *Æneas* had obey'd
What *Dido* rather then what *Jove* had said.
If funerall Rites can give a Ghost repose,
Your Muse so justly has discharged those,
Elisa's shade may now its wandring cease,   65
And claim a title to the fields of peace.
But if *Æneas* be oblig'd, no lesse
Your kindnesse great *Achilles* doth confesse,
Who dress'd by *Statius* in too bold a look,
Did ill become those Virgin's Robes he took.   70
To understand how much we owe to you,
We must your Numbers with your Author's view;

Then we shall see his work was lamely rough,
Each figure stiffe as if design'd in buffe;
His colours laid so thick on every place,   75
As onely shew'd the paint, but hid the face:
But as in Perspective we Beauties see,
Which in the Glasse, not in the Picture be;
So here our sight obligeingly mistakes
That wealth which his your bounty onely makes.   80
Thus vulgar dishes are by Cooks disguis'd,
More for their dressing than their substance priz'd.
Your curious *Notes so search into that Age,
When all was fable but the sacred Page,
That since in that dark night we needs must stray,   85
We are at least misled in pleasant way.
But what we most admire, your Verse no lesse
The Prophet than the Poet doth confesse.
Ere our weak eyes discern'd the doubtfull streak
Of light, you saw great *Charls* his morning break.   90
So skilfull Sea-men ken the Land from far,
Which shews like mists to the dul Passenger.
To *Charls* your Muse first pays her dutious love,
As still the Antients did begin from *Jove*.
With *Monck* you end, whose name preserv'd shall be,   95
As *Rome* recorded †*Rufus* memory,
Who thought it greater honor to obey
His Countrey's interest than the world to sway.
But to write worthy things of worthy men
Is the peculiar talent of your Pen: 100
Yet let me take your Mantle up, and I
Will venture in your right to prophesy.

"This Work by merit first of Fame secure
"Is likewise happy in its Geniture:
"For since 'tis born when *Charls* ascends the Throne,   105
"It shares at once his Fortune and its own."

* *Annotations on* Statius
† Hic situs est *Rufus* qui pulso vindice quondam, Imperium asseruit non sibi sed
Patriæ

Astræa Redux
A POEM On the Happy Restoration
and Return Of His Sacred Majesty
Charles the Second

Iam Redit & Virgo, Redeunt Saturnia Regna. Virgil.

Now with a general Peace the World was blest,
    While Ours, a World divided from the rest,
A dreadful Quiet felt, and worser farre
Then Armes, a sullen Intervall of Warre:
Thus when black Clouds draw down the lab'ring Skies,   5
Ere yet abroad the winged Thunder flyes
An horrid Stillness first invades the ear,
And in that silence Wee the Tempest fear.
Th' Ambitious *Swede* like restless Billowes tost,
On this hand gaining what on that he lost,   10
Though in his life he Blood and Ruine breath'd,
To his now guideless Kingdome Peace bequeath'd.
And Heaven that seem'd regardless of our Fate,
For *France* and *Spain* did Miracles create,
Such mortal Quarrels to compose in Peace   15
As Nature bred and Int'rest did encrease.
We sigh'd to hear the fair *Iberian* Bride
Must grow a Lilie to the Lilies side,
While Our cross Stars deny'd us *Charles* his Bed
Whom Our first Flames and Virgin Love did wed.   20
For his long absence Church and State did groan;
Madness the Pulpit, Faction seiz'd the Throne:
Experienc'd Age in deep despair was lost
To see the Rebel thrive, the Loyal crost:
Youth that with Joys had unacquainted been   25
Envy'd gray hairs that once good days had seen:
We thought our Sires, not with their own content,
Had ere we came to age our Portion spent.
Nor could our Nobles hope their bold Attempt

Astræa Redux. Text from the first edition of 1660, collated with the second edition, 1688

Who ruin'd Crowns would Coronets exempt: 30
For when by their designing Leaders taught
To strike at Pow'r which for themselves they sought,
The Vulgar gull'd into Rebellion, arm'd,
Their blood to action by the Prize was warm'd.
The Sacred Purple then and Scarlet Gown   35
Like sanguine Dye to Elephants was shown.
Thus when the bold *Typhoeus* scal'd the Sky,
And forc'd great *Jove* from his own Heaven to fly,
(What King, what Crown from Treasons reach is free,
If *Jove* and *Heaven* can violated be?)   40
The lesser Gods that shar'd his prosp'rous State
All suffer'd in the Exil'd Thund'rers Fate.
The Rabble now such Freedom did enjoy,
As Winds at Sea that use it to destroy:
Blind as the *Cyclops*, and as wild as he,   45
They own'd a lawless salvage Libertie,
Like that our painted Ancestours so priz'd
Ere Empires Arts their Breasts had Civiliz'd.
How Great were then Our *Charles* his Woes, who thus
Was forc'd to suffer for Himself and us!   50
He toss'd by Fate, and hurried up and down,
Heir to his Fathers Sorrows, with his Crown,
Could tast no sweets of youths desired Age,
But found his life too true a Pilgrimage.
Unconquer'd yet in that forlorne Estate   55
His Manly Courage overcame his Fate.
His wounds he took like *Romans* on his brest,
Which by his Vertue were with Lawrells drest.
As Souls reach Heav'n while yet in Bodies pent,
So did he live above his Banishment.   60
That Sun which we beheld with cous'ned eyes
Within the water, mov'd along the skies.
How easie 'tis when Destiny proves kind
With full spread Sails to run before the wind,
But those that 'gainst stiff gales laveering go   65
Must be at once resolv'd and skilful too.
He would not like soft *Otho* hope prevent
But stay'd and suffer'd Fortune to repent.
These Vertues *Galba* in a stranger sought;

And *Piso* to Adopted Empire brought.   70
How shall I then my doubtful thoughts express
That must his suff'rings both regret and bless!
For when his early Valour Heav'n had crost,
And all at *Worc'ster* but the honour lost,
Forc'd into exile from his rightful Throne   75
He made all Countries where he came his own.
And viewing Monarchs secret Arts of sway
A Royal Factor for their Kingdomes lay.
Thus banish'd *David* spent abroad his time,
When to be Gods Anointed was his Crime;   80
And when restor'd made his proud Neighbours rue
Those choice Remarques he from his Travels drew:
Nor is he onely by afflictions shown
To conquer others Realms but rule his own:
Recov'ring hardly what he lost before,   85
His right indears it much, his purchase more.
Inur'd to suffer ere he came to raigne
No rash procedure will his actions stain.
To bus'ness ripened by digestive thought
His future rule is into Method brought: 90
As they who first Proportion understand
With easie Practice reach a Masters hand.
Well might the Ancient Poets then confer
On Night the honour'd name of *Counseller*,
Since struck with rayes of prosp'rous fortune blind   95
We light alone in dark afflictions find.
In such adversities to Scepters train'd
The name of *Great* his famous Grandsire gain'd:
Who yet a King alone in Name and Right,
With hunger, cold and angry *Jove* did fight;   100
Shock'd by a Covenanting Leagues vast Pow'rs
As holy and as Catholique as ours:
Till Fortunes fruitless spight had made it known
Her blowes not shook but riveted his Throne.
    Some lazy Ages lost in sleep and ease   105
No action leave to busie Chronicles;
Such whose supine felicity but makes
In story *Chasmes*, in *Epoche's* mistakes;
O're whom *Time* gently shakes his wings of Down

Till with his silent sickle they are mown: 110
Such is not *Charles* his too too active age,
Which govern'd by the wild distemper'd rage
Of some black Star infecting all the Skies,
Made him at his own cost like *Adam* wise.
Tremble ye Nations who secure before 115
Laught at those Armes that 'gainst our selves we bore;
Rous'd by the lash of his own stubborn tail
Our Lyon now will forraign Foes assail.
With *Alga* who the sacred altar strowes?
To all the Sea-Gods *Charles* an Off'ring owes: 120
A Bull to thee *Portunus* shall be slain,
A Lamb to you the Tempests of the Main:
For those loud stormes that did against him rore
Have cast his shipwrack'd Vessel on the shore.
Yet as wise Artists mix their colours so 125
That by degrees they from each other go,
Black steals unheeded from the neighb'ring white
Without offending the well cous'ned sight:
So on us stole our blessed change; while we
Th' effect did feel but scarce the manner see. 130
Frosts that constrain the ground, and birth deny
To flow'rs, that in its womb expecting lye,
Do seldom their usurping Pow'r withdraw,
But raging floods pursue their hasty thaw:
Our thaw was mild, the cold not chas'd away 135
But lost in kindly heat of lengthned day.
Heav'n would no bargain for its blessings drive
But what we could not pay for, freely give.
The Prince of Peace would like himself confer
A gift unhop'd without the price of war. 140
Yet as he knew his blessings worth, took care
That we should know it by repeated pray'r;
Which storm'd the skies and ravish'd *Charles* from thence
As Heav'n it self is took by violence.
Booth's forward Valour only serv'd to show 145
He durst that duty pay we all did owe:
Th' Attempt was fair; but Heav'ns prefixed hour
Not come; so like the watchful travellour
That by the Moons mistaken light did rise,

Lay down again, and clos'd his weary eyes.   150
'Twas *MONCK* whom Providence design'd to loose
Those real bonds false freedom did impose.
The blessed Saints that watch'd this turning Scene
Did from their Stars with joyful wonder leane,
To see small clues draw vastest weights along,   155
Not in their bulk but in their order strong.
Thus Pencils can by one slight touch restore
Smiles to that changed face that wept before.
With ease such fond *Chymæra's* we pursue
As fancy frames for fancy to subdue,   160
But when our selves to action we betake
It shuns the Mint like gold that Chymists make:
How hard was then his task, at once to be
What in the body natural we see
Mans Architect distinctly did ordain   165
The charge of Muscles, Nerves, and of the Brain;
Through viewless Conduits Spirits to dispense,
The Springs of Motion from the Seat of Sense.
'Twas not the hasty product of a day,
But the well ripened fruit of wise delay.   170
He like a patient Angler, e're he strooke
Would let them play a while upon the hook.
Our healthful food the Stomach labours thus,
At first embracing what it strait doth crush.
Wise Leeches will not vain Receipts obtrude,   175
While growing pains pronounce the humours crude;
Deaf to complaints they wait upon the ill
Till some safe *Crisis* authorise their skill.
Nor could his Acts too close a vizard wear
To scape their eyes whom guilt had taught to fear,   180
And guard with caution that polluted nest
Whence Legion twice before was dispossest,
Once sacred house which when they enter'd in
They thought the place could sanctifie a sin;
Like those that vainly hop'd kind Heav'n would wink   185
While to excess on Martyrs tombs they drink.
And as devouter *Turks* first warn their souls
To part, before they tast forbidden bowls,
So these when their black crimes they went about

First timely charm'd their useless conscience out. 190
Religions name against it self was made;
The shadow serv'd the substance to invade:
Like Zealous Missions they did care pretend
Of souls in shew, but made the Gold their end.
Th' incensed Pow'rs beheld with scorn from high 195
An Heaven so far distant from the sky,
Which durst with horses hoofs that beat the ground
And Martial brass bely the thunders sound.
'Twas hence at length just Vengeance thought it fit
To speed their ruine by their impious wit. 200
Thus *Sforza* curs'd with a too fertile brain
Lost by his wiles the Pow'r his wit did gain.
Henceforth their Fogue must spend at lesser rate
Then in its flames to wrap a Nations Fate.
Suffer'd to live, they are like *Helots* set 205
A vertuous shame within us to beget.
For by example most we sinn'd before,
And glass-like, clearness mixt with frailty bore.
But since reform'd by what we did amiss,
We by our suff'rings learn to prize our bliss: 210
Like early Lovers whose unpractis'd hearts
Were long the May-game of malicious arts,
When once they find their Jealousies were vain
With double heat renew their fires again.
'Twas this produc'd the joy that hurried o're 215
Such swarmes of *English* to the Neighb'ring shore,
To fetch that prize, by which *Batavia* made
So rich amends for our impoverish'd Trade.
Oh had you seen from *Schevelines* barren shore
(Crowded with troops, and barren now no more,) 220
Afflicted *Holland* to his farewell bring
True Sorrow, *Holland* to regret a King;
While waiting him his Royal Fleet did ride
And willing winds to their low'rd sayles deny'd.
The wavering Streamers, Flags, and Standart out, 225
The merry Seamens rude but chearful shout,

---

195 beheld *60 (some copies)* 88: behold *60 (some copies)*   208 And glass-like,] And
glass-like *60 (some copies)* 88: Like glass we *60 (some copies)*

And last the Cannons voice that shook the skies
And, as it fares in sudden Extasies
At once bereft us both of ears and eyes.
The *Naseby* now no longer *Englands* shame   230
But better to be lost in *Charles* his name
(Like some unequal Bride in nobler sheets)
Receives her Lord: the joyful *London* meets
The Princely *York*, himself alone a freight;
The *Swift-sure* groans beneath Great *Gloc'sters* weight.   235
Secure as when the *Halcyon* breeds, with these
He that was born to drown might cross the Seas.
Heav'n could not own a Providence and take
The wealth three Nations ventur'd at a stake.
The same indulgence *Charles* his Voyage bless'd   240
Which in his right had Miracles confess'd.
The winds that never Moderation knew
Afraid to blow too much, too faintly blew;
Or out of breath with joy could not enlarge
Their straightned lungs, or conscious of their Charge.   245
The British *Amphitryte* smooth and clear
In richer Azure never did appear;
Proud her returning Prince to entertain
With the submitted Fasces of the Main.

    And welcome now (*Great Monarch*) to your own;   250
Behold th' approaching cliffes of *Albion*;
It is no longer Motion cheats your view,
As you meet it, the Land approacheth you.
The Land returns, and in the white it wears
The marks of penitence and sorrow bears.   255
But you, whose goodness your discent doth show,
Your Heav'nly Parentage and earthly too;
By that same mildness which your Fathers Crown
Before did ravish, shall secure your own.
Not ty'd to rules of Policy, you find   260
Revenge less sweet then a forgiving mind.
Thus when th' Almighty would to *Moses* give
A sight of all he could behold and live;
A voice before his entry did proclaim
Long-Suff'ring, Goodness, Mercy in his Name.   265

Your Pow'r to Justice doth submit your Cause,
Your Goodness only is above the Laws;
Whose rigid letter while pronounc'd by you
Is softer made. So winds that tempests brew
When through *Arabian* Groves they take their flight   270
Made wanton with rich Odours, lose their spight.
And as those Lees that trouble it, refine
The agitated Soul of Generous Wine,
So tears of joy for your returning spilt,
Work out and expiate our former guilt.   275
Methinks I see those Crowds on *Dovers* Strand
Who in their hast to welcome you to Land
Choak'd up the Beach with their still growing store,
And made a wilder Torrent on the shore.
While spurr'd with eager thoughts of past delight   280
Those who had seen you, court a second sight;
Preventing still your steps, and making hast
To meet you often where so e're you past.
How shall I speak of that triumphant Day
When you renew'd the expiring Pomp of *May*!   285
(A Month that owns an Intrest in your Name:
You and the Flow'rs are its peculiar Claim.)
That Star that at your Birth shone out so bright
It stain'd the duller Suns Meridian light,
Did once again its potent Fires renew   290
Guiding our eyes to find and worship you.
    And now times whiter Series is begun
Which in soft Centuries shall smoothly run;
Those Clouds that overcast your Morne shall fly
Dispell'd to farthest corners of the sky.   295
Our Nation with united Int'rest blest
Not now content to poize, shall sway the rest.
Abroad your Empire shall no Limits know,
But like the Sea in boundless Circles flow.
Your much lov'd Fleet shall with a wide Command   300
Besiege the petty Monarchs of the Land:
And as Old Time his Off-spring swallow'd down
Our Ocean in its depths all Seas shall drown.
Their wealthy Trade from Pyrates Rapine free
Our Merchants shall no more Advent'rers be: 305

Nor in the farthest East those Dangers fear
Which humble *Holland* must dissemble here.
Spain to your Gift alone her *Indies* owes;
For what the Pow'rful takes not he bestowes.
And *France* that did an Exiles presence fear   310
May justly apprehend you still too near.
At home the hateful names of Parties cease
And factious Souls are weary'd into peace.
The discontented now are only they
Whose Crimes before did your Just Cause betray: 315
Of those your Edicts some reclaim from sins,
But most your Life and Blest Example wins.
Oh happy Prince whom Heav'n hath taught the way
By paying Vowes, to have more Vowes to pay!
Oh Happy Age! Oh times like those alone   320
By Fate reserv'd for Great *Augustus* Throne!
When the joint growth of Armes and Arts foreshew
The World a Monarch, and that Monarch *You*.

TO HIS SACRED MAIESTY,
A PANEGYRICK ON HIS CORONATION

IN that wild Deluge where the World was drownd,
When life and sin one common tombe had found,
The first small prospect of a rising hill
With various notes of Joy the Ark did fill:
Yet when that flood in its own depths was drownd   5
It left behind it false and slipp'ry ground;
And the more solemn pomp was still deferr'd
Till new-born Nature in fresh looks appeard:
Thus (Royall Sir) to see you landed here
Was cause enough of triumph for a year: 10
Nor would your care those glorious Joyes repeat
Till they at once might be secure and great:
Till your kind beams by their continu'd stay
Had warm'd the ground, and call'd the Damps away.

To His Sacred Maiesty. Text from the first edition of 1661, collated with the editions of 1662 and 1688.

Such vapours while your pow'rfull influence dryes 15
Then soonest vanish when they highest rise.
Had greater hast these sacred rights prepar'd
Some guilty Moneths had in your triumphs shar'd:
But this untainted year is all your own,
Your glory's may without our crimes be shown. 20
We had not yet exhausted all our store
When you refresh'd our joyes by adding more:
As Heav'n of old dispenc'd Cælestial dew,
You give us Manna and still give us new.

Now our sad ruines are remov'd from sight, 25
The Season too comes fraught with new delight;
Time seems not now beneath his years to stoop
Nor do his wings with sickly feathers droop:
Soft western winds waft ore the gaudy spring
And opend Scenes of flow'rs and blossoms bring 30
To grace this happy day, while you appear
Not King of us alone but of the year.
All eyes you draw, and with the eyes the heart,
Of your own pomp your self the greatest part:
Loud shouts the Nations happiness proclaim 35
And Heav'n this day is feasted with your name.
Your Cavalcade the fair Spectators view
From their high standings, yet look up to you.
From your brave train each singles out a prey,
And longs to date a Conquest from your day. 40
Now charg'd with blessings while you seek repose,
Officious slumbers hast your eyes to close:
And glorious dreams stand ready to restore
The pleasing shapes of all you saw before.
Next to the sacred Temple you are led, 45
Where waites a Crown for your more sacred Head:
How justly from the Church that Crown is due,
Preserv'd from ruine and restor'd by you!
The gratefull quire their harmony employ
Not to make greater but more solemn joy. 50
Wrapt soft and warm your Name is sent on high,
As flames do on the wings of Incense fly:
Musique her self is lost, in vain she brings

32 Not . . . alone *61 (some copies)* 88: Not only King of us *61 (some copies)* 62

Her choisest notes to praise the best of Kings:
Her melting strains in you a tombe have found,   55
And lye like Bees in their own sweetnesse drown'd.
He that brought peace and discord could attone,
His Name is Musick of it self alone.
Now while the sacred Oyl annoints your head,
And fragrant scents, begun from you, are spread   60
Through the large Dome, the peoples joyful sound
Sent back, is still preserv'd in hallow'd ground:
Which in one blessing mixt descends on you,
As heightned spirits fall in richer dew.
Not that our wishes do increase your store,   65
Full of your self you can admit no more:
We add not to your glory, but employ
Our time like Angels in expressing joy.
Nor is it duty or our hopes alone
Create that joy, but full fruition;   70
We know those blessings which we must possesse,
And judge of future by past happinesse.
No promise can oblige a Prince so much
Still to be good as long to have been such.
A noble Emulation heats your breast,   75
And your own fame now robbs you of your rest:
Good actions still must be maintain'd with good,
As bodies nourish'd with resembling food.
You have already quench'd seditions brand;
And zeal (which burnt it) only warms the Land.   80
The jealous Sects that dare not trust their cause
So farre from their own will as to the Laws,
You for their Umpire and their Synod take,
And their appeal alone to *Cæsar* make.
Kind Heav'n so rare a temper did provide   85
That guilt repenting might in it confide.
Among our crimes oblivion may be set,
But 'tis our Kings perfection to forget.
Virtues unknown to these rough Northern climes
From milder heav'ns you bring, without their crimes: 90
Your calmnesse does no after storms provide,
Nor seeming patience mortal anger hide.

78 *Text ends in 62 (some copies)*

When Empire first from families did spring,
Then every Father govern'd as a King;
But you that are a Soveraign Prince, allay   95
Imperial pow'r with your paternal sway.
From those great cares when ease your soul unbends
Your pleasures are design'd to noble ends:
Born to command the Mistress of the Seas,
Your thoughts themselves in that blue Empire please.   100
Hither in Summer ev'nings you repair
To take the fraischeur of the purer air:
Vndaunted here you ride when Winter raves,
With *Cæsars* heart that rose above the waves.
More I could sing but fear my Numbers stayes;   105
No Loyal Subject dares that courage praise.
In stately Frigats most delight you find,
Where well-drawn Battels fire your martial mind.
What to your cares we owe is learnt from hence,
When ev'n your pleasures serve for our defence.   110
Beyond your Court flows in th' admitted tide,
Where in new depths the wondring fishes glide:
Here in a Royal bed the waters sleep,
When tir'd at Sea within this bay they creep.
Here the mistrustfull foul no harm suspects,   115
So safe are all things which our King protects.
From your lov'd *Thames* a blessing yet is due,
Second alone to that it brought in you;
A Queen, from whose chast womb, ordain'd by Fate,
The souls of Kings unborn for bodies wait.   120
It was your Love before made discord cease:
Your love is destin'd to your Countries peace.
Both *Indies* (Rivalls in your bed) provide
With Gold or Jewels to adorn your Bride.
This to a mighty King presents rich ore,   125
While that with Incense does a God implore.
Two Kingdomes wait your doom, and as you choose,
This must receive a Crown, or that must loose.
Thus from your Royal Oke, like *Jove*'s of old,
Are answers sought, and destinies fore-told: 130
Propitious Oracles are beg'd with vows,
And Crowns that grow upon the sacred boughs.

Your Subjects, while you weigh the Nations fate,
Suspend to both their doubtfull love or hate:
Choose only, (Sir,) that so they may possesse   135
With their own peace their Childrens happinesse.

TO MY LORD CHANCELLOR
Presented on New-years-day

My Lord,

W HILE flattering crouds officiously appear
  To give themselves, not you, an happy year;
And by the greatness of their Presents prove
How much they hope, but not how well they love;
The Muses (who your early courtship boast,   5
Though now your flames are with their beauty lost)
Yet watch their time, that if you have forgot
They were your Mistresses, the World may not:
Decay'd by time and wars, they only prove
Their former beauty by your former love;   10
And now present, as antient Ladies do
That courted long at length are forc'd to woo.
For still they look on you with such kind eyes
As those that see the Churches Soveraign rise
From their own Order chose, in whose high State   15
They think themselves the second choice of Fate.
When our Great Monarch into Exile went
Wit and Religion suffer'd banishment:
Thus once when *Troy* was wrapt in fire and smoak
The helpless Gods their burning shrines forsook;   20
They with the vanquisht Prince and party go,
And leave their Temples empty to the fo:
At length the Muses stand restor'd again
To that great charge which Nature did ordain;

To My Lord Chancellor. Text from the first edition, 1662, collated with the edition of 1688

And their lov'd Druyds seem reviv'd by Fate 25
While you dispence the Laws and guide the State.
The Nations soul (our Monarch) does dispence
Through you to us his vital influence;
You are the Chanel where those spirits flow,
And work them higher as to us they go. 30

   In open prospect nothing bounds our eye
Until the Earth seems joyn'd unto the Sky:
So in this Hemisphær our utmost view
Is only bounded by our King and you:
Our sight is limited where you are joyn'd 35
And beyond that no farther Heav'n can find.
So well your Vertues do with his agree
That though your Orbs of different greatness be,
Yet both are for each others use dispos'd,
His to inclose, and yours to be inclos'd. 40
Nor could another in your room have been
Except an Emptinesse had come between.
Well may he then to you his Cares impart,
And share his burden where he shares his heart.
In you his sleep still wakes; his pleasures find 45
Their share of bus'nesse in your lab'ring mind:
So when the weary Sun his place resigns
He leaves his light and by reflection shines.

   Justice that sits and frowns where publick Laws
Exclude soft mercy from a private cause, 50
In your Tribunal most her self does please;
There only smiles because she lives at ease;
And like young *David* finds her strength the more
When disincumberd from those arms she wore:
Heav'n would your Royal Master should exceed 55
Most in that Vertue which we most did need,
And his mild Father (who too late did find
All mercy vain but what with pow'r was joyn'd,)
His fatal goodnesse left to fitter times,
Not to increase but to absolve our Crimes: 60
But when the Heir of this vast treasure knew
How large a Legacy was left to you,
(Too great for any Subject to retain)
He wisely ti'd it to the Crown again:

Yet passing through your hands it gathers more,   65
As streams through Mines bear tincture of their Ore.
While Emp'rique politicians use deceipt,
Hide what they give, and cure but by a cheat;
You boldly show that skill which they pretend,
And work by means as noble as your end: 70
Which, should you veil, we might unwind the clue
As men do Nature, till we came to you.
And as the *Indies* were not found before
Those rich perfumes, which from the happy shore
The winds upon their balmy wings convay'd,   75
Whose guilty sweetnesse first their World betray'd;
So by your Counsels we are brought to view
A rich and undiscover'd World in you.
By you our Monarch does that fame assure
Which Kings must have or cannot live secure: 80
For prosp'rous Princes gain their Subjects heart,
Who love that praise in which themselves have part:
By you he fits those Subjects to obey,
As Heavens Eternal Monarch does convey
His pow'r unseen, and man to his designs,   85
By his bright Ministers the Stars, inclines.
   Our setting Sun from his declining seat
Shot beams of kindnesse on you, not of heat:
And when his love was bounded in a few,
That were unhappy that they might be true;   90
Made you the favo'rite of his last sad times,
That is a suff'rer in his Subjects crimes:
Thus those first favours you receiv'd were sent
Like Heav'ns rewards, in earthly punishment.
Yet Fortune conscious of your destiny   95
Ev'n then took care to lay you softly by:
And wrapt your fate among her precious things,
Kept fresh to be unfolded with your Kings.
Shown all at once you dazled so our eyes,
As new-born *Pallas* did the Gods surprise;   100
When springing forth from *Jove*'s new-closing wound
She struck the Warlick Spear into the ground;
Which sprouting leaves did suddenly inclose,

                    81 their *88*: the *62*

And peaceful Olives shaded as they rose.
How strangely active are the arts of Peace,   105
Whose restlesse motions lesse than Wars do cease!
Peace is not freed from labour but from noise;
And War more force but not more pains employs;
Such is the mighty swiftnesse of your mind
That (like the earth's) it leaves our sence behind;   110
While you so smoothly turn and roul our Sphear,
That rapid motion does but rest appear.
For as in Natures swiftnesse, with the throng
Of flying Orbs while ours is born along,
All seems at rest to the deluded eye: 115
(Mov'd by the Soul of the same harmony)
So carry'd on by your unwearied care
We rest in Peace and yet in motion share.
Let Envy then those Crimes within you see
From which the Happy never must be free;   120
(Envy that does with misery reside,
The joy and the revenge of ruin'd Pride;)
Think it not hard if at so cheap a rate
You can secure the constancy of Fate,
Whose kindnesse sent, what does their malice seem,   125
By lesser ills the greater to redeem.
Nor can we this weak show'r a tempest call
But drops of heat that in the Sun-shine fall.
You have already weary'd Fortune so
She can not farther be your friend or fo;   130
But sits all breathlesse, and admires to feel
A Fate so weighty that it stops her wheel.
In all things else above our humble fate
Your equal mind yet swells not into state,
But like some mountain in those happy Isles   135
Where in perpetual Spring young Nature smiles,
Your greatnesse shows: no horrour to afright
But Trees for shade, and Flow'rs to court the sight;
Sometimes the Hill submits itself a while
In small descents, which do its height beguile;   140
And sometimes mounts, but so as billows play
Whose rise not hinders but makes short our way.
Your brow which does no fear of thunder know

Sees rouling tempests vainly beat below;
And (like *Olympus* top,) th' impression wears   145
Of Love and Friendship writ in former years.
Yet unimpair'd with labours or with time
Your age but seems to a new youth to climb.
Thus Heav'nly bodies do our time beget;
And measure Change, but share no part of it.   150
And still it shall without a weight increase,
Like this New-year, whose motions never cease;
For since the glorious Course you have begun
Is led by *CHARLS*, as that is by the Sun,
It must both weightlesse and immortal prove,   155
Because the Center of it is above.

To my Honour'd Friend, Dᵣ Charleton,
on his learned and useful Works;
and more particularly this of STONE-HENG,
by him Restored to the true Founders

THE longest Tyranny that ever sway'd,
     Was that wherein our Ancestors betray'd
Their free-born *Reason* to the *Stagirite*,
And made his Torch their universal Light.
So *Truth*, while onely one suppli'd the State,   5
Grew scarce, and dear, and yet sophisticate,
Until 'twas bought, like Emp'rique Wares, or Charms,
Hard words seal'd up with *Aristotle*'s Armes.
Columbus was the first that shook his Throne;
And found a *Temp'rate* in a *Torrid* Zone: 10
The fevrish aire fann'd by a cooling breez,
The fruitful Vales set round with shady Trees;

To my Honour'd Friend, Dʳ Charleton. Text from Charleton's Chorea Gigantum, *1663, collated with* Poetical Miscellanies: The Fifth Part, *1704*

And guiltless *Men*, who danc'd away their time,
Fresh as their *Groves*, and *Happy* as their *Clime*.
Had we still paid that homage to a *Name*,   15
Which onely *God* and *Nature* justly claim;
The *Western* Seas had been our utmost bound,
Where *Poets* still might dream the *Sun* was drown'd:
And all the *Starrs*, that shine in *Southern* Skies,
Had been admir'd by none but *Salvage* Eyes.   20

   Among th' *Assertors* of free Reason's claim,
Th' *English* are not the least in Worth, or Fame.
The World to *Bacon* does not onely owe
Its *present* Knowledge, but its *future* too.
Gilbert shall live, till *Load-stones* cease to draw,   25
Or *British* Fleets the boundless Ocean awe.
And noble *Boyle*, not less in *Nature* seen,
Than his great *Brother* read in *States* and *Men*.
The *Circling* streams, once thought but pools, of blood
(Whether Life's fewel, or the Bodie's food)   30
From dark Oblivion *Harvey*'s name shall save;
While *Ent* keeps all the honour that he gave.
Nor are *You*, Learned Friend, the least renown'd;
Whose Fame, not circumscrib'd with *English* ground,
Flies like the nimble journeys of the Light;   35
And is, like that, unspent too in its flight.
What ever *Truths* have been, by *Art*, or *Chance*,
Redeem'd from *Error*, or from *Ignorance*,
Thin in their *Authors*, (like rich veins of Ore)
Your Works unite, and still discover more.   40
Such is the healing virtue of Your Pen,
To perfect Cures on *Books*, as well as *Men*.
Nor is This Work the least: You well may give
To *Men* new vigour, who make *Stones* to live.
Through You, the *DANES* (their short Dominion lost)   45
A longer Conquest than the *Saxons* boast.
STONE-HENG, once thought a *Temple*, You have found
A *Throne*, where Kings, our Earthly Gods, were Crown'd,
Where by their wondring Subjects They were seen,

13 who *63* (*some copies*) *04*: that *63* (*some copies*)   22 Th' *English* are not the
least *63* (*some copies*): The *English* are not least *63* (*some copies*): Our Nation's not
the least *04*   39 of *63* (*some copies*) *04*: in *63* (*some copies*)

Joy'd with their Stature, and their Princely meen.   50
Our *Soveraign* here above the rest might stand;
And here be chose again to rule the Land.

These Ruines sheltred once *His* Sacred Head,
Then when from *Wor'sters* fatal Field *He* fled;
Watch'd by the Genius of this Royal place,   55
And mighty Visions of the *Danish* Race.
His *Refuge* then was for a *Temple* shown:
But, *He* Restor'd, 'tis now become a *Throne.*

PROLOGUE To the RIVAL-LADIES

'TIS much Desir'd, you Judges of the Town
    Would pass a Vote to put all *Prologues* down;
For who can show me, since they first were Writ,
They e'r Converted one hard-hearted Wit?
Yet the World's mended well; in former Days   5
Good *Prologues* were as scarce, as now good *Plays.*
For the reforming Poets of our Age,
In this first Charge, spend their Poetique rage:
Expect no more when once the *Prologue's* done;
The Wit is ended e'r the *Play's* begun.   10
You now have Habits, Dances, Scenes, and Rhymes;
High Language often; I, and Sense, sometimes:
As for a clear Contrivance doubt it not;
They blow out Candles to give Light to th' Plot.
And for Surprize, two Bloody-minded Men   15
Fight till they Dye, then rise and Dance agen:
Such deep Intrigues you'r welcome to this Day:
But blame your Selves, not him who Writ the Play;
Though his Plot's Dull, as can be well desir'd,
Wit stiff as any you have e'r admir'd: 20
He's bound to please, not to Write well; and knows
There is a mode in Plays as well as Cloaths:
Therefore kind Judges——

50 Joy'd with *63 (some copies) 04*: Chose by *63 (some copies)*   52 rule *63 (some copies) 04*: sway *63 (some copies)*   54 Then . . . fled] When *He* from *Wor'sters* fatal Battle fled *04*   55 Royal *63 (some copies) 04*: Kingly *63 (some copies)*
Prologue. Text from The Rival Ladies. A Tragi-Comedy, *1664.*

A SECOND PROLOGUE
Enters.

2.——Hold; Would you admit
For Judges all you see within the Pit?
  1. Whom would he then Except, or on what Score?   25
  2. All, who (like him) have Writ ill Plays before:
For they, like Thieves condemn'd, are Hang-men made,
To execute the Members of their Trade.
All that are Writing now he would disown;
But then he must Except, ev'n all the Town.   30
All Chol'rique, losing Gamesters, who in spight
Will Damn to Day, because they lost last Night.
All Servants whom their Mistress's scorn upbraids;
All Maudlin Lovers, and all Slighted Maids:
All who are out of Humour, or Severe;   35
All, that want Wit, or hope to find it here.

PROLOGUE, EPILOGUE
and SONGS from
THE INDIAN-QUEEN, A Tragedy
PROLOGUE

As the Musick plays a soft Air, the Curtain rises softly, and discovers an Indian
*Boy and Girl sleeping under two Plantain-Trees; and when the Curtain is
almost up, the Musick turns into a Tune expressing an Alarm, at which the
Boy wakes and speaks.*

  Boy. WAKE, wake, *Quevira;* our soft Rest must cease,
       And fly together with our Country's Peace;
No more must we sleep under Plantain shade,
Which neither Heat could pierce, nor Cold invade;

Prologue, Epilogue and Songs. Text from Four New Plays . . . Written by the Honourable
Sir Robert Howard, *1665*

Where bounteous Nature never feels decay,   5
And op'ning Buds drive falling Fruits away.

Que.   Why should men quarrel here, where all possess
As much as they can hope for by success?

.   None can have most, where Nature is so kind
As to exceed Man's Use, though not his Mind.   10

Boy.   By ancient Prophesies we have been told
Our World shall be subdu'd by one more old;
And see that World already's hither come.

Que.   If these be they, we welcom then our Doom.
Their Looks are such, that Mercy flows from thence,   15
More gentle than our Native Innocence.

Boy.   Why should we then fear these are Enemies,
That rather seem to us like Deities?

Que.   By their protection let us beg to live;
They came not here to Conquer, but Forgive.   20
If so, your Goodness may your Pow'r express;
And we shall judg both best by our success.

EPILOGUE TO THE INDIAN QUEEN
Spoken by Montezuma

YOU see what Shifts we are inforc'd to try
To help out Wit with some Variety;
Shows may be found that never yet were seen,
'Tis hard to finde such Wit as ne're has been:
You have seen all that this old World cou'd do,   5
We therefore try the fortune of the new,
And hope it is below your aim to hit
At untaught Nature with your practic'd Wit:
Our naked Indians then, when Wits appear,
Wou'd as soon chuse to have the Spaniards here: 10
'Tis true, y'have marks enough, the Plot, the Show,
The Poets Scenes, nay, more the Painters too;
If all this fail, considering the cost,
'Tis a true Voyage to the Indies lost:
But if you smile on all, then these designs,   15
Like the imperfect Treasure of our Mindes,

'Twill pass for currant wheresoe're they go,
When to your bounteous hands their stamps they owe.

SONGS

I

Ism. YOU twice Ten Hundred Deities,
    To whom we daily Sacrifice;
    You Powers that dwell with Fate below,
    And see what men are doom'd to do;
    Where Elements in discord dwell;   5
    Thou God of Sleep arise and tell
    Great *Zempoalla* what strange Fate
    Must on her dismal Vision wait.

    By the croaking of the Toad,
    In their Caves that make aboad,   10
    Earthy *Dun* that pants for breath,
    With her swell'd sides full of death;
    By the Crested Adders Pride
    That along the Clifts do glide;
    By thy visage fierce and black;   15
    By the Deaths-head on thy Back;
    By the twisted Serpents plac'd
    For a Girdle round thy Waste.
    By the Hearts of Gold that deck
    Thy Brest, thy Shoulders, and thy Neck: 20
    From thy sleepy Mansion rise,
    And open thy unwilling Eyes,
    While bubling Springs their Musick keep,
    That use to lull thee in thy sleep.

II

SONG is suppos'd sung by Aerial-Spirits

POOR Mortals that are clog'd with Earth below
    Sink under Love and Care,
    While we that dwell in Air
Such heavy Passions never know.

Why then shou'd Mortals be   5
Unwilling to be free
From Blood, that sullen Cloud,
Which shining Souls does shroud?
Then they'l shew bright,
And like us light,   10
When leaving Bodies with their Care,
They slide to us and Air.

III

SONG

You to whom Victory we owe,
Whose glories rise
By sacrifice,
And from our fates below;
Never did yet your Altars shine   5
Feasted with Blood so nere divine;
Princes to whom we bow,
As they to you,
These you can ravish from a throne,
And by their loss of power declare your own.   10

PROLOGUE, EPILOGUE and SONGS
from *THE INDIAN EMPEROUR*

PROLOGUE

Almighty Critiques! whom our *Indians* here
Worship, just as they do the Devil, for fear.
In reverence to your pow'r I come this day
To give you timely warning of our Play.

Prologue, Epilogue and Songs. Text from The Indian Emperour, or, The Conquest of
Mexico by the Spaniards, *1667, collated with the editions of 1668–1696*

The Scenes are old, the Habits are the same,   5
We wore last year, before the *Spaniards* came.
Now if you stay, the blood that shall be shed
From this poor Play, be all upon your head.
We neither promise you one Dance, or Show,
Then Plot and Language they are wanting too: 10
But you, kind Wits, will those light faults excuse:
Those are the common frailties of the Muse;
Which who observes he buys his place too dear:
For 'tis your business to be couz'ned here.
These wretched spies of wit must then confess   15
They take more pains to please themselves the less.
Grant us such Judges, *Phœbus* we request,
As still mistake themselves into a jest;
Such easie Judges, that our Poet may
Himself admire the fortune of his Play.   20
And arrogantly, as his fellows do,
Think he writes well, because he pleases you.
This he conceives not hard to bring about
If all of you would join to help him out.
Would each man take but what he understands,   25
And leave the rest upon the Poets hands.

EPILOGUE
By a Mercury

To all and singular in this full meeting,
 Ladies and Gallants, *Phœbus* sends me greeting.
To all his Sons by what e're Title known,
Whether of Court, of Coffee-house, or Town;
From his most mighty Sons, whose confidence   5
Is plac'd in lofty sound, and humble sence,
Ev'n to his little Infants of the Time
Who Write new Songs, and trust in Tune and Rhyme.

Prologue. Additional after l. 6 in 67 only:
        Our Prologue, th'old-cast too—
        For to observe the new it should at least
        Be spoke, by some ingenious Bird or Beast.

Epilogue.   8 Who 68-96: That 67

Be't known that *Phœbus* (being daily griev'd
To see good Plays condemn'd, and bad receiv'd,)   10
Ordains your judgement upon every Cause,
Henceforth be limited by wholesome Laws.
He first thinks fit no Sonnettier advance
His censure, farther then the Song or Dance.
Your Wit Burlesque may one step higher climb,   15
And in his sphere may judge all Doggrel Rhyme:
All proves, and moves, and Loves, and Honours too:
All that appears high sence, and scarce is low.
As for the Coffee-wits he says not much,
Their proper bus'ness is to Damn the *Dutch*:   20
For the great *Dons* of Wit—
Phœbus gives them full priviledge alone
To Damn all others, and cry up their own.
Last, for the Ladies, 'tis *Apollo*'s will,
They should have pow'r to save, but not to kill: 25
For Love and He long since have thought it fit,
Wit live by Beauty, Beauty raign by Wit.

SONGS

I

Kalib ascends all in White in the shape of a Woman and Sings

Kalib. I LOOK'D and saw within the Book of Fate,
        Where many days did lower,
        When lo one happy hour
Leapt up, and smil'd to save thy sinking State;
        A day shall come when in thy power   5
        Thy cruel Foes shall be;
        Then shall thy Land be free,
        And thou in Peace shalt Raign:
But take, O take that opportunity,
Which once refus'd will never come again.   10

Songs. I. 8 shalt 68–96: shall 67

II

A pleasant Grotto discover'd: in it a Fountain spouting; round about it Vasquez, Pizarro, *and other* Spaniards *lying carelessly un-arm'd, and by them many* Indian *Women, one of which Sings the following Song.*

SONG

A H fading joy, how quickly art thou past?
      Yet we thy ruine haste:
As if the cares of Humane Life were few
      We seek out new:
And follow Fate which would too fast pursue.   5

See how on every bough the Birds express
      In their sweet notes their happiness.
    They all enjoy, and nothing spare;
      But on their Mother Nature lay their care:
Why then should Man, the Lord of all below   10
      Such troubles chuse to know
As none of all his Subjects undergo?

Hark, hark, the Waters fall, fall, fall;
And with a Murmuring sound
Dash, dash, upon the ground,   15
      To gentle slumbers call.

After the Song two Spaniards *arise and Dance a* Saraband *with* Castanieta's . . .

Songs. II. 5 which would 68–96: that does 67

ANNUS MIRABILIS

The Year of WONDERS, 1666.
AN HISTORICAL POEM: CONTAINING
The Progress and various Successes of
our Naval War with *Holland,* under the
Conduct of His Highness Prince RUPERT,
and His Grace the Duke of ALBEMARL.
And describing THE FIRE OF LONDON

Multum interest res poscat, an homines latius imperare velint.
TRAJAN. Imperator. ad Plin.
Urbs antiqua ruit, multos dominata per annos. VIRG.

TO THE METROPOLIS OF GREAT BRITAIN,

The most Renowned and late Flourishing
CITY of LONDON, In its REPRESENTATIVES
The LORD MAYOR *and Court of* ALDERMEN,
the SHERIFS *and* COMMON COUNCIL *of it*

As perhaps I am the first who ever presented a work of this nature
to the Metropolis of any Nation, so is it likewise consonant to
Justice, that he who was to give the first Example of such a Dedication
should begin it with that City, which has set a pattern to all others
of true Loyalty, invincible Courage and unshaken Constancy. Other 5
Cities have been prais'd for the same Virtues, but I am much deceiv'd
if any have so dearly purchas'd their reputation; their fame has been
won them by cheaper trials then an expensive, though necessary, War,
a consuming Pestilence, and a more consuming Fire. To submit your
selves with that humility to the Judgments of Heaven, and at the same 10
time to raise your selves with that vigour above all humane Enemies;
to be combated at once from above and from below, to be struck

Annus Mirabilis. Text from the first edition, 1667, collated with the editions of 1668 and 1688

down and to triumph; I know not whether such trials have been
ever parallel'd in any Nation, the resolution and successes of them
never can be. Never had Prince or People more mutual reason to love 15
each other, if suffering for each other can indear affection. You have
come together a pair of matchless Lovers, through many difficulties;
He, through a long Exile, various traverses of Fortune, and the inter-
position of many Rivals, who violently ravish'd and with-held You
from Him: And certainly you have had your share in sufferings. But 20
Providence has cast upon you want of Trade, that you might appear
bountiful to your Country's necessities; and the rest of your afflictions
are not more the effects of God's displeasure, (frequent examples of
them having been in the Reign of the most excellent Princes) then
occasions for the manifesting of your Christian and Civil virtues. To 25
you therefore this Year of Wonders is justly dedicated, because you
have made it so: You who are to stand a wonder to all Years and Ages,
and who have built your selves an immortal Monument on your own
ruines. You are now a *Phœnix* in her ashes, and, as far as Humanity can
approach, a great Emblem of the suffering Deity. But Heaven never 30
made so much Piety and Vertue to leave it miserable. I have heard
indeed of some vertuous persons who have ended unfortunately, but
never of any vertuous Nation: Providence is engag'd too deeply, when
the cause becomes so general. And I cannot imagine it has resolv'd the
ruine of that people at home, which it has blessed abroad with such 35
successes. I am therefore to conclude, that your sufferings are at an
end; and that one part of my Poem has not been more an History of
your destruction, then the other a Prophecy of your restoration. The
accomplishment of which happiness, as it is the wish of all true *English-*
men, so is by none more passionately desired then by 40

> The greatest of your Admirers, and
> most humble of your Servants,
> JOHN DRYDEN.

An account of the ensuing Poem,
in a LETTER to the Honorable,
Sir ROBERT HOWARD

SIR,

I Am so many ways oblig'd to you, and so little able to return your favours, that,
like those who owe too much, I can onely live by getting farther into your debt.

You have not onely been careful of my Fortune, which was the effect of your Nobleness, but you have been sollicitous of my Reputation, which is that of your Kindness. It is not long since I gave you the trouble of perusing a Play for me, 5 *and now, instead of an acknowledgment, I have given you a greater, in the correction of a Poem. But since you are to bear this persecution, I will at least give you the encouragement of a Martyr, you could never suffer in a nobler cause. For I have chosen the most heroick Subject which any Poet could desire: I have taken upon me to describe the motives, the beginning, progress and successes of a* 10 *most just and necessary War; in it, the care, management and prudence of our King; the conduct and valour of a Royal Admiral, and of two incomparable Generals; the invincible courage of our Captains and Sea-men, and three glorious Victories, the result of all. After this I have, in the Fire, the most deplorable, but withall the greatest Argument that can be imagin'd: the destruction being* 15 *so swift, so sudden, so vast and miserable, as nothing can parallel in Story. The former part of this Poem, relating to the War, is but a due expiation for my not serving my King and Country in it. All Gentlemen are almost oblig'd to it: And I know no reason we should give that advantage to the* Commonalty *of* England *to be formost in brave actions, which the* Noblesse *of* France *would never suffer* 20 *in their Peasants. I should not have written this but to a Person, who has been ever forward to appear in all employments, whither his Honour and Generosity have call'd him. The latter part of my Poem, which describes the Fire, I owe first to the Piety and Fatherly Affection of our Monarch to his suffering Subjects; and, in the second place, to the courage, loyalty and magnanimity of the City:* 25 *both which were so conspicuous, that I have wanted words to celebrate them as they deserve. I have call'd my Poem* Historical, *not* Epick, *though both the Actions and Actors are as much Heroick, as any Poem can contain. But since the Action is not properly one, nor that accomplish'd in the last successes, I have judg'd it too bold a Title for a few Stanza's, which are little more in number* 30 *then a single* Iliad, *or the longest of the* Æneids. *For this reason, (I mean not of length, but broken action, ti'd too severely to the Laws of History) I am apt to agree with those who rank* Lucan *rather among Historians in Verse, then Epique Poets: In whose room, if I am not deceiv'd,* Silius Italicus, *though a worse Writer, may more justly be admitted. I have chosen to write my Poem in* 35 *Quatrains or Stanza's of four in alternate rhyme, because I have ever judg'd them more noble, and of greater dignity, both for the sound and number, then any other Verse in use amongst us; in which I am sure I have your approbation. The learned Languages have, certainly, a great advantage of us, in not being tied to the slavery of any Rhyme; and were less constrain'd in the quantity of* 40 *every syllable, which they might vary with* Spondæes *or* Dactiles, *besides so many other helps of Grammatical Figures, for the lengthning or abbreviation of them, then the Modern are in the close of that one Syllable, which often confines, and more often corrupts the sense of all the rest. But in this necessity of our Rhymes, I have always found the couplet Verse most easie, (though not so proper* 45 *for this occasion) for there the work is sooner at an end, every two lines concluding the labour of the Poet: but in Quattrains he is to carry it farther on; and not onely so, but to bear along in his head the troublesome sense of four lines together. For those who write correctly in this kind must needs acknowledge, that the last line of the Stanza is to be consider'd in the composition of the first. Neither can we* 50 *give our selves the liberty of making any part of a Verse for the sake of Rhyme, or concluding with a word which is not currant* English, *or using the variety of Female Rhymes, all which our Fathers practis'd; and for the Female Rhymes, they are still in use amongst other Nations: with the* Italian *in every line, with the* Spaniard *promiscuously, with the* French *alternately, as those who have* 55 *read the* Alarique, *the* Pucelle, *or any of their latter Poems, will agree with me. And besides this, they write in* Alexandrins, *or Verses of six feet, such as amongst us is the old Translation of* Homer, *by* Chapman; *all which, by lengthning of their Chain, makes the sphere of their activity the larger. I have dwelt too long upon the choice of my Stanza, which you may remember is much* 60 *better defended in the Preface to* Gondibert, *and therefore I will hasten to acquaint you with my endeavours in the writing. In general I will onely say, I have never yet seen the description of any Naval Fight in the proper terms which are us'd at Sea; and if there be any such in another Language, as that of* Lucan *in the third of his* Pharsalia, *yet I could not prevail my self of it in the* English; 65 *the terms of Arts in every Tongue bearing more of the Idiom of it then any other words. We hear, indeed, among our Poets, of the thundring of Guns, the smoke, the disorder and the slaughter; but all these are common notions. And certainly as those who, in a Logical dispute, keep in general terms, would hide a fallacy, so those who do it in any Poetical description would vail their ignorance.* 70

Descriptas servare vices operumque colores
Cur ego, si nequeo ignoroque, poeta salutor?

For my own part, if I had little knowledge of the Sea, yet I have thought it no shame to learn: and if I have made some few mistakes, 'tis onely, as you can bear me witness, because I have wanted opportunity to correct them, the whole Poem 75 *being first written, and now sent you from a place, where I have not so much as the converse of any Sea-man. Yet, though the trouble I had in writing it was great, it was more then recompens'd by the pleasure; I found my self so warm in celebrating the praises of military men, two such especially as the* Prince *and* General, *that it is no wonder if they inspir'd me with thoughts above my ordinary* 80 *level. And I am well satisfi'd, that as they are incomparably the best subject I*

have ever had, excepting onely the Royal Family; *so also, that this I have
written of them is much better then what I have perform'd on any other. I have
been forc'd to help out other Arguments, but this has been bountiful to me; they
have been low and barren of praise, and I have exalted them, and made them fruit-* 85
*ful: but here—*Omnia sponte suâ reddit justissima tellus. *I have had a
large, a fair and a pleasant field, so fertile, that, without my cultivating, it has
given me two Harvests in a Summer, and in both oppress'd the Reaper. All other
greatness in subjects is onely counterfeit, it will not endure the test of danger; the
greatness of Arms is onely real: other greatness burdens a Nation with its weight,* 90
*this supports it with its strength. And as it is the happiness of the Age, so is it the
peculiar goodness of the best of Kings, that we may praise his Subjects without
offending him: doubtless it proceeds from a just confidence of his own vertue,
which the lustre of no other can be so great as to darken in him: for the Good or
the Valiant are never safely prais'd under a bad or a degenerate Prince. But to* 95
*return from this digression to a farther account of my Poem, I must crave leave
to tell you, that as I have endeavour'd to adorn it with noble thoughts, so much
more to express those thoughts with elocution. The composition of all Poems is or
ought to be of wit, and wit in the Poet, or wit writing, (if you will give me leave
to use a School distinction) is no other then the faculty of imagination in the* 100
*writer, which, like a nimble Spaniel, beats over and ranges through the field of
Memory, till it springs the Quarry it hunted after; or, without metaphor, which
searches over all the memory for the species or Idea's of those things which it
designs to represent. Wit written, is that which is well defin'd, the happy result of
thought, or product of that imagination. But to proceed from wit in the general* 105
*notion of it, to the proper wit of an Heroick or Historical Poem, I judge it chiefly
to consist in the delightful imaging of persons, actions, passions, or things. 'Tis not
the jerk or sting of an Epigram, nor the seeming contradiction of a poor Anti-
thesis, (the delight of an ill judging Audience in a Play of Rhyme) nor the gingle
of a more poor* Paranomasia: *neither is it so much the morality of a grave* 110
sentence, affected by Lucan, *but more sparingly used by* Virgil; *but it is some
lively and apt description, dress'd in such colours of speech, that it sets before your
eyes the absent object, as perfectly and more delightfully then nature. So then, the
first happiness of the Poet's imagination is properly Invention, or finding of the
thought; the second is Fancy, or the variation, deriving or moulding of that* 115
*thought, as the judgment represents it proper to the subject; the third is Elocution,
or the Art of clothing and adorning that thought so found and varied, in apt,
significant and sounding words: the quickness of the Imagination is seen in the
Invention, the fertility in the Fancy, and the accuracy in the Expression. For the
two first of these* Ovid *is famous amongst the Poets, for the latter* Virgil. Ovid 120

images more often the movements and affections of the mind, either combating between two contrary passions, or extremely discompos'd by one: his words therefore are the least part of his care, for he pictures Nature in disorder, with which the study and choice of words is inconsistent. This is the proper wit of Dialogue or Discourse, and, consequently, of the Drama, *where all that is said is to be sup-* 125 *pos'd the effect of sudden thought; which, though it excludes not the quickness of wit in repartees, yet admits not a too curious election of words, too frequent allusions, or use of Tropes, or, in fine, any thing that showes remoteness of thought, or labour in the Writer. On the other side,* Virgil *speaks not so often to us in the person of another, like* Ovid, *but in his own; he relates almost all things as from* 130 *himself, and thereby gains more liberty then the other, to express his thoughts with all the graces of elocution, to write more figuratively, and to confess, as well the labour as the force of his imagination. Though he describes his* Dido *well and naturally, in the violence of her passions, yet he must yield in that to the* Myrrha, *the* Biblis, *the* Althæa, *of* Ovid; *for, as great an admirer of him as I am, I must* 135 *acknowledge, that, if I see not more of their Souls then I see of* Dido's, *at least I have a greater concernment for them: and that convinces me that* Ovid *has touch'd those tender strokes more delicately then* Virgil *could. But when Action or Persons are to be describ'd, when any such Image is to be set before us, how bold, how masterly are the strokes of* Virgil! *we see the objects he represents us* 140 *with in their native figures, in their proper motions; but we so see them, as our own eyes could never have beheld them so beautiful in themselves. We see the Soul of the Poet, like that universal one of which he speaks, informing and moving through all his Pictures,* Totamque infusa per artus mens agitat molem, & magno se corpore miscet; *we behold him embellishing his Images, as he* 145 *makes* Venus *breathing beauty upon her son* Æneas.

> —lumenque juventæ
> Purpureum, & lætos oculis afflârat honores:
> Quale manus addunt Ebori decus, aut ubi flavo
> Argentum, Pariusve lapis circundatur auro.   150

See his Tempest, *his* Funeral Sports, *his* Combat *of* Turnus *and* Æneas, *and in his* Georgicks, *which I esteem the Divinest part of all his writings, the* Plague, *the* Country, *the* Battel *of* Bulls, *the labour of the* Bees, *and those many other excellent Images of Nature, most of which are neither great in themselves, nor have any natural ornament to bear them up: but the words wherewith he describes* 155 *them are so excellent, that it might be well appli'd to him which was said by* Ovid, Materiam superabat opus: *the very sound of his words has often somewhat that is connatural to the subject, and while we read him, we sit, as in a Play, beholding the Scenes of what he represents. To perform this, he made frequent use*

of Tropes, which you know change the nature of a known word, by applying it to 160
some other signification; and this is it which Horace *means in his Epistle to the*
Pisos.

> Dixeris egregie notum si callida verbum
> Reddiderit junctura novum—

But I am sensible I have presum'd too far, to entertain you with a rude discourse 165
of that Art, which you both know so well, and put into practise with so much
happiness. Yet before I leave Virgil, *I must own the vanity to tell you, and by you*
the world, that he has been my Master in this Poem: I have followed him every
where, I know not with what success, but I am sure with diligence enough: my
Images are many of them copied from him, and the rest are imitations of him. My 170
expressions also are as near as the Idioms of the two Languages would admit of in
translation. And this, Sir, I have done with that boldness, for which I will stand
accomptable to any of our little Criticks, who, perhaps, are not better acquainted
with him then I am. Upon your first perusal of this Poem, you have taken notice
of some words which I have innovated (if it be too bold for me to say refin'd) upon 175
his Latin; which, as I offer not to introduce into English *prose, so I hope they*
are neither improper, nor altogether unelegant in Verse; and, in this, Horace
will again defend me.

> Et nova, fictaque nuper habebunt verba fidem, si
> Græco fonte cadant, parcè detorta—   180

The inference is exceeding plain; for if a Roman *Poet might have liberty to coin*
a word, supposing onely that it was derived from the Greek, *was put into a* Latin
termination, and that he us'd this liberty but seldom, and with modesty: How
much more justly may I challenge that privilege to do it with the same præ-
requisits, from the best and most judicious of Latin *Writers? In some places,* 185
where either the fancy, or the words, were his, or any others, I have noted it in
the Margin, that I might not seem a Plagiary: in others I have neglected it, to
avoid as well the tediousness, as the affectation of doing it too often. Such descrip-
tions or images, well wrought, which I promise not for mine, are, as I have said,
the adequate delight of heroick Poesie, for they beget admiration, which is its 190
proper object; as the images of the Burlesque, which is contrary to this, by the
same reason beget laughter; for the one shows Nature beautified, as in the picture
of a fair Woman, which we all admire; the other shows her deformed, as in that
of a Lazar, or of a fool with distorted face and antique gestures, at which we
cannot forbear to laugh, because it is a deviation from Nature. But though the 195
same images serve equally for the Epique Poesie, and for the Historique and
Panegyrique, which are branches of it, yet a several sort of Sculpture is to be used
in them: if some of them are to be like those of Juvenal, Stantes in curribus

Æmiliani, *Heroes drawn in their triumphal Chariots, and in their full propor-*
tion; others are to be like that of Virgil, *Spirantia mollius æra: there is some-* 200
what more of softness and tenderness to be shown in them. You will soon find I write
not this without concern. Some who have seen a paper of Verses which I wrote
last year to her Highness the Dutchess, *have accus'd them of that onely thing*
I could defend in them; they have said I did humi serpere, *that I wanted not*
onely height of fancy, but dignity of words to set it off; I might well answer with 205
that of Horace, Nunc non erat his locus, *I knew I address'd them to a Lady,*
and accordingly I affected the softness of expression, and the smoothness of
measure, rather then the height of thought; and in what I did endeavour, it is no
vanity to say, I have succeeded. I detest arrogance, but there is some difference
betwixt that and a just defence. But I will not farther bribe your candour, or the 210
Readers. I leave them to speak for me, and, if they can, to make out that character,
not pretending to a greater, which I have given them.

Verses to her Highness *the* DUTCHESS,
on the memorable Victory *gain'd by the* DUKE
against the Hollanders, June *the* 3. 1665.
and on Her Journey afterwards into the North

MADAM,

W HEN, for our sakes, your *Heroe* you resign'd
    To swelling Seas, and every faithless wind;
When you releas'd his courage, and set free
A valour fatal to the Enemy,
You lodg'd your Countries cares within your breast;   5
(The mansion where soft Love should onely rest:)
And ere our foes abroad were overcome,
The noblest conquest you had gain'd at home.
Ah, what concerns did both your Souls divide!
Your Honour gave us what your Love deni'd: 10
And 'twas for him much easier to subdue
Those foes he fought with, then to part from you.
That glorious day, which two such Navies saw,
As each, unmatch'd, might to the world give Law,

Neptune, yet doubtful whom he should obey,   15
Held to them both the Trident of the Sea:
The winds were hush'd, the waves in ranks were cast,
As awfully as when God's people past:
Those, yet uncertain on whose sails to blow,
These, where the wealth of Nations ought to flow.   20
Then with the Duke your Highness rul'd the day:
While all the brave did his command obey,
The fair and pious under you did pray.
How pow'rful are chast vows! the wind and tyde
You brib'd to combat on the *English* side.   25
Thus to your much lov'd Lord you did convey
An unknown succour, sent the nearest way.
New vigour to his wearied arms you brought;
(So *Moses* was upheld while *Israel* fought.)
While, from afar, we heard the Canon play,   30
Like distant Thunder on a shiny day,
For absent friends we were asham'd to fear,
When we consider'd what you ventur'd there.
Ships, Men and Arms our Country might restore,
But such a Leader could supply no more.   35
With generous thoughts of conquest he did burn,
Yet fought not more to vanquish then return.
Fortune and Victory he did pursue,
To bring them, as his Slaves, to wait on you.
Thus Beauty ravish'd the rewards of Fame,   40
And the Fair triumph'd when the Brave o'rcame.
Then, as you meant to spread another way
By Land your Conquests far as his by Sea,
Leaving our Southern Clime, you march'd along
The stubborn North, ten thousand *Cupid's* strong.   45
Like Commons the Nobility resort
In crowding heaps, to fill your moving Court:
To welcome your approach the Vulgar run,
Like some new Envoy from the distant Sun.
And Country Beauties by their Lovers go,   50
Blessing themselves, and wondring at the show.
So when the new-born *Phœnix* first is seen,
Her feather'd Subjects all adore their Queen.
And, while she makes her progress through the East,

From every grove her numerous train's increase:
Each Poet of the air her glory sings,
And round him the pleas'd Audience clap their wings.

And now, Sir, 'tis time I should relieve you from the tedious length of this
account. You have better and more profitable employment for your hours, and I
wrong the Publick to detain you longer. In conclusion, I must leave my Poem to 215
you with all its faults, which I hope to find fewer in the printing by your emenda-
tions. I know you are not of the number of those, of whom the younger Pliny
speaks, Nec sunt parum multi qui carpere amicos suos judicium vocant;
I am rather too secure of you on that side. Your candour in pardoning my errors
may make you more remiss in correcting them; if you will not withall consider 220
that they come into the world with your approbation, and through your hands.
I beg from you the greatest favor you can confer upon an absent person, since I
repose upon your management what is dearest to me, my Fame and Reputation;
and therefore I hope it will stir you up to make my Poem fairer by many of your
blots; if not, you know the story of the Gamester who married the rich man's 225
daughter, and when her father denyed the portion, christned all the children by his
sirname, that if, in conclusion, they must beg, they should do so by one name, as
well as by the other. But since the reproach of my faults will light on you, 'tis
but reason I should do you that justice to the Readers, to let them know that if
there be any thing tolerable in this Poem, they owe the Argument to your choice, 230
the writing to your encouragement, the correction to your judgment, and the care
of it to your friendship, to which he must ever acknowledge himself to owe all
things, who is,

SIR,

The most obedient and most
faithful of your Servants,
JOHN DRYDEN.

From Charleton *in* Wiltshire,
Novem. 10. 1666.

ANNUS MIRABILIS
The YEAR of WONDERS, MDCLXVI

1

IN thriving Arts long time had *Holland* grown,
   Crouching at home, and cruel when abroad:
Scarce leaving us the means to claim our own.
   Our King they courted, and our Merchants aw'd.

2

Trade, which like bloud should circularly flow,
   Stop'd in their Channels, found its freedom lost   5
Thither the wealth of all the world did go,
   And seem'd but shipwrack'd on so base a Coast.

3

For them alone the Heav'ns had kindly heat,
   ªIn Eastern Quarries ripening precious Dew:
For them the *Idumæan* Balm did sweat,   10
   And in hot *Ceilon* Spicy Forrests grew.

(a) *In Eastern Quarries, &c.* Precious Stones at first are Dew,
condens'd and harden'd by the warmth of the Sun, or subterranean
Fires.

4

The Sun but seem'd the Lab'rer of their Year;
   ᵇEach wexing Moon suppli'd her watry store,
To swell those Tides, which from the Line did bear   15
   Their brim-full Vessels to the *Belg'an* shore.

(b) *Each wexing, &c. according to their opinion, who think that*
great heap of waters under the Line is depressed into Tydes by the
Moon, towards the Poles.

5

Thus mighty in her Ships, stood *Carthage* long,
    And swept the riches of the world from far;
Yet stoop'd to *Rome*, less wealthy, but more strong:
    And this may prove our second Punick War.   20

6

What peace can be where both to one pretend?
    (But they more diligent, and we more strong)
Or if a peace, it soon must have an end
    For they would grow too pow'rful were it long.

7

Behold two Nations then, ingag'd so far,   25
    That each seav'n years the fit must shake each Land:
Where *France* will side to weaken us by War,
    Who onely can his vast designs withstand.

8

See how he feeds th' °*Iberian* with delays,
    To render us his timely friendship vain;   30
And, while his secret Soul on *Flanders* preys,
    He rocks the Cradle of the Babe of *Spain*.

(c) *Th'* Iberian, *the* Spaniard.

9

Such deep designs of Empire does he lay
    O're them whose cause he seems to take in hand:
And, prudently, would make them Lords at Sea,   35
    To whom with ease he can give Laws by Land.

10

This saw our King; and long within his breast
    His pensive counsels ballanc'd too and fro;
He griev'd the Land he freed should be oppress'd,
    And he less for it then Usurpers do.   40

11

His gen'rous mind the fair Idea's drew
    Of Fame and Honour which in dangers lay;
Where wealth, like fruit on precipices, grew,
    Not to be gather'd but by Birds of prey.

12

The loss and gain each fatally were great;   45
    And still his Subjects call'd aloud for war:
But peaceful Kings o'r martial people set,
    Each others poize and counter-ballance are.

13

He, first, survey'd the charge with careful eyes,
    Which none but mighty Monarchs could maintain;   50
Yet judg'd, like vapours that from Limbecks rise,
    It would in richer showers descend again.

14

At length resolv'd t' assert the watry Ball,
    He in himself did whole Armado's bring:
Him, aged Sea-men might their Master call,   55
    And choose for General were he not their King.

15

It seems as every Ship their Sovereign knows,
    His awful summons they so soon obey;
So hear the skaly Herd when ᵈ*Proteus* blows,
    And so to pasture follow through the Sea.   60

(d) *When* Proteus *blows, or* Cæruleus Proteus immania
ponti armenta, & magnas pascit sub gurgite Phocas. *Virg*.

16

To see this Fleet upon the Ocean move
    Angels drew wide the Curtains of the skies:
And Heav'n, as if there wanted Lights above,
    For Tapers made two glareing Comets rise.

17

Whether they unctuous Exhalations are,   65
    Fir'd by the Sun, or seeming so alone,
Or each some more remote and slippery Star,
    Which looses footing when to Mortals shown.

18

Or one that bright companion of the Sun,
    Whose glorious aspect seal'd our new-born King;   70
And now a round of greater years begun,
    New influence from his walks of light did bring.

19

Victorious *York* did, first, with fam'd success,
    To his known valour make the *Dutch* give place:
Thus Heav'n our Monarch's fortune did confess,   75
    Beginning conquest from his Royal Race.

20

But since it was decreed, Auspicious King,
    In *Britain*'s right that thou should'st wed the Main,
Heav'n, as a gage, would cast some precious thing
    And therefore doom'd that *Lawson* should be slain.   80

21

Lawson amongst the formost met his fate,
    Whom Sea-green *Syrens* from the Rocks lament:
Thus as an off'ring for the *Grecian* State,
    He first was kill'd who first to Battel went.

22

*Their Chief blown up, in air, not waves expir'd,   85
     To which his pride presum'd to give the Law:
The *Dutch* confess'd Heav'n present, and retir'd,
     And all was *Britain* the wide Ocean saw.

* *The Admiral of* Holland.

23

To nearest Ports their shatter'd Ships repair,
     Where by our dreadful Canon they lay aw'd: 90
So reverently men quit the open air
     When thunder speaks the angry Gods abroad.

24

And now approach'd their Fleet from *India*, fraught
     With all the riches of the rising Sun:
And precious Sand from ᵉSouthern Climates brought,   95
     (The fatal Regions where the War begun.)

The attempt at Berghen.
(e) *Southern Climates*, Guinny.

25

Like hunted *Castors*, conscious of their store,
     Their way-laid wealth to *Norway*'s coasts they bring:
There first the North's cold bosome Spices bore,
     And Winter brooded on the Eastern Spring.   100

26

By the rich scent we found our perfum'd prey,
     Which flanck'd with Rocks did close in covert lie:
And round about their murdering Canon lay,
     At once to threaten and invite the eye.

27

Fiercer then Canon, and then Rocks more hard,   105
    The *English* undertake th' unequal War:
Seven Ships alone, by which the Port is barr'd,
    Besiege the *Indies*, and all *Denmark* dare.

28

These fight like Husbands, but like Lovers those:
    These fain would keep, and those more fain enjoy: 110
And to such height their frantick passion grows,
    That what both love, both hazard to destroy.

29

Amidst whole heaps of Spices lights a Ball,
    And now their Odours arm'd against them flie:
Some preciously by shatter'd Porc'lain fall,   115
    And some by Aromatick splinters die.

30

And though by Tempests of the prize bereft,
    In Heavens inclemency some ease we find:
Our foes we vanquish'd by our valour left,
    And onely yielded to the Seas and Wind.   120

31

Nor wholly lost we so deserv'd a prey;
    For storms, repenting, part of it restor'd:
Which, as a tribute from the *Balthick* Sea,
    The *British* Ocean sent her mighty Lord.

32

Go, Mortals, now, and vex your selves in vain   125
    For wealth, which so uncertainly must come:
When what was brought so far, and with such pain,
    Was onely kept to lose it neerer home.

33

The Son, who, twice three month's on th' Ocean tost,
　Prepar'd to tell what he had pass'd before,   130
Now sees, in *English* Ships the *Holland* Coast,
　And Parents arms in vain stretch'd from the shore.

34

This carefull Husband had been long away,
　Whom his chast wife and little children mourn;
Who on their fingers learn'd to tell the day   135
　On which their Father promis'd to return.

35

ᶠSuch are the proud designs of human kind,
　And so we suffer Shipwrack every where!
Alas, what Port can such a Pilot find,
　Who in the night of Fate must blindly steer!   140

(f) *Such are*, &c. *from* Petronius. Si, bene calculum ponas
ubique fit naufragium.

36

The undistinguish'd seeds of good and ill
　Heav'n, in his bosom, from our knowledge hides;
And draws them in contempt of human skill,
　Which oft, for friends, mistaken foes provides.

37

Let *Munsters* Prelate ever be accurst,   145
　In whom we seek the ᵍ*German* faith in vain:
Alas, that he should teach the *English* first
　That fraud and avarice in the Church could reign!

(g) *The* German *faith.* Tacitus *saith of them,* Nullos mortalium
fide aut armis ante Germanos esse.

38

Happy who never trust a Strangers will,
    Whose friendship's in his interest understood!   150
Since money giv'n but tempts him to be ill
    When pow'r is too remote to make him good.

39

Till now, alone the Mighty Nations strove:
    The rest, at gaze, without the Lists did stand:
And threatning *France*, plac'd like a painted *Jove*,   155
    Kept idle thunder in his lifted hand.

War declar'd by France.

40

That Eunuch Guardian of rich *Hollands* trade,
    Who envies us what he wants pow'r t' enjoy!
Whose noisefull valour does no foe invade,
    And weak assistance will his friends destroy.   160

41

Offended that we fought without his leave,
    He takes this time his secret hate to show:
Which *Charles* does with a mind so calm receive
    As one that neither seeks, nor shuns his foe.

42

With *France*, to aid the *Dutch*, the *Danes* unite: 165
    France as their Tyrant, *Denmark* as their Slave.
But when with one three Nations joyn to fight,
    They silently confess that one more brave.

43

Lewis had chas'd the *English* from his shore;
    But *Charles* the *French* as Subjects does invite.   170
Would Heav'n for each some *Salomon* restore,
    Who, by their mercy, may decide their right.

44

Were Subjects so but onely by their choice,
   And not from Birth did forc'd Dominion take,
Our Prince alone would have the publique voice;   175
   And all his Neighbours Realms would desarts make.

45

He without fear a dangerous War pursues,
   Which without rashness he began before.
As Honour made him first the danger choose,
   So still he makes it good on virtues score.   180

46

The doubled charge his Subjects love supplies,
   Who, in that bounty, to themselves are kind:
So glad *Egyptians* see their *Nilus* rise,
   And in his plenty their abundance find.

47

With equal pow'r he does two Chiefs create,   185
   Two such, as each seem'd worthiest when alone:
Each able to sustain a Nations fate,
   Since both had found a greater in their own.

Prince Rupert *and Duke* Albemarl *sent to sea.*

48

Both great in courage, Conduct and in Fame,
   Yet neither envious of the others praise;   190
Their duty, faith, and int'rest too the same,
   Like mighty Partners equally they raise.

49

The Prince long time had courted Fortune's love,
    But once possess'd did absolutely reign;
Thus with their *Amazons* the *Heroes* strove,   195
    And conquer'd first those Beauties they would gain.

50

The Duke beheld, like *Scipio*, with disdain
    That *Carthage*, which he ruin'd, rise once more:
And shook aloft the Fasces of the Main,
    To fright those Slaves with what they felt before.   200

51

Together to the watry Camp they haste,
    Whom Matrons passing, to their children show:
Infants first vows for them to Heav'n are cast,
    And ^h^future people bless them as they go.

(h) *Future people*, Examina infantium futurusque populus.
Plin. Jun. in pan. ad Traj.

52

With them no riotous pomp, nor *Asian* train,   205
    T' infect a Navy with their gawdy fears:
To make slow fights, and victories but vain;
    But war, severely, like it self, appears.

53

Diffusive of themselves, where e'r they pass,
    They make that warmth in others they expect: 210
Their valour works like bodies on a glass,
    And does its Image on their men project.

54

Our Fleet divides, and straight the *Dutch* appear,
  In number, and a fam'd Commander, bold:
The Narrow Seas can scarce their Navy bear,   215
  Or crowded Vessels can their Soldiers hold.

Duke of Albemarl'*s Battel, first day.*

55

The Duke, less numerous, but in courage more.
  On wings of all the winds to combat flies:
His murdering Guns a loud defiance roar,
  And bloudy Crosses on his Flag-staffs rise.   220

56

Both furl their sails, and strip them for the fight,
  Their folded sheets dismiss the useless air:
[i]Th' *Elean* Plains could boast no nobler sight,
  When strugling Champions did their bodies bare.

(i) *Th'* Elean, *&c. Where the Olimpick Games were celebrated.*

57

Born each by other in a distant Line,   225
  The Sea-built Forts in dreadful order move:
So vast the noise, as if not Fleets did joyn,
  [k]But Lands unfix'd, and floating Nations, strove.

(k) *Lands unfix'd, from* Virgil: *Credas innare revulsas Cycladas,*
&c.

58

Now pass'd, on either side they nimbly tack,
  Both strive to intercept and guide the wind: 230
And, in its eye, more closely they come back
  To finish all the deaths they left behind.

59

On high-rais'd Decks the haughty *Belgians* ride,
   Beneath whose shade our humble Fregats go:
Such port the *Elephant* bears, and so defi'd   235
   By the *Rhinocero's* her unequal foe.

60

And as the built, so different is the fight;
   Their mounting shot is on our sails design'd:
Deep in their hulls our deadly bullets light,
   And through the yielding planks a passage find.   240

61

Our dreaded Admiral from far they threat,
   Whose batter'd rigging their whole war receives.
All bare, like some old Oak which tempests beat,
   He stands, and sees below his scatter'd leaves.

62

Heroes of old, when wounded, shelter sought,   245
   But he, who meets all danger with disdain,
Ev'n in their face his ship to Anchor brought,
   And Steeple high stood propt upon the Main.

63

At this excess of courage, all amaz'd,
   The foremost of his foes a while withdraw.   250
With such respect in enter'd *Rome* they gaz'd,
   Who on high Chairs the God-like Fathers saw.

64

And now, as where *Patroclus* body lay,
   Here *Trojan* Chiefs advanc'd, and there the *Greek*:
Ours o'r the Duke their pious wings display,   255
   And theirs the noblest spoils of *Britain* seek.

65

Mean time, his busie Marriners he hasts,
  His shatter'd sails with rigging to restore:
And willing Pines ascend his broken Masts,
  Whose lofty heads rise higher then before.   260

66

Straight to the *Dutch* he turns his dreadful prow,
  More fierce th' important quarrel to decide.
Like Swans, in long array his Vessels show,
  Whose creasts, advancing, do the waves divide.

67

They charge, re-charge, and all along the Sea   265
  They drive, and squander the huge *Belgian* Fleet.
Berkley alone, who neerest Danger lay,
  Did a like fate with lost *Creüsa* meet.

68

The night comes on, we, eager to pursue
  The Combat still, and they asham'd to leave: 270
Till the last streaks of dying day withdrew,
  And doubtful Moon-light did our rage deceive.

69

In th' *English* Fleet each ship resounds with joy,
  And loud applause of their great Lead'rs fame.
In fiery dreams the *Dutch* they still destroy,   275
  And, slumbring, smile at the imagin'd flame.

70

Not so the *Holland* Fleet, who tir'd and done,
  Stretch'd on their decks like weary Oxen lie:
Faint sweats all down their mighty members run,
  (Vast bulks which little souls but ill supply.)   280

267 who neerest Danger lay *67 (some copies)* 88: not making equal way *67 (some copies)*
274 Lead'rs *67 (some copies)* 88: Leader's *67 (some copies)* 68

71

In dreams they fearful precipices tread,
  Or, shipwrack'd, labour to some distant shore:
Or in dark Churches walk among the dead:
  They wake with horrour, and dare sleep no more.

72

The morn they look on with unwilling eyes,   285
  Till, from their Main-top, joyful news they hear
Of ships, which by their mould bring new supplies,
  And in their colours *Belgian* Lions bear.

Second days Battel.

73

Our watchful General had discern'd, from far,
  This mighty succour which made glad the foe.   290
He sigh'd, but, like a Father of the War,
  [1]His face spake hope, while deep his sorrows flow.

(1) *His face, &c.* Spem vultu simulat, premit alto corde
dolorem. *Virg.*

74

His wounded men he first sends off to shore:
  (Never, till now, unwilling to obey.)
They, not their wounds but want of strength deplore,   295
  And think them happy who with him can stay.

75

Then, to the rest, Rejoyce, (said he) to day
  In you the fortune of *Great Britain* lies:
Among so brave a people you are they
  Whom Heav'n has chose to fight for such a Prize.   300

76

If number *English* courages could quell,
    We should at first have shun'd, not met our foes;
Whose numerous sails the fearful onely tell:
    Courage from hearts, and not from numbers grows.

77

He said; nor needed more to say: with hast   305
    To their known stations chearfully they go:
And all at once, disdaining to be last,
    Sollicite every gale to meet the foe.

78

Nor did th' incourag'd *Belgians* long delay,
    But, bold in others, not themselves, they stood: 310
So thick, our Navy scarce could sheer their way,
    But seem'd to wander in a moving wood.

79

Our little Fleet was now ingag'd so far,
    That, like the Sword-fish in the Whale, they fought.
The Combat onely seem'd a Civil War,   315
    Till through their bowels we our passage wrought.

80

Never had valour, no not ours before,
    Done ought like this upon the Land or Main:
Where not to be o'rcome was to do more
    Then all the Conquests former Kings did gain.   320

81

The mighty Ghosts of our great *Harries* rose,
    And armed *Edwards* look'd, with anxious eyes,
To see this Fleet among unequal foes,
    By which fate promis'd them their *Charls* should rise.

82

Mean time the *Belgians* tack upon our Reer,   325
   And raking Chace-guns through our sterns they send:
Close by, their Fire-ships, like *Jackals*, appear,
   Who on their Lions for the prey attend.

83

Silent in smoke of Canons they come on:
   (Such vapours once did fiery *Cacus* hide.)   330
In these the height of pleas'd revenge is shown,
   Who burn contented by another's side.

84

Sometimes, from fighting Squadrons of each Fleet,
   (Deceiv'd themselves, or to preserve some friend)
Two grapling *Ætna's* on the Ocean meet,   335
   And *English* fires with *Belgian* flames contend.

85

Now, at each Tack, our little Fleet grows less;
   And, like maim'd fowl, swim lagging on the Main.
Their greater loss their numbers scarce confess
   While they lose cheaper then the *English* gain.   340

86

Have you not seen when, whistled from the fist,
   Some Falcon stoops at what her eye design'd,
And, with her eagerness, the quarry miss'd,
   Straight flies at check, and clips it down the wind,

87

The dastard Crow, that to the wood made wing,   345
   And sees the Groves no shelter can afford,
With her loud Kaws her Craven kind does bring,
   Who, safe in numbers cuff the noble Bird?

88

Among the *Dutch* thus *Albemarl* did fare:
　He could not conquer, and disdain'd to flie.
Past hope of safety, 'twas his latest care,
　Like falling *Cesar*, decently to die.

350

89

Yet pity did his manly spirit move
　To see those perish who so well had fought:
And, generously, with his dispair he strove,
　Resolv'd to live till he their safety wrought.

355

90

Let other Muses write his prosp'rous fate,
　Of conquer'd Nations tell, and Kings restor'd:
But mine shall sing of his eclips'd estate,
　Which, like the Sun's, more wonders does afford.

360

91

He drew his mighty Fregates all before,
　On which the foe his fruitless force employes:
His weak ones deep into his Reer he bore,
　Remote from Guns as sick men are from noise.

92

His fiery Canon did their passage guide,
　And foll'wing smoke obscur'd them from the foe.
Thus *Israel* safe from the *Egyptian*'s pride,
　By flaming pillars, and by clouds did go.

365

93

Elsewhere the *Belgian* force we did defeat,
　But here our courages did theirs subdue:
So *Xenophon* once led that fam'd retreat,
　Which first the *Asian* Empire overthrew.

370

94

The foe approach'd: and one, for his bold sin,
Was sunk, (as he that touch'd the Ark was slain;)
The wild waves master'd him, and suck'd him in,   375
And smiling Eddies dimpled on the Main.

(o) *The third of* June, *famous for two former Victories.*

95

This seen, the rest at awful distance stood;
As if they had been there as servants set,
To stay, or to go on, as he thought good,
And not persue, but wait on his retreat.   380

96

So *Lybian* Huntsmen, on some sandy plain,
From shady coverts rouz'd, the Lion chace:
The Kingly beast roars out with loud disdain,
   ᵐAnd slowly moves, unknowing to give place.

(m) *The simile is* Virgil's, Vestigia retro improperata refert,
&c.

97

But if some one approach to dare his force,   385
He swings his tail, and swiftly turns him round:
With one paw seizes on his trembling Horse,
And with the other tears him to the ground.

98

Amidst these toils succeeds the balmy night,
Now hissing waters the quench'd guns restore;   390
ⁿAnd weary waves, withdrawing from the fight,
Lie lull'd and panting on the silent shore.

(n) *Weary waves, from* Statius Sylv. Nec trucibus fluviis
idem sonus: occidit horror æquoris, ac terris maria ac-
clinata quiescunt.

99

The Moon shone clear on the becalmed floud,
   Where, while her beams like glittering silver play,
Upon the Deck our careful General stood,
   And deeply mus'd on the °succeeding day.   395

(o) *The third of* June, *famous for two former Victories.*

100

That happy Sun, said he, will rise again,
   Who twice victorious did our Navy see:
And I alone must view him rise in vain,
   Without one ray of all his Star for me.   400

101

Yet, like an *English* Gen'ral will I die,
   And all the Ocean make my spatious grave.
Women and Cowards on the Land may lie,
   The Sea's a Tomb that's proper for the brave.

102

Restless he pass'd the remnants of the night,   405
   Till the fresh air proclaim'd the morning nigh,
And burning ships, the Martyrs of the fight,
   With paler fires beheld the Eastern sky.

103

But now, his Stores of Ammunition spent,
   His naked valour is his onely guard:
Rare thunders are from his dumb Cannon sent,   410
   And solitary Guns are scarcely heard.

Third day.

104

Thus far had Fortune pow'r, here forc'd to stay,
 Nor longer durst with vertue be at strife:
This, as a Ransome *Albemarl* did pay
 For all the glories of so great a life.   415

105

For now brave *Rupert* from afar appears,
 Whose waving Streamers the glad General knows:
With full spread Sails his eager Navy steers,
 And every Ship in swift proportion grows.   420

106

The anxious Prince had heard the Cannon long,
 And from that length of time dire *Omens* drew
Of *English* over-match'd, and *Dutch* too strong,
 Who never fought three days but to pursue.

107

Then, as an Eagle, (who, with pious care,   425
 Was beating widely on the wing for prey)
To her now silent Eiry does repair,
 And finds her callow Infants forc'd away;

108

Stung with her love she stoops upon the plain,
 The broken air loud whistling as she flies: 430
She stops, and listens, and shoots forth again,
 And guides her pinions by her young ones cries:

417-20 For now ... grows. *67* (some copies) *88*: *67* (some copies) *and 68 have*:
    For now brave *Rupert*'s Navy did appear,
    Whose waving streamers from afar he knows:
    As in his fate something divine there were,
    Who dead and buried the third day arose.

109

With such kind passion hastes the Prince to fight,
    And spreads his flying canvass to the sound:
Him, whom no danger, were he there, could fright,   435
    Now, absent, every little noise can wound.

110

As, in a drought, the thirsty creatures cry,
    And gape upon the gather'd clowds for rain,
And first the Martlet meets it in the sky,
    And, with wet wings, joys all the feather'd train,   440

111

With such glad hearts did our dispairing men
    Salute th' appearance of the Princes Fleet:
And each ambitiously would claim the Ken
    That with first eyes did distant safety meet.

112

The *Dutch*, who came like greedy Hinds before,   445
    To reap the harvest their ripe ears did yield,
Now look like those, when rowling thunders roar,
    And sheets of Lightning blast the standing field.

113

Full in the Princes passage, hills of sand
    And dang'rous flats in secret ambush lay,   450
Where the false tides skim o'r the cover'd Land,
    And Sea-men with dissembled depths betray:

114

The wily *Dutch*, who, like fall'n Angels, fear'd
    This new *Messiah*'s coming, there did wait,
And round the verge their braving Vessels steer'd,   455
    To tempt his courage with so fair a bait.

115

But he, unmov'd, contemns their idle threat,
  Secure of fame when ere he please to fight:
His cold experience tempers all his heat,
  And inbred worth does boasting valour slight.   460

116

Heroique virtue did his actions guide,
  And he the substance not th' appearance chose:
To rescue one such friend he took more pride
  Than to destroy whole thousands of such foes.

117

But, when approach'd, in strict embraces bound,   465
  Rupert and *Albemarl* together grow:
He joys to have his friend in safety found,
  Which he to none but to that friend would owe.

118

The chearful Souldiers, with new stores suppli'd,
  Now long to execute their spleenfull will;   470
And, in revenge for those three days they tri'd,
  Wish one, like *Joshuah*'s, when the Sun stood still.

119

Thus re-inforc'd, against the adverse Fleet
  Still doubling ours, brave *Rupert* leads the way.
With the first blushes of the Morn they meet,   475
  And bring night back upon the new-born day.

Fourth days Battel.

120

His presence soon blows up the kindling fight,
  And his loud Guns speak thick like angry men:
It seem'd as slaughter had been breath'd all night,
  And death new pointed his dull dart agen.   480

121

The *Dutch*, too well his mighty Conduct knew,
    And matchless Courage since the former fight:
Whose Navy like a stiff stretch'd cord did show
    Till he bore in, and bent them into flight.

122

The wind he shares while half their Fleet offends   485
    His open side, and high above him shows,
Upon the rest at pleasure he descends,
    And, doubly harm'd, he double harms bestows.

123

Behind, the Gen'ral mends his weary pace,
    And sullenly to his revenge he sails: 490
ᵖSo glides some trodden Serpent on the grass,
    And long behind his wounded vollume trails.

(p) *So glides, &c. from* Virgil. Quum medii nexus, extremæ-
que agmina caudæ solvuntur; tardosque trahit sinus
ultimus orbes, &c.

124

Th' increasing sound is born to either shore,
    And for their stakes the throwing Nations fear.
Their passions double with the Cannons roar,
    And with warm wishes each man combats there.   495

125

Pli'd thick and close as when the fight begun,
    Their huge unwieldy Navy wasts away:
So sicken waning Moons too neer the Sun,
    And blunt their crescents on the edge of day.   500

495 passions] passion, *67 68 88*

126

And now reduc'd on equal terms to fight,
　　Their Ships like wasted Patrimonies show:
Where the thin scatt'ring Trees admit the light,
　　And shun each others shadows as they grow.

127

The warlike Prince had sever'd from the rest　　505
　　Two giant ships, the pride of all the Main;
Which, with his one, so vigorously he press'd,
　　And flew so home they could not rise again.

128

Already batter'd, by his Lee they lay,
　　In vain upon the passing winds they call:　　510
The passing winds through their torn canvass play,
　　And flagging sails on heartless Sailors fall.

129

Their open'd sides receive a gloomy light,
　　Dreadful as day let in to shades below:
Without, grim death rides bare-fac'd in their sight,　　515
　　And urges ent'ring billows as they flow.

130

When one dire shot, the last they could supply,
　　Close by the board the Prince's Main-mast bore:
All three now, helpless, by each other lie,
　　And this offends not, and those fear no more.　　520

131

So have I seen some fearful Hare maintain
　　A Course, till tir'd before the Dog she lay:
Who, stretch'd behind her, pants upon the plain,
　　Past pow'r to kill as she to get away.

132

With his loll'd tongue he faintly licks his prey,   525
   His warm breath blows her flix up as she lies:
She, trembling, creeps upon the ground away,
   And looks back to him with beseeching eyes.

133

The Prince unjustly does his Stars accuse,
   Which hinder'd him to push his fortune on: 530
For what they to his courage did refuse,
   By mortal valour never must be done.

134

This lucky hour the wise *Batavian* takes,
   And warns his tatter'd Fleet to follow home:
Proud to have so got off with equal stakes,   535
   qWhere 'twas a triumph not to be o'r-come.

(q) *From* Horace: Quos opimus fallere & effugere est triumphus.

135

The General's force, as kept alive by fight,
   Now, not oppos'd, no longer can persue:
Lasting till Heav'n had done his courage right,
   When he had conquer'd he his weakness knew.   540

136

He casts a frown on the departing foe,
   And sighs to see him quit the watry field:
His stern fix'd eyes no satisfaction show,
   For all the glories which the Fight did yield.

137

Though, as when Fiends did Miracles avow,   545
   He stands confess'd ev'n by the boastful *Dutch*,
He onely does his conquest disavow,
   And thinks too little what they found too much.

138

Return'd, he with the Fleet resolv'd to stay,
  No tender thoughts of home his heart divide: 550
Domestick joys and cares he puts away,
  For Realms are housholds which the Great must guide.

139

As those who unripe veins in Mines explore,
  On the rich bed again the warm turf lay,
Till time digests the yet imperfect Ore,   555
  And know it will be Gold another day:

140

So looks our Monarch on this early fight,
  Th' essay, and rudiments of great success,
Which all-maturing time must bring to light,
  While he, like Heav'n, does each days labour bless.   560

141

Heav'n ended not the first or second day,
  Yet each was perfect to the work design'd:
God and Kings work, when they their work survey,
  And passive aptness in all subjects find.

142

In burden'd Vessels, first, with speedy care,   565
  His plenteous Stores do season'd timber send;
Thither the brawny Carpenters repair,
  And as the Surgeons of maim'd ships attend.

His Majesty repairs the Fleet.

143

With Cord and Canvass from rich *Hamburgh* sent,
  His Navies molted wings he imps once more: 570
Tall *Norway* Fir, their Masts in Battel spent,
  And *English* Oak sprung leaks and planks restore.

144

All hands employ'd, ^rthe Royal work grows warm,
   Like labouring Bees on a long Summers day,
Some sound the Trumpet for the rest to swarm,   575
   And some on bells of tasted Lillies play:

(r) Fervet opus: *the same similitude in* Virgil.

145

With glewy wax some new foundation lay
   Of Virgin combs, which from the roof are hung:
Some arm'd within doors, upon duty stay,
   Or tend the sick, or educate the young.   580

146

So here, some pick out bullets from the sides,
   Some drive old Okum through each seam and rift:
Their left-hand does the Calking-iron guide,
   The ratling Mallet with the right they lift.

147

With boiling Pitch another near at hand   585
   (From friendly *Sweden* brought) the seams instops:
Which well paid o'r the salt-Sea waves withstand,
   And shakes them from the rising beak in drops.

148

Some the gall'd ropes with dawby Marling bind,
   Or sear-cloth Masts with strong Tarpawling coats: 590
To try new shrouds one mounts into the wind,
   And one, below, their ease or stifness notes.

149

Our careful Monarch stands in Person by,
   His new-cast Canons firmness to explore:
The strength of big-corn'd powder loves to try,   595
   And Ball and Cartrage sorts for every bore.

150

Each day brings fresh supplies of Arms and Men,
    And Ships which all last Winter were abrode:
And such as fitted since the Fight had been,
    Or new from Stocks were fall'n into the Road.   600

151

The goodly *London* in her gallant trim,
    (The *Phœnix* daughter of the vanish'd old:)
Like a rich Bride does to the Ocean swim,
    And on her shadow rides in floating gold.

Loyal London *describ'd.*

152

Her Flag aloft spread ruffling to the wind,   605
    And sanguine Streamers seem the floud to fire:
The Weaver charm'd with what his Loom design'd,
    Goes on to Sea, and knows not to retire.

153

With roomy decks, her Guns of mighty strength,
    (Whose low-laid mouthes each mounting billow laves:)   610
Deep in her draught, and warlike in her length,
    She seems a Sea-wasp flying on the waves.

154

This martial Present, piously design'd,
    The Loyal City give their best-lov'd King:
And with a bounty ample as the wind,   615
    Built, fitted and maintain'd to aid him bring.

155

By viewing Nature, Natures Hand-maid, Art,
    Makes mighty things from small beginnings grow:
Thus fishes first to shipping did impart
    Their tail the Rudder, and their head the Prow.   620

Digression concerning Shipping and Navigation.

156

Some Log, perhaps, upon the waters swam
An useless drift, which, rudely cut within,
And hollow'd, first a floating trough became,
And cross some Riv'let passage did begin.

157

In shipping such as this the *Irish Kern*,
And untaught *Indian*, on the stream did glide:
Ere sharp-keel'd Boats to stem the floud did learn,
Or fin-like Oars did spread from either side.

158

Adde but a Sail, and *Saturn* so appear'd,
When, from lost Empire, he to Exile went,
And with the Golden age to *Tyber* steer'd,
Where Coin and first Commerce he did invent.

159

Rude as their Ships was Navigation, then;
No useful Compass or Meridian known:
Coasting, they kept the Land within their ken,
And knew no North but when the Pole-star shone.

160

Of all who since have us'd the open Sea,
Then the bold *English* none more fame have won:
ᵉBeyond the Year, and out of Heav'ns high-way,
They make discoveries where they see no Sun.

(s) Extra anni solisque vias. *Virg.*

161

But what so long in vain, and yet unknown,
By poor man-kinds benighted wit is sought,
Shall in this Age to *Britain* first be shown,
And hence be to admiring Nations taught.

162

The Ebbs of Tydes, and their mysterious flow,
  We, as Arts Elements shall understand:
And as by Line upon the Ocean go,
  Whose paths shall be familiar as the Land.

163

'Instructed ships shall sail to quick Commerce;
  By which remotest Regions are alli'd:
Which makes one City of the Universe,
  Where some may gain, and all may be suppli'd.

(t) *By a more exact measure of Longitude.*

164

Then, we upon our Globes last verge shall go,
  And view the Ocean leaning on the sky:
From thence our rolling Neighbours we shall know,
  And on the Lunar world securely pry.

165

This I fore-tel, from your auspicious care,
  Who great in search of God and Nature grow:
Who best your wise Creator's praise declare,
  Since best to praise his works is best to know.

Apostrophe to the Royal Society.

166

O truly Royal! who behold the Law,
  And rule of beings in your Makers mind,
And thence, like Limbecks, rich Idea's draw,
  To fit the levell'd use of humane kind.

649 note *measure of Longitude* 88: *knowledge of Longitudes* 67 68

167

But first the toils of war we must endure,   665
   And, from th' Injurious *Dutch* redeem the Seas.
War makes the valiant of his right secure,
   And gives up fraud to be chastis'd with ease.

168

Already were the *Belgians* on our coast,
   Whose Fleet more mighty every day became,   670
By late success, which they did falsly boast,
   And now, by first appearing seem'd to claim.

169

Designing, subtil, diligent, and close,
   They knew to manage War with wise delay:
Yet all those arts their vanity did cross,   675
   And, by their pride, their prudence did betray.

170

Nor staid the *English* long: but, well suppli'd,
   Appear as numerous as th' insulting foe.
The Combat now by courage must be tri'd,
   And the success the braver Nation show.   680

171

There was the *Plimouth* Squadron new come in,
   Which in the *Straights* last Winter was abroad:
Which twice on *Biscay*'s working Bay had been,
   And on the Mid-land Sea the *French* had aw'd.

172

Old expert *Allen*, loyal all along,   685
   Fam'd for his action on the *Smirna* Fleet,
And *Holmes*, whose name shal live in Epique Song,
   While Musick Numbers, or while Verse has Feet.

173

Holmes, the *Achates* of the Gen'rals fight,
    Who first bewitch'd our eyes with *Guinny* Gold: 690
As once old *Cato* in the *Roman*'s sight
    The tempting fruits of *Africk* did unfold.

174

With him went *Sprag*, as bountiful as brave,
    Whom his high courage to command had brought:
Harman, who did the twice fir'd *Harry* save,   695
    And in his burning ship undaunted fought.

175

Young Hollis, on a *Muse* by *Mars* begot
    Born, *Cesar*-like, to write and act great deeds:
Impatient to revenge his fatal shot,
    His right hand doubly to his left succeeds.   700

176

Thousands were there in darker fame that dwell,
    Whose deeds some nobler Poem shall adorn:
And, though to me unknown, they, sure, fought well,
    Whom *Rupert* led, and who were *British* born.

177

Of every size an hundred fighting Sail,   705
    So vast the Navy now at Anchor rides,
That underneath it the press'd waters fail,
    And, with its weight, it shoulders off the Tydes.

178

Now Anchors weigh'd, the Sea-men shout so shrill,
    That Heav'n and Earth and the wide Ocean rings: 710
A breeze from Westward waits their sails to fill,
    And rests, in those high beds, his downy wings.

179

The wary *Dutch* this gathering storm foresaw,
 And durst not bide it on the *English* coast:
Behind their treach'rous shallows they withdraw,   715
 And their lay snares to catch the *British* Hoast.

180

So the false Spider, when her Nets are spread,
 Deep ambush'd in her silent den does lie:
And feels, far off, the trembling of her thread,
 Whose filmy cord should bind the strugling Fly.   720

181

Then, if at last, she find him fast beset,
 She issues forth, and runs along her Loom:
She joys to touch the Captive in her Net,
 And drags the little wretch in triumph home.

182

The *Belgians* hop'd that, with disorder'd haste,   725
 Our deep-cut keels upon the sands might run:
Or, if with caution leisurely were past,
 Their numerous gross might charge us one by one

183

But, with a fore-wind pushing them above,
 And swelling tyde that heav'd them from below,   730
O'r the blind flats our warlike Squadrons move,
 And, with spread sails, to welcome Battel go.

184

It seem'd as there the *British Neptune* stood,
 With all his host of waters at command,
Beneath them to submit th' officious floud: 735
 "And, with his Trident, shov'd them off the sand.

(u) Levat ipse Tridenti, & vastas aperit Syrtes, &c. *Virg.*

185

To the pale foes they suddenly draw near,
      And summon them to unexpected fight:
They start like Murderers when Ghosts appear,
      And draw their Curtains in the dead of night.   740

186

Now Van to Van the formost Squadrons meet,
      The midmost Battels hasting up behind,
Who view, far off, the storm of falling Sleet,
      And hear their thunder ratling in the wind.
Second Battel.

187

At length the adverse Admirals appear;   745
      (The two bold Champions of each Countries right)
Their eyes describe the lists as they come near,
      And draw the lines of death before they fight.

188

The distance judg'd for shot of every size,
      The Linstocks touch, the pond'rous ball expires: 750
The vig'rous Sea-man every port-hole plies,
      And adds his heart to every Gun he fires.

189

Fierce was the fight on the proud *Belgians* side,
      For honour, which they seldome sought before:
But now they by their own vain boasts were ti'd,   755
      And forc'd, at least in show, to prize it more.

190

But sharp remembrance on the *English* part,
      And shame of being match'd by such a foe,
Rouze conscious vertue up in every heart,
      ʷAnd seeming to be stronger makes them so.   760

(w) Possunt quia posse videntur. *Virg.*

191

Nor long the *Belgians* could that Fleet sustain,
    Which did two Gen'rals fates, and *Cesar*'s bear.
Each several Ship a victory did gain,
    As *Rupert* or as *Albemarl* were there.

192

Their batter'd Admiral too soon withdrew,   765
    Unthank'd by ours for his unfinish'd fight:
But he the minds of his *Dutch* Masters knew,
    Who call'd that providence which we call'd flight.

193

Never did men more joyfully obey,
    Or sooner understood the sign to flie: 770
With such alacrity they bore away,
    As if to praise them all the States stood by.

194

O famous Leader of the *Belgian* Fleet,
    Thy Monument inscrib'd such praise shall wear
As *Varro*, timely flying, once did meet,   775
    Because he did not of his *Rome* despair.

195

Behold that Navy which a while before
    Provok'd the tardy *English* to the fight,
Now draw their beaten vessels close to shore,
    As Larks lie dar'd to shun the Hobbies flight.   780

196

Who ere would *English* Monuments survey,
    In other records may our courage know:
But let them hide the story of this day,
    Whose fame was blemish'd by too base a foe.

197

Or if too busily they will enquire
    Into a victory which we disdain:
Then let them know, the *Belgians* did retire
    ˣBefore the Patron Saint of injur'd *Spain*.

785

(x) *Patron Saint:* St. James, *on whose day this victory was gain'd.*

198

Repenting *England* this revengeful day
    ʸTo *Philip*'s Manes did an off'ring bring:
England, which first, by leading them astray,
    Hatch'd up Rebellion to destroy her King.

790

(y) *Philip's Manes:* Philip *the second, of* Spain, *against whom the* Hollanders *rebelling, were aided by Queen* Elizabeth.

199

Our Fathers bent their baneful industry
    To check a Monarchy that slowly grew:
But did not *France* or *Holland*'s fate foresee,
    Whose rising pow'r to swift Dominion flew.

795

200

In fortunes Empire blindly thus we go,
    And wander after pathless destiny:
Whose dark resorts since prudence cannot know
    In vain it would provide for what shall be.

800

201

But what ere *English* to the bless'd shall go,
    And the fourth *Harry* or first *Orange* meet:
Find him disowning of a *Burbon* foe,
    And him detesting a *Batavian* Fleet.

202

Now on their coasts our conquering Navy rides,   805
   Way-lays their Merchants, and their Land besets:
Each day new wealth without their care provides,
   They lie asleep with prizes in their nets.

(x) *Patron Saint; St. James; on whose day this victory was gain'd.*

203

So, close behind some Promontory lie
   The huge Leviathans t' attend their prey: 810
And give no chace, but swallow in the frie,
   Which through their gaping jaws mistake the way.

204

Nor was this all; in Ports and Roads remote,
   Destructive Fires among whole Fleets we send:
Triumphant flames upon the water flote,   815
   And out-bound ships at home their voyage end.

Burning of the Fleet in the Vly *by Sir* Robert Holmes.

205

Those various Squadrons, variously design'd,
   Each vessel fraighted with a several load:
Each Squadron waiting for a several wind,
   All find but one, to burn them in the Road.   820

206

Some bound for *Guinny*, golden sand to find,
   Bore all the gawds the simple Natives wear:
Some for the pride of *Turkish* Courts design'd,
   For folded *Turbans* finest *Holland* bear.

207

Some *English* Wool, vex'd in a *Belgian* Loom,   825
   And into Cloth of spungy softness made:
Did into *France* or colder *Denmark* doom,
   To ruine with worse ware our staple Trade.

208

Our greedy Sea-men rummage every hold,
  Smile on the booty of each wealthier Chest:
And, as the Priests who with their gods make bold,
  Take what they like, and sacrifice the rest.

209

But ah! how unsincere are all our joys!
  Which, sent from Heav'n, like Lightning make no stay:
Their palling taste the journeys length destroys,
  Or grief, sent post, o'r-takes them on the way.

Transitum *to the Fire of* London.

210

Swell'd with our late successes on the Foe,
  Which *France* and *Holland* wanted power to cross:
We urge an unseen Fate to lay us low,
  And feed their envious eyes with *English* loss.

211

Each Element his dread command obeys,
  Who makes or ruines with a smile or frown;
Who as by one he did our Nation raise,
  So now he with another pulls us down.

212

Yet, *London*, Empress of the Northern Clime,
  By an high fate thou greatly didst expire;
'Great as the worlds, which at the death of time
  Must fall, and rise a nobler frame by fire.

(z) Quum mare quum tellus correptaque regia Cœli,
ardeat, &c. *Ovid.*

830

835

840

845

213

As when some dire Usurper Heav'n provides,
 To scourge his Country with a lawless sway: 850
His birth, perhaps, some petty Village hides,
 And sets his Cradle out of Fortune's way:

214

Till fully ripe his swelling fate breaks out,
 And hurries him to mighty mischiefs on:
His Prince surpriz'd at first, no ill could doubt,   855
 And wants the pow'r to meet it when 'tis known:

215

Such was the rise of this prodigious fire,
 Which in mean buildings first obscurely bred,
From thence did soon to open streets aspire,
 And straight to Palaces and Temples spread.   860

216

The diligence of Trades and noiseful gain,
 And luxury, more late, asleep were laid:
All was the nights, and in her silent reign,
 No sound the rest of Nature did invade.

217

In this deep quiet, from what source unknown,   865
 Those seeds of fire their fatal birth disclose:
And first, few scatt'ring sparks about were blown,
 Big with the flames that to our ruine rose.

218

Then, in some close-pent room it crept along,
 And, smouldring as it went, in silence fed:
Till th' infant monster, with devouring strong,   870
 Walk'd boldly upright with exalted head.

219

Now, like some rich or mighty Murderer,
　　Too great for prison, which he breaks with gold:
Who fresher for new mischiefs does appear,　　　　875
　　And dares the world to tax him with the old:

220

So scapes th' insulting fire his narrow Jail,
　　And makes small out-lets into open air:
There the fierce winds his tender force assail,
　　And beat him down-ward to his first repair.　　880

221

ᵃThe winds, like crafty Courtezans, with-held
　　His flames from burning, but to blow them more:
And, every fresh attempt, he is repell'd
　　With faint denials, weaker then before.

(a) *Like crafty, &c.* Hæc arte tractabat cupidum virum,
ut illius animum inopia accenderet.

222

And now, no longer letted of his prey,　　　　885
　　He leaps up at it with inrag'd desire:
O'r-looks the neighbours with a wide survey,
　　And nods at every house his threatning fire.

223

The Ghosts of Traitors, from the *Bridge* descend,
　　With bold Fanatick Spectres to rejoyce:　　890
About the fire into a Dance they bend,
　　And sing their Sabbath Notes with feeble voice.

224

Our Guardian Angel saw them where he sate
    Above the Palace of our slumbring King,
He sigh'd, abandoning his charge to Fate,   895
    And, drooping, oft lookt back upon the wing.

225

At length the crackling noise and dreadful blaze,
    Call'd up some waking Lover to the sight:
And long it was ere he the rest could raise,
    Whose heavy eye-lids yet were full of night.   900

226

The next to danger, hot pursu'd by fate,
    Half cloth'd, half naked, hastily retire:
And frighted Mothers strike their breasts, too late,
    For helpless Infants left amidst the fire.

227

Their cries soon waken all the dwellers near: 905
    Now murmuring noises rise in every street:
The more remote run stumbling with their fear,
    And, in the dark, men justle as they meet.

228

So weary Bees in little Cells repose:
    But if night-robbers lift the well-stor'd Hive,   910
An humming through their waxen City grows,
    And out upon each others wings they drive.

229

Now streets grow throng'd and busie as by day:
    Some run for Buckets to the hallow'd Quire:
Some cut the Pipes, and some the Engines play,   915
    And some more bold mount Ladders to the fire.

896 lookt 88: look 67 68   903 Mothers 88: Mother 67 68

230

In vain: for, from the East, a *Belgian* wind,
  His hostile breath through the dry rafters sent:
The flames impell'd, soon left their foes behind,
  And forward, with a wanton fury went.   920

231

A Key of fire ran all along the shore,
  [b]And lighten'd all the River with the blaze:
The waken'd Tydes began again to roar,
  And wond'ring Fish in shining waters gaze.

(b) Sigæa igni freta lata relucent. *Virg.*

232

Old Father *Thames* rais'd up his reverend head,   925
  But fear'd the fate of *Simoeis* would return:
Deep in his *Ooze* he sought his sedgy bed,
  And shrunk his waters back into his Urn.

233

The fire, mean time, walks in a broader gross,
  To either hand his wings he opens wide: 930
He wades the streets, and straight he reaches cross,
  And plays his longing flames on th' other side.

234

At first they warm, then scorch, and then they take:
  Now with long necks from side to side they feed:
At length, grown strong, their Mother fire forsake,   935
  And a new Collony of flames succeed.

235

To every nobler portion of the Town,
  The curling billows roul their restless Tyde:
In parties now they straggle up and down,
  As Armies, unoppos'd, for prey divide.   940

236

One mighty Squadron, with a side wind sped,
    Through narrow lanes his cumber'd fire does haste:
By pow'rful charms of gold and silver led,
    The *Lombard* Banquers and the *Change* to waste.

237

Another backward to the *Tow'r* would go,   945
    And slowly eats his way against the wind:
But the main body of the marching foe
    Against th' Imperial Palace is design'd.

238

Now day appears, and with the day the King,
    Whose early care had robb'd him of his rest: 950
Far off the cracks of falling houses ring,
    And shrieks of subjects pierce his tender breast.

239

Near as he draws, thick harbingers of smoke,
    With gloomy pillars, cover all the place:
Whose little intervals of night are broke   955
    By sparks that drive against his Sacred Face.

240

More then his Guards his sorrows made him known,
    And pious tears which down his cheeks did show'r:
The wretched in his grief forgot their own:
    (So much the pity of a King has pow'r.)   960

241

He wept the flames of what he lov'd so well,
    And what so well had merited his love.
For never Prince in grace did more excel,
    Or Royal City more in duty strove.

242

Nor with an idle care did he behold: 965
    (Subjects may grieve, but Monarchs must redress.)
He chears the fearful, and commends the bold,
    And makes despairers hope for good success.

243

Himself directs what first is to be done,
    And orders all the succours which they bring.   970
The helpful and the good about him run,
    And form an Army worthy such a King.

244

He sees the dire contagion spread so fast,
    That where it seizes, all relief is vain:
And therefore must unwillingly lay waste   975
    That Country which would, else, the foe maintain.

245

The powder blows up all before the fire:
    Th' amazed flames stand gather'd on a heap;
And from the precipices brinck retire,
    Afraid to venture on so large a leap.   980

246

Thus fighting fires a while themselves consume,
    But straight, like *Turks*, forc'd on to win or die,
They first lay tender bridges of their fume,
    And o'r the breach in unctuous vapours flie.

247

Part stays for passage till a gust of wind   985
    Ships o'r their forces in a shining sheet:
Part, creeping under ground, their journey blind,
    And, climbing from below, their fellows meet.

248

Thus, to some desart plain, or old wood side,
    Dire night-hags come from far to dance their round;
And o'r brode Rivers on their fiends they ride,
    Or sweep in clowds above the blasted ground.

    990

249

No help avails: for, *Hydra*-like, the fire,
    Lifts up his hundred heads to aim his way.
And scarce the wealthy can one half retire,
    Before he rushes in to share the prey.

    995

250

The rich grow suppliant, and the poor grow proud:
    Those offer mighty gain, and these ask more.
So void of pity is th' ignoble crowd,
    When others ruine may increase their store.

    1000

251

As those who live by shores with joy behold
    Some wealthy vessel split or stranded nigh;
And, from the Rocks, leap down for shipwrack'd Gold,
    And seek the Tempest which the others flie:

252

So these but wait the Owners last despair,
    And what's permitted to the flames invade:
Ev'n from their jaws they hungry morsels tear,
    And, on their backs, the spoils of *Vulcan* lade.

    1005

253

The days were all in this lost labour spent;
    And when the weary King gave place to night,
His Beams he to his Royal Brother lent,
    And so shone still in his reflective light.

    1010

254

Night came, but without darkness or repose,
  A dismal picture of the gen'ral doom:
Where Souls distracted when the Trumpet blows,   1015
  And half unready with their bodies come.

255

Those who have homes, when home they do repair
  To a last lodging call their wand'ring friends.
Their short uneasie sleeps are broke with care,
  To look how near their own destruction tends.   1020

256

Those who have none sit round where once it was,
  And with full eyes each wonted room require:
Haunting the yet warm ashes of the place,
  As murder'd men walk where they did expire.

257

Some stir up coals and watch the Vestal fire,   1025
  Others in vain from sight of ruine run:
And, while through burning Lab'rinths they retire,
  With loathing eyes repeat what they would shun.

258

The most, in fields, like herded beasts lie down;
  To dews obnoxious on the grassie floor: 1030
And while their Babes in sleep their sorrows drown,
  Sad Parents watch the remnants of their store.

259

While by the motion of the flames they ghess
  What streets are burning now, and what are near:
An Infant, waking, to the paps would press,   1035
  And meets, instead of milk, a falling tear.

260

No thought can ease them but their Sovereign's care,
    Whose praise th' afflicted as their comfort sing:
Ev'n those whom want might drive to just despair,
    Think life a blessing under such a King.   1040

261

Mean time he sadly suffers in their grief,
    Out-weeps an Hermite, and out-prays a Saint:
All the long night he studies their relief,
    How they may be suppli'd, and he may want.

262

O God, said he, thou Patron of my days,   1045
    Guide of my youth in exile and distress!
Who me unfriended, brought'st by wondrous ways
    The Kingdom of my Fathers to possess:

King's Prayer.

263

Be thou my Judge, with what unwearied care
    I since have labour'd for my People's good:
To bind the bruises of a Civil War,   1050
    And stop the issues of their wasting bloud.

264

Thou, who hast taught me to forgive the ill,
    And recompense, as friends, the good misled;
If mercy be a Precept of thy will,
    Return that mercy on thy Servant's head.   1055

265

Or, if my heedless Youth has stept astray,
    Too soon forgetful of thy gracious hand:
On me alone thy just displeasure lay,
    But take thy judgments from this mourning Land.   1060

266

We all have sinn'd, and thou hast laid us low,
    As humble Earth from whence at first we came:
Like flying shades before the clowds we show,
    And shrink like Parchment in consuming flame.

267

O let it be enough what thou hast done,   1065
    When spotted deaths ran arm'd through every street,
With poison'd darts, which not the good could shun,
    The speedy could out-fly, or valiant meet.

268

The living few, and frequent funerals then,
    Proclam'd thy wrath on this forsaken place: 1070
And now those few who are return'd agen
    Thy searching judgments to their dwellings trace.

269

O pass not, Lord, an absolute decree,
    Or bind thy sentence unconditional:
But in thy sentence our remorce foresee,   1075
    And, in that foresight, this thy doom recall.

270

Thy threatnings, Lord, as thine, thou maist revoke:
    But, if immutable and fix'd they stand,
Continue still thy self to give the stroke,
    And let not foreign foes oppress thy Land.   1080

271

Th' Eternal heard, and from the Heav'nly Quire,
    Chose out the Cherub with the flaming sword:
And bad him swiftly drive th' approaching fire
    From where our Naval Magazins were stor'd.

272

The blessed Minister his wings displai'd,
    And like a shooting Star he cleft the night:
He charg'd the flames, and those that disobey'd,
    He lash'd to duty with his sword of light.   1085

273

The fugitive flames, chastis'd, went forth to prey
    On pious Structures, by our Fathers rear'd:
By which to Heav'n they did affect the way,   1090
    Ere Faith in Church-men without Works was heard.

274

The wanting Orphans saw, with watry eyes,
    Their Founders charity in dust laid low:
And sent to God their ever-answer'd cries,   1095
    (For he protects the poor who made them so.)

275

Nor could thy Fabrick, *Paul*'s, defend thee long,
    Though thou wert Sacred to thy Makers praise:
Though made immortal by a Poet's Song;
    And Poets Songs the *Theban* walls could raise.   1100

276

The dareing flames peep't in and saw from far,
    The awful beauties of the Sacred Quire:
But, since it was prophan'd by Civil War,
    Heav'n thought it fit to have it purg'd by fire.

277

Now down the narrow streets it swiftly came,   1105
    And, widely opening, did on both sides prey.
This benefit we sadly owe the flame,
    If onely ruine must enlarge our way.

278

And now four days the Sun had seen our woes,
    Four nights the Moon beheld th' incessant fire: 1110
It seem'd as if the Stars more sickly rose,
    And farther from the feav'rish North retire.

279

In th' Empyrean Heaven, (the bless'd abode)
    The Thrones and the Dominions prostrate lie,
Not daring to behold their angry God: 1115
    And an hush'd silence damps the tuneful sky.

280

At length th' Almighty cast a pitying eye,
    And mercy softly touch'd his melting breast:
He saw the Town's one half in rubbish lie,
    And eager flames give on to storm the rest.   1120

281

An hollow chrystal Pyramid he takes,
    In firmamental waters dipt above;
Of it a brode Extinguisher he makes,
    And hoods the flames that to their quarry strove.

282

The vanquish'd fires withdraw from every place,   1125
    Or full with feeding, sink into a sleep:
Each houshold Genius shows again his face,
    And, from the hearths, the little Lares creep.

283

Our King this more then natural change beholds;
    With sober joy his heart and eyes abound: 1130
To the All-good his lifted hands he folds,
    And thanks him low on his redeemed ground.

284

As when sharp frosts had long constrain'd the earth,
  A kindly thaw unlocks it with mild rain:
And first the tender blade peeps up to birth,   1135
  And straight the green fields laugh with promis'd grain:

285

By such degrees, the spreading gladness grew
  In every heart, which fear had froze before:
The standing streets with so much joy they view,
  That with less grief the perish'd they deplore.   1140

286

The Father of the people open'd wide
  His stores, and all the poor with plenty fed:
Thus God's Annointed God's own place suppli'd,
  And fill'd the empty with his daily bread.

287

This Royal bounty brought its own reward,   1145
  And, in their minds, so deep did print the sense:
That if their ruines sadly they regard,
  'Tis but with fear the sight might drive him thence.

288

But so may he live long, that Town to sway,
  Which by his Auspice they will nobler make,   1150
As he will hatch their ashes by his stay,
  And not their humble ruines now forsake.

Cities request to the King not to leave them.

289

They have not lost their Loyalty by fire;
  Nor is their courage or their wealth so low,
That from his Wars they poorly would retire,   1155
  Or beg the pity of a vanquish'd foe.

290

Not with more constancy the *Jews* of old,
   By *Cyrus* from rewarded Exile sent:
Their Royal City did in dust behold,
   Or with more vigour to rebuild it went.   1160

291

The utmost malice of their Stars is past,
   And two dire Comets which have scourg'd the Town,
In their own Plague and Fire have breath'd their last,
   Or, dimly, in their sinking sockets frown.

292

Now frequent Trines the happier lights among,   1165
   And high-rais'd *Jove* from his dark prison freed:
(Those weights took off that on his Planet hung)
   Will gloriously the new laid work succeed.

293

Me-thinks already, from this Chymick flame,
   I see a City of more precious mold: 1170
Rich as the Town which gives the ᶜ*Indies* name,
   With Silver pav'd, and all divine with Gold.

(c) *Mexico*.

294

Already, Labouring with a mighty fate,
   She shakes the rubbish from her mounting brow,
And seems to have renew'd her Charters date,   1175
   Which Heav'n will to the death of time allow.

295

More great then humane, now, and more ᵈ*August*,
   New deifi'd she from her fires does rise:
Her widening streets on new foundations trust,
   And, opening, into larger parts she flies.   1180

(d) Augusta, *the old name of* London.

296

Before, she like some Shepherdess did show,
  Who sate to bathe her by a River's side:
Not answering to her fame, but rude and low,
  Nor taught the beauteous Arts of Modern pride.

297

Now, like a Maiden Queen, she will behold,   1185
  From her high Turrets, hourly Sutors come:
The East with Incense, and the West with Gold,
  Will stand, like Suppliants, to receive her doom.

298

The silver *Thames*, her own domestick Floud,
  Shall bear her Vessels, like a sweeping Train;   1190
And often wind (as of his Mistress proud)
  With longing eyes to meet her face again.

299

The wealthy *Tagus*, and the wealthier *Rhine*,
  The glory of their Towns no more shall boast:
And *Sein*, That would with *Belgian* Rivers joyn,   1195
  Shall find her lustre stain'd, and Traffick lost.

300

The vent'rous Merchant, who design'd more far,
  And touches on our hospitable shore:
Charm'd with the splendour of this Northern Star,
  Shall here unlade him, and depart no more.   1200

301

Our pow'rful Navy shall no longer meet,
  The wealth of *France* or *Holland* to invade:
The beauty of this Town, without a Fleet,
  From all the world shall vindicate her Trade.

302

And, while this fam'd Emporium we prepare,   1205
    The *British* Ocean shall such triumphs boast,
That those who now disdain our Trade to share,
    Shall rob like Pyrats on our wealthy Coast.

303

Already we have conquer'd half the War,
    And the less dang'rous part is left behind: 1210
Our trouble now is but to make them dare,
    And not so great to vanquish as to find.

304

Thus to the Eastern wealth through storms we go;
    But now, the Cape once doubled, fear no more:
A constant Trade-wind will securely blow,   1215
    And gently lay us on the Spicy shore.

PROLOGUE and SONG
from *SECRET-LOVE*

PROLOGUE

I

H_E who writ this, not without pains and thought
From *French* and *English* Theaters has brought
Th' exactest Rules by which a Play is wrought.

II

The Unities of Action, Place, and Time;
The Scenes unbroken; and a mingled chime
Of *Johnsons* humour, with *Corneilles* rhyme.   5

III

But while dead colours he with care did lay,
He fears his Wit, or Plot he did not weigh,
Which are the living Beauties of a Play.

IV

Plays are like Towns, which howe're fortifi'd   10
By Engineers, have still some weaker side
By the o'reseen Defendant unespy'd.

V

And with that Art you make approaches now;
Such skilful fury in Assaults you show,
That every Poet without shame may bow.   15

Prologue and Song. Text from Secret-Love, or The Maiden-Queen, 1668, *collated with the editions of 1669, 1679, 1691, 1698*

VI

Ours therefore humbly would attend your doom,
If Souldier-like, he may have termes to come
With flying colours, and with beat of Drum.

The Prologue goes out, and stayes while a Tune is play'd, after which
be returnes again.

Second *PROLOGUE*

I HAD forgot one half I do protest,
And now am sent again to speak the rest.   20
He bowes to every great and noble Wit,
But to the little Hectors of the Pit
Our Poet 's sturdy, and will not submit.
He'll be before-hand with 'em, and not stay
To see each peevish Critick stab his Play: 25
Each Puny Censor, who his skill to boast,
Is cheaply witty on the Poets cost.
No Criticks verdict, should, of right, stand good,
They are excepted all as men of blood:
And the same Law should shield him from their fury   30
Which has excluded Butchers from a Jury.
You'd all be Wits—
But writing's tedious, and that way may fail;
The most compendious method is to rail:
Which you so like, you think your selves ill us'd   35
When in smart Prologues you are not abus'd.
A civil Prologue is approv'd by no man;
You hate it as you do a Civil woman:
Your Fancy's pall'd, and liberally you pay
To have it quicken'd, e're you see a Play.   40
Just as old Sinners worn from their delight,
Give money to be whip'd to appetite.
But what a Pox keep I so much ado
To save our Poet? he is one of you;
A Brother Judgment, and as I hear say,   45

Prologue. 30 should shield him] should shield them *69 (some copies) 98*: shall shield
them *69 (some copies) 79 91*

A cursed Critick as e're damn'd a Play.
Good salvage Gentlemen your own kind spare,
He is, like you, a very Wolf, or Bear;
Yet think not he'll your ancient rights invade,
Or stop the course of your free damning trade: 50
For he, (he vows) at no friends Play can sit
But he must needs find fault to shew his Wit:
Then, for his sake, ne're stint your own delight,
Throw boldly, for he sets to all that write;
With such he ventures on an even lay,   55
For they bring ready money into Play.
Those who write not, and yet all Writers nick,
Are Bankrupt Gamesters, for they damn on Tick.

SONG

I FEED a flame within which so torments me
  That it both pains my heart, and yet contents me:
'Tis such a pleasing smart, and I so love it,
That I had rather die, then once remove it.

Yet he for whom I grieve shall never know it,   5
My tongue does not betray, nor my eyes show it:
Not a sigh nor a tear my pain discloses,
But they fall silently like dew on Roses.

Thus to prevent my love from being cruel,
My heart's the sacrifice as 'tis the fuel: 10
And while I suffer this to give him quiet,
My faith rewards my love, though he deny it.

On his eyes will I gaze, and there delight me;
While I conceal my love, no frown can fright me:
To be more happy I dare not aspire;   15
Nor can I fall more low, mounting no higher.

PROLOGUE, EPILOGUE and SONGS
from *SIR MARTIN MAR-ALL*
PROLOGUE

FOOLS, which each man meets in his Dish each day,
  Are yet the great Regalios of a Play;
In which to Poets you but just appear,
To prize that highest which cost them so dear:
Fops in the Town more easily will pass;   5
One story makes a statutable Ass:
But such in Plays must be much thicker sown,
Like yolks of Eggs, a dozen beat to one.
Observing Poets all their walks invade,
As men watch Woodcocks gliding through a Glade: 10
And when they have enough for Comedy,
They stow their several Bodies in a Pye:
The Poet 's but the Cook to fashion it,
For, Gallants, you your selves have found the wit.
To bid you welcome would your bounty wrong,   15
None welcome those who bring their chear along.

EPILOGUE

AS Country Vicars, when the Sermon's done,
  Run hudling to the Benediction;
Well knowing, though the better sort may stay,
The Vulgar Rout will run unblest away:
So we, when once our Play is done, make haste   5
With a short Epilogue to close your taste.
In thus withdrawing we seem mannerly,
But when the Curtain's down we peep, and see
A Jury of the Wits who still stay late,
And in their Club decree the poor Plays fate;   10

Prologue, Epilogue and Songs. Text from Sr Martin Mar-all, or The Feign'd Innocence:
A Comedy, 1668 (a), collated with the second edition, 1668 (b) and the editions of 1678,
1691, 1697
  Prologue. 4 cost 68b–97: costs 68a

Their Verdict back is to the Boxes brought,
Thence all the Town pronounces it their thought.
Thus, Gallants, we like *Lilly* can foresee,
But if you ask us what our doom will be,
We by to morrow will our Fortune cast,   15
As he tells all things when the Year is past.

SONGS

I

[WARNER] *SINGS*

MAKE ready fair Lady to night,
   And stand at the Door below,
For I will be there
To receive you with care,
   And to your true Love you shall go.   5

[MILLISENT] *SINGS*

And when the Stars twinckle so bright,
   Then down to the Door will I creep,
   To my Love will I flye,
   E're the jealous can spye,
And leave my old daddy asleep.   10

II

The SONG

BLIND Love to this hour
Had never like me, a Slave under his power.
   Then blest be the Dart
   That he threw at my heart,
For nothing can prove   5
A joy so great as to be wounded with love.

My Days and my Nights
Are fill'd to the purpose with sorrows and frights;
   From my heart still I sigh
   And my Eyes are ne're dry,   10

So that *Cupid* be prais'd,
I am to the top of Love's happiness rais'd.

My Soul's all on fire,
So that I have the pleasure to doat and desire,
  Such a pretty soft pain   15
  That it tickles each vein;
   'Tis the dream of a smart,
Which makes me breathe short when it beats at my heart.

Sometimes in a Pet,
When I am despis'd, I my freedom would get; 20
  But streight a sweet smile
  Does my anger beguile,
   And my heart does recall,
Then the more I do struggle, the lower I fall.

Heaven does not impart   25
Such a grace as to love unto ev'ry ones heart;
  For many may wish
  To be wounded and miss:
   Then blest be loves Fire,
And more blest her Eyes that first taught me desire. 30

PROLOGUES and EPILOGUES
to *THE WILD GALLANT*

PROLOGUE to the WILD GALLANT
as it was first Acted

Is it not strange, to hear a Poet say,
He comes to ask you, how you like the Play?
You have not seen it yet! alas 'tis true,
But now your Love and Hatred judge, not You.
And cruel Factions (brib'd by Interest) come, 5
Not to weigh Merit, but to give their Doome:

Prologues and Epilogues. Text from The Wild Gallant: A Comedy, *1669*

Our Poet therefore, jealous of th' Event,
And (though much boldness takes) not confident,
Has sent me, whither you, fair Ladies, too
Sometimes upon as small occasions goe,   10
And from this Scheme, drawn for the hour and day,
Bid me inquire the fortune of his Play.

*The Curtain drawn discovers two Astrologers; The Prologue
is presented to them.*

First Astrol. reads. A Figure of the heavenly Bodies in their several
Apartments, *Feb.* the 5*th*. half an hour after three after Noon, from
whence you are to judge the success of a new Play called the *Wild* 15
Gallant.

2. Astrol. Who must Judge of it, we, or these Gentlemen? We'l not
meddle with it, so tell your Poet. Here are in this House the ablest
Mathematicians in *Europe* for his purpose.

They will resolve the question e'r they part.   20

1. Ast. Yet let us judge it by the rules of Art.
First *Jupiter*, the Ascendants Lord disgrac'd,
In the twelfth House, and near grim *Saturn* plac'd,
Denote short life unto the Play:—

2. Ast.   *Jove* yet,   25
In his Apartment *Sagitary*, set
Under his own Roof, canot take much wrong;

1. Ast. Why then the Lifes not very short, nor long;

2. Ast. The Luck not very good, nor very ill,

Prolo. That is to say, 'tis as 'tis taken still.   30

1. Ast. But, Brother, *Ptolomy* the Learned says,
'Tis the fifth house from whence we judge of Plays.
Venus the Lady of that House I find
Is *Peregrine*, your Play is ill design'd,
It should have been but one continued Song,   35
Or at the least a Dance of 3 hours long.

2. Ast. But yet the greatest Mischief does remain,
The twelfth apartment bears the Lord of *Spain*;
Whence I conclude it is your Authors lot,
To be indanger'd by a *Spanish* Plot.   40

Prolo. Our Poet yet protection hopes from you,
But bribes you not with any thing that's new.
Nature is old, which Poets imitate,
And for Wit, those that boast their own estate,
Forget *Fletcher* and *Ben* before them went,   45
Their Elder Brothers, and that vastly spent:
So much 'twill hardly be repair'd again,
Not, though supply'd with all the wealth of *Spain*:
This Play is *English*, and the growth your own;
As such it yields to *English* Plays alone.   50
He could have wish'd it better for your sakes;
But that in Plays he finds you love mistakes:
Besides he thought it was in vain to mend
What you are bound in honour to defend,
That *English* Wit (how e'r despis'd by some)   55
Like *English* Valour still may overcome.

EPILOGUE *to the WILD GALLANT,*
as it was first Acted

THE *Wild Gallant* has quite playd out his game;
He's marry'd now, and that will make him tame;
Or if you think Marriage will not reclaim him,
The Critiques swear they'll damn him, but they'll tame him.
Yet though our Poet 's threatned most by these,   5
They are the only People he can please:
For he to humour them, has shown to day,
That which they only like, a wretched Play:
But though his Play be ill, here have been shown
The greatest Wits and Beauties of the Town.   10
And his Occasion having brought you here
You are too grateful to become severe.
There is not any Person here so mean,
But he may freely judge each Act and Scene:
But if you bid him choose his Judges then,   15
He boldly names true English Gentlemen:
For he ne'r thought a handsome Garb or Dress,
So great a Crime to make their Judgement less:

And with these Gallants he these Ladies joyns,
To judge that Language their Converse refines.   20
But if their Censures should condemn his Play,
Far from Disputing, he does only pray
He may *Leanders* Destiny obtain:
Now spare him, drown him when he comes again.

PROLOGUE *to the* WILD-GALLANT
Reviv'd

As some raw Squire, by tender Mother bred,
Till one and Twenty keeps his Maidenhead,
(Pleas'd with some Sport which he alone does find,
And thinks a secret to all Humane kind;)
Till mightily in love, yet halfe afraid,   5
He first attempts the gentle Dairymaid:
Succeeding there, and led by the renown
Of *Whetstones Park*, he comes at length to Town,
Where enter'd, by some School-fellow, or Friend,
He grows to break Glass-Windows in the end: 10
His valour too, which with the Watch began,
Proceeds to duell, and he kills his Man.
By such degrees, while knowledge he did want,
Our unfletch'd Author, writ a *Wild Gallant*.
He thought him monstrous leud (I'l lay my life)   15
Because suspected with his Landlords Wife:
But since his knowledge of the Town began,
He thinks him now a very civil man:
And, much asham'd of what he was before,
Has fairly play'd him at three Wenches more.   20
'Tis some amends his frailties to confess;
Pray pardon him his want of wickedness:
He's towardly, and will come on apace;
His frank confession shows he has some grace.
You balk'd him when he was a young beginner,   25
And almost spoyl'd a very hopeful sinner:
But, if once more you slight his weak indeavour;
For ought I know, he may turn taile for ever.

EPILOGUE to the WILD GALLANT reviv'd

OF all Dramatique Writing, Comick Wit,
As 'tis the best, so 'tis most hard to hit.
For it lies all in level to the eye,
Where all may judge, and each defect may spye.
Humour is that which every day we meet,   5
And therefore known as every publick street;
In which, if e'r the Poet go astray
You all can point, 'twas there he lost his way.
But, What's so common, to make pleasant too,
Is more than any wit can alwayes do.   10
For 'tis, like *Turkes*, with Hen and Rice to treat;
To make regallio's out of common meat.
But, in your Diet you grow Salvages:
Nothing but Humane flesh your taste can please:
And, as their Feasts with slaughter'd slaves began,   15
So you, at each new Play, must have a Man.
Hither you come, as to see Prizes fought;
If no Blood's drawn, you cry the Prize is naught.
But fooles grow wary now; and when they see
A Poet eyeing round the Company,   20
Straight each man for himself begins to doubt;
They shrink like Seamen when a Press comes out.
Few of 'em will be found for Publick use,
Except you charge an Oph upon each house,
Like the Traind-Bands, and every man ingage   25
For a sufficient Foole to serve the Stage.
And, when with much adoe you get him there,
Where he in all his glory shou'd appear,
Your Poets make him such rare things to say,
That he's more wit than any Man ith' Play.   30
But of so ill a mingle with the rest,
As when a Parrat's taught to break a jeast.
Thus aiming to be fine, they make a show
As tawdry Squires in Country Churches do.
Things well consider'd, 'tis so hard to make   35
A Comedy, which should the knowing take:
That our dull Poet, in despair to please,
Does humbly beg by me his writ of ease.

'Tis a Land-tax which he's too poor to pay;
You, therefore, must some other impost lay.   40
Would you but change for serious Plot and Verse
This mottley garniture of Fool and Farce,
Nor scorn a Mode, because 'tis taught at home,
Which does, like Vests, our Gravity become;
Our Poet yields you should this Play refuse,   45
As Tradesmen, by the change of fashions, lose
With some content their fripperies of *France*,
In hope it may their staple Trade advance.

PROLOGUE and EPILOGUE
to *THE TEMPEST*

PROLOGUE *to the* Tempest, *or the* Enchanted Island

As when a Tree's cut down the secret root
Lives under ground, and thence new Branches shoot;
So, from old *Shakespear*'s honour'd dust, this day
Springs up and buds a new reviving Play.
Shakespear, who (taught by none) did first impart   5
To *Fletcher* Wit, to labouring *Johnson* Art.
He Monarch-like gave those his subjects law,
And is that Nature which they paint and draw.
Fletcher reach'd that which on his heights did grow,
Whilst *Johnson* crept and gather'd all below.   10
This did his Love, and this his Mirth digest:
One imitates him most, the other best.
If they have since out-writ all other men,
'Tis with the drops which fell from *Shakespear*'s Pen.
The Storm which vanish'd on the Neighb'ring shore,   15
Was taught by *Shakespear*'s Tempest first to roar.
That innocence and beauty which did smile
In *Fletcher*, grew on this *Enchanted Isle*.

Prologue and Epilogue. Text from The Tempest, or The Enchanted Island. A Comedy, 1670

But *Shakespear*'s Magick could not copy'd be,
Within that Circle none durst walk but he. 20
I must confess 'twas bold, nor would you now,
That liberty to vulgar Wits allow,
Which works by Magick supernatural things:
But *Shakespear*'s pow'r is sacred as a King's.
Those Legends from old Priest-hood were receiv'd, 25
And he then writ, as people then believ'd.
But, if for *Shakespear* we your grace implore,
We for our Theatre shall want it more:
Who by our dearth of Youths are forc'd t' employ
One of our Women to present a Boy. 30
And that's a transformation you will say
Exceeding all the Magick in the Play.
Let none expect in the last Act to find,
Her Sex transform'd from man to Woman-kind.
What e're she was before the Play began, 35
All you shall see of her is perfect man.
Or if your fancy will be farther led,
To find her Woman, it must be abed.

EPILOGUE

GALLANTS, by all good signs it does appear,
That Sixty Seven's a very damning year,
For Knaves abroad, and for ill Poets here.

Among the Muses there's a gen'ral rot,
The Rhyming Mounsieur and the Spanish Plot: 5
Defie or Court, all's one, they go to Pot.

The Ghosts of Poets walk within this place,
And haunt us Actors wheresoe're we pass,
In Visions bloodier than King *Richard*'s was.

For this poor wretch he has not much to say, 10
But quietly brings in his part o'th' Play,
And begs the favour to be damn'd to day.

He sends me only like a Sh'riffs man here
To let you know the Malefactor's neer;
And that he means to dye, *en Cavalier*.   15

For if you shou'd be gracious to his Pen,
Th' Example will prove ill to other men,
And you'll be troubled with 'em all agen.

PROLOGUE, EPILOGUE and SONGS
from *TYRANNICK LOVE*

PROLOGUE

SELF-LOVE (which never rightly understood)
Makes Poets still conclude their Plays are good:
And malice in all Criticks raigns so high,
That for small Errors, they whole Plays decry;
So that to see this fondness, and that spite,   5
You'd think that none but Mad-men judge or write.
Therefore our Poet, as he thinks not fit
T' impose upon you, what he writes for Wit,
So hopes that leaving you your censures free,
You equal Judges of the whole will be: 10
They judge but half who only faults will see.
Poets like Lovers should be bold and dare,
They spoil their business with an over-care.
And he who servilely creeps after sence,
Is safe, but ne're will reach an Excellence.   15
Hence 'tis our Poet in his conjuring,
Allow'd his Fancy the full scope and swing.
But when a Tyrant for his Theme he had,
He loos'd the Reins, and bid his Muse run mad:
And though he stumbles in a full career;   20
Yet rashness is a better fault than fear.
He saw his way; but in so swift a pace,
To chuse the ground, might be to lose the race.
They then who of each trip th' advantage take,
Find but those Faults which they want Wit to make.   25

Prologue, Epilogue and Songs. Text from Tyrannick Love, or The Royal Martyr. A
Tragedy, *1670.*

EPILOGUE

Spoked by Mrs. Ellen, *when she was to be carried off dead by the Bearers*

To the Bearer. HOLD, are you mad? you damn'd confounded Dog,
I am to rise, and speak the Epilogue.

To the Audience. I come, kind Gentlemen, strange news to tell ye,
I am the Ghost of poor departed *Nelly*.
Sweet Ladies, be not frighted, I'le be civil,   5
I'm what I was, a little harmless Devil.
For after death, we Sprights, have just such Natures,
We had for all the World, when humane Creatures;
And therefore I that was an Actress here,
Play all my Tricks in Hell, a Goblin there.   10
Gallants, look to't, you say there are no Sprights;
But I'le come dance about your Beds at nights.
And faith you'l be in a sweet kind of taking,
When I surprise you between sleep and waking.
To tell you true, I walk because I dye   15
Out of my Calling in a Tragedy.
O Poet, damn'd dull Poet, who could prove
So sensless! to make *Nelly* dye for Love,
Nay, what's yet worse, to kill me in the prime
Of *Easter*-Term, in Tart and Cheese-cake time!   20
I'le fit the Fopp; for I'le not one word say
T'excuse his godly out of fashion Play.
A Play which if you dare but twice sit out,
You'l all be slander'd, and be thought devout.
But, farewel Gentlemen, make haste to me,   25
I'm sure e're long to have your company.
As for my Epitaph when I am gone,
I'le trust no Poet, but will write my own.

Here Nelly *lies, who, though she liv'd a Slater'n,*
Yet dy'd a Princess, acting in S. Cathar'n.   30

SONGS

I

Nakar and *Damilcar* descend in Clouds, and sing

Nakar. HARK, my *Damilcar*, we are call'd below!

Dam. Let us go, let us go!
    Go to relieve the care
    Of longing Lovers in despair!

Nakar. Merry, merry, merry, we sail from the East   5
    Half tippled at a Rain-bow Feast.

Dam. In the bright Moon-shine while winds whistle loud,
    Tivy, tivy, tivy, we mount and we fly,
    All racking along in a downy white Cloud:
    And lest our leap from the Skie should prove too far,   10
    We slide on the back of a new-falling Star.

Nakar. And drop from above,
    In a Gelly of Love!

Dam. But now the Sun's down, and the Element's red,
    The Spirits of Fire against us make head!   15

Nakar. They muster, they muster, like Gnats in the Air:
    Alas! I must leave thee, my Fair;
    And to my light Horse-men repair.

Dam. O stay, for you need not to fear 'em to night;
    The wind is for us, and blows full in their sight: 20
    And o're the wide Ocean we fight!
    Like leaves in the Autumn our Foes will fall down;
    And hiss in the Water—

Both. And hiss in the Water and drown!

Nakar. But their men lye securely intrench'd in a Cloud: 25
    And a Trumpeter-Hornet to battel sounds loud.

Dam. Now Mortals that spie
    How we tilt in the Skie
    With wonder will gaze;
    And fear such events as will ne're come to pass!   30

Nakar. Stay you to perform what the man will have done.

Dam. Then call me again when the Battel is won.

Both. So ready and quick is a Spirit of Air
    To pity the Lover, and succour the fair,

That, silent and swift, the little soft God   35
Is here with a wish, and is gone with a nod.

The Clouds part, *Nakar* flies up, and *Damilcar* down.

II

Damilcar stamps, and the Bed arises with S. *Catharine* in it

Dam. singing. YOU pleasing dreams of Love and sweet delight,
          Appear before this slumbring Virgins sight:
          Soft visions set her free
          From mournful piety.
          Let her sad thoughts from Heav'n retire;   5
          And let the Melancholy Love
          Of those remoter joys above
          Give place to your more sprightly fire.
          Let purling streams be in her fancy seen;
          And flowry Meads, and Vales of chearful green: 10
          And in the midst of deathless Groves
          Soft sighing wishes ly,
          And smiling hopes fast by,
          And just beyond 'em ever laughing Loves.

          A Scene of a *Paradise* is discovered.

III

SONG

Dam. AH how sweet it is to love,
          Ah how gay is young desire!
          And what pleasing pains we prove
          When we first approach Loves fire!
               Pains of Love be sweeter far   5
               Than all other pleasures are.

          Sighs which are from Lovers blown,
          Do but gently heave the Heart:
          Ev'n the tears they shed alone
          Cure, like trickling Balm their smart.   10
               Lovers when they lose their breath,
               Bleed away in easie death.

Love and Time with reverence use,
Treat 'em like a parting friend:
Nor the golden gifts refuse   15
Which in youth sincere they send:
    For each year their price is more,
    And they less simple than before.

Love, like Spring-tides full and high,
Swells in every youthful vein: 20
But each Tide does less supply,
Till they quite shrink in again:
    If a flow in Age appear,
    'Tis but rain, and runs not clear.

At the end of the Song a Dance of Spirits. . . .

PROLOGUE, EPILOGUE and SONGS
from *AN EVENING'S LOVE*

PROLOGUE

WHEN first our Poet set himself to write,
    Like a young Bridegroom on his Wedding-night
He layd about him, and did so bestir him,
His Muse could never lye in quiet for him:
But now his Honey-moon is gone and past,   5
Yet the ungrateful drudgery must last:
And he is bound, as civil Husbands do,
To strain himself, in complaisance to you:
To write in pain, and counterfeit a bliss,
Like the faint smackings of an after kiss.   10
But you, like Wives ill pleas'd, supply his want;
Each writing Monsieur is a fresh Gallant:
And though, perhaps, 'twas done as well before,
Yet still there's something in a new amour.
Your several Poets work with several tools,   15
One gets you wits, another gets you fools:

Prologue, Epilogue and Songs. Text from An Evening's Love, or The Mock-Astrologer, *1671*

This pleases you with some by-stroke of wit,
This finds some cranny, that was never hit.
But should these janty Lovers daily come
To do your work, like your good man at home,   20
Their fine small timber'd wits would soon decay;
These are Gallants but for a Holiday.
Others you had who oftner have appear'd,
Whom, for meer impotence you have cashier'd:
Such as at first came on with pomp and glory,   25
But, overstraining, soon fell flat before yee.
Their useless weight with patience long was born,
But at the last you threw 'em off with scorn.
As for the Poet of this present night,
Though now he claims in you an Husbands right,   30
He will not hinder you of fresh delight.
He, like a Seaman, seldom will appear;
And means to trouble home but thrice a year:
That only time from your Gallants he'll borrow;
Be kind to day, and Cuckold him to morrow.   35

EPILOGUE

M Y part being small, I have had time to day,
To mark your various censures of our Play:
First, looking for a Judgement or a Wit,
Like *Jews* I saw 'em scatter'd through the Pit:
And where a knot of Smilers lent an eare   5
To one that talk'd, I knew the foe was there.
The Club of jests went round; he who had none
Borrow'd oth' next, and told it for his own:
Among the rest they kept a fearfull stir,
In whisp'ring that he stole th' *Astrologer*;   10
And said, betwixt a *French* and *English* Plot
He eas'd his half-tir'd Muse, on pace and trot.
Up starts a Monsieur new come o're; and warm
In the *French* stoop; and the pull-back oth' arm;
Morbleu dit il, and cocks, I am a rogue   15
But he has quite spoil'd the feint *Astrologue*.
Pox, sayes another; here's so great a stir
With a son of a whore Farce that's regular,

A rule where nothing must decorum shock!
Dam'me 'ts as dull as dining by the clock.   20
An Evening! why the devil should we be vext
Whither he gets the Wench this night or next?
When I heard this, I to the Poet went,
Told him the house was full of discontent,
And ask'd him what excuse he could invent.   25
He neither swore nor storm'd as Poets do,
But, most unlike an Author, vow'd 'twas true.
Yet said, he us'd the *French* like Enemies,
And did not steal their Plots, but made 'em prize.
But should he all the pains and charges count   30
Of taking 'em, the bill so high wou'd mount,
That, like Prize-goods, which through the Office come,
He could have had 'em much more cheap at home.
He still must write; and Banquier-like, each day
Accept new Bills, and he must break, or pay.   35
When through his hands such sums must yearly run,
You cannot think the Stock is all his own.
His haste his other errors might excuse;
But there's no mercy for a guilty Muse:
For like a Mistress, she must stand or fall,   40
And please you to a height, or not at all.

SONGS

I

SONG

You charm'd me not with that fair face
    Though it was all divine:
To be anothers is the Grace,
    That makes me wish you mine.
The Gods and Fortune take their part   5
    Who like young Monarchs fight;
And boldly dare invade that heart
    Which is anothers right.
First mad with hope we undertake
    To pull up every barr;   10

But once possess'd, we faintly make
　　A dull defensive warr.
Now every friend is turn'd a foe
　　In hope to get our store:
And passion makes us Cowards grow,   15
　　Which made us brave before.

II

SONG

AFTER the pangs of a desperate Lover,
When day and night I have sigh'd all in vain,
Ah what a pleasure it is to discover
In her eyes pity, who causes my pain!

2

When with unkindness our love at a stand is,   5
And both have punish'd our selves with the pain,
Ah what a pleasure the touch of her hand is,
Ah what a pleasure to press it again!

3

When the denyal comes fainter and fainter,
And her eyes give what her tongue does deny,   10
Ah what a trembling I feel when I venture,
Ah what a trembling does usher my joy!

4

When, with a Sigh, she accords me the blessing,
And her eyes twinkle 'twixt pleasure and pain;
Ah what a joy 'tis beyond all expressing,   15
Ah what a joy to hear, shall we again!

III

SONG

CALM was the Even, and cleer was the Skie,
    And the new budding flowers did spring,
When all alone went *Amyntas* and I
    To hear the sweet Nightingale sing;
I sate, and he laid him down by me;   5
    But scarcely his breath he could draw;
For when with a fear he began to draw near,
    He was dash'd with A ha ha ha ha!

2

He blush'd to himself, and lay still for a while,
    And his modesty curb'd his desire;   10
But streight I convinc'd all his fear with a smile,
    Which added new flames to his fire.
O *Sylvia*, said he, you are cruel,
    To keep your poor Lover in awe;
Then once more he prest with his hand to my brest,   15
    But was dash'd with A ha ha ha ha.

3

I knew 'twas his passion that caus'd all his fear;
    And therefore I pity'd his case:
I whisper'd him softly there's no body near,
    And layd my cheek close to his face: 20
But as he grew bolder and bolder,
    A Shepherd came by us and saw;
And just as our bliss we began with a kiss,
    He laughd out with A ha ha ha ha.

IV

SONG

Damon. CELIMENA, of my heart,
    None shall e're bereave you:
    If, with your good leave, I may
    Quarrel with you once a day,
    I will never leave you.   5

2

Celimena. Passion's but an empty name
         Where respect is wanting:
         Damon you mistake your ayme;
         Hang your heart, and burn your flame,
         If you must be ranting.   10

3

Damon. Love as dull and muddy is,
        As decaying liquor:
        Anger sets it on the lees,
        And refines it by degrees,
        Till it workes it quicker.   15

4

Celimena. Love by quarrels to beget
         Wisely you endeavour;
         With a grave Physician's wit
         Who to cure an Ague fit
         Put me in a Feavor.   20

5

Damon. Anger rouzes love to fight,
        And his only bayt is,
        'Tis the spurre to dull delight,
        And is but an eager bite,
        When desire at height is.   25

6

Celimena. If such drops of heat can fall
         In our wooing weather;
         If such drops of heat can fall,
         We shall have the Devil and all
         When we come together.   30

PROLOGUES, EPILOGUES and SONGS
from *THE CONQUEST OF GRANADA*

PROLOGUE to the First Part

Spoken by Mris. Ellen Guyn *in a broad-brim'd hat, and wast-belt*

THIS jeast was first of t'other houses making,
And, five times try'd, has never fail'd of taking.
For 'twere a shame a Poet shoud be kill'd
Under the shelter of so broad a shield.
This is that hat whose very sight did win yee   5
To laugh and clap, as though the Devil were in yee.
As then, for *Nokes*, so now, I hope, you'l be
So dull, to laugh, once more, for love of me.
I'll write a Play, sayes one, for I have got
A broad-brim'd hat, and wastbelt tow'rds a Plot.   10
Sayes t'other, I have one more large than that:
Thus they out-write each other with a hat.
The brims still grew with every Play they writ;
And grew so large, they cover'd all the wit.
Hat was the Play: 'twas language, wit and tale: 15
Like them that find, Meat, drink, and cloth, in Ale.
What dulness do these Mungrill-wits confess
When all their hope is acting of a dress!
Thus two, the best Comedians of the Age
Must be worn out, with being blocks o'th' Stage.   20
Like a young Girl, who better things has known,
Beneath their Poets Impotence they groan.
See now, what Charity it was to save!
They thought you lik'd, what onely you forgave:
And brought you more dull sence.—dull sence, much worse   25
Than brisk, gay Non-sence; and the heavyer Curse.
They bring old Ir'n, and glass upon the Stage,
To barter with the Indians of our Age.

Prologues, Epilogues and Songs. Text from The Conquest of Granada by the Spaniards: In Two Parts, *1672, collated with the editions of 1673, 1678, 1687, 1695*

Still they write on; and like great Authors show:
But 'tis as Rowlers in wet gardens grow;
Heavy with dirt, and gath'ring as they goe.   } 30
May none who have so little understood
To like such trash, presume to praise what's good!
And may those drudges of the Stage, whose fate
Is, damn'd dull farce more dully to translate,   35
Fall under that excise the State thinks fit
To set on all French wares, whose worst, is wit.
French farce worn out at home, is sent abroad;
And, patch'd up here, is made our English mode.
Hence forth, let Poets, 'ere allow'd to write,   40
Be search'd, like Duellists, before they fight,
For wheel-broad hats, dull humour, all that chaffe,
Which makes you mourn, and makes the Vulgar laugh.
For these, in Playes, are as unlawful Arms,
As, in a Combat, Coats of Mayle, and Charms.   45

EPILOGUE

SUCCESS, which can no more than beauty last,
Makes our sad Poet mourn your favours past:
For, since without desert he got a name,
He fears to loose it now with greater shame.
Fame, like a little Mistriss of the town,   5
Is gaind with ease; but then she's lost as soon.
For, as those taudry Misses, soon or late
Jilt such as keep 'em at the highest rate:
(And oft the Lacquey, or the Brawny Clown,
Gets what is hid in the loose body'd gown;)   10
So, Fame is false to all that keep her long;
And turns up to the Fop that's brisk and young.
Some wiser Poet now would leave Fame first:
But elder wits are like old Lovers, curst;
Who, when the vigor of their youth is spent,   15
Still grow more fond as they grow impotent.
This, some years hence, our Poets case may prove;
But, yet, he hopes, he's young enough to love.

When forty comes, if 'ere he live to see
That wretched, fumbling age of poetry;   20
T'will be high time to bid his Muse adieu:
Well he may please him self, but never you.
Till then he'l do as well as he began;
And hopes you will not finde him less a man.

Think him not duller for this years delay;   25
He was prepar'd, the women were away;
And men, without their parts, can hardly play.
If they, through sickness, seldome did appear,
Pity the virgins of each Theatre!
For, at both houses, 'twas a sickly year!   30
And pity us, your servants, to whose cost,
In one such sickness, nine whole Mon'ths are lost.
Their stay, he fears, has ruin'd what he writ:
Long waiting both disables love and wit.
They thought they gave him leisure to do well: 35
But when they forc'd him to attend, he fell!
Yet though he much has faild, he begs to day
You will excuse his unperforming Play:
Weakness sometimes great passion does express;
He had pleas'd better, had he lov'd you less.   40

SONGS

I

SONG

I

BENEATH a Myrtle shade
Which Love for none but happy Lovers made,
I slept, and straight my Love before me brought
Phillis the object of my waking thought;
Undress'd she came my flames to meet,   5
While Love strow'd flow'rs beneath her feet;
Flow'rs, which so press'd by her, became more sweet.

Epilogue 23–24, 31–32, 35–36 *the transcript in Bodl. MS. Don. B. 8 has* not spoke *in margin*
Songs. I. *Two versions are printed in* Westminster-Drollery I, *1671:* (*a*) A Song at the
Kings house, (*b*) A Vision

2

From the bright Visions head
A careless vail of Lawn was loosely spread:
From her white temples fell her shaded hair,   10
Like cloudy sunshine not too brown nor fair:
Her hands, her lips did love inspire;
Her every grace my heart did fire:
But most her eyes which languish'd with desire.

3

Ah, Charming fair, said I,   15
How long can you my bliss and yours deny?
By Nature and by love this lonely shade
Was for revenge of suffring Lovers made:
Silence and shades with love agree:
Both shelter you and favour me;   20
You cannot blush because I cannot see.

4

No, let me dye, she said,
Rather than loose the spotless name of Maid:
Faintly me thought she spoke, for all the while
She bid me not believe her, with a smile.
Then dye, said I, she still deny'd: 25
And, is it thus, thus, thus she cry'd
You use a harmless Maid, and so she dy'd!

5

I wak'd, and straight I knew
I lov'd so well it made my dream prove true: 30
Fancy, the kinder Mistress of the two,
Fancy had done what *Phillis* wou'd not do!
Ah, Cruel Nymph, cease your disdain,
While I can dream you scorn in vain;
Asleep or waking you must ease my pain.   35

II

SONG

1

WHEREVER I am, and whatever I doe;
    My *Phillis* is still in my mind:
When angry I mean not to *Phillis* to goe,
    My Feet of themselves the way find:
Unknown to my self I am just at her door,   5
And when I would raile, I can bring out no more,
    Than *Phillis* too fair and unkind!

2

When *Phillis* I see, my Heart bounds in my Breast,
    And the Love I would stifle is shown:
But asleep, or awake, I am never at rest   10
    When from my Eyes *Phillis* is gone!
Sometimes a sweet Dream does delude my sad mind,
But, alas, when I wake and no *Phillis* I find
    How I sigh to my self all alone.

3

Should a King be my Rival in her I adore   15
    He should offer his Treasure in vain:
O let me alone to be happy and poor,
    And give me my *Phillis* again:
Let *Phillis* be mine, and for ever be kind
I could to a Desart with her be confin'd,   20
    And envy no Monarch his Raign.

4

Alas, I discover too much of my Love,
    And she too well knows her own power!
She makes me each day a new Martyrdom prove,
    And makes me grow jealous each hour: 25
But let her each minute torment my poor mind
I had rather love *Phillis* both False and Unkind,
    Then ever be freed from her Pow'r.

Songs. II. *A version is printed in* Westminster-Drollery I, *1672*   12 sweet *W*D:
sad *72–95*   19 for *73 78*: but *72 87 95*

PROLOGUE To the Second Part,
of The CONQUEST OF GRANADA

THEY who write Ill, and they who ne'r durst write,
   Turn Critiques, out of meer Revenge and Spight:
A *Play-house* gives 'em Fame; and up there starts,
From a mean Fifth-rate Wit, a Man of Parts.
(So Common Faces on the Stage appear: 5
We take 'em in; and they turn Beauties here.)
Our Authour fears those Critiques as his Fate:
And those he Fears, by consequence, must Hate.
For they the Trafficque of all Wit, invade;
As Scriv'ners draw away the Bankers Trade.   10
Howe're, the Poet's safe enough to day:
They cannot censure an unfinish'd Play.
But, as when Vizard Masque appears in Pit,
Straight, every man who thinks himself a Wit,
Perks up; and, managing his Comb, with grace,   15
With his white Wigg sets off his Nut-brown Face:
That done, bears up to th' prize, and views each Limb,
To know her by her Rigging and her Trimm:
Then, the whole noise of Fopps to wagers go,
Pox on her, 't must be she; and *Damm'ee* no: 20
Just so I Prophecy, these Wits to day,
Will blindly guess at our imperfect Play:
With what new Plots our Second Part is fill'd;
Who must be kept alive, and who be kill'd.
And as those Vizard Masques maintain that Fashion,   25
To sooth and tickle sweet Imagination:
So, our dull Poet keeps you on with Masquing;
To make you think there's something worth your asking:
But when 'tis shown, that which does now delight you,
Will prove a Dowdy, with a Face to fright you.   30

Prologue To the Second Part. 10 *In the transcript in Bodl. MS. Don. B. 8 additional line
follow:*

> Some of them seeme indeede yᵉ Poetts freinds;
> But 'tis, as France courts England, for her ends.
> They build up this Lampoone, & th' other Songe,
> And Court him, to lye still, while they grow stronge.

EPILOGUE to the
Second Part of GRANADA

THEY, who have best succeeded on the Stage,
　Have still conform'd their Genius to their Age.
Thus *Jonson* did Mechanique humour show,
When men were dull, and conversation low.
Then, Comedy was faultless, but 'twas course:　　　　　5
Cobbs Tankard was a jest, and *Otter*'s horse.
And as their Comedy, their love was mean:
Except, by chance, in some one labour'd Scene,
Which must attone for an ill-written Play.
They rose; but at their height could seldome stay.　　10
Fame then was cheap, and the first commer sped;
And they have kept it since, by being dead.
But were they now to write when Critiques weigh
Each Line, and ev'ry word, throughout a Play,
None of 'em, no not *Jonson,* in his height　　　　　15
Could pass, without allowing grains for weight.
Think it not envy that these truths are told,
Our Poet's not malicious, though he's bold.
'Tis not to brand 'em that their faults are shown,
But, by their errours, to excuse his own.　　　　　　20
If Love and Honour now are higher rais'd,
'Tis not the Poet, but the Age is prais'd.
Wit's now arriv'd to a more high degree;
Our native Language more refin'd and free.
Our Ladies and our men now speak more wit　　　　25
In conversation, than those Poets writ.
Then, one of these is, consequently, true;
That what this Poet writes comes short of you,
And imitates you ill, (which most he fears)
Or else his writing is not worse than theirs.　　　　　30
Yet, though you judge, (as sure the Critiques will)
That some before him writ with greater skill,
In this one praise he has their fame surpast,
To please an Age more Gallant than the last.

SONG, *In two Parts*

He. HOW unhappy a Lover am I
    While I sigh for my *Phillis* in vain;
All my hopes of Delight
Are another man's Right,
    Who is happy while I am in pain!   5

2

She. Since her Honour allows no Relief,
    But to pity the pains which you bear,
'Tis the best of your Fate,
(In a hopeless Estate,)
    To give o're, and betimes to despair.   10

3

He. I have try'd the false Med'cine in vain;
    For I wish what I hope not to win:
From without, my desire
Has no Food to its Fire,
    But it burns and consumes me within.   15

4

She. Yet at least 'tis a pleasure to know
    That you are not unhappy alone:
For the Nymph you adore
Is as wretched and more,
    And accounts all your suff'rings her own.   20

5

He. O ye Gods, let me suffer for both;
    At the feet of my *Phillis* I'le lye:
I'le resign up my Breath,
And take pleasure in Death,
    To be pity'd by her when I dye.   25

6

She. What her Honour deny'd you in Life
    In her Death she will give to your Love.
    Such a Flame as is true
    After Fate will renew,
     For the Souls to meet closer above.   30

A SONG

1

FAREWEL, fair *Armeda*, my Joy and my Grief;
In vain I have Lov'd you, and find no Relief:
Undone by your Vertue, too strict and severe,
Your Eyes gave me Love, and you gave me Despair.
Now, call'd by my Honour, I seek, with Content,   5
A Fate which in pity you wou'd not prevent:
    To languish in Love, were to find by delay
    A Death, that's more welcom the speediest way.

2

On Seas, and in Battels, in Bullets and Fire,
The Danger is less than in Hopeless Desire.   10
My Deaths Wound you gave me, though far off I bear
My Fate from your sight, not to cost you a Tear.
But if the kind Flood on a Wave should convey,
And under your Window my Body should lay,
    The Wound on my Breast when you happen to see,   15
    You'll say with a Sigh,—*It was given by me.*

A Song. Text from New Court-Songs, and Poems. By R. *V*. Gent., *1672*

POEMS FROM
COVENT GARDEN DROLERY

PROLOGUE and EPILOGUE to *SECRET-LOVE*
Spoken by the Women

PROLOGUE

Spoken by Mrs. Boutell *to the Maiden Queen, in mans Cloathes*

WOMEN like us (passing for men) you'l cry,
    Presume too much upon your Secresie.
There's not a fop in town but will pretend,
To know the cheat himself, or by his friend;
Then make no words on 't, Gallants, tis e'ne true,   5
We are condemn'd to look, and strut, like you.
Since we thus freely, our hard fate confess,
Accept us these bad times in any dress.
You'l find the sweet on 't, now old Pantaloons,
Will go as far, as formerly new Gowns,   10
And from your own cast Wigs, expect no frowns.
The Ladies we shall not so easily please.
They'l say what impudent bold things are these,
That dare provoke, yet cannot do us right,
Like men with huffing looks, that dare not fight.   15
But this reproach, our courage must not daunt,
The Bravest Souldier may a Weapon want,
Let Her that doubts us still, send her Gallant.
Ladies in us, you'l Youth and Beauty find,
All things but one, according to your mind.   20
And when your Eyes and Ears, are feasted here,
Rise up and make out the short Meal, elsewhere.

Poems. Text from Covent Garden Drolery, *1672 (CGDa), collated with* The Second
Impression *1672(b), the transcript in BM. Eg. MS. 2623, ff. 43-44,* Westminster
Drolery. The Second Part, *1672 (WD), and* Miscellany Poems, *1684 and 1692*
   Prologue. Heading: 'in mans Cloathes' added in *CGDb*

EPILOGUE

Spoken by Mrs. Reeves *to the Maiden Queen, in mans Cloathes*

WHAT think you Sirs, was't not all well enough,
  Will you not grant that we can strut, and huff.
Men may be proud, but faith for ought I see,
They neither walk, nor cock, so well as we.
And for the fighting Part we may in time,   5
Grow up to swagger in heroick Rhime.
For though we cannot boast of equal force,
Yet at some Weapon's men have still the worse.
Why should not then we Women act alone,
Or whence are men so necessary grown,   10
Our's are so old, they are as good as none.
Some who have tri'd 'em, if you'l take their Oaths,
Swear they're as arrant tinsell as their Cloaths.
Imagine us but what we represent,
And we could e'ne give you as good content.   15
Our faces, shapes, all's better that you see,
And for the rest they want as much as we.
Oh would the higher Powers be kind to us,
And grant us to set up a female house;
We'l make our selves to please both Sexes then, 20
To the Men Women, to the Women Men.
Here we presume, our Legs are no ill sight,
And they will give you no ill Dreams at night.
In Dream's both Sexes may their passions ease,
You make us then as civil as you please.   25
This would prevent the houses joyning too,
At which we are as much displeas'd as you.
For all our Women most devoutly swear,
Each would be rather a poor Actress here,
Then to be made a *Mamamouchi* there.   30

Epilogue. Heading: '*in mans Cloathes*' added in *CGDb* 11 so] too *MS* 16 that
MS: than *CGDa CGDb*   23 will *CGDb MS*: would *CGDa* 26 too *CGDb*
MS: two *CGDa*

The Prologue to *Witt without Money*
being the first Play acted after the Fire

So shipwrack't Passengers escape to Land,
So look they, when on the bare Beach they stand,
Dropping and cold; and their first fear scarce o're,
Expecting Famine on a Desart Shore;
From that hard Climate, we must wait for Bread,   5
Whence even the Natives forc't by hunger fled.
Our Stage does humane chance present to view,
But ne're before was seen so sadly true,
You are chang'd too, and your pretence to see
Is but a nobler name for charity.   10
Your own provisions furnish out our Feasts
While you the Founders make your selves the guests.
Of all mankind beside Fate had some care,
But for poor Wit no portion did prepare,
'Tis left a rent-charge to the brave and fair.   15
You cherish'd it, and now its fall you mourn,
Which blind unmanner'd *Zealots* make their scorn,
Who think that Fire a judgement on the Stage,
Which spar'd not *Temples* in its furious rage.
But as our new-built City rises higher,   20
So from old Theaters *may new aspire,*
Since Fate contrives magnificence by fire.
Our great *Metropolis*, does far surpass
What e're is now, and equals all that was:
Our wit as far, does Forreign wit excell;   25
And, like a King, should in a Palace dwell,
But we with golden hopes, are vainly fed,
Talk high, and entertain you in a Shed.
Your presence here (for which we humbly sue)
Will grace old Theatres, and build up new.   30

The Prologue to Witt without Money.   2 the *84 92: om. CGD WD*   4 on *84
92:* from *CGD WD*   10 for *84 92:* of *CGD WD*   12 While *84 92:* Whilst
CGD WD   the guests *84 92:* our guests *CGD WD*   13 beside *84 92:* besides
CGD WD   16 cherish'd *84 92 WD:* cherish *CGD*   18 that] the *CGDa WD*
23–30 *added in CGDb WD 84 92*   23 does far *84 92:* does so far *CGDb:* doth farr
WD   24 equals] equald *WD*   25 does] doth *WD*

Prologue to Albumazar

To say this Commedy pleas'd long ago,
  Is not enough, to make it pass you now:
Yet gentlemen, your Ancestors had witt,
When few men censurd, and when fewer writ.
And *Johnson* (of those few the best) chose this,   5
As the best modell of his master piece;
Subtle was got by our *Albumazar*,
That *Alchamist* by this Astrologer.
Here he was fashion'd, and we may suppose,
He lik'd the Fashion well, who wore the Cloaths.   10
But *Ben* made nobly his, what he did mould,
What was another's Lead, becomes his Gold;
Like an unrighteous Conquerer he raigns,
Yet rules that well, which he unjustly gains.
But this our age such Authors does afford,   15
As make whole Playes, and yet scarce write one word:
Who in this Anarchy of witt, rob all,
And what's their Plunder, their Possession call.
Who like bold Padders scorn by night to prey,
But Rob by Sun-shine, in the face of day;   20
Nay scarce the common Ceremony use,
Of stand, Sir, and deliver up your Muse;
But knock the Poet down; and, with a grace,
Mount *Pegasus* before the owners Face.
Faith if you have such Country *Toms*, abroad,   25
Tis time for all true men to leave that Road.
Yet it were modest, could it but be sed,
They strip the living, but these rob the dead:
Dare with the Mummyes of the Muses Play,
And make love to 'em, the *Ægyptian*, way.   30
Or as a Rhyming Authour would have sed,
Joyn the dead living, to the living dead.

Prologue to Albumazar.   4 when *84 92:* om. *CGD*   6 As *84 92:* And *CGD*   9 we
may *84 92:* I should *CGD*   10 He . . . Cloaths *84 92:* He likes my fashion well,
that wears my Cloaths *CGD*   12 becomes *84 92:* became *CGD*   16 one
84 92: a *CGD*   21 Nay *84 92:* Who *CGD*   28 strip *84 92:* stript *CGD*   these *84
92:* they *CGD*   29 Dare *84 92:* 'Twill *CGD*   Mummyes *84 92:* mummey *CGD*

Such Men in Poetry may claim some part,
They have the Licence, though they want the Art,
And might, where Theft was prais'd, for Lawreats stand   35
Poets, not of the head, but of the hand;
They make the benefits of others studying,
Much like the meales of Politick *Jack Pudding*:
Whose dish to challenge, no Man has the courage,
'Tis all his own, when once h' has spit i'th' Porredge.   40
But Gentlemen, y'are all concernd in this,
You are in fault for what they do amiss:
For they their thefts still undiscover'd think,
And durst not steal unless you please to winck.
Perhaps, You may award by Your Decree,   45
They shou'd refund, but that can never be.
For should You Letters of reprizall seal,
These men write that, which no man else would steale.

Prologue to Iulius Cæsar

IN Country Beauties as we often see,
Something that takes in their simplicity;
Yet while they charm, they know not they are fair,
And take without the spreading of the snare;
Such Artless beauty lies in *Shakespears* wit,   5
'Twas well in spight of him what ere he writ.
His Excellencies came and were not sought,
His words like casual Atoms made a thought:
Drew up themselves in Rank and File, and writ,
He wondring how the Devil it was such wit.   10
Thus like the drunken Tinker, in his Play,
He grew a Prince, and never knew which way.
He did not know what trope or Figure meant,
But to perswade is to be eloquent,

---

33 Such Men *84 92*: Yet such *CGD*   35 And ... stand *84 92*: Such as in *Sparta* weight for Laurels stand, *CGDa*: Such ... might ... stand *CGDb*   37 the benefits *84 92*: their benefit *CGD*   39 Whose ... Man *84 92*: Where Broth to claim, there's no one *CGD*   40 when once h'has *84 92*: after he has *CGD*   43 still *84 92*: will *CGD*   *45–46 added in 84 92*   47 For sbould You *84 92*: Now should we *CGD*

Prologue.   4 the *CGDb*: their *CGDa*   10 was *CGDb*: were *CGDa*

So in this *Cæsar* which to day you see,   15
  Tully ne'r spoke as he makes *Anthony*.
Those then that tax his Learning are to blame,
He knew the thing, but did not know the Name:
Great *Iohnson* did that Ignorance adore,
And though he envi'd much, admir'd him more;   20
The faultless *Iohnson* equally writ well,
Shakespear made faults; but then did more excel.
One close at Guard like some old Fencer lay,
T'other more open, but he shew'd more play.
In Imitation *Iohnsons* wit was shown,   25
Heaven made his men; but *Shakespear* made his own.
Wise *Iohnson*'s talent in observing lay,
But others follies still made up his play.
He drew the life in each elaborate line,
But *Shakespear* like a Master did design.   30
Iohnson with skill dissected humane kind,
And show'd their faults that they their faults might find:
But then as all Anatomists must do,
He to the meanest of mankind did go,
And took from Gibbets such as he would show.   35
Both are so great that he must boldly dare,
Who both of 'em does judge and both compare.
If amongst Poets one more bold there be,
The man that dare attempt in either way, is he.

15 to *CGDb*: this *CGDa*   29 life] like *CGD*

PROLOGUE, EPILOGUE and SONGS
from *MARRIAGE A-LA-MODE*

PROLOGUE

LORD, how reform'd and quiet we are grown,
  Since all our Braves and all our Wits are gone:
Fop-corner now is free from Civil War:
White-Wig and Vizard make no longer jar.
France, and the Fleet, have swept the Town so clear,   5
That we can Act in peace, and you can hear.
'Twas a sad sight, before they march'd from home,
To see our Warriours, in Red Wastecoats, come,
With hair tuck'd up, into our Tireing-room.
But 'twas more sad to hear their last Adieu,   10
The Women sob'd, and swore they would be true;
And so they were, as long as e're they cou'd:
But powerful *Guinnee* cannot be withstood,
And they were made of Play house flesh and bloud.
Fate did their Friends for double use ordain,   15
In Wars abroad, they grinning Honour gain,
And Mistresses, for all that stay, maintain.
Now they are gone, 'tis dead Vacation here,
For neither Friends nor Enemies appear.
Poor pensive Punk now peeps ere Plays begin,   20
Sees the bare Bench, and dares not venture in:
But manages her last Half-crown with care,
And trudges to the *Mall*, on foot, for Air.
Our City Friends so far will hardly come,
They can take up with Pleasures nearer home;   25
And see gay Shows, and gawdy Scenes elsewhere:
For we presume they seldom come to hear.
But they have now ta'n up a glorious Trade,
And cutting *Moorcraft*, struts in Masquerade.
There's all our hope, for we shall show to day,   30
A Masquing Ball, to recommend our Play:

Prologue, Epilogue and Songs. Text from Marriage a-la-Mode. A Comedy, *1673*

Nay, to endear 'em more, and let 'em see,
We scorn to come behind in Courtesie,
We'll follow the new Mode which they begin,
And treat 'em with a Room, and Couch within: 35
For that's one way, how e're the Play fall short,
T' oblige the Town, the City, and the Court.

EPILOGUE

THUS have my Spouse and I inform'd the Nation,
And led you all the way to Reformation.
Not with dull Morals, gravely writ, like those,
Which men of easie Phlegme, with care compose.
Your Poet's of stiff words, and limber sense,   5
Born on the confines of indifference.
But by examples drawn, I dare to say,
From most of you, who hear, and see the Play.
There are more *Rhodophils* in this Theatre,
More *Palamedes*, and some few Wives, I fear.   10
But yet too far our Poet would not run,
Though 'twas well offer'd, there was nothing done.
He would not quite the Woman's frailty bare,
But stript 'em to the waste, and left 'em there.
And the men's faults are less severely shown,   15
For he considers that himself is one.
Some stabbing Wits, to bloudy Satyr bent,
Would treat both Sexes with less complement:
Would lay the Scene at home, of Husbands tell,
For Wenches, taking up their Wives i'th' *Mell*,   20
And a brisk bout which each of them did want,
Made by mistake of Mistris and Gallant.
Our modest Authour, thought it was enough
To cut you off a Sample of the stuff:
He spar'd my shame, which you, I'm sure, would not,   25
For you were all for driving on the Plot:
You sigh'd when I came in to break the sport,
And set your teeth when each design fell short.
To Wives, and Servants all good wishes lend,
But the poor Cuckold seldom finds a friend.   30

Since therefore Court and Town will take no pity,
I humbly cast my self upon the City.

SONGS

I

1

WHY should a foolish Marriage Vow
    Which long ago was made,
Oblige us to each other now
    When Passion is decay'd?
We lov'd, and we lov'd, as long as we cou'd,   5
    Till our love was lov'd out in us both:
But our Marriage is dead, when the Pleasure is fled:
    'Twas Pleasure first made it an Oath.

2

If I have Pleasures for a Friend,
    And farther love in store,   10
What wrong has he whose joys did end,
    And who cou'd give no more?

'Tis a madness that he
Should be jealous of me,
Or that I shou'd bar him of another: 15
For all we can gain,
Is to give our selves pain,
When neither can hinder the other.

II

SONG

1

WHIL'ST *Alexis* lay prest
In her Arms he lov'd best,
With his hands round her neck,
And his head on her breast,

He found the fierce pleasure too hasty to stay,   5
And his soul in the tempest just flying away.

2

When *Cœlia* saw this,
With a sigh, and a kiss,
She cry'd, Oh my dear, I am robb'd of my bliss;
'Tis unkind to your Love, and unfaithfully done,   10
To leave me behind you, and die all alone.

3

The Youth, though in haste,
And breathing his last,
In pity dy'd slowly, while she dy'd more fast;
Till at length she cry'd, Now, my dear, now let us go,   15
Now die, my *Alexis*, and I will die too.

4

Thus intranc'd they did lie,
Till *Alexis* did try
To recover new breath, that again he might die:
Then often they di'd; but the more they did so,   20
The Nymph di'd more quick, and the Shepherd more slow.

PROLOGUE, EPILOGUE and SONG
from *THE ASSIGNATION*

PROLOGUE

*P*ROLOGUES, like Bells to Churches, toul you in
    With Chimeing Verse; till the dull Playes begin:
With this sad difference though, of Pit and Pue;
You damn the *Poet*, but the *Priest* damns you.
But Priests can treat you at your own expence: 5
And, gravely, call you Fooles, without offence.
Poets, poor Devils, have ne'r your Folly shown
But, to their cost, you prov'd it was their own.
For, when a Fop's presented on the Stage,
Straight all the Coxcombs in the Town ingage: 10
For his deliverance, and revenge they joyn:
And grunt, like Hogs, about their Captive Swine.
Your Poets daily split upon this shelfe:
You must have Fooles, yet none will have himself.
Or, if in kindness, you that leave would give,   15
No man could write you at that rate you live:
For some of you grow Fops with so much haste,   )
Riot in nonsence, and commit such waste,   }
'Twould Ruine Poets should they spend so fast.)
He who made this, observ'd what Farces hit,   20
And durst not disoblige you now with wit.
But, Gentlemen, you overdo the Mode:
You must have Fooles out of the common Rode.
Th' unnatural strain'd Buffoon is onely taking:
No Fop can please you now of Gods own making.   25
Pardon our Poet if he speaks his Mind,
You come to Plays with your own Follies lin'd:
Small Fooles fall on you, like small showers, in vain:
Your own oyl'd Coates keep out all common raine.
You must have Mamamouchi, such a Fop   30
As would appear a Monster in a Shop:

Prologue, Epilogue and Song. Text from The Assignation: or, Love in a Nunnery, *1673*

Hee'l fill your Pit and Boxes to the brim,
Where, Ram'd in Crowds, you see your selves in him.
Sure there's some spell our Poet never knew,
In hullibabilah da, and Chu, chu, chu.   35
But Marabarah sahem most did touch you,
That is: Oh how we love the Mamamouchi!
Grimace and habit sent you pleas'd away:
You damn'd the Poet, and cry'd up the Play.

  This thought had made our Author more uneasie,   40
But that he hopes I'm Fool enough to please ye:
But here's my griefe; though Nature joyn'd with art,
Have cut me out to act a Fooling Part;
Yet, to your praise, the few wits here will say,
'Twas imitating you taught *Haynes* to Play.   45

EPILOGUE

SOME have expected from our Bills to day
To find a *Satyre* in our *Poet*'s *Play*.
The *Zealous Rout* from *Coleman-street* did run,
To see the Story of the *Fryer* and *Nun*.
Or Tales, yet more Ridiculous to hear,   5
Vouch'd by their Vicar of Ten pounds a year;
Of Nuns, who did against Temptation Pray,
And Discipline laid on the Pleasant way:
Or that to please the Malice of the Town,
Our *Poet* should in some close Cell have shown   ⎫
Some Sister, Playing at Content alone: ⎬ 10
This they did hope; the other side did fear,   ⎭
And both you see alike are Couzen'd here.
Some thought the Title of our Play to blame,
They lik'd the thing, but yet abhor'd the Name: 15
Like Modest *Puncks*, who all you ask afford,
But, for the *World*, they would not name that word.
Yet, if you'll credit what I heard him say,
Our *Poet* meant no Scandal in his *Play*;
His Nuns are good which on the Stage are shown,   20
And, sure, behind our *Scenes* you'll look for none.

SONG and DANCE

LONG betwixt Love and fear *Phillis* tormented,
Shun'd her own wish yet at last she consented:
But loath that day shou'd her blushes discover,
    Come gentle Night She said,
    Come quickly to my aid,   5
    And a poor Shamefac'd Maid
    Hide from her Lover.

Now cold as Ice I am, now hot as Fire,
I dare not tell my self my own desire;
But let Day fly away, and let Night hast her: 10
    Grant yee kind Powers above,
    Slow houres to parting Love,
    But when to Bliss we move,
    Bid 'em fly faster.

How sweet it is to Love when I discover,   15
That Fire which burns my Heart, warming my Lover;
'Tis pitty Love so true should be mistaken:
    But if this Night he be
    False or unkinde to me,
    Let me dye ere I see   20
    That I'me forsaken.

PROLOGUE, EPILOGUE and SONGS
from *AMBOYNA*

PROLOGUE To AMBOYNA

As needy Gallants in the Scriv'ners hands,
  Court the rich Knave that gripes their Mortgag'd Lands,
The first fat Buck of all the Season's sent
And Keeper takes no Fee in Complement:

Prologue, Epilogue and Songs. Text from Amboyna: A Tragedy, 1673; *collated with the edition of 1691 and the transcript in* Bodl. MS. Don. B. 8, pp. 463–4

The doteage of some *Englishmen* is such   5
To fawn on those who ruine them; the *Dutch*.
They shall have all rather then make a War
With those who of the same Religion are.
The *Streights*, the *Guiney* Trade, the Herrings too,
Nay, to keep friendship, they shall pickle you: 10
Some are resolv'd not to find out the Cheat,
But Cuckold like, love him who does the Feat:
What injuries soe'r upon us fall,
Yet still the same Religion answers all:
Religion wheedled you to Civil War,   15
Drew *English* Blood, and *Dutchmens* now wou'd spare:
Be gull'd no longer, for you'l find it true,
They have no more Religion, faith—then you;
Interest's the God they worship in their State,
And you, I take it, have not much of that.   20
Well Monarchys may own Religions name,
But States are Atheists in their very frame.
They share a sin, and such proportions fall
That like a stink, 'tis nothing to 'em all.
How they love *England*, you shall see this day: 25
No Map shews *Holland* truer then our Play:
Their Pictures and Inscriptions well we know;
We may be bold one Medal sure to show.
View then their Falshoods, Rapine, Cruelty;
And think what once they were, they still would be: 30
But hope not either Language, Plot, or Art,
'Twas writ in haste, but with an *English* Heart:
And lest Hope, Wit; in *Dutchmen* that would be
As much improper as would Honesty.

Prologue.   12 love *MS*: loves *73 91*   16 *Additional couplet follows in MS:*
    One would haue thought, you should haue growne more wise,
    Then to be caught with ye same bargaine twice.
19–20 *om. in MS*

EPILOGUE

A POET once the *Spartans* led to fight,
And made 'em Conquer in the Muses right:
So wou'd our Poet lead you on this day:
Showing your tortur'd Fathers in his Play.
To one well born, th' affront is worse and more,   5
When he's abus'd, and baffled by a Bore:
With an ill Grace the *Dutch* their mischiefs do,
They've both ill Nature and ill Manners too.
Well may they boast themselves an antient Nation,
For they were bred e're Manners, were in fashion: 10
And their new Common-wealth has set 'em free,
Onely from Honour and Civility.
Venetians do not more uncouthly ride,
Than did their Lubber-State Mankind bestride.
Their sway became 'em with as ill a Meen,   15
As their own Paunches swell above their Chin:
Yet is their Empire no true Growth but Humour,
And onely two Kings Touch can cure the Tumor.
As *Cato* did his *Affricque* Fruits display:
So we before your Eies their *Indies* lay: 20
All Loyal *English* will like him conclude,
Let *Cæsar* Live, and *Carthage* be subdu'd.

SONGS

I

Epithalamium

THE day is come, I see it rise,
Betwixt the Bride's and Bridegroom's Eyes,
That Golden day they wish'd so long,
Love pick'd it out amidst the throng;
He destin'd to himself this Sun,   5
And took the Reins and drove him on;
In his own Beams he drest him bright,
Yet bid him bring a better night.

The day you wish'd arriv'd at last,
You wish as much that it were past,   10
One Minute more and night will hide,
The Bridegroom and the blushing Bride.
The Virgin now to Bed do's goe:
Take care oh Youth, she rise not soe;
She pants and trembles at her doom,   15
And fears and wishes thou wou'dst come.

The Bridegroom comes, He comes apace
With Love and Fury in his Face;
She shrinks away, He close pursues,
And Prayers and Threats, at once do's use,   20
She softly sighing begs delay,
And with her hand puts his away,
Now out a loud for help she cryes,
And now despairing shuts her Eyes.

II

The Sea Fight

Who ever saw a noble sight,
That never view'd a brave Sea Fight:
Hang up your bloody Colours in the Aire,
Up with your Fights and your Nettings prepare,
Your Merry Mates chear, with a lusty bold spright,   5
Now each Man his brindice, and then to the Fight,
St. George, St. George we cry,
The shouting *Turks* reply.
Oh now it begins, and the Gunroom grows hot,
Plie it with Culverin and with small shot;   10
Heark do's it not Thunder, no 'tis the Guns roar,
The Neighbouring Billows are turn'd into Gore,
Now each man must resolve to dye,
For here the Coward cannot flye.
Drums and Trumpets toll the Knell,   15
And Culverins the Passing Bell.
Now now they Grapple, and now board a Main,
Blow up the Hatches, they're off all again:

Epithalamium. 22 puts 91: put 73

Give 'em a broadside, the Dice run at all,
Down comes the Mast and Yard, and tacklings fall,   20
She grows giddy now like blind fortunes wheel,
She sinks there, she sinks, she turns up her Keel.
Who ever beheld so noble a sight
As this so brave, so bloody Sea Fight.

TO THE Lady *CASTLEMAIN*,
UPON *Her incouraging his first Play*

As Sea-men shipwrackt on some happy shore,
    Discover Wealth in Lands unknown before;
And what their Art had labour'd long in vain,
By their misfortunes happily obtain:
So my much-envy'd Muse by Storms long tost,   5
Is thrown upon your Hospitable Coast;
And finds more favour by her ill success,
Than she could hope for by her happiness.
Once *Cato*'s Vertue did the Gods oppose,
While they the Victor, he the Vanquish'd chose: 10
But you have done what *Cato* could not do,
To chuse the Vanquish'd, and restore him too.
Let others still triumph, and gain their cause
By their deserts, or by the Worlds applause;
Let Merit Crowns, and Justice Laurels give,   15
But let me Happy by your Pity live.
True Poets empty Fame, and Praise despise;
Fame is the Trumpet, but your Smile the Prize.
You sit above, and see vain men below
Contend for what you only can bestow: 20
But those great Actions others do by chance,
Are, like your Beauty, your Inheritance.
So great a Soul, such sweetness joyn'd in One,
Could only spring from Noble *Grandison*;
You, like the Stars, not by reflexion bright,   25

To the Lady Castlemain. Text from A New Collection of Poems and Songs. . . . Collected
by John Bulteel, *1674, collated with* Examen Poeticum, *1693*
Heading To the Lady Castlemain . . . 93: To the Dutchess of *Cleaveland* 74   3 long
93: for 74   6 thrown 93: cast 74   9 Vertue 93: Virtues 74   10 While
93: When 74   17 Fame, and Praise 93: Praise and Fame 74   18 Smile 93:
Smiles 74

Are born to your own Heav'n, and your own Light:
Like them are good, but from a Nobler Cause,
From your own Knowledg, not from Natures Laws.
Your pow'r you never use, but for Defence,
To guard your own, or others Innocence.   30
Your Foes are such as they, not you, have made;
And Virtue may repel, though not invade.
Such courage did the Ancient *Hero's* show,
Who, when they might prevent, wou'd wait the blow:
With such assurance, as they meant to say,   35
We will o'recome, but scorn the safest way.

    Well may I rest secure in your great Fate,
And dare my Stars to be unfortunate.
What further fear of danger can there be?
Beauty, which captives all things, sets me free.   40
Posterity will judge by my success,
I had the *Grecian* Poets happiness,
Who waving Plots, found out a better way;
Some God descended and preserv'd the Play.

    When first the Triumphs of your Sex were sung   45
By those old Poets, Beauty was but young;
And few admir'd the native red and white,
Till Poets drest them up to charm the sight.
So Beauty took on trust, and did engage
For sums of praises, till she came to age: 50
But this long growing Debt to Poesie,
You justly (Madam) have discharg'd to me,
When your applause and favour did infuse
New life to my condemn'd and dying Muse;
Which, that the World as well as you may see,   55
Let these rude Verses your Acquittance be.

    Receiv'd in full this present day and year,
    One soveraign smile from Beauties general Heir.

29 never use, but for *93*: use but for your own *74*   34 wou'd wait *93*: did
wait *74*   35 such *93*: that *74*   37-38 Well . . . unfortunate. *om. 93*
40 which *93*: that *74*   41 will *93*: would *74*   47 the *93*: her *74*   48
them *93*: her *74*   50 to *93*: of *74*. *Cf.* Astræa Redux, *l.* 28   51 this long
growing *93*: this vast growing *74*   to *93*: of *74*   52 You justly (Madam)
93: You, Madam, justly *74*   55-58 *om. 93*

PROLOGUE and EPILOGUE
to *AURENG-ZEBE*

PROLOGUE

OUR Author by experience finds it true,
'Tis much more hard to please himself than you:
And out of no feign'd modesty, this day,
Damns his laborious Trifle of a Play:
Not that its worse than what before he writ,   5
But he has now another taste of Wit;
And to confess a truth, (though out of time)
Grows weary of his long-lov'd Mistris, Rhyme.
Passion's too fierce to be in Fetters bound,
And Nature flies him like Enchanted Ground.   10
What Verse can do, he has perform'd in this,
Which he presumes the most correct of his:
But spite of all his pride a secret shame,
Invades his breast at *Shakespear*'s sacred name:
Aw'd when he hears his Godlike *Romans* rage,   15
He, in a just despair, would quit the Stage.
And to an Age less polish'd, more unskill'd,
Does, with disdain the foremost Honours yield.
As with the greater Dead he dares not strive,
He wou'd not match his Verse with those who live: 20
Let him retire, betwixt two Ages cast,
The first of this, and hindmost of the last.
A losing Gamester, let him sneak away;
He bears no ready Money from the Play.
The Fate which governs Poets, thought it fit,   25
He shou'd not raise his Fortunes by his Wit.
The Clergy thrive, and the litigious Bar;
Dull Heroes fatten with the spoils of War:
All Southern Vices, Heav'n be prais'd, are here;
But Wit's a luxury you think too dear.   30
When you to cultivate the Plant are loath,

Prologue and Epilogue. Text from Aureng-Zebe: A Tragedy, *1676*

'Tis a shrewd sign 'twas never of your growth:
And Wit in Northern Climates will not blow,
Except, like *Orange-trees*, 'tis hous'd from Snow.
There needs no care to put a Play-house down,   35
'Tis the most desart place of all the Town.
We and our Neighbours, to speak proudly, are
Like Monarchs, ruin'd with expensive War.
While, like wise *English*, unconcern'd, you sit,
And see us play the Tragedy of Wit.   40

EPILOGUE

A PRETTY task! and so I told the Fool,
   Who needs would undertake to please by Rule:
He thought that, if his Characters were good,
The Scenes entire, and freed from noise and bloud;
The Action great, yet circumscrib'd by Time,   5
The Words not forc'd, but sliding into Rhime,
The Passions rais'd and calm'd by just Degrees,
As Tides are swell'd, and then retire to Seas;
He thought, in hitting these, his bus'ness done,
Though he, perhaps, has fail'd in ev'ry one: 10
But, after all, a Poet must confess,
His Art's like Physick, but a happy ghess.
Your Pleasure on your Fancy must depend:
The Lady's pleas'd, just as she likes her Friend.
No Song! no Dance! no Show! he fears you'l say,   15
You love all naked Beauties, but a Play.
He much mistakes your methods to delight;
And, like the French, abhors our Target-fight:
But those damn'd Dogs can never be i'th' right.
True English hate your Monsieur's paltry Arts;   20
For you are all Silk-weavers, in your hearts.
Bold Brittons, at a brave Bear-garden Fray,
Are rouz'd: and, clatt'ring Sticks, cry, *Play, play, play*.
Mean time, your filthy Forreigner will stare,
And mutter to himself, *Ha gens Barbare!*   25
And, Gad, 'tis well he mutters; well for him;
Our Butchers else would tear him limb from limb.

'Tis true, the time may come, your Sons may be
Infected with this French civility;
But this in. After-ages will be done: 30
Our Poet writes a hundred years too soon.
This Age comes on too slow, or he too fast:
And early Springs are subject to a blast!
Who would excel, when few can make a Test
Betwixt indiff'rent Writing and the best?   35
For Favours cheap and common, who wou'd strive,
Which, like abandon'd Prostitutes, you give?
Yet scatter'd here and there I some behold,
Who can discern the Tinsel from the Gold:
To these he writes; and, if by them allow'd,   40
'Tis their Prerogative to rule the Crowd.
For he more fears (like a presuming Man)
Their Votes who cannot judge, than theirs who can.

EPILOGUE to *THE MAN OF MODE*

Most Modern Wits, such monstrous Fools have shown,
    They seem'd not of heav'ns making but their own.
Those Nauseous Harlequins in Farce may pass,
But there goes more to a substantial Ass!
Something of man must be expos'd to View,   5
That, Gallants, it may more resemble you:
Sir *Fopling* is a Fool so nicely writ,
The Ladies wou'd mistake him for a Wit,
And when he sings, talks lowd, and cocks; wou'd cry,
I now methinks he's pretty Company,   10
So brisk, so gay, so travail'd, so refin'd!
As he took pains to graff upon his kind.
True Fops help Natures work, and go to school,
To file and finish god-a'mighty's fool.
Yet none Sir *Fopling* him, or him can call;   15
He's Knight o'th' Shire, and represents ye all.
From each he meets, he culls what e're he can,

Epilogue. Text from Etherege's The Man of Mode, or, Sᵣ Fopling Flutter. A Comedy, *1676, collated with the editions of 1684 and 1693 and the transcript in Bodl. MS. Don. B. 8, pp. 558–9*
6 it *MS*: they *76 84 93*

Sir *Fopling* is a Fool so nicely writ,
The Ladies wou'd mistake him for a Wit,
And when he sings, talks lowd, and cocks; wou'd cry,
I now methinks he's pretty Company,   10
So brisk, so gay, so travail'd, so refin'd!
As he took pains to graff upon his kind.
True Fops help Natures work, and go to school,
To file and finish god-a'mighty's fool.
Yet none Sir *Fopling* him, or him can call;   15
He's Knight o'th' Shire, and represents ye all.
From each he meets, he culls what e're he can,
Legion's his name, a people in a Man.
His bulky folly gathers as it goes,
And, rolling o're you, like a Snow-ball growes. 20
His various modes from various Fathers follow,
One taught the Toss, and one the new *French* Wallow.
His Sword-knot, this; his Crevat, this design'd,
And this, the yard long Snake he twirls behind.
From one the sacred Perriwig he gain'd,   25
Which Wind ne're blew, nor touch of Hat prophan'd.
Anothers diving Bow he did adore,
Which with a shog casts all the hair before:
Till he with full Decorum brings it back,
And rises with a Water Spaniel shake.   30
As for his Songs (the Ladies dear delight)
Those sure he took from most of you who Write.
Yet every man is safe from what he fear'd,
For no one fool is hunted from the herd.

10 I now] I vow *76 84 93*: I, now *MS* 14 *Additional lines follow in MS*:
  Labour, to put in more, as Master Bayes
  Thrumms in Additions to his ten-yeares playes

PROLOGUE *to CIRCE,* A *Tragedy*

(A) THE PROLOGUE

WERE you but half so wise as you're severe,
  Our youthful Poet shou'd not need to fear;
To his green years your Censures you wou'd suit,
Not blast the Blossom, but expect the Fruit.
The Sex that best does pleasure understand,
Will always chuse to err on t'other hand.
They check not him that's Aukward in delight,
But clap the young Rogues Cheek, and set him right.
Thus heartn'd well, and flesh't upon his Prey,
The youth may prove a man another day;   10
For your own sakes, instruct him when he's out,
You'l find him mend his work at every bout.
When some young lusty Thief is passing by,
How many of your tender Kind will cry,
A proper Fellow, pity he shou'd dye.   15
He might be sav'd, and thank us for our pains,
There's such a stock of Love within his Veins.
These Arguments the Women may perswade,
But move not you, the Brothers of the Trade,
Who scattering your Infection through the Pit,   20
With aking hearts and empty Purses sit,
To take your dear Five Shillings worth of Wit.
The praise you give him in your kindest mood,
Comes dribling from you, just like drops of blood;
And then you clap so civilly, for fear   25
The loudness might offend your Neighbours ear;
That we suspect your Gloves are lin'd within,
For silence sake, and Cotten'd next the skin.
From these Usurpers we appeal to you,
The only knowing, only judging few;   30
You who in private have this Play allow'd,
Ought to maintain your Suffrage to the Crowd.
The Captive once submitted to your Bands,
You shou'd protect from Death by Vulgar hands.

Prologue. Version (A): text from Charles D'Avenant's Circe, A Tragedy, *1677. Version (B):*
text from Miscellany Poems, *1684*

(B) An EPILOGUE

WERE you but half so Wise as y'are Severe,
Our youthful Poet shou'd not need to fear:
To his green Years your Censures you would suit,
Not blast the Blossom, but expect the Fruit.
The Sex that best does pleasure understand,   5
Will always chuse to err on t'other hand.
They check not him that's awkard in delight,
But Clap the young Rogues Cheek, and set him right.
Thus heart'nd well and flesh'd upon his prey,
The Youth may prove a Man another day.   10
Your *Ben* and *Fletcher* in their first young flight
Did no *Volpone*, no *Arbaces* write.
But hopp'd about, and short excursions made
From Bough to Bough, as if they were afraid,
And each were guilty of some *slighted Maid*.   } 15
Shakespear's own Muse her *Pericles* first bore,
The Prince of *Tyre* was elder than the *Moore*:
'Tis miracle to see a first good Play,
All Hawthorns do not bloom on *Christmas-day*.
A slender Poet must have time to grow,   20
And spread and burnish as his Brothers do.
Who still looks lean, sure with some Pox is curst,
But no Man can be *Falstaff* fat at first.
Then damn not, but indulge his stew'd essays,
Encourage him, and bloat him up with praise,   25
That he may get more bulk before he dyes;
He's not yet fed enough for Sacrifice.
Perhaps if now your Grace you will not grudge,
He may grow up to Write, and you to Judge.

To Mr. *Lee*, on his *Alexander*

THE Blast of common Censure cou'd I fear,
    Before your Play my Name shou'd not appear;
For 'twill be thought, and with some colour too,
I pay the Bribe I first receiv'd from You:

To Mr. Lee. Text from The Rival Queens, or The Death of Alexander the Great, *1677*

That mutual Vouchers for our Fame we stand,   5
To play the Game into each others Hand;
And as cheap Pen'orths to our selves afford
As *Bessus*, and the Brothers of the Sword.
Such Libels private Men may well endure,
When States, and Kings themselves are not secure: 10
For ill Men, conscious of their inward guilt,
Think the best Actions on By-ends are built.
And yet my silence had not scap'd their spight,
Then envy had not suffer'd me to write:
For, since I cou'd not Ignorance pretend,   15
Such worth I must or envy or commend.
So many Candidates there stand for Wit,
A place in Court is scarce so hard to get;
In vain they croud each other at the Door;
For ev'n Reversions are all beg'd before: 20
Desert, how known so e're, is long delay'd;
And, then too, Fools and Knaves are better pay'd.
Yet, as some Actions bear so great a Name,
That Courts themselves are just, for fear of shame:
So has the mighty Merit of your Play   25
Extorted praise, and forc'd it self a Way.
'Tis here, as 'tis at Sea; who farthest goes,
Or dares the most, makes all the rest his Foes;
Yet, when some Virtue much out-grows the rest,
It shoots too fast, and high, to be opprest;   30
As his Heroic worth struck Envy dumb
Who took the *Dutchman*, and who cut the Boom:
Such praise is yours, while you the Passions move,
That 'tis no longer feign'd; 'tis real Love:
Where Nature Triumphs over wretched Art;   35
We only warm the Head, but you the Heart.
Always you warm! and if the rising Year,
As in hot Regions, bring the Sun too near,
Tis but to make your Fragrant Spices blow,
Which in our colder Climates will not grow.   40
They only think you animate your Theme
With too much Fire, who are themselves all Phle'me:
Prizes wou'd be for Lags of slowest pace,
Were Cripples made the Judges of the Race.

Despise those Drones, who praise while they accuse   45
The too much vigour of your youthful Muse:
That humble Stile which they their Virtue make
Is in your pow'r; you need but stoop and take.
Your beauteous Images must be allow'd
By all, but some vile Poets of the Crowd;   50
But how shou'd any Sign-post-dawber know
The worth of *Titian*, or of *Angelo*?
Hard Features every Bungler can command;
To draw true Beauty shews a Masters Hand.

EPILOGUE to
MITHRIDATES KING OF PONTUS

YO'VE seen a Pair of faithful Lovers die:
   And much you care; for, most of you will cry,
'Twas a just Judgment on their Constancy.
For, Heav'n be thank'd, we live in such an Age
When no man dies for Love, but on the Stage: 5
And ev'n those Martyrs are but rare in Plays;
A cursed sign how much true Faith decays.
Love is no more a violent desire;
'Tis a meer Metaphor, a painted Fire.
In all our Sex, the name examin'd well,   10
Is Pride, to gain; and Vanity to tell:
In Woman, 'tis of subtil int'rest made,
Curse on the Punk that made it first a Trade!
She first did Wits Prerogative remove,
And made a Fool presume to prate of Love.   15
Let Honour and Preferment go for Gold;
But glorious Beauty is not to be sold:
Or, if it be, 'tis at a rate so high,
That nothing but adoring it shou'd buy.
Yet the rich Cullies may their boasting spare;   20
They purchase but sophisticated Ware.
'Tis Prodigality that buys deceit;

Epilogue. Text from Mithridates King of Pontus, A Tragedy, *1678*

Where both the Giver, and the Taker cheat.
Men but refine on the old Half-Crown way:
And Women fight, like *Swizzers*, for their Pay.   25

PROLOGUE and EPILOGUE
to *ALL FOR LOVE*

PROLOGUE to Anthony *and* Cleopatra

WHAT Flocks of Critiques hover here to day,
   As Vultures wait on Armies for their Prey,
All gaping for the Carcass of a Play!
With Croaking Notes they bode some dire event;
And follow dying Poets by the scent.   5
Ours gives himself for gone; y'have watch'd your time!
He fights this day unarm'd; without his Rhyme.
And brings a Tale which often has been told;
As sad as *Dido*'s; and almost as old.
His Heroe, whom you Wits his Bully call,   10
Bates of his mettle; and scarce rants at all:
He's somewhat lewd; but a well-meaning mind;
Weeps much; fights little; but is wond'rous kind.
In short, a Pattern, and Companion fit,
For all the keeping Tonyes of the Pit.   15
I cou'd name more: A Wife, and Mistress too;
Both (to be plain) too good for most of you:
The Wife well-natur'd, and the Mistress true.
   Now, Poets, if your fame has been his care;
Allow him all the candour you can spare.   20
A brave Man scorns to quarrel once a day;
Like Hectors, in at every petty fray.
Let those find fault whose Wit's so very small,
They've need to show that they can think at all:
Errours like Straws upon the surface flow;   25
He who would search for Pearls must dive below.
Fops may have leave to level all they can;

Prologue and Epilogue. Text from All for Love: or, The World well Lost. A Tragedy, *1678*.

As Pigmies wou'd be glad to lopp a Man.
Half-Wits are Fleas; so little and so light;
We scarce cou'd know they live, but that they bite.   30
But, as the Rich, when tir'd with daily Feasts,
For change, become their next poor Tenants Ghests;
Drink hearty Draughts of Ale, from plain brown Bowls,
And snatch the homely Rasher from the Coals:
So you, retiring from much better Cheer,   35
For once, may venture to do penance here.
And since that plenteous Autumn now is past,
Whose Grapes and Peaches have Indulg'd your taste,
Take in good part from our poor Poets boord,
Such rivell'd Fruits as Winter can afford.   40

EPILOGUE

POETS, like Disputants, when Reasons fail,
   Have one sure Refuge left; and that's to rail.
Fop, Coxcomb, Fool, are thunder'd through the Pit;
And this is all their Equipage of Wit.
We wonder how the Devil this diff'rence grows,   5
Betwixt our Fools in Verse, and yours in Prose:
For, 'Faith, the quarrel rightly understood,
'Tis *Civil War* with their own Flesh and Blood.
The thread-bare Author hates the gawdy Coat;
And swears at the Guilt Coach, but swears a foot: 10
For 'tis observ'd of every Scribling Man,
He grows a Fop as fast as e'er he can;
Prunes up, and asks his Oracle the Glass,
If Pink or Purple best become his face.
For our poor Wretch, he neither rails nor prays;   ⎫   15
Nor likes your Wit just as you like his Plays;   ⎬
He has not yet so much of Mr. *Bays*.   ⎭
He does his best; and, if he cannot please,
Wou'd quietly sue out his *Writ of Ease*.
Yet, if he might his own Grand Jury call,   20
By the Fair Sex he begs to stand or fall.
Let *Cæsar*'s Pow'r the Mens ambition move,
But grace You him who lost the World for Love.

Yet if some antiquated Lady say,
The last Age is not Copy'd in his Play;   25
Heav'n help the Man who for that face must drudge,
Which only has the wrinkles of a Judge.
Let not the Young and Beauteous join with those;
For shou'd you raise such numerous Hosts of Foes,
Young Wits and Sparks he to his aid must call;   30
'Tis more than one Man's work to please you all.

PROLOGUE to *A TRUE WIDOW*

HEAV'N save ye Gallants, and this hopeful Age,
Y'are welcome to the downfal of the Stage:
The Fools have labour'd long in their Vocation;
And Vice, (the Manufacture of the Nation)
O're-stocks the Town so much, and thrives so well,   5
That Fopps and Knaves grow Druggs, and will not sell.
In vain our Wares on Theaters are shown,
When each has a Plantation of his own.
His Cruse ne'r fails; for whatsoe're he spends,
There's still God's plenty for himself and friends.   10
Shou'd Men be rated by Poetick Rules,
Lord what a Poll would there be rais'd from Fools!
Mean time poor Wit prohibited must lye,
As if 'twere made some *French* Commodity.
Fools you will have, and rais'd at vast expence,   15
And yet as soon as seen, they give offence.
Time was, when none would cry, that Oaf was mee,
But now you strive about your Pedigree:
Bawble and Cap no sooner are thrown down,
But there's a Muss of more than half the Town.   20
Each one will challenge a Child's part at least,
A sign the Family is well increas'd.
Of Forreign Cattle! there's no longer need,
When w' are supply'd so fast with *English* Breed.
Well! Flourish, Countrymen: drink swear and roar,   25

Prologue. Text from Shadwell's A True Widow. A Comedy, *1679*

Let every free-born Subject keep his Whore;
And wandring in the Wilderness about,
At end of 40 years not wear her out.
But when you see these Pictures, let none dare
To own beyond a Limb, or single share: 30
For where the Punk is common! he's a Sot,
Who needs will Father what the Parish got.

PROLOGUE, EPILOGUE and SONGS
from *OEDIPUS*

PROLOGUE

WHEN *Athens* all the *Græcian* State did guide,
  And *Greece* gave Laws to all the World beside,
Then *Sophocles* with *Socrates* did sit,
Supreme in Wisdom one, and one in Wit:
And Wit from Wisdom differ'd not in those,   5
But as 'twas Sung in Verse, or said in Prose.
Then, *Oedipus*, on Crowded Theaters,
Drew all admiring Eyes and listning Ears;
The pleas'd Spectator shouted every Line,
The noblest, manliest, and the best Design!   10
And every Critick of each learned Age
By this just Model has reform'd the Stage.
Now, should it fail, (as Heav'n avert our fear!)
Damn it in silence, lest the World should hear.
For were it known this Poem did not please,   15
You might set up for perfect Salvages:
Your Neighbours would not look on you as men:
But think the Nation all turn'd *Picts* agen.
Faith, as you manage matters, 'tis not fit
You should suspect your selves of too much Wit.   20
Drive not the jeast too far, but spare this piece;

Prologue, Epilogue and Songs. Text from Oedipus: A Tragedy, *1679*

And, for this once, be not more Wise than *Greece*.
See twice! Do not pell-mell to Damning fall,
Like true born *Brittains*, who ne're think at all:
Pray be advis'd; and though at *Mons* you won,   25
On pointed Cannon do not always run.
With some respect to antient Wit proceed;
You take the four first Councils for your Creed.
But, when you lay Tradition wholly by,
And on the private Spirit alone relye,   } 30
You turn Fanaticks in your Poetry.
If, notwithstanding all that we can say,
You needs will have your pen'worths of the Play: }
And come resolv'd to Damn, because you pay,
   Record it, in memorial of the Fact,   35
   The first Play bury'd since the Wollen Act.

EPILOGUE

WHAT *Sophocles* could undertake alone,
   Our Poets found a Work for more than one;
And therefore Two lay tugging at the piece,
With all their force, to draw the pondrous Mass from *Greece*.
A weight that bent ev'n *Seneca*'s strong Muse,   5
And which *Corneille*'s Shoulders did refuse.
So hard it is th' *Athenian* Harp to string!
So much two Consuls yield to one just King.
Terrour and pity this whole Poem sway;
The mightiest Machines that can mount a Play;   10
How heavy will those Vulgar Souls be found,
Whom two such Engines cannot move from ground?
When *Greece* and *Rome* have smil'd upon this Birth,
You can but Damn for one poor spot of Earth;
And when your Children find your judgment such,   15
They'll scorn their Sires, and wish themselves born *Dutch*;
Each haughty Poet will infer with ease,
How much his Wit must under-write to please.
As some strong Churle would brandishing advance
The monumental Sword that conquer'd *France*;   20

So you, by judging this, your judgments teach
Thus far you like, that is, thus far you reach.
Since then the Vote of full two Thousand years
Has Crown'd this Plot, and all the Dead are theirs;
Think it a Debt you pay, not Alms you give,   25
And in your own defence, let this Play live.
Think 'em not vain, when *Sophocles* is shown,
To praise his worth, they humbly doubt their own.
Yet as weak States each others pow'r assure,
Weak Poets by Conjunction are secure.   30
Their Treat is what your Pallats rellish most,
Charm! Song! and Show! a Murder and a Ghost!
We know not what you can desire or hope,
To please you more, but burning of a *Pope*.

SONGS

I

SONG to Apollo

PHŒBUS, God belov'd by men;
At thy dawn, every Beast is rouz'd in his Den;
At thy setting, all the Birds of thy absence complain,
And we dye, all dye till the morning comes again,
          Phœbus, God belov'd by men!   5
          Idol of the Eastern Kings,
          Awful as the God who flings
          His Thunder round, and the Lightning wings;
          God of Songs, and *Orphean* strings,
          Who to this mortal bosom brings,   10
          All harmonious heav'nly things!
          Thy drouzie Prophet to revive,
Ten thousand thousand forms before him drive;
With Chariots and Horses all o' fire awake him,
Convulsions, and Furies, and Prophesies shake him: 15
Let him tell it in groans, tho' he bend with the load,
Tho' he burst with the weight of the terrible God.

II

Tir.   Chuse the darkest part o' th' Grove;
      Such as Ghosts at noon-day love.
      Dig a Trench, and dig it nigh
      Where the bones of *Lajus* lye.
      Altars rais'd of Turf or Stone,   5
      Will th' Infernal Pow'rs have none.
      Answer me, if this be done?
All Pr. 'Tis done.

Tir.   Is the Sacrifice made fit?   10
      Draw her backward to the pit:
      Draw the barren Heyfer back;
      Barren let her be and black.
      Cut the curled hair that grows
      Full betwixt her horns and brows:
      And turn your faces from the Sun: 15
      Answer me, if this be done?
All Pr. 'Tis done.

Tir.   Pour in blood, and blood like wine,
      To Mother Earth and *Proserpine*:   20
      Mingle Milk into the stream;
      Feast the Ghosts that love the steam;
      Snatch a brand from funeral pile;
      Toss it in to make 'em boil;
      And turn your faces from the Sun;
      Answer me, if all be done?   25
All Pr. All is done.

III

1. Hear, ye sullen Pow'rs below:
      Hear, ye taskers of the dead.
2. You that boiling Cauldrons blow,
      You that scum the molten Lead.
3. You that pinch with Red-hot Tongs;   5
1.   You that drive the trembling hosts
      Of poor, poor Ghosts,
    With your Sharpen'd Prongs;

2. You that thrust 'em off the Brim.

3. You that plunge 'em when they Swim: 10

1. Till they drown;

    Till they go

      On a row

Down, down, down

Ten thousand thousand, thousand fadoms low.   15

Chorus. Till they drown, *&c.*

1. Musick for a while

    Shall your cares beguile:

    Wondring how your pains were eas'd.

2. And disdaining to be pleas'd;   20

3. Till *Alecto* free the dead

    From their eternal bands;

    Till the snakes drop from her head,

      And whip from out her hands.

1. Come away   25

    Do not stay,

    But obey

    While we play,

For Hell 's broke up, and Ghosts have holy-day.

Chorus. Come away, *&c.*   30

[*A flash of Lightning: the Stage is made bright; and the Ghosts are seen passing betwixt the Trees.*

1 Lajus! 2 Lajus! 3 Lajus!

    1 Hear! 2 Hear! 3 Hear!

Tir. Hear and appear:

    By the Fates that spun thy thread;

Cho. Which are three,   35

Tir. By the Furies fierce, and dread!

Cho. Which are three,

Tir. By the Judges of the dead!

Cho. Which are three,

    Three times three!   40

Tir. By Hells blew flame:

    By the *Stygian* Lake:

And by *Demogorgon*'s name,

    At which Ghosts quake,

Hear and appear.   45

PROLOGUE, EPILOGUE and SONG
from *TROILUS and CRESSIDA*

THE PROLOGUE

Spoken by Mr. Betterton, *Representing the Ghost of* Shakespear

SEE, my lov'd *Britons*, see your *Shakespeare* rise,
An awfull ghost confess'd to human eyes!
Unnam'd, methinks, distinguish'd I had been
From other shades, by this eternal green,
About whose wreaths the vulgar Poets strive,   5
And with a touch, their wither'd Bays revive.
Untaught, unpractis'd, in a barbarous Age,
I found not, but created first the Stage.
And, if I drain'd no *Greek* or *Latin* store,
'Twas, that my own abundance gave me more.   10
On foreign trade I needed not rely
Like fruitfull *Britain*, rich without supply.
In this my rough-drawn Play, you shall behold
Some Master-strokes, so manly and so bold
That he, who meant to alter, found 'em such   15
He shook; and thought it Sacrilege to touch.
Now, where are the Successours to my name?
What bring they to fill out a Poets fame?
Weak, short-liv'd issues of a feeble Age;
Scarce living to be Christen'd on the Stage!   20
For Humour farce, for love they rhyme dispence,
That tolls the knell, for their departed sence.
Dulness might thrive in any trade but this:
'T wou'd recommend to some fat Benefice.
Dulness, that in a Playhouse meets disgrace   25
Might meet with Reverence, in its proper place.
The fulsome clench that nauseats the Town
Wou'd from a Judge or Alderman go down!
Such virtue is there in a Robe and gown!

Prologue, Epilogue and Song. Text from Troilus and Cressida, or, Truth Found too Late. A Tragedy, *1679*

And that insipid stuff which here you hate   30
Might somewhere else be call'd a grave debate:
Dulness is decent in the Church and State.
But I forget that still 'tis understood
Bad Plays are best decry'd by showing good:
Sit silent then, that my pleas'd Soul may see   35
A Judging Audience once, and worthy me:
My faithfull Scene from true Records shall tell
How *Trojan* valour did the *Greek* excell;
Your great forefathers shall their fame regain,
And *Homers* angry Ghost repine in vain.   40

THE EPILOGUE

Spoken by *Thersites*

THESE cruel Critiques put me into passion;
    For in their lowring looks I reade damnation:
Ye expect a Satyr, and I seldom fail,
When I'm first beaten, 'tis my part to rail.
You *British* fools, of the Old *Trojan* stock,   5
That stand so thick one cannot miss the flock,
Poets have cause to dread a keeping Pit,
When Womens Cullyes come to judge of Wit.
As we strow Rats-bane when we vermine fear,
'Twere worth our cost to scatter fool-bane here.   10
And after all our judging Fops were serv'd,
Dull Poets too shou'd have a dose reserv'd,
Such Reprobates, as past all sence of shaming
Write on, and nere are satisfy'd with damming,
Next, those, to whom the Stage does not belong,   15
Such whose Vocation onely is to Song;
At most to Prologue, when for want of time
Poets take in for Journywork in Rhime.
But I want curses for those mighty shoales,
Of scribling *Chlorisses*, and *Phillis* fools,   20
Those Ophs shou'd be restraind, during their lives,
From Pen and Ink, as Madmen are from knives:

I cou'd rayl on, but 'twere a task as vain
As Preaching truth at *Rome*, or wit in *Spain*,
Yet to huff out our Play was worth my trying,   25
John Lilbourn scap'd his Judges by defying:
If guilty, yet I'm sure oth' Churches blessing,
By suffering for the Plot, without confessing.

SONG

CAN life be a blessing,
Or worth the possessing,
Can life be a blessing if love were away?
Ah no! though our love all night keep us waking,
And though he torment us with cares all the day,   5
Yet he sweetens he sweetens our pains in the taking,
There's an hour at the last, there's an hour to repay.

2

In every possessing,
The ravishing blessing,
In every possessing the fruit of our pain,   10
Poor lovers forget long ages of anguish,
Whate're they have suffer'd and done to obtain;
'Tis a pleasure, a pleasure to sigh and to languish,
When we hope, when we hope to be happy again.

PROLOGUE, EPILOGUE and SONGS
from *THE KIND KEEPER*

PROLOGUE

TRUE Wit has seen its best days long ago,
It ne're look'd up, since we were dipt in Show:
When Sense in Dogrel Rhimes and Clouds was lost,
And Dulness flourish'd at the Actors cost.

Prologue, Epilogue and Songs. Text from The Kind Keeper; or, Mr. Limberham: A Comedy, *1680*

Nor stopt it here, when Tragedy was done,   5
Satyre and Humour the same Fate have run;
And Comedy is sunk to Trick and Pun.
Now our Machining Lumber will not sell,
And you no longer care for Heav'n or Hell;
What Stuff will please you next, the Lord can tell.   10
Let them, who the Rebellion first began,
To wit, restore the Monarch if they can;
Our Author dares not be the first bold Man.
He, like the prudent Citizen, takes care,
To keep for better Marts his Staple Ware,   15
His Toys are good enough for *Sturbridge* Fair.
Tricks were the Fashion; if it now be spent,
'Tis time enough at *Easter* to invent;
No Man will make up a new Suit for *Lent*:
If now and then he takes a small pretence   20
To forrage for a little Wit and Sense,
Pray pardon him, he meant you no offence.
Next Summer *Nostradamus* tells, they say,
That all the *Criticks* shall be shipt away,
And not enow be left to damn a Play.   25
To every Sayl beside, good Heav'n be kind;
But drive away that Swarm with such a Wind,
That not one *Locust* may be left behind.

EPILOGUE

Spoken by LIMBERHAM

I BEG a Boon, that e're you all disband,
Some one would take my Bargain off my hand;
To keep a Punk is but a common evil,
To find her false, and Marry, that's the Devil.
Well, I ne're Acted Part in all my life,   5
But still I was fobb'd off with some such Wife:
I find the Trick; these Poets take no pity
Of one that is a Member of the City.
We Cheat you lawfully, and in our Trades,
You Cheat us basely with your Common Jades.   10

Now I am Married, I must sit down by it;
But let me keep my Dear-bought Spouse in quiet:
Let none of you Damn'd *Woodalls* of the Pit,
Put in for Shares to mend our breed, in Wit;
We know your Bastards from our Flesh and Blood,   15
Not one in ten of yours e're comes to good.
In all the Boys their Fathers Vertues shine,
But all the Female Fry turn *Pugs* like mine.
When these grow up, Lord with what Rampant Gadders
Our Counters will be throng'd, and Roads with Padders.   20
This Town two Bargains has, not worth one farthing,
A *Smithfield* Horse, and Wife of *Covent-Garden*.

SONGS

I

A SONG

1

'GAINST Keepers we petition,
Who wou'd inclose the Common:
'Tis enough to raise Sedition
In the free-born subject Woman.
Because for his gold   5
I my body have sold,
He thinks I'm a Slave for my life;
He rants, domineers,
He swaggers and swears,
And wou'd keep me as bare as his Wife.   10

2

'Gainst Keepers we petition, *&c.*
'Tis honest and fair,
That a Feast I prepare;
But when his dull appetite's o're,
I'le treat with the rest   15
Some welcomer Ghest,
For the Reck'ning was paid me before.

II

A SONG from the ITALIAN

By a dismal Cypress lying,
Damon cry'd, all pale and dying,
Kind is Death that ends my pain,
But cruel She I lov'd in vain.
The Mossy Fountains   5
Murmure my trouble,
And hollow Mountains
My groans redouble:
Every Nymph mourns me,
Thus while I languish;   10
She only scorns me,
Who caus'd my anguish.
No Love returning me, but all hope denying;
By a dismal Cypress lying,
Like a *Swan*, so sung he dying: 15
Kind is Death that ends my pain,
But cruel She I lov'd in vain.

PROLOGUE to *CÆSAR BORGIA*

TH' unhappy man, who once has trail'd a Pen,
  Lives not to please himself but other men:
Is always drudging, wasts his Life and Blood,
Yet only eats and drinks what you think good:
What praise soe're the Poetry deserve,   5
Yet every Fool can bid the Poet starve:
That fumbling Lecher to revenge is bent,
Because he thinks himself or Whore is meant:
Name but a Cuckold, all the City swarms,
From *Leaden-hall* to *Ludgate* is in Arms.   10
Were there no fear of *Antichrist* or *France*,
In the best times poor Poets live by chance.
Either you come not here, or as you grace
Some old acquaintance, drop into the place,   ⎫
Careless and qualmish with a yawning Face.   ⎬ 15
You sleep o're Wit, and by my troth you may, ⎭
Most of your Talents lye another way.
You love to hear of some prodigious Tale,
The Bell that toll'd alone, or *Irish* Whale.
News is your Food, and you enough provide,   20
Both for your selves and all the World beside.
One Theatre there is of vast resort,
Which whilome of Requests was call'd the Court.
But now the great *Exchange* of News 'tis hight,
And full of hum and buzz from Noon till Night: 25
Up Stairs and down you run as for a Race,
And each man wears three Nations in his Face.
So big you look, tho' Claret you retrench,
That arm'd with bottled Ale, you huff the *French*:
But all your Entertainment still is fed   30
By Villains, in our own dull Island bred:
Would you return to us, we dare engage
To show you better Rogues upon the Stage:
You know no Poison but plain Rats-bane here,
Death 's more refind, and better bred elsewhere.   35

Prologue. Text from Lee's Cæsar Borgia; Son of Pope Alexander the Sixth: A Tragedy, *1680*

They have a civil way in *Italy*
By smelling a perfume to make you dye,
A Trick would make you lay your Snuff-box by.
Murder's a Trade—so known and practis'd there,
That 'tis Infallible as is the Chair—   40
But mark their Feasts, you shall behold such Pranks,
The Pope says Grace, but 'tis the Devil gives Thanks.

PROLOGUE to *THE LOYAL GENERAL*

IF yet there be a few that take delight
In that which reasonable Men should write;
To them Alone we Dedicate this Night.
The Rest may satisfie their curious Itch
With City Gazets or some Factious Speech,   5
Or what-ere Libel for the Publick Good,
Stirs up the Shrove-tide Crew to Fire and Blood!
Remove your Benches you apostate Pit,
And take Above, twelve penny-worth of Wit;
Go back to your dear Dancing on the Rope,   10
Or see what's worse the Devil and the Pope!
The Plays that take on our Corrupted Stage,
Methinks resemble the distracted Age;
Noise, Madness, all unreasonable Things,
That strike at Sense, as Rebels do at Kings!   15
The stile of Forty One our Poets write,
And you are grown to judge like Forty Eight.
Such Censures our mistaking Audience make,
That 'tis almost grown Scandalous to Take!
They talk of Feavours that infect the Brains,   20
But Non-sence is the new Disease that reigns.
Weak Stomacks with a long Disease opprest,
Cannot the Cordials of strong Wit digest:
Therfore thin Nourishment of Farce ye choose,
Decoctions of a Barly-water Muse: 25
A Meal of Tragedy wou'd make ye Sick,
Unless it were a very tender Chick.
Some Scenes in Sippets wou'd be worth our time,
Those wou'd go down; some Love that's poach'd in Rime:

Prologue. Text from Tate's The Loyal General, A Tragedy, *1680*

If these shou'd fail—   30
We must lie down, and after all our cost,
Keep Holy-day, like Water-men in Frost,
Whil'st you turn Players on the Worlds great Stage,
And Act your selves the Farce of your own Age.

PROLOGUE and SONGS
from *THE SPANISH FRYAR*

PROLOGUE

Now Luck for us, and a kind hearty Pit;
    For he who pleases, never failes of Wit:
Honour is yours:
And you, like Kings, at City Treats bestow it;
The Writer kneels, and is bid rise a Poet: 5
But you are fickle Sovereigns, to our Sorrow,
You dubb to day, and hang a man to morrow;
You cry the same Sense up, and down again,
Just like brass mony once a year in *Spain*:
Take you i'th' mood, what e'er base metal come,   10
You coin as fast as Groats at *Bromingam*:
Though 'tis no more like Sense in ancient Plays,
Than *Rome*'s Religion like St. *Peter*'s days.
In short, so swift your Judgments turn and wind,
You cast our fleetest Wits a mile behind.   15
'Twere well your Judgments but in Plays did range,
But ev'n your Follies and Debauches change
With such a Whirl, the Poets of your age
Are tyr'd, and cannot score 'em on the Stage,
Unless each Vice in short-hand they indite,   20
Ev'n as notcht Prentices whole Sermons write.
The heavy *Hollanders* no Vices know   ⎫
But what they us'd a hundred years ago,   ⎬
Like honest Plants, where they were stuck, they grow; ⎭

Prologue and Songs. Text from The Spanish Fryar or, The Double Discovery, *1681*,
collated with the editions of 1686, 1690, 1695
    Prologue. 12–13 om. *86*

They cheat, but still from cheating Sires they come;   25
They drink, but they were christ'ned first in Mum.
Their patrimonial Sloth the *Spaniards* keep,
And *Philip* first taught *Philip* how to sleep.
The *French* and we still change, but here's the Curse,
They change for better, and we change for worse;   30
They take up our old trade of Conquering,
And we are taking theirs, to dance and sing:
Our Fathers did for change to *France* repair,
And they for change will try our *English* Air.
As Children, when they throw one Toy away,   35
Strait a more foolish Gugaw comes in play:
So we, grown penitent, on serious thinking,
Leave Whoring, and devoutly fall to Drinking.
Scowring the Watch grows out of fashion wit
Now we set up for Tilting in the Pit,   40
Where 'tis agreed by Bullies, chicken-hearted,
To fright the Ladies first, and then be parted.
A fair Attempt has twice or thrice been made,
To hire Night-murth'rers, and make Death a Trade.
When Murther's out, what Vice can we advance?   45
Unless the new found Pois'ning Trick of *France*:
And when their Art of *Rats-bane* we have got,
By way of thanks, we'll send 'em o'er our *Plot*.

SONGS

I

A Procession of Priests and Choristers in white, with Tapers, follow'd by the Queen and Ladies, goes over the Stage: the Choristers singing.

LOOK down, ye bless'd above, look down,
   Behold our weeping Matron's Tears,
   Behold our tender Virgins Fears,
And with success our Armies crown.

Look down, ye bless'd above, look down: 5
   Oh! save us, save us, and our State restore;
   For Pitty, Pitty, Pitty, we implore;
For Pitty, Pitty, Pitty, we implore.

II

A SONG

I

FARWELL ungratefull Traytor,
   Farwell my perjur'd Swain,
Let never injur'd Creature
   Believe a Man again.
The Pleasure of Possessing   5
Surpasses all Expressing,
But 'tis too short a Blessing,
   And Love too long a Pain.

II

'Tis easie to deceive us
   In pity of your Pain,   10
But when we love you leave us
   To rail at you in vain.
Before we have descry'd it
There is no Bliss beside it,
But she that once has try'd it   15
   Will never love again.

III

The Passion you pretended
   Was onely to obtain,
But when the Charm is ended
   The Charmer you disdain.   20
Your Love by ours we measure
Till we have lost our Treasure,
But Dying is a Pleasure,
   When Living is a Pain.

Songs. II. 10 your *86 90 95*: our *81*

EPILOGUE to
TAMERLANE THE GREAT

LADIES, the Beardless Author of this Day,
Commends to you the Fortune of his Play.
A Woman Wit has often grac'd the Stage,
But he's the first Boy-Poet of our Age.
Early as is the Year his Fancies blow,   5
Like young *Narcissus* peeping through the Snow;
Thus *Cowley* Blossom'd soon, yet Flourish'd long,
This is as forward, and may prove as strong.
Youth with the Fair shou'd always Favour find,
Or we are damn'd Dissemblers of our kind.   10
What's all this Love they put into our Parts?
'Tis but the pit-a-pat of Two Young Hearts.
Shou'd Hag and Gray-Beard make such tender moan,
Faith you'd e'en trust 'em to themselves alone,
And cry let's go, here's nothing to be done.   15
Since Love's our Business, as 'tis your Delight,
The Young, who best can practise, best can Write.
What though he be not come to his full Pow'r,
He's mending and improving every hour.
You sly She-Jockies of the Box and Pit,   20
Are pleas'd to find a hot unbroken Wit,
By management he may in time be made,
But there's no hopes of an old batter'd Jade;
Faint and unnerv'd he runs into a Sweat,
And always fails you at the Second Heat.   25

Epilogue. Text from Saunders's Tamerlane the Great. A Tragedy, *1681*

THE EPILOGUE

Spoken to the KING at the opening the
PLAY-House at *Oxford* on Saturday last.
Being *March* the Nineteenth 1681

As from a darkn'd Roome some Optick glass
Transmits the distant Species as they pass;
The worlds large Landschape is from far descry'd,
And men contracted on the Paper glide;
Thus crowded *Oxford* represents Mankind,   5
And in these Walls *Great Brittain* seems Confin'd.
Oxford is now the publick *Theater*;
And you both Audience are, and Actors here.
The gazing World on the New Scene attend,
Admire the turns, and wish a prosp'rous end.   10
This Place the seat of Peace, the quiet Cell
Where Arts remov'd from noisy buisness dwell,
Shou'd calm your Wills, unite the jarring parts,
And with a kind Contagion seize your hearts:
Oh! may its Genius, like soft Musick move,   15
And tune you all to Concord and to Love.
Our Ark that has in Tempests long been tost,
Cou'd never land on so secure a Coast.
From hence you may look back on Civil Rage,
And view the ruines of the former Age.   20
Here a New World its glories may unfold,
And here be sav'd the remnants of the Old.
But while your daies on publick thoughts are bent
Past ills to heal, and future to prevent;
Some vacant houres allow to your delight,   ⎞ 25
Mirth is the pleasing buisness of the Night,   ⎟
The Kings Prerogative, the Peoples right.   ⎠
Were all your houres to sullen cares confind,
The Body wou'd be Jaded by the Mind.
'Tis Wisdoms part betwixt extreams to Steer: 30
Be Gods in Senates, but be Mortals here.

The Epilogue. Text from the Oxford print

The Prologue at OXFORD, 1680

*T*HESPIS, the first Professor of our Art,
 At Country Wakes, Sung Ballads from a Cart.
To prove this true, if Latin be no Trespass,
Dicitur & Plaustris, vexisse Poemata Thespis.
But *Escalus,* says *Horace* in some Page,   5
Was the first Mountebank that trod the Stage:
Yet *Athens* never knew your Learned sport,
Of Tossing Poets in a *Tennis-Court*;
But 'tis the Talent of our *English* Nation,
Still to be Plotting some New Reformation: 10
And few years hence, if Anarchy goes on,
Jack Presbyter shall here Erect his Throne.
Knock out a Tub with Preaching once a day,
And every Prayer be longer than a Play.
Then all you Heathen Wits shall go to Pot,   15
For disbelieving of a Popish Plot:
Your Poets shall be us'd like Infidels,
And worst the Author of the *Oxford Bells*:
Nor shou'd we scape the Sentence, to Depart,
Ev'n in our first Original, A Cart.   20
No Zealous Brother there wou'd want a Stone,
To Maul Us Cardinals, and pelt Pope *Joan*:
Religion, Learning, Wit, wou'd be supprest,
Rags of the Whore, and Trappings of the Beast:
Scot, Swarez, Tom of Aquin, must go down,   25
As chief Supporters of the Triple Crown;
And *Aristotle*'s for destruction ripe,
Some say He call'd the Soul an Organ-Pipe,
Which by some little help of Derivation,
Shall then be prov'd a Pipe of Inspiration.   30

The Prologue. Text from Miscellany Poems, *1684 and 1692* (MP), *collated with Lee's*
Sophonisba: or, Hannibal's Overthrow, a Tragedy, *1681, 1685, 1691, 1693 and 1697*
2 from] in *81–97* 6 that] e're *81–97* 11 few] some *81–97* goes]
go *81–93* 12 shall] will *81–97* 17–18 om. *81–97* 19 scape]
want *81–97* 21–24 om. *81–97* 25 Scot . . . must] Occam, Dun, Scotus
must, though learn'd, *81–97* 27 Aristotle's] Aristotle, *81–97* 30 then
be prov'd] thence be call'd *81–97*

[Your wiser Judgments farther penetrate,
Who late found out one Tare amongst the Wheat.
This is our comfort, none e're cry'd us down,
But who dislik'd both *Bishop* and a *Crown*.]

PROLOGUE and EPILOGUE
spoken at *MITHRIDATES*

A PROLOGUE spoken at *MITHRIDATES* King of *PONTUS*, the First Play Acted at the *THEATRE ROYAL* this Year, 1681

AFTER a four Months Fast we hope at length
Your queasie Stomachs have recover'd strength
That You can taste a Play (your old coarse Messe)
As honest and as plain as an Addresse.
And therefore Welcome from your several Parts,   5
You that have gain'd kind Country Wenches Hearts:
Have watch'd returning Milk-maids in the Dark,
And sinn'd against the Pales of every Park.
Welcom fair Ladies of unblemish'd Faith,
That left Town Bagnio's for the fruitful Bath;   10
For when the Season's Hot, and Lover's there,
The Waters never fail to get an Heir.
Welcom kind Men that did your Wives attend,
And Welcom He that was the Husbands Friend,
Who holding Chat did silently Encroach,   15
With Treacherous Hand to grabble in the Coach.
Hail you New-Market Brothers of the Switch,
That leap left Strumpets, full of Pox and Itch,
A leap more dangerous than the Devil's Ditch.
Last Welcom you who never did appear;   20
Gave out i'th' Country, but lay fluxing here.
Now Crawl abroad with Stick, lean-chapt and thin,
And Fair as Lady that hath new lain in;

31-34 Your . . . *Crown 81-97: not in MP*
Prologue and Epilogue. Text from the edition of 1681. L: Luttrell's corrections to his copy

This Winter let us reckon you our own,
For all Wise Men will let the State alone: 25
The Plot's remov'd, a Witness of Renown
Has lodg'd it safe, at t'other End o'th' Town,
And that it ne're may fail, some pious Whore
Has cast her Mite, and fairly at his Dore
Laid two small squalling Evidences more;   30
Which well instructed, if we take their words,
In time may grow to hang two Popish Lords;
Heav'n Grant the Babes may Live, for Faith there's need,
Swearers fall off so fast, if none succeed
The Land's in danger quite to loose the breed.   35
Unless you break an Act, which were a Sin,
And for recruit let Irish Cattle in.
Well; after all 'twere better to Compound,
Then let the foolish Frolick still go round,
Both sides have lost and by my Computation   40
None but *Jack Ketch* has gained in the Nation.

EPILOGUE

Pox on this Play-house, 'tis an old tir'd Jade,
'Twill do no longer, we must force a Trade;
What if we all turn Witness of the Plot?
That's overstockt, there's nothing to be got.
Shall we take Orders? That will Parts require,   5
Our Colledges give no Degrees for Hire,
Would *Salamancha* was a little nigher.
Will nothing do? Oh now 'tis found I hope;
Have not you seen the Dancing of the Rope?
When *Andrew*'s Wit was clean run off the Score,   10
And *Jacob*'s Cap'ring Tricks could do no more,
A Damsel does to the Ladders Top advance
And with two heavy Buckets drags a Dance;
The Yawning Crowd perk't up to see the sight,
And slav'r'd at the Mouth for vast Delight: 15
Oh Friends there's nothing to Enchant the Mind,
Nothing like that cleft Sex to draw Mankind:

The Foundred Horse that switching will not stir,
Trots to the Mare, afore without a Spur.
Faith I'le go scoure the Scene-room and Engage   20
Some Toy within to save the falling Stage.   *Exit.*

    Re-Enters with Mrs. Cox.

Who have we here again, what Nump's i'th' Stocks?
Your most Obedient Slave, sweet Madam *Cox.*
You'd best be Coy, and Blush for a pretence,
For Shame say something in your own Defence.   25

Mrs. Cox. What shall I say? I have been hence so long
I've e'ne almost forgot my Mother Tongue;
If I can Act I wish I were ten Fathom
Beneath—

M. Goodman. —Oh Lord, Pray, no swearing, Madam;

Mrs. Cox. Why Sir, If I had sworn, to save the Nation   30
I could find out some Mental Reservation.
Well in plain Termes, Gallants, without a Shamm,
Will you be pleas'd to take me as I am.
Quite out of Countenance, with a down cast look,
Just like a Truant that returnes to Book: 35
Yet I'me not old, but if I were this place
Ne're wanted Art to peice a ruin'd Face.
When Grey-Beards Govern'd I forsook the Stage,
You know 'tis piteous work to Act with Age;
Though there's no sence amongst these Beardless Boys, 40
There's what we Women love, that's Mirth and Noise,
These young Beginners may grow up in time,
And the Devil's in't if I'me past my Prime.

22 Nump's *L:* Nymphs *81* 23 Slave *L:* Servant *81* 40 sence *L:* sex *81*

ABSALOM AND ACHITOPHEL

A POEM

—*Si Propiùs stes*
Te Capiet Magis—

TO THE READER

'TIS not my intention to make an Apology for my Poem: Some will think it needs no Excuse; and others will receive none. The Design, I am sure, is honest: but he who draws his Pen for one Party, must expect to make Enemies of the other. For, Wit and Fool, are Consequents of Whig and Tory: And every man is a Knave or an Ass to the contrary side. There's a Treasury of Merits in 5 the Phanatick Church, as well as in the Papist; and a Pennyworth to be had of Saintship, Honesty, and Poetry, for the Leud, the Factious, and the Blockheads: But the longest Chapter in Deuteronomy, has not Curses enow for an Anti-Bromingham. My Comfort is, their manifest Prejudice to my Cause, will render their Judgment of less Authority against me. Yet if a Poem have a 10 Genius, it will force its own reception in the World. For there's a sweetness in good Verse, which Tickles even while it Hurts: And, no man can be heartily angry with him, who pleases him against his will. The Commendation of Adversaries, is the greatest Triumph of a Writer; because it never comes unless Extorted. But I can be satisfied on more easy termes: If I happen to please the more 15 Moderate sort, I shall be sure of an honest Party; and, in all probability, of the best Judges; for, the least Concern'd, are commonly the least Corrupt: And, I confess, I have laid in for those, by rebating the Satyre, (where Justice woud allow it) from carrying too sharp an Edge. They, who can Criticize so weakly, as to imagine I have done my Worst, may be Convinc'd, at their own Cost, that 20 I can write Severely, with more ease, than I can Gently. I have but laught at some mens Follies, when I coud have declaim'd against their Vices; and, other mens Vertues I have commended, as freely as I have tax'd their Crimes. And now, if you are a Malitious Reader, I expect you should return upon me, that I affect to be thought more Impartial than I am. But, if men are not to be judg'd by their 25 Professions, God forgive you Common-wealths-men, for professing so plausibly for the Government. You cannot be so Unconscionable, as to charge me for not

---

Absalom and Achitophel. Text from the first edition, 1681 (A), collated with the subsequent London editions of 1681 (B and C), 1682 (D, E and F), Miscellany Poems 1684 (G) and 1692 (H), and the separate edition of 1692 (I)

Subscribing of my Name; for that woud reflect too grosly upon your own Party,
who never dare, though they have the advantage of a Jury to secure them. If you
like not my Poem, the fault may, possibly, be in my Writing: (though 'tis hard 30
for an Authour to judge against himself;) But, more probably, 'tis in your
Morals, which cannot bear the truth of it. The Violent, on both sides, will con-
demn the Character of Absalom, *as either too favourably, or too hardly drawn.*
But, they are not the Violent, whom I desire to please. The fault, on the right
hand, is to Extenuate, Palliate and Indulge; and, to confess freely, I have en- 35
deavour'd to commit it. Besides the respect which I owe his Birth, I have a greater
for his Heroique Vertues; and, David *himself, coud not be more tender of the*
Young-man's Life, than I woud be of his Reputation. But, since the most excellent
Natures are always the most easy; and, as being such, are the soonest perverted
by ill Counsels, especially when baited with Fame and Glory; 'tis no more a 40
wonder that he withstood not the temptations of Achitophel, *than it was for*
Adam, *not to have resisted the two Devils; the Serpent, and the Woman. The*
conclusion of the Story, I purposely forbore to prosecute; because, I coud not
obtain from my self, to shew Absalom *Unfortunate. The Frame of it, was cut*
out, but for a Picture to the Wast; and, if the Draught be so far true, 'tis as 45
much as I design'd.

Were I the Inventour, who am only the Historian, I shoud certainly conclude
the Piece, with the Reconcilement of Absalom *to* David. *And, who knows but*
this may come to pass? Things were not brought to an Extremity where I left the
Story: There seems, yet, to be room left for a Composure; hereafter, there may 50
only be for pity. I have not, so much as an uncharitable Wish against Achitophel;
but, am content to be Accus'd of a good natur'd Errour; and, to hope with
Origen, *that the Devil himself may, at last, be sav'd. For which reason, in this*
Poem, he is neither brought to set his House in order, nor to dispose of his Person
afterwards, as he in Wisedom shall think fit. God is infinitely merciful; and his 55
Vicegerent is only not so, because he is not Infinite.

The true end of Satyre, *is the amendment of Vices by correction. And he who*
writes Honestly, is no more an Enemy to the Offendour, than the Physician to the
Patient, when he prescribes harsh Remedies to an inveterate Disease: for those,
are only in order to prevent the Chyrurgeon's work of an Ense rescindendum, 60
which I wish not to my very Enemies. To conclude all, If the Body Politique have
any Analogy to the Natural, in my weak judgment, an Act of Oblivion *were*
as necessary in a Hot, Distemper'd State, as an Opiate *woud be in a Raging*
Fever.

ABSALOM AND ACHITOPHEL

A Poem

IN pious times, e'r Priest-craft did begin,
Before *Polygamy* was made a sin;
When man, on many, multiply'd his kind,
E'r one to one was, cursedly, confind:
When Nature prompted, and no law deny'd   5
Promiscuous use of Concubine and Bride;
Then, *Israel*'s Monarch, after Heaven's own heart,
His vigorous warmth did, variously, impart
To Wives and Slaves: And, wide as his Command,
Scatter'd his Maker's Image through the Land.   10
Michal, of Royal blood, the Crown did wear,
A Soyl ungratefull to the Tiller's care:
Not so the rest; for several Mothers bore
To Godlike *David*, several Sons before.
But since like slaves his bed they did ascend,   15
No True Succession could their seed attend.
Of all this Numerous Progeny was none
So Beautifull, so brave as *Absolon*:
Whether, inspir'd by some diviner Lust,
His Father got him with a greater Gust;   20
Or that his Conscious destiny made way
By manly beauty to Imperiall sway.
Early in Foreign fields he won Renown,
With Kings and States ally'd to *Israel*'s Crown:
In Peace the thoughts of War he coud remove,   25
And seem'd as he were only born for love.
What e'r he did was done with so much ease,
In him alone, 'twas Natural to please.
His motions all accompanied with grace;
And *Paradise* was open'd in his face.   30
With secret Joy, indulgent *David* view'd
His Youthfull Image in his Son renew'd:
To all his wishes Nothing he deny'd,
And made the Charming *Annabel* his Bride.

Absalom and Achitophel.   19 by *C–I*: with *A B*

What faults he had (for who from faults is free?)   35
His Father coud not, or he woud not see.
Some warm excesses, which the Law forbore,
Were constru'd Youth that purg'd by boyling o'r:
And *Amnon*'s Murther, by a specious Name,
Was call'd a Just Revenge for injur'd Fame.   40
Thus Prais'd, and Lov'd, the Noble Youth remain'd,
While *David*, undisturb'd, in *Sion* raign'd.
But Life can never be sincerely blest:
Heaven punishes the bad, and proves the best.
The *Jews*, a Headstrong, Moody, Murmuring race,   45
As ever try'd th' extent and stretch of grace;
God's pamper'd people whom, debauch'd with ease,
No King could govern, nor no God could please;
(Gods they had tri'd of every shape and size
That God-smiths could produce, or Priests devise:)   50
These *Adam*-wits, too fortunately free,
Began to dream they wanted libertie;
And when no rule, no president was found
Of men, by Laws less circumscrib'd and bound,
They led their wild desires to Woods and Caves,   55
And thought that all but Savages were Slaves.
They who when *Saul* was dead, without a blow,
Made foolish *Ishbosheth* the Crown forgo;
Who banisht *David* did from *Hebron* bring,
And, with a Generall Shout, proclaim'd him King: 60
Those very *Jewes*, who, at their very best,
Their Humour more than Loyalty exprest,
Now, wondred why, so long, they had obey'd
An Idoll Monarch which their hands had made:
Thought they might ruine him they could create;   65
Or melt him to that Golden Calf, a State.
But these were randome bolts: No form'd Design,
Nor Interest made the Factious Croud to joyn:
The sober part of *Israel*, free from stain,
Well knew the value of a peacefull raign: 70
And, looking backward with a wise afright,
Saw Seames of wounds, dishonest to the sight;
In contemplation of whose ugly Scars,
They Curst the memory of Civil Wars.

The moderate sort of Men, thus qualifi'd,   75
Inclin'd the Ballance to the better side:
And *David*'s mildness manag'd it so well,
The Bad found no occasion to Rebell.
But, when to Sin our byast Nature leans,
The carefull Devil is still at hand with means;   80
And providently Pimps for ill desires:
The Good old Cause reviv'd, a Plot requires.
Plots, true or false, are necessary things,
To raise up Common-wealths, and ruin Kings.

    Th' inhabitants of old *Jerusalem*   85
Were *Jebusites*: the Town so call'd from them;
And their's the Native right—
But when the chosen people grew more strong,
The rightfull cause at length became the wrong:
And every loss the men of *Jebus* bore,   90
They still were thought God's enemies the more.
Thus, worn and weaken'd, well or ill content,
Submit they must to *David*'s Government:
Impoverisht, and depriv'd of all Command,
Their Taxes doubled as they lost their Land,   95
And, what was harder yet to flesh and blood,
Their Gods disgrac'd, and burnt like common wood.
This set the Heathen Priesthood in a flame;
For Priests of all Religions are the same:
Of whatsoe'r descent their Godhead be,   100
Stock, Stone, or other homely pedigree,
In his defence his Servants are as bold
As if he had been born of beaten gold.
The *Jewish Rabbins* thô their Enemies,
In this conclude them honest men and wise: 105
For 'twas their duty, all the Learned think,
T'espouse his Cause by whom they eat and drink.
From hence began that Plot, the Nation's Curse,
Bad in it self, but represented worse.
Rais'd in extremes, and in extremes decry'd;   110
With Oaths affirm'd, with dying Vows deny'd.
Not weigh'd, or winnow'd by the Multitude;
But swallow'd in the Mass, unchew'd and Crude.
Some Truth there was, but dash'd and brew'd with Lyes;

To please the Fools, and puzzle all the Wise.   115
Succeeding times did equal folly call,
Believing nothing, or believing all.
Th' *Egyptian* Rites the *Jebusites* imbrac'd;
Where Gods were recommended by their Tast.
Such savory Deities must needs be good,   120
As serv'd at once for Worship and for Food.
By force they could not Introduce these Gods;
For Ten to One, in former days was odds.
So Fraud was us'd, (the Sacrificers trade,)
Fools are more hard to Conquer than Perswade.   125
Their busie Teachers mingled with the *Jews*;
And rak'd, for Converts, even the Court and Stews:
Which *Hebrew* Priests the more unkindly took,
Because the Fleece accompanies the Flock.
Some thought they God's Anointed meant to Slay   130
By Guns, invented since full many a day:
Our Authour swears it not; but who can know
How far the Devil and *Jebusites* may go?
This Plot, which fail'd for want of common Sense,
Had yet a deep and dangerous Consequence: 135
For, as when raging Fevers boyl the Blood,
The standing Lake soon floats into a Flood;
And every hostile Humour, which before
Slept quiet in its Channels, bubbles o'r:
So, several Factions from this first Ferment,   140
Work up to Foam, and threat the Government.
Some by their Friends, more by themselves thought wise,
Oppos'd the Power, to which they could not rise.
Some had in Courts been Great, and thrown from thence,
Like Feinds, were harden'd in Impenitence.   145
Some by their Monarch's fatal mercy grown,
From Pardon'd Rebels, Kinsmen to the Throne;
Were rais'd in Power and publick Office high:
Strong Bands, if Bands ungratefull men could tye.
Of these the false *Achitophel* was first: 150
A Name to all succeeding Ages Curst.
For close Designs, and crooked Counsels fit;

Sagacious, Bold, and Turbulent of wit:
Restless, unfixt in Principles and Place;
In Power unpleas'd, impatient of Disgrace.   155
A fiery Soul, which working out its way,
Fretted the Pigmy Body to decay:
And o'r inform'd the Tenement of Clay.
A daring Pilot in extremity;
Pleas'd with the Danger, when the Waves went high   160
He sought the Storms; but for a Calm unfit,
Would Steer too nigh the Sands, to boast his Wit.
Great Wits are sure to Madness near ally'd;
And thin Partitions do their Bounds divide:
Else, why should he, with Wealth and Honour blest,   165
Refuse his Age the needful hours of Rest?
Punish a Body which he coud not please;
Bankrupt of Life, yet Prodigal of Ease?
And all to leave, what with his Toyl he won,
To that unfeather'd, two Leg'd thing, a Son: 170
Got, while his Soul did hudled Notions try;
And born a shapeless Lump, like Anarchy.
In Friendship False, Implacable in Hate:
Resolv'd to Ruine or to Rule the State.
To Compass this the Triple Bond he broke;   175
The Pillars of the publick Safety shook:
And fitted *Israel* for a Foreign Yoke.
Then, seiz'd with Fear, yet still affecting Fame,
Usurp'd a Patriott's All-attoning Name.
So easie still it proves in Factious Times,   180
With publick Zeal to cancel private Crimes:
How safe is Treason, and how sacred ill,
Where none can sin against the Peoples Will:
Where Crouds can wink; and no offence be known,
Since in anothers guilt they find their own.   185
Yet, Fame deserv'd, no Enemy can grudge;
The Statesman we abhor, but praise the Judge.
In *Israels* Courts ne'r sat an *Abbethdin*
With more discerning Eyes, or Hands more clean:

---

154 Principles *C–I*: Principle *A B*   179 Usurp'd *C–I*: Assum'd *A B*
Patriott's *B–I*: Patron's *A* (*some copies*)   180–91 *added in* C. *D–I. Text from* C

Unbrib'd, unsought, the Wretched to redress;   190
Swift of Dispatch, and easie of Access.
Oh, had he been content to serve the Crown,
With vertues only proper to the Gown;
Or, had the rankness of the Soyl been freed
From Cockle, that opprest the Noble seed: 195
David, for him his tunefull Harp had strung,
And Heaven had wanted one Immortal song.
But wilde Ambition loves to slide, not stand;
And Fortunes Ice prefers to Vertues Land:
Achitophel, grown weary to possess   200
A lawfull Fame, and lazy Happiness;
Disdain'd the Golden fruit to gather free,
And lent the Croud his Arm to shake the Tree.
Now, manifest of Crimes, contriv'd long since,
He stood at bold Defiance with his Prince: 205
Held up the Buckler of the Peoples Cause,
Against the Crown; and sculk'd behind the Laws.
The wish'd occasion of the Plot he takes,
Some Circumstances finds, but more he makes.
By buzzing Emissaries, fills the ears   210
Of listning Crowds, with Jealosies and Fears
Of Arbitrary Counsels brought to light,
And proves the King himself a *Jebusite*:
Weak Arguments! which yet he knew full well,
Were strong with People easie to Rebell.   215
For, govern'd by the *Moon*, the giddy *Jews*
Tread the same track when she the Prime renews:
And once in twenty Years, their Scribes Record,
By natural Instinct they change their Lord.
Achitophel still wants a Chief, and none   220
Was found so fit as Warlike *Absolon*:
Not, that he wish'd his Greatness to create,
(For Polititians neither love nor hate:)
But, for he knew, his Title not allow'd,
Would keep him still depending on the Crowd: 225
That Kingly power, thus ebbing out, might be
Drawn to the dregs of a Democracy.
Him he attempts, with studied Arts to please,
And sheds his Venome, in such words as these.

Achitophel:

"Auspicious Prince! at whose Nativity   230
Some Royal Planet rul'd the Southern sky;
Thy longing Countries Darling and Desire;
Their cloudy Pillar, and their guardian Fire:
Their second *Moses*, whose extended Wand
Divides the Seas, and shews the promis'd Land: 235
Whose dawning Day, in every distant age,
Has exercis'd the Sacred Prophets rage:
The Peoples Prayer, the glad Deviners Theam,
The Young-mens Vision, and the Old mens Dream!
Thee, *Saviour*, Thee, the Nations Vows confess;   240
And, never satisfi'd with seeing, bless:
Swift, unbespoken Pomps, thy steps proclaim,
And stammerring Babes are taught to lisp thy Name.
How long wilt thou the general Joy detain;
Starve, and defraud the People of thy Reign?   245
Content ingloriously to pass thy days
Like one of Vertues Fools that feeds on Praise;
Till thy fresh Glories, which now shine so bright,
Grow Stale and Tarnish with our daily sight.
Believe me, Royal Youth, thy Fruit must be,   250
Or gather'd Ripe, or rot upon the Tree.
Heav'n, has to all allotted, soon or late,
Some lucky Revolution of their Fate:
Whose Motions, if we watch and guide with Skill,
(For humane Good depends on humane Will,)   255
Our Fortune rolls, as from a smooth Descent,
And, from the first Impression, takes the Bent:
But, if unseiz'd, she glides away like wind;
And leaves repenting Folly far behind.
Now, now she meets you, with a glorious prize,   260
And spreads her Locks before her as she flies.
Had thus Old *David*, from whose Loyns you spring,
Not dar'd, when Fortune call'd him, to be King,
At *Gath* an Exile he might still remain,
And heavens Anointing Oyle had been in vain.   265
Let his successfull Youth your hopes engage,
But shun th' example of Declining Age:
Behold him setting in his Western Skies,

The Shadows lengthning as the Vapours rise.
He is not now, as when on *Jordan*'s Sand 270
The Joyfull People throng'd to see him Land,
Cov'ring the *Beach*, and blackning all the *Strand*:
But, like the Prince of Angels from his height,
Comes tumbling downward with diminish'd light;
Betray'd by one poor Plot to publick Scorn, 275
(Our only blessing since his Curst Return:)
Those heaps of People which one Sheaf did bind,
Blown off and scatter'd by a puff of Wind.
What strength can he to your Designs oppose,
Naked of Friends, and round beset with Foes? 280
If *Pharaoh*'s doubtfull Succour he shoud use,
A Foreign Aid woud more Incense the *Jews*:
Proud *Egypt* woud dissembled Friendship bring;
Foment the War, but not support the King:
Nor woud the Royal Party e'r unite 285
With *Pharaoh*'s Arms, t'assist the *Jebusite*;
Or if they shoud, their Interest soon woud break,
And with such odious Aid make *David* weak.
All sorts of men by my successfull Arts,
Abhorring Kings, estrange their alter'd Hearts 290
From *David*'s Rule: And 'tis the general Cry,
Religion, Common-wealth, and Liberty.
If you as Champion of the publique Good,
Add to their Arms a Chief of Royal Blood;
What may not *Israel* hope, and what Applause 295
Might such a General gain by such a Cause?
Not barren Praise alone, that Gaudy Flower,
Fair only to the sight, but solid Power:
And Nobler is a limited Command,
Giv'n by the Love of all your Native Land, 300
Than a Successive Title, Long, and Dark,
Drawn from the Mouldy Rolls of *Noah*'s Ark.
   What cannot Praise effect in Mighty Minds,
When Flattery Sooths, and when Ambition Blinds!
Desire of Power, on Earth a Vitious Weed, 305
Yet, sprung from High, is of Cælestial Seed:
In God 'tis Glory: And when men Aspire,
'Tis but a Spark too much of Heavenly Fire.

Th' Ambitious Youth, too Covetous of Fame,
Too full of Angells Metal in his Frame;   310
Unwarily was led from Vertues ways;
Made Drunk with Honour, and Debauch'd with Praise.
Half loath, and half consenting to the Ill,
(For Loyal Blood within him strugled still)
He thus reply'd—And what Pretence have I   315
To take up Arms for Publick Liberty?
My Father Governs with unquestion'd Right;
The Faiths Defender, and Mankinds Delight:
Good, Gracious, Just, observant of the Laws;
And Heav'n by Wonders has Espous'd his Cause.   320
Whom has he Wrong'd in all his Peaceful Reign?
Who sues for Justice to his Throne in Vain?
What Millions has he Pardon'd of his Foes,
Whom Just Revenge did to his Wrath expose?
Mild, Easy, Humble, Studious of our Good;   325
Enclin'd to Mercy, and averse from Blood.
If Mildness Ill with Stubborn *Israel* Suite,
His Crime is God's beloved Attribute.
What could he gain, his People to Betray,
Or change his Right, for Arbitrary Sway?   330
Let Haughty *Pharaoh* Curse with such a Reign,
His Fruitfull *Nile*, and Yoak a Servile Train.
If *David*'s Rule *Jerusalem* Displease,
The *Dog-star* heats their Brains to this Disease.
Why then shoud I, Encouraging the Bad,   335
Turn Rebell, and run Popularly Mad?
Were he a Tyrant who, by Lawless Might,
Opprest the *Jews*, and Rais'd the *Jebusite*,
Well might I Mourn; but Natures Holy Bands
Woud Curb my Spirits, and Restrain my Hands: 340
The People might assert their Liberty;
But what was Right in them, were Crime in me.
His Favour leaves me nothing to require;
Prevents my Wishes, and outruns Desire.
What more can I expect while *David* lives,   345
All but his Kingly Diadem he gives;
And that: But there he Paus'd; then Sighing, said,
Is Justly Destin'd for a Worthier Head.

For when my Father from his Toyls shall Rest,
And late Augment the Number of the Blest: 350
His Lawfull Issue shall the Throne ascend,
Or the *Collateral* Line where that shall end.
His Brother, though Opprest with Vulgar Spight,
Yet Dauntless and Secure of Native Right,
Of every Royal Vertue stands possest;   355
Still Dear to all the Bravest, and the Best.
His Courage Foes, his Friends his Truth Proclaim;
His Loyalty the King, the World his Fame.
His Mercy even th' Offending Crowd will find,
For sure he comes of a Forgiving Kind.   360
Why shoud I then Repine at Heavens Decree;
Which gives me no Pretence to Royalty?
Yet oh that Fate Propitiously Enclind,
Had rais'd my Birth, or had debas'd my Mind;
To my large Soul, not all her Treasure lent,   365
And then Betray'd it to a mean Descent.
I find, I find my mounting Spirits Bold,
And *David*'s Part disdains my Mothers Mold.
Why am I Scanted by a Niggard Birth?
My Soul Disclaims the Kindred of her Earth: 370
And made for Empire, Whispers me within;
Desire of Greatness is a Godlike Sin. "
    Him Staggering so when Hells dire Agent found,
While fainting Vertue scarce maintain'd her Ground,
He pours fresh Forces in, and thus Replies: 375
 ·' Th' Eternal God Supreamly Good and Wise,   *Achitophel*
Imparts not these Prodigious Gifts in vain;
What Wonders are Reserv'd to bless your Reign?
Against your will your Arguments have shown,
Such Vertue's only given to guide a Throne.   380
Not that your Father's Mildness I contemn;
But Manly Force becomes the Diadem.
'Tis true, he grants the People all they crave;
And more perhaps than Subjects ought to have:
For Lavish grants suppose a Monarch tame,   385
And more his Goodness than his Wit proclaim.
But when shoud People strive their Bonds to break,

    381 contemn *C–I:* condemn *A B*

If not when Kings are Negligent or Weak?
Let him give on till he can give no more,
The Thrifty Sanhedrin shall keep him poor: 390
And every Sheckle which he can receive,
Shall cost a Limb of his Prerogative.
To ply him with new Plots, shall be my care,
Or plunge him deep in some Expensive War;
Which when his Treasure can no more Supply,   395
He must, with the Remains of Kingship, buy.
His faithful Friends, our Jealousies and Fears,
Call *Jebusites*; and *Pharaoh*'s Pentioners:
Whom, when our Fury from his Aid has torn,
He shall be Naked left to publick Scorn.   400
The next Successor, whom I fear and hate,
My Arts have made Obnoxious to the State;
Turn'd all his Vertues to his Overthrow,
And gain'd our Elders to pronounce a Foe.
His Right, for Sums of necessary Gold,   405
Shall first be Pawn'd, and afterwards be Sold:
Till time shall Ever-wanting *David* draw,
To pass your doubtfull Title into Law:
If not; the People have a Right Supreme
To make their Kings; for Kings are made for them.   410
All Empire is no more than Pow'r in Trust,
Which when resum'd, can be no longer Just.
Succession, for the general Good design'd,
In its own wrong a Nation cannot bind:
If altering that, the People can relieve,   415
Better one Suffer, than a Nation grieve.
The *Jews* well know their power: e'r *Saul* they Chose,
God was their King, and God they durst Depose.
Urge now your Piety, your Filial Name,
A Father's Right, and fear of future Fame;   420
The publick Good, that Universal Call,
To which even Heav'n Submitted, answers all.
Nor let his Love Enchant your generous Mind;
'Tis Natures trick to Propagate her Kind.
Our fond Begetters, who woud never dye,   425
Love but themselves in their Posterity.

Or let his Kindness by th' Effects be try'd,
Or let him lay his vain Pretence aside.
God said he lov'd your Father; coud he bring
A better Proof, than to Anoint him King? 430
It surely shew'd he lov'd the Shepherd well,
Who gave so fair a Flock as *Israel*.
Woud *David* have you thought his Darling Son?
What means he then, to Alienate the Crown?
The name of Godly he may blush to bear: 435
'Tis after God's own heart to Cheat his Heir.
He to his Brother gives Supreme Command;
To you a Legacy of Barren Land:
Perhaps th' old Harp, on which he thrums his Layes:
Or some dull *Hebrew* Ballad in your Praise. 440
Then the next Heir, a Prince, Severe and Wise,
Already looks on you with Jealous Eyes;
Sees through the thin Disguises of your Arts,
And markes your Progress in the Peoples Hearts.
Though now his mighty Soul its Grief contains; 445
He meditates Revenge who least Complains.
And like a Lyon, Slumbring in the way,
Or Sleep-dissembling, while he waits his Prey,
His fearless Foes within his Distance draws;
Constrains his Roaring, and Contracts his Paws; 450
Till at the last, his time for Fury found,
He shoots with suddain Vengeance from the Ground:
The Prostrate Vulgar, passes o'r, and Spares;
But with a Lordly Rage, his Hunters teares.
Your Case no tame Expedients will afford; 455
Resolve on Death, or Conquest by the Sword,
Which for no less a Stake than Life, you Draw;
And Self-defence is Natures Eldest Law.
Leave the warm People no Considering time;
For then Rebellion may be thought a Crime. 460
Prevail your self of what Occasion gives,
But try your Title while your Father lives:
And that your Arms may have a fair Pretence,
Proclaim, you take them in the King's Defence:
Whose Sacred Life each minute woud Expose, 465
To Plots, from seeming Friends, and secret Foes.

And who can sound the depth of *David*'s Soul?
Perhaps his fear, his kindness may Controul.
He fears his Brother, though he loves his Son,
For plighted Vows too late to be undone.　　　　　　470
If so, by Force he wishes to be gain'd,
Like womens Leachery, to seem Constrain'd:
Doubt not, but when he most affects the Frown,
Commit a pleasing Rape upon the Crown.
Secure his Person to secure your Cause;　　　　　　475
They who possess the Prince, possess the Laws.
　　He said, And this Advice above the rest,
With *Absalom*'s Mild nature suited best;
Unblam'd of Life (Ambition set aside,)
Not stain'd with Cruelty, nor puft with Pride;　　　480
How happy had he been, if Destiny
Had higher plac'd his Birth, or not so high!
His Kingly Vertues might have claim'd a Throne,
And blest all other Countries but his own:
But charming Greatness, since so few refuse;　　　485
'Tis Juster to Lament him, than Accuse.
Strong were his hopes a Rival to remove,
With blandishments to gain the publick Love;
To Head the Faction while their Zeal was hot,
And Popularly prosecute the Plot.　　　　　　490
To farther this, *Achitophel* Unites
The Malecontents of all the *Israelites*;
Whose differing Parties he could wisely Joyn,
For several Ends, to serve the same Design.
The Best, and of the Princes some were such,　　　495
Who thought the power of Monarchy too much:
Mistaken Men, and Patriots in their Hearts;
Not Wicked, but Seduc'd by Impious Arts.
By these the Springs of Property were bent,
And wound so high, they Crack'd the Government.　　500
The next for Interest sought t' embroil the State,
To sell their Duty at a dearer rate;
And make their *Jewish* Markets of the Throne,
Pretending publick Good, to serve their own.
Others thought Kings an useless heavy Load,　　　505
Who Cost too much, and did too little Good.

These were for laying Honest *David* by,
On Principles of pure good Husbandry.
With them Joyn'd all th' Haranguers of the Throng,
That thought to get Preferment by the Tongue.   510
Who follow next, a double Danger bring,
Not only hating *David,* but the King,
The *Solymæan* Rout; well Verst of old,
In Godly Faction, and in Treason bold;
Cowring and Quaking at a Conqueror's Sword,   515
But Lofty to a Lawfull Prince Restor'd;
Saw with Disdain an *Ethnick* Plot begun,
And Scorn'd by *Jebusites* to be Out-done.
Hot *Levites* Headed these; who pul'd before
From th' *Ark*, which in the Judges days they bore,   520
Resum'd their Cant, and with a Zealous Cry,
Pursu'd their old belov'd Theocracy.
Where Sanhedrin and Priest inslav'd the Nation,
And justifi'd their Spoils by Inspiration;
For who so fit for Reign as *Aaron*'s Race,   525
If once Dominion they could found in Grace?
These led the Pack; tho not of surest scent,
Yet deepest mouth'd against the Government.
A numerous Host of dreaming Saints succeed;
Of the true old Enthusiastick breed: 530
'Gainst Form and Order they their Power employ;
Nothing to Build and all things to Destroy.
But far more numerous was the herd of such,
Who think too little, and who talk too much.
These, out of meer instinct, they knew not why,   535
Ador'd their fathers God, and Property:
And, by the same blind benefit of Fate,
The Devil and the *Jebusite* did hate:
Born to be sav'd, even in their own despight;
Because they could not help believing right.   540
Such were the tools; but a whole Hydra more
Remains, of sprouting heads too long, to score.
   Some of their Chiefs were Princes of the Land:
In the first Rank of these did *Zimri* stand:
A man so various, that he seem'd to be   545
Not one, but all Mankinds Epitome.

Stiff in Opinions, always in the wrong;
Was every thing by starts, and nothing long:
But, in the course of one revolving Moon,
Was Chymist, Fidler, States-Man, and Buffoon: 550
Then all for Women, Painting, Rhiming, Drinking;
Besides ten thousand freaks that dy'd in thinking.
Blest Madman, who coud every hour employ,
With something New to wish, or to enjoy!
Rayling and praising were his usual Theams;   555
And both (to shew his Judgment) in Extreams:
So over Violent, or over Civil,
That every man, with him, was God or Devil.
In squandring Wealth was his peculiar Art:
Nothing went unrewarded, but Desert.   560
Begger'd by Fools, whom still he found too late:
He had his Jest, and they had his Estate.
He laught himself from Court, then sought Relief
By forming Parties, but coud ne're be Chief:
For, spight of him, the weight of Business fell   565
On *Absalom* and wise *Achitophel*:
Thus, wicked but in will, of means bereft,
He left not Faction, but of that was left.

   Titles and Names 'twere tedious to Reherse
Of Lords, below the Dignity of Verse.   570
Wits, warriors, Common-wealthsmen, were the best:
Kind Husbands and meer Nobles all the rest.
And, therefore in the name of Dulness, be
The well hung *Balaam* and cold *Caleb* free.
And Canting *Nadab* let Oblivion damn,   575
Who made new porridge for the Paschal Lamb.
Let Friendships holy band some Names assure:
Some their own Worth, and some let Scorn secure.
Nor shall the Rascall Rabble here have Place,
Whom Kings no Titles gave, and God no Grace: 580
Not Bull-fac'd *Jonas*, who could Statutes draw
To mean Rebellion, and make Treason Law.
But he, tho bad, is follow'd by a worse,
The wretch, who Heavens Annointed dar'd to Curse.
Shimei, whose Youth did early Promise bring   585

585 Youth did early *C–I*: early Youth did *A B*

Of Zeal to God, and Hatred to his King;
Did wisely from Expensive Sins refrain,
And never broke the Sabbath, but for Gain:
Nor ever was he known an Oath to vent,
Or Curse unless against the Government.   590
Thus, heaping Wealth, by the most ready way
Among the *Jews*, which was to Cheat and Pray;
The City, to reward his pious Hate
Against his Master, chose him Magistrate:
His Hand a Vare of Justice did uphold;   595
His Neck was loaded with a Chain of Gold.
During his Office, Treason was no Crime.
The Sons of *Belial* had a glorious Time:
For *Shimei*, though not prodigal of pelf,
Yet lov'd his wicked Neighbour as himself: 600
When two or three were gather'd to declaim
Against the Monarch of *Jerusalem*,
Shimei was always in the midst of them.
And, if they Curst the King when he was by,
Woud rather Curse, than break good Company.   605
If any durst his Factious Friends accuse,
He pact a Jury of dissenting *Jews*:
Whose fellow-feeling, in the godly Cause,
Would free the suffring Saint from Humane Laws.
For Laws are only made to Punish those,   610
Who serve the King, and to protect his Foes.
If any leisure time he had from Power,
(Because 'tis Sin to misimploy an hour;)
His business was, by Writing, to Persuade,
That Kings were Useless, and a Clog to Trade: 615
And, that his noble Stile he might refine,
No *Rechabite* more shund the fumes of Wine.
Chast were his Cellars, and his Shrieval Board
The Grossness of a City Feast abhor'd:
His Cooks, with long disuse, their Trade forgot;   620
Cool was his Kitchen, tho his Brains were hot.
Such frugal Vertue Malice may accuse,
But sure 'twas necessary to the *Jews*:
For Towns once burnt, such Magistrates require
As dare not tempt Gods Providence by fire.   625

With Spiritual food he fed his Servants well,
But free from flesh, that made the *Jews* Rebel:
And *Moses*'s Laws he held in more account,
For forty days of Fasting in the Mount.

  To speak the rest, who better are forgot,   630
Would tyre a well breath'd Witness of the Plot:
Yet, *Corah*, thou shalt from Oblivion pass;
Erect thy self thou Monumental Brass:
High as the Serpent of thy mettall made,
While Nations stand secure beneath thy shade.   635
What tho his Birth were base, yet Comets rise
From Earthy Vapours ere they shine in Skies.
Prodigious Actions may as well be done
By Weavers issue, as by Princes Son.
This Arch-Attestor for the Publick Good,   640
By that one Deed Enobles all his Bloud.
Who ever ask'd the Witnesses high race,
Whose Oath with Martyrdom did *Stephen* grace?
Ours was a *Levite*, and as times went then,
His Tribe were Godalmightys Gentlemen.   645
Sunk were his Eyes, his Voyce was harsh and loud,
Sure signs he neither Cholerick was, nor Proud:
His long Chin prov'd his Wit; his Saintlike Grace
A Church Vermilion, and a *Moses*'s Face;
His Memory, miraculously great,   650
Could Plots, exceeding mans belief, repeat;
Which, therefore cannot be accounted Lies,
For humane Wit could never such devise.
Some future Truths are mingled in his Book;
But, where the witness faild, the Prophet Spoke: 655
Some things like Visionary flights appear;
The Spirit caught him up, the Lord knows where:
And gave him his *Rabinical* degree
Unknown to Foreign University.
His Judgment yet his Memory did excel;   660
Which peic'd his wondrous Evidence so well:
And suited to the temper of the times;
Then groaning under *Jebusitick* Crimes.
Let *Israels* foes suspect his heav'nly call,

And rashly judge his Writ Apocryphal;   665
Our Laws for such affronts have forfeits made:
He takes his life, who takes away his trade.
Were I my self in witness *Corahs* place,
The wretch who did me such a dire disgrace,
Should whet my memory, though once forgot,   670
To make him an Appendix of my Plot.
His Zeal to heav'n, made him his Prince despise,
And load his person with indignities:
But Zeal peculiar priviledg affords;
Indulging latitude to deeds and words.   675
And *Corah* might for *Agag*'s murther call,
In terms as course as *Samuel* us'd to *Saul*.
What others in his Evidence did Joyn,
(The best that could be had for love or coyn,)
In *Corah*'s own predicament will fall: 680
For *witness* is a Common Name to all.
   Surrounded thus with Freinds of every sort,
Deluded *Absalom*, forsakes the Court:
Impatient of high hopes, urg'd with renown,
And Fir'd with near possession of a Crown: 685
Th' admiring Croud are dazled with surprize,
And on his goodly person feed their eyes:
His joy conceal'd, he sets himself to show;
On each side bowing popularly low:
His looks, his gestures, and his words he frames,   690
And with familiar ease repeats their Names.
Thus, form'd by Nature, furnish'd out with Arts,
He glides unfelt into their secret hearts:
Then with a kind compassionating look,
And sighs, bespeaking pity ere he spoak,   695
Few words he said; but easy those and fit:
More slow than Hybla drops, and far more sweet.
   I mourn, my Countrymen, your lost Estate;
Tho far unable to prevent your fate:
Behold a Banisht man, for your dear cause   700
Expos'd a prey to Arbitrary laws!
Yet oh! that I alone cou'd be undone,

665 Writ *C–I*: Wit *A B. Cf.* The Second Part, *l. 95*   688 His joy conceal'd *C–I*:
Dissembling Joy *A B*

Cut off from Empire, and no more a Son!
Now all your Liberties a spoil are made;
Ægypt and Tyrus intercept your Trade,   705
And Jebusites your Sacred Rites invade.
My Father, whom with reverence yet I name,
Charm'd into Ease, is careless of his Fame:
And, brib'd with petty summs of Forreign Gold,
Is grown in Bathsheba's Embraces old: 710
Exalts his Enemies, his Freinds destroys:
And all his pow'r against himself employs.
He gives, and let him give my right away:
But why should he his own, and yours betray?
He only, he can make the Nation bleed,   715
And he alone from my revenge is freed.
Take then my tears (with that he wip'd his Eyes)
'Tis all the Aid my present power supplies:
No Court Informer can these Arms accuse,
These Arms may Sons against their Fathers use,   720
And, tis my wish, the next Successors Reign
May make no other Israelite complain.

   Youth, Beauty, Graceful Action, seldom fail:
But Common Interest always will prevail:
And pity never Ceases to be shown   725
To him, who makes the peoples wrongs his own.
The Croud, (that still believe their Kings oppress)
With lifted hands their young Messiah bless:
Who now begins his Progress to ordain;
With Chariots, Horsemen, and a numerous train: 730
From East to West his Glories he displaies:
And, like the Sun, the promis'd land survays.
Fame runs before him, as the morning Star;
And shouts of Joy salute him from afar:
Each house receives him as a Guardian God;   735
And Consecrates the Place of his aboad:
But hospitable treats did most Commend
Wise Issachar, his wealthy western friend.
This moving Court, that caught the peoples Eyes,
And seem'd but Pomp, did other ends disguise: 740
Achitophel had form'd it, with intent

               727 believe *C–I*: believes *A B*

To sound the depths, and fathom where it went,
The Peoples hearts; distinguish Friends from Foes;
And try their strength, before they came to blows:
Yet all was colour'd with a smooth pretence 745
Of specious love, and duty to their Prince.
Religion, and Redress of Grievances,
Two names, that always cheat and always please,
Are often urg'd; and good King *David*'s life
Indanger'd by a Brother and a Wife. 750
Thus, in a Pageant Show, a Plot is made;
And Peace it self is War in Masquerade.
Oh foolish *Israel*! never warn'd by ill,
Still the same baite, and circumvented still!
Did ever men forsake their present ease, 755
In midst of health Imagine a desease;
Take pains Contingent mischiefs to foresee,
Make Heirs for Monarks, and for God decree?
What shall we think! can People give away
Both for themselves and Sons, their Native sway? 760
Then they are left Defensless, to the Sword
Of each unbounded Arbitrary Lord:
And Laws are vain, by which we Right enjoy,
If Kings unquestiond can those laws destroy.
Yet, if the Crowd be Judge of fit and Just, 765
And Kings are onely Officers in trust,
Then this resuming Cov'nant was declar'd
When Kings were made, or is for ever bar'd:
If those who gave the Scepter, coud not tye
By their own deed their own Posterity, 770
How then coud *Adam* bind his future Race?
How coud his forfeit on mankind take place?
Or how coud heavenly Justice damn us all,
Who nere consented to our Fathers fall?
Then Kings are slaves to those whom they Command, 775
And Tenants to their Peoples pleasure stand.
Add, that the Pow'r for Property allowd,
Is mischeivously seated in the Crowd:
For who can be secure of private Right,

742 depths *C–I*: depth *A B*   went, *C–I*: went: 777 Add, that the Pow'r *C–I*:
That Pow'r, which is *A B*

If Sovereign sway may be dissolv'd by might?   780
Nor is the Peoples Judgment always true:
The most may err as grosly as the few.
And faultless Kings run down, by Common Cry,
For Vice, Oppression, and for Tyranny.
What Standard is there in a fickle rout,   785
Which, flowing to the mark, runs faster out?
Nor only Crowds, but Sanhedrins may be
Infected with this publick Lunacy:
And Share the madness of Rebellious times,
To Murther Monarchs for Imagin'd crimes.   790
If they may Give and Take when e'r they please,
Not Kings alone, (the Godheads Images,)
But Government it self at length must fall
To Natures state; where all have Right to all.
Yet, grant our Lords the People Kings can make,   795
What Prudent men a setled Throne woud shake?
For whatsoe'r their Sufferings were before,
That Change they Covet makes them suffer more.
All other Errors but disturb a State;
But Innovation is the Blow of Fate.   800
If ancient Fabricks nod, and threat to fall,
To Patch the Flaws, and Buttress up the Wall,
Thus far 'tis Duty; but here fix the Mark:
For all beyond it is to touch our Ark.
To change Foundations, cast the Frame anew,   805
Is work for Rebels who base Ends pursue:
At once Divine and Humane Laws controul;
And mend the Parts by ruine of the Whole.
The Tampering World is subject to this Curse,
To Physick their Disease into a worse.   810
     Now what Relief can Righteous *David* bring?
How Fatall 'tis to be too good a King!
Friends he has few, so high the Madness grows,
Who dare be such, must be the Peoples Foes:
Yet some there were, ev'n in the worst of days;   815
Some let me name, and Naming is to praise.
     In this short File *Barzillai* first appears;
Barzillai crown'd with Honour and with Years:
Long since, the rising Rebells he withstood

In Regions Waste, beyond the *Jordans* Flood:　　　　820
Unfortunately Brave to buoy the State;
But sinking underneath his Masters Fate:
In Exile with his Godlike Prince he Mourn'd;
For him he Suffer'd, and with him Return'd.
The Court he practis'd, not the Courtier's art:　　　　825
Large was his Wealth, but larger was his Heart:
Which, well the Noblest Objects knew to choose,
The Fighting Warriour, and Recording Muse.
His Bed coud once a Fruitfull Issue boast:
Now more than half a Father's Name is lost.　　　　830
His Eldest Hope, with every Grace adorn'd,
By me (so Heav'n will have it) always Mourn'd,
And always honour'd, snatcht in Manhoods prime
By' unequal Fates, and Providences crime:
Yet not before the Goal of Honour won,　　　　835
All parts fulfill'd of Subject and of Son;
Swift was the Race, but short the Time to run.
Oh Narrow Circle, but of Pow'r Divine,
Scanted in Space, but perfect in thy Line!
By Sea, by Land, thy Matchless Worth was known;　　　　840
Arms thy Delight, and War was all thy Own:
Thy force, Infus'd, the fainting *Tyrians* prop'd:
And Haughty *Pharaoh* found his Fortune stop'd.
Oh Ancient Honour, Oh Unconquer'd Hand,
Whom Foes unpunish'd never coud withstand!　　　　845
But *Israel* was unworthy of thy Name:
Short is the date of all Immoderate Fame.
It looks as Heaven our Ruine had design'd,
And durst not trust thy Fortune and thy Mind.
Now, free from Earth, thy disencumbred Soul　　　　850
Mounts up, and leaves behind the Clouds and Starry Pole:
From thence thy kindred legions mayst thou bring
To aid the guardian Angel of thy King.
Here stop my Muse, here cease thy painfull flight;
No Pinions can pursue Immortal height:　　　　855
Tell good *Barzillai* thou canst sing no more,
And tell thy Soul she should have fled before;
Or fled she with his life, and left this Verse

846 thy Name: *C*: thy Birth; *A B*: his Name: *D–I*　　　847 Fame *C–I*: Worth *A B*

To hang on her departed Patron's Herse?
Now take thy steepy flight from heaven, and see   860
If thou canst find on earth another *He*;
Another He would be too hard to find,
See then whom thou canst see not far behind.
Zadock the Priest, whom, shunning Power and Place,
His lowly mind advanc'd to *David*'s Grace: 865
With him the *Sagan* of *Jerusalem*,
Of hospitable Soul and noble Stem;
Him of the Western dome, whose weighty sense
Flows in fit words and heavenly eloquence.
The Prophets Sons by such example led,   870
To Learning and to Loyalty were bred:
For *Colleges* on bounteous Kings depend,
And never Rebell was to Arts a friend.
To these succeed the Pillars of the Laws,
Who best cou'd plead and best can judge a Cause.   875
Next them a train of Loyal Peers ascend:
Sharp judging *Adriel* the Muses friend,
Himself a Muse—In Sanhedrins debate
True to his Prince; but not a Slave of State.
Whom *David*'s love with Honours did adorn,   880
That from his disobedient Son were torn.
Jotham of piercing wit and pregnant thought,
Indew'd by nature, and by learning taught
To move Assemblies, who but onely try'd
The worse awhile, then chose the better side;   885
Nor chose alone, but turn'd the balance too;
So much the weight of one brave man can doe.
Hushai the friend of *David* in distress,
In publick storms of manly stedfastness;
By foreign treaties he inform'd his Youth;   890
And join'd experience to his native truth.
His frugal care supply'd the wanting Throne,
Frugal for that, but bounteous of his own:
'Tis easy conduct when Exchequers flow,
But hard the task to manage well the low: 895
For Soveraign power is too deprest or high,
When Kings are forc'd to sell, or Crowds to buy.

861 *He*; *C–I*: He, *A B*   882 piercing *C–I*: ready *A B*

Indulge one labour more my weary Muse,
For *Amiel*, who can *Amiel*'s praise refuse?
Of ancient race by birth, but nobler yet   900
In his own worth, and without Title great:
The Sanhedrin long time as chief he rul'd,
Their Reason guided and their Passion coold;
So dexterous was he in the Crown's defence,
So form'd to speak a Loyal Nation's Sense,   905
That as their band was *Israel*'s Tribes in small,
So fit was he to represent them all.
Now rasher Charioteers the Seat ascend,
Whose loose Carriers his steady Skill commend:
They like th' unequal Ruler of the Day,   910
Misguide the Seasons and mistake the Way;
While he withdrawn at their mad Labour smiles,
And safe enjoys the Sabbath of his Toyls.

    These were the chief, a small but faithful Band
Of Worthies, in the Breach who dar'd to stand,   915
And tempt th' united Fury of the Land.
With grief they view'd such powerful Engines bent,
To batter down the lawful Government.
A numerous Faction with pretended frights,
In Sanhedrins to plume the Regal Rights.   920
The true Successour from the Court remov'd:
The Plot, by hireling Witnesses improv'd.
These Ills they saw, and as their Duty bound,
They shew'd the King the danger of the Wound:
That no Concessions from the Throne woud please,   925
But Lenitives fomented the Disease:
That *Absalom*, ambitious of the Crown,
Was made the Lure to draw the People down:
That false *Achitophel*'s pernitious Hate,
Had turn'd the Plot to Ruine Church and State: 930
The Councill violent, the Rabble worse
That *Shimei* taught *Jerusalem* to Curse.

    With all these loads of Injuries opprest,
And long revolving, in his carefull Breast,
Th' event of things; at last his patience tir'd,   935
Thus from his Royal Throne by Heav'n inspir'd,
The <u>God-like</u> *David* spoke: with awfull fear

His Train their Maker in their Master hear.

David: " Thus long have I, by native mercy sway'd,
My wrongs dissembl'd, my revenge delay'd: 940
So willing to forgive th' Offending Age,
So much the Father did the King asswage.
But now so far my Clemency they slight,
Th' Offenders question my Forgiving Right.
That one was made for many, they contend: 945
But 'tis to Rule, for that's a Monarch's End.
They call my tenderness of Blood, my Fear:
Though Manly tempers can the longest bear.
Yet, since they will divert my Native course,
'Tis time to shew I am not Good by Force.   950
Those heap'd Affronts that haughty Subjects bring,
Are burthens for a Camel, not a King:
Kings are the publick Pillars of the State,
Born to sustain and prop the Nations weight:
If my Young *Samson* will pretend a Call   955
To shake the Column, let him share the Fall:
But oh that yet he woud repent and live!
How easie 'tis for Parents to forgive!
With how few Tears a Pardon might be won
From Nature, pleading for a Darling Son!   960
Poor pitied Youth, by my Paternal care,
Rais'd up to all the Height his Frame coud bear:
Had God ordain'd his fate for Empire born,
He woud have given his Soul another turn:
Gull'd with a Patriots name, whose Modern sense   965
Is one that would by Law supplant his Prince:
The Peoples Brave, the Politicians Tool;
Never was Patriot yet, but was a Fool.
Whence comes it that Religion and the Laws
Should more be *Absalom*'s than *David*'s Cause?   970
His old Instructor, e're he lost his Place,
Was never thought indu'd with so much Grace.
Good Heav'ns, how Faction can a Patriot Paint!
My Rebel ever proves my Peoples Saint:
Would *They* impose an Heir upon the Throne?   975
Let Sanhedrins be taught to give their Own.

957–60 *added in* C, D–I   966 supplant *C–I*: destroy *A B*

A King's at least a part of Government,
And mine as requisite as their Consent:
Without my Leave a future King to choose,
Infers a Right the Present to Depose: 980
True, they Petition me t' approve their Choise,
But *Esau*'s Hands suite ill with *Jacob*'s Voice.
My Pious Subjects for my Safety pray,
Which to Secure they take my Power away.
From Plots and Treasons Heaven preserve my years,   985
But Save me most from my Petitioners.
Unsatiate as the barren Womb or Grave;
God cannot Grant so much as they can Crave.
What then is left but with a Jealous Eye
To guard the Small remains of Royalty?   990
The Law shall still direct my peacefull Sway,
And the same Law teach Rebels to Obey:
Votes shall no more Establish'd Pow'r controul,
Such Votes as make a Part exceed the Whole:
No groundless Clamours shall my Friends remove,   995
Nor Crowds have power to Punish e're they Prove:
For Gods, and Godlike Kings their Care express,
Still to Defend their Servants in distress.
Oh that my Power to Saving were confin'd:
Why am I forc'd, like Heaven, against my mind,   1000
To make Examples of another Kind?
Must I at length the Sword of Justice draw?
Oh curst Effects of necessary Law!
How ill my Fear they by my Mercy scan,
Beware the Fury of a Patient Man.   1005
They coud not be content to look on Grace,
Her hinder parts, but with a daring Eye
To tempt the terror of her Front, and Dye.
By their own arts 'tis Righteously decreed,   1010
Those dire Artificers of Death shall bleed.
Against themselves their Witnesses will Swear,
Till Viper-like their Mother Plot they tear:
And suck for Nutriment that bloody gore
Which was their Principle of Life before.   1015
Their *Belial* with their *Belzebub* will fight;
Thus on my Foes, my Foes shall do me Right:

Nor doubt th' event: for Factious crowds engage
In their first Onset, all their Brutal Rage;
Then, let 'em take an unresisted Course,   1020
Retire and Traverse, and Delude their Force:
But when they stand all Breathless, urge the fight,
And rise upon 'em with redoubled might:
For Lawfull Pow'r is still Superiour found,
When long driven back, at length it stands the ground.   1025
  He said. Th' Almighty, nodding, gave Consent;
And Peals of Thunder shook the Firmament.
Henceforth a Series of new time began,
The mighty Years in long Procession ran:
Once more the Godlike *David* was Restor'd,   1030
And willing Nations knew their Lawfull Lord.

PROLOGUE and EPILOGUE
to *THE UNHAPPY FAVOURITE*

PROLOGUE

Spoken to the King and Queen at their coming to the House,
and Written on purpose

WHEN first the Ark was Landed on the Shore,
 And Heaven had vow'd to curse the Ground no more,
When Tops of Hills the Longing Patriark saw,
And the new Scene of Earth began to draw;
The Dove was sent to View the Waves Decrease,   5
And first brought back to Man the Pledge of Peace:
'Tis needless to apply when those appear
Who bring the Olive, and who Plant it here.
We have before our eyes the Royal Dove,
Still Innocence is Harbinger to Love,   10
The Ark is open'd to dismiss the Train,
And People with a better Race the Plain.
Tell me you Powers, why should vain Man pursue,
With endless Toyl, each object that is new,
And for the seeming substance leave the true—   15
Why should he quit for hopes his certain good,
And loath the Manna of his dayly food?
Must *England* still the Scene of Changes be,
Tost and Tempestuous like our Ambient Sea?
Must still our Weather and our Wills agree?   20
Without our Blood our Liberties we have,
Who that is Free would Fight to be a Slave?
Or what can Wars to after Times Assure,
Of which our Present Age is not secure?
All that our Monarch would for us Ordain,   25
Is but t' Injoy the Blessings of his Reign.
Our Land's an *Eden*, and the Main's our Fence,
While we Preserve our State of Innocence;

Prologue and Epilogue. Text from Banks's The Unhappy Favourite: or The Earl of Essex.
A Tragedy, *1682, collated with the editions of 1685, 1693, and (Epilogue only) Miscellany*
Poems, *1684 and 1692*

That lost, then Beasts their Brutal Force employ,
And first their Lord, and then themselves destroy: 30
What Civil Broils have cost we know too well,
Oh let it be enough that once we fell,
And every Heart conspire with every Tongue,
Still to have such a King, and this King Long.

EPILOGUE

WE Act by Fits and Starts, like drowning Men,
        But just Peep up, and then Dop down again;
Let those who call us Wicked change their Sence,
For never Men liv'd more on Providence,
Not Lott'ry Cavaliers are half so poor,   5
Nor Broken Cits, nor a Vacation Whore,
Not Courts nor Courtiers living on the Rents,
Of the Three last ungiving Parliaments.
So wretched that if *Pharoah* could Divine,
He might have spar'd his Dream of Seven lean Kine,   } 10
And chang'd his Vision for the Muses Nine.
The Comet that they say Portends a Dearth,
Was but a Vapour drawn from Play-house Earth,
Pent there since our last Fire, and *Lilly* sayes,
Fore-shows our change of State and thin Third dayes.   15
'Tis not our want of Wit that keeps us Poor,
For then the Printers Press would suffer more:
Their Pamphleteers each day their Venom spit,
They thrive by Treason and we starve by Wit.
Confess the truth, which of you has not laid [*To the Upper Gallery.* 20
Four Farthings out to buy the *Hatfield* Maid?
Or which is duller yet, and more wou'd spight us,
Democritus his Wars with *Heraclitus*?
Such are the Authors who have run us down,
And Exercis'd you Critticks of the Town;   25

Prologue. 31 know *85 93*: knew *82*
Epilogue.
11 his *84 92*: the *82 85 93*   12 that *84 92*: which *82 85 93*   14 there *84 92*:
here *82 85 93*   18 each day their Venom *84 92*: their Venom dayly *82 85 93*
20 Stage direction. *Looking above. 84 92*   22 which *84 92*: what *82 85 93*
wou'd *84 92*: to *82*: does *85 93*   24 Such *84 92*: These *82 85 93*   who *84*
92: that *82 85 93*   25 Exercis'd *84 92*: Exercise *82 85 93*

Yet these are Pearls to your Lampooning Rhimes,
Y'abuse your selves more dully than the Times;
Scandal, the Glory of the *English* Nation,
Is worn to Rags and Scribled out of Fashion;
Such harmless thrusts, as if like Fencers Wise,   30
They had agreed their Play before their Prize.
Faith they may hang their Harps upon the Willows,
'Tis just like Children when they Box with Pillows.
Then put an end to Civil Wars for shame,
Let each Knight Errant who has wrong'd a Dame,   35
Throw down his Pen, and give her as he can,
The satisfaction of a Gentleman.

PROLOGUE and EPILOGUE
to *THE LOYAL BROTHER*

A PROLOGUE

Written by Mr. Dryden, *to a New Play, call'd,*
The Loyal Brother, *&c.*

Poets, like Lawfull Monarchs, rul'd the Stage,
Till Criticks, like Damn'd Whiggs, debauch'd our Age.
Mark how they jump: Criticks wou'd regulate
Our Theatres, and Whiggs reform our State:
Both pretend love, and both (Plague rot 'em) hate.   5
The Critick humbly seems Advice to bring,
The fawning Whigg Petitions to the King:
But ones advice into a Satyr slides;
T'others Petition a Remonstrance hides.
These will no Taxes give, and those no Pence: 10
Criticks wou'd starve the Poet, Whiggs the Prince.

31 They . . . their . . . their *84 92*: You . . . your . . . the *82 85 93*   32 they
. . . their *84 92*: you . . . your *82 85 93*   36 as *84 92*: if *82 85 93*
*Prologue and Epilogue. Text from the separate edition of 1682, collated with the first edition
of Southerne's* The Loyal Brother *or* The Persian Prince. A Tragedy

The Critick all our troops of friends discards;
Just so the Whigg wou'd fain pull down the Guards.
Guards are illegal, that drive foes away,
As watchfull Shepherds, that fright beasts of prey.   15
Kings, who Disband such needless Aids as these,
Are safe—as long as e're their Subjects please.
And that wou'd be till next Queen *Besses* night:
Which thus, grave penny Chroniclers endite.
Sir *Edmond-berry*, first, in wofull wise,   20
Leads up the show, and Milks their Maudlin eyes.
There's not a Butcher's Wife but Dribs her part,
And pities the poor Pageant from her heart;
Who, to provoke revenge, rides round the fire,
And, with a civil congee, does retire.   25
But guiltless blood to ground must never fall:
There's *Antichrist* behind, to pay for all.
The Punk of *Babylon* in Pomp appears,
A lewd Old Gentleman of Seventy years.
Whose Age in vain our Mercy wou'd implore;   30
For few take pity on an Old-cast Whore.
The Devil, who brought him to the shame, takes part; ⎫
Sits cheek by jowl, in black, to cheer his heart: ⎬
Like Theef and Parson in a *Tyburn*-Cart.   ⎭
The word is giv'n; and with a loud Huzzaw   35
The Miter'd Moppet from his Chair they draw:
On the slain Corps contending Nations fall;
Alas, what's one poor Pope among 'em all!
He burns; now all true hearts your Triumphs ring;
And next (for fashion) cry, *God save the King*.   40
A needful Cry in midst of such Alarms:
When Forty thousand Men are up in Arms.
But after he's once sav'd, to make amends,   ⎫
In each succeeding Health they Damn his Friends: ⎬
So God begins, but still the Devil ends.   ⎭   45
What if some one inspir'd with Zeal, shou'd call,
Come let's go cry, God save him at *White-Hall*?
His best friends wou'd not like this over-care:
Or think him e're the safer for that pray'r.
Five Praying Saints are by an Act allow'd;   50
But not the whole Church-Militant, in crowd.

Yet, should heav'n all the true Petitions drain
Of *Presbyterians*, who wou'd Kings maintain;
Of Forty thousand, five wou'd scarce remain.

The EPILOGUE *by the same Hand*

Spoken by Mrs. Sarah Cook

A VIRGIN Poet was serv'd up to day;
　Who till this hour, ne're cackled for a Play:
He's neither yet a Whigg nor Tory-Boy;
But, like a Girl, whom several wou'd enjoy,
Begs leave to make the best of his own natural Toy.　5
Were I to play my callow Author's game,
The King's House wou'd instruct me, by the Name:
There's Loyalty to one: I wish no more:
A Commonwealth sounds like a Common Whore.
Let Husband or Gallant be what they will,　10
One part of Woman is true Tory still.
If any Factious spirit shou'd rebell,
Our Sex, with ease, can every rising quell.
Then, as you hope we shou'd your failings hide,
An honest Jury for our play provide:　15
Whiggs, at their Poets never take offence;
They save dull Culpritts who have Murther'd Sense:
Tho Nonsense is a nauseous heavy Mass,
The Vehicle call'd Faction makes it pass.
Faction in Play's the Commonwealths man's bribe:　20
The leaden farthing of the Canting Tribe:
Though void in payment Laws and Statutes make it,
The Neighbourhood, that knows the Man, will take it.
'Tis Faction buys the Votes of half the Pit;
Theirs is the Pention-Parliament of wit.　25
In City-Clubs their venom let 'em vent;
For there 'tis safe, in its own Element:
Here, where their madness can have no pretence,
Let 'em forget themselves an hour in sense.
In one poor Isle, why shou'd two Factions be?　30
Small diff'rence in your Vices I can see;
In Drink and Drabs both sides too well agree.

Wou'd there were more Preferments in the Land;
If Places fell, the party cou'd not stand.
Of this damn'd grievance ev'ry Whigg complains;   35
They grunt like Hogs, till they have got their Grains.
Mean time you see what Trade our Plots advance,
We send each year good Money into *France*:
And they, that know what Merchandise we need,
Send o're true Protestants, to mend our breed.   40

THE MEDALL

A SATYRE AGAINST SEDITION

Per Graiûm populos, mediæque per Elidis Urbem
Ibat ovans; Divumque sibi poscebat Honores

EPISTLE To the WHIGS

*F*OR *to whom can I dedicate this Poem, with so much justice as to you?'Tis*
the representation of your own Heroe:'tis the Picture drawn at length, which
you admire and prize so much in little. None of your Ornaments are wanting;
neither the Landscap of the Tower, nor the Rising Sun; nor the Anno Domini
of your New Sovereign's Coronation. This must needs be a gratefull undertaking 5
to your whole Party: especially to those who have not been so happy as to purchase
the Original. I hear the Graver *has made a good Market of it: all his Kings are*
bought up already; or the value of the remainder so inhanc'd, that many a poor
Polander *who would be glad to worship the Image, is not able to go to the cost*
of him: But must be content to see him here. I must confess I am no great Artist; 10
but Sign-post painting will serve the turn to remember a Friend by; especially
when better is not to be had. Yet for your comfort the lineaments are true: and
though he sate not five times to me, as he did to B. yet I have consulted History;
as the Italian *Painters doe, when they wou'd draw a* Nero *or a* Caligula;
though they have not seen the Man, they can help their Imagination by a Statue 15
of him, and find out the Colouring from Suetonius *and* Tacitus. *Truth is, you*
might have spar'd one side of your Medall: the Head wou'd be seen to more
advantage, if it were plac'd on a Spike of the Tower; a little nearer to the Sun.
Which wou'd then break out to better purpose. You tell us in your Preface to the
No-protestant Plot, *that you shall be forc'd hereafter to leave off your* 20
Modesty: I suppose you mean that little which is left you: for it was worn to rags
when you put out this Medall. Never was there practis'd such a piece of notorious
Impudence in the face of an Establish'd Government. I believe, when he is dead,
you will wear him in Thumb-Rings, as the Turks *did* Scanderbeg; *as if there*
were virtue in his Bones to preserve you against Monarchy. Yet all this while 25
you pretend not onely zeal for the Publick good; but a due veneration for the
person of the King. But all men who can see an inch before them, may easily
detect those gross fallacies. That it is necessary for men in your circumstances
to pretend both, is granted you; for without them there could be no ground to
raise a Faction. But I would ask you one civil question, what right has any man 30

The Medall. Text from the first edition, 1682

*among you, or any Association of men, (to come nearer to you,) who out of
Parliament, cannot be consider'd in a publick Capacity, to meet, as you daily doe,
in Factious Clubs, to vilify the Government, in your Discourses, and to libel it in
all your Writings? who made you Judges in* Israel? *or how is it consistent with
your Zeal of the publick Welfare, to promote Sedition? Does your definition of* 35
*loyal, which is to serve the King according to the Laws, allow you the licence of
traducing the Executive Power, with which you own he is invested? You complain
that his Majesty has lost the love and confidence of his People; and by your very
urging it, you endeavour what in you lies, to make him lose them. All good
Subjects abhor the thought of Arbitrary Power, whether it be in one or many:* 40
*if you were the Patriots you would seem, you would not at this rate incense the
Multitude to assume it; for no sober man can fear it, either from the King's
Disposition, or his Practice; or even, where you would odiously lay it, from his
Ministers. Give us leave to enjoy the Government and the benefit of Laws under
which we were born, and which we desire to transmit to our Posterity. You are* 45
*not the Trustees of the publick Liberty: and if you have not right to petition in
a Crowd, much less have you to intermeddle in the management of Affairs; or to
arraign what you do not like: which in effect is every thing that is done by the
King and Council. Can you imagine that any reasonable man will believe you
respect the person of his Majesty, when 'tis apparent that your Seditious Pamphlets* 50
*are stuff'd with particular Reflexions on him? If you have the confidence to deny
this, 'tis easy to be evinc'd from a thousand Passages, which I onely forbear to
quote, because I desire they should die and be forgotten. I have perus'd many of
your Papers; and to show you that I have, the third part of your* No-protestant
Plot *is much of it stolen, from your dead Authour's Pamphlet call'd, the* Growth 55
of Popery; *as manifestly as* Milton's *defence of the* English *People, is from*
Buchanan, de jure regni apud Scotos: *or your first Covenant, and new
Association, from the holy League of the* French Guisards. *Any one who reads*
Davila, *may trace your Practices all along. There were the same pretences for
Reformation, and Loyalty, the same Aspersions of the King, and the same grounds* 60
*of a Rebellion. I know not whether you will take the Historian's word, who says
it was reported, that* Poltrot *a Hugonot, murther'd Francis Duke of* Guise
by the instigations of Theodore Beza: *or that it was a* Hugonot *Minister,
otherwise call'd a* Presbyterian, *(for our Church abhors so devilish a Tenent)
who first writ a Treatise of the lawfulness of deposing and murthering Kings,* 65
*of a different Perswasion in Religion: But I am able to prove from the Doctrine
of* Calvin, *and Principles of* Buchanan, *that they set the People above the
Magistrate; which if I mistake not, is your own Fundamental; and which carries
your Loyalty no farther than your likeing. When a Vote of the House of
Commons goes on your side, you are as ready to observe it, as if it were pass'd into* 70

a Law: But when you are pinch'd with any former, and yet unrepealed Act of
Parliament, *you declare that in some cases, you will not be oblig'd by it. The
Passage is in the same third part of the* No-protestant Plot; *and is too plain to
be denied. The late Copy of your intended Association, you neither wholly justify
nor condemn; But, as the Papists, when they are unoppos'd, fly out into all the* 75
Pageantry's *of Worship; but in times of War, when they are hard press'd by
Arguments, lie close intrench'd behind the* Council of Trent: *So, now, when
your Affairs are in a low condition, you dare not pretend that to be a legal
Combination, but whensoever you are afloat, I doubt not but it will be maintain'd
and justify'd to purpose. For indeed there is nothing to defend it but the Sword:* 80
'tis the proper time to say any thing, when men have all things in their power.

In the mean time *you wou'd fain be nibbling at a parallel betwixt this
Association, and that in the time of* Queen Elizabeth. *But there is this small
difference betwixt them, that the ends of the one are directly opposite to the other:
one with the Queen's approbation, and conjunction, as head of it; the other without* 85
*either the consent, or knowledge of the King, against whose Authority it is mani-
festly design'd. Therefore you doe well to have recourse to your last Evasion, that
it was contriv'd by your Enemies, and shuffled into the Papers that were seiz'd:
which yet you see the Nation is not so easy to believe as your own Jury; But the
matter is not difficult, to find twelve men in* New-gate, *who wou'd acquit a* 90
Malefactour.

*I have one onely favour to desire of you at parting, that when you think of answer-
ing this* Poem, *you wou'd employ the same Pens against it, who have combated
with so much success against* Absalom and Achitophel: *for then you may
assure your selves of a clear Victory, without the least reply. Raile at me* 95
*abundantly; and, not to break a Custome, doe it without wit: By this method
you will gain a considerable point, which is wholly to wave the answer of my
Arguments. Never own the botome of your Principles, for fear they shou'd be
Treason. Fall severely on the miscarriages of Government; for if scandal be not
allow'd, you are no freeborn subjects. If God has not bless'd you with the Talent* 100
*of Rhiming, make use of my poor Stock and wellcome: let your Verses run upon
my feet: and for the utmost refuge of notorious Block-heads, reduc'd to the last
extremity of sense, turn my own lines upon me, and in utter despaire of your own
Satyre, make me Satyrize my self. Some of you have been driven to this Bay
already; But above all the rest commend me to the Non-conformist Parson, who* 105
writ the Whip and Key. *I am afraid it is not read so much as the Piece deserves,
because the Bookseller is every week crying help at the end of his* Gazette, *to get
it off. You see I am charitable enough to doe him a kindness, that it may be
publish'd as well as printed; and that so much skill in* Hebrew *Derivations, may
not lie for* Wast-paper *in the Shop. Yet I half suspect he went no farther for his* 110

*learning, than the Index of Hebrew Names and Etymologies, which is printed at
the end of some* English *Bibles. If* Achitophel *signify the Brother of a Fool, the
Authour of that Poem will pass with his Readers for the next of kin. And perhaps
'tis the Relation that makes the kindness. Whatever the Verses are; buy 'em up I
beseech you out of pity; for I hear the Conventicle is shut up, and the Brother of* 115
Achitophel *out of service.*

*Now Footmen, you know, have the generosity to make a Purse, for a Member
of their Society, who has had his Livery pull'd over his Ears: and even Protestant
Socks are bought up among you, out of veneration to the name. A Dissenter in
Poetry from Sense and* English, *will make as good a Protestant Rhymer, as a* 120
Dissenter from the Church of England *a Protestant Parson. Besides, if you
encourage a young Beginner, who knows but he may elevate his stile a little,
above the vulgar Epithets of prophane, and sawcy* Jack, *and Atheistick Scribler,
with which he treats me, when the fit of Enthusiasm is strong upon him: by which
well-manner'd and charitable Expressions, I was certain of his Sect, before I knew* 125
*his name. What wou'd you have more of a man? he has damn'd me in your Cause
from* Genesis *to the* Revelations: *And has half the Texts of both the* Testaments *against me, if you will be so civil to your selves as to take him for your
Interpreter; and not to take them for* Irish *Witnesses. After all, perhaps you will
tell me, that you retain'd him onely for the opening of your Cause, and that your* 130
*main Lawyer is yet behind. Now if it so happen he meet with no more reply than
his Predecessours, you may either conclude, that I trust to the goodness of my
Cause, or fear my Adversary, or disdain him, or what you please, for the short on't
is, 'tis indifferent to your humble servant, whatever your Party says or thinks of him.*

THE MEDALL
A Satyre Against Sedition

OF all our Antick Sights, and Pageantry
    Which *English* Ideots run in crowds to see,
The *Polish Medall* bears the prize alone:
A Monster, more the Favourite of the Town
Than either Fayrs or Theatres have shown.   5
Never did Art so well with Nature strive;
Nor ever Idol seem'd so much alive:

So like the Man; so golden to the sight,
So base within, so counterfeit and light.
One side is fill'd with Title and with Face;   10
And, lest the King shou'd want a regal Place,
On the reverse, a Tow'r the Town surveys;
O'er which our mounting Sun his beams displays.
The Word, pronounc'd aloud by Shrieval voice,
Lætamur, which, in *Polish*, is *rejoyce*.   15
The Day, Month, Year, to the great Act are join'd:
And a new Canting Holiday design'd.
Five daies he sate, for every cast and look;
Four more than God to finish *Adam* took.
But who can tell what Essence Angels are,   20
Or how long Heav'n was making *Lucifer*?
Oh, cou'd the Style that copy'd every grace,
And plough'd such furrows for an Eunuch face,
Cou'd it have form'd his ever-changing Will,
The various Piece had tir'd the Graver's Skill!   25
A Martial Heroe first, with early care,
Blown, like a Pigmee by the Winds, to war.
A beardless Chief, a Rebel, e'r a Man:
(So young his hatred to his Prince began.)
Next this, (How wildly will Ambition steer!)   30
A Vermin, wriggling in th' Usurper's Ear.
Bart'ring his venal wit for sums of gold
He cast himself into the Saint-like mould;
Groan'd, sigh'd and pray'd, while Godliness was gain;
The lowest Bagpipe of the squeaking Train.   35
But, as 'tis hard to cheat a Juggler's Eyes,
His open lewdness he cou'd ne'er disguise.
There split the Saint: for Hypocritique Zeal
Allows no Sins but those it can conceal.
Whoring to Scandal gives too large a scope: 40
Saints must not trade; but they may interlope.
Th' ungodly Principle was all the same;
But a gross Cheat betrays his Partner's Game.
Besides, their pace was formal, grave and slack:
His nimble Wit outran the heavy Pack.   45
Yet still he found his Fortune at a stay;
Whole droves of Blockheads choaking up his way;

They took, but not rewarded, his advice;
Villain and Wit exact a double price.
Pow'r was his aym: but, thrown from that pretence,⎫   50
The Wretch turn'd loyal in his own defence;   ⎬
And Malice reconcil'd him to his Prince.   ⎭
Him, in the anguish of his Soul he serv'd;
Rewarded faster still than he deserv'd,
Behold him now exalted into trust;   55
His Counsel's oft convenient, seldom just.
⌈ Ev'n in the most sincere advice he gave
⌊ He had a grudging still to be a Knave.
The Frauds he learnt in his Fanatique years
Made him uneasy in his lawfull gears.   60
At best as little honest as he cou'd:
And, like white Witches, mischievously good.
To his first byass, longingly he leans;
And *rather* wou'd be great by wicked means.
Thus, fram'd for ill, he loos'd our Triple hold;   65
(Advice unsafe, precipitous, and bold.)
From hence those tears! that *Ilium* of our woe!
Who helps a pow'rfull Friend, fore-arms a Foe.
What wonder if the Waves prevail so far
When He cut down the Banks that made the bar?   70
Seas follow but their Nature to invade;
But He by Art our native Strength betray'd.
So *Sampson* to his Foe his force confest;
And, to be shorn, lay slumb'ring on her breast.
But, when this fatal Counsel, found too late,   75
Expos'd its Authour to the publique hate;
When his just Sovereign, by no impious way,
Cou'd be seduc'd to Arbitrary sway;
Forsaken of that hope, he shifts the sayle;⎫
Drives down the Current with a pop'lar gale;⎬   80
And shews the Fiend confess'd, without a vaile.⎭
⌈ He preaches to the Crowd, that Pow'r is lent,
⌊ But not convey'd to Kingly Government;
That Claimes successive bear no binding force;
That Coronation Oaths are things of course;   85
Maintains the Multitude can never err;
And sets the People in the Papal Chair.

The reason's obvious; *Int'rest never lyes;*
The most have still their Int'rest in their eyes;
The pow'r is always theirs, and pow'r is ever wise. } 90 (6)
Almighty Crowd, thou shorten'st all dispute;
Pow'r is thy Essence; Wit thy Attribute!
Nor Faith nor Reason make thee at a stay,
Thou leapst o'r all eternal truths, in thy *Pindarique* way! (6)
Athens, no doubt, did righteously decide, 95
When *Phocion* and when *Socrates* were try'd:
As righteously they did those dooms repent;
Still they were wise, what ever way they went.
Crowds err not, though to both extremes they run;
To kill the Father, and recall the Son. 100
Some think the Fools were most, as times went then;
But now the World's o'r stock'd with prudent men.
The common Cry is ev'n Religion's Test;
The *Turk*'s is, at *Constantinople,* best;
Idols in *India,* Popery at *Rome;* 105
And our own Worship onely true at home.
And true, but for the time, 'tis hard to know
How long we please it shall continue so.
This side to day, and that to morrow burns;
So all are God-a'mighties in their turns. 110
A Tempting Doctrine, plausible and new:
What Fools our Fathers were, if this be true!
Who, to destroy the seeds of Civil War,
Inherent right in Monarchs did declare:
And, that a lawfull Pow'r might never cease, 115
Secur'd Succession, to secure our Peace.
Thus, Property and Sovereign Sway, at last
In equal Balances were justly cast:
But this new *Jehu* spurs the hot mouth'd horse;
Instructs the Beast to know his native force; 120
To take the Bit between his teeth and fly
To the next headlong Steep of Anarchy.
Too happy *England,* if our good we knew;
Wou'd we possess the freedom we pursue!
The lavish Government can give no more: 125
Yet we repine; and plenty makes us poor.
God try'd us once; our Rebel-fathers fought;

He glutted 'em with all the pow'r they sought:
Till, master'd by their own usurping Brave,
The free-born Subject sunk into a Slave.   130
We loath our Manna, and we long for Quails;
Ah, what is man, when his own wish prevails!
How rash, how swift to plunge himself in ill;
Proud of his Pow'r, and boundless in his Will!
That Kings can doe no wrong we must believe: 135
None can they doe, and must they all receive?
Help Heaven! or sadly we shall see an hour,
When neither wrong nor right are in their pow'r!
Already they have lost their best defence,
The benefit of Laws, which they dispence.   140
No justice to their righteous Cause allow'd;
But baffled by an Arbitrary Crowd.
And Medalls grav'd, their Conquest to record,
The Stamp and Coyn of their adopted Lord.

     The Man who laugh'd but once, to see an Ass   145
Mumbling to make the cross-grain'd Thistles pass;
Might laugh again, to see a Jury chaw
The prickles of unpalatable Law.
The Witnesses, that, Leech-like, liv'd on bloud,
Sucking for them were med'cinally good;   150
But, when they fasten'd on *their* fester'd Sore,
Then, Justice and Religion they forswore;
Their Mayden Oaths debauch'd into a Whore.
Thus Men are rais'd by Factions, and decry'd;
And Rogue and Saint distinguish'd by their Side.   155
They rack ev'n Scripture to confess their Cause;
And plead a Call to preach, in spight of Laws.
But that's no news to the poor injur'd Page;
It has been us'd as ill in every Age:
And is constrain'd, with patience, all to take;   160
For what defence can Greek and Hebrew make?
Happy who can this talking Trumpet seize;
They make it speak whatever Sense they please!
'Twas fram'd, at first, our Oracle t' enquire;
But, since our Sects in prophecy grow higher,   165
The Text inspires not them; but they the Text inspire.
     London, thou great *Emporium* of our Isle,

O, thou too bounteous, thou too fruitfull *Nile*,
How shall I praise or curse to thy desert!
Or separate thy sound, from thy corrupted part!   170
I call'd thee *Nile*; the parallel will stand:
Thy tydes of Wealth o'rflow the fattend Land;
Yet Monsters from thy large increase we find;
Engender'd on the Slyme thou leav'st behind.
Sedition has not wholly seiz'd on thee;   175
Thy nobler Parts are from infection free.
Of *Israel*'s Tribes thou hast a numerous band;
But still the *Canaanite* is in the Land.
Thy military Chiefs are brave and true;
Nor are thy disinchanted Burghers few.   180
The Head is loyal which thy Heart commands;
But what's a Head with two such gouty Hands?
The wise and wealthy love the surest way;
And are content to thrive and to obey.
But Wisedom is to Sloath too great a Slave;   185
None are so busy as the Fool and Knave.
Those let me curse; what vengeance will they urge,
Whose Ordures neither Plague nor Fire can purge;
Nor sharp Experience can to duty bring,
Nor angry Heav'n, nor a forgiving King!   190
In Gospel phrase their Chapmen they betray:
Their Shops are Dens, the Buyer is their Prey.
The Knack of Trades is living on the Spoyl;
They boast, ev'n when each other they beguile.
Customes to steal is such a trivial thing,   195
That 'tis their Charter, to defraud their King.
All hands unite of every jarring Sect;
They cheat the Country first, and then infect.
They, for God's Cause their Monarchs dare dethrone;
And they'll be sure to make his Cause their own.   200
Whether the plotting Jesuite lay'd the plan
Of murth'ring Kings, or the *French* Puritan,
Our Sacrilegious Sects their Guides outgo;
And Kings and Kingly Pow'r wou'd murther too.
     What means their Trait'rous Combination less,   205

174 Engender'd on] *Noyes records a copy of 82 with* Enlivend by   179–80, 181–2
transposed in Noyes's copy   182 a] the Noyes's copy

Too plain t'evade, too shamefull to confess.
But Treason is not own'd when tis descry'd;
Successfull Crimes alone are justify'd.
The Men, who no Conspiracy wou'd find,   210
Who doubts, but had it taken, they had join'd.
Joyn'd, in a mutual Cov'nant of defence;
At first without, at last against their Prince.
If Sovereign Right by Sovereign Pow'r they scan,
The same bold Maxime holds in God and Man: 215
God were not safe, his Thunder cou'd they shun
He shou'd be forc'd to crown another Son.
Thus, when the Heir was from the Vineyard thrown,
The rich Possession was the Murth'rers own.
In vain to Sophistry they have recourse:
By proving theirs no Plot, they prove 'tis worse;   220
Unmask'd Rebellion, and audacious Force.
Which, though not Actual, yet all Eyes may see
'Tis working, in th' immediate Pow'r to be;
For, from pretended Grievances they rise,
First to dislike, and after to despise.   225
Then, *Cyclop*-like in humane Flesh to deal;
Chop up a Minister, at every meal:
Perhaps not wholly to melt down the King;
But clip his regal Rights within the Ring.
From thence, t'assume the pow'r of Peace and War;   230
And ease him by degrees of publique Care.
Yet, to consult his Dignity and Fame,
He shou'd have leave to exercise the Name;
And hold the Cards, while Commons play'd the game.
For what can Pow'r give more than Food and Drink,   235
To live at ease, and not be bound to think?
These are the cooler methods of their Crime;
But their hot Zealots think 'tis loss of time:
On utmost bounds of Loyalty they stand;
And grinn and whet like a *Croatian* Band;   240
That waits impatient for the last Command.
Thus Out-laws open Villany maintain:
They steal not, but in Squadrons scoure the Plain:
And, if their Pow'r the Passengers subdue;
The Most have right, the wrong is in the Few.   245

Such impious Axiomes foolishly they show;
For, in some Soyles Republiques will not grow:
Our Temp'rate Isle will no extremes sustain,
Of pop'lar Sway, or Arbitrary Reign:
But slides between them both into the best;   250
Secure in freedom, in a Monarch blest.
And though the Clymate, vex't with various Winds,
Works through our yielding Bodies, on our Minds,
The wholsome Tempest purges what it breeds;
To recommend the Calmness that succeeds.   255
  But thou, the Pander of the Peoples hearts,
(O Crooked Soul, and Serpentine in Arts,)
Whose blandishments a Loyal Land have whor'd,
And broke the Bonds she plighted to her Lord;
What Curses on thy blasted Name will fall!   260
Which Age to Age their Legacy shall call;
For all must curse the Woes that must descend on all.
Religion thou hast none: thy *Mercury*
Has pass'd through every Sect, or theirs through Thee.
But what thou giv'st, that Venom still remains;   265
And the pox'd Nation feels Thee in their Brains.
What else inspires the Tongues, and swells the Breasts
Of all thy bellowing Renegado Priests,
That preach up Thee for God; dispence thy Laws;
And with thy Stumm ferment their fainting Cause?   270
Fresh Fumes of Madness raise; and toile and sweat
To make the formidable Cripple great.
Yet, shou'd thy Crimes succeed, shou'd lawless Pow'r
Compass those Ends thy greedy Hopes devour,
Thy Canting Friends thy Mortal Foes wou'd be;   275
Thy God and Theirs will never long agree.
For thine, (if thou hast any,) must be one
That lets the World and Humane-kind alone:
A jolly God, that passes hours too well
To promise Heav'n, or threaten us with Hell.   280
That unconcern'd can at Rebellion sit;
And Wink at Crimes he did himself commit.
A Tyrant theirs; the Heav'n their Priesthood paints
A Conventicle of gloomy sullen Saints;
A Heav'n, like *Bedlam*, slovenly and sad;   285

Fore-doom'd for Souls, with false Religion, mad.
    Without a Vision Poets can fore-show
What all but Fools, by common Sense may know:
If true Succession from our Isle shou'd fail,
And Crowds profane, with impious Arms prevail,
Not Thou, nor those thy Factious Arts ingage   290
Shall reap that Harvest of Rebellious Rage,
With which thou flatter'st thy decrepit Age.
The swelling Poyson of the sev'ral Sects,
Which wanting vent, the Nations Health infects   295
Shall burst its Bag; and fighting out their way
The various Venoms on each other prey.
The *Presbyter*, puft up with spiritual Pride,
Shall on the Necks of the lewd Nobles ride:
His Brethren damn, the Civil Pow'r defy;   300
And parcel out Republique Prelacy.
But short shall be his Reign: his rigid Yoke
And Tyrant Pow'r will puny Sects provoke;
And Frogs and Toads, and all the Tadpole Train
Will croak to Heav'n for help, from this devouring Crane.   305
The Cut-throat Sword and clamorous Gown shall jar,
In shareing their ill-gotten Spoiles of War:
Chiefs shall be grudg'd the part which they pretend;
Lords envy Lords, and Friends with every Friend
About their impious Merit shall contend.   310
The surly Commons shall respect deny;
And justle Peerage out with Property.
Their Gen'ral either shall his Trust betray,
And force the Crowd to Arbitrary sway;
Or they suspecting his ambitious Aym,   315
In hate of Kings shall cast anew the Frame;
And thrust out *Collatine* that bore their Name.
    Thus inborn Broyles the Factions wou'd ingage;
Or Wars of Exil'd Heirs, or Foreign Rage,
Till halting Vengeance overtook our Age:
And our wild Labours, wearied into Rest,   320
Reclin'd us on a rightfull Monarch's Breast.
        —*Pudet hæc opprobria, vobis*
Et dici potuisse, & non potuisse refelli.

        323–4 Added in 82, second issue

PROLOGUE To His *ROYAL HIGHNESS*
Upon His first appearance at the *DUKE'S THEATRE* since his Return from *SCOTLAND*

Spoken by Mr. Smith

IN those cold Regions which no Summers chear,
When brooding darkness covers half the year,
To hollow Caves the shivering Natives go;
Bears range abroad, and hunt in tracks of Snow:
But when the tedious Twilight wears away, 5
And Stars grow paler at th' approach of Day,
The longing Crowds to frozen Mountains run,
Happy who first can see the glimmering Sun!
The surly Salvage Off-spring disappear;
And curse the bright Successour of the Year. 10
Yet, though rough Bears in Covert seek defence,
White Foxes stay, with seeming Innocence:
That crafty kind with day-light can dispense.
Still we are throng'd so full with *Reynard*'s race,
That Loyal Subjects scarce can find a place: 15
Thus modest Truth is cast behind the Crowd:
Truth speaks too Low; Hypocrisie too Loud.
Let 'em be first, to flatter in success;
Duty can stay; but Guilt has need to press.
Once, when true Zeal the Sons of God did call, 20
To make their solemn show at Heaven's *White-hall*,
The fawning Devil appear'd among the rest,
And made as good a Courtier as the best.
The Friends of *Job*, who rail'd at him before,
Came Cap in hand when he had three times more. 25
Yet, late Repentance may, perhaps, be true;
Kings can forgive if Rebels can but sue:
A Tyrant's Pow'r in rigour is exprest:
The Father yearns in the true Prince's Breast.
We grant an O'regrown Whig no grace can mend; 30
But most are Babes, that know not they offend.

Prologue To His Royal Highness. Text from the first edition, 1682

The Crowd, to restless motion still enclin'd,
Are Clouds, that rack according to the Wind.
Driv'n by their Chiefs they storms of Hail-stones pour:
Then mourn, and soften to a silent showre.   35
O welcome to this much offending Land
The Prince that brings forgiveness in his hand!
Thus Angels on glad Messages appear:
Their first Salute commands us not to fear:
Thus Heav'n, that cou'd constrain us to obey,   ⎫
(With rev'rence if we might presume to say,)   ⎬ 40
Seems to relax the rights of Sov'reign sway: ⎭
Permits to Man the choice of Good and Ill;
And makes us Happy by our own Free-will.

PROLOGUE To The Dutchess
On Her Return from SCOTLAND

WHEN Factious Rage to cruel Exile, drove
    The Queen of Beauty, and the Court of Love;
The Muses Droop'd, with their forsaken Arts,
And the sad *Cupids* broke their useless Darts.
Our fruitfull Plains to Wilds and Desarts turn'd,   5
Like *Edens* Face when banish'd Man it mourn'd:
Love was no more when Loyalty was gone,
The great Supporter of his Awfull Throne.
Love cou'd no longer after Beauty stay,   ⎫
But wander'd Northward to the verge of day,   ⎬ 10
As if the Sun and He had lost their way.   ⎭
But now th' Illustrious Nymph return'd again,
Brings every Grace triumphant in her Train:
The wondring *Nereids*, though they rais'd no storm,
Foreslow'd her passage to behold her form: 15
Some cry'd a *Venus*, some a *Thetis* past:
But this was not so fair, nor that so chast.
Far from her sight flew Faction, Strife and Pride:
And Envy did but look on her, and dy'd.

Prologue To The Dutchess. *Text from the first edition, 1682*

What e'er we suffer'd from our sullen Fate,   20
Her sight is purchas'd at an easy rate:
Three gloomy Years against this day were set:
But this one mighty Sum has clear'd the Debt.
Like *Joseph*'s Dream, but with a better doom;
The Famine past, the Plenty still to come.   25
For Her the weeping Heav'ns become serene,
For Her the Ground is clad in cheerfull green:
For Her the Nightingales are taught to sing,
And Nature has for her delay'd the Spring.
The Muse resumes her long-forgotten Lays,   ⎤ 30
And Love, restor'd, his Ancient Realm surveys;   ⎬
Recalls our Beauties, and revives our Plays.   ⎦
His Wast Dominions peoples once again,
And from Her presence dates his Second Reign.
But awfull Charms on her fair Forehead sit,   35
Dispensing what she never will admit.
Pleasing, yet cold, like *Cynthia*'s silver Beam,
The Peoples Wonder, and the Poets Theam.
Distemper'd Zeal, Sedition, canker'd Hate,
No more shall vex the Church, and tear the State;   40
No more shall Faction civil Discords move,
Or onely discords of too tender love:
Discord like that of Musicks various parts,
Discord that makes the harmony of Hearts,
Discord that onely this dispute shall bring,   45
Who best shall love the Duke, and serve the King.

MAC FLECKNOE

ALL humane things are subject to decay,
    And, when Fate summons, Monarchs must obey:
This *Fleckno* found, who, like *Augustus*, young
Was call'd to Empire, and had govern'd long:
In Prose and Verse, was own'd, without dispute   5
Through all the Realms of *Non-sense*, absolute.
This aged Prince now flourishing in Peace,
And blest with issue of a large increase,
Worn out with business, did at length debate
To settle the succession of the State: 10
And pond'ring which of all his Sons was fit
To Reign, and wage immortal War with Wit;
Cry'd, 'tis resolv'd; for Nature pleads that He
Should onely rule, who most resembles me:
Sh—— alone my perfect image bears,   15
Mature in dullness from his tender years.
Sh—— alone, of all my Sons, is he
Who stands confirm'd in full stupidity.
The rest to some faint meaning make pretence,
But *Sh——* never deviates into sense.   20
Some Beams of Wit on other souls may fall,
Strike through and make a lucid intervall;
But *Sh——*'s genuine night admits no ray,
His rising Fogs prevail upon the Day:
Besides his goodly Fabrick fills the eye,   25
And seems design'd for thoughtless Majesty:
Thoughtless as Monarch Oakes, that shade the plain,
And, spread in solemn state, supinely reign.
Heywood and *Shirley* were but Types of thee,
Thou last great Prophet of Tautology: 30
Even I, a dunce of more renown than they,
Was sent before but to prepare thy way;
And coursly clad in *Norwich* Drugget came
To teach the Nations in thy greater name.
My warbling Lute, the Lute I whilom strung   35

When to King *John* of *Portugal* I sung,
Was but the prelude to that glorious day,
When thou on silver *Thames* did'st cut thy way,
With well tim'd Oars before the Royal Barge,
Swell'd with the Pride of thy Celestial charge;   40
And big with Hymn, Commander of an Host,
The like was ne'er in *Epsom* Blankets tost.
Methinks I see the new *Arion* Sail,
The Lute still trembling underneath thy nail.
At thy well sharpned thumb from Shore to Shore   45
The Treble squeaks for fear, the Bases roar:
Echoes from *Pissing-Ally*, *Sh——* call,
And *Sh——* they resound from *A—— Hall*.
About thy boat the little Fishes throng,
As at the Morning Toast, that Floats along.   50
Sometimes as Prince of thy Harmonious band
Thou weild'st thy Papers in thy threshing hand.
St. *Andre*'s feet ne'er kept more equal time,
Not ev'n the feet of thy own *Psyche*'s rhime:
Though they in number as in sense excell;   55
So just, so like tautology they fell,
That, pale with envy, *Singleton* forswore
The Lute and Sword which he in Triumph bore,
And vow'd he ne'er would act *Villerius* more.
Here stopt the good old *Syre*; and wept for joy   60
In silent raptures of the hopefull boy.
All arguments, but most his Plays, perswade,
That for anointed dullness he was made.

    Close to the Walls which fair *Augusta* bind,
(The fair *Augusta* much to fears inclin'd)   65
An ancient fabrick, rais'd t'inform the sight,
There stood of yore, and *Barbican* it hight:
A watch Tower once; but now, so Fate ordains,
Of all the Pile an empty name remains.
From its old Ruins Brothel-houses rise,   70
Scenes of lewd loves, and of polluted joys.
Where their vast Courts the Mother-Strumpets keep,
And, undisturb'd by Watch, in silence sleep.
Near these a Nursery erects its head,
Where Queens are form'd, and future Hero's bred;   75

Where unfledg'd Actors learn to laugh and cry,
Where infant Punks their tender Voices try,
And little *Maximins* the Gods defy.
Great *Fletcher* never treads in Buskins here,
Nor greater *Johnson* dares in Socks appear.   (Jonson)   80
But gentle *Simkin* just reception finds
Amidst this Monument of vanisht minds:
Pure Clinches, the suburbian Muse affords;
And *Panton* waging harmless War with words.
Here *Fleckno*, as a place to Fame well known,   85
Ambitiously design'd his *Sh*——'s Throne.
For ancient *Decker* prophesi'd long since,
That in this Pile should Reign a mighty Prince,
Born for a scourge of Wit, and flayle of Sense:
To whom true dulness should some *Psyches* owe,   90
But Worlds of *Misers* from his pen should flow;
Humorists and *Hypocrites* it should produce,
Whole *Raymond* families, and Tribes of *Bruce*.
Now Empress *Fame* had publisht the Renown
Of *Sh*——'s Coronation through the Town.   95
Rows'd by report of Fame, the Nations meet,
From near *Bun-Hill*, and distant *Watling-street*.
No *Persian* Carpets spread th' Imperial way,
But scatter'd Limbs of mangled Poets lay:
From dusty shops neglected Authors come,   100
Martyrs of Pies, and Reliques of the Bum.
Much *Heywood*, *Shirly*, *Ogleby* there lay,
But loads of *Sh*—— almost choakt the way.
Bilk't *Stationers* for Yeomen stood prepar'd,
And *H*—— was Captain of the Guard.   105
The hoary Prince in Majesty appear'd,
High on a Throne of his own Labours rear'd.
At his right hand our young *Ascanius* sate
Rome's other hope, and pillar of the State.
His Brows thick fogs, instead of glories, grace,   110
And lambent dullness plaid arround his face.
As *Hannibal* did to the Altars come,
Sworn by his *Syre* a mortal Foe to *Rome*;
So *Sh*—— swore, nor should his Vow bee vain,

108 sate   92: sat   84

That he till Death true dullness would maintain;   115
And in his father's Right, and Realms defence,
Ne'er to have peace with Wit, nor truce with Sense.
The King himself the sacred Unction made,
As King by Office, and as Priest by Trade:
In his sinister hand, instead of Ball,   120
He plac'd a mighty Mug of potent Ale;
Love's Kingdom to his right he did convey,
At once his Sceptre and his rule of Sway;
Whose righteous Lore the Prince had practis'd young,
And from whose Loyns recorded *Psyche* sprung.   125
His Temples last with Poppies were o'erspread,
That nodding seem'd to consecrate his head:
Just at that point of time, if Fame not lye,
On his left hand twelve reverend *Owls* did fly.
So *Romulus*, 'tis sung, by *Tyber's Brook*,   130
Presage of Sway from twice six Vultures took.
Th' admiring throng loud acclamations make,
And Omens of his future Empire take.
The *Syre* then shook the honours of his head,
And from his brows damps of oblivion shed   135
Full on the filial dullness: long he stood,
Repelling from his Breast the raging God;
At length burst out in this prophetick mood:
    Heavens bless my Son, from *Ireland* let him reign
To farr *Barbadoes* on the Western main;   140
Of his Dominion may no end be known,
And greater than his Father's be his Throne.
Beyond loves Kingdom let him stretch his Pen;
He paus'd, and all the people cry'd *Amen*.
Then thus, continu'd he, my Son advance   145
Still in new Impudence, new Ignorance.
Success let others teach, learn thou from me
Pangs without birth, and fruitless Industry.
Let *Virtuoso's* in five years be Writ;
Yet not one thought accuse thy toyl of wit.   150
Let gentle *George* in triumph tread the Stage,
Make *Dorimant* betray, and *Loveit* rage;
Let *Cully*, *Cockwood*, *Fopling*, charm the Pit,
And in their folly shew the Writers wit.

Yet still thy fools shall stand in thy defence,   155
And justifie their Author's want of sense.
Let 'em be all by thy own model made
Of dullness, and desire no foreign aid:
That they to future ages may be known,
Not Copies drawn, but Issue of thy own.   160
Nay let thy men of wit too be the same,
All full of thee, and differing but in name;
But let no alien *S—dl—y* interpose
To lard with wit thy hungry *Epsom* prose.
And when false flowers of *Rhetorick* thou would'st cull,   165
Trust Nature, do not labour to be dull;
But write thy best, and top; and in each line,
Sir *Formal*'s oratory will be thine.
Sir *Formal*, though unsought, attends thy quill,
And does thy *Northern Dedications* fill.   170
Nor let false friends seduce thy mind to fame,
By arrogating *Johnson*'s Hostile name.
Let Father *Fleckno* fire thy mind with praise,
And Uncle *Ogleby* thy envy raise.
Thou art my blood, where *Johnson* has no part;   175
What share have we in Nature or in Art?
Where did his wit on learning fix a brand,
And rail at Arts he did not understand?
Where made he love in Prince *Nicander*'s vein,
Or swept the dust in *Psyche*'s humble strain?   180
Where sold he Bargains, Whip-stitch, kiss my Arse,
Promis'd a Play and dwindled to a Farce?
When did his Muse from *Fletcher* scenes purloin,
As thou whole *Eth'ridg* dost transfuse to thine?
But so transfus'd as Oyl on Waters flow,   185
His always floats above, thine sinks below.
This is thy Province, this thy wondrous way,
New Humours to invent for each new Play:
This is that boasted Byas of thy mind,
By which one way, to dullness, 'tis inclin'd.   190
Which makes thy writings lean on one side still,
And in all changes that way bends thy will.
Nor let thy mountain belly make pretence
Of likeness; thine 's a tympany of sense.

A Tun of Man in thy Large bulk is writ,   195
But sure thou'rt but a Kilderkin of wit.
Like mine thy gentle numbers feebly creep,
Thy Tragick Muse gives smiles, thy Comick sleep.
With whate'er gall thou sett'st thy self to write,
Thy inoffensive Satyrs never bite.   200
In thy fellonious heart, though Venom lies,
It does but touch thy *Irish* pen, and dyes.
Thy Genius calls thee not to purchase fame
In keen Iambicks, but mild Anagram:
Leave writing Plays, and chuse for thy command   205
Some peacefull Province in Acrostick Land.
There thou maist wings display and Altars raise,
And torture one poor word Ten thousand ways.
Or if thou would'st thy diff'rent talents suit,
Set thy own Songs, and sing them to thy lute.   210
He said, but his last words were scarcely heard,
For *Bruce* and *Longvil* had a *Trap* prepar'd,
And down they sent the yet declaiming Bard.
Sinking he left his Drugget robe behind,
Born upwards by a subterranean wind.   215
The Mantle fell to the young Prophet's part,
With double portion of his Father's Art.

THE SECOND PART OF

ABSALOM AND ACHITOPHEL

A POEM

—Si Quis tamen Hæc quoque, Si Quis
Captus Amore Leget—

SINCE Men like Beasts, each others Prey were made,
Since Trade began, and Priesthood grew a Trade,
Since Realms were form'd, none sure so curst as those
That madly their own Happiness oppose;
There Heaven it self, and Godlike Kings, in vain   5
Showr down the *Manna* of a gentle Reign;
While pamper'd Crowds to mad Sedition run,
And Monarchs by Indulgence are undone.
Thus *David*'s Clemency was fatal grown,
While wealthy Faction aw'd the wanting Throne.   10
For now their Sov'reigns Orders to contemn
Was held the Charter of *Jerusalem*,
His Rights t' invade, his Tributes to refuse,
A Privilege peculiar to the *Jews*;
As if from Heav'nly Call this Licence fell,   15
And *Jacob*'s Seed were chosen to rebell!
   Achitophel with triumph sees his Crimes
Thus suited to the madness of the Times;
And *Absalom*, to make his hopes succeed,
Of Flattering Charms no longer stands in need;   20
While fond of Change, though ne'er so dearly bought,
Our Tribes out-strip the Youth's Ambitious Thought;
His swiftest Hopes with swifter Homage meet,
And crowd their servile Necks beneath his Feet.
Thus to his aid while pressing Tides repair,   25
He mounts and spreads his Streamers in the Air.
The Charms of Empire might his Youth mis-lead,
But what can our besotted *Israel* plead?
Sway'd by a Monarch whose serene Command,

---

*The Second Part, &c. Text from the first edition, 1682 (A), collated with the second edition
1682 (B)*

  9 Clemency was *B*: Goodness was e'en *A*   20 Flattering *B*: Flatterie's *A*

Seems half the Blessing of our promis'd Land,   30
Whose onely Grievance is excess of Ease,
Freedome our Pain, and Plenty our Disease!
Yet, as all Folly wou'd lay claim to Sense,
And Wickedness ne'er wanted a Pretence,
With Arguments they'd make their Treason good,   35
And righteous *David*'s self with Slanders load:
That Arts of foreign Sway he did affect,
And guilty *Jebusites* from Law protect,
Whose very Chiefs, convict, were never freed,
Nay, we have seen their Sacrificers bleed!   40
Accusers Infamy is urg'd in vain,
While in the bounds of Sense they did contain,
But soon they launcht into th' unfathom'd Tide,
And in the Depths they knew disdain'd to Ride,
For probable Discoveries to dispence,   45
Was thought below a pention'd Evidence;
Mere Truth was dull, nor suited with the port
Of pamper'd *Corah*, when advanc't to Court.
No less than Wonders now they will impose,
And Projects void of Grace or Sense disclose.   50
Such was the Charge on pious *Michal* brought,
Michal that ne'er was cruel e'en in thought,
The best of Queens, and most obedient Wife,
Impeach'd of curst Designs on *David*'s Life!
His Life, the Theam of her eternal Pray'r,   55
'Tis scarce so much his Guardian Angels Care.
Not Summer Morns such Mildness can disclose,
The *Hermon* Lilly, nor the *Sharon* Rose.
Neglecting each vain Pomp of Majesty,
Transported *Michal* feeds her thoughts on high.   60
She lives with Angels, and as Angels do,
Quits Heav'n sometimes to bless the World below.
Where cherisht by her Bounties plenteous Spring,
Reviving Widows smile, and Orphans sing.
Oh! when rebellious *Israel*'s Crimes at height,   65
Are threatned with her Lord's approaching Fate,
The Piety of *Michal* then remain
In Heav'ns Remembrance, and prolong his Reign.

33 as *B*: since *A*

Less Desolation did the Pest persue,
That from *Dan*'s limits to *Beersheba* slew,   70
Less fatal the repeated Wars of *Tyre*,
And less *Jerusalem*'s avenging Fire.
With gentler terrour these our State o'erran,
Than since our Evidencing Days began!
On every Cheek a pale Confusion sat,   75
Continu'd Fear beyond the worst of Fate!
Trust was no more, Art, Science useless made,
All occupations lost but *Corah*'s Trade.
Mean while a Guard on modest *Corah* wait,
If not for safety, needfull yet for State.   80
Well might he deem each Peer and Prince his Slave:
And Lord it o'er the Tribes which he could save:
E'en Vice in him was Vertue—what sad Fate
But for his Honesty had seiz'd our State?
And with what Tyranny had we been curst,   85
Had *Corah* never prov'd a Villain first?
T' have told his knowledge of th' Intrigue in gross
Had been alas to our Deponent's loss:
The travell'd Levite had th' Experience got,
To husband well, and make the best of's Plot;   90
And therefore like an Evidence of skill,
With wise Reserves secur'd his Pension still;
Nor quite of future Pow'r himself bereft,
But Limbo's large for unbelievers left.
And now his Writ such Reverence had got,   95
'Twas worse than Plotting to suspect his Plot.
Some were so well convinc't, they made no doubt,
Themselves to help the founder'd Swearers out.
Some had their Sense impos'd on by their Fear,
But more for Int'rest sake believe and swear: 100
E'en to that height with some the Frenzy grew,
They rag'd to find their danger not prove true.
    Yet, than all these a viler Crew remain,
Who with *Achitophel* the Cry maintain;
Not urg'd by Fear, nor through misguided Sense,   105
(Blind Zeal, and starving Need had some pretence)
But for the *Good Old Cause* that did excite

95 And *B*: For *A*

Th' Original Rebells Wiles, Revenge and Spight.
These raise the Plot to have the Scandal thrown
Upon the bright Successor of the Crown,   110
Whose Vertue with such wrongs they had persu'd,
As seem'd all hope of pardon to exclude.
Thus, while on private Ends their Zeal is built
The cheated Crowd applaud and share their Guilt.

   Such Practices as These, too gross to lye   115
Long unobserv'd by each discerning Eye,
The more judicious *Israelites* Unspell'd,
Though still the Charm the giddy Rabble held.
Ev'n *Absalom* amidst the dazling Beams
Of Empire, and Ambitions flattering Dreams,   120
Perceives the Plot (too foul to be excus'd)
To aid Designs, no less pernicious, us'd.
And (Filial Sense yet striving in his Breast)
Thus to *Achitophel* his Doubts exprest.

Absolom: "Why are my Thoughts upon a Crown employ'd,   125
Which once obtain'd, can be but half Enjoy'd?
Not so when Virtue did my Arms require,
And to my Father's Wars I flew Intire.
My Regal Pow'r how will my Foes resent,
When I my Self have scarce my own Consent?   130
Give me a Son's unblemisht Truth again,
Or quench the Sparks of Duty that remain.
How slight to force a Throne that Legions guard
The Task to me; to prove Unjust, how hard!
And if th' imagin'd Guilt thus wound my Thought,   135
What will it when the tragick Scene is wrought?
Dire War must first be conjur'd from below,
The Realm we'd Rule we first must Overthrow.
And when the Civil Furies are on wing
That blind and undistinguisht Slaughters fling,   140
Who knows what impious chance may reach the King?
Oh! rather let me Perish in the Strife,
Than have my Crown the Price of *David*'s Life!
Or if the Tempest of the War he stand,
In Peace, some vile officious Villain's hand   145
His Soul's anointed Temple may invade,

Or, prest by clamorous Crowds, my Self be made
His Murtherer; rebellious Crowds, whose Guilt
Shall dread his vengeance till his Bloud be spilt.
Which if my filial Tenderness oppose,   150
Since to the Empire by their Arms I rose,
Those very Arms on Me shall be employ'd,
A new Usurper Crown'd, and I Destroy'd:
The same Pretence of Publick Good will hold,
And new *Achitophels* be found, as bold   } 155
To urge the needfull Change, perhaps the Old. "
    He said. The Statesman with a Smile replies,
(A smile that did his rising Spleen disguise.)
" My thoughts presum'd our labours at an End,
And are we still with Conscience to contend?   160
Whose Want in Kings, as needfull is allow'd,
As 'tis for them to find it in the Crowd.
Far in the doubtfull Passage you are gone,
And onely can be Safe by pressing on.
The Crowns true Heir, a Prince severe, and wise,   165
Has view'd your Motions long with Jealous Eyes;
Your Persons Charms, your more prevailing Arts,
And mark't your Progress in the Peoples Hearts:
Whose Patience is th' effect of stinted Pow'r,
But treasures Vengeance for the fatal hour,   170
And if remote the Perill He can bring,
Your Present Danger's greater from the King.
Let not a Parent's name deceive your Sense,
Nor trust the Father in a Jealous Prince!
Your trivial Faults if he could so resent,   175
To doom you little less than Banishment,
What rage must your Presumption Since inspire?
Against his Orders your Return from *Tyre*?
Nor onely so, but with a Pomp more high,
And open Court of Popularity,   180
The Factious Tribes—And this Reproof from Thee?
(The Prince replies) O Statesman's winding Skill,
They first Condemn that first Advis'd the Ill!
Illustrious Youth (returned *Achitophel*)
Misconstrue not the Words that mean you well.   185
The Course you steer I worthy Blame conclude,

But 'tis because you leave it Unpersu'd.
A Monarch's Crown with Fate surrounded lyes,
Who reach, lay hold on Death that miss the Prize.
Did you for this expose your self to Show,   190
And to the Crowd bow popluarly low?
For this your Glorious Progress next ordain,
With Chariots, Horsemen, and a numerous Train,
With Fame before you like the Morning Starr,
And Shouts of Joy saluting from afarr?   195
Oh from the Heights you've reach't but take a View,
Scarce leading *Lucifer* cou'd Fall like You!
And must I here my Ship-wrackt Arts bemoan?
Have I for this so oft made *Israel* groan!
Your single Interest with the Nation weigh'd,   200
And turn'd the Scale where your Desires were laid?
Ev'n when at Helm a Course so dang'rous mov'd
To Land your Hopes, as my Removal prov'd.
" I not dispute (the Royal Youth replyes)
The known Perfection of your Policies,   205
Nor in *Achitophel* yet grudge, or blame,
The Priviledge that Statesmen ever claim;
Who private Interest never yet persu'd,
But still pretended 'twas for Others good:
What Polititian yet e'er scap't his Fate,   210
Who saving his own Neck not sav'd the State?
From hence on ev'ry hum'rous Wind that veer'd,
With shifted Sayls a sev'ral Course you Steer'd.
What Form of Sway did *David* e'er persue
That seem'd like Absolute but sprung from You?   215
Who at your instance quasht each penal Law,
That kept dissenting factious *Jews* in awe;
And who suspends fixt Laws, may abrogate,
That done, form New, and so enslave the State.
Ev'n Property, whose Champion now you stand,   220
And seem for this the Idol of the Land,
Did ne'er sustain such Violence before,
As when your Counsel shut the Royal Store;
Advice, that Ruine to whole Tribes procur'd,
But secret kept till your own Banks secur'd.   225
Recount with this the tripple Cov'nant broke,

And *Israel* fitted for a Foreign Yoke;
Nor here your Counsels fatal Progress staid,
But sent our levied Pow'rs to *Pharaoh*'s Aid.
Hence *Tyre* and *Israel*, low in Ruins laid,   230
And *Egypt* once their Scorn, their common Terrour made.
Ev'n yet of such a Season we can dream,
When Royal Rights you made your darling Theam.
For Pow'r unlimited could Reasons draw,
And place Prerogative above the Law;   235
Which on your fall from Office grew Unjust,
The Laws made King, the King a Slave in Trust:
Whom with State-craft (to Int'rest onely True)
You now Accuse of ills contriv'd by You.

Achitophel :   To this Hell's Agent—Royal Youth fix here,   240
Let Int'rest be the Star by which I Steer.
Hence to repose your Trust in Me was wise,
Whose Int'rest most in your Advancement lies.
A Tye so firm as always will avail
When Friendship, Nature and Religion fail;   245
On ours the Safety of the Crowd depends,
Secure the Crowd and we obtain our Ends,
Whom I will cause so far our Guilt to share
Till they are made our Champions by their Fear.
What Opposition can your Rival bring,   250
While Sanhedrims are Jealous of the King?
His Strength as yet in *David*'s Friendship lies,
And what can *David*'s Self without Supplies?
Who with Exclusive Bills must now Dispence,
Debarr the Heir, or Starve in his Defence.   255
Conditions which our Elders ne'er will quit,
And *David*'s Justice never can admit.
Or forc't by Wants his Brother to betray,
To your Ambition next he clears the Way;
For if Succession once to Nought they bring,   260
Their next Advance removes the present King:
Persisting else his Senates to dissolve,
In equal Hazzard shall his Reign involve.
Our Tribes, whom *Pharaoh*'s Pow'r so much Alarms,
Shall rise without their Prince t' oppose his Arms;   265
Nor boots it on what Cause at first they Joyn,

Their Troops once up, are Tools for our Design.
At least such subtle Covenants shall be made,
Till Peace it self is War in Masquerade.
Associations of Mysterious Sense,   270
Against, but seeming for the King's Defence:
Ev'n on their Courts of Justice Fetters draw,
And from our Agents Muzzle up their Law.
By which, a Conquest if we fail to make,
'Tis a drawn Game at worst, and we secure our Stake.   275
 He said, and for the dire Success depends
On various Sects, by common Guilt made Friends:
Whose Heads, though ne'er so diff'ring in their Creed,
I' th' point of Treason yet were well Agreed.
'Mongst these, Extorting *Ishban* first appears,   280
Persu'd b' a meager Troop of Bankrupt Heirs.
Blest times, when *Ishban*, He whose Occupation
So long has been to Cheat, Reformes the Nation!
Ishban of Conscience suited to his Trade,
As good a Saint as Usurer e'er made.   285
Yet *Mammon* has not so engrost him quite,
But *Belial* lays as large a Claim of Spight;
Who, for those Pardons from his Prince he draws,
Returns Reproaches, and cries up the Cause.
That Year in which the City he did sway,   290
He left Rebellion in a hopefull way.
Yet his Ambition once was found so bold,
To offer Talents of Extorted Gold;
Cou'd *David*'s Wants have So been brib'd to shame
And scandalize our Peerage with his Name;   295
For which, his dear Sedition he'd forswear,
And e'en turn Loyal to be made a Peer.
Next him, let Railing *Rabsheka* have place,
So full of Zeal He has no need of Grace;
A Saint that can both Flesh and Spirit use,   300
Alike haunt Conventicles and the Stews:
Of whom the Question difficult appears,
If most i' th' Preachers or the Bawds Arrears.
What Caution cou'd appear too much in Him
That keeps the Treasure of *Jerusalem*!   305
Let *David*'s Brother but approach the Town,

Double our Guards, (He cries) *We are undone.*
Protesting that He dares not Sleep in's Bed
Lest he shou'd rise next Morn without his Head.

Next these, a Troop of buisy Spirits press,   310
Of little Fortunes, and of Conscience Less;
With them the Tribe, whose Luxury had drain'd
Their Banks, in former Sequestrations gain'd:
Who Rich and Great by past Rebellions grew,
And long to fish the troubled Streams anew.   315
Some future Hopes, some present Payment draws,
To Sell their Conscience and espouse the Cause,
Such Stipends those vile Hirelings best befit,
Priests without Grace, and Poets without Wit.
Shall that false *Hebronite* escape our Curse,   320
Judas that keeps the Rebells Pension-Purse;
Judas that pays the Treason-writers Fee,
Judas that well deserves his Namesake's Tree;
Who at *Jerusalem*'s own Gates Erects
His College for a Nursery of Sects.   325
Young Prophets with an early Care secures,
And with the Dung of his own Arts manures.
What have the Men of *Hebron* here to doe?
What part in *Israel*'s promis'd Land have you?
Here *Phaleg* the Lay *Hebronite* is come,   330
'Cause like the rest he could not live at Home;
Who from his own Possessions cou'd not drain
An *Omer* even of *Hebronitish* Grain,
Here Struts it like a Patriot, and talks high
Of Injur'd Subjects, alter'd Property: 335
An Emblem of that buzzing Insect Just,
That mounts the Wheell, and thinks she raises Dust.
Can dry Bones Live? or *Skeletons* produce
The Vital Warmth of Cuckoldizing Juice?
Slim *Phaleg* cou'd, and at the Table fed,   340
Return'd the gratefull product to the Bed.
A Waiting-man to Trav'ling Nobles chose,
He, his own Laws, wou'd Sawcily impose;
Till Bastinado'd back again he went,
To Learn those Manners he to Teach was sent.   345

315 Streams *B:* Waves *A*

Chastiz'd, he ought to have retreated Home,
But He reads Politicks to *Absalom*.
For never *Hebronite* though Kickt and Scorn'd,
To his own Country willingly return'd.
— But leaving famish'd *Phaleg* to be fed,   350
And to talk Treason for his daily Bread,
Let *Hebron*, nay let Hell produce a Man
So made for Mischief as *Ben-Jochanan*.
A *Jew* of Humble Parentage was He,
By Trade a Levite though of low Degree: 355
His Pride no higher than the Desk aspir'd,
But for the Drudgery of Priests was hir'd
To Reade and Pray in Linen Ephod brave,
And pick up single Sheckles from the Grave.
Married at last, and finding Charge come faster,   360
He cou'd not live by God, but chang'd his Master:
Inspir'd by Want, was made a Factious Tool,
They Got a Villain, and we lost a Fool.
Still Violent, whatever Cause he took,
But most against the Party he forsook,   365
For Renegadoes, who ne'er turn by halves,
Are bound in Conscience to be double Knaves.
So this Prose-Prophet took most monstrous Pains,
To let his Masters see he earn'd his Gains.
But as the Dev'l ows all his Imps a Shame,   370
He chose th' *Apostate* for his proper Theme;
With little Pains he made the Picture true,
And from Reflexion took the Rogue he drew.
A wondrous Work to prove the *Jewish* Nation,
In every Age a Murmuring Generation;   375
To trace 'em from their Infancy of Sinning,
And shew 'em Factious from their First Beginning.
To prove they cou'd Rebell, and Rail, and Mock,
Much to the Credit of the Chosen Flock;
A strong Authority which must Convince,   380
That Saints own no Allegiance to their Prince.
As 'tis a Leading-Card to make a Whore,
To prove her Mother had turn'd up before.
But, tell me, did the Drunken Patriarch Bless

384 Patriarch *B*: Patriot *A*

The Son that shew'd his Father's Nakedness?   385
Such Thanks the present Church thy Pen will give,
Which proves Rebellion was so Primitive.
Must Ancient Failings be Examples made?
Then Murtherers from *Cain* may learn their Trade.
As thou the Heathen and the Saint hast drawn,   390
Methinks th' Apostate was the better man:
And thy hot *Father* (waving my respect)
Not of a mother Church, but of a Sect.
And Such he needs must be of thy Inditing,
This Comes of drinking Asses milk and writing.   395
If *Balack* should be cal'd to leave his place
(As profit is the loudest call of Grace,)
His Temple dispossess'd of one, wou'd be
Replenish'd with seven Devils more by thee.
    Levi, thou art a load, I'll lay thee down,   400
And shew Rebellion bare, without a Gown;
Poor Slaves in metre, dull and adle-pated,
Who Rhime below ev'n *David*'s Psalms translated.
Some in my Speedy pace I must outrun,
As lame *Mephibosheth* the Wisard's Son: 405
To make quick way I'll Leap o'er heavy blocks,
Shun rotten *Uzza* as I wou'd the Pox;
And hasten *Og* and *Doeg* to rehearse,
Two Fools that Crutch their Feeble sense on Verse;
Who by my Muse, to all succeeding times,   410
Shall live in spight of their own Dogrell Rhimes.
    Doeg, though without knowing how or why,
Made still a blund'ring kind of Melody;
Spurd boldly on, and Dash'd through Thick and Thin,
Through Sense and Non-sense, never out nor in;   415
Free from all meaning, whether good or bad,
And in one word, Heroically mad:
He was too warm on Picking-work to dwell,
But Faggotted his Notions as they fell,
And if they Rhim'd and Rattl'd all was well.   420
Spightfull he is not, though he wrote a Satyr,
For still there goes some *thinking* to ill-Nature:
He needs no more than Birds and Beasts to think,
All his occasions are to eat and drink.

If he call Rogue and Rascal from a Garrat,   425
He means you no more Mischief than a Parat:
The words for Friend and Foe alike were made,
To Fetter 'em in Verse is all his Trade.
For Almonds he'll cry Whore to his own Mother:
And call Young *Absalom* King *David*'s Brother.   430
Let him be Gallows-Free by my consent,
And nothing suffer since he nothing meant;
Hanging Supposes humane Soul and reason,
This Animal's below committing Treason:
Shall he be hang'd who never cou'd Rebell?   435
That's a preferment for *Achitophel*.
The Woman that Committed Buggary,
Was rightly Sentenc'd by the Law to die;
But 'twas hard Fate that to the Gallows led,
The Dog that never heard the Statute read.   440
Railing in other Men may be a crime,
But ought to pass for mere instinct in him;
Instinct he follows and no farther knows,
For to write Verse with him is to *Transprose*.
'Twere pity treason at his Door to lay,   445
Who makes Heaven's gate a Lock to its own Key:
Let him rayl on, let his invective muse
Have four and Twenty letters to abuse,
Which if he Jumbles to one line of Sense,
Indict him of a Capital Offence.   450
In Fire-works give him leave to vent his spight,
Those are the onely Serpents he can write;
The height of his Ambition is we know
But to be Master of a Puppet-show:
On that one Stage his works may yet appear,   455
And a months Harvest keeps him all the Year.
     Now stop your noses Readers, all and some,
For here's a tun of Midnight-work to come,
Og from a Treason Tavern rowling home.
Round as a Globe, and Liquor'd ev'ry chink,   460
Goodly and Great he Sayls behind his Link;
With all this Bulk there's nothing lost in *Og*
For ev'ry inch that is not Fool is Rogue:
A Monstrous mass of foul corrupted matter,

As all the Devils had spew'd to make the batter.   465
When wine has given him courage to Blaspheme,
He Curses God, but God before Curst him;
And if man cou'd have reason none has more,
That made his Paunch so rich and him so poor.
With wealth he was not trusted, for Heav'n knew   470
What 'twas of Old to pamper up a *Jew*;
To what wou'd he on Quail and Pheasant swell,
That ev'n on Tripe and Carrion cou'd rebell?
But though Heav'n made him poor, (with rev'rence
    speaking,)
He never was a Poet of God's making;   475
The Midwife laid her hand on his Thick Skull,
With this Prophetick blessing—*Be thou Dull;*
Drink, Swear and Roar, forbear no lew'd delight
Fit for thy Bulk, doe any thing but write:
Thou art of lasting Make like thoughtless men,   480
A strong Nativity—but for the Pen;
Eat Opium, mingle Arsenick in thy Drink,
Still thou mayst live avoiding Pen and Ink.
I see, I see 'tis Counsell given in vain,
For Treason botcht in Rhime will be thy bane;   485
Rhime is the Rock on which thou art to wreck,
'Tis fatal to thy Fame and to thy Neck:
Why shoud thy Metre good King *David* blast?
A Psalm of his will Surely be thy last.
Dar'st thou presume in verse to meet thy foes,   490
Thou whom the Penny Pamphlet foil'd in prose?
Doeg, whom God for Mankinds mirth has made,
O'er-tops thy tallent in thy very Trade;
Doeg to thee, thy paintings are so Course,
A Poet is, though he's the Poets Horse.   495
A Double Noose thou on thy Neck dost pull,
For Writing Treason, and for Writing dull;
To die for Faction is a Common evil,
But to be hang'd for Non-sense is the Devil:
Had'st thou the Glories of thy King exprest,   500
Thy praises had been Satyr at the best;
But thou in Clumsy verse, unlickt, unpointed,
Hast Shamefully defi'd the Lord's Anointed:

I will not rake the Dunghill of thy Crimes,
For who wou'd reade thy Life that reads thy rhimes? 505
But of King *David*'s Foes be this the Doom,
May all be like the Young-man *Absalom*;
And for my Foes may this their Blessing be,
To talk like *Doeg*, and to Write like Thee.

Achitophel each Rank, Degree and Age, 510
For various Ends neglects not to Engage;
The Wise and Rich for Purse and Counsell brought,
The Fools and Beggars for their Number sought:
Who yet not onely on the Town depends,
For Ev'n in Court the Faction had its Friends; 515
These thought the Places they possest too small,
And in their Hearts wisht Court and King to fall:
Whose Names the Muse disdaining holds i' th' Dark,
Thrust in the Villain Herd without a Mark;
With Parasites and Libell-spawning Imps, 520
Intriguing Fopps, dull Jesters and worse Pimps.
Disdain the Rascal Rabble to persue,
Their Sett Caballs are yet a viler Crew;
See where involv'd in Common Smoak they sit;
Some for our Mirth, some for our Satyr fit: 525
These Gloomy, Thoughtfull and on Mischief bent,
While those for mere good Fellowship frequent
Th' Appointed Clubb, can let Sedition pass,
Sense, Non-sence, anything t' employ the Glass;
And who believe in their dull honest Hearts, 530
The Rest talk Treason but to shew their Parts;
Who n'er had Wit or Will for Mischief yet,
But pleas'd to be reputed of a Set.

But in the Sacred Annals of our Plot,
Industrious *AROD* never be forgot: 535
The Labours of this Midnight-Magistrate,
May Vie with *Corah*'s to preserve the State;
In search of Arms, He fail'd not to lay hold
On War's most powerfull dang'rous Weapon, *GOLD*.
And last, to take from *Jebusites*, all Odds, 540
Their Altars pillag'd, stole their very Gods;
Oft wou'd He Cry, when Treasure He surpriz'd,
'*Tis* Baalish *Gold in* David's *Coyn Disguiz'd*.

Which to his House with *richer Relicts* came,
While Lumber Idols onely fed the Flame: 545
For our wise Rabble ne'er took pains t' enquire,
What 'twas he burnt, so 't made a rousing Fire.
With which our Elder was enricht no more
Than False *Gehazi* with the *Syrian*'s Store;
So Poor, that when our Choosing-Tribes were met,   550
Ev'n for his Stinking Votes He ran in Debt;
For Meat the Wicked, and as Authours think,
The Saints He Chous'd for His Electing Drink;
Thus, ev'ry Shift and subtle Method past,
And All to be no *Zaken* at the Last.   555
    Now, rais'd on *Tyre*'s sad Ruines, *Pharaoh*'s Pride
Soar'd high, his Legions threatning far and wide;
As when a battring Storm ingendred high,
By Winds upheld, hangs hov'ring in the Skye,
Is gaz'd upon by ev'ry trembling Swain,   560
This for his Vineyard fears, and that his Grain:
For blooming Plants, and Flow'rs new Opening, These
For Lambs ean'd lately, and far-lab'ring Bees;
To Guard his Stock each to the Gods does call,
Uncertain where the Fire-charg'd Clouds will Fall: 565
Ev'n so the doubtfull Nations watch his Arms,
With Terrour each expecting his Alarms.
Where *Judah*, where was now, thy Lyons Roar?
Thou onely cou'dst the Captive Lands restore;
But Thou, with inbred Broils, and Faction prest,   570
From *Egypt* needst a Guardian with the Rest.
Thy Prince from Sanhedrims no Trust allow'd,
Too much the Representers of the Crow'd,
Who for their own Defence give no Supply,
But what the Crowns Prerogatives must buy: 575
As if their Monarch's Rights to violate,
More needfull were than to preserve the State!
From present Dangers they divert their Care,
And all their Fears are of the Royal Heir;
Whom now the reigning Malice of his Foes   580
Unjudg'd wou'd Sentence, and e'er Crown'd, Depose.
Religion the Pretence, but their Decree
To barr his Reign, whate'er his Faith shall be!

By Sanhedrims, and clam'rous Crowds, thus prest
What passions rent the Righteous *David*'s Breast?   585
Who knows not how t' oppose, or to comply,
Unjust to Grant, and dangerous to Deny!
How near in this dark Juncture *Israel*'s Fate,
Whose Peace one sole Expedient cou'd create,
Which yet th' extremest Virtue did require,   590
Ev'n of that Prince whose Downfall they conspire!
His Absence *David* does with Tears advise,
T' appease their Rage, Undaunted He Complies;
Thus he who prodigal of Bloud, and Ease,
A Royal Life expos'd to Winds and Seas,   595
At once contending with the Waves and Fire,
And heading Danger in the Wars of *Tyre*,
Inglorious now forsakes his Native Sand,
And like an Exile quits the promis'd Land!
Our Monarch scarce from pressing Tears refrains,   600
And painfully his Royal State maintains,
Who now embracing on th' extremest Shore
Almost Revokes what he Injoyn'd before:
Concludes at last more Trust to be allow'd,
To Storms and Seas, than to the raging Crow'd!   605
Forbear, rash Muse, the parting Scene to draw,
With Silence charm'd as deep as theirs that saw!
Not onely our attending Nobles weep,
But hardy Saylers swell with Tears the Deep!
The Tyde restrain'd her Course, and more amaz'd,   610
The Twyn-Stars on the Royal Brothers gaz'd:
While this sole Fear—
Does Trouble to our suff'ring Heroe bring
Lest next the Popular Rage oppress the King!
Thus parting, each for th' others Danger griev'd,   615
The Shore the King, and Seas the Prince receiv'd.
Go injur'd Heroe while propitious Gales,
Soft as thy Consorts breath, inspire thy Sails;
Well may She trust her Beauties on a Flood,
Where thy Triumphant Fleets so oft have rode!   620
Safe on thy Breast reclin'd her Rest be deep,
Rockt like a *Nereid* by the Waves asleep;
While happiest Dreams her Fancy entertain,

And to *Elysian Fields* convert the Main!
Go injur'd Heroe while the Shores of *Tyre*,   625
At thy Approach so Silent shall admire,
Who on thy Thunder still their Thoughts imploy,
And greet thy Landing with a trembling Joy.
   On Heroes thus the Prophet's Fate is thrown,
Admir'd by ev'ry Nation but their Own;   630
Yet while our factious *Jews* his Worth deny,
Their Aking Conscience gives their Tongue the Lye.
Ev'n in the worst of Men the noblest Parts
Confess him, and he Triumphs in their Hearts,
Whom to his King the best Respects commend   635
Of Subject, Souldier, Kinsman, Prince and Friend;
All Sacred Names of most divine Esteem,
And to Perfection all sustain'd by Him,
Wise, Just and Constant, Courtly without Art,
Swift to discern and to reward Desert;   640
No Hour of His in fruitless Ease destroy'd,
But on the noblest Subjects still employ'd:
Whose steddy Soul ne'er learnt to Separate
Between his Monarch's Int'rest and the State,
But heaps those Blessings on the Royal Head,   645
Which He well knows must be on Subjects shed.
   On what Pretence cou'd then the Vulgar Rage
Against his Worth, and native Rights engage?
Religious Fears their Argument are made,
Religious Fears his Sacred Rights invade!   650
Of future Superstition They complain,
And *Jebusitick* Worship in His Reign;
With such Alarms his Foes the Crowd deceive,
With Dangers fright, which not Themselves believe.
   Since nothing can our Sacred Rites remove,   655
Whate'er the Faith of the Successour prove:
Our *Jews* their Ark shall undisturb'd retain,
At least while their Religion is their Gain,
Who know by old Experience *Baal*'s Commands
Not onely claim'd their Conscience, but their Lands;   660
They grutch God's Tythes, how therefore shall they yield
An Idol full possession of the Field?
Grant such a Prince enthron'd, we must confess

The People's Suff'rings than that Monarch's less,
Who must to hard Conditions still be bound,   665
And for his Quiet with the Crowd compound;
Or shou'd his thoughts to Tyranny incline,
Where are the means to compass the design?
Our Crowns Revenues are too short a Store,
And Jealous Sanedrims wou'd give no more!   670
    As vain our Fears of *Egypt*'s potent Aid,
Not so has *Pharaoh* learnt Ambition's Trade,
Nor ever with such Measures can comply,
As Shock the common Rules of Policy;
None dread like Him the Growth of *Israel*'s King,   675
And He alone sufficient Aids can bring;
Who knows that Prince to *Egypt* can give Law,
That on our Stubborn Tribes his Yoak cou'd draw,
At such profound Expence He has not stood,
Nor dy'd for this his Hands so deep in Blood;   680
Wou'd nere through Wrong and Right his Progress take,
Grudge his own Rest, and keep the World awake,
To fix a Lawless Prince on *Judah*'s Throne,
First to Invade our Rights, and then his Own;
His dear-gaind Conquests cheaply to despoil,   685
And Reap the Harvest of his Crimes and Toil.
We grant his Wealth Vast as our Ocean's Sand,
And Curse its Fatal Influence on our Land,
Which our Brib'd *Jews* so num'rously pertake,
That even an Host his Pensioners wou'd make;   690
From these Deceivers our Divisions spring,
Our Weakness, and the Growth of *Egypt*'s King;
These with pretended Friendship to the State,
Our Crowd's Suspition of their Prince Create,
Both pleas'd and frighten'd with the specious Cry,   695
To Guard their Sacred Rights and Property;
To Ruin, thus, the Chosen Flock are Sold,
While Wolves are tane for Guardians of the Fold;
Seduc'd by these, we groundlesly complain,
And loath the Manna of a gentle Reign: 700
Thus our Fore-fathers crooked Paths are trod,
We trust our Prince, no more then They their God.
But all in vain our Reasoning Prophets Preach,

To those whom sad Experience ne're cou'd Teach,
Who can commence new Broils in Bleeding Scars,   705
And fresh Remembrance of Intestine Wars;
When the same Houshold Mortal Foes did yeild,
And Brothers stain'd with Brothers Blood the Feild;
When Sons Curst Steel the Fathers Gore did Stain,
And Mothers Mourn'd for Sons by Fathers Slain!   710
When thick, as *Egypt*'s Locusts on the Sand,
Our Tribes lay Slaughter'd through the promis'd Land,
Whose few Survivers with worse Fate remain,
To drag the Bondage of a Tyrants Reign:
Which Scene of Woes, unknowing We renew,   715
And madly, ev'n those ills we Fear, persue;
While *Pharaoh* laughs at our Domestick Broils,
And safely crowds his Tents with Nations Spoils.
Yet our fierce Sanedrim in restless Rage,
Against our absent Heroe still engage,   720
And chiefly urge, (such did their frenzy prove),
The only Suit their Prince forbids to move,
Which till obtain'd, they cease Affairs of State,
And real Dangers wave, for groundless Hate.
Long *David*'s patience waits Relief to bring,   725
With all th' Indulgence of a lawful King,
Expecting till the troubled Waves wou'd cease,
But found the raging Billows still increase.
The Crowd, whose Insolence Forbearance swells,
While he forgives too far, almost Rebels.   730
At last his deep Resentments silence broke,
Th' Imperial Pallace shook, while thus he spoke,
" Then Justice wake, and Rigour take her time,
For Lo! Our Mercy is become our Crime.
While haulting Punishment her stroke delays,   735
Our Sov'reign Right, Heav'ns Sacred Trust, decays;
For whose support ev'n Subjects Interest calls,
Wo! to that Kingdom where the Monarch Falls.
That Prince who yields the least of Regal Sway,
So far his Peoples Freedom does Betray.   740
Right lives by Law, and Law subsists by Pow'r,
Disarm the Shepherd, Wolves the Flock devour.
Hard Lot of Empire o're a stubborn Race,

Which Heav'n it Self in vain has try'd with Grace!
When will our Reasons long-charm'd Eyes unclose,   745
And *Israel* judge between her Friends and Foes?
When shall we see expir'd Deceivers Sway,
And credit what our God and Monarchs say?
Dissembled Patriots brib'd with *Egypts* Gold,
Ev'n Sanedrims in blind Obedience hold;   750
Those Patriots Falshood in their Actions see,
And judge by the pernicious Fruit the Tree;
If ought for which so loudly they declaim
Religion, Laws, and Freedom were their Aim;
Our Senates in due Methods they had led,   755
T' avoid those Mischeifs which they seem'd to dread;
But first e're yet they propt the sinking State,
T' impeach and charge, as urg'd by private Hate;
Proves that they ne're beleiv'd the Fears they prest,
But Barb'rously destroy'd the Nations Rest!   760
O! Whither will ungovern'd Senates drive,
And to what Bounds licentious Votes arrive?
When their Injustice We are prest to share,
The Monarch urg'd t' exclude the lawful Heir;
Are Princes thus distinguish'd from the Crowd,   765
And this the Priviledge of Royal Blood?
But grant we shou'd Confirm the Wrongs they press,
His Sufferings yet were, than the Peoples, less;
Condem'd for Life the Murdring Sword to weild,
And on their Heirs entail a Bloody Feild: 770
Thus madly their own Freedom they betray,
And for th' Oppression which they fear, make way;
Succession fixt by Heav'n the Kingdoms Bar,
Which once dissolv'd, admits the Flood of War;
Wast, Rapine, Spoil, without th' Assault begin,   775
And our mad Tribes Supplant the Fence within.
Since then their Good they will not understand,
'Tis time to take the Monarchs Pow'r in hand;
Authority, and Force to joyn with Skill, ⎤
And save the Lunaticks against their Will. ⎦   780
The same rough Means that swage the Crowd, appease
Our Senates raging with the Crowds Disease.
Henceforth unbiass'd Measures let 'em draw

From no false Gloss, but Genuine Text of Law;
Nor urge those Crimes upon Religions score   785
Themselves so much, in *Jebusites* abhor.
Whom Laws convict (and only they) shall Bleed,
Nor Pharisees by Pharisees be Freed.
Impartial Justice from our Throne shall Shou'r,
All shall have Right, and We our Sov'reign Pow'r.   790

    He said, th' Attendants heard with awful Joy,
And glad Presages their fixt Thoughts employ;
From *Hebron* now the suffering Heir Return'd,
A Realm that long with Civil Discor'd Mourn'd;
Till his Approach, like some Arriving God,   795
Compos'd, and heal'd the place of his Aboad;
The Deluge checkt that to *Judea* spread,
And stopt Sedition at the Fountain's Head.
Thus in forgiving *David*'s Paths he drives,
And chas'd from *Israel*, *Israels* Peace contrives.   800
The Feild confest his Pow'r in Arms before,
And Seas proclaim'd his Tryumphs to the Shore;
As nobly has his Sway in *Hebron* shown,
How fit t' Inherit Godlike *Davids* Throne.
Through *Sion*'s-Streets his glad Arrivals spread,   805
And Conscious Faction shrinks her snaky head;
His Train their Sufferings think o'repaid, to see
The Crowds Applause with Vertue once agree.
Success charms All, but Zeal for Worth distrest
A Virtue proper to the Brave and Best;   810
'Mongst whom was *Jothran*, *Jothran* always bent
To serve the Crown and Loyal by Descent.
Whose Constancy so Firm, and Conduct Just,
Deserv'd at once Two Royal Masters Trust;
Who *Tyre*'s proud Arms had Manfully withstood   815
On Seas, and gather'd Lawrels from the Flood;
Of Learning yet no Portion was deny'd,
Friend to the Muses, and the Muses Pride.
Nor can *Benaiah*'s Worth forgotten lie,
Of steddy Soul when Publick Storms were high;   820
Whose Conduct, while the *Moor* fierce Onsets made,
Secur'd at once our Honour and our Trade.
Such were the Chiefs, who most his Suff'rings mourn'd,

And view'd with silent Joy the Prince return'd;
While those that sought his Absence to Betray,   825
Press first their Nauseous False Respects to pay;
Him still th' officious Hypocrites Molest,
And with malicious Duty break his Rest.

   While real Transports thus his Friends Employ,
And Foes are Loud in their dissembled Joy,   830
His Tryumphs so resounded far and near,
Mist not his Young Ambitious Rival's Ear;
And as when joyful Hunters clam'rous Train,
Some Slumbring Lion Wakes in *Moab*'s Plain,
Who oft had forc'd the bold Assailants Yeild,   835
And scatter'd his Persuers through the Feild,
Disdaining, furls his Main, and tears the Ground,
His Eyes enflaming all the Desart Round,
With Roar of Seas directs his Chasers Way,
Provokes from far, and dares them to the Fray: 840
Such Rage storm'd now in *Absalom*'s fierce Breast,
Such Indignation his fir'd Eyes Confest;
Where now was the Instructer of his Pride?
Slept the Old Pilot in so rough a Tide?
Whose Wiles had from the happy Shore betray'd,   845
And thus on Shelves the cred'lous Youth convey'd.
In deep revolving Thoughts He weighs his State,
Secure of Craft, nor doubts to baffle Fate,
At least, if his storm'd Bark must go adrift,
To baulk his Charge, and for himself to shift,   850
In which his dextrous Wit had oft been shown,
And in the wreck of Kingdoms sav'd his own;
But now with more then Common Danger prest,
Of various Resolutions stands possest,
Perceives the Crowds unstable Zeal decay,   855
Least their Recanting Chief the Cause betray,
Who on a Father's Grace his Hopes may ground,
And for his Pardon with their Heads compound.
Him therefore, e're his Fortune slip her Time,
The Statesman Plots t' engage in some bold Crime   860
Past Pardon, whether to Attempt his Bed,
Or Threat with open Arms the Royal Head,
Or other daring Method, and Unjust,

That may confirm him in the Peoples Trust.
But failing thus t' ensnare him, nor secure   865
How long his foil'd Ambition may endure,
Plots next to lay him by, as past his Date,
And try some new Pretenders luckier Fate;
Whose Hopes with equal Toil he wou'd persue,
Nor cares what Claimer's Crownd, except the True.   870
Wake *Absalom*, approaching Ruin shun,
And see, O see, for whom thou art Undone!
How are thy Honours and thy Fame betray'd,
The Property of desp'rate Villains made?
Lost Pow'r and Conscious Fears their Crimes Create,   875
And Guilt in them was little less than Fate;
But why shou'dst Thou, from ev'ry Grievance free,
Forsake thy Vineyards for their Stormy Sea?
For Thee did *Canaan*'s Milk and Honey flow,
Love drest thy Bow'rs, and Lawrels sought thy Brow,   880
Preferment, Wealth and Pow'r thy Vassals were,
And of a Monarch all things but the Care.
Oh shou'd our Crimes, again, that Curse draw down,
And Rebel-Arms once more attempt the Crown,
Sure Ruin waits unhappy *Absalon*,   885
Alike by Conquest or Defeat undone;
Who cou'd relentless see such Youth and Charms,
Expire with wretched Fate in Impious Armes?
A Prince so form'd with Earth's, and Heav'ns Applause,
To Tryumph ore Crown'd Heads in *David*'s Cause: 890
Or grant him Victor, still his Hopes must fail,
Who, Conquering, wou'd not for himself prevail;
The Faction whom He trusts for future Sway,
Him and the Publique wou'd alike Betray;
Amongst themselves divide the Captive State,   895
And found their *Hydra*-Empire in his Fate!
Thus having beat the Clouds with painful Flight,
The pitty'd Youth, with Scepters in his Sight,
(So have their Cruel Politicks Decreed,)
Must by that Crew that made him Guilty, Bleed!   900
For cou'd their Pride brook any Prince's Sway,
Whom but mild *David* wou'd they choose t' Obey?

                864 confirm *B*: secure *A*

Who once at such a gentle Reign Repine,
The Fall of Monarchy it self Design;
From Hate to That their Reformations spring,   905
And *David* not their Grievance, but the King.
Seiz'd now with pannick Fear the Faction lies,
Least this clear Truth strike *Absaloms* charm'd Eyes,
Least He percieve, from long Enchantment free,
What all, beside the flatter'd Youth, must see.   910
But whate're doubts his troubled Bosome swell,
Fair Carriage still became *Achitophel*.
Who now an envious Festival enstalls,
And to survey their Strength the Faction calls,
Which Fraud, Religious Worship too must Guild;   915
But oh how weakly does Sedition Build!
For Lo! the Royal Mandate Issues forth,
Dashing at once their Treason, Zeal, and Mirth!
So have I seen disastrous Chance Invade,
Where careful Emmits had their Forrage laid,   920
Whether fierce *Vulcan*'s Rage, the Furzy Plain
Had seiz'd, Engendred by some careless Swain;
Or swelling *Neptune* lawless Inroads made,
And to their Cell of Store his Flood convey'd;
The Common-Wealth broke up distracted go,   925
And in wild Hast their loaded Mates o'rethrow:
Ev'n so our scatter'd Guests confus'dly meet,
With Boil'd, Bak'd, Roast, all Justling in the Street;
Dejected all, and rufully dismai'd,
For *Sheckle* without Treat, or Treason paid.   930
   Seditions dark Eclipse now fainter shows,
More bright each Hour the Royal Plannet grows,
Of Force the Clouds of Envy to disperse,
In kind Conjunction of Assisting Stars.
Here lab'ring Muse those Glorious Chiefs relate,   935
That turn'd the doubtful Scale of *David*'s Fate;
The rest of that Illustrious Band rehearse,
Immortalliz'd in Lawrell'd *Asaph*'s Verse:
Hard task! yet will I not thy Flight recall,
View Heav'n and then enjoy thy glorious Fall.   940
   First Write *Bezaliel*, whose Illustrious Name
Forestals our Praise, and gives his Poet Fame.

The *Kenites* Rocky Province his Command,
A barren Limb of Fertile *Canaans* Land;
Which for its gen'rous Natives yet cou'd be   945
Held Worthy such a President as He!
Bezaliel with each Grace, and Virtue Fraught,
Serene his Looks, Serene his Life and Thought,
On whom so largly Nature heapt her Store,
There scarce remain'd for Arts to give him more!   950
To Aid the Crown and State his greatest Zeal,
His Second Care that Service to Conceal;
Of Dues Observant, Firm in ev'ry Trust,
And to the Needy always more than Just.
Who Truth from specious falshood can divide,   955
Has all the Gown-mens Skill without their Pride;
Thus crown'd with worth from heights of honor won,
Sees all his Glories copied in his Son,
Whose forward Fame should every Muse engage:
Whose Youth boasts skill denyed to others Age.   960
Men, Manners, Language, Books of noblest kind
Already are the Conquest of his Mind.
Whose Loyalty before its Date was prime;
Nor waited the dull course of rowling Time:
The Monster *Faction* early he dismaid,   965
And *David*'s Cause long since confest his Aid.
     Brave *Abdael* o're the Prophets School was plac'd;
Abdael with all his Fathers Virtue grac'd;
A Heroe, who, while Stars look'd wondring down,
Without one *Hebrew*'s Bloud restor'd the Crown.   970
That Praise was His; what therefore did remain
For following Chiefs, but boldly to maintain
That Crown restor'd; and in this Rank of Fame,
Brave *Abdael* with the First a place must claim.
Proceed illustrious, happy Chief, proceed,   975
Foreseize the Garlands for thy Brow decreed,
While th' inspir'd Tribe attend with noblest strein
To Register the Glories thou shalt gain:
For sure, the Dew shall *Gilboah*'s Hills forsake,
And *Jordan* mix his Streams with *Sodom*'s Lake;   980
Or Seas retir'd their secret Stores disclose,
And to the Sun their scaly Brood expose,

Or swell'd above the Clifts, their Billows raise,
Before the Muses leave their Patron's Praise.

    Eliab our next Labour does invite,   985
And hard the Task to doe *Eliab* right:
Long with the royal Wanderer he rov'd,
And firm in all the Turns of Fortune prov'd!
Such ancient Service and Desert so large,
Well claim'd the Royal Houshold for his Charge.   990
His Age with only one mild Heiress blest,
In all the Bloom of smiling Nature drest,
And blest again to see his Flow'r ally'd
To *David*'s Stock, and made young *Othniel*'s Bride!
The bright Restorer of his Father's Youth,   995
Devoted to a Son's and Subject's Truth:
Resolv'd to bear that prize of Duty home,
So bravely sought (while sought) by *Absalom*.
Ah Prince! th' illustrious Planet of thy Birth,
And thy more powerful Virtue guard thy worth;   1000
That no *Achitophel* thy Ruine boast;
Israel too much in one such Wreck has lost.

    Ev'n Envy must consent to *Helon*'s Worth,
Whose Soul (though *Egypt* glories in his Birth)
Cou'd for our Captive-Ark its Zeal retain,   1005
And *Pharaoh*'s Altars in their Pomp disdain:
To slight his Gods was small; with nobler pride,
He all th' Allurements of his Court defi'd.
Whom Profit nor Example cou'd betray,
But *Israel*'s Friend and true to *David*'s Sway.   1010
What acts of favour in his Province fall;
On Merit he confers, and Freely all.

    Our List of Nobles next let *Amri* grace,
Whose Merits claim'd the *Abethdins* high place;
Who, with a Loyalty that did excell,   1015
Brought all th' endowments of *Achitophel*.
Sincere was *Amri*, and not only knew,
But *Israel*'s Sanctions into practice drew;
Our Laws, that did a boundless Ocean seem,
Were coasted all, and fathom'd all by Him.   1020
No *Rabbin* speaks like him their mystick Sense,

So just, and with such Charms of Eloquence:
To whom the double Blessing does belong,
With *Moses* Inspiration, *Aaron*'s Tongue.
  Than *Sheva*, none more loyal Zeal have shown, 1025
Wakefull, as *Judah*'s Lion for the Crown,
Who for that Cause still combats in his Age,
For which his Youth with danger did engage.
In vain our factious Priests the Cant revive,
In vain seditious Scribes with Libels strive 1030
T' enflame the Crow'd, while He with watchfull Eye
Observes, and shoots their Treasons as They fly.
Their weekly Frauds his keen Replies detect,
He undeceives more fast than they infect.
So *Moses* when the Pest on *Legions* prey'd, 1035
Advanc'd his Signal and the Plague was stay'd.
  Once more, my fainting Muse, thy Pinnions try,
And Strengths exhausted store let *Love* supply.
What Tribute, *Asaph*, shall we render Thee?
We'll crown thee with a Wreath from thy own Tree! 1040
Thy Lawrell Grove no Envye's flash can blast.
The Song of *Asaph* shall for ever last!
With wonder late Posterity shall dwell
On *Absalom*, and false *Achitophel*:
Thy streins shall be our slumbring Prophets dream, 1045
And when our *Sion* Virgins sing, their Theam.
Our *Jubilees* shall with thy Verse be grac't,
The Song of *Asaph* shall for ever last!
How fierce his Satyr loos'd, restrain'd how tame,
How tender of th' offending *Young man*'s Fame! 1050
How well his worth, and brave Adventures still'd,
Just to his Vertues, to his Errour mild.
No Page of thine that fears the strictest view,
But teems with just Reproof, or Praise, as due;
Not *Eden* cou'd a fairer Prospect yield, 1055
All *Paradise* without one barren Field:
Whose Wit the Censure of his Foes has past,
The Song of *Asaph* shall for ever last!
What Praise for such rich Strains shall we allow?
What just Rewards the gratefull Crown bestow? 1060
While Bees in Flow'rs rejoyce, and Flow'rs in Dew,

While Stars and Fountains to their Course are true;
While *Judah*'s Throne, and *Sion*'s Rock stand fast,
The Song of *Asaph* and the Fame shall last.

    Still *Hebrons* honour'd happy Soil Retains   1065
Our Royal Heroes beauteous dear remains;
Who now sails off with Winds nor Wishes slack,
To bring his Suff'rings bright Companion back:
But e're such Transport can our sense employ
A bitter grief must poyson half our Joy;   1070
Nor can our Coasts restor'd those Blessings see
Without a Bribe to envious Destiny!
Curs'd *Sodom*'s Doom for ever fix the Tyde
Where by inglorious Chance the Valiant dy'd.
Give not insulting *Askalon* to know,   1075
Nor let *Gath*'s Daughters triumph in our Woe!
No Sailer with the News swell *Egypt*'s Pride,
By what inglorious Fate our Valiant dy'd!
Weep *Arnon*! *Jordan* weep thy Fountains dry
While *Sion*'s Rock dissolves for a Supply!   1080
Calm were the Elements, Night's silence deep,
The Waves scarce murm'ring, and the Winds asleep;
Yet Fate for Ruine takes so still an hour,
And treacherous Sands the Princely Barque devour;
Then Death unworthy seiz'd a gen'rous Race,   1085
To Virtues scandal, and the Stars disgrace!
Oh! had th' Indulgent Pow'rs vouchsaf't to yield,
Instead of faithless Shelves, a listed Field;
A listed Field of Heav'ns and *David*'s Foes,
Fierce as the Troops that did his Youth oppose,   1090
Each Life had on his slaughter'd heap retir'd,
Not Tamely, and Unconqu'ring thus expir'd:
But Destiny is now their only Foe,
And dying, ev'n o're that they tryumph too;
With loud last Breaths their Master's 'Scape applaud,   1095
Of whom kind Force cou'd scarce the Fates defraud;
Who for such Followers lost, O matchless Mind!
At his own Safety now almost repin'd!
Say Royal Sir, by all your Fame in Arms,
Your Praise in Peace, and by *Urania*'s Charms;   1100
If all your Suff'rings past so nearly prest,

Or pierct with half so painful Grief your Breast?
   Thus some Diviner Muse her *Heroe* forms,
Not sooth'd with soft Delights, but tost in storms.
Not stretcht on Roses in the Myrtle Grove,   1105
Nor Crowns his Days with Mirth, his Nights with Love,
But far remov'd in Thundring Camps is found,
His Slumbers short, his Bed the herbless Ground:
In Tasks of Danger always seen the First,
Feeds from the Hedg, and slakes with Ice his Thirst.   1110
Long must his Patience strive with Fortunes Rage
And long, opposing Gods themselves engage,
Must see his Country Flame, his Friends destroy'd,
Before the promis'd Empire be enjoy'd,
Such Toil of Fate must build a Man of Fame,   1115
And such, to *Israel*'s Crown, the God-like *David* came.
   What suddain Beams dispel the Clouds so fast,
Whose drenching Rains laid all our Vineyards waste?
The Spring so far behind her Course delay'd,
On th' Instant is in all her Bloom array'd,   1120
The Winds breath low, the Element serene;
Yet mark what Motion in the Waves is seen!
Thronging and busie as *Hyblæan* Swarms,
Or stragled Souldiers Summon'd to their Arms.
See where the Princely Barque in loosest Pride,   1125
With all her Guardian Fleet, Adorns the Tide!
High on her Deck the Royal Lovers stand,
Our Crimes to Pardon e're they toucht our Land.
Welcome to *Israel* and to *David*'s Breast!
Here all your Toils, here all your Suff'rings Rest.   1130
   This year did *Ziloah* Rule *Jerusalem*,
And boldly all Sedition's Syrges stem,
How e're incumbred with a viler Pair
Than *Ziph* or *Shimei* to assist the Chair;
Yet *Ziloah*'s loyal Labours so prevail'd   1135
That Faction at the next Election fail'd,
When ev'n the common Cry did Justice Sound,
And Merit by the Multitude was Crown'd:
With *David* then was *Israel*'s peace restor'd,
Crowds Mournd their Errour and Obey'd their Lord.   1140

RELIGIO LAICI

or A Laymans Faith

A POEM

Ornari res ipsa negat; contenta doceri

THE PREFACE

A POEM with so bold a Title, and a Name prefix'd, from which the handling of so serious a Subject wou'd not be expected, may reasonably oblige the Author, to say somewhat in defence both of himself, and of his undertaking. In the first place, if it be objected to me that being a *Layman*, I ought not to have concern'd my self with 5 Speculations, which belong to the Profession of *Divinity*; I cou'd Answer, that perhaps, Laymen, with equal advantages of Parts and Knowledge, are not the most incompetent Judges of Sacred things; But in the due sense of my own weakness and want of Learning, I plead not this: I pretend not to make my self a Judge of Faith, in others, but 10 onely to make a Confession of my own; I lay no unhallow'd hand upon the Ark; but wait on it, with the Reverence that becomes me at a distance: In the next place I will ingenuously confess, that the helps I have us'd in this small Treatise, were many of them taken from the Works of our own Reverend Divines of the Church of *England*; so that 15 the Weapons with which I Combat Irreligion, are already Consecrated; though I suppose they may be taken down as lawfully as the Sword of *Goliah* was by *David*, when they are to be employed for the common Cause, against the Enemies of Piety. I intend not by this to intitle them to any of my errours; which, yet, I hope are only those of Charity to 20 Mankind; and such as my *own* Charity has caus'd me to commit, that of *others* may more easily excuse. Being naturally inclin'd to Scepticism in Philosophy, I have no reason to impose my Opinions, in a Subject which is above it: But whatever they are, I submit them with all reverence to my Mother Church, accounting them no further mine, 25 than as they are Authoriz'd, or at least, uncondemn'd by her. And, indeed, to secure my self on this side, I have us'd the necessary Pre-

Religio Laici. Text from the first edition, 1682 (82a), collated with the second edition, 1682 (82b).

caution, of showing this Paper before it was Publish'd to a judicious and learned Friend, a Man indefatigably zealous in the service of the Church and State: and whose Writings, have highly deserv'd of both. He was 30 pleas'd to approve the body of the Discourse, and I hope he is more my Friend, than to do it out of Complaisance: 'Tis true he had too good a tast to like it all; and amongst some other faults recommended to my second view, what I have written, perhaps too boldly on St. *Athanasius*: which he advised me wholy to omit. I am sensible enough that I had 35 done more *prudently* to have follow'd his opinion: But then I could not have satisfied my self, that I had done honestly not to have written what was my own. It has always been my *thought*, that Heathens, who never did, nor without Miracle cou'd hear of the name of Christ were yet in a possibility of Salvation. Neither will it enter easily into my 40 belief, that before the coming of our Saviour, the whole World, except- ing only the Jewish Nation, shou'd lye under the inevitable necessity of everlasting Punishment, for want of that Revelation, which was confin'd to so small a spot of ground as that of *Palæstine*. Among the Sons of *Noah* we read of one onely who was accurs'd; and if a blessing 45 in the ripeness of time was reserv'd for *Japhet*, (of whose Progeny we are,) it seems unaccountable to me, why so many Generations of the same Offspring, as preceeded our Saviour in the Flesh, shou'd be all involv'd in one common condemnation, and yet that their Posterity shou'd be Intitled to the hopes of Salvation: As if a Bill of Exclusion had 50 passed only on the Fathers, which debar'd not the Sons from their Suc- cession. Or that so many Ages had been *deliver'd over* to Hell, and so many *reserv'd* for Heaven, and that the Devil had the first choice, and God the next. Truly I am apt to think, that the revealed Religion which was taught by *Noah* to all his Sons, might continue for some Ages 55 in the whole Posterity. That afterwards it was included wholly in the Family of *Sem* is manifest: but when the Progenies of *Cham* and *Japhet* swarm'd into Colonies, and those Colonies were subdivided into many others; in process of time their Descendants lost by little and little the Primitive and Purer Rites of Divine Worship, retaining onely the notion 60 of one Deity; to which succeeding Generations added others: (for Men took their Degrees in those Ages from Conquerours to Gods.) Revela- tion being thus Eclipsed to almost all Mankind, the light of Nature as the next in Dignity was substituted; and that is it which St. *Paul* con- cludes to be the Rule of the Heathens; and by which they are hereafter 65 to be judg'd. If my supposition be true, then the consequence which I have assum'd in my Poem may be also true; namely, that Deism, or the

Principles of Natural Worship, are onely the faint remnants or dying
flames of reveal'd Religion in the Posterity of *Noah*: And that our
Modern Philosophers, nay and some of our Philosophising Divines have 70
too much exalted the faculties of our Souls, when they have maintain'd
that by their force, mankind has been able to find out that there is one
Supream Agent or Intellectual Being which we call God: that Praise
and Prayer are his due Worship; and the rest of those deducements,
which I am confident are the remote effects of Revelation, and un- 75
atainable by our Discourse, I mean as simply considerd, and without
the benefit of Divine Illumination. So that we have not lifted up our
selves to God, by the weak Pinions of our Reason, but he has been
pleasd to descend to us: and what *Socrates* said of him, what *Plato* writ,
and the rest of the Heathen Philosophers of several Nations, is all no 80
more than the Twilight of Revelation, after the Sun of it was set in the
Race of *Noah*. That there is some thing above us, some Principle of
motion, our Reason can apprehend, though it cannot discover what it
is, by its own Vertue. And indeed 'tis very improbable, that we, who
by the strength of our faculties cannot enter into the knowledg of any 85
Beeing, not so much as of our *own*, should be able to find out by them,
that Supream Nature, which we cannot otherwise define, than by
saying it is Infinite; as if Infinite were definable, or Infinity a Subject for
our narrow understanding. They who wou'd prove Religion by Reason,
do but weaken the cause which they endeavour to support: 'tis to take 90
away the Pillars from our Faith, and to prop it onely with a twig: 'tis
to design a Tower like that of *Babel*, which if it were possible (as it is
not) to reach Heaven, would come to nothing by the confusion of the
Workmen. For every man is Building a several way; impotently con-
ceipted of his own Model, and his own Materials: Reason is always 95
striving, and always at a loss, and of necessity it must so come to pass,
while 'tis exercis'd about that which is not its proper object. Let us be
content at last, to know God, by his own Methods; at least so much
of him, as he is pleas'd to reveal to us, in the sacred Scriptures; to
apprehend them to be the word of God, is all our Reason has to do; for 100
all beyond it is the work of Faith, which is the Seal of Heaven impress'd
upon our humane understanding.

And now for what concerns the Holy Bishop *Athanasius*, the Preface
of whose Creed seems inconsistent with my opinion; which is, That
Heathens may possibly be sav'd; in the first place I desire it may be 105
consider'd that it is the Preface onely, not the Creed it self, which, (till
I am better inform'd) is of too hard a digestion for my Charity. 'Tis not

that I am ignorant how many several Texts of Scripture seemingly
support that Cause; but neither am I ignorant how all those Texts may
receive a kinder, and more mollified Interpretation. Every man who is   110
read in Church History, knows *that* Belief was drawn up after a long
contestation with *Arrius*, concerning the Divinity of our Blessed
Saviour, and his being one Substance with the Father; and that thus
compild, it was sent abroad among the Christian Churches, as a kind
of Test, which whosoever took, was look'd on as an Orthodox Believer.   115
'Tis manifest from hence, that the Heathen part of the Empire was not
concerned in it: for its business was not to distinguish betwixt Pagans
and Christians, but betwixt Heriticks and true Believers. This, well
consider'd, takes off the heavy weight of Censure, which I wou'd willingly avoid from so venerable a Man; for if this Proportion, *whosoever*   120
will be sav'd, be restrained onely, to those to whom it was intended, and
for whom it was compos'd, I mean the Christians; then the Anathema,
reaches not the Heathens, who had never heard of Christ, and were
nothing interessed in that dispute. After all, I am far from blaming even
that Prefatory addition to the Creed, and as far from cavilling at the   125
continuation of it in the Liturgy of the Church; where on the days
appointed, 'tis publickly read: For I suppose there is the same reason
for it now, in opposition to the Socinians, as there was then against the
Arrians; the one being a Heresy, which seems to have been refin'd out
of the other; and with how much more plausibility of Reason it combats   130
our Religion, with so much more caution to be avoided: and therefore the prudence of our Church is to be commended which has interpos'd her Authority for the recommendation of this Creed. Yet to such
as are grounded in the true belief, those explanatory Creeds, the *Nicene*
and this of *Athanasius* might perhaps be spar'd: for what is supernatural,   135
will always be a mystery in spight of Exposition: and for my own part
the plain Apostles Creed, is most sutable to my weak understanding;
as the simplest diet is the most easy of Digestion.

I have dwelt longer on this Subject than I intended; and longer than,
perhaps, I ought; for having laid down, as my Foundation, that the   140
Scripture is a Rule; that in all things needfull to Salvation, it is clear,
sufficient, and ordain'd by God Almighty for that purpose, I have left
my self no right to interpret obscure places, such as concern the possibility of eternal happiness to Heathens: because whatsoever is obscure
is concluded not necessary to be known.   145

But, by asserting the Scripture to be the Canon of our Faith, I have
unavoidably created to my self two sorts of Enemies: The Papists in-

deed, more directly, because they have kept the Scripture from us, what
they cou'd; and have reserv'd to themselves a right of Interpreting
what they have deliver'd under the pretence of Infalibility: and the 150
Fanaticks more collaterally, because they have assum'd what amounts
to an Infalibility, in the private Spirit: and have detorted those Texts
of Scripture, which are not necessary to Salvation, to the damnable
uses of Sedition, disturbance and destruction of the Civil Government.
To begin with the Papists, and to speak freely, I think them the less 155
dangerous (at least in appearance) to our present State; for not onely
the Penal Laws are in Force against them, and their number is con-
temptible; but also their Peerage and Commons are excluded from
Parliaments, and consequently those Laws in no probability of being
Repeal'd. A General and Uninterrupted Plot of their Clergy, ever since 160
the Reformation, I suppose all Protestants believe. For 'tis not reasonable to think but that so many of their Orders, as were outed from their
fat possessions, wou'd endeavour a reentrance against those whom they
account Hereticks. As for the late design, Mr. *Colemans* Letters, for
ought I know are the best Evidence; and what they discover, without 165
wyre-drawing their Sence, or malicious Glosses, all Men of reason conclude credible. If there be any thing more than this requir'd of me, I
must believe it as well as I am able, in spight of the Witnesses, and out
of a decent conformity to the Votes of Parliament: For I suppose the
Fanaticks will not allow the private Spirit in this Case: Here the In- 170
fallibility is at least in one part of the Government; and our under-
standings as well as our wills are represented. But to return to the
Roman Catholicks, how can we be secure from the practice of Jesuited
Papists in that Religion? For not two or three of that Order, as some of
them would impose upon us, but almost the whole Body of them are 175
of opinion, that their Infallible Master has a right over Kings, not onely
in Spirituals but Temporals. Not to name *Mariana, Bellarmine, Emanuel
Sa, Molina, Santarel, Simancha,* and at the least twenty others of Foreign
Countries; we can produce of our own Nation, *Campian,* and *Doleman* or
Parsons, besides many are nam'd whom I have not read, who all of them 180
attest this Doctrine, that the Pope can Depose and give away the Right
o fany Sovereign Prince, *si vel paulum deflexerit,* if he shall never so little
Warpe: but if he once comes to be Excommunicated, then the Bond of
obedience is taken off from Subjects; and they may and ought to drive
him like another *Nebuchadnezzar, ex hominum Christianorum Dominatu,* 185
from exercising Dominion over Christians: and to this they are bound
by virtue of Divine Precept, and by all the tyes of Conscience under no

less Penalty than Damnation. If they answer me (as a Learned Priest has lately Written,) that this Doctrine of the Jesuits is not *de fide*, and that consequently they are not oblig'd by it, they must pardon me, if 190 I think they have said nothing to the purpose; for 'tis a Maxim in their Church, where Points of Faith are not decided, and that Doctors are of contrary opinions, they may follow which part they please; but more safely the most receiv'd and most Authoriz'd. And their Champion *Bellarmine* has told the World, in his Apology, that the King of *England* 195 is a Vassal to the Pope, *ratione directi Dominii*, and that he holds in Villanage of his Roman Landlord. Which is no new claim put in for *England*. Our Chronicles are his Authentique Witnesses, that, King *John* was depos'd by the same Plea, and *Philip Augustus* admitted Tenant. And which makes the more for *Bellarmine*, the French King 200 was again ejected when our King submitted to the Church, and the Crown receiv'd under the sordid Condition of a Vassalage.

'Tis not sufficient for the more moderate and well-meaning Papists, (of which I doubt not there are many) to produce the Evidences of their Loyalty to the late King, and to declare their Innocency in this Plot; 205 I will grant their behaviour in the first, to have been as Loyal and as brave as they desire; and will be willing to hold them excus'd as to the second, (I mean when it comes to my turn, and after my betters; for 'tis a madness to be sober alone, while the Nation continues Drunk:) but that saying of their Father *Cres:* is still running in my head, that 210 they may be dispens'd with in their Obedience to an Heretick Prince, while the necessity of the times shall oblige them to it: (for that (as another of them tells us,) is onely the effect of Christian Prudence) but when once they shall get power to shake him off, an Heretick is no lawful King, and consequently to rise against him is no Rebellion. I 215 should be glad therefore, that they wou'd follow the advice which was charitably given them by a Reverend Prelate of our Church; namely, that they would joyn in a publick Act of disowning and detesting those Jesuitick Principles; and subscribe to all Doctrines which deny the Popes Authority of Deposing Kings, and releasing Subjects from their 220 Oath of Allegiance: to which I shou'd think they might easily be in-duc'd, if it be true that this present Pope has condemn'd the Doctrine of King-killing (a Thesis of the Jesuites) amongst others *ex Cathedra* (as they call it) or in open consistory.

Leaving them, therefore, in so fair a way (if they please themselves) 225 of satisfying all reasonable Men, of their sincerity and good meaning to the Government, I shall make bold to consider that other extream of

our Religion, I mean the Fanaticks, or Schismaticks, of the English
Church. Since the Bible has been Translated into our Tongue, they
have us'd it so, as if their business was not to be sav'd but to be damnd 230
by its Contents. If we consider onely them, better had it been for the
English Nation, that it had still remain'd in the original Greek and
Hebrew, or at least in the honest Latine of St. *Jerome*, than that several
Texts in it, should have been prevaricated to the destruction of that
Government, which put it into so ungrateful hands. 235

How many Heresies the first Translation of *Tyndal* produced in few
years, let my Lord *Herbert*'s History of *Henry* the Eighth inform you;
Insomuch that for the gross errours in it, and the great mischiefs it
occasion'd, a Sentence pass'd on the first Edition of the Bible, too shamefull almost to be repeated. After the short Reign of *Edward* the Sixth 240
(who had continued to carry on the Reformation, on other principles
than it was begun) every one knows that not onely the chief promoters
of that work, but many others, whose Consciences wou'd not dispence
with Popery, were forc'd, for fear of persecution, to change Climates:
from whence returning at the beginning of Queen *Elizabeth*'s Reign, 245
many of them who had been in *France*, and at *Geneva*, brought back the
rigid opinions and imperious discipline of *Calvin*, to graffe upon our
Reformation. Which, though they cunningly conceal'd at first, (as
well knowing how nauseously that Drug wou'd go down in a lawfull
Monarchy, which was prescrib'd for a rebellious Common-wealth) yet 250
they always kept it in reserve; and were never wanting to themselves
either in Court or Parliament, when either they had any prospect of a
numerous Party of Fanatique Members in the one, or the encouragement of any Favourite in the other, whose Covetousness was gaping
at the Patrimony of the Church. They who will consult the Works of 255
our venerable *Hooker*, or the account of his Life, or more particularly the
Letter written to him on this Subject, by *George Cranmer*, may see by
what gradations they proceeded; from the dislike of Cap and Surplice,
the very next step was Admonitions to the Parliament against the
whole Government Ecclesiastical: then came out Volumes in English 260
and Latin in defence of their Tenets: and immediately, practices were
set on foot to erect their Discipline without Authority. Those not succeeding, Satyre and Rayling was the next: And *Martin Mar-Prelate* (the
Marvel of those times) was the first Presbyterian Scribler, who sanctify'd
Libels and Scurrility to the use of the Good Old Cause. Which was done 265
(says my Authour) upon this account; that (their serious Treatises
having been fully answered and refuted) they might compass by rayling

what they had lost by reasoning; and when their Cause was sunk in
Court and Parliament, they might at least hedge in a stake amongst the
Rabble: for to their ignorance all things are Wit which are abusive; but 270
if Church and State were made the Theme, then the Doctoral Degree
of Wit was to be taken at *Billingsgate*: even the most Saintlike of the
Party, though they durst not excuse this contempt and villifying of the
Government, yet were pleas'd, and grin'd at it with a pious smile; and
call'd it a judgment of God against the Hierarchy. Thus Sectaries, we 275
may see, were born with teeth, foul-mouth'd and scurrilous from their
Infancy: and if Spiritual Pride, Venome, Violence, Contempt of
Superiours and Slander had been the marks of Orthodox Belief; the
Presbytery and the rest of our Schismaticks, which are their Spawn,
were always the most visible Church in the Christian World.   280

'Tis true, the Government was too strong at that time for a Rebellion; but to shew what proficiency they had made in *Calvin*'s School,
even *Then* their mouths water'd at it: for two of their gifted Brotherhood (*Hacket* and *Coppinger*) as the Story tells us, got up into a Pease-
Cart, and harangued the People, to dispose them to an insurrection, 285
and to establish their Discipline by force: so that however it comes
about, that now they celebrate Queen *Elizabeth*'s Birth-night, as that
of their Saint and Patroness; yet then they were for doing the work of
the Lord by Arms against her; and in all probability, they wanted but
a Fanatique Lord Mayor and two Sheriffs of their Party to have com- 290
pass'd it.

Our venerable *Hooker*, after many Admonitions which he had given
them, toward the end of his Preface, breaks out into this Prophetick
speech. "*There is in every one of these Considerations most just cause to fear*,
"*lest our hastiness to embrace a thing of so perilous Consequence* (meaning the 295
"Presbyterian Discipline) *should cause Postery to feel those Evils, which as yet*
"*are more easy for us to prevent, than they would be for them to remedy.*

How fatally this *Cassandra* has foretold we know too well by sad
experience: the Seeds were sown in the time of Queen *Elizabeth*, the
bloudy Harvest ripened in the Reign of King *Charles* the Martyr: and 300
because all the Sheaves could not be carried off without shedding some
of the loose Grains, another Crop is too like to follow; nay I fear 'tis
unavoidable if the Conventiclers be permitted still to scatter.

A man may be suffer'd to quote an Adversary to our Religion, when
he speaks Truth: and 'tis the observation of *Meimbourg* in his History of 305
Calvinism, that where-ever that Discipline was planted and embrac'd,
Rebellion, Civil War and Misery attended it. And how indeed should

it happen otherwise? Reformation of Church and State has always been the ground of our Divisions in *England*. While we were Papists, our Holy Father rid us, by pretending authority out of the Scriptures to 310 depose Princes, when we shook off his Authority, the Sectaries furnish'd themselves with the same Weapons, and out of the same Magazine, the Bible. So that the Scriptures, which are in themselves the greatest security of Governours, as commanding express obedience to them, are now turn'd to their destruction; and never since the Reformation has 315 there wanted a Text of their interpreting to authorize a Rebel. And 'tis to be noted by the way, that the Doctrines of King-killing and Depos-ing, which have been taken up onely by the worst Party of the Papists, the most frontless Flatterers of the Pope's Authority, have been espous'd, defended and are still maintain'd by the whole Body of Non- 320 conformists and Republicans. 'Tis but dubbing themselves the People of God, which 'tis the interest of their Preachers to tell them they are, and their own interest to believe; and after that, they cannot dip into the Bible, but one Text or another will turn up for their purpose: If they are under Persecution (as they call it,) then that is a mark of their 325 Election; if they flourish, then God works Miracles for their Deliver-ance, and the Saints are to possess the Earth.

They may think themselves to be too roughly handled in this Paper; but I who know best how far I could have gone on this Subject, must be bold to tell them they are spar'd: though at the same time I am not 330 ignorant that they interpret the mildness of a Writer to them, as they do the mercy of the Government; in the one they think it Fear, and conclude it Weakness in the other. The best way for them to confute me, is, as I before advis'd the Papists, to disclaim their Principles, and renounce their Practices. We shall all be glad to think them true 335 Englishmen when they obey the King, and true Protestants when they conform to the Church Discipline.

It remains that I acquaint the Reader, that the Verses were written for an ingenious young Gentleman my Friend; upon his Translation of *The Critical History of the Old Testament*, compos'd by the learned Father 340 *Simon*: The Verses therefore are address'd to the Translatour of that Work, and the style of them is, what it ought to be, Epistolary.

If any one be so lamentable a Critique as to require the Smoothness, the Numbers and the Turn of Heroick Poetry in this Poem; I must tell

311–12 *after* Princes, *82a* (*first issue only*) *has* (a Doctrine which, though some Papists may reject, no Pope has hitherto deny'd, nor ever will,) 340 compos'd *82a* (*second issue*) *82b*: written *82a* (*first issue*) *83*

him, that if he has not read *Horace*, I have studied him, and hope the 345
style of his Epistles is not ill imitated here. The Expressions of a Poem,
design'd purely for Instruction, ought to be Plain and Natural, and yet
Majestick: for here the Poet is presum'd to be a kind of Law-giver, and
those three qualities which I have nam'd are proper to the Legislative
style. The Florid, Elevated and Figurative way is for the Passions; for 350
Love and Hatred, Fear and Anger, are begotten in the Soul by shewing
their Objects out of their true proportion; either greater than the Life,
or less; but Instruction is to be given by shewing them what they
naturally are. A Man is to be cheated into Passion, but to be reason'd
into Truth. 355

RELIGIO LAICI

D IM, as the borrow'd beams of Moon and Stars
    To *lonely, weary, wandring* Travellers,
Is *Reason* to the *Soul*: And as on high,
Those rowling Fires *discover* but the Sky
Not light us *here*; So *Reason*'s glimmering Ray   5
Was lent, not to *assure* our *doubtfull* way,
But *guide* us upward to a *better Day*.
And as those nightly Tapers disappear
When Day's bright Lord ascends our Hemisphere;
So pale grows *Reason* at *Religions* sight;   10
So *dyes*, and so *dissolves* in *Supernatural Light*.
Some few, whose Lamp shone brighter, have been led
From Cause to Cause, to *Natures* secret head;
And found that *one first principle* must be:
But *what*, or *who*, that *UNIVERSAL HE*;   15
Whether some *Soul* incompassing this Ball
Unmade, unmov'd; yet *making, moving All*;
Or various *Atoms* interfering Dance
Leapt into *Form*, (the Noble work of *Chance*;)

Or this great *All* was from *Eternity*;   } 20
Not ev'n the *Stagirite* himself could see;
And *Epicurus Guess'd* as well as He:
As *blindly grop'd* they for a *future State*;
As *rashly Judg'd* of *Providence* and *Fate*:
But least of all could their Endeavours find   *Opinions of*
What most concern'd the good of Humane kind: *the several*
For *Happiness* was never to be found;   *Sects of*
But vanish'd from 'em, like Enchanted ground.   *Philosophers*
One thought *Content* the Good to be enjoy'd: *concerning*
This, every little *Accident* destroy'd: *the* Sum-
                                                                  mum Bo-
                                                                  num.
The *wiser Madmen* did for *Vertue* toyl: 30
A Thorny, or at best a barren Soil:
In *Pleasure* some their glutton Souls would steep;   }
But found their Line too short, the Well too deep;   } 35
And leaky Vessels which no *Bliss* cou'd keep.   }
Thus, *anxious Thoughts* in *endless Circles* roul,
Without a *Centre* where to fix the *Soul*:
In this wilde Maze their vain Endeavours end.
How can the *less* the *Greater* comprehend?
Or *finite Reason* reach *Infinity*?   40
For what cou'd *Fathom GOD* were *more* than He.

    The *Deist* thinks he stands on firmer ground;   *Systeme of*
Cries ἕυρεκα: the mighty Secret's found: *Deisme.*
God is that *Spring* of *Good*; *Supreme*, and *Best*;
We, made to *serve*, and in that *Service blest*;   45
If so, some *Rules* of Worship must be given,
Distributed alike to all by Heaven:
Else *God* were *partial*, and to *some* deny'd
The Means his Justice shou'd for *all* provide.
This *general Worship* is to *PRAISE*, and *PRAY*:   50
One part to *borrow* Blessings, one to *pay*:
And when frail Nature slides into *Offence*,
The *Sacrifice* for *Crimes* is *Penitence*.
Yet, since th' Effects of Providence, we find
Are variously dispens'd to Humane kind;   55
That *Vice Triumphs*, and *Vertue suffers* here,
(A Brand that Sovereign Justice cannot bear;)
Our Reason prompts us to a *future State*:
The *last Appeal* from *Fortune*, and from *Fate*:

Where God's all-righteous ways will be declar'd;   60
The *Bad* meet *Punishment*, the *Good*, *Reward*.

    Thus Man by his own strength to Heaven wou'd soar:
And wou'd not be Oblig'd to God for more.
Vain, wretched Creature, how art thou misled
To think thy Wit these God-like Notions bred!   65
These Truths are not the product of thy Mind,
But dropt from Heaven, and of a Nobler kind.
Reveal'd Religion first inform'd thy Sight,
And *Reason* saw not, till *Faith* sprung the Light.
Hence all thy *Natural Worship* takes the *Source*:   70
'Tis *Revelation* what thou thinkst *Discourse*.
Else, how com'st *Thou* to see these truths so clear,
Which so obscure to *Heathens* did appear?
Not *Plato* these, nor *Aristotle* found:

Nor He whose Wisedom *Oracles* renown'd.
Hast thou a Wit so deep, or so sublime,
Or canst thou lower dive, or higher climb?
Canst *Thou*, by *Reason*, more of *God-head* know
Than *Plutarch*, *Seneca*, or *Cicero*?
Those *Gyant* Wits, in happyer Ages born,   80
(When *Arms*, and *Arts* did *Greece* and *Rome* adorn)
Knew no such *Systeme*: no such Piles cou'd raise
Of *Natural Worship*, built on *Pray'r* and *Praise*,
To One sole GOD.
Nor did Remorse, to Expiate Sin, prescribe: 85
But slew their fellow Creatures for a Bribe:
The guiltless *Victim* groan'd for their Offence;
And *Cruelty*, and *Blood* was *Penitence.*
If *Sheep* and *Oxen* cou'd Attone for Men
Ah! at how cheap a rate the *Rich* might Sin!   90
And great Oppressours might Heavens Wrath beguile
By offering his own Creatures for a Spoil!
    Dar'st thou, poor Worm, offend *Infinity*?
And must the Terms of Peace be given by *Thee*?
Then *Thou* art *Justice* in the *last Appeal*;   95
Thy easie God instructs Thee to *rebell*:
And, like a King remote, and weak, must take
What Satisfaction *Thou* art pleas'd to make.
    But if there be a *Pow'r* too *Just*, and *strong*

To wink at *Crimes*, and bear unpunish'd *Wrong*;　　100
Look humbly upward, see his Will disclose:
The *Forfeit* first, and then the *Fine* impose:
A *Mulct thy* Poverty cou'd never pay
Had not *Eternal Wisedom* found the way:
And with *Cœlestial* Wealth supply'd thy Store:　　105
His Justice makes the *Fine*, *his Mercy* quits the *Score*.
See God descending in thy Humane Frame;
Th' *offended*, suff'ring in th' *Offenders* Name:
All thy Misdeeds to him imputed see,
And all his Righteousness devolv'd on thee.　　110

　　For granting we have Sin'd, and that th' offence
Of *Man*, is made against *Omnipotence*,
Some Price, that bears *proportion*, must be paid;
And *Infinite* with *Infinite* be weigh'd.
See then the *Deist lost: Remorse* for *Vice*,　　115
Not paid, or *paid*, *inadequate* in price:
What farther means can *Reason* now direct,
Or what Relief from *humane Wit* expect?
That shews us *sick*; and sadly are we sure
Still to be *Sick*, till *Heav'n* reveal the *Cure*:　　120
If then *Heaven*'s *Will* must needs be understood,
(Which must, if we want *Cure*, and *Heaven*, be *Good*)
Let all Records of *Will reveal'd* be shown;
With *Scripture*, all in equal ballance thrown,
And *our one Sacred Book* will be *That one*.　　125

　　Proof needs not here, for whether we compare
That Impious, Idle, Superstitious Ware
Of *Rites*, *Lustrations*, *Offerings*, (which before,
In various Ages, various Countries bore)
With *Christian Faith* and *Vertues*, we shall find　　130
None answ'ring the great ends of humane kind
But *This one Rule of Life: That* shews us best
How *God* may be *appeas'd*, and *Mortals blest*.
Whether from length of *Time* its worth we draw,
The *World* is scarce more *Ancient* than the *Law*:　　135
Heav'ns early Care prescrib'd for every Age;
First, in the *Soul*, and after, in the *Page*.
Or, whether more abstractedly we look,
Or on the *Writers*, or the *written Book*,

Whence, but from *Heav'n*, cou'd men unskill'd in Arts,   140
In several Ages born, in several parts,
Weave such *agreeing Truths*? or *how*, or *why*
Shou'd *all* conspire to cheat us with a *Lye*?
Unask'd their *Pains*, *ungratefull* their *Advice*,
Starving their *Gain*, and *Martyrdom* their *Price*.   145

    If on the Book it self we cast our view,
Concurrent Heathens prove the Story *True*:
The *Doctrine*, *Miracles*; which must convince,
For *Heav'n* in *Them* appeals to *humane Sense*:
And though they *prove* not, they *Confirm* the Cause,   150
When what is *Taught* agrees with *Natures Laws*.

    Then for the *Style*; *Majestick* and *Divine*,
It speaks no less than God in every Line:
Commanding words; whose *Force* is still the same
As the first *Fiat* that produc'd our *Frame*.   155
All Faiths *beside*, or did by *Arms* ascend;
Or *Sense* indulg'd has made *Mankind* their *Friend*:
This *onely* Doctrine does our *Lusts* oppose:
Unfed by Natures Soil, in which it grows;
Cross to our *Interests*, curbing Sense, and Sin;   160
Oppress'd without, and undermin'd within,
It thrives through pain; its own Tormentours tires;
And with a stubborn patience still aspires.
To what can *Reason* such Effects assign
Transcending *Nature*, but to *Laws Divine*?   165
Which in that Sacred Volume are contain'd;
Sufficient, clear, and for that use ordain'd.

*Objection of
the Deist.*

    But stay: the *Deist* here will urge anew,
No *Supernatural Worship* can be *True*:
Because a *general Law* is that alone   170
Which must to *all*, and every *where* be known:
A *Style* so large as not *this* Book can claim
Nor ought that bears *reveal'd* Religions *Name*.
'Tis said the sound of a *Messiah's Birth*
Is gone through all the habitable Earth: 175
But still that Text must be confin'd alone
To what was *Then* inhabited, and known:
And what Provision cou'd from *thence* accrue
To *Indian* Souls, and Worlds discover'd *New*?

In other parts it helps, that Ages past,   180
The Scriptures there were *known*, and were *imbrac'd*,
Till Sin spread once again the Shades of Night:
What's that to these who never *saw* the Light?   *The Objection answer'd.*
   Of all Objections this indeed is chief
To startle Reason, stagger frail Belief: 185
We grant, 'tis true, that Heav'n from humane Sense
Has hid the secret paths of *Providence*:
But *boundless Wisedom*, *boundless Mercy*, may
Find ev'n for those *be-wildred* Souls, a *way*:
If from his *Nature Foes* may Pity claim,   190
Much more may *Strangers* who ne'er heard his *Name*.
And though *no Name* be for *Salvation* known,
But that of his *Eternal Sons* alone;
Who knows how far transcending Goodness can
Extend the *Merits* of *that Son* to *Man*?   195
Who knows what *Reasons* may his *Mercy* lead;
Or *Ignorance invincible* may plead?
Not onely *Charity* bids hope the *best*,
But *more* the great Apostle has exprest:
That, if the Gentiles, (whom no Law inspir'd,)   200
By Nature did what was by *Law requir'd*;
They, who the written Rule had never known,
Were to themselves both Rule and Law alone:
To Natures plain indictment they shall plead;
And, by their Conscience, be condemn'd or freed.   205
Most righteous Doom! because a *Rule reveal'd*
Is *none* to *Those*, from whom it was *conceal'd*.
Then those who follow'd *Reasons* Dictates right;
Liv'd up, and lifted high their *Natural Light*;
With *Socrates* may see their Maker's Face,   210
While Thousand *Rubrick-Martyrs* want a place.
   Nor does it baulk my *Charity*, to find
Th' *Egyptian* Bishop of another mind:
For, though his *Creed Eternal Truth* contains,
'Tis hard for *Man* to doom to *endless pains*   215
All who believ'd not all, his *Zeal* requir'd;
Unless he first cou'd prove he was inspir'd.
Then let us either think he meant to say
This Faith, where *publish'd*, was the onely way;

Or else conclude that, *Arius* to confute,   220
The good old Man, too eager in dispute,
Flew high; and as his *Christian* Fury rose
Damn'd all for *Hereticks* who durst *oppose.*

*Digression
to the
Translatour
of Father
Simon's
Critical
History of
the Old
Testament.*

    Thus far my Charity this path has try'd;
(A much unskilfull, but well meaning guide:)
Yet what they are, ev'n these crude thoughts were bred
By reading that, which better thou hast read,
Thy Matchless Author's work: which thou, my Friend,
By well translating better dost commend:
Those youthfull hours which, of thy Equals most   230
In *Toys* have *squander'd*, or in *Vice* have *lost*,
Those hours hast thou to Nobler use employ'd;
And the severe Delights of Truth enjoy'd.
Witness this weighty Book, in which appears
The crabbed Toil of many thoughtfull years,   235
Spent by thy Authour, in the Sifting Care
Of *Rabbins* old Sophisticated Ware
From Gold Divine; which he who well can sort
May afterwards make *Algebra* a Sport.
A Treasure, which if *Country-Curates* buy,   240
They *Junius*, and *Tremellius* may defy:
Save pains in various readings, and Translations;
And without *Hebrew* make most learn'd quotations.
A Work so full with various Learning fraught,
So nicely pondred, yet so strongly wrought,   245
As Natures height and Arts last hand requir'd:
As much as Man cou'd compass, uninspir'd.
Where we may see what *Errours* have been made
Both in the *Copiers* and *Translaters Trade*:
How *Jewish*, *Popish*, Interests have prevail'd,   250
And where *Infallibility* has *fail'd.*
    For some, who have his secret meaning ghes'd,
Have found our Authour not too *much* a *Priest*:
For *Fashion-sake* he seems to have recourse
To *Pope*, and *Councils*, and *Traditions* force: 255
But he that *old* Traditions cou'd subdue,
Cou'd not but find the weakness of the *New*:
If *Scripture*, though deriv'd from *heav'nly birth*,
Has been but carelesly preserv'd on *Earth*;

If *God's own People*, who of *God* before   260
Knew what we know, and had been promis'd more,
In fuller Terms, of Heaven's assisting Care,
And who did neither *Time*, nor *Study* spare
To keep this Book *untainted*, *unperplext*;
Let in gross *Errours* to corrupt the *Text*:   265
Omitted *paragraphs*, embroyl'd the *Sense*;
With vain *Traditions* stopt the gaping Fence,
Which every common hand pull'd up with ease:
What Safety from such *brushwood-helps* as these?
If *written words* from time are not secur'd,   270
How can we think have *oral Sounds* endur'd?
Which *thus* transmitted, if *one* Mouth has fail'd,
Immortal Lyes on *Ages* are intail'd:
And that some such have been, is prov'd too plain;
If we consider *Interest*, *Church*, and *Gain*.   275

    Oh but says one, *Tradition* set aside,   *Of the In-*
Where can we hope for an *unerring Guid*?   *fallibility*
For since th' *original* Scripture has been lost, *of Tradi-*
All Copies *disagreeing*, *maim'd* the *most*,   *tion, in*
Or *Christian Faith* can have no *certain* ground, *General.* 280
Or *Truth* in *Church Tradition* must be found.

    Such an *Omniscient* Church we wish indeed;
'Twere worth *Both Testaments*, and cast in the *Creed*:
But if *this Mother* be a *Guid* so sure,
As can all *doubts resolve*, all *truth secure*,   285
Then her *Infallibility*, as well
Where Copies are *corrupt*, or *lame*, can tell;
Restore *lost Canon* with as little pains,
As *truly explicate* what still *remains*:
Which yet no *Council* dare *pretend* to doe;   290
Unless like *Esdras*, they cou'd *write* it new:
Strange Confidence, still to *interpret* true,
Yet not be sure that all they have explain'd,
Is in the blest *Original* contain'd.
More Safe, and much more modest 'tis, to say   295
God wou'd not leave Mankind without a way:
And that the *Scriptures*, though not *every where*
Free from Corruption, or intire, or clear,
Are uncorrupt, sufficient, clear, intire,

In *all* things which our needfull *Faith* require.   300
If *others* in the *same Glass better* see
'Tis for *Themselves* they look, but not for *me*:
For *MY* Salvation must its Doom receive
Not from what *OTHERS*, but what *I* believe.

    Must *all Tradition* then be set aside?
This to affirm were Ignorance, or Pride.
Are there not many points, some needfull sure
To saving Faith, that Scripture leaves obscure?
Which every Sect will wrest a several way
(For what *one* Sect Interprets, *all* Sects *may*:)   310
We hold, and say we prove from Scripture plain,
That *Christ* is *GOD*; the bold *Socinian*
From the *same* Scripture urges he's but *MAN*.
Now what Appeal can end th' important Suit;
Both parts *talk* loudly, but the *Rule* is *mute*?   315

    Shall I speak plain, and in a Nation free
Assume an honest *Layman's Liberty*?
I think (according to my little Skill,
To my own Mother-Church submitting still:)
That many have been sav'd, and many may,   320
Who never heard this Question brought in play.
Th' *unletter'd* Christian, who believes in *gross*,
Plods on to *Heaven*; and ne'er is at a loss:
For the *Streight-gate* wou'd be made *streighter* yet,
Were *none* admitted there but men of *Wit*.   325
The few, by Nature form'd, with Learning fraught,
Born to instruct, as others to be taught,
Must Study well the Sacred Page; and see
Which Doctrine, this, or that, does best agree
With the whole Tenour of the Work Divine: 330
And plainlyest points to Heaven's reveal'd Design:
Which Exposition flows from *genuine Sense*;
And which is *forc'd* by *Wit* and *Eloquence*.
Not that Traditions parts are useless here:
When general, old, disinteress'd and clear: 335
That Ancient Fathers thus expound the Page,
Gives *Truth* the reverend Majesty of *Age*:
Confirms its force, by biding every *Test*;
For best *Authority's* next *Rules* are best.

Objecti
behalf
Tradit
urg'd
Father
Simon

And still the nearer to the Spring we go   340
More limpid, more unsoyl'd the Waters flow.
Thus, *first Traditions* were a proof alone;
Cou'd we be *certain* such they *were*, so *known*:
But since some Flaws in long descent may be,
They make not *Truth* but *Probability*.   345
Even *Arius* and *Pelagius* durst provoke
To what the *Centuries preceding* spoke.
Such difference is there in an oft-told Tale:
But Truth by its own Sinews will prevail.
Tradition written therefore more commends   350
Authority, than what from *Voice* descends:
And this, as perfect as its kind can be,
Rouls down to us the Sacred History:
Which, from the *Universal Church receiv'd*,
Is *try'd*, and *after*, for its *self* believ'd.   355

    The partial *Papists* wou'd infer from hence   *The Second Objection.*
Their Church, in last resort, shou'd Judge the *Sense*.
But first they wou'd assume, with wondrous Art,   *Answer to the Objection.*
Themselves to be the *whole*, who are but *part*
Of that vast Frame, the Church; yet grant they were   360
The handers down, can they from thence infer
A right t' interpret? or wou'd they alone
Who brought the Present, claim it for their own?
The *Book*'s a *Common Largess* to *Mankind*;
Not more for *them*, than *every* Man design'd: 365
The *welcome News* is in the *Letter* found;
The *Carrier*'s not Commission'd to *expound*.
It *speaks* it *Self*, and what it does contain,
In all things *needfull* to be *known*, is *plain*.

    In times o'ergrown with Rust and Ignorance,   370
A gainfull Trade their Clergy did advance:
When want of Learning kept the *Laymen* low,
And none but *Priests* were *Authoriz'd* to *know*:
When what small Knowledge was, in them did dwell;
And he a *God* who cou'd but *Reade* or *Spell*;   375
Then *Mother Church* did mightily prevail:
She parcel'd out the Bible by *retail*:
But still *expounded* what She *sold* or *gave*;
To keep it in *her Power* to *Damn* and *Save*:

Scripture was *scarce*, and as the Market went,   380
Poor *Laymen* took *Salvation* on *Content*;
As needy men take Money, good or bad:
God's Word they had not, but the *Priests* they had.
Yet, whate'er *false Conveyances* they made,
The *Lawyer* still was *certain* to be paid.   385
In those dark times they learn'd their knack so well,
That by long use they grew *Infallible*:
At last, a knowing Age began t' enquire
If *they* the *Book*, or *That* did *them* inspire:
And, making narrower search they found, thô late,   390
That what they thought the *Priest*'s, was *Their* Estate:
Taught by the *Will produc'd*, (the written Word)
How long they had been *cheated* on *Record*.
Then, every man who saw the Title fair,
Claim'd a Child's part, and put in for a Share: 395
Consulted Soberly his private good;
And sav'd himself as cheap as e'er he cou'd.
  'Tis true, my Friend, (and far be Flattery hence)
This good had full as bad a Consequence:
The Book thus put in every vulgar hand,   400
Which each presum'd he best cou'd understand,
The *Common Rule* was made the *common Prey*;
And at the mercy of the *Rabble* lay.
The tender Page with horney Fists was gaul'd;
And he was gifted most that loudest baul'd: 405
The *Spirit* gave the *Doctoral Degree*:
And every member of a *Company*
Was of *his Trade*, and of the *Bible free*.
Plain *Truths* enough for needfull *use* they found;
But men wou'd still be itching to *expound*:   410
Each was ambitious of th' obscurest place,
No measure ta'n from *Knowledge*, all from GRACE.
Study and *Pains* were now no more their Care;
Texts were explain'd by *Fasting*, and by *Prayer*:
This was the Fruit the *private Spirit* brought;   415
Occasion'd by *great Zeal*, and *little Thought*.
While Crouds unlearn'd, with rude Devotion warm,
About the Sacred Viands buz and swarm,
The *Fly-blown Text* creates a *crawling Brood*;

And turns to *Maggots* what was meant for *Food.*   420
A Thousand daily Sects rise up, and dye;
A Thousand more the perish'd Race supply.
So all we make of Heavens discover'd Will
Is, not to have it, or to use it ill.
The Danger's much the same; on several Shelves   425
If *others* wreck *us*, or *we* wreck our *selves.*

    What then remains, but, waving each Extreme,
The Tides of Ignorance, and Pride to stem?
Neither so rich a Treasure to forgo;
Nor proudly seek beyond our pow'r to know: 430
Faith is not built on disquisitions vain;
The things we *must* believe, are *few*, and *plain*:
But since men *will* believe more than they *need*;
And every man will make *himself* a Creed:
In doubtfull questions 'tis the safest way   435
To learn what unsuspected Ancients say:
For 'tis not likely *we* shou'd higher Soar
In search of Heav'n, than *all the Church before*:
Nor can we be deceiv'd, unless we see
The *Scripture*, and the *Fathers disagree.*   440
If after all, they stand suspected still,
(For no man's Faith depends upon his Will;)
'Tis some Relief, that points not clearly known,
Without much hazard may be let alone:
And, after hearing what our Church can say,   445
If still our Reason runs another way,
That private Reason 'tis more Just to curb,
Than by Disputes the publick Peace disturb.
For points obscure are of small use to learn:
But *Common quiet* is *Mankind's concern.*   450
    Thus have I made my own Opinions clear:
Yet neither Praise expect, nor Censure fear:
And this unpolish'd, rugged Verse, I chose;
As fittest for Discourse, and nearest Prose:
For, while from *Sacred Truth* I do not swerve,   455
Tom Sternhold's, or *Tom Shadwell's Rhimes* will serve.

PROLOGUE and EPILOGUE
To the King and Queen

PROLOGUE TO THE King and Queen,
AT THE OPENING OF Their THEATRE

Spoken by Mr. *Batterton*

SINCE Faction ebbs, and Rogues grow out of Fashion,
Their penny-Scribes take care t' inform the Nation,
How well men thrive in this or that Plantation.

How *Pensilvania*'s Air agrees with Quakers,
And *Carolina*'s with Associators: 5
Both e'en too good for Madmen and for Traitors.

Truth is, our Land with Saints is so run o'er,
And every Age produces such a store,
That now there's need of two *New-Englands* more.

What's this, you'll say, to Us and our Vocation?   10
Onely thus much, that we have left our Station,
And made this Theatre our new Plantation.

The Factious Natives never cou'd agree;
But aiming, as they call'd it, to be Free,
Those Play-house Whiggs set up for Property.   15

Some say they no Obedience paid of late;
But wou'd new Fears and Jealousies create;
Till topsy-turvy they had turn'd the State.

Plain Sense, without the Talent of Foretelling,
Might guess 'twou'd end in down-right knocks and quelling: 20
For seldome comes there better of Rebelling.

When Men will, needlesly, their Freedom barter
For Lawless Pow'r, sometimes they catch a Tartar:
(There's a damn'd word that rhimes to this call'd Charter.)

But, since the Victory with Us remains,   25
You shall be call'd to Twelve in all our Gains:
(If you'll not think us sawcy for our pains.)

Prologue and Epilogue. Text from the first edition, 1683

Old Men shall have good old Plays to delight 'em:
And you, fair Ladys and Gallants that slight 'em,
We'll treat with good new Plays; if our new Wits can   30
  write 'em.

We'll take no blundring Verse, no fustian Tumour,
No dribling Love, from this or that Presumer:
No dull fat Fool shamm'd on the Stage for humour.

For, faith, some of 'em such vile stuff have made,
As none but Fools or Fairies ever Play'd;   35
But 'twas, as Shopmen say, to force a Trade.

We've giv'n you Tragedies, all Sense defying:
And singing men, in wofull Metre dying;
This 'tis when heavy Lubbers will be flying.

All these disasters we well hope to weather;   40
We bring you none of our old Lumber hether:
Whigg Poets and Whigg Sheriffs may hang together.

EPILOGUE

Spoken by Mr. *Smith*

NEW Ministers, when first they get in place
  Must have a care to Please; and that's our Case:
Some Laws for publick Welfare we design,
If You, the Power supreme, will please to joyn:
There are a sort of Pratlers in the Pit,   5
Who either have, or who pretend to Wit:
These noisie Sirs so loud their Parts rehearse,
That oft the Play is silenc'd by the Farce:
Let such be dumb, this Penalty to shun,
Each to be thought my Lady's Eldest Son.   10
But stay: methinks some Vizard Masque I see,
Cast out her Lure from the mid Gallery:
About her all the flutt'ring Sparks are rang'd;
The Noise continues though the Scene is chang'd:
Now growling, sputtring, wauling, such a clutter,   15
'Tis just like Puss defendant in a Gutter:
Fine Love no doubt, but e'er two days are o'er ye,
The Surgeon will be told a wofull story.

Let Vizard Masque her naked Face expose,
On pein of being thought to want a Nose: 20
Then for your Lacqueys, and your Train beside,
(By what e'er Name or Title dignify'd)
They roar so loud, you'd think behind the Stairs
Tom Dove, and all the Brotherhood of Bears:
They're grown a Nuisance, beyond all Disasters,   25
We've none so great but their unpaying Masters.
We beg you, Sirs, to beg your Men, that they
Wou'd please to give you leave to hear the Play.
Next, in the Play-house spare your pretious Lives;
Think, like good Christians, on your Bearns and Wives: 30
Think on your Souls; but by your lugging forth,
It seems you know how little they are Worth:
If none of these will move the Warlike Mind,
Think on the helpless Whore you leave behind!
We beg you last, our Scene-room to forbear,   35
And leave our Goods and Chattels to our Care:
Alas, our Women are but washy Toys,
And wholly taken up in Stage employs:
Poor willing Tits they are: but yet I doubt
This double Duty soon will wear 'em out.   40
Then you are watcht besides, with jealous care;
What if my Lady's Page shoud find you there?
My Lady knows t'a tittle what there's in ye;
No passing your guilt Shilling for a Guiney.
Thus, Gentlemen, we have summ'd up in short,   45
Our Grievances, from Country, Town and Court:
Which humbly we submit to your good pleasure;
But first vote Money, then Redress at leasure.

PROLOGUE, EPILOGUES and SONG
from *THE DUKE OF GUISE*

PROLOGUE
TO THE Duke of GUISE

Spoken by Mr. *Smith*

OUR Play's a Parallel: The Holy League
   Begot our Cov'nant: Guisards got the Whigg:
Whate'er our hot-brain'd Sheriffs did advance,
Was, like our Fashions, first produc'd in *France*:
And, when worn out, well scourg'd, and banish'd there,   5
Sent over, like their godly Beggars here.
Cou'd the same Trick, twice play'd, our Nation gull?
It looks as if the Devil were grown dull;
Or serv'd us up, in scorn, his broken Meat,
And thought we were not worth a better Cheat.   10
The fulsome Cov'nant, one wou'd think in reason,
Had giv'n us all our Bellys-full of Treason:
And yet, the Name but chang'd, our nasty Nation
Chaws its own Excrement, th' Association.
'Tis true we have not learn'd their pois'ning way,   15
For that's a mode but newly come in play;
Besides, your Drug's uncertain to prevail;
But your true Protestant can never fail,
With that compendious Instrument, a Flail.
Go on; and bite, ev'n though the Hook lies bare;   20
Twice in one Age expell the lawfull Heir:
Once more decide Religion by the Sword;
And purchase for us a new Tyrant Lord.
Pray for your King; but yet your Purses spare;
Make him not two-Pence richer by your Prayer.   25
To show you love him much, chastise him more;
And make him very Great, and very Poor.
Push him to Wars, but still no Pence advance;

Let him lose *England* to recover *France*.
Cry Freedom up with Popular noisy Votes: 30
And get enough to cut each others Throats.
Lop all the Rights that fence your Monarch's Throne;
For fear of too much Pow'r, pray leave him none.
A noise was made of Arbitrary Sway;
But in Revenge, you Whiggs, have found a way,   35
An Arbitrary Duty now to pay.
Let his own Servants turn, to save their stake;
Glean from his plenty, and his wants forsake.
But let some *Judas* near his Person stay,
To swallow the last Sop, and then betray.   40
Make *London* independant of the Crown:
A Realm apart; the Kingdom of the Town.
Let *Ignoramus* Juries find no Traitors:
And *Ignoramus* Poets scribble Satyres.
And, that your meaning none may fail to scan,   45
Doe, what in Coffee-houses you began;
Pull down the Master, and Set up the Man.

EPILOGUE

Spoken by Mrs. *Cooke*

MUCH Time and Trouble this poor Play has cost;
And, faith, I doubted once the Cause was lost.
Yet no one Man was meant; nor Great nor Small;
Our Poets, like frank Gamesters, threw at all.
They took no single Aim:—   5
But, like bold Boys, true to their Prince and hearty,
Huzza'd, and fir'd Broad-sides at the whole Party.
Duells are Crimes; but when the Cause is right,
In Battel, every Man is bound to fight.
For what shou'd hinder Me to sell my Skin
Dear as I cou'd, if once my hand were in?   10
Se defendendo never was a Sin.
'Tis a fine World, my Masters, right or wrong,
The Whiggs must talk, and Tories hold their tongue.
They must doe all they can—   15
But We, forsooth, must bear a Christian mind;

And fight, like Boys, with one Hand ty'd behind;
Nay, and when one Boy's down, 'twere wondrous wise,
To cry, Box fair, and give him time to rise.
When Fortune favours, none but Fools will dally: 20
Wou'd any of you Sparks, if *Nan* or *Mally*
Tipt you th' inviting Wink, stand shall I, shall I?
A *Trimmer* cry'd, (that heard me tell this Story)
Fie, Mistress *Cooke*! faith you're too rank a Tory!
Wish not Whiggs hang'd, but pity their hard Cases;   25
You Women love to see Men make wry Faces.
Pray, Sir, said I, don't think me such a *Jew*;
I say no more, but give the Dev'l his due.
Lenitives, says he, suit best with our Condition.
Jack Ketch, says I, 's an excellent Physician.   30
I love no Bloud—. Nor I, Sir, as I breath;
But hanging is a fine dry kind of Death.
We *Trimmers* are for holding all things even:
Yes—just like him that hung 'twixt Hell and Heaven.
Have we not had Mens Lives enow already?   35
Yes sure:—but you're for holding all things steddy:
Now since the Weight hangs all on one side, Brother,
You *Trimmers* shou'd, to poize it, hang on t'other.
Damn'd Neuters, in their middle way of steering,
Are neither Fish, nor Flesh, nor good Red-Herring: 40
Not Whiggs, nor Tories they; nor this, nor that;
Not Birds, nor Beasts; but just a kind of Bat:
A Twilight Animal; true to neither Cause,
With Tory Wings, but Whiggish Teeth and Claws.

ANOTHER EPILOGUE

Intended to have been Spoken to the PLAY, before it was forbidden, last Summer

Two Houses joyn'd, two Poets to a Play?
 You noisy Whiggs will sure be pleas'd to day;
It looks so like two Shrieves the City way.

But since our Discords and Divisions cease,
You, Bilbo Gallants, learn to keep the Peace: 5
Make here no Tilts: let our Poor Stage alone;
Or if a decent Murther must be done,
Pray take a Civil turn to *Marybone*.
If not, I swear we'll pull up all our Benches;
Not for your sakes, but for our Orange-Wenches: 10
For you thrust wide sometimes; and many a Spark,
That misses one, can hit the other Mark.
This makes our Boxes full; for Men of Sense
Pay their four Shillings in their own defence:
That safe behind the Ladies they may stay,   15
Peep o'er the Fan, and Judg the bloudy Fray.
But other Foes give Beauty worse alarms;
The *Posse Poetarum*'s up in Arms:
No Womans Fame their Libells has escap'd;
Their Ink runs Venome, and their Pens are Clap'd.   20
When Sighs and Pray'rs their Ladies cannot move,
They Rail, write Treason, and turn Whiggs to love.
Nay, and I fear they worse Designs advance,
There's a damn'd Love-trick new brought o'er from *France*,
We charm in vain, and dress, and keep a Pother,   25
While those false Rogues are Ogling one another.
All Sins besides, admit some expiation;
But this against our Sex is plain Damnation.
They joyn for Libells too, these Women-haters;
And as they club for Love, they club for Satyrs: 30
The best on't is they hurt not: for they wear
Stings in their Tayls; their onely Venom's there.
'Tis true, some Shot at first the Ladies hit,
Which able Markesmen made and Men of Wit:
But now the Fools give fire, whose Bounce is louder;   35
And yet, like mere Train-bands, they shoot but Powder.
Libells, like Plots, sweep all in their first Fury;
Then dwindle like an *Ignoramus* Jury:
Thus Age begins with Towzing and with Tumbling;
But Grunts, and Groans, and ends at last in Fumbling.   40

A SONG in the Fifth ACT of the
DUKE of GUISE

Shepherdess.	TELL me *Thirsis*, tell your Anguish,
	why you Sigh, and why you Languish;
	when the Nymph whom you Adore,
	grants the Blessing of Possessing,
	what can Love and I do more? 5
	what can Love, what can Love and I do more?

Shepherd.	Think it's Love beyond all measure,
	makes me faint away with Pleasure;
	strength of Cordial may destroy,
	and the Blessing of Possessing 10
	kills me with excess of Joy.

Shepherdess.	*Thirsis*, how can I believe you?
	but confess, and I'le forgive you;
	Men are false, and so are you;
	never Nature fram'd a Creature 15
	to enjoy, and yet be true;
	never Nature fram'd a Creature
	to enjoy, and yet be true;
	to enjoy, and yet be true,
Soft.	and yet be true. 20

Shepherd.	Mine's a Flame beyond expiring,
	still possessing, still desiring,
	fit for Love's Imperial Crown;
	ever shining, and refining,
	still the more 'tis melted down. 25

Chorus together.	Mine's a Flame beyond expiring,
	still possessing, still desiring,
	fit for Love's Imperial Crown;
	ever shining, and refining,
	still the more 'tis melted down. 30

A Song. Text from The Duke of Guise. A Tragedy, *1683, collated with the editions of 1687 and 1699*
6, 17–20 *om. 87* 99   20 *Soft.*] *Direction in the music*   26–30 *om. 87* 99

[*An Epigram of* Agathias]

*C*HERONEAN *PLUTARCH*, to thy deathless praise,
  Does Martial *Rome* this grateful Statue raise:
Because both *Greece* and she thy fame have shar'd;
(Their Heroes written, and their Lives compar'd:)
But thou thy self cou'dst never write thy own;   5
Their Lives have Parallels but thine has none.

An Epigram. Text from Plutarchs Lives. Translated From the Greek by Several Hands
... 1683.

THE EPILOGUE TO
CONSTANTINE the *GREAT*

OUR Hero's happy in the Plays Conclusion,
  The holy Rogue at last has met Confusion:
Tho' *Arius* all along appear'd a Saint,
The last Act shew'd him a true Protestant.
Eusebius, (for you know I read Greek Authors,)   5
Reports, that after all these Plots and Slaughters,
The Court of *Constantine* was full of Glory,
And every *Trimmer* turn'd Addressing *Tory*;
They follow'd him in Heards as they were mad:
When *Clause* was King, then all the World was glad.   10
Whigs kept the Places they possest before,
And most were in a Way of getting more;
Which was as much as saying, Gentlemen,
Here 's Power and Money to be Rogues again.
Indeed there were a sort of peaking Tools,   15
Some call them Modest, but I call 'em Fools,
Men much more Loyal, tho' not half so loud;
But these poor Devils were cast behind the Croud.
For bold Knaves thrive without one grain of Sence,
But good men starve for want of Impudence.   20
Besides all these, there were a sort of Wights,
(I think my Author calls them *Teckelites*;)
Such hearty Rogues, against the King and Laws,
They favour'd even a Foreign Rebel's Cause.
When their own damn'd Design was quash'd and aw'd,   25
At least they gave it their good Word abroad.
As many a Man, who, for a quiet Life,
Breeds out his Bastard, not to nose his Wife;
Thus o're their Darling Plot, these *Trimmers* cry;
And tho' they cannot keep it in their Eye,   } 30
They bind it Prentice to Count *Teckely*.
They believe not the last Plot; may I be curst,
If I believe they e're believ'd the first;
No wonder their own Plot, no Plot they think;
The Man that makes it, never smells the Stink.   35
And, now it comes into my Head, I'le tell

The Epilogue. Text from A True Coppy of the Epilogue to Constantine the Great.

Why these damn'd *Trimmers* lov'd the *Turks* so well.
The Original *Trimmer*, tho' a Friend to no man,
Yet in his heart ador'd a pretty Woman:
He knew that *Mahomet* laid up for ever,   40
Kind black-eyed Rogues, for every true Believer:
And, which was more than mortal Man e're tasted,
One Pleasure that for threescore Twelve-months lasted:
To turn for this, may surely be forgiven:
Who'd not be circumcis'd for such a Heav'n!   45

POEMS FROM
MISCELLANY POEMS
By the most Eminent Hands
(*1684*)

PROLOGUE, To the University of *Oxon*.

Spoken by Mr. Hart, *at the Acting of the* Silent Woman

WHAT *Greece*, when Learning flourish'd, onely Knew,
    (*Athenian* Judges,) you this day Renew.
Here too are Annual Rites to *Pallas* done,
And here Poetique prizes lost or won.
Methinks I see you, Crown'd with Olives sit,   5
And strike a sacred Horrour from the Pit.
A Day of Doom is this of your Decree,
Where even the Best are but by Mercy free:
A Day which none but *Johnson* durst have wish'd to see.
Here they who long have known the usefull Stage,   10
Come to be taught themselves to teach the Age.
As your Commissioners our Poets goe,
To Cultivate the Virtue which you sow:
In your *Lycæum*, first themselves refind,
And Delegated thence to Humane kind.   15
But as Embassadours, when long from home,
For new Instructions to their Princes come;
So Poets who your Precepts have forgot,
Return, and beg they may be better taught:
Follies and Faults elsewhere by them are shown,   20
But by your Manners they Correct their Own.
Th' illiterate Writer, Emperique like, applies
To minds diseas'd, unsafe, chance Remedies:
The Learn'd in Schools, where Knowledge first began,
Studies with Care th' Anatomy of Man;   25
Sees Vertue, Vice, and Passions in their Cause,
And Fame from Science, not from Fortune draws.

Poems. Text from the first edition, 1684,

So Poetry, which is in *Oxford* made
An Art, in *London* onely is a Trade.
There Haughty Dunces whose unlearned Pen   30
Could ne'er Spell Grammar, would be reading Men.
Such build their Poems the *Lucretian* way,
So many Huddled Atoms make a Play,
And if they hit in Order by some Chance,
They call that Nature, which is Ignorance.   35
To such a Fame let mere Town-Wits aspire,
And their Gay Nonsense their own Citts admire.
Our Poet, could he find Forgiveness here
Would wish it rather than a *Plaudit* there.
He owns no Crown from those *Prætorian* bands,   40
But knows *that* Right is in this Senates hands.
Not Impudent enough to hope your Praise,
Low at the Muses feet, his Wreath he lays,
And where he took it up Resigns his Bays.
Kings make their Poets whom themselves think fit, 45
But 'tis your Suffrage makes Authentique Wit.

EPILOGUE, *Spoken by the same*

No poor *Dutch* Peasant, wing'd with all his Fear,
   Flies with more haste, when the *French* arms draw near,
Than We with our Poetique train come down
For refuge hither, from th' infected Town;
Heaven for our Sins this Summer has thought fit   5
To visit us with all the Plagues of Wit.
   A *French* Troop first swept all things in its way,
But those Hot *Monsieurs* were too quick to stay;
Yet, to our Cost in that short time, we find
They left their Itch of Novelty behind.   10
   Th' *Italian* Merry-Andrews took their place,
And quite Debauch'd the Stage with lewd Grimace;
Instead of Wit, and Humours, your Delight
Was there to see two Hobby-horses Fight,
Stout *Scaramoucha* with Rush Lance rode in,   15
And ran a Tilt at Centaure *Arlequin*.
For Love you heard how amorous Asses bray'd,

And Cats in Gutters gave their Serenade.
Nature was out of Countenance, and each Day
Some new born Monster shewn you for a Play.   20
  But when all fail'd, to strike the Stage quite Dumb,
Those wicked Engines call'd Machines are come.
Thunder and Lightning now for Wit are Play'd,
And shortly Scenes in *Lapland* will be Lay'd:
Art Magique is for Poetry profest,   25
And Cats and Dogs, and each obscener Beast
To which *Ægyptian* Dotards once did Bow,
Upon our *English* stage are worship'd now.
Witchcraft reigns there, and raises to Renown
Macbeth, the *Simon Magus* of the Town.   30
Fletcher's despis'd, your *Johnson* out of Fashion,
And Wit the onely Drug in all the Nation.
In this low Ebb our Wares to you are shown,
By you those Staple Authours worth is known,
For Wit's a Manufacture of your Own.   35
When you, who onely can, their Scenes have prais'd,
We'll boldly back, and say their Price is rais'd.

PROLOGUE, *to the University of* Oxford, 1674

Spoken by Mr. Hart

POETS, your Subjects, have their Parts assign'd
    T' unbend, and to divert their Sovereign's mind;
When tyr'd with following Nature, you think fit
To seek repose in the cool shades of Wit,
And from the sweet Retreat, with Joy survey   5
What rests, and what is conquer'd, of the way.
Here free your selves, from Envie, Care and Strife,
You view the various turns of humane Life:
Safe in our Scene, through dangerous Courts you go,
And Undebauch'd, the Vice of Cities know.   10
Your Theories are here to Practice brought,
As in Mechanick operations wrought;
And Man the Little world before you set,
As once the Sphere of Chrystal, shew'd the Great:
Blest sure are you above all Mortal kind,   15
If to your Fortunes you can Suit your Mind.

Content to see, and shun, those Ills we show,
And Crimes, on Theatres alone, to know:
With joy we bring what our dead Authours writ,
And beg from you the value of their Wit.   20
That *Shakespear*'s, *Fletcher*'s, and great *Johnson*'s claim
May be Renew'd from those, who gave them fame.
None of our living Poets dare appear,
For Muses so severe are worshipt here;
That conscious of their Faults they shun the Eye,   } 25
And as Prophane, from Sacred places fly,
Rather than see th' offended God, and dye.
We bring no Imperfections, but our own,
Such Faults as made, are by the Makers shown.
And you have been so kind, that we may boast,   30
The greatest Judges still can Pardon most.
Poets must stoop, when they would please our Pit,
Debas'd even to the Level of their Wit.
Disdaining that, which yet they know, will Take,
Hating themselves, what their Applause must make: 35
But when to Praise from you they would Aspire
Though they like Eagles Mount, your *Jove* is Higher.
So far your Knowledge, all their Pow'r transcends,
As what *should* be, beyond what *Is*, extends.

EPILOGUE To *OXFORD*

Spoken by *Mrs. Marshal*

OFT has our Poet wisht, this happy Seat
Might prove his fading Muses last retreat:
I wonder'd at his wish, but now I find
He sought for quiet, and content of mind;
Which noisfull Towns, and Courts can never know,   5
And onely in the shades like Laurels grow.
Youth, e'er it sees the World, here studies rest,
And Age returning thence concludes it best.
What wonder if we court that happiness
Yearly to share, which hourly you possess,   10
Teaching ev'n you, (while the vext World we show,)

Your Peace to value more, and better know?
'Tis all we can return for favours past,
Whose holy Memory shall ever last,
For Patronage from him whose care presides   15
O'er every noble Art, and every Science guides:
Bathurst, a name the learn'd with reverence know,
And scarcely more to his own *Virgil* owe.
Whose Age enjoys but what his Youth deserv'd,
To rule those Muses whom before he serv'd.   20
His Learning, and untainted Manners too
We find (*Athenians*) are deriv'd to you;
Such Ancient hospitality there rests   ⎫
In yours, as dwelt in the first *Grecian* Breasts, ⎬
Whose kindness was Religion to their Guests.   ⎭   25
Such Modesty did to our sex appear,   ⎫
As had there been no Laws we need not fear,   ⎬
Since each of you was our Protector here.   ⎭
Converse so chast, and so strict Vertue shown,
As might *Apollo* with the Muses own.   30
Till our return we must despair to find
Judges so just, so knowing, and so kind.

Prologue *to the University of* Oxford

DISCORD, and Plots which have undone our Age
With the same ruine, have o'erwhelm'd the Stage.
Our House has suffer'd in the common Woe,
We have been troubled with *Scotch* Rebels too;
Our Brethren, are from *Thames* to *Tweed* departed,   ⎫
And of our Sisters, all the kinder hearted,   ⎬   5
To *Edenborough* gone, or Coacht, or Carted.   ⎭
With bonny Blewcap there they act all night
For *Scotch* half Crown, in *English* Three-pence hight.
One Nymph, to whom fat *Sir John Falstaff*'s lean,   10
There with her single Person fills the Scene.
Another, with long use, and Age decay'd,
Div'd here old Woman, and rose there a Maid.
Our Trusty Door-keepers of former time,
There strutt and swagger in Heroique rhime: 15
Tack but a Copper-lace to Drugget sute,

25 Whose] Where *84b*

And there's a Heroe made without dispute.
And that which was a Capons tayl before,
Becomes a plume for *Indian* Emperour.
But all his Subjects, to express the care   20
Of Imitation, go, like *Indians*, bare;
Lac'd Linen there wou'd be a dangerous thing,
It might perhaps a new Rebellion bring,
The *Scot* who wore it, wou'd be chosen King.
But why shou'd I these Renegades describe,   25
When you your selves have seen a lewder Tribe.
Teg has been here, and to this learned Pit,
With *Irish* action slander'd *English* Wit.
You have beheld such barb'rous *Mac's* appear,
As merited a second Massacre.   30
Such as like *Cain* were branded with disgrace,
And had their Country stampt upon their Face.

When Stroulers durst presume to pick your purse,
We humbly thought our broken Troop not worse,
How ill soe'er our action may deserve,   35
Oxford's a place, where Wit can never sterve.

PROLOGUE TO THE University of *OXFORD*

Tho' Actors cannot much of Learning boast,
    Of all who want it, we admire it most.
We love the Praises of a Learned Pit,
As we remotely are ally'd to Wit.
We speak our Poets Wit, and Trade in Ore,   5
Like those who touch upon the Golden Shore:
Betwixt our Judges can distinction make,
Discern how much, and why, our Poems take.
Mark if the Fools, or Men of Sence, rejoyce,
Whether th' Applause be only Sound or Voice.   10
When our Fop Gallants, or our City Folly
Clap over-loud, it makes us melancholy:
We doubt that Scene which does their wonder raise,
And, for their ignorance contemn their Praise.

Judge then, if We who Act, and They who Write,   15
Shou'd not be proud of giving You delight.
London likes grossly, but this nicer Pit
Examines, Fathoms all the depths of Wit:
The ready Finger lays on every Blot,
Knows what shou'd justly please, and what shou'd not.   20
Nature her self lies open to your view,
You judge by Her what draught of Her is true,
Where out lines false, and Colours seem too faint,
Where Bunglers dawb, and where True Poets Paint.
But by the Sacred Genius of this Place,   25
By every Muse, by each Domestick Grace,
Be kind to Wit, which but endeavours well,
And, where you judge, presumes not to excel.
Our Poets hither for Adoption come,
As Nations su'd to be made Free of *Rome*.   30
Not in the suffragating Tribes to stand,
But in your utmost, last, Provincial Band.
If His Ambition may those Hopes pursue,
Who with Religion loves Your Arts and You,
Oxford to Him a dearer Name shall be,   35
Than His own Mother University.
Thebes did His Green, unknowing Youth ingage,
He chuses *Athens* in His Riper Age.

Prologue to ARVIRAGUS REVIV'D

Spoken by Mr. *Hart*

WITH sickly Actors and an old House too,
We're match'd with Glorious Theatres and New,
And with our Alehouse Scenes, and Cloaths bare worn,
Can neither raise Old Plays, nor New adorn.
If all these ills could not undo us quite,   5
A Brisk *French* Troop is grown your dear delight.
Who with broad bloody Bills call you each day,
To laugh, and break your Buttons at their Play.
Or see some serious Piece, which we presume
Is fal'n from some incomparable Plume;   10

And therefore, *Messieurs*, if you'l do us grace,
Send Lacquies early to preserve your Place.
We dare not on your Priviledge intrench,
Or ask you why you like 'em? They are *French*.
Therefore some go with Courtesie exceeding,   15
Neither to Hear nor See, but show their Breeding.
Each Lady striving to out-laugh the rest,
To make it seem they understood the Jest:
Their Countrymen come in, and nothing pay,
To teach Us *English* where to Clap the Play: 20
Civil *Igad*: Our Hospitable Land,
Bears all the charge for them to understand:
Mean time we Languish, and neglected lye,
Like Wives, while You keep better Company;
And wish for our own sakes, without a Satyr,   25
You'd less good Breeding, or had more good Nature.

Prologue for the Women,
when they Acted at the Old THEATRE
in LINCOLNS-INN-FIELDS

WERE none of you Gallants e're driven so hard,
    As when the poor kind Soul was under guard
And could not do't at home, in some by-street,
To take a Lodging, and in private meet?
Such is our Case, We can't appoint our House,   5
The Lovers old and wonted Rendezvouz.
But hither to this trusty Nook remove,
The worse the Lodging is, the more the Love.
For much good Pastime, many a dear sweet hug
Is stoln in Garrets on the humble Rugg.   10
Here's good Accommodation in the Pit,
The Grave demurely in the midst may Sit.
And so the hot *Burgundian* on the Side,
Ply Vizard Masque, and o're the Benches stride:

Prologue. 6 wonted] wanted *84*

Here are convenient upper Boxes too,   } 15
For those that make the most triumphant show,
All that keep Coaches must not Sit below.

There Gallants, You betwixt the Acts retire,
And at dull Plays have something to admire:
We who look up, can Your Addresses mark;   20
And see the Creatures Coupled in the Ark:
So we expect the *Lovers*, *Braves*, and *Wits*;
The Gaudy House with Scenes, will serve for *Citts*.

A Prologue spoken at the Opening of the NEW HOUSE, *Mar.* 26. 1674

A PLAIN Built House after so long a stay,
    Will send you half unsatisfy'd away;
When, fal'n from your expected Pomp, you find
A bare convenience only is design'd.
You who each day can Theatres behold,   5
Like *Nero*'s Palace, shining all with Gold,
Our mean ungilded Stage will scorn, we fear,
And for the homely Room, disdain the Chear.
Yet now cheap Druggets to a Mode are grown,
And a plain Sute (since we can make but one)   } 10
Is better than to be by tarnisht gawdry known.
They who are by Your Favours wealthy made,
With mighty Sums may carry on the Trade:
We, broken Banquers, half destroy'd by Fire,
With our small Stock to humble Roofs retire;   } 15
Pity our Loss, while you their Pomp admire.
For Fame and Honour we no longer strive,
We yield in both, and only beg to Live.
Unable to support their vast Expence,
Who Build, and Treat with such Magnificence;   20
That like th' Ambitious Monarchs of the Age,
They give the Law to our Provincial Stage:
Great Neighbours enviously promote Excess,
While they impose their Splendor on the less.

But only Fools, and they of vast Estate,   25
Th' extremity of Modes will imitate,
The dangling Knee-fringe, and the Bib-Cravat.
Yet if some Pride with want may be allow'd,
We in our plainness may be justly proud:
Our Royal Master will'd it should be so,   30
What e're He's pleas'd to own, can need no show:
That Sacred Name gives Ornament and Grace,
And, like his stamp, makes basest Mettals pass.
'Twere Folly now a stately Pile to raise,
To build a Play-House while You throw down Plays.   35
Whilst Scenes, Machines, and empty *Opera's* reign,
And for the Pencil You the Pen disdain.
While Troops of famisht *Frenchmen* hither drive,
And laugh at those upon whose Alms they live:
Old *English* Authors vanish, and give place   40
To these new Conqu'rors of the *Norman* Race;
More tamely, than your Fathers You submit,
You'r now grown Vassals to 'em in your wit:
Mark, when they Play, how our fine Fops advance
The mighty Merits of these Men of *France*,   45
Keep Time, cry *Ben*, and humour the Cadence:
Well, please your selves, but sure 'tis understood,
That *French* Machines have ne'r done *England* good:
I wou'd not prophesie our Houses Fate:
But while vain Shows and Scenes you over-rate,   50
'Tis to be fear'd—
That as a Fire the former House o'rethrew,
Machines and Tempests will destroy the new.

Epilogue by the same Author

THOUGH what our Prologue said was sadly true,
      Yet, Gentlemen, our homely House is new,
A Charm that seldom fails with, wicked, You.
A Country Lip may have the Velvet touch,
Tho' She's no Lady, you may think her such,   5
A strong imagination may do much.
But you, loud Sirs, who thro' your Curls look big,
Epilogue. 7 thro'] tho' *84 92*

Criticks in Plume and white vallancy Wig,
Who lolling on our foremost Benches sit,
And still charge first, (the true forlorn of Wit)   10
Whose favours, like the Sun, warm where you roul,
Yet you like him, have neither heat nor Soul;
So may your Hats your Foretops never press,
Untouch'd your Ribbonds, sacred be your dress;
So may you slowly to Old Age advance,   15
And have th' excuse of Youth for Ignorance.
So may Fop corner full of noise remain,
And drive far off the dull attentive train;
So may your Midnight Scowrings happy prove,
And Morning Batt'ries force your way to Love;   20
So may not *France* your Warlike Hands recall,
But leave you by each others Swords to fall:
As you come here to ruffle Vizard Punk,
When sober, rail and roar when you are drunk.
But to the Wits we can some merit plead,   25
And urge what by themselves has oft been said:
Our House relieves the Ladies from the frights
Of ill pav'd Streets, and long dark Winter Nights;
The *Flanders* Horses from a cold bleak Road,
Where Bears in Furs dare scarcely look abroad: 30
The Audience from worn Plays and Fustian Stuff
Of Rhyme, more nauseous than three Boys in Buff.
Though in their House the Poets Heads appear,
We hope we may presume their Wits are here.
The best which they reserv'd they now will Play,   35
For, like kind Cuckolds, tho' w' have not the way
To please, we'l find you Abler Men who may.
If they shou'd fail, for last recruits we breed
A Troop of frisking Monsieurs to succeed:
(You know the *French* sure cards at time of need.)   40

Prologue to the Princess of CLEVES

LADIES! (I hope there's none behind to hear,)
   I long to whisper something in your Ear:
A Secret, which does much my Mind perplex,

There's Treason in the Play against our Sex.
A Man that's false to Love, that Vows and cheats,   5
And kisses every living thing he meets!
A Rogue in Mode, I dare not speak too broad,
One that does something to the very Bawd.
Out on him, Traytor, for a filthy Beast,
Nay, and he's like the pack of all the rest;   10
None of 'em stick at mark: They all deceive,
Some *Jew* has chang'd the Text, I half believe,
Their *Adam* cozen'd our poor Grandame *Eve*.
To hide their faults they rap out Oaths and tear:
Now tho' we Lye, w're too well bred to Swear.   15
So we compound for half the Sin we owe,
But men are dipt for Soul and Body too.
And when found out excuse themselves, Pox cant 'em,
With Latin stuff, *perjuria ridet Amantum*.
I'm not Book Learn'd, to know that word in vogue,   20
But I suspect 'tis Latin for a Rogue.
I'me sure I never heard that Schritch owl hollow'd
In my poor ears, but Separation follow'd.
How can such perjur'd Villains e're be Saved,
Achitophel's not half so false to *David*.   25
With Vows and soft expressions to allure,
They stand like Foremen of a Shop, demure,
No sooner out of sight, but they are gadding,
And for the next new Face Ride out a padding.
Yet, by their favour when they have bin Kissing,   30
We can perceive the ready Mony missing:
Well! we may rail, but 'tis as good e'en wink,
Something we find, and something they will sink.
But since they'r at Renouncing, 'tis our parts,
To trump their Diamonds, as they trump our Hearts.   35

Epilogue to the Princess of *Cleves*

A QUALM of Conscience brings me back agen
    To make amends to you bespatter'd Men!
We Women Love like Cats, that hide their Joys,
By growling, squaling, and a hideous noise.

I rail'd at wild young Sparks, but without lying,   5
Never was Man worse thought on for high-flying;
The prodigal of Love gives each her part,
And squandring shows, at least, a noble Heart.
I've heard of Men, who in some lew'd Lampoon,
Have hir'd a Friend, to make their valour known.   10
That Accusation straight, this question brings,
What is the Man that does such naughty things?
The Spaniel Lover, like a sneaking Fop,
Lyes at our Feet. He's scarce worth taking up;
'Tis true, such Hero's in a Play go far,   15
But Chamber practice, is not like the Bar.
When Men such vile, such faint Petitions make,
We fear to give, because they fear to take;
Since Modesty's the Vertue of our kind,
Pray let it be to our own Sex confin'd.   20
When Men usurp it from the Female Nation,
'Tis but a work of Supererrogation.—
We show'd a Princess in the Play, 'tis true,
Who gave her *Cæsar* more than all his due.
Told her own Faults, but I shou'd much abhor,   25
To choose a Husband for my Confessor.
You see what Fate follow'd the Saint-like Fool,
For telling Tales from out the Nuptial School.
    Our Play a merry Comedy had prov'd,
    Had she Confess't as much to him she lov'd.   30
    True *Presbyterian*-Wives, the *means* wou'd try,
    But damn'd Confessing is flat Popery.

The Tears of AMYNTA, for the Death of DAMON

SONG

ON a bank, beside a Willow,
    Heav'n her Cov'ring, Earth her Pillow,
Sad *Amynta* sigh'd alone:
From the chearless Dawn of Morning
Till the Dew's of Night returning   5

Singing thus she made her mone:
          Hope is banish'd
          Joys are vanish'd;
Damon, my belov'd is gone!

2

Time, I dare thee to discover   10
Such a Youth, and such a Lover,
Oh so true, so kind was he!
Damon was the Pride of Nature,
Charming in his every Feature,
Damon liv'd alone for me: 15
          Melting Kisses
          Murmuring Blisses,
Who so liv'd and lov'd as we!

3

Never shall we curse the Morning,
Never bless the Night returning,   20
Sweet Embraces to restore:
Never shall we both ly dying
Nature failing, Love supplying
All the Joyes he drain'd before:
          Death, come end me   25
          To befriend me;
Love and *Damon* are no more.

EPILOGUE intended to have been spoken by
the Lady Henr. Mar. Wentworth
when Calisto *was acted at Court*

As *Jupiter* I made my Court in vain,
   I'le now assume my native shape again.
I'm weary to be so unkindly us'd,
And would not be a God to be refus'd.
State grows uneasie when it hinders love,   5
A glorious burden, which the Wise remove.
Now as a Nymph I need not sue nor try
The force of any lightning but the eye.

Beauty and youth more then a God Command;
No *Jove* could e're the force of these withstand.   10
Tis here that Sovereign Pow'r admits dispute,
Beauty sometimes is justly absolute.

Our sullen *Catoes*, whatsoe're they say,
Even while they frown and dictate Laws, obey.
You, mighty Sir, our Bonds more easie make   15
And gracefully what all must suffer take.
Above those forms the Grave affect to wear;
For 'tis not to be wise to be severe.
True wisdom may some gallantry admit,
And soften business with the charms of wit.   20
These peaceful Triumphs with your cares you bought,
And from the midst of fighting Nations brought.
You only hear it thunder from afar,
And sit in peace the Arbiter of War.
Peace, the loath'd Manna, which hot brains despise,   25
You knew its worth, and made it early prize:
And in its happy leisure sit and see
The promises of more felicity:
Two glorious Nymphs of your one Godlike line,
Whose Morning Rays like Noontide strike and shine;   30
Whom you to suppliant Monarchs shall dispose,
To bind your Friends and to disarm your Foes.

PROLOGUE To a NEW PLAY, Call'd,
The Disappointment: or, The Mother in Fashion.

Spoken by Mr. BETTERTON

How comes it, Gentlemen, that now aday's
  When all of you so shrewdly judge of Plays,
Our Poets tax you still with want of Sence?
All Prologues treat you at your own Expence.
Sharp Citizens a wiser way can go;   5
They make you Fools, but never call you so.
They, in good Manners, seldom make a Slip,
But, Treat a Common Whore with Ladyship:
But here each sawcy Wit at Random writes,
And uses Ladies as he uses Knights.   10
Our Author, Young, and Grateful in his Nature,
Vow's, that from him no Nymph deserves a Satyr.
Nor will he ever Draw—I mean his Rhime,
Against the sweet Partaker of his Crime.
Nor is he yet so bold an Undertaker   15
To call MEN Fools, 'tis Railing at their MAKER.
Besides, he fears to split upon that Shelf;
He's young enough to be a FOPP himself.
And, if his Praise can bring you all A-bed,
He swears such hopeful Youth no Nation ever bred.   20
Your Nurses, we presume, in such a Case,
Your Father chose, because he lik'd the Face;
And, often, they supply'd your Mothers place.
The Dry Nurse was your Mothers ancient Maid,
Who knew some former Slip she ne're betray'd.   25
Betwixt 'em both, for Milk and Sugar Candy,
Your sucking Bottles were well stor'd with Brandy.
Your Father to initiate your Discourse
Meant to have taught you first to Swear and Curse;
But was prevented by each careful Nurse.   30
For, leaving Dad and Mam, as Names too common,
They taught you certain parts of Man and Woman.
I pass your Schools, for there when first you came,

Prologue To a New Play, &c. Text from the separate edition, 1684

You wou'd be sure to learn the Latin name.
In Colledges you scorn'd their Art of thinking,   35
But learn'd all Moods and Figures of good Drinking:
Thence, come to Town you practise Play, to know
The Vertues of the High Dice, and the Low.
Each thinks himself a SHARPER most profound:
He cheats by Pence; is cheated by the Pound: 40
With these Perfections, and what else he Gleans,   ⎫
The SPARK sets up for Love behind our Scenes;   ⎬
Hot in pursuit of Princesses and Queens.   ⎭
There, if they know their Man, with cunning Carriage,
Twenty to one but it concludes in Marriage.   45
He hires some Homely Room, Love's Fruits to gather,
And, Garret-high, Rebels against his Father.
But he once dead—
Brings her in Triumph, with her Portion down,
A Twillet, Dressing-Box, and Half a Crown.   50
Some Marry first, and then they fall to Scowring,
Which is, Refining Marriage into Whoring.
Our Women batten well on their good Nature,
All they can rap and rend for the dear Creature.
But while abroad so liberal the DOLT is,   55
Poor SPOUSE at Home as Ragged as a Colt is.
Last, some there are, who take their first Degrees
Of Lewdness, in our Middle Galleries:
The Doughty BULLIES enter Bloody Drunk,
Invade and grubble one another's PUNK: 60
They Caterwaul, and make a dismal Rout,
Call SONS of WHORES, and strike, but ne're lugg-out:
Thus while for *Paultry Punk* they roar and stickle,
They make it *Bawdier* than a CONVENTICLE.

To the Earl of *Roscomon*, on his
Excellent *Essay* on *Translated Verse*

WHETHER the fruitful *Nile*, or *Tyrian* Shore,
The seeds of Arts and Infant Science bore,
'Tis sure the noble Plant, translated first,
Advanc'd its head in *Grecian* Gardens nurst.
The *Grecians* added Verse, their tuneful Tongue   5
Made Nature first, and Nature's God their song.
Nor stopt Translation here: For conquering *Rome*
With *Grecian* Spoils brought *Grecian* Numbers home;
Enrich'd by those *Athenian* Muses more,
Than all the vanquish'd World cou'd yield before.   10
'Till barb'rous Nations, and more barb'rous Times
Debas'd the majesty of Verse to Rhymes;
Those rude at first: a kind of hobbling Prose:
That limp'd along, and tinckl'd in the close:
But *Italy*, reviving from the trance,   15
Of *Vandal*, *Goth*, and *Monkish* ignorance,
With pauses, cadence, and well vowell'd Words,
And all the Graces a good Ear affords,
Made Rhyme an Art: and *Dante*'s polish'd page
Restor'd a silver, not a golden Age: 20
Then *Petrarch* follow'd, and in him we see,
What Rhyme improv'd in all its height can be;
At best a pleasing Sound, and fair barbarity:
The *French* pursu'd their steps; and *Brittain*, last
In Manly sweetness all the rest surpass'd.   25
The Wit of *Greece*, the Gravity of *Rome*
Appear exalted in the *Brittish* Loome;
The Muses Empire is restor'd agen,
In *Charles* his Reign, and by *Roscomon*'s Pen.
Yet modestly he does his Work survey,   30
And calls a finish'd Poem an *ESSAY*;
For all the needful Rules are scatter'd here;
Truth smoothly told, and pleasantly severe;
(So well is Art disguis'd, for Nature to appeare.)

To the Earl of Roscomon. Text from An Essay on Translated Verse, *1684, collated with the edition of 1685*

Nor need those Rules, to give Translation light;   35
His own example is a flame so bright;
That he, who but arrives to copy well,
Unguided will advance; unknowing will excel.
Scarce his own *Horace* cou'd such Rules ordain;
Or his own *Virgil* sing a nobler strain.   40
How much in him may rising *Ireland* boast,
How much in gaining him has *Britain* lost!
Their Island in revenge has ours reclaim'd,
The more instructed we, the more we still are sham'd.
'Tis well for us his generous bloud did flow   45
Deriv'd from *British* Channels long ago;
That here his conquering Ancestors were nurst;
And *Ireland* but translated *England* first:
By this Reprisal we regain our right;
Else must the two contending Nations fight,   50
A nobler quarrel for his Native earth,
Than what divided *Greece* for *Homer*'s birth.
To what perfection will our Tongue arrive,
How will Invention and Translation thrive
When Authors nobly born will bear their part   55
And not disdain th' inglorious praise of Art!
Great Generals thus descending from command,
With their own toil provoke the Souldiers hand.
How will sweet *Ovid*'s Ghost be pleas'd to hear
His Fame augmented by an *English* Peer,   The Earl   60
How he embellishes His *Helen*'s loves,   of Mul-
Out does his softness, and his sense improves?   grave.
When these translate, and teach Translators too,
Nor Firstling Kid, nor any vulgar vow
Shou'd at *Apollo*'s grateful Altar stand;   ⎫ 65
Roscomon writes, to that auspicious hand,   ⎬
Muse feed the Bull that spurns the yellow sand.   ⎭
Roscomon, whom both Court and Camps commend,
True to his Prince, and faithful to his friend;
Roscomon first in Fields of Honour known,   ⎫ 70
First in the peaceful Triumphs of the Gown;   ⎬
He both *Minerva*'s justly makes his own.   ⎭

47 were *85*: was *84*   60 English *85*: Brittish *84*

Now let the few belov'd by *Jove*, and they,
Whom infus'd *Titan* form'd of better Clay,
On equal terms with ancient Wit ingage,   75
Nor mighty *Homer* fear, nor sacred *Virgil*'s page:
Our *English* Palace opens wide in state;
And without stooping they may pass the Gate.

To the MEMORY of Mr. *OLDHAM*

FAREWEL, too little and too lately known,
   Whom I began to think and call my own;
For sure our Souls were near ally'd; and thine
Cast in the same Poetick mould with mine.
One common Note on either Lyre did strike,   5
And Knaves and Fools we both abhorr'd alike:
To the same Goal did both our Studies drive,
The last set out the soonest did arrive.
Thus *Nisus* fell upon the slippery place,
While his young Friend perform'd and won the Race.   10
O early ripe! to thy abundant store
What could advancing Age have added more?
It might (what Nature never gives the young)
Have taught the numbers of thy native Tongue.
But Satyr needs not those, and Wit will shine   15
Through the harsh cadence of a rugged line.
A noble Error, and but seldom made,
When Poets are by too much force betray'd.
Thy generous fruits, though gather'd ere their prime ⎫
Still shew'd a quickness; and maturing time ⎬   20
But mellows what we write to the dull sweets of Rime. ⎭
Once more, hail and farewel; farewel thou young,
But ah too short, *Marcellus* of our Tongue;
Thy Brows with Ivy, and with Laurels bound;
But Fate and gloomy Night encompass thee around.   25

To the Memory of Mr. Oldham. Text from Remains of Mr. John Oldham in Verse and
Prose, *1684,*

A New SONG

SYLVIA the fair, in the bloom of Fifteen,
  Felt an innocent warmth, as she lay on the green;
She had heard of a pleasure, and something she guest
By the towzing and tumbling and touching her Breast;
She saw the men eager, but was at a loss,   5
What they meant by their sighing, and kissing so close;
       By their praying and whining
       And clasping and twining,
       And panting and wishing,
       And sighing and kissing   10
       And sighing and kissing so close.

II

Ah she cry'd, ah for a languishing Maid
In a Country of Christians to die without aid!
Not a Whig, or a Tory, or Trimmer at least,
Or a Protestant Parson, or Catholick Priest,   15
To instruct a young Virgin, that is at a loss
What they meant by their sighing, and kissing so close!
       By their praying and whining
       And clasping and twining,
       And panting and wishing,   20
       And sighing and kissing
       And sighing and kissing so close.

III

Cupid in Shape of a Swayn did appear,
He saw the sad wound, and in pity drew near,
Then show'd her his Arrow, and bid her not fear,   25
For the pain was no more than a Maiden may bear;
When the balm was infus'd she was not at a loss,
What they meant by their sighing and kissing so close;
       By their praying and whining,
       And clasping and twining,   30
       And panting and wishing,
       And sighing and kissing,
       And sighing and kissing so close.

A New Song. Text from Sylvæ, or the Second Part of Poetical Miscellanies *1685*

SONG

Go tell *Amynta* gentle Swain,
I wou'd not die nor dare complain,
Thy tuneful Voice with numbers joyn,
Thy words will more prevail than mine;
To Souls oppress'd and dumb with grief,   5
The Gods ordain this kind relief;
That Musick shou'd in sounds convey,
What dying Lovers dare not say.

II

A Sigh or Tear perhaps she'll give,
But love on pitty cannot live.   10
Tell her that Hearts for Hearts were made,
And love with love is only paid.
Tell her my pains so fast encrease,
That soon they will be past redress;
But ah! the Wretch that speechless lyes,   15
Attends but Death to close his Eyes.

Song. Text from Sylvæ, 1685

THRENODIA AUGUSTALIS

A Funeral-Pindarique

POEM Sacred to the Happy Memory
of King CHARLES II

Fortunati Ambo, si quid mea Carmina possunt,
Nulla dies unquam memori vos eximet ævo!

I

THUS long my Grief has kept me dumb:
    Sure there's a Lethargy in mighty Woe,
  Tears stand congeal'd, and cannot flow;
And the sad Soul retires into her inmost Room:
Tears, for a Stroke foreseen, afford Relief;   5
    But, unprovided for a sudden Blow,
    Like *Niobe* we Marble grow;
      And Petrifie with Grief.
Our *British* Heav'n was all Serene,
    No threatning Cloud was nigh,   10
    Not the least wrinkle to deform the Sky;
  We liv'd as unconcern'd and happily
As the first Age in Natures golden Scene;
    Supine amidst our flowing Store,
We slept securely, and we dream't of more: 15
  When suddenly the Thunder-clap was heard,
  It took us unprepar'd and out of guard,
  Already lost before we fear'd.
Th' amazing News of *Charles* at once were spread,
  At once the general Voice declar'd,   20
    Our Gracious Prince was dead.
No Sickness known before, no slow Disease,
  To soften Grief by Just Degrees:
But, like an Hurricane on *Indian* Seas,
    The Tempest rose;   25
    An unexpected Burst of Woes:

Threnodia Augustalis. Text from the Harvard copy of the first edition (H), 1685, collated with the subsequent London editions (A, B), 1685

With scarce a breathing space betwixt,
This *Now* becalm'd, and perishing the next.
As if great *Atlas* from his Height
Shou'd sink beneath his heavenly Weight,   30
And, with a mighty Flaw, the flaming Wall
    (As once it shall)
Shou'd gape immense and rushing down, o'erwhelm this neather Ball;
So swift and so surprizing was our Fear:
Our *Atlas* fell indeed; But *Hercules* was near.   35

          II

   His Pious Brother, sure the best
     Who ever bore that Name,
  Was newly risen from his Rest,
     And, with a fervent Flame,
  His usual morning Vows had just addrest   40
    For his dear Sovereign's Health;
      And hop'd to have 'em heard,
     In long increase of years,
In Honour, Fame and Wealth:
    Guiltless of Greatness thus he always pray'd,   45
    Nor knew nor wisht those Vows he made,
    On his own Head shou'd be repay'd.
Soon as th' ill omen'd Rumor reacht his Ear,
   (Ill News is wing'd with Fate, and flies apace)
   Who can describe th' Amazement in his Face!   50
Horrour in all his Pomp was there,
Mute and magnificent without a Tear:
And then the *Hero* first was seen to fear.
Half unarray'd he ran to his Relief,
So hasty and so artless was his grief: 55
Approaching Greatness met him with her Charms
    Of Pow'r and future State;
     But look'd so ghastly in a Brother's Fate,
     He shook her from his Armes.
Arriv'd within the mournful Room, he saw   60
   A wild Distraction, void of Awe,
And arbitrary Grief unbounded by a Law.
   God's Image, God's Anointed lay

Without Motion, Pulse or Breath,
A Senseless Lump of sacred Clay, 65
An Image, now, of Death.
Amidst his sad Attendants Grones and Cryes,
The Lines of that ador'd, forgiving Face,
Distorted from their native grace;
An Iron Slumber sat on his Majestick Eyes. 70
The Pious Duke—forbear audacious Muse,
No Terms thy feeble Art can use
Are able to adorn so vast a Woe;
The grief of all the rest like subject-grief did show,
His like a Sovereign did transcend; 75
No Wife, no Brother, such a Grief cou'd know,
Nor any name, but Friend.

III

O wondrous Changes of a fatal Scene,
Still varying to the last!
Heav'n, though its hard Decree was past, 80
Seem'd pointing to a gracious Turn agen:
And Death's up-lifted Arme arrested in its hast.
Heav'n half repented of the doom,
And almost griev'd it had foreseen,
What by Foresight it will'd eternally to come. 85
Mercy above did hourly plead
For her Resemblance here below:
And mild Forgiveness intercede
To stop the coming blow.
New Miracles approach'd th' Etherial Throne, 90
Such as his wondrous Life had oft and lately known,
And urg'd that still they might be shown.
On Earth his Pious Brother pray'd and vow'd,
Renouncing Greatness at so dear a rate,
Himself defending what he cou'd, 95
From all the Glories of his future Fate.
With him th' innumerable Croud
Of armed Prayers
Knock'd at the Gates of Heav'n, and knock'd aloud;
The first, well meaning rude Petitioners. 100

All for his Life assayl'd the Throne,
All wou'd have brib'd the Skyes by offring up their own.
So great a Throng not Heav'n it self cou'd bar;
'Twas almost born by force as in the Giants War.
The Pray'rs, at least, for his Reprive were heard;   105
His Death, like *Hezekiah*'s, was deferr'd:
    Against the Sun the Shadow went;
    Five days, those five Degrees, were lent
    To form our Patience and prepare th' Event.
The second Causes took the swift Command,   110
The med'cinal Head, the ready Hand,
All eager to perform their Part,
All but Eternal Doom was conquer'd by their Art:
Once more the fleeting Soul came back
    T' inspire the mortal Frame,   115
And in the Body took a doubtful Stand,
    Doubtful and hov'ring like expiring Flame,
That mounts and falls by turns, and trembles o'er the Brand.

IV

The joyful short-liv'd news soon spread around,
Took the same Train, the same impetuous bound: 120
The drooping Town in smiles again was drest,
Gladness in every Face exprest,
Their Eyes before their Tongues confest.
Men met each other with erected look,
The steps were higher that they took,   125
Friends to congratulate their friends made haste;
And long inveterate Foes saluted as they past:
Above the rest Heroick *James* appear'd
Exalted more, because he more had fear'd:
His manly heart, whose Noble pride   130
Was still above
Dissembled hate or varnisht Love,
Its more then common transport cou'd not hide;
But like an *Eagre rode in triumph o're the tide.

    * *An* Eagre *is a Tyde swelling above another Tyde, which I have my self observ'd on the River* Trent.

---

105 were *A B*: was *H*   125 that *A B*: then *H*   126 Friends . . . their friends *B*: Each . . . his friend *H A*

Thus, in alternate Course, 135
  The Tyrant passions, hope and fear,
  Did in extreams appear,
And flasht upon the Soul with equal force.
Thus, at half Ebb, a rowling Sea
Returns and wins upon the shoar; 140
The watry Herd, affrighted at the roar,
Rest on their Fins a while, and stay,
Then backward take their wondring way:
The Prophet wonders more than they,
At Prodigies but rarely seen before, 145
And cries a *King* must fall, or Kingdoms change their sway.
Such were our counter-tydes at land, and so
Presaging of the fatal blow,
In their prodigious Ebb and flow.
The Royal Soul, that like the labouring Moon, 150
By Charms of Art was hurried down,
Forc'd with regret to leave her Native Sphear,
Came but a while on liking here:
Soon weary of the painful strife,
And made but faint Essays of Life: 155
An Evening light
Soon shut in Night;
A strong distemper, and a weak relief,
Short intervals of joy, and long returns of grief.

V

The Sons of Art all Med'cines try'd 160
And every Noble remedy apply'd;
With emulation each essay'd
His utmost skill, nay more they pray'd:
Never was losing game with better conduct plaid.
Death never won a stake with greater toyl, 165
Nor e're was Fate so near a foil:
But, like a fortress on a Rock,
Th' impregnable Disease their vain attempts did mock;
They min'd it near, they batter'd from a far
With all the Cannon of the Med'cinal War; 170

164 Never was *B*: Was never *H A*

No gentle means cou'd be essay'd,
Twas beyond parly when the siege was laid:
Th' extreamest ways they first ordain,
Prescribing such intollerable pain,
As none but *Cæsar* cou'd sustain: 175
Undaunted *Cæsar* underwent
The malice of their Art, nor bent
Beneath what e'r their pious rigour cou'd invent:
In five such dayes he suffer'd more
Then any suffer'd in his reign before;   180
More, infinitely more, than he,
Against the worst of Rebels, cou'd decree,
A Traytor or twice pardon'd Enemy.
Now Art was tir'd without success,
No Racks cou'd make the stubborn malady confess.   185
The vain *Insurancers* of Life,
And He who most perform'd and promis'd less,
Even *Short* himself forsook th' unequal strife.
Death and despair was in their looks,
No longer they consult their memories or books;   190
Like helpless friends, who view from shoar
The labouring Ship, and hear the tempest roar,
So stood they with their arms across;
Not to assist; but to deplore
Th' inevitable loss.   195

VI

Death was denounc'd; that frightful sound
Which even the best can hardly bear,
He took the Summons void of fear;
And, unconcern'dly, cast his eyes around;
As if to find and dare the griesly Challenger.   200
What death cou'd do he lately try'd,
When in four days he more then dy'd.
The same assurance all his words did grace;
The same Majestick mildness held its place;
Nor lost the Monarch in his dying face.   205
Intrepid, pious, merciful, and brave,
He lookt as when he conquer'd and forgave.

VII

As if some Angel had been sent
To lengthen out his Government,
And to foretel as many years again, 210
As he had number'd in his happy reign,
So chearfully he took the doom
Of his departing breath;
Nor shrunk nor stept aside for death:
But, with unalter'd pace, kept on; 215
Providing for events to come,
When he resign'd the Throne.
Still he maintain'd his Kingly State;
And grew familiar with his fate.
Kind, good and gracious to the last, 220
On all he lov'd before, his dying beams he cast:
Oh truly good, and truly great,
For glorious as he rose benignly so he set!
All that on earth he held most dear,
He recommended to his Care, 225
To whom both heav'n
The right had giv'n
And his own Love bequeath'd supream command:
He took and prest that ever loyal hand,
Which cou'd in Peace secure his Reign, 230
Which cou'd in wars his Pow'r maintain,
That hand on which no plighted vows were ever vain.
Well for so great a trust, he chose
A Prince who never disobey'd:
Not when the most severe commands were laid; 235
Nor want, nor Exile with his duty weigh'd:
A Prince on whom (if Heav'n its Eyes cou'd close)
The Welfare of the World it safely might repose.

VIII

That King who liv'd to Gods own heart,
Yet less serenely died than he: 240

232 on *A B*: in *H*

Charles left behind no harsh decree
For Schoolmen with laborious art
To salve from cruelty:
Those, for whom love cou'd no excuses frame,
He graciously forgot to name.   245
Thus far my Muse, though rudely, has design'd
Some faint resemblance of his Godlike mind:
But neither Pen nor Pencil can express
The parting Brothers *tenderness*:
Though thats a term too mean and low;   250
(The blest above a kinder word may know:)
But what they did, and what they said,
The Monarch who Triumphant went,
The Militant who staid,
Like Painters, when their heigthning arts are spent,   255
I cast into a shade.
That all forgiving King,
The type of him above,
That inexhausted spring
Of clemency and Love;   260
Himself to his next self accus'd,
And ask'd that Pardon which he ne're refus'd:
For faults not his, for guilt and Crimes
Of Godless men, and of Rebellious times:
For an hard Exile, kindly meant,   265
When his ungrateful Country sent
Their best *Camillus* into banishment:
And forc'd their Sov'raigns Act, they cou'd not his consent.
Oh how much rather had that injur'd Chief
Repeated all his sufferings past,   270
Then hear a pardon beg'd at last,
Which giv'n cou'd give the dying no relief:
He bent, he sunk beneath his grief:
His dauntless heart wou'd fain have held
From weeping, but his eyes rebell'd.   275
Perhaps the Godlike Hero in his breast
Disdain'd, or was asham'd to show
So weak, so womanish a woe,
Which yet the Brother and the Friend so plenteously confest.

259 inexhausted *A B*: inexhausting *H*

IX

Amidst that silent show'r, the Royal mind   280
An Easy passage found,
And left its sacred earth behind:
Nor murm'ring groan exprest, nor labouring sound,
Nor any least tumultuous breath;
Calm was his life, and quiet was his death.   285
Soft as those gentle whispers were,
In which th' Almighty did appear;
By the still Voice, the Prophet knew him there.
That Peace which made thy Prosperous Reign to shine,
That Peace thou leav'st to thy Imperial Line,   290
That Peace, oh happy Shade, be ever thine!

X

For all those Joys thy Restauration brought,
For all the Miracles it wrought,
For all the healing Balm thy Mercy pour'd
Into the Nations bleeding Wound,   295
And Care that after kept it sound,
For numerous Blessings yearly shour'd,
And Property with Plenty crown'd;
For Freedom, still maintain'd alive,
Freedom which in no other Land will thrive,   300
Freedom an *English* Subject's sole Prerogative,
Without whose Charms ev'n Peace wou'd be
But a dull quiet Slavery:
For these and more, accept our Pious Praise;
'Tis all the Subsidy   305
The present Age can raise,
The rest is charg'd on late Posterity.
Posterity is charg'd the more,
Because the large abounding store
To them and to their Heirs, is still entail'd by thee.   310
Succession, of a long Descent,
Which Chastly in the Channells ran,
And from our Demi-gods began,
Equal almost to time in its extent,

288 Voice *B*: Sound *H A*

Through Hazzards numberless and great,   315
Thou hast deriv'd this mighty Blessing down,
And fixt the fairest Gemm that decks th' Imperial Crown:
Not Faction, when it shook thy Regal Seat,
Not Senates, insolently loud,
(Those Ecchoes of a thoughtless Croud)   320
Not Foreign or Domestick Treachery,
Could warp thy Soul to their Unjust Decree.
So much thy Foes thy manly Mind mistook,
Who judg'd it by the Mildness of thy look:
Like a well temper'd Sword, it bent at will;   325
But kept the Native toughness of the Steel.

XI

Be true, O *Clio*, to thy Hero's Name!
But draw him strictly so
That all who view, the Piece may know,
He needs no Trappings of fictitious Fame: 330
The Load's too weighty: Thou may'st chuse
Some Parts of Praise, and some refuse:
Write, that his Annals may be thought more lavish than the Muse.
In scanty Truth thou hast confin'd
The Vertues of a Royal Mind,
Forgiving, bounteous, humble, just and kind: 335
His Conversation, Wit, and Parts,
His Knowledge in the Noblest, useful Arts,
Were such, Dead Authors cou'd not give;
But habitudes of those who live;
Who, lighting him, did greater lights receive: 340
He drain'd from all, and all they knew;
His Apprehension quick, his Judgment true:
That the most Learn'd, with shame, confess
His Knowledge more, his Reading only less.   345

XII

Amidst the peaceful Triumphs of his Reign,
What wonder if the kindly beams he shed
Reviv'd the drooping Arts again,
If Science rais'd her Head,

347 he *A B*: be *H*

And soft Humanity that from Rebellion fled;   350
Our Isle, indeed, too fruitful was before;
But all uncultivated lay
Out of the *Solar* walk and Heav'ns high way;
With rank *Geneva* Weeds run o're,
And Cockle, at the best, amidst the Corn it bore: 355
The Royal Husbandman appear'd,
And Plough'd, and Sow'd, and Till'd,
The Thorns he rooted out, the Rubbish clear'd,
And blest th' obedient Field.
When, straight, a double Harvest rose;   360
Such as the swarthy *Indian* mowes;
Or happier Climates near the Line,
Or Paradise Manur'd, and drest by hands Divine.

XIII

As when the New-born Phœnix takes his way,
His rich Paternal Regions to Survey,   365
Of airy Choristers a numerous Train
Attend his wondrous Progress o're the Plain;
So, rising from his Fathers Urn,
So Glorious did our *Charles* return;
Th' officious Muses came along,   370
A gay Harmonious Quire like Angels ever Young:
(The Muse that mourns him now his happy Triumph sung)
Even *they* cou'd thrive in his Auspicious reign;
And such a plenteous Crop they bore
Of purest and well winow'd Grain,   375
As *Britain* never knew before.
Tho little was their Hire, and light their Gain,
Yet somewhat to their share he threw;
Fed from his Hand, they sung and flew,
Like Birds of Paradise, that liv'd on Morning dew.   380
Oh never let their Lays his Name forget!
The Pension of a Prince's praise is great.
Live then thou great Encourager of Arts,
Live ever in our Thankful Hearts;
Live blest Above, almost invok'd Below;   385
Live and receive this Pious Vow,

371 like B: of H A

Our Patron once, our Guardian Angel now.
Thou *Fabius* of a sinking State,
Who didst by wise delays, divert our Fate,
When Faction like a Tempest rose,   390
In Death's most hideous form,
Then, Art to Rage thou didst oppose,
To weather out the Storm:
Not quitting thy Supream command,
Thou heldst the Rudder with a steady hand,   395
Till safely on the Shore the Bark did land:
The Bark that all our Blessings brought,
Charg'd with thy Self and *James*, a doubly Royal fraught.

XIV

Oh frail Estate of Humane things,
And slippery hopes below!   400
Now to our Cost your Emptiness we know,
(For 'tis a Lesson dearly bought)
Assurance here is never to be sought.
The Best, and best belov'd of Kings,
And best deserving to be so,   405
When scarce he had escap'd the fatal blow
Of Faction and Conspiracy,
Death did his promis'd hopes destroy:
He toyl'd, He gain'd, but liv'd not to enjoy.
What mists of Providence are these   410
Through which we cannot see!
So Saints, by supernatural Pow'r set free,
Are left at last in Martyrdom to dye;
Such is the end of oft repeated Miracles.
Forgive me Heav'n that Impious thought,   415
'Twas Grief for *Charles*, to Madness wrought,
That Question'd thy Supream Decree!
Thou didst his gracious Reign prolong,
Even in thy Saints and Angels wrong,
His Fellow Citizens of Immortality: 420
For Twelve long years of Exile, born,
Twice twelve we number'd since his blest Return:
So strictly wer't thou Just to pay,
Even to the driblet of a day.

Yet still we murmur, and Complain, 425
The Quails and Manna shou'd no longer rain;
Those Miracles 'twas needless to renew;
The Chosen Flock has now the Promis'd Land in view.

XV

A Warlike Prince ascends the Regal State,
A Prince, long exercis'd by Fate: 430
Long may he keep, tho he obtains it late.
Heroes, in Heaven's peculiar Mold are cast,
They and their Poets are not form'd in hast;
Man was the first in God's design, and Man was made the last.
False Heroes made by Flattery so, 435
Heav'n can strike out, like Sparkles, at a blow;
But e'r a Prince is to Perfection brought,
He costs Omnipotence a second thought.
With Toyl and Sweat,
With hardning Cold, and forming Heat, 440
The Cyclops did their strokes repeat,
Before th' impenetrable Shield was wrought.
It looks as if the Maker wou'd not own
The Noble work for his,
Before 'twas try'd and found a Masterpiece. 445

XVI

View then a *Monarch* ripen'd for a Throne.
Alcides thus his race began,
O're Infancy he swiftly ran;
The future God, at first was more than Man:
Dangers and Toils, and *Juno*'s Hate 450
Even o're his Cradle lay in wait;
And there he grappled first with Fate:
In his young Hands the hissing Snakes he prest,
So early was the Deity confest;
Thus, by degrees, he rose to *Jove*'s Imperial Seat; 455
Thus difficulties prove a Soul *legitimately* great.
Like his, our Hero's Infancy was try'd;
Betimes the Furies did their Snakes provide;

And, to his Infant Arms oppose
His Father's Rebels, and his Brother's Foes;   460
The more opprest the higher still he rose:
Those were the Preludes of his Fate,
That form'd his Manhood, to subdue
The *Hydra* of the many-headed, hissing Crew.

XVII

As after *Numa*'s peaceful Reign,   465
The Martial *Ancus* did the Scepter wield,
Furbish'd the rusty Sword again,
Resum'd the long forgotten Shield,
And led the *Latins* to the dusty Field;
So *James* the drowsy *Genius* wakes   470
Of *Britain* long entranc'd in Charms,
Restiff and slumbring on its Arms:
'Tis rows'd and with a new strung Nerve, the Spear already shakes.
No Neighing of the Warriour Steeds,
No Drum, or louder Trumpet, needs   475
T' inspire the Coward, warm the Cold,
His Voice, his sole Appearance makes 'em bold.
Gaul and *Batavia* dread th' impending blow;
Too well the Vigour of that Arm they know;
They lick the dust, and Crouch beneath their fatal Foe.   480
Long may they fear this awful Prince,
And not Provoke his lingring Sword;
Peace is their only sure Defence,
Their best Security his Word:
In all the Changes of his doubtful State,   485
His Truth, like Heav'ns, was kept inviolate,
For him to Promise is to make it Fate.
His *Valour* can Triumph o'r Land and Main;
With broken Oaths his Fame he will not stain;
With Conquest basely bought, and with Inglorious gain.   490

XVIII

For once, O Heav'n, unfold thy Adamantine Book;
And let his wondring *Senate* see,
If not thy firm Immutable Decree,

484 Their *A B*: The H

At least the second Page, of strong contingency;
Such as consists with wills, Originally free: 495
   Let them, with glad amazement, look
   On what their happiness may be:
Let them not still be obstinately blind,
Still to divert the Good thou hast design'd,
Or with Malignant penury, 500
To sterve the Royal Vertues of his Mind.
Faith is a Christian's and a Subject's Test,
Oh give them to believe, and they are surely blest!
   They do; and, with a distant view, I see
   Th' amended Vows of *English* Loyalty. 505
And all beyond that Object, there appears
The long Retinue of a Prosperous Raign,
A Series of Successful years,
In Orderly Array, a Martial, manly Train.
Behold ev'n to remoter Shores 510
A Conquering Navy proudly spread;
The *British* Cannon formidably roars,
While starting from his Oozy Bed,
Th' asserted Ocean rears his reverend Head;
To View and Recognize his ancient Lord again: 515
And with a willing hand, restores
The *Fasces* of the Main.

PROLOGUE and EPILOGUE
to *ALBION AND ALBANIUS*

PROLOGUE *To the* OPERA

FULL twenty years and more, our lab'ring Stage
Has lost, on this incorrigible age:
Our Poets, the *John Ketches* of the Nation,
Have seem'd to lash yee, ev'n to excoriation:

494 strong B: great H A
Prologue and Epilogue. Text from Albion and Albanius: An Opera, *1685,*

But still no sign remains; which plainly notes,   5
You bore like Hero's, or you brib'd like *Oates*.
What can we do, when mimicking a Fop,
Like beating Nut-trees, makes a larger Crop?
Faith we'll e'en spare our pains: and to content you,
Will fairly leave you what your Maker meant you.   10
Satyre was once your Physick, Wit your Food;
One nourisht not, and t'other drew no Blood.
Wee now prescribe, like Doctors in despair,
The Diet your weak appetites can bear.
Since hearty Beef and Mutton will not do,   15
Here's Julep dance, Ptisan of Song and show:
Give you strong Sense, the Liquor is too heady;
You're come to farce, that's Asses milk, already.
Some hopeful Youths there are, of callow Wit,
Who one Day may be Men, if Heav'n think fit;   20
Sound may serve such, ere they to Sense are grown;
Like leading strings, till they can walk alone:
But yet to keep our Friends in count'nance, know,
The Wise *Italians* first invented show;
Thence, into *France* the Noble Pageant past;   25
'Tis *England*'s Credit to be cozn'd last.
Freedom and Zeal have chous'd you o'er and o'er;   ⎫
'Pray' give us leave to bubble you once more;   ⎬
You never were so cheaply fool'd before.   ⎭
Wee bring you change, to humour your Disease;   30
Change for the worse has ever us'd to please:
Then 'tis the mode of *France*, without whose Rules,
None must presume to set up here for Fools:
In *France*, the oldest Man is always young,   ⎫
Sees *Opera*'s daily, learns the Tunes so long,   ⎬ 35
Till Foot, Hand, Head, keep time with ev'ry Song.   ⎭
Each sings his part, echoing from Pit and Box,
With his hoarse Voice, half Harmony, half Pox.
Le plus grand Roy du Monde, is always ringing;
They show themselves good Subjects by their singing.   40
On that condition, set up every Throat;
You Whiggs may sing, for you have chang'd your Note.
Cits and Citesses, raise a joyful strain,
'Tis a good Omen to begin a Reign:

Voices may help your Charter to restoring;   45
And get by singing, what you lost by roaring.

EPILOGUE *To the* OPERA

AFTER our *Æsop*'s Fable, shown to day,
    I come to give the Moral of the Play.
Feign'd Zeal, you saw, set out the speedier pace;
But, the last heat, *Plain Dealing* won the Race:
Plain Dealing for a Jewel has been known;   5
But ne'er till now the Jewel of a Crown.
When Heav'n made Man, to show the work Divine,
Truth was his Image, stampt upon the Coin:
And, when a King is to a God refin'd,
On all he says and does, he stamps his Mind: 10
This proves a Soul without allay, and pure;
Kings, like their Gold, should every touch endure.
To dare in Fields is Valour; but how few
Dare be so throughly Valiant to be true?
The Name of Great, let other Kings affect: 15
He's Great indeed, the Prince that is direct.
His Subjects know him now, and trust him more,
Than all their Kings, and all their Laws before.
What safety could their publick Acts afford?
Those he can break; but cannot break his Word.   20
So great a Trust to him alone was due;
Well have they trusted whom so well they knew.
The Saint, who walk'd on Waves, securely trod,
While he believ'd the beckning of his God;
But, when his Faith no longer bore him out,   25
Began to sink, as he began to doubt.
Let us our native Character maintain,
'Tis of our growth, to be sincerely plain.
T' excel in Truth, we Loyally may strive;
Set Privilege against Prerogative: 30
He Plights his Faith; and we believe him just;
His Honour is to Promise, ours to Trust.
Thus *Britain*'s Basis on a Word is laid,
As by a Word the World it self was made.

To my Friend Mr. J. Northleigh,
Author of the Parallel.
On his Triumph of the British Monarchy

So *Joseph* yet a youth, expounded well
  The bodeing Dream, and did th' event foretell,
Judg'd by the past, and drew the Parallel.
Thus early *Solomon* the Truth explor'd,
The Right awarded, and the Babe restor'd.   5
Thus *Daniel*, e're to Prophecy he grew,
The perjur'd Presbyters did first subdue,
And freed *Susannah* from the canting Crew.
Well may our Monarchy Triumphant stand
While warlike *JAMES* protects both Sea and Land,   10
And under covert of his sev'n-fold shield,
Thou send'st thy shafts to scowre the distant Field.
By Law thy powerful Pen has set us free,
Thou study'st that, and that may study thee.

To the Pious Memory
Of the Accomplisht Young LADY
Mrs Anne Killigrew,
Excellent in the two Sister-Arts of
Poësie, and Painting.
An ODE

I

Thou Youngest Virgin-Daughter of the Skies,
  Made in the last Promotion of the Blest;
Whose Palmes, new pluckt from Paradise,
In spreading Branches more sublimely rise,
Rich with Immortal Green above the rest: 5
Whether, adopted to some Neighbouring Star,

To my Friend, &c. Text from The Triumph of Our Monarchy, *1685*
To the Pious Memory, &c. Text from Poems by Mrs Anne Killigrew, *1686, collated with*
Examen Poeticum, *1693*

Thou rol'st above us, in thy wand'ring Race,
   Or, in Procession fixt and regular,
   Mov'd with the Heavens Majestick Pace;
   Or, call'd to more Superiour Bliss,   10
Thou tread'st, with Seraphims, the vast Abyss:
What ever happy Region is thy place,
Cease thy Celestial Song a little space;
(Thou wilt have Time enough for Hymns Divine,
   Since Heav'ns Eternal Year is thine.)   15
Hear then a Mortal Muse thy Praise rehearse,
     In no ignoble Verse;
But such as thy own voice did practise here,
When thy first Fruits of Poesie were giv'n;
To make thy self a welcome Inmate there: 20
   While yet a young Probationer,
     And Candidate of Heav'n.

II

   If by Traduction came thy Mind,
   Our Wonder is the less to find
A Soul so charming from a Stock so good;   25
Thy Father was transfus'd into thy Blood:
So wert thou born into the tuneful strain,
(An early, rich, and inexhausted Vain.)
   But if thy Præexisting Soul
   Was form'd, at first, with Myriads more,   30
It did through all the Mighty Poets roul,
   Who *Greek* or *Latine* Laurels wore,
And was that *Sappho* last, which once it was before.
   If so, then cease thy flight, *O Heav'n-born Mind!*
   Thou hast no Dross to purge from thy Rich Ore: 35
   Nor can thy Soul a fairer Mansion find,
   Than was the Beauteous Frame she left behind:
Return, to fill or mend the Quire, of thy Celestial kind.

III

   May we presume to say, that at thy Birth,
New joy was sprung in Heav'n, as well as here on Earth.   40

12 is *93*: be *86*

For sure the Milder Planets did combine
On thy Auspicious Horoscope to shine,
And ev'n the most Malicious were in Trine. }
   Thy Brother-Angels at thy Birth
    Strung each his Lyre, and tun'd it high,   45
   That all the People of the Skie
Might know a Poetess was born on Earth.
     And then if ever, Mortal Ears
     Had heard the Musick of the Spheres!
     And if no clust'ring Swarm of Bees   50
On thy sweet Mouth distill'd their golden Dew,
   'Twas that, such vulgar Miracles,
   Heav'n had not Leasure to renew:
For all the Blest Fraternity of Love
Solemniz'd there thy Birth, and kept thy Holyday above.   55

IV

O Gracious God! How far have we
Prophan'd thy Heav'nly Gift of Poesy?
Made prostitute and profligate the Muse,
Debas'd to each obscene and impious use,
Whose Harmony was first ordain'd Above   60
For Tongues of Angels, and for Hymns of Love?
O wretched We! why were we hurry'd down
   This lubrique and adult'rate age,
   (Nay added fat Pollutions of our own)
T' increase the steaming Ordures of the Stage?   65
What can we say t' excuse our *Second Fall*?
Let this thy *Vestal*, Heav'n, attone for all!
   Her *Arethusian* Stream remains unsoil'd,
   Unmixt with Forreign Filth, and undefil'd,
Her Wit was more than Man, her Innocence a Child!   70

V

   Art she had none, yet wanted none:
   For Nature did that Want supply,
   So rich in Treasures of her Own,
   She might our boasted Stores defy:
Such Noble Vigour did her Verse adorn,   75
That it seem'd borrow'd, where 'twas only born.

Her Morals too were in her Bosome bred
 By great Examples daily fed,
What in the best of Books, her Fathers Life, she read.
 And to be read her self she need not fear,   80
 Each Test, and ev'ry Light, her Muse will bear,
 Though *Epictetus* with his Lamp were there.
Ev'n Love (for Love sometimes her Muse exprest)
Was but a *Lambent-flame* which play'd about her Brest:
 Light as the Vapours of a Morning Dream,   85
 So cold herself, whilst she such Warmth exprest,
 'Twas *Cupid* bathing in *Diana*'s Stream.

VI

 Born to the Spacious Empire of the *Nine*,
 One would have thought, she should have been content
 To manage well that Mighty Government: 90
 But what can young ambitious Souls confine?
  To the next Realm she stretcht her Sway,
  For *Painture* neer adjoyning lay,
 A plenteous Province, and alluring Prey.
A Chamber of Dependences was fram'd,   95
 (As Conquerors will never want Pretence,
  When arm'd, to justifie the Offence)
And the whole Fief, in right of Poetry she claim'd.
 The Country open lay without Defence:
 For Poets frequent In-rodes there had made,   100
  And perfectly could represent
 The Shape, the Face, with ev'ry Lineament;
And all the large Demains which the *Dumb-sister* sway'd,
  All bow'd beneath her Government,
  Receiv'd in Triumph wheresoe're she went.   105
 Her Pencil drew, what e're her Soul design'd,
And oft the happy Draught surpass'd the Image in her Mind.
 The *Sylvan* Scenes of Herds and Flocks,
 And fruitful Plains and barren Rocks,
 Of shallow Brooks that flow'd so clear,   110
 The Bottom did the Top appear;
 Of deeper too and ampler Flouds,
 Which as in Mirrors, shew'd the Woods;
 Of lofty Trees with Sacred Shades,

And Perspectives of pleasant Glades,   115
Where Nymphs of brightest Form appear,
And shaggy Satyrs standing neer,
Which them at once admire and fear.
The Ruines too of some Majestick Piece,
Boasting the Pow'r of ancient *Rome* or *Greece*,   120
Whose Statues, Freezes, Columns broken lie,
And though deface't, the Wonder of the Eie,
What Nature, Art, bold Fiction e're durst frame,
Her forming Hand gave Feature to the Name.
So strange a Concourse ne're was seen before,   125
But when the peopl'd Ark the whole Creation bore.

VII

The Scene then chang'd, with bold Erected Look
Our Martial King the sight with Reverence strook:
For not content t' express his Outward Part,
Her hand call'd out the Image of his Heart,   130
His Warlike Mind, his Soul devoid of Fear,
His High-designing Thoughts, were figur'd there,
As when, by Magick, Ghosts are made appear.
Our Phenix Queen was portrai'd too so bright,
Beauty alone could Beauty take so right: 135
Her Dress, her Shape, her matchless Grace,
Were all observ'd, as well as heav'nly Face.
With such a Peerless Majesty she stands,
As in that Day she took the Crown from Sacred hands:
Before a Train of Heroins was seen,   140
In *Beauty* foremost, as in Rank, the Queen!
Thus nothing to her *Genius* was deny'd,
But like a Ball of Fire the further thrown,
Still with a greater Blaze she shone,
And her bright Soul broke out on ev'ry side.   145
What next she had design'd, Heaven only knows,
To such Immod'rate Growth her Conquest rose,

124 Feature to *93*: Shape unto *86*   128 sight *93*:   Eye *86*
139–41 As . . . the Queen! *93*: *86* has
                As in that Day she took from Sacred hands
                The Crown; 'mong num'rous Heroins was seen,
                More yet in Beauty, than in Rank, the Queen!

That Fate alone its Progress could oppose.

VIII

Now all those Charmes, that blooming Grace,
The well-proportion'd Shape, and beauteous Face,   150
Shall never more be seen by Mortal Eyes;
In Earth the much lamented Virgin lies!
   Not Wit, nor Piety could Fate prevent;
   Nor was the cruel *Destiny* content
     To finish all the Murder at a Blow,   155
To sweep at once her Life, and Beauty too;
But, like a hardn'd Fellon, took a pride
     To work more Mischievously slow,
     And plunder'd first, and then destroy'd.
O double Sacriledge on things Divine,   160
To rob the Relique, and deface the Shrine!
    But thus *Orinda* dy'd:
Heav'n, by the same Disease, did both translate,
As equal were their Souls, so equal was their Fate.

IX

Mean time her Warlike Brother on the Seas   165
His waving Streamers to the Winds displays,
And vows for his Return, with vain Devotion, pays.
   Ah, Generous Youth, that Wish forbear,
   The Winds too soon will waft thee here!
   Slack all thy Sailes, and fear to come,   170
Alas, thou know'st not, Thou art wreck'd at home!
No more shalt thou behold thy Sisters Face,
Thou hast already had her last Embrace.
But look aloft, and if thou ken'st from far,
Among the *Pleiad's* a New-kindl'd Star,   175
If any sparkles, than the rest, more bright,
'Tis she that shines in that propitious Light.

X

When in mid-Aire, the Golden Trump shall sound,
   To raise the Nations under ground;

148 its *93*: their *86*

When in the Valley of *Jehosaphat*,   180
The Judging God shall close the Book of Fate;
   And there the last Assizes keep,
   For those who Wake, and those who Sleep;
   When ratling Bones together fly,
From the four Corners of the Skie,   185
When Sinews o're the Skeletons are spread,
Those cloath'd with Flesh, and Life inspires the Dead:
The Sacred Poets first shall hear the Sound,
   And formost from the Tomb shall bound:
For they are cover'd with the lightest Ground   190
And streight, with in-born Vigour, on the Wing,
Like mounting Larkes, to the New Morning sing.
There *Thou*, Sweet Saint, before the Quire shalt go,
As Harbinger of Heav'n, the Way to show,
The Way which thou so well hast learn'd below.   195

To my Ingenious Friend, Mr. Henry Higden, Esq;
On his Translation of the Tenth
SATYR OF JUVENAL

THE *Grecian* Wits, who *Satyr* first began,
   Were Pleasant *Pasquins* on the Life of Man:
At Mighty Villains, who the State opprest,
They durst not Rail; perhaps, they Laugh'd at least,
And turn'd 'em out of Office with a Jest.   5
No Fool could peep abroad, but ready stand
The *Drolls*, to clap a *Bauble* in his Hand:
Wise *Legislators* never yet could draw
A *Fopp* within the Reach of Common-Law;
For Posture, Dress, Grimace, and Affectation,   10
Tho' Foes to *Sence*, are Harmless to the *Nation*.
Our last Redress is Dint of *Verse* to try;
And Satyr is our *Court of Chancery*.
This Way took *Horace* to reform an Age
Not Bad enough to need an Author's Rage: 15

To my Ingenious Friend, &c. *Text from Higden's* A Modern Essay on the Tenth Satyr of Juvenal, *1687*

But Yours,* who liv'd in more degen'rate Times,   **Juvenal.*
Was forc'd to fasten Deep, and woorry Crimes:
Yet You, my Friend, have temper'd him so well,
You make him Smile in spight of all his Zeal:
An Art peculiar to your Self alone,   20
To joyn the Vertues of Two Stiles in One.

    Oh! were your Author's Principle receiv'd,
Half of the lab'ring World wou'd be reliev'd;
For not to Wish, is not to be Deceiv'd!
Revenge wou'd into *Charity* be chang'd,   25
Because it costs too Dear to be *Reveng'd*:
It costs our *Quiet* and *Content of Mind*;
And when 'tis compass'd, leaves a Sting behind.
Suppose I had the better End o' th' Staff,
Why shou'd I help th' ill-natur'd World to laugh?   30
'Tis all alike to them, who gets the Day;
They Love the Spight and Mischief of the *Fray*.
No; I have Cur'd my Self of that *Disease*;
Nor will I be provok'd, but when I please:
But let me half that *Cure* to You restore;   35
You gave the *Salve*, I laid it to the *Sore*.

    Our kind Relief against a Rainy Day,
Beyond a Tavern, or a tedious Play;
We take your Book, and laugh our Spleen away.
If all Your *Tribe*, (too studious of *Debate*)   40
Wou'd cease false Hopes and Titles to create,
Led by the *Rare Example* you begun,
Clyents wou'd fail, and *Lawyers* be undone.

THE HIND
AND THE PANTHER

A POEM, In Three Parts

—Antiquam exquirite matrem. ⎫
Et vera, incessu, patuit Dea.— ⎭ VIRG.

TO THE READER

*T*HE *Nation is in too high a Ferment, for me to expect either fair War, or
even so much as fair Quarter from a Reader of the opposite Party. All Men
are engag'd either on this side or that: and tho' Conscience is the common* Word,
*which is given by both, yet if a Writer fall among Enemies, and cannot give the
Marks of* Their *Conscience, he is knock'd down before the Reasons of his own are* 5
heard. A Preface, *therefore, which is but a bespeaking of Favour, is altogether
useless. What I desire the* Reader *should know concerning me, he will find in the
Body of the Poem; if he have but the patience to peruse it. Only this Advertise-
ment let him take before hand, which relates to the Merits of the Cause. No
general Characters of Parties, (call 'em either Sects or Churches) can be so fully* 10
*and exactly drawn, as to Comprehend all the several Members of 'em; at least all
such as are receiv'd under that Denomination. For example; there are some of the
Church by Law Establish'd, who envy not Liberty of Conscience to Dissenters;
as being well satisfied that, according to their own Principles, they ought not to
persecute them. Yet these, by reason of their fewness, I could not distinguish from* 15
*the Numbers of the rest with whom they are Embodied in one common Name: On
the other side there are many of our Sects, and more indeed then I could reasonably
have hop'd, who have withdrawn themselves from the Communion of the* Panther;
*and embrac'd this Gracious Indulgence of His Majesty in point of Toleration. But
neither to the one nor the other of these is this Satyr any way intended: 'tis* 20
*aim'd only at the refractory and disobedient on either side. For those who are come
over to the Royal Party are consequently suppos'd to be out of Gunshot. Our
Physicians have observ'd, that in Process of Time, some Diseases have abated of
their Virulence, and have in a manner worn out their Malignity, so as to be no
longer Mortal: and why may not I suppose the same concerning some of those who* 25
*have formerly been Enemies to Kingly Government, As well as Catholick Religion?
I hope they have now another Notion of both, as having found, by Comfort-*

The Hind and the Panther. Text from the first edition, 1687 (A), collated with the second (B)
and third (C) editions, 1687

able Experience, that the Doctrine of Persecution is far from being an Article of our Faith.

'*Tis not for any Private Man to Censure the Proceedings of a Foreign Prince:* 30 *but, without suspicion of Flattery, I may praise our own, who has taken contrary Measures, and those more suitable to the Spirit of Christianity. Some of the Dissenters in their Addresses to His Majesty have said* That he has restor'd God to his Empire over Conscience: *I Confess I dare not stretch the Figure to so great a boldness: but I may safely say, that Conscience is the Royalty and Pre-* 35 *rogative of every Private man. He is absolute in his own Breast, and accountable to no Earthly Power, for that which passes only betwixt God and Him. Those who are driven into the Fold are, generally speaking, rather made Hypocrites then Converts.*

This Indulgence being granted to all the Sects, it ought in reason to be expected, 40 *that they should both receive it, and receive it thankfully. For at this time of day to refuse the Benefit, and adhere to those whom they have esteem'd their Persecutors, what is it else, but publickly to own that they suffer'd not before for Conscience sake; but only out of Pride and Obstinacy to separate from a Church for those Impositions, which they now judge may be lawfully obey'd? After they* 45 *have so long contended for their Classical Ordination, (not to speak of Rites and Ceremonies) will they at length submit to an Episcopal? If they can go so far out of Complaisance to their old Enemies, methinks a little reason should perswade 'em to take another step, and see whether that wou'd lead 'em.*

Of the receiving this Toleration thankfully, I shall say no more, than that 50 *they ought, and I doubt not they will consider from what hands they receiv'd it. 'Tis not from a* Cyrus, *a Heathen Prince, and a Foreigner, but from a Christian King, their Native Sovereign: who expects a Return in* Specie *from them; that the Kindness which He has Graciously shown them, may be retaliated on those of his own perswasion.* 55

As for the Poem in general, I will only thus far satisfie the Reader: *That it was neither impos'd on me, nor so much as the Subject given me by any man. It was written during the last Winter and the beginning of this Spring; though with long interruptions of ill health, and other hindrances. About a Fortnight before I had finish'd it, His Majesties Declaration for Liberty of Conscience came* 60 *abroad: which, if I had so soon expected, I might have spar'd my self the labour of writing many things which are contain'd in the third part of it. But I was alwayes in some hope, that the Church of* England *might have been perswaded to have taken off the* Penal Lawes *and the* Test, *which was one Design of the Poem when I propos'd to my self the writing of it.* 65

'*Tis evident that some part of it was only occasional, and not first intended. I mean that defence of my self, to which every honest man is bound, when he is*

*injuriously attacqu'd in Print: and I refer my self to the judgment of those who
have read the* Answer to the Defence of the late Kings Papers, *and that of
the* Dutchess, *(in which last I was concerned) how charitably I have been* 70
*represented there. I am now inform'd both of the Author and Supervisers of his
Pamphlet: and will reply when I think he can affront me: for I am of* Socrates's
*Opinion that all Creatures cannot. In the mean time let him consider, whether he
deserv'd not a more severe reprehension then I gave him formerly; for using so
little respect to the Memory of those whom he pretended to answer: and, at his* 75
*leisure look out for some Original Treatise of Humility, written by any Protestant
in English, (I believe I may say in any other Tongue:) for the magnified Piece of*
Duncomb *on that Subject, which either he must mean or none, and with which
another of his Fellows has upbraided me, was Translated from the Spanish of*
Rodriguez: *tho' with the Omission of the* 17th, *the* 24th, *the* 25th, *and the* 80
last Chapter, which will be found in comparing of the Books.

He would have insinuated to the World that Her late Highness died not a
Roman Catholick: He declares himself to be now satisfied to the contrary; in
which he has giv'n up the Cause: for matter of Fact was the Principal
Debate betwixt us. In the mean time he would dispute the Motives of her 85
Change: how prepostrously let all men judge, when he seem'd to deny the Subject
of the Controversy, the Change it self. And because I would not take up this
ridiculous Challenge, he tells the World I cannot argue: but he may as well infer
that a Catholick cannot fast, because he will not take up the Cudgels against Mrs.*
James, *to confute the Protestant Religion.*   90

I *have but one word more to say concerning the Poem as such, and abstracting
from the Matters either Religious or Civil which are handled in it. The* first
part, *consisting most in general Characters and Narration, I have endeavour'd
to raise, and give it the Majestick Turn of Heroick Poesie. The* second, *being
Matter of Dispute, and chiefly concerning Church Authority, I was oblig'd to* 95
*make as plain and perspicuous as possibly I cou'd: yet not wholly neglecting the
Numbers, though I had not frequent occasions for the Magnificence of Verse.
The* third, *which has more of the Nature of Domestick Conversation, is, or
ought to be more free and familiar than the two former.*

There are in it two *Episodes, or Fables, which are interwoven with the main* 100
*Design; so that they are properly parts of it, though they are also distinct Stories
of themselves. In both of these I have made use of the Common Places of Satyr,
whether true or false, which are urg'd by the Members of the one Church against
the other. At which I hope no Reader of either Party will be scandaliz'd;
because they are not of my Invention: but as old, to my knowledge, as the Times* 105
of Boccace *and* Chawcer *on the one side, and as those of the Reformation on the
other.*

THE HIND AND THE PANTHER

THE FIRST PART

A MILK white *Hind*, immortal and unchang'd,
Fed on the lawns, and in the forest rang'd;
Without unspotted, innocent within,
She fear'd no danger, for she knew no sin.
Yet had she oft been chas'd with horns and hounds, 5
And Scythian shafts; and many winged wounds
Aim'd at Her heart; was often forc'd to fly,
And doom'd to death, though fated not to dy.
Not so her young, for their unequal line
Was Heroe's make, half humane, half divine. 10
Their earthly mold obnoxious was to fate,
Th' immortal part assum'd immortal state.
Of these a slaughtered army lay in bloud,
Extended o'er the *Caledonian* wood,
Their native walk; whose vocal bloud arose, 15
And cry'd for pardon on their perjur'd foes;
Their fate was fruitfull, and the sanguin seed
Endu'd with souls, encreas'd the sacred breed.
So Captive *Israel* multiply'd in chains
A numerous Exile, and enjoy'd her pains. 20
With grief and gladness mixt, their mother view'd
Her martyr'd offspring, and their race renew'd;
Their corps to perish, but their kind to last,
So much the deathless plant the dying fruit surpass'd.
Panting and pensive now she rang'd alone, 25
And wander'd in the kingdoms, once Her own.
The common Hunt, though from their rage restrain'd
By sov'reign pow'r, her company disdain'd:
Grin'd as They pass'd, and with a glaring eye
Gave gloomy signs of secret enmity. 30
'Tis true, she bounded by, and trip'd so light
They had not time to take a steady sight.
For truth has such a face and such a meen
As to be lov'd needs onely to be seen.

The bloudy *Bear* an *Independent* beast,   83
Unlick'd to form, in groans her hate express'd.
Among the timorous kind the *Quaking Hare*
Profess'd neutrality, but would not swear.
Next her the *Buffoon Ape*, as Atheists use,
Mimick'd all Sects, and had his own to chuse: 40
Still when the Lyon look'd, his knees he bent,
And pay'd at Church a Courtier's Complement.

   The bristl'd *Baptist Boar*, impure as He,
(But whitn'd with the foam of sanctity)
With fat pollutions fill'd the sacred place,   45
And mountains levell'd in his furious race,
So first rebellion founded was in grace.
But since the mighty ravage which he made
In *German* Forests, had his guilt betrayd,
With broken tusks, and with a borrow'd name   50
He shun'd the vengeance, and conceal'd the shame;
So lurk'd in Sects unseen. With greater guile
False *Reynard* fed on consecrated spoil:
The graceless beast by *Athanasius* first
Was chas'd from *Nice*; then by *Socinus* nurs'd   55
His impious race their blasphemy renew'd,
And natures King through natures opticks view'd.
Revers'd they view'd him lessen'd to their eye,
Nor in an Infant could a God descry:
New swarming Sects to this obliquely tend,   60
Hence they began, and here they all will end.

   What weight of antient witness can prevail
If private reason hold the publick scale?
But, gratious God, how well dost thou provide
For erring judgments an unerring Guide?   65
Thy throne is darkness in th' abyss of light,
A blaze of glory that forbids the sight;
O teach me to believe Thee thus conceal'd,
And search no farther than thy self reveal'd;
But her alone for my Directour take   70
Whom thou hast promis'd never to forsake!
My thoughtless youth was wing'd with vain desires,
My manhood, long misled by wandring fires,
Follow'd false lights; and when their glimps was gone,

My pride struck out new sparkles of her own.   75
Such was I, such by nature still I am,
Be thine the glory, and be mine the shame.
Good life be now my task: my doubts are done,
(What more could fright my faith, than Three in One?)
Can I believe eternal God could lye   80
Disguis'd in mortal mold and infancy?
That the great maker of the world could dye?
And after that, trust my imperfect sense
Which calls in question his omnipotence?
Can I my reason to my faith compell,   85
And shall my sight, and touch, and taste rebell?
Superiour faculties are set aside,
Shall their subservient organs be my guide?
Then let the moon usurp the rule of day,
And winking tapers shew the sun his way;   90
For what my senses can themselves perceive
I need no revelation to believe.
Can they who say the Host should be descry'd
By sense, define a body glorify'd?
Impassible, and penetrating parts?   95
Let them declare by what mysterious arts
He shot that body through th' opposing might
Of bolts and barrs impervious to the light,
And stood before his train confess'd in open sight.

For since thus wondrously he pass'd, 'tis plain   100
One single place two bodies did contain,
And sure the same omnipotence as well
Can make one body in more places dwell.
Let reason then at Her own quarry fly,
But how can finite grasp infinity?   105
    'Tis urg'd again that faith did first commence
By miracles, which are appeals to sense,
And thence concluded that our sense must be
The motive still of credibility.
For latter ages must on former wait,   110
And what began belief, must propagate.

    But winnow well this thought, and you shall find,
'Tis light as chaff that flies before the wind.
Were all those wonders wrought by pow'r divine

As means or ends of some more deep design?   115
Most sure as means, whose end was this alone,
To prove the god-head of th' eternal Son.
God thus asserted: man is to believe
Beyond what sense and reason can conceive.
And for mysterious things of faith rely   120
On the Proponent, heav'ns authority.
If then our faith we for our guide admit,
Vain is the farther search of humane wit,
As when the building gains a surer stay,
We take th' unusefull scaffolding away: 125
Reason by sense no more can understand,
The game is play'd into another hand.
Why chuse we then like *Bilanders* to creep   ⎫
Along the coast, and land in view to keep,   ⎬
When safely we may launch into the deep?   ⎭ 130
In the same vessel which our Saviour bore   ⎫
Himself the Pilot, let us leave the shoar,   ⎬
And with a better guide a better world explore.   ⎭
Could He his god-head veil with flesh and bloud
And not veil these again to be our food?   135
His grace in both is equal in extent,
The first affords us life, the second nourishment.
And if he can, why all this frantick pain   ⎫
To construe what his clearest words contain,   ⎬
And make a riddle what He made so plain?   ⎭ 140
To take up half on trust, and half to try,
Name it not faith, but bungling biggottry.
Both knave and fool the Merchant we may call   ⎫
To pay great summs, and to compound the small.   ⎬
For who wou'd break with heav'n, and wou'd not break for all?⎭ 145
Rest then, my soul, from endless anguish freed;
Nor sciences thy guide, nor sense thy creed.
Faith is the best ensurer of thy bliss;
The Bank above must fail before the venture miss.
But heav'n and heav'n-born faith are far from Thee   150
Thou first Apostate to Divinity.
Unkennel'd range in thy *Polonian* Plains;
A fiercer foe th' insatiate *Wolfe* remains.
    Too boastfull *Britain* please thy self no more,

That beasts of prey are banish'd from thy shoar: 155
The *Bear*, the *Boar*, and every salvage name,
Wild in effect, though in appearance tame,
Lay waste thy woods, destroy thy blissfull bow'r,
And muzl'd though they seem, the mutes devour.
More haughty than the rest the *wolfish* race,   160
Appear with belly Gaunt, and famish'd face:
Never was so deform'd a beast of Grace.

His ragged tail betwixt his leggs he wears
Close clap'd for shame, but his rough crest he rears,
And pricks up his predestinating ears.   165

His wild disorder'd walk, his hagger'd eyes,
Did all the bestial citizens surprize.

Though fear'd and hated, yet he ruled awhile
As Captain or Companion of the spoil.

Full many a year his hatefull head had been   170
For tribute paid, nor since in *Cambria* seen:
The last of all the litter scap'd by chance,
And from *Geneva* first infested *France*.

Some authours thus his pedigree will trace,
But others write him of an upstart race: 175
Because of *Wickliff*'s brood no mark he brings
But his innate antipathy to kings.

These last deduce him from th' *Helvetian* kind
Who near the *Leman lake* his Consort lin'd.

That fi'ry *Zuynglius* first th' affection bred,   180
And meagre *Calvin* blest the nuptial bed.

In *Israel* some believe him whelp'd long since   *Vid. Pref.*
When the proud *Sanhedrim* oppress'd the Prince.   *to* Heyl.
                                                        Hist. of
Or, since he will be *Jew*, derive him high'r   *Presb.*
When *Corah* with his brethren did conspire,   185
From *Moyses* hand the Sov'reign sway to wrest,
And *Aaron* of his Ephod to devest:

Till opening Earth made way for all to pass,
And cou'd not bear the burd'n of a *class*.

The *Fox* and he came shuffl'd in the dark,   190
If ever they were stow'd in *Noah*'s ark:
Perhaps not made; for all their barking train
The *Dog* (a common species) will contain.

And some wild currs, who from their masters ran
Abhorring the supremacy of man,   ⎞
In woods and caves the rebel-race began.   ⎠ 195

  O happy pair, how well have you increas'd,
What ills in Church and State have you redress'd!
With teeth untry'd, and rudiments of claws
Your first essay was on your native laws: 200
Those having torn with ease, and trampl'd down   ⎞
Your Fangs you fastn'd on the miter'd crown,   ⎟
And freed from God and monarchy your town.   ⎠
What though your native kennel still be small
Bounded betwixt a puddle and a wall,   205
Yet your victorious colonies are sent
Where the north ocean girds the continent.
Quickn'd with fire below your monsters breed,
In Fenny *Holland* and in fruitfull *Tweed*.
And like the first the last affects to be   210
Drawn to the dreggs of a Democracy.
As where in fields the fairy rounds are seen,
A rank sow'r herbage rises on the green,
So, springing where these mid-night Elves advance,
Rebellion prints the foot-steps of the Dance.   215
Such are their doctrines, such contempt they show   ⎞
To heav'n above, and to their Prince below,   ⎟
As none but Traytours and Blasphemers know.   ⎠
God, like the Tyrant of the skyes is plac'd,
And kings like slaves beneath the crowd debas'd.   220
So fulsome is their food, that flocks refuse
To bite, and onely dogs for physick use.
As where the lightning runs along the ground,
No husbandry can heal the blasting wound,
Nor bladed grass, nor bearded corn succeeds,   225
But scales of scurf, and putrefaction breeds:
Such warrs, such waste, such fiery tracks of dearth
Their zeal has left, and such a teemless earth.
But as the Poisons of the deadliest kind
Are to their own unhappy coasts confin'd,   230
As onely *Indian* shades of sight deprive,
And magick plants will but in *Colchos* thrive;
So Presbyt'ry and pestilential zeal

Can onely flourish in a common-weal.

From *Celtique* woods is chas'd the *wolfish* crew;   235
But ah! some pity e'en to brutes is due:
Their native walks, methinks, they might enjoy
Curb'd of their native malice to destroy.
Of all the tyrannies on humane kind
The worst is that which persecutes the mind.   240
Let us but weigh at what offence we strike,
'Tis but because we cannot think alike.
In punishing of this, we overthrow
The laws of nations and of nature too.
Beasts are the subjects of tyrannick sway,   245
Where still the stronger on the weaker prey.
Man onely of a softer mold is made;
Not for his fellows ruine, but their aid.
Created kind, beneficent and free,
The noble image of the Deity.   250
   One portion of informing fire was giv'n
To Brutes, th' inferiour family of heav'n:
The Smith divine, as with a careless beat,
Struck out the mute creation at a heat:
But, when arriv'd at last to humane race,   255
The god-head took a deep consid'ring space:
And, to distinguish man from all the rest,
Unlock'd the sacred treasures of his breast:
And mercy mix'd with reason did impart;
One to his head, the other to his heart: 260
Reason to rule, but mercy to forgive:
The first is law, the last prerogative.
And like his mind his outward form appear'd;
When issuing naked, to the wondring herd,
He charm'd their eyes, and for they lov'd, they fear'd.   265
Not arm'd with horns of arbitrary might,
Or claws to seize their furry spoils in fight,
Or with increase of feet t' o'ertake 'em in their flight.
Of easie shape, and pliant ev'ry way;
Confessing still the softness of his clay,   270
And kind as kings upon their coronation day:
With open hands, and with extended space
Of arms, to satisfie a large embrace.

Thus kneaded up with milk, the new made man
His kingdom o'er his kindred world began: 275
Till knowledge misapply'd, misunderstood,
And pride of Empire sour'd his balmy bloud.

Then, first rebelling, his own stamp he coins;
The murth'rer *Cain* was latent in his loins,
And bloud began its first and loudest cry   280
For diff'ring worship of the Deity.
Thus persecution rose, and farther space
Produc'd the mighty hunter of his race.

Not so the blessed *Pan* his flock encreas'd,
Content to fold 'em from the famish'd beast: 285
Mild were his laws; the Sheep and harmless Hind
Were never of the persecuting kind.

Such pity now the pious Pastor shows,
Such mercy from the *British* Lyon flows,
That both provide protection for their foes.   290

   Oh happy Regions, *Italy* and *Spain*,
Which never did those monsters entertain!
The *Wolfe*, the *Bear*, the *Boar*, can there advance
No native claim of just inheritance.

And self-preserving laws, severe in show,   295
May guard their fences from th' invading foe.
Where birth has plac'd 'em let 'em safely share
The common benefit of vital air.

Themselves unharmfull, let them live unharm'd;
Their jaws disabl'd, and their claws disarm'd: 300
Here, onely in nocturnal howlings bold,
They dare not seize the Hind nor leap the fold.

More pow'rfull, and as vigilant as they,
The *Lyon* awfully forbids the prey.

Their rage repress'd, though pinch'd with famine sore,   305
They stand aloof, and tremble at his roar;
Much is their hunger, but their fear is more.

   These are the chief; to number o'er the rest,
And stand, like *Adam*, naming ev'ry beast,
Were weary work; nor will the Muse describe   310
A slimy-born and sun-begotten Tribe:
Who, far from steeples and their sacred sound,

In fields their sullen conventicles found:
These gross, half-animated lumps I leave;
Nor can I think what thoughts they can conceive. 315
But if they think at all, 'tis sure no high'r
Than matter, put in motion, may aspire.
Souls that can scarce ferment their mass of clay;
So drossy, so divisible are They,
As wou'd but serve pure bodies for allay: 320
Such souls as *Shards* produce, such beetle things
As onely buz to heav'n with ev'ning wings;
Strike in the dark, offending but by chance,
Such are the blind-fold blows of ignorance.
They know not beings, and but hate a name, 325
To them the *Hind* and *Panther* are the same.
   The *Panther* sure the noblest, next the *Hind*,
And fairest creature of the spotted kind;
Oh, could her in-born stains be wash'd away,
She were too good to be a beast of Prey! 330
How can I praise, or blame, and not offend,
Or how divide the frailty from the friend!
Her faults and vertues lye so mix'd, that she
Nor wholly stands condemn'd, nor wholly free.
Then, like her injur'd *Lyon*, let me speak, 335
He can not bend her, and he would not break.
Unkind already, and estrang'd in part,
The *Wolfe* begins to share her wandring heart.
Though unpolluted yet with actual ill,
She half commits, who sins but in Her will. 340
If, as our dreaming *Platonists* report,
There could be spirits of a middle sort,
Too black for heav'n, and yet too white for hell,
Who just dropt half way down, nor lower fell;
So pois'd, so gently she descends from high, 345
It seems a soft dismission from the sky.
Her house not ancient, whatsoe'er pretence
Her clergy Heraulds make in her defence.
A second century not half-way run
Since the new honours of her bloud begun. 350
A *Lyon* old, obscene, and furious made
By lust, compress'd her mother in a shade.

Then, by a left-hand marr'age weds the Dame,
Cov'ring adult'ry with a specious name:
So schism begot; and sacrilege and she,   355
A well-match'd pair, got graceless heresie.
God's and kings rebels have the same good cause,
To trample down divine and humane laws:
Both would be call'd Reformers, and their hate,
Alike destructive both to church and state: 360
The fruit proclaims the plant; a lawless Prince
By luxury reform'd incontinence,
By ruins, charity; by riots, abstinence.
Confessions, fasts and penance set aside;
Oh with what ease we follow such a guide!   365
Where souls are starv'd, and senses gratify'd.
Where marr'age pleasures, midnight pray'r supply,
And mattin bells (a melancholy cry)
Are tun'd to merrier notes, *encrease* and *multiply*.
Religion shows a Rosie colour'd face;   370
Not hatter'd out with drudging works of grace;
A down-hill Reformation rolls apace.
What flesh and bloud wou'd croud the narrow gate,
Or, till they waste their pamper'd paunches, wait?
All wou'd be happy at the cheapest rate.   375
      Though our lean faith these rigid laws has giv'n,
The full fed *Musulman* goes fat to heav'n;
For his *Arabian* Prophet with delights
Of sense, allur'd his eastern Proselytes.
The jolly *Luther*, reading him, began   380
T' interpret Scriptures by his *Alcoran*;
To grub the thorns beneath our tender feet,
And make the paths of *Paradise* more sweet:
Bethought him of a wife e'er half way gone,
(For 'twas uneasy travailing alone;)   385
And in this masquerade of mirth and love,
Mistook the bliss of heav'n for *Bacchanals* above.
Sure he presum'd of praise, who came to stock
Th' etherial pastures with so fair a flock,
Burnish'd, and bat'ning on their food, to show   390
The diligence of carefull herds below.
      Our *Panther* though like these she chang'd her head,

Yet, as the mistress of a monarch's bed,
Her front erect with majesty she bore,
The Crozier weilded, and the Miter wore. 395
Her upper part of decent discipline
Shew'd affectation of an ancient line:
And fathers, councils, church and churches head,
Were on her reverend *Phylacteries* read.
But what disgrac'd and disavow'd the rest, 400
Was *Calvin*'s brand, that stigmatiz'd the beast.
Thus, like a creature of a double kind,
In her own labyrinth she lives confin'd.
To foreign lands no sound of Her is come,
Humbly content to be despis'd at home. 405
Such is her faith, where good cannot be had,
At least she leaves the refuse of the bad.
Nice in her choice of ill, though not of best,
And least deform'd, because reform'd the least.
In doubtfull points betwixt her diff'ring friends, 410
Where one for substance, one for sign contends,
Their contradicting terms she strives to join,
Sign shall be substance, substance shall be sign.
A real presence all her sons allow,
And yet 'tis flat Idolatry to bow, 415
Because the god-head's there they know not how.
Her Novices are taught that bread and wine
Are but the visible and outward sign
Receiv'd by those who in communion join.
But th' inward grace, or the thing signify'd, 420
His bloud and body, who to save us dy'd;
The faithfull this thing signify'd receive.
What is't those faithfull then partake or leave?
For what is signify'd and understood,
Is, by her own confession, flesh and blood. 425
Then, by the same acknowledgement, we know
They take the sign, and take the substance too.
The lit'ral sense is hard to flesh and blood,
But nonsense never can be understood.
    Her wild belief on ev'ry wave is tost, 430
But sure no church can better morals boast.
True to her king her principles are found;

Oh that her practice were but half so sound!
Stedfast in various turns of state she stood,
And seal'd her vow'd affection with her bloud;   435
Nor will I meanly tax her constancy,
That int'rest or obligement made the tye,
(Bound to the fate of murdr'd Monarchy:)
(Before the sounding Ax so falls the Vine,
Whose tender branches round the Poplar twine.)   440
She chose her ruin, and resign'd her life,
In death undaunted as an *Indian* wife:
A rare example: but some souls we see
Grow hard, and stiffen with adversity:
Yet these by fortunes favours are undone,   445
Resolv'd into a baser form they run,
And bore the wind, but cannot bear the sun.
Let this be natures frailty or her fate,
Or *Isgrim*'s counsel, her new chosen mate;   * The Wolfe.
Still she's the fairest of the fallen crew,   450
No mother more indulgent but the true.

    Fierce to her foes, yet fears her force to try,
Because she wants innate auctority;
For how can she constrain them to obey
Who has herself cast off the lawfull sway?   455
Rebellion equals all, and those who toil
In common theft, will share the common spoil.
Let her produce the title and the right
Against her old superiours first to fight;
If she reform by Text, ev'n that's as plain   460
For her own Rebels to reform again.
As long as words a diff'rent sense will bear,
And each may be his own Interpreter,
Our ai'ry faith will no foundation find:
The word's a weathercock for ev'ry wind: 465
The *Bear*, the *Fox*, the *Wolfe*, by turns prevail,
The most in pow'r supplies the present gale.
The wretched *Panther* crys aloud for aid
To church and councils, whom she first betray'd;
No help from Fathers or traditions train,   470
Those ancient guides she taught us to disdain.
And by that scripture which she once abus'd

To Reformation, stands herself accus'd.
What bills for breach of laws can she prefer,
Expounding which she owns herself may err? 475
And, after all her winding ways are try'd,
If doubts arise she slips herself aside,
And leaves the private conscience for the guide.
If then that conscience set th' offender free,
It barrs her claim to church auctority. 480
How can she censure, or what crime pretend,
But Scripture may be constru'd to defend?
Ev'n those whom for rebellion she transmits
To civil pow'r, her doctrine first acquits;
Because no disobedience can ensue, 485
Where no submission to a Judge is due.
Each judging for himself, by her consent,
Whom thus absolv'd she sends to punishment.
Suppose the Magistrate revenge her cause,
'Tis onely for transgressing humane laws. 490
How answ'ring to its end a church is made,
Whose pow'r is but to counsell and persuade?
O solid rock, on which secure she stands!
Eternal house, not built with mortal hands!
Oh sure defence against th' infernal gate, 495
A patent during pleasure of the state!
 Thus is the *Panther* neither lov'd nor fear'd,
A mere mock Queen of a divided Herd;
Whom soon by lawfull pow'r she might controll,
Her self a part submitted to the whole. 500
Then, as the Moon who first receives the light
By which she makes our nether regions bright,
So might she shine, reflecting from afar
The rays she borrow'd from a better star:
Big with the beams which from her mother flow 505
And reigning o'er the rising tides below:
Now, mixing with a salvage croud, she goes
And meanly flatters her invet'rate foes.
Rul'd while she rules, and losing ev'ry hour
Her wretched remnants of precarious pow'r. 510
 One evening while the cooler shade she sought,
Revolving many a melancholy thought,

Alone she walk'd, and look'd around in vain,
With rufull visage for her vanish'd train:
None of her sylvan subjects made their court;   515
Levées and couchées pass'd without resort.

So hardly can Usurpers manage well
Those, whom they first instructed to rebell:
More liberty begets desire of more,
The hunger still encreases with the store.   520

Without respect they brush'd along the wood
Each in his clan, and fill'd with loathsome food
Ask'd no permission to the neighb'ring flood.

The *Panther* full of inward discontent
Since they wou'd goe, before 'em wisely went: 525
Supplying want of pow'r by drinking first,
As if she gave 'em leave to quench their thirst.

Among the rest, the *Hind*, with fearfull face
Beheld from far the common wat'ring place,
Nor durst approach; till with an awfull roar   530
The sovereign *Lyon* bad her fear no more.

Encourag'd thus she brought her younglings nigh,
Watching the motions of her Patron's eye,
And drank a sober draught; the rest amaz'd
Stood mutely still, and on the stranger gaz'd: 535
Survey'd her part by part, and sought to find
The ten-horn'd monster in the harmless *Hind*,
Such as the *Wolfe* and *Panther* had design'd.

They thought at first they dream'd, for 'twas offence
With them, to question certitude of sense,   540

Their guide in faith; but nearer when they drew,
And had the faultless object full in view,
Lord, how they all admir'd her heav'nly hiew!

Some, who before her fellowship disdain'd,
Scarce, and but scarce, from in-born rage restrain'd,   545
Now frisk'd about her, and old kindred feign'd.

Whether for love or int'rest, ev'ry sect
Of all the salvage nation shew'd respect:
The Vice-roy *Panther* could not awe the herd,
The more the company the less they fear'd.   550

The surly *Wolfe* with secret envy burst,
Yet cou'd not howl, the *Hind* had seen him first:
But what he durst not speak, the *Panther* durst.

    For when the herd suffis'd did late repair
To ferny heaths, and to their forest lare,   555
She made a mannerly excuse to stay,
Proff'ring the *Hind* to wait her half the way:
That since the Sky was clear, an hour of talk,
Might help her to beguile the tedious walk.
With much good-will the motion was embrac'd,   560
To chat awhile on their adventures pass'd:
Nor had the gratefull *Hind* so soon forgot
Her friend and fellow-suff'rer in the plot.
Yet wondring how of late she grew estrang'd,
Her forehead cloudy, and her count'nance chang'd,   565
She thought this hour th' occasion would present
To learn her secret cause of discontent,
Which, well she hop'd, might be with ease redress'd,
Consid'ring Her a well-bred civil beast,
And more a Gentlewoman than the rest.   570
After some common talk what rumours ran,
The Lady of the spotted-muff began.

THE HIND AND THE PANTHER

THE SECOND PART

DAME, said the *Panther*, times are mended well
Since late among the *Philistines* you fell,
The toils were pitch'd, a spacious tract of ground
With expert hunts-men was encompass'd round;
Th' Enclosure narrow'd; the sagacious pow'r   5
Of hounds, and death drew nearer ev'ry hour.
'Tis true, the younger *Lyon* scap'd the snare,
But all your priestly calves lay strugling there;
As sacrifices on their Altars laid;
While you their carefull mother wisely fled   10
Not trusting destiny to save your head.
For, what e'er promises you have apply'd
To your unfailing church, the surer side
Is four fair leggs in danger to provide.
And what e'er tales of *Peter*'s chair you tell,   15
Yet, saving reverence of the miracle,
The better luck was yours to 'scape so well.

   As I remember, said the sober *Hind*,
Those toils were for your own dear self design'd,
As well as me; and, with the self same throw,   20
To catch the quarry, and the vermin too,
(Forgive the sland'rous tongues that call'd you so.)
How e'er you take it now, the common cry
Then ran you down for your rank loyalty;
Besides, in Popery they thought you nurst,   25
(As evil tongues will ever speak the worst,)
Because some forms, and ceremonies some
You kept, and stood in the main question dumb.
Dumb you were born indeed, but thinking long
The *Test* it seems at last has loos'd your tongue.   30
And, to explain what your forefathers meant,
By real presence in the sacrament,

(After long fencing push'd, against a wall,)
Your *salvo* comes, that he's not there at all:
There chang'd your faith, and what may change may fall. } 35
Who can believe what varies every day,
Nor ever was, nor will be at a stay?
  Tortures may force the tongue untruths to tell,
And I ne'er own'd my self infallible,
Reply'd the *Panther*; grant such Presence were,   40
Yet in your sense I never own'd it there.
A real *vertue* we by faith receive,
And that we in the sacrament believe.
  Then said the *Hind*, as you the matter state
Not onely *Jesuits* can equivocate;   45
For *real*, as you now the word expound,
From solid substance dwindles to a sound.
Methinks an *Æsop*'s fable you repeat,
You know who took the shadow for the meat:
Your churches substance thus you change at will,   50
And yet retain your former figure still.
I freely grant you spoke to save your life,
For then you lay beneath the butcher's knife.
Long time you fought, redoubl'd batt'ry bore,
But, after all, against your self you swore;   55
Your former self, for ev'ry hour your form
Is chop'd and chang'd, like winds before a storm.
Thus fear and int'rest will prevail with some,
For all have not the gift of martyrdome.
  The *Panther* grin'd at this, and thus reply'd;   60
That men may err was never yet deny'd.
But, if that common principle be true,
The Cannon, Dame, is level'd full at you.
But, shunning long disputes, I fain wou'd see
That wond'rous wight infallibility.   65
Is he from heav'n this mighty champion come,
Or lodg'd below in subterranean *Rome*?
First, seat him somewhere, and derive his race,
Or else conclude that nothing has no place.
  Suppose (though I disown it) said the *Hind*,   70
The certain mansion were not yet assign'd,
The doubtfull residence no proof can bring

Against the plain existence of the thing.
Because *Philosophers* may disagree,
If sight b' emission or reception be,   75
Shall it be thence inferr'd, I do not see?
But you require an answer positive,
Which yet, when I demand, you dare not give,
For fallacies in Universals live.
I then affirm that this unfailing guide   80
In Pope and gen'ral councils must reside;
Both lawfull, both combin'd, what one decrees
By numerous votes, the other ratifies:
On this undoubted sense the church relies.
'Tis true, some Doctours in a scantier space,   85
I mean in each apart, contract the place.
Some, who to greater length extend the line,
The churches after acceptation join.
This last circumference appears too wide,
The church diffus'd is by the council ty'd;   90
As members by their representatives
Oblig'd to laws which Prince and Senate gives:
Thus some contract, and some enlarge the space;
In Pope and council who denies the place,
Assisted from above with God's unfailing grace?   95
Those Canons all the needfull points contain;
Their sense so obvious, and their words so plain,
That no disputes about the doubtfull Text
Have, hitherto, the lab'ring world perplex'd:
If any shou'd in after times appear,   100
New Councils must be call'd, to make the meaning clear.
Because in them the pow'r supreme resides;
And all the promises are to the guides.
This may be taught with sound and safe defence:
But mark how sandy is your own pretence,   105
Who setting Councils, Pope, and Church aside,
Are ev'ry man his own presuming guide.
The sacred books, you say, are full and plain,
And ev'ry needfull point of truth contain:
All who can read, Interpreters may be: 110
Thus though your sev'ral churches disagree,
Yet ev'ry Saint has to himself alone

The secret of this Philosophick stone.
These principles your jarring sects unite,
When diff'ring Doctours and disciples fight.   115
Though *Luther, Zuinglius, Calvin,* holy chiefs
Have made a battel Royal of beliefs;
Or like wild horses sev'ral ways have whirl'd
The tortur'd Text about the Christian World;
Each *Jehu* lashing on with furious force,   120
That *Turk* or *Jew* cou'd not have us'd it worse.
No matter what dissention leaders make
Where ev'ry private man may save a stake,
Rul'd by the Scripture and his own advice
Each has a blind by-path to Paradise;   125
Where driving in a circle slow or fast,
Opposing sects are sure to meet at last.
A wondrous charity you have in store
For all reform'd to pass the narrow door:
So much, that *Mahomet* had scarcely more.   130
For he, kind Prophet, was for damning none,
But *Christ* and *Moyses* were to save their own:
Himself was to secure his chosen race,
Though reason good for *Turks* to take the place,
And he allow'd to be the better man   135
In virtue of his holier *Alcoran.*
    True, said the *Panther,* I shall ne'er deny
My breth'ren may be sav'd as well as I:
Though *Huguenots* contemn our ordination,
Succession, ministerial vocation,   140
And *Luther,* more mistaking what he read,
Misjoins the sacred Body with the Bread;
Yet, *Lady,* still remember I maintain,
The Word in needfull points is onely plain.
    Needless or needfull I not now contend,   145
For still you have a loop-hole for a friend,
(Rejoyn'd the Matron) but the rule you lay
Has led whole flocks, and leads them still astray
In weighty points, and full damnation's way.
For did not *Arius* first, *Socinus* now,   150
The Son's eternal god-head disavow,
And did not these by Gospel Texts alone

Condemn our doctrine, and maintain their own?
Have not all hereticks the same pretence
To plead the Scriptures in their own defence?   155
How did the *Nicene* council then decide
That strong debate, was it by Scripture try'd?
No, sure to those the Rebel would not yield,
Squadrons of Texts he marshal'd in the field;
That was but civil war, an equal set,   160
Where Piles with piles, and eagles Eagles met.
With Texts point-blank and plain he fac'd the Foe:
And did not *Sathan* tempt our Saviour so?
The good old Bishops took a simpler way,
Each ask'd but what he heard his Father say,   165
Or how he was instructed in his youth,
And by traditions force upheld the truth.

   The *Panther* smil'd at this, and when, said she,
Were those first Councils disallow'd by me?
Or where did I at sure tradition strike,   170
Provided still it were Apostolick?

   Friend, said the *Hind*, you quit your former ground,
Where all your Faith you did on Scripture found;
Now 'tis tradition join'd with holy writ,
But thus your memory betrays your wit.   175

   No, said the *Panther*, for in that I view,
When your tradition's forg'd, and when 'tis true.
I set 'em by the rule, and as they square
Or deviate from undoubted doctrine there
This Oral fiction, that old Faith declare.   180

   (*Hind.*) The Council steer'd it seems a diff'rent course,
They try'd the Scripture by tradition's force;
But you tradition by the Scripture try;
Pursu'd, by Sects, from this to that you fly,
Nor dare on one foundation to rely.   185
The word is then depos'd, and in this view,
You rule the Scripture, not the Scripture you.
Thus said the *Dame*, and, smiling, thus pursu'd,
I see tradition then is disallow'd,
When not evinc'd by Scripture to be true,   190
And Scripture, as interpreted by you.
But here you tread upon unfaithfull ground;

Unless you cou'd infallibly expound.
Which you reject as odious Popery,
And throw that doctrine back with scorn on me.   195
Suppose we on things traditive divide,
And both appeal to Scripture to decide;
By various texts we both uphold our claim,
Nay, often ground our titles on the same:
After long labour lost, and times expence,   200
Both grant the words, and quarrel for the sense.
Thus all disputes for ever must depend;
For no dumb rule can controversies end.
Thus when you said tradition must be try'd
By Sacred Writ, whose sense your selves decide,   205
You said no more, but that your selves must be
The judges of the Scripture sense, not we.
Against our church tradition you declare
And yet your Clerks wou'd sit in *Moyses* chair:
At least 'tis prov'd against your argument,   210
The rule is far from plain, where all dissent.
   If not by Scriptures how can we be sure
(Reply'd the *Panther*) what tradition's pure?
For you may palm upon us new for old,
All, as they say, that glitters is not gold.   215
   How but by following her, reply'd the Dame,
To whom deriv'd from sire to son they came;
Where ev'ry age do's on another move,
And trusts no farther than the next above;
Where all the rounds like *Jacob*'s ladder rise,   220
The lowest hid in earth, the topmost in the skyes.
   Sternly the salvage did her answer mark,
Her glowing eye-balls glitt'ring in the dark,
And said but this, since lucre was your trade,
Succeeding times such dreadfull gaps have made   225
'Tis dangerous climbing: to your sons and you
I leave the ladder, and its omen too.
   (*Hind.*) The *Panther*'s breath was ever fam'd for sweet,
But from the *Wolfe* such wishes oft I meet:
You learn'd this language from the blatant beast,   230
Or rather did not speak, but were possess'd.
As for your answer 'tis but barely urg'd;

You must evince tradition to be forg'd;
Produce plain proofs; unblemish'd authours use
As ancient as those ages they accuse;   235
Till when 'tis not sufficient to defame:
An old possession stands, till Elder quitts the claim.
Then for our int'rest which is nam'd alone
To load with envy, we retort your own.
For when traditions in your faces fly,   240
Resolving not to yield, you must decry:
As when the cause goes hard, the guilty man
Excepts, and thins his jury all he can;
So when you stand of other aid bereft,
You to the twelve Apostles would be left.   245
Your friend the *Wolfe* did with more craft provide
To set those toys traditions quite aside:
And *Fathers* too, unless when reason spent
He cites 'em but sometimes for ornament.
But, Madam *Panther*, you, though more sincere,   250
Are not so wise as your Adulterer:
The private spirit is a better blind
Than all the dodging tricks your authours find.
For they, who left the Scripture to the crowd, ⎫
Each for his own peculiar judge allow'd;   ⎬   255
The way to please 'em was to make 'em proud. ⎭
Thus, with full sails, they ran upon the shelf;
Who cou'd suspect a couzenage from himself?
On his own reason safer 'tis to stand,
Than be deceiv'd and damn'd at second hand.   260
But you who *Fathers* and traditions take,
And garble some, and some you quite forsake,
Pretending church auctority to fix,
And yet some grains of private spirit mix,
Are like a *Mule* made up of diff'ring seed,   265
And that's the reason why you never breed;
At least not propagate your kind abroad,
For home-dissenters are by statutes aw'd.
And yet they grow upon you ev'ry day,   ⎫
While you (to speak the best) are at a stay, ⎬   270
For sects that are extremes, abhor a middle way. ⎭

Like tricks of state, to stop a raging flood,
Or mollify a mad-brain'd Senate's mood:
Of all expedients never one was good.
Well may they argue, (nor can you deny) 275
If we must fix on church auctority,
Best on the best, the fountain, not the flood,
That must be better still, if this be good.
Shall she command, who has herself rebell'd?
Is *Antichrist* by *Antichrist* expell'd? 280
Did we a lawfull tyranny displace,
To set aloft a bastard of the race?
Why all these wars to win the Book, if we
Must not interpret for our selves, but she?
Either be wholly slaves or wholly free. 285
For *purging* fires traditions must not fight;
But they must prove Episcopacy's right:
Thus those led horses are from service freed;
You never mount 'em but in time of need.
Like mercenary's, hir'd for home defence, 290
They will not serve against their native Prince.
Against domestick foes of *Hierarchy*
These are drawn forth, to make fanaticks fly,
But, when they see their countrey-men at hand,
Marching against 'em under church-command, 295
Straight they forsake their colours, and disband.
  Thus she, nor cou'd the *Panther* well enlarge
With weak defence against so strong a charge;
But said, for what did *Christ* his Word provide,
If still his church must want a living guide? 300
And if all saving doctrines are not there,
Or sacred Pen-men cou'd not make 'em clear,
From after ages we should hope in vain
For truths, which men inspir'd, cou'd not explain.
  Before the Word was written, said the *Hind*: 305
Our Saviour preach'd his Faith to humane kind;
From his Apostles the first age receiv'd
Eternal truth, and what they taught, believ'd.
Thus by tradition faith was planted first,
Succeeding flocks succeeding Pastours nurs'd. 310

This was the way our wise Redeemer chose,
(Who sure could all things for the best dispose,)
To fence his fold from their encroaching foes.
He cou'd have writ himself, but well foresaw
Th' event would be like that of *Moyses* law;   315
Some difference wou'd arise, some doubts remain,
Like those, which yet the jarring *Jews* maintain.
No written laws can be so plain, so pure,
But wit may gloss, and malice may obscure,
Not those indited by his first command,   320
A Prophet grav'd the text, an Angel held his hand.
Thus faith was e'er the written word appear'd,
And men believ'd, not what they read, but heard.
But since th' Apostles cou'd not be confin'd,
To these, or those, but severally design'd   325
Their large commission round the world to blow;
To spread their faith they spread their labours too.
Yet still their absent flock their pains did share,
They hearken'd still, for love produces care.
And as mistakes arose, or discords fell,   330
Or bold seducers taught 'em to rebell,
As charity grew cold, or faction hot,
Or long neglect, their lessons had forgot,
For all their wants they wisely did provide,
And preaching by Epistles was supply'd: 335
So great Physicians cannot all attend,
But some they visit, and to some they send.
Yet all those letters were not writ to all;
Nor first intended, but occasional,
Their absent sermons; nor if they contain   340
All needfull doctrines, are those doctrines plain.
Clearness by frequent preaching must be wrought,
They writ but seldome, but they daily taught.
And what one Saint has said of holy *Paul*,
He darkly writ, is true apply'd to all.   345
For this obscurity could heav'n provide
More prudently than by a living guide,
As doubts arose, the difference to decide?
A guide was therefore needfull, therefore made,
And, if appointed, sure to be obey'd.   350

Thus, with due rev'rence, to th' Apostles writ,
By which my sons are taught, to which, submit;
I think, those truths their sacred works contain,
The church alone can certainly explain,
That following ages, leaning on the past,   355
May rest upon the Primitive at last.
Nor wou'd I thence the word no rule infer,
But none without the church interpreter.
Because, as I have urg'd before, 'tis mute,
And is it self the subject of dispute.   360
But what th' Apostles their successours taught,
They to the next, from them to us is brought,
Th' undoubted sense which is in scripture sought.
From hence the church is arm'd, when errours rise,
To stop their entrance, and prevent surprise;   365
And safe entrench'd within, her foes without defies.
By these all festring sores her councils heal,
Which time or has disclos'd, or shall reveal,
For discord cannot end without a last appeal.
Nor can a council national decide   370
But with subordination to her Guide:
(I wish the cause were on that issue try'd.)
Much less the scripture; for suppose debate
Betwixt pretenders to a fair estate,
Bequeath'd by some Legator's last intent;   375
(Such is our dying Saviour's Testament:)
The will is prov'd, is open'd, and is read;
The doubtfull heirs their diff'ring titles plead:
All vouch the words their int'rest to maintain,
And each pretends by those his cause is plain.   380
Shall then the testament award the right?
No, that's the *Hungary* for which they fight;
The field of battel, subject of debate;
The thing contended for, the fair estate.
The sense is intricate, 'tis onely clear   385
What vowels and what consonants are there.
Therefore 'tis plain, its meaning must be try'd
Before some judge appointed to decide.
    Suppose, (the fair Apostate said,) I grant,
The faithfull flock some living guide should want,   390

Your arguments an endless chase persue:
Produce this vaunted Leader to our view,
This mighty *Moyses* of the chosen crew.

    The Dame, who saw her fainting foe retir'd,
With force renew'd, to victory aspir'd;   395
(And looking upward to her kindred sky,
As once our Saviour own'd his Deity,
Pronounc'd his words—*she whom ye seek am I.*)
Nor less amaz'd this voice the *Panther* heard,
Than were those *Jews* to hear a god declar'd.   400
Then thus the matron modestly renew'd:
Let all your prophets and their sects be view'd,
And see to which of 'em your selves think fit
The conduct of your conscience to submit:
Each Proselyte wou'd vote his Doctor best,   405
With absolute exclusion to the rest:
Thus wou'd your *Polish* Diet disagree,
And end as it began in Anarchy:
Your self the fairest for election stand,
Because you seem crown-gen'ral of the land;   410
But soon against your superstitious lawn
Some Presbyterian Sabre wou'd be drawn:
In your establish'd laws of sov'raignty
The rest some fundamental flaw wou'd see,
And call Rebellion gospel-liberty.   415
To church-decrees your articles require
Submission modify'd, if not entire;
Homage deny'd, to censures you proceed;
But when *Curtana* will not doe the deed,
You lay that pointless clergy-weapon by,   420
And to the laws, your sword of justice, fly.
Now this your sects the more unkindly take
(Those prying varlets hit the blots you make)
Because some ancient friends of yours declare,
Your onely rule of faith the Scriptures are,   425
Interpreted by men of judgment sound,
Which ev'ry sect will for themselves expound:
Nor think less rev'rence to their doctours due
For sound interpretation, than to you.

401 modestly, *B C*: modesty, *A*

If then, by able heads, are understood　　　　　　　430
Your brother prophets, who reform'd abroad,
Those able heads expound a wiser way,
That their own sheep their shepherd shou'd obey.

But if you mean your selves are onely sound,
That doctrine turns the reformation round,　　　　435
And all the rest are false reformers found.

Because in sundry points you stand alone,
Not in communion join'd with any one;
And therefore must be all the church, or none.

Then, till you have agreed whose judge is best,　440
Against this forc'd submission they protest:
While *sound* and *sound* a diff'rent sense explains
Both play at hard-head till they break their brains:
And from their chairs each others force defy,
While unregarded thunders vainly fly.　　　　　445
I pass the rest, because your church alone
Of all usurpers best cou'd fill the throne.

But neither you, nor any sect beside
For this high office can be qualify'd,
With necessary gifts requir'd in such a guide.　　450

For that which must direct the whole, must be
Bound in one bond of faith and unity:
But all your sev'ral churches disagree.

The *Consubstantiating* church and Priest
Refuse communion to the *Calvinist*;　　　　　455
The *French* reform'd, from preaching you restrain,
Because you judge their ordination vain;
And so they judge of yours, but Donors must ordain.

In short, in doctrine, or in discipline
Not one reform'd, can with another join:　　　　460
But all from each, as from damnation fly;
No union, they pretend, but in *Non-Popery*.

Nor shou'd their members in a synod meet,
Cou'd any church presume to mount the seat
Above the rest, their discords to decide;　　　　465
None wou'd obey, but each wou'd be the guide:
And face to face dissentions wou'd encrease;
For onely distance now preserves the peace.

All in their turns accusers, and accus'd:
Babel was never half so much confus'd.   470
What one can plead, the rest can plead as well;
For amongst equals lies no last appeal,
And all confess themselves are fallible.
Now since you grant some necessary guide,
All who can err are justly laid aside: 475
Because a trust so sacred to confer
Shows want of such a sure interpreter:
And how can he be needfull who can err?
Then, granting that unerring guide we want,
That such there is you stand oblig'd to grant: 480
Our Saviour else were wanting to supply
Our needs, and obviate that necessity.
It then remains that church can onely be
The guide, which owns unfailing certainty;
Or else you slip your hold, and change your side,   485
Relapsing from a necessary guide.
But this annex'd condition of the crown,
Immunity from errours, you disown,
Here then you shrink, and lay your weak pretensions down.
For petty royalties you raise debate;   490
But this unfailing universal state
You shun; nor dare succeed to such a glorious weight.
And for that cause those promises detest
With which our Saviour did his Church invest:
But strive t' evade, and fear to find 'em true,   495
As conscious they were never meant to you:
All which the mother church asserts her own,
And with unrivall'd claim ascends the throne.
So when of old th' Almighty father sate
In Council, to redeem our ruin'd state,   500
Millions of millions at a distance round,
Silent the sacred Consistory crown'd,
To hear what mercy mixt with justice cou'd propound.
All prompt with eager pity, to fulfill
The full extent of their Creatour's will: 505
But when the stern conditions were declar'd,
A mournfull whisper through the host was heard,
And the whole hierarchy with heads hung down

Submissively declin'd the pondrous proffer'd crown.
Then, not till then, th' eternal Son from high   510
Rose in the strength of all the Deity;
Stood forth t' accept the terms, and underwent
A weight which all the frame of heav'n had bent,
Nor he Himself cou'd bear, but as omnipotent.

Now, to remove the least remaining doubt,   515
That ev'n the blear-ey'd sects may find her out,
Behold what heav'nly rays adorn her brows,
What from his Wardrobe her belov'd allows
To deck the wedding-day of his unspotted spouse.

Behold what marks of majesty she brings;   520
Richer than ancient heirs of Eastern kings:
Her right hand holds the sceptre and the keys,
To shew whom she commands, and who obeys:
With these to bind, or set the sinner free,
With that t' assert spiritual Royalty.   525

   One in herself not rent by schism, but sound,   *Marks of*
Entire, one solid shining Diamond,   *the Catho-*
Not sparkles shatter'd into sects like you,   *lick Church*
One is the church, and must be to be true: *from the*
One central principle of unity.   *Nicene*
                                                      Creed.
As undivided, so from errours free,   530
As one in faith, so one in sanctity.

Thus she, and none but she, th' insulting rage
Of Hereticks oppos'd from age to age:
Still when the Gyant-brood invades her throne   535
She stoops from heav'n, and meets 'em half way down,
And with paternal thunder vindicates her crown.
But like *Ægyptian* Sorcerers you stand,
And vainly lift aloft your magick wand,
To sweep away the swarms of vermin from the land: 540
You cou'd like them, with like infernal force
Produce the plague, but not arrest the course.
But when the boils and botches, with disgrace
And publick scandal sat upon the face,
Themselves attack'd, the *Magi* strove no more,   545
They saw God's finger, and their fate deplore;
Themselves they cou'd not cure of the dishonest sore.

Thus one, thus pure, behold her largely spread
Like the fair ocean from her mother bed;
From East to West triumphantly she rides,   550
All shoars are water'd by her wealthy Tides.

The Gospel-sound diffus'd from Pole to Pole,
Where winds can carry, and where waves can roll.
The self same doctrine of the Sacred page
Convey'd to ev'ry clime in ev'ry age.   555

Here let my sorrow give my satyr place,
To raise new blushes on my *British* race;
Our sayling ships like common shoars we use,
And through our distant colonies diffuse
The draughts of Dungeons, and the stench of stews.   560
Whom, when their home-bred honesty is lost,
We disembogue on some far *Indian* coast:
Thieves, Pandars, Palliards, sins of ev'ry sort,
Those are the manufactures we export;
And these the Missionaires our zeal has made: 565
For, with my countrey's pardon be it said,
Religion is the least of all our trade.

Yet some improve their traffick more than we,
For they on gain, their onely God, rely:
And set a publick price on piety.   570
Industrious of the needle and the chart
They run full sail to their *Japponian* Mart:
Prevention fear, and prodigal of fame
Sell all of Christian to the very name;
Nor leave enough of that, to hide their naked shame.   575

Thus, of three marks which in the Creed we view,
Not one of all can be apply'd to you:
Much less the fourth; in vain alas you seek
Th' ambitious title of Apostolick:
God-like descent! 'tis well your bloud can be   580
Prov'd noble, in the third or fourth degree:
For all of ancient that you had before
(I mean what is not borrow'd from our store)
Was Errour fulminated o'er and o'er.
Old Heresies condemn'd in ages past,   585
By care and time recover'd from the blast.

552 Gospel-sound *B C*: Golspel's-sound *A*

'Tis said with ease, but never can be prov'd,
The church her old foundations has remov'd,
And built new doctrines on unstable sands:
Judge that ye winds and rains; you prov'd her, yet she stands.   590
Those ancient doctrines charg'd on her for new,
Shew when, and how, and from what hands they grew.
We claim no pow'r when Heresies grow bold
To coin new faith, but still declare the old.
How else cou'd that obscene disease be purg'd   595
When controverted texts are vainly urg'd?
To prove tradition new, there's somewhat more
Requir'd, than saying, 'twas not us'd before.
Those monumental arms are never stirr'd
Till Schism or Heresie call down *Goliah*'s sword.   600
    Thus, what you call corruptions, are in truth,
The first plantations of the gospel's youth,
Old standard faith: but cast your eyes again
And view those errours which new sects maintain
Or which of old disturb'd the churches peacefull reign,   605
And we can point each period of the time,
When they began, and who begot the crime;
Can calculate how long th' eclipse endur'd,
Who interpos'd, what digits were obscur'd:
Of all which are already pass'd away,   610
We know the rise, the progress and decay.
    Despair at our foundations then to strike
Till you can prove your faith Apostolick;
A limpid stream drawn from the native source;
Succession lawfull in a lineal course.   615
Prove any church oppos'd to this our head,
So one, so pure, so unconfin'dly spread,
Under one chief of the spiritual state,
The members all combin'd, and all subordinate.
Shew such a seamless coat, from schism so free,   620
In no communion join'd with heresie:
If such a one you find, let truth prevail:
Till when your weights will in the balance fail:
A church unprincipl'd kicks up the scale.
    But if you cannot think, (nor sure you can   625
Suppose in God what were unjust in man,)

That he, the fountain of eternal grace,
Should suffer falshood for so long a space
To banish truth, and to usurp her place:
That seav'n successive ages should be lost   630
And preach damnation at their proper cost;
That all your erring ancestours should dye,
Drown'd in th' Abyss of deep Idolatry;
If piety forbid such thoughts to rise,
Awake and open your unwilling eyes: 635
God has left nothing for each age undone
From this to that wherein he sent his Son:
Then think but well of him, and half your work is done.

  See how his church adorn'd with ev'ry grace
With open arms, a kind forgiving face,   640
Stands ready to prevent her long lost sons embrace.
Not more did *Joseph* o'er his brethren weep,
Nor less himself cou'd from discovery keep,
When in the croud of suppliants they were seen,
And in their crew his best beloved *Benjamin*.   645
That pious *Joseph* in the church behold,
To feed your famine, and refuse your gold;
The *Joseph* you exil'd, the *Joseph* whom you sold.

  Thus, while with heav'nly charity she spoke,
A streaming blaze the silent shadows broke:
Shot from the skyes a chearfull azure light;   650
The birds obscene to forests wing'd their flight,
And gaping graves receiv'd the wandring guilty spright.

  Such were the pleasing triumphs of the sky
For *James* his late nocturnal victory;   655
The pledge of his Almighty patron's love,
The fire-works which his angel made above.
I saw my self the lambent easie light
Guild the brown horrour and dispell the night;
The messenger with speed the tidings bore,   660
News which three lab'ring nations did restore,
But heav'ns own *Nuncius* was arriv'd before.

  By this, the *Hind* had reach'd her lonely cell;
And vapours rose, and dews unwholsome fell.

*The re-
nunciation
of the Bene-
dictines to
the Abby
Lands.*

*Poëta
loquitur.*

When she, by frequent observation wise,
As one who long on heav'n had fix'd her eyes,
Discern'd a change of weather in the skyes. 665
The Western borders were with crimson spread,
The moon descending look'd all flaming red,
She thought good manners bound her to invite 670
The stranger Dame to be her guest that night.
'Tis true, course dyet and a short repast,
(She said) were weak inducements to the tast
Of one so nicely bred, and so unus'd to fast.
But what plain fare her cottage cou'd afford, 675
A hearty welcome at a homely board
Was freely hers; and, to supply the rest,
An honest meaning and an open breast.
Last, with content of mind, the poor man's Wealth;
A grace-cup to their common Patron's health. 680
This she desir'd her to accept and stay,
For fear she might be wilder'd in her way,
Because she wanted an unerring guide;
And then the dew-drops on her silken hide
Her tender constitution did declare, 685
Too Lady-like a long fatigue to bear,
And rough inclemencies of raw nocturnal air.
But most she fear'd that travelling so late,
Some evil minded beasts might lye in wait;
And without witness wreak their hidden hate. 690
    The *Panther*, though she lent a list'ning ear,
Had more of *Lyon* in her than to fear:
Yet wisely weighing, since she had to deal
With many foes, their numbers might prevail,
Return'd her all the thanks she cou'd afford; 695
And took her friendly hostess at her word.
Who ent'ring first her lowly roof, (a shed
With hoary moss and winding Ivy spread,
Honest enough to hide an humble Hermit's head,)
Thus graciously bespoke her welcome guest: 700
So might these walls, with your fair presence blest
Become your dwelling-place of everlasting rest,
Not for a night, or quick revolving year,
Welcome an owner, not a sojourner.

This peacefull Seat my poverty secures,   705
War seldom enters but where wealth allures;
Nor yet despise it, for this poor aboad
Has oft receiv'd, and yet receives a god;
A god victorious of the Stygian race
Here laid his sacred limbs, and sanctified the place.   710
This mean retreat did mighty *Pan* contain;
Be emulous of him, and pomp disdain,
And dare not to debase your soul to gain.

    The silent stranger stood amaz'd to see
Contempt of wealth, and wilfull poverty: 715
And, though ill habits are not soon controll'd,
A while suspended her desire of gold.
But civily drew in her sharpn'd paws,
Not violating hospitable laws,
And pacify'd her tail, and lick'd her frothy jaws.   720
    The *Hind* did first her country Cates provide;
Then couch'd her self securely by her side.

THE HIND AND THE PANTHER

THE THIRD PART

MUCH malice mingl'd with a little wit
Perhaps may censure this mysterious writ,
Because the Muse has peopl'd *Caledon*
With *Panthers*, *Bears*, and *Wolves*, and Beasts unknown,
As if we were not stock'd with monsters of our own.   5
Let *Æsop* answer, who has set to view,
Such kinds as *Greece* and *Phrygia* never knew;
And mother *Hubbard* in her homely dress
Has sharply blam'd a *British Lioness*,
That *Queen*, whose feast the factious rabble keep,   10
Expos'd obscenely naked and a-sleep.
Led by those great examples, may not I
The wanted organs of their words supply?
If men transact like brutes 'tis equal then
For brutes to claim the privilege of men.   15
    Others our *Hind* of folly will endite,
To entertain a dang'rous guest by night.

Let those remember that she cannot dye
Till rolling time is lost in round eternity;
Nor need she fear the *Panther*, though untam'd,   20
Because the *Lyon's* peace was now proclam'd;
The wary salvage would not give offence,
To forfeit the protection of her *Prince*;
But watch'd the time her vengeance to compleat,
When all her furry sons in frequent Senate met.   25
Mean while she quench'd her fury at the floud,
And with a Lenten sallad cool'd her bloud.
Their commons, though but course, were nothing scant,
Nor did their minds an equal banquet want.

    For now the *Hind*, whose noble nature strove   30
T' express her plain simplicity of love,
Did all the honours of her house so well,
No sharp debates disturb'd the friendly meal.
She turn'd the talk, avoiding that extreme,
To common dangers past, a sadly pleasing theam;   35
Remembring ev'ry storm which toss'd the state,
When both were objects of the publick hate,
And drop'd a tear betwixt for her own childrens fate.

    Nor fail'd she then a full review to make
Of what the *Panther* suffer'd for her sake.   40
Her lost esteem, her truth, her loyal care,
Her faith unshaken to an exil'd Heir,
Her strength t' endure, her courage to defy;
Her choice of honourable infamy.
On these prolixly thankfull, she enlarg'd,   45
Then with acknowledgments herself she charg'd:
For friendship of it self, an holy tye,
Is made more sacred by adversity.
Now should they part, malicious tongues wou'd say,
They met like chance companions on the way,   50
Whom mutual fear of robbers had possess'd;
While danger lasted, kindness was profess'd;
But that once o'er, the short-liv'd union ends:
The road divides, and there divide the friends.

    The *Panther* nodded when her speech was done,   55
And thank'd her coldly in a hollow tone.
But said her gratitude had gone too far

For common offices of Christian care.
If to the lawfull Heir she had been true,
She paid but *Cæsar* what was *Cæsar*'s due.   60
I might, she added, with like praise describe
Your suff'ring sons, and so return your bribe;
But incense from my hands is poorly priz'd,
For gifts are scorn'd where givers are despis'd.
I serv'd a turn, and then was cast away;   65
You, like the gawdy fly, your wings display,
And sip the sweets, and bask in your Great *Patron*'s day.
   This heard, the *Matron* was not slow to find
What sort of malady had seiz'd her mind;
Disdain, with gnawing envy, fell despight,   70
And canker'd malice stood in open sight.
Ambition, int'rest, pride without controul,
And jealousie, the jaundice of the soul;
Revenge, the bloudy minister of ill,
With all the lean tormenters of the will.   75
'Twas easie now to guess from whence arose
Her new made union with her ancient foes,
Her forc'd civilities, her faint embrace,
Affected kindness with an alter'd face:
Yet durst she not too deeply probe the wound,   80
As hoping still the nobler parts were sound;
But strove with Anodynes t' asswage the smart,
And mildly thus her med'cine did impart.
   Complaints of Lovers help to ease their pain,
It shows a Rest of kindness to complain,   85
A friendship loth to quit its former hold,
And conscious merit may be justly bold.
But much more just your jealousie would show,
If others good were injury to you:
Witness ye heav'ns how I rejoice to see   90
Rewarded worth, and rising loyalty.
Your Warrier Offspring that upheld the crown,
The scarlet honours of your peacefull gown,
Are the most pleasing objects I can find,
Charms to my sight, and cordials to my mind: 95
When vertue spoomes before a prosp'rous gale
My heaving wishes help to fill the sail,

And if my pray'rs for all the brave were heard,
Cæsar should still have such, and such should still reward.
    The labour'd earth your pains have sow'd and till'd: 100
'Tis just you reap the product of the field.
Yours be the harvest, 'tis the beggars gain
To glean the fallings of the loaded wain.
Such scatter'd ears as are not worth your care,
Your charity for alms may safely spare,   105
And alms are but the vehicles of pray'r.
My daily bread is litt'rally implor'd,
I have no barns nor granaries to hoard;
If *Cæsar* to his own his hand extends,
Say which of yours his charity offends: 110
You know he largely gives to more than are his friends.
Are you defrauded when he feeds the poor?
Our mite decreases nothing of your store;
I am but few, and by your fare you see
My crying sins are not of luxury.   115
Some juster motive sure your mind withdraws,
And makes you break our friendships holy laws,
For barefac'd envy is too base a cause.
    Show more occasion for your discontent,
Your love, the *Wolf,* wou'd help you to invent,   120
Some *German* quarrel, or, as times go now,
Some *French,* where force is uppermost, will doe.
When at the fountains head, as merit ought
To claim the place, you take a swilling draught,
How easie 'tis an envious eye to throw,   125
And tax the sheep for troubling streams below,
Or call her, (when no farther cause you find,)
An enemy profess'd of all your kind.
But then, perhaps, the wicked World wou'd think,
The *Wolf* design'd to eat as well as drink.   130
    This last allusion gaul'd the *Panther* more,
Because indeed it rubb'd upon the sore.
Yet seem'd she not to winch, though shrewdly pain'd:
But thus her Passive character maintain'd.
    I never grudg'd, whate're my foes report,   135
Your flaunting fortune in the *Lyon*'s court.
You have your day, or you are much bely'd,

But I am always on the suff'ring side:
You know my doctrine, and I need not say
I will not, but I cannot disobey.   140
On this firm principle I ever stood:
He of my sons who fails to make it good,
By one rebellious act renounces to my bloud.

  Ah, said the *Hind*, how many sons have you
Who call you mother, whom you never knew!   145
But most of them who that relation plead
Are such ungratious youths as wish you dead.
They gape at rich revenues which you hold,
And fain would nible at your grandame gold;
Enquire into your years, and laugh to find   150
Your crazy temper shews you much declin'd.
Were you not dim, and doted, you might see
A pack of cheats that claim a pedigree,
No more of kin to you, than you to me.
Do you not know, that for a little coin,   155
Heralds can foist a name into the line;
They ask you blessing but for what you have,
But once possess'd of what with care you save,
The wanton boyes wou'd piss upon your grave.

  Your sons of Latitude that court your grace,   160
Though most resembling you in form and face,
Are far the worst of your pretended race.
And, but I blush your honesty to blot,
Pray god you prove 'em lawfully begot:
For, in some *Popish* libells I have read,   165
The *Wolf* has been too busie in your bed.
At least their hinder parts, the belly piece,
The paunch, and all that *Scorpio* claims are his.
Their malice too a sore suspicion brings;
For though they dare not bark, they snarl at kings: 170
Nor blame 'em for intruding in your line,
Fat Bishopricks are still of right divine.

  Think you your new *French* Proselytes are come
To starve abroad, because they starv'd at home?
Your benefices twinckl'd from afar,   175
They found the new *Messiah* by the star:
Those *Swisses* fight on any side for pay,

And 'tis the living that conforms, not they.
Mark with what management their tribes divide,
Some stick to you, and some to t'other side,   180
That many churches may for many mouths provide.
More vacant pulpits wou'd more converts make,
All wou'd have latitude enough to take;
The rest unbenefic'd, your sects maintain:
For ordinations without cures are vain,   185
And chamber practice is a silent gain.
Your sons of breadth at home, are much like these,
Their soft and yielding metals run with ease,
They melt, and take the figure of the mould:
But harden, and preserve it best in gold.   190
    Your *Delphick* Sword, the *Panther* then reply'd,
Is double edg'd, and cuts on either side.
Some sons of mine who bear upon their shield,
Three steeples Argent in a sable field,
Have sharply tax'd your converts, who unfed   195
Have follow'd you for miracles of bread;
Such who themselves of no religion are,
Allur'd with gain, for any will declare.
Bare lyes with bold assertions they can face,
But dint of argument is out of place.   200
The grim Logician puts 'em in a fright,
'Tis easier far to flourish than to fight.
Thus our eighth *Henry*'s marriage they defame;
They say the schism of beds began the game,
Devorcing from the *Church* to wed the Dame: 205
Though largely prov'd, and by himself profess'd
That conscience, conscience wou'd not let him rest,
I mean, not till possess'd of her he lov'd,
And old, uncharming *Catherine* was remov'd.
For sundry years before did he complain,   210
And told his ghostly Confessour his pain.
With the same impudence, without a ground,
They say, that look the reformation round,
No *Treatise of Humility* is found.
But if none were, the Gospel does not want,   215
Our *Saviour* preach'd it, and I hope you grant,
The Sermon in the mount was *Protestant*:

No doubt, reply'd the *Hind*, as sure as all
The writings of Saint *Peter* and Saint *Paul*.
On that decision let it stand or fall.   220
Now for my converts, who you say unfed
Have follow'd me for miracles of bread,
Iudge not by hear-say, but observe at least,
If since their change, their loaves have been increast.
The *Lyon* buyes no Converts, if he did,   225
Beasts wou'd be sold as fast as he cou'd bid.
Tax those of int'rest who conform for gain,
Or stay the market of another reign.
Your broad-way sons wou'd never be too nice
To close with *Calvin*, if he paid their price;   230
But rais'd three steeples high'r, wou'd change their note,
And quit the Cassock for the Canting-coat.
Now, if you damn this censure, as too bold,
Judge by your selves, and think not others sold.

   Mean-time my sons accus'd, by fames report   235
Pay small attendance at the *Lyon*'s court,
Nor rise with early crowds, nor flatter late,
(For silently they beg who daily wait.)
Preferment is bestow'd that comes unsought,
Attendance is a bribe, and then 'tis bought.   240
How they shou'd speed, their fortune is untry'd,
For not to ask, is not to be deny'd.
For what they have, their *God* and *King* they bless,
And hope they shou'd not murmur, had they less.
But, if reduc'd subsistence to implore,   245
In common prudence they wou'd pass your door;
Unpitty'd *Hudibrass*, your Champion friend,
Has shown how far your charities extend.
This lasting verse shall on his tomb be read,
He sham'd you living, and upbraids you dead.   250

   With odious *Atheist* names you load your foes,
Your lib'ral *Clergy* why did I expose?
It never fails in charities like those.
In climes where true religion is profess'd,
That imputation were no laughing jest.   255
But *Imprimatur*, with a Chaplain's name,
Is here sufficient licence to defame.

What wonder is't that black detraction thrives,
The Homicide of names is less than lives;
And yet the perjur'd murtherer survives.   260
   This said, she paus'd a little, and suppress'd
The boiling indignation of her breast;
She knew the vertue of her blade, nor wou'd
Pollute her satyr with ignoble bloud:
Her panting foes she saw before her lye,   265
And back she drew the shining weapon dry:
So when the gen'rous *Lyon* has in sight
His equal match, he rouses for the fight;
But when his foe lyes prostrate on the plain,
He sheaths his paws, uncurls his angry mane;   270
And, pleas'd with bloudless honours of the day,
Walks over, and disdains th' inglorious Prey.
So *JAMES*, if great with less we may compare,
Arrests his rowling thunder-bolts in air;
And grants ungratefull friends a lengthn'd space,   275
T' implore the remnants of long suff'ring grace.
   This breathing-time the *Matron* took; and then,
Resum'd the thrid of her discourse agen.
Be vengeance wholly left to pow'rs divine,
And let heav'n judge betwixt your sons and mine: 280
If joyes hereafter must be purchas'd here
With loss of all that mortals hold so dear,
Then welcome infamy and publick shame,
And, last, a long farwell to worldly fame.
'Tis said with ease, but oh, how hardly try'd   285
By haughty souls to humane honour ty'd!
O sharp convulsive pangs of agonizing pride!
Down then thou rebell, never more to rise,
And what thou didst, and do'st so dearly prize,
That fame, that darling fame, make that thy sacrifice.   290
'Tis nothing thou hast giv'n, then add thy tears
For a long race of unrepenting years:
'Tis nothing yet; yet all thou hast to give,
Then add those *may-be* years thou hast to live.
Yet nothing still: then poor, and naked come,   295
Thy father will receive his unthrift home,
And thy blest Saviour's bloud discharge the mighty sum.

Thus (she pursu'd) I discipline a son
Whose uncheck'd fury to revenge wou'd run:
He champs the bit, impatient of his loss,   300
And starts a-side, and flounders at the cross.
Instruct him better, gracious God, to know,
As thine is vengeance, so forgiveness too.
That suff'ring from ill tongues he bears no more
Than what his Sovereign bears, and what his Saviour bore.   305
    It now remains for you to school your child,
And ask why *God*'s anointed he revil'd;
A *King* and *Princess* dead! did *Shimei* worse?
The curser's punishment should fright the curse:
Your son was warn'd, and wisely gave it o're,   310
But he who councell'd him, has paid the score:
The heavy malice cou'd no higher tend,
But wo to him on whom the weights descend:
So to permitted ills the *Dæmon* flyes:
His rage is aim'd at him who rules the skyes;   315
Constrain'd to quit his cause, no succour found,
The foe discharges ev'ry Tyre around,
In clouds of smoke abandoning the fight,
But his own thundring peals proclaim his flight.

    In *Henry*'s change his charge as ill succeeds,   320
To that long story little answer needs,
Confront but *Henry*'s words with *Henry*'s deeds.
Were space allow'd, with ease it might be prov'd,
What springs his blessed reformation mov'd.
The dire effects appear'd in open sight,   325
Which from the cause, he calls a distant flight,
And yet no larger leap than from the sun to light.
    Now last your sons a double *Pæan* sound,
A Treatise of Humility is found.
'Tis found, but better had it ne'er been sought   330
Than thus in Protestant procession brought.
The fam'd original through *Spain* is known,
Rodriguez work, my celebrated son,
Which yours, by ill-translating made his own,
Conceal'd its authour, and usurp'd the name,   335
The basest and ignoblest theft of fame.
My Altars kindl'd first that living coal,

Restore, or practice better what you stole:
That vertue could this humble verse inspire,
'Tis all the restitution I require.   340

   Glad was the *Panther* that the charge was clos'd,
And none of all her fav'rite sons expos'd.
For laws of arms permit each injur'd man,
To make himself a saver where he can.
Perhaps the plunder'd merchant cannot tell   345
The names of Pirates in whose hands he fell:
But at the den of thieves he justly flies,
And ev'ry *Algerine* is lawfull prize.
No private person in the foes estate
Can plead exemption from the publick fate.   350
Yet Christian laws allow not such redress;
Then let the greater supersede the less.
But let th' Abbettors of the *Panther*'s crime
Learn to make fairer wars another time.
Some characters may sure be found to write   355
Among her sons, for 'tis no common sight
A spotted Dam, and all her offspring white.

   The *Salvage*, though she saw her plea controll'd,
Yet wou'd not wholly seem to quit her hold,
But offer'd fairly to compound the strife;   360
And judge conversion by the convert's life.
'Tis true, she said, I think it somewhat strange
So few shou'd follow profitable change:
For present joys are more to flesh and bloud,
Than a dull prospect of a distant good.   365
'Twas well alluded by a son of mine,
(I hope to quote him is not to purloin.)
Two magnets, heav'n and earth, allure to bliss,
The larger loadstone that, the nearer this:
The weak attraction of the greater fails,   370
We nodd a-while, but neighbourhood prevails:
But when the greater proves the nearer too,
I wonder more your converts come so slow.
Methinks in those who firm with me remain,
It shows a nobler principle than gain.   375

   Your inf'rence wou'd be strong (the *Hind* reply'd)
If yours were in effect the suff'ring side:

Your clergy sons their own in peace possess,
Nor are their prospects in reversion less.
My Proselytes are struck with awfull dread,   380
Your bloudy Comet-laws hang blazing o're their head.
The respite they enjoy but onely lent,
The best they have to hope, protracted punishment.
Be judge your self, if int'rest may prevail,
Which motives, yours or mine, will turn the scale.   385
While pride and pomp allure, and plenteous ease,
That is, till man's predominant passions cease, }
Admire no longer at my slow encrease.

    By education most have been misled,
So they believe, because they so were bred.   390
The *Priest* continues what the nurse began,
And thus the child imposes on the man.
The rest I nam'd before, nor need repeat:
But int'rest is the most prevailing cheat,
The sly seducer both of age and youth;   395
They study that, and think they study truth:
When int'rest fortifies an argument
Weak reason serves to gain the wills assent; }
For souls already warp'd receive an easie bent.

    Add long prescription of establish'd laws,   400
And picque of honour to maintain a cause,
And shame of change, and fear of future ill,
And Zeal, the blind conductor of the will;
And chief among the still mistaking crowd,
The fame of teachers obstinate and proud, }   405
And more than all, the private Judge allow'd.
Disdain of Fathers which the daunce began,
And last, uncertain who's the narrower span, }
The clown unread, and half-read gentleman.

    To this the *Panther*, with a scornfull smile: 410
Yet still you travail with unwearied toil,
And range around the realm without controll
Among my sons, for Proselytes to prole, }
And here and there you snap some silly soul.
You hinted fears of future change in state,   415
Pray heav'n you did not prophesie your fate;

Perhaps you think your time of triumph near,
But may mistake the season of the year;
The *Swallows* fortune gives you cause to fear.

    For charity (reply'd the *Matron*) tell   420
What sad mischance those pretty birds befell.

    Nay, no mischance, (the salvage Dame reply'd)
But want of wit in their unerring guide,
And eager haste, and gaudy hopes, and giddy pride.
Yet, wishing timely warning may prevail,   425
Make you the moral, and I'll tell the tale.

    The *Swallow*, privileg'd above the rest
Of all the birds, as man's familiar Guest,
Pursues the Sun in summer brisk and bold,
But wisely shuns the persecuting cold: 430
Is well to chancels and to chimneys known,
Though 'tis not thought she feeds on smoak alone.
From hence she has been held of heav'nly line,
Endu'd with particles of soul divine.
This merry Chorister had long possess'd   435
Her summer seat, and feather'd well her nest:
Till frowning skys began to change their chear
And time turn'd up the wrong side of the year;
The shedding trees began the ground to strow
With yellow leaves, and bitter blasts to blow.   440
Sad auguries of winter thence she drew,
Which by instinct, or Prophecy, she knew:
When prudence warn'd her to remove betimes
And seek a better heav'n, and warmer clymes.

    Her sons were summon'd on a steeples height,   445
And, call'd in common council, vote a flight;
The day was nam'd, the next that shou'd be fair,
All to the gen'ral rendezvouz repair,
They try their flutt'ring wings and trust themselves in air.
But whether upward to the moon they go,   450
Or dream the winter out in caves below,
Or hawk at flies elsewhere, concerns us not to know.

    Southwards, you may be sure, they bent their flight,
And harbour'd in a hollow rock at night:
Next morn they rose and set up ev'ry sail,   455

The wind was fair, but blew a *mackrel* gale:
The sickly young sat shivring on the shoar,
Abhorr'd salt-water never seen before,
And pray'd their tender mothers to delay
The passage, and expect a fairer day.   460

With these the *Martyn* readily concurr'd,
A church-begot, and church-believing bird;
Of little body, but of lofty mind,
Round belly'd, for a dignity design'd,
And much a dunce, as *Martyns* are by kind.   465
Yet often quoted Cannon-laws, and *Code*,
And Fathers which he never understood,
But little learning needs in noble bloud.
For, sooth to say, the *Swallow* brought him in,
Her houshold Chaplain, and her next of kin.   470
In Superstition silly to excess,
And casting Schemes, by planetary guess:
In fine, shortwing'd, unfit himself to fly,
His fear foretold foul weather in the sky.

Besides, a *Raven* from a wither'd Oak,   475
Left of their lodging, was observ'd to croke.
That omen lik'd him not, so his advice
Was present safety, bought at any price:
(A seeming pious care, that cover'd cowardise.)
To strengthen this, he told a boding dream,   480
Of rising waters, and a troubl'd stream,
Sure signs of anguish, dangers and distress,
With something more not lawfull to express:
By which he slyly seem'd to intimate
Some secret revelation of their fate.   485
For he concluded, once upon a time,
He found a leaf inscrib'd with sacred rime,
Whose antique characters did well denote
The *Sibyl*'s hand of the *Cumæan* Grott:
The mad Divineress had plainly writ,   490
A time shou'd come (but many ages yet,)
In which, sinister destinies ordain,
A *Dame* shou'd drown with all her feather'd train,
And seas from thence be call'd the *Chelidonian* main.

At this, some shook for fear, the more devout   495
Arose, and bless'd themselves from head to foot.
   'Tis true, some stagers of the wiser sort
Made all these idle wonderments their sport:
They said, their onely danger was delay,
And he who heard what ev'ry fool cou'd say,   500
Wou'd never fix his thoughts, but trim his time away.
The passage yet was good, the wind, 'tis true,
Was somewhat high, but that was nothing new,
Nor more than usual *Equinoxes* blew.
The Sun (already from the scales declin'd)   505
Gave little hopes of better days behind,
But change from bad to worse of weather and of wind.
Nor need they fear the dampness of the Sky
Should flag their wings, and hinder them to fly,
'Twas onely water thrown on sails too dry.   510
But, least of all *Philosophy* presumes
Of truth in dreams, from melancholy fumes:
Perhaps the *Martyn*, hous'd in holy ground,
Might think of Ghosts that walk their midnight round,
Till grosser atoms tumbling in the stream   515
Of fancy, madly met and clubb'd into a dream.
As little weight his vain presages bear,
Of ill effect to such alone who fear.
Most prophecies are of a piece with these,
Each *Nostradamus* can foretell with ease: 520
Not naming persons, and confounding times,
One casual truth supports a thousand lying rimes.
   Th' advice was true, but fear had seiz'd the most,
And all good counsel is on cowards lost.
The question crudely put, to shun delay,   525
'Twas carry'd by the *major* part to stay.
   His point thus gain'd, Sir *Martyn* dated thence
His pow'r, and from a Priest became a Prince.
He order'd all things with a busie care,
And cells, and refectories did prepare,   530
And large provisions lay'd of winter fare.
But now and then let fall a word or two
Of hope, that heav'n some miracle might show,
And, for their sakes, the sun shou'd backward go;

Against the laws of nature upward climb,   535
And, mounted on the *Ram*, renew the prime:
For which two proofs in Sacred story lay,
Of *Ahaz* dial, and of *Joshuah*'s day.
In expectation of such times as these
A chapell hous'd 'em, truly call'd of ease: 540
For *Martyn* much devotion did not ask,
They pray'd sometimes, and that was all their task.

   It happen'd (as beyond the reach of wit
Blind prophecies may have a lucky hit)
That, this accomplish'd, or at least in part,   545
Gave great repute to their new *Merlin*'s art.
Some *Swifts, the Gyants of the *Swallow* kind,   * *Other-*
Large limb'd, stout-hearted, but of stupid mind,   *wise call'd*
(For *Swisses*, or for *Gibeonites* design'd,)   Martlets.
These Lubbers, peeping through a broken pane,   550
To suck fresh air, survey'd the neighbouring plain,
And saw (but scarcely cou'd believe their eyes)
New blossoms fiourish, and new flow'rs arise;
As God had been abroad, and walking there,
Had left his foot-steps, and reform'd the year: 555
The sunny hills from far were seen to glow
With glittering beams, and in the meads below
The burnish'd brooks appear'd with liquid gold to flow.
At last they heard the foolish *Cuckow* sing,
Whose note proclaim'd the holy day of spring.   560

   No longer doubting, all prepare to fly,
And repossess their patrimonial sky.
The *Priest* before 'em did his wings display;
And, that good omens might attend their way,
As luck wou'd have it, 'twas St. *Martyn*'s day.   565

   Who but the *Swallow* now triumphs alone,
The Canopy of heaven is all her own,
Her youthfull offspring to their haunts repair;
And glide along in glades, and skim in air,
And dip for insects in the purling springs,   570
And stoop on rivers to refresh their wings.
Their mothers think a fair provision made,
That ev'ry son can live upon his trade,
And now the carefull charge is off their hands,

Look out for husbands, and new nuptial bands: 575
The youthfull widow longs to be supply'd;
But first the lover is by Lawyers ty'd
To settle jointure-chimneys on the bride.
So thick they couple, in so short a space,
That *Martyns* marr'age offrings rise apace;   580
Their ancient houses, running to decay,
Are furbish'd up, and cemented with clay;
They teem already; store of eggs are laid,
And brooding mothers call *Lucina*'s aid.
Fame spreads the news, and foreign fowls appear   585
In flocks to greet the new returning year,
To bless the founder, and partake the cheer.

  And now 'twas time (so fast their numbers rise)
To plant abroad, and people colonies;
The youth drawn forth, as *Martyn* had desir'd,   590
(For so their cruel destiny requir'd)
Were sent far off on an ill fated day;
The rest wou'd need conduct 'em on their way,
And *Martyn* went, because he fear'd alone to stay.

  So long they flew with inconsiderate haste   595
That now their afternoon began to waste;
And, what was ominous, that very morn
The Sun was entr'd into *Capricorn*;
Which, by their bad Astronomers account,
That week the virgin balance shou'd remount;   600
An infant moon eclips'd him in his way,
And hid the small remainders of his day:
The crowd amaz'd, pursu'd no certain mark;
But birds met birds, and justled in the dark;
Few mind the publick in a Panick fright;   605
And fear increas'd the horrour of the night.
Night came, but unattended with repose,
Alone she came, no sleep their eyes to close,
Alone, and black she came, no friendly stars arose.

  What shou'd they doe, beset with dangers round,   610
No neighb'ring Dorp, no lodging to be found,
But bleaky plains, and bare unhospitable ground.
The latter brood, who just began to fly

Sick-feather'd, and unpractis'd in the sky,
For succour to their helpless mother call,   615
She spread her wings; some few beneath 'em craul,
She spread 'em wider yet, but cou'd not cover all.
T' augment their woes, the winds began to move
Debate in air, for empty fields above,
Till *Boreas* got the skyes, and powr'd amain   620
His ratling hail-stones mix'd with snow and rain.

    The joyless morning late arose, and found
A dreadfull desolation reign a-round,
Some buried in the Snow, some frozen to the ground:
The rest were strugling still with death, and lay   625
The *Crows* and *Ravens* rights, an undefended prey;
Excepting *Martyn*'s race, for they and he
Had gain'd the shelter of a hollow tree,
But soon discover'd by a sturdy clown,
He headed all the rabble of a town,   630
And finish'd 'em with bats, or poll'd 'em down.

Martyn himself was caught a-live, and try'd
For treas'nous crimes, because the laws provide
No *Martyn* there in winter shall abide.
High on an Oak which never leaf shall bear,   635
He breath'd his last, expos'd to open air,
And there his corps, unbless'd, are hanging still,
To show the change of winds with his prophetick bill.

    The patience of the *Hind* did almost fail,
For well she mark'd the malice of the tale: 640
Which Ribbald art their church to *Luther* owes,
In malice it began, by malice grows,
He sow'd the *Serpent*'s teeth, an iron-harvest rose.
But most in *Martyn*'s character and fate,
She saw her slander'd sons, the *Panther*'s hate,   645
The people's rage, the persecuting state:
Then said, I take th' advice in friendly part,
You clear your conscience, or at least your heart:
Perhaps you fail'd in your fore-seeing skill,
For *Swallows* are unlucky birds to kill: 650
As for my sons, the family is bless'd,

Whose ev'ry child is equal to the rest:
No church reform'd can boast a blameless line;
Such *Martyns* build in yours, and more than mine:
Or else an old fanatick Authour lyes 655
Who summ'd their Scandals up by Centuries.
But, through your parable I plainly see
The bloudy laws, the crowds barbarity:
The sun-shine that offends the purblind sight,
Had some their wishes, it wou'd soon be night. 660
Mistake me not, the charge concerns not you,
Your sons are male-contents, but yet are true,
As far as non-resistance makes 'em so,
But that's a word of neutral sense you know,
A passive term which no relief will bring, 665
But trims betwixt a rebell and a king.
    Rest well assur'd the *Pardelis* reply'd,
My sons wou'd all support the regal side,
Though heav'n forbid the cause by battel shou'd be try'd.
    The Matron answer'd with a loud Amen, 670
And thus pursu'd her argument agen.
If as you say, and as I hope no less,
Your sons will practise what your self profess,
What angry pow'r prevents our present peace?
The *Lyon*, studious of our common good, 675
Desires, (and Kings desires are ill withstood,)
To join our Nations in a lasting love;
The barrs betwixt are easie to remove,
For sanguinary laws were never made above.
If you condemn that Prince of Tyranny 680
Whose mandate forc'd your *Gallick* friends to fly,
Make not a worse example of your own,
Or cease to rail at causeless rigour shown,
And let the guiltless person throw the stone.
His blunted sword, your suff'ring brotherhood 685
Have seldom felt, he stops it short of bloud:
But you have ground the persecuting knife,
And set it to a razor edge on life.
Curs'd be the wit which cruelty refines,
Or to his father's rod the *Scorpion* joins; 690
Your finger is more gross than the great Monarch's loins.

But you perhaps remove that bloudy note,
And stick it on the first Reformers coat.
Oh let their crime in long oblivion sleep,
'Twas theirs indeed to make, 'tis yours to keep.   695
Unjust, or just, is all the question now,
'Tis plain, that not repealing you allow.

    To name the Test wou'd put you in a rage,
You charge not that on any former age,
But smile to think how innocent you stand   700
Arm'd by a weapon put into your hand.
Yet still remember that you weild a sword
Forg'd by your foes against your Sovereign Lord.
Design'd to hew th' imperial Cedar down,
Defraud Succession, and dis-heir the Crown.   705
T' abhor the makers, and their laws approve,
Is to hate Traytors, and the treason love.
What means it else, which now your children say,
We made it not, nor will we take away.

    Suppose some great Oppressour had by slight   710
Of law, disseis'd your brother of his right,
Your common sire surrendring in a fright;
Would you to that unrighteous title stand,
Left by the villain's will to heir the land?
More just was *Judas*, who his Saviour sold;   715
The sacrilegious bribe he cou'd not hold,
Nor hang in peace, before he rendr'd back the gold.
What more could you have done, than now you doe,
Had *Oates* and *Bedlow*, and their Plot been true?
Some specious reasons for those wrongs were found;   720
The dire Magicians threw their mists around,
And wise men walk'd as on inchanted ground.
But now when time has made th' imposture plain,
(Late though he follow'd truth, and limping held her train,)
What new delusion charms your cheated eyes again?   725
The painted Harlot might awhile bewitch,
But why the Hag uncas'd, and all obscene with itch?

    The first Reformers were a modest race,
Our Peers possess'd in peace their native place:
And when rebellious arms o'return'd the state,   730
They suffer'd onely in the common fate;

But now the Sov'reign mounts the regal chair
And mitr'd seats are full, yet *David*'s bench is bare:
Your answer is, they were not dispossess'd,
They need but rub their mettle on the Test
To prove their ore: 'twere well if gold alone   735
Were touch'd and try'd on your discerning stone;
But that unfaithfull Test, unsound will pass
The dross of Atheists, and sectarian brass:
As if th' experiment were made to hold
For base productions, and reject the gold: 740
Thus men ungodded may to places rise,
And sects may be preferr'd without disguise:
No danger to the church or state from these,
The Papist onely has his Writ of ease.   745
No gainfull office gives him the pretence
To grind the Subject or defraud the Prince.
Wrong conscience, or no conscience may deserve
To thrive, but ours alone is privileg'd to sterve.

    Still thank your selves you cry, your noble race   750
We banish not, but they forsake the place.
Our doors are open: true, but e'er they come,
You toss your censing Test, and fume the room;
As if 'twere *Toby*'s rival to expell,
And fright the fiend who could not bear the smell.   755

    To this the *Panther* sharply had reply'd,
But, having gain'd a Verdict on her side,
She wisely gave the loser leave to chide;
Well satisfy'd to have the But and peace,
And for the Plaintiff's cause she car'd the less,   760
Because she su'd *in formâ Pauperis;*
Yet thought it decent something shou'd be said,
For secret guilt by silence is betray'd:
So neither granted all, nor much deny'd,
But answer'd with a yawning kind of pride.   765

    Methinks such terms of proferr'd peace you bring
As once *Æneas* to th' *Italian* King:
By long possession all the land is mine,
You strangers come with your intruding line,
To share my sceptre, which you call to join.   770
You plead like him an ancient Pedigree,

And claim a peacefull seat by fates decree.
In ready pomp your Sacrificer stands,
T' unite the *Trojan* and the *Latin* bands,
And that the League more firmly may be ty'd,   775
Demand the fair *Lavinia* for your bride.
Thus plausibly you veil th' intended wrong,
But still you bring your exil'd gods along;
And will endeavour in succeeding space,
Those houshold Poppits on our hearths to place.   780
Perhaps some barb'rous laws have been preferr'd,
I spake against the *Test*, but was not heard;
These to rescind, and Peerage to restore,
My gracious Sov'reign wou'd my vote implore:
I owe him much, but owe my conscience more.   785

   Conscience is then your Plea, reply'd the Dame,
Which well-inform'd will ever be the same.
But yours is much of the *Camelion* hew,
To change the dye with ev'ry diff'rent view.
When first the *Lyon* sat with awfull sway   790
Your conscience taught you duty to obey:
He might have had your Statutes and your Test,
No conscience but of subjects was profess'd.
He found your temper, and no farther try'd,
But on that broken reed your church rely'd.   795
In vain the sects assay'd their utmost art
With offer'd treasure to espouse their part,
Their treasures were a bribe too mean to move his heart.
But when by long experience you had proov'd,
How far he cou'd forgive, how well he lov'd;   800
A goodness that excell'd his godlike race,
And onely short of heav'ns unbounded grace:
A floud of mercy that o'erflowed our Isle,
Calm in the rise, and fruitfull as the *Nile*:
Forgetting whence your *Ægypt* was supply'd,   805
You thought your Sov'reign bound to send the tide:
Nor upward look'd on that immortal spring,
But vainly deem'd, he durst not be a king:
Then conscience, unrestrain'd by fear, began
To stretch her limits, and extend the span,   810
Did his indulgence as her gift dispose,

And made a wise Alliance with her foes.
Can conscience own th' associating name,
And raise no blushes to conceal her shame?
For sure she has been thought a bashfull Dame.   815
But if the cause by battel shou'd be try'd,
You grant she must espouse the regal side:
O *Proteus* Conscience, never to be ty'd!
What *Phœbus* from the *Tripod* shall disclose,
Which are in last resort, your friends or foes?   820
Homer, who learn'd the language of the sky,
The seeming *Gordian* knot wou'd soon unty;
Immortal pow'rs the term of conscience know,
But int'rest is her name with men below.

    Conscience or int'rest be't, or both in one;   825
(The *Panther* answer'd in a surly tone,)
The first commands me to maintain the Crown,
The last forbids to throw my barriers down.
Our penal laws no sons of yours admit,
Our *Test* excludes your Tribe from benefit.   830
These are my banks your ocean to withstand,
Which proudly rising overlooks the land:
And once let in, with unresisted sway
Wou'd sweep the Pastors and their flocks away.
Think not my judgment leads me to comply   835
With laws unjust, but hard necessity:
Imperious need which cannot be withstood
Makes ill authentick, for a greater good.
Possess your soul with patience, and attend:
A more auspicious Planet may ascend;   840
Good fortune may present some happier time,
With means to cancell my unwilling crime;
(Unwilling, witness all ye Pow'rs above)
To mend my errours and redeem your love:
That little space you safely may allow,   845
Your all-dispensing pow'r protects you now.

    Hold, said the *Hind*, 'tis needless to explain;
You wou'd *postpone* me to another reign:
Till when you are content to be unjust,
Your part is to possess, and mine to trust.   850
A fair exchange propos'd of future chance,

For present profit and inheritance:
Few words will serve to finish our dispute,
Who will not now repeal wou'd persecute;
To ripen green revenge your hopes attend,   855
Wishing that happier Planet wou'd ascend:
For shame let Conscience be your Plea no more,
To will hereafter, proves she might before;
But she's a Bawd to gain, and holds the Door.

    Your care about your Banks, infers a fear   860
Of threatning Floods, and Inundations near;
If so, a just Reprise would only be
Of what the Land usurp'd upon the Sea;
And all your Jealousies but serve to show
Your Ground is, like your Neighbour-Nation, low.   865
T' intrench in what you grant unrighteous Laws,
Is to distrust the justice of your Cause;
And argues that the true Religion lyes
In those weak Adversaries you despise.

    Tyrannick force is that which least you fear,   870
The sound is frightfull in a Christian's ear;
Avert it, Heav'n; nor let that Plague be sent
To us from the dispeopled Continent.

    But Piety commands me to refrain;
Those Pray'rs are needless in this Monarch's Reign.   875
Behold! how he protects your Friends opprest,
Receives the Banish'd, succours the Distress'd:
Behold, for you may read an honest open Breast.
He stands in Day-light, and disdains to hide
An Act to which, by Honour he is ty'd,   880
A generous, laudable, and Kingly Pride.
Your Test he would repeal, his Peers restore,
This when he says he means, he means no more.
    Well, said the *Panther*, I believe him just,
And yet—
        And yet, 'Tis but because you must,   885
You would be trusted, but you would not trust.
The *Hind* thus briefly, and disdain'd t' inlarge
On Pow'r of *Kings*, and their Superiour charge,
As Heav'ns Trustees before the Peoples choice:
Tho' sure the *Panther* did not much rejoyce   890
To hear those *Echo's* giv'n of her once Loyal voice.

The *Matron* woo'd her Kindness to the last,
But cou'd not win; her hour of Grace was past.
Whom thus persisting when she could not bring
To leave the *Woolf*, and to believe her King,   895
She gave Her up, and fairly wish'd her Joy
Of her late Treaty with her new Ally:
Which well she hop'd wou'd more successfull prove,
Than was the *Pigeons*, and the *Buzzards* love.
The *Panther* ask'd, what concord there cou'd be   900
Betwixt two kinds whose Natures disagree?
The *Dame* reply'd, 'Tis sung in ev'ry Street,
The common chat of Gossips when they meet:
But, since unheard by you, 'tis worth your while
To take a wholesome Tale, tho' told in homely stile.   905

    A Plain good Man, whose Name is understood,
(So few deserve the name of Plain and Good)
Of three fair lineal Lordships stood possess'd,
And liv'd, as reason was, upon the best;
Inur'd to hardships from his early Youth,   910
Much had he done, and suffer'd for his truth:
At Land, and Sea, in many a doubtfull Fight,
Was never known a more advent'rous Knight,
Who oftner drew his Sword, and always for the right.

    As Fortune wou'd (his fortune came tho' late)   915
He took Possession of his just Estate:
Nor rack'd his Tenants with increase of Rent,
Nor liv'd too sparing, nor too largely spent;
But overlook'd his Hinds, their Pay was just,
And ready, for he scorn'd to go on trust: 920
Slow to resolve, but in performance quick;
So true, that he was awkard at a trick.
For little Souls on little shifts rely,
And coward Arts of mean Expedients try:
The noble Mind will dare do anything but lye.   925
False Friends, (his deadliest foes,) could find no way
But shows of honest bluntness to betray;
That unsuspected plainness he believ'd,
He look'd into Himself, and was deceiv'd.
Some lucky Planet sure attends his Birth,   930
Or Heav'n wou'd make a Miracle on Earth;

For prosp'rous Honesty is seldom seen:
To bear so dead a weight, and yet to win.
It looks as Fate with Nature's Law would strive,
To shew Plain dealing once an age may thrive: 935
And, when so tough a frame she could not bend,
Exceeded her Commission to befriend.

   This gratefull man, as Heav'n encreas'd his Store,
Gave *God* again, and daily fed his Poor;
His House with all convenience was purvey'd,   940
The rest he found, but rais'd the Fabrick where he pray'd;
And in that Sacred Place, his beauteous Wife
Employ'd Her happiest hours of Holy Life.

   Nor did their Alms extend to those alone
Whom common Faith more strictly made their own;   945
A sort of *Doves* were hous'd too near their Hall,
Who cross the Proverb, and abound with Gall.
Tho' some 'tis true, are passively inclin'd,
The greater Part degenerate from their kind;
Voracious Birds, that hotly Bill and breed,   950
And largely drink, because on Salt they feed.
Small Gain from them their Bounteous Owner draws,
Yet, bound by Promise, he supports their Cause,
As Corporations priviledg'd by Laws.

   That House which harbour to their kind affords   955
Was built, long since, God knows, for better Birds;
But flutt'ring there they nestle near the Throne,
And lodge in Habitations not their own,
By their high Crops, and Corny Gizzards known.
Like *Harpy's* they could scent a plenteous board,   960
Then to be sure they never fail'd their Lord.
The rest was form, and bare Attendance paid,
They drunk, and eat, and grudgingly obey'd.
The more they fed, they raven'd still for more,
They drain'd from *Dan*, and left *Beersheba* poor;   965
All this they had by Law, and none repin'd,
The pref'rence was but due to *Levi*'s Kind,
But when some Lay-preferment fell by chance
The Gourmands made it their Inheritance.
When once possess'd, they never quit their Claim,   970
For then 'tis sanctify'd to Heav'ns high Name;

And Hallow'd thus they cannot give Consent,
The Gift should be prophan'd by Worldly management.
　　Their Flesh was never to the Table serv'd,
Tho' 'tis not thence inferr'd the Birds were starv'd; 　　975
But that their Master did not like the Food,
As rank, and breeding Melancholy Blood.
Nor did it with His Gracious Nature suite,
Ev'n tho' they were not Doves, to persecute:
Yet He refus'd, (nor could they take Offence) 　　980
Their Glutton Kind should teach him abstinence.
Nor Consecrated Grain their Wheat he thought,
Which new from treading in their Bills they brought:
But left his Hinds each in his Private Pow'r,
That those who like the Bran might leave the Flow'r. 　　985
He for himself, and not for others chose,
Nor would He be impos'd on, nor impose;
But in their Faces His Devotion paid,
And Sacrifice with Solemn Rites was made,
And Sacred Incense on His Altars laid. 　　990
　　Besides these jolly Birds whose Crops impure,
Repay'd their Commons with their Salt Manure;
Another Farm he had behind his House,
Not overstock't, but barely for his use;
Wherein his poor Domestick Poultry fed, 　　995
And from His Pious Hands receiv'd their Bread.
Our pamper'd Pigeons with malignant Eyes,
Beheld these Inmates, and their Nurseries:
Tho' hard their fare, at Ev'ning, and at Morn
A Cruise of Water and an Ear of Corn; 　　1000
Yet still they grudg'd that Modicum, and thought
A Sheaf in ev'ry single Grain was brought;
Fain would they filch that little Food away,
While unrestrain'd those happy Gluttons prey.
And much they griev'd to see so nigh their Hall, 　　1005
The Bird that warn'd St. *Peter* of his Fall;
That he should raise his miter'd Crest on high,
And clap his Wings, and call his Family
To Sacred Rites; and vex th' Etherial Pow'rs
With midnight Mattins, at uncivil Hours: 　　1010
Nay more, his quiet Neighbours should molest,

Just in the sweetness of their Morning rest.
   Beast of a Bird, supinely when he might
Lye snugg and sleep, to rise before the light:
What if his dull Forefathers us'd that cry,   1015
Cou'd he not let a Bad Example dye?
The World was fall'n into an easier way,
This Age knew better, than to Fast and Pray.
Good Sense in Sacred Worship would appear
So to begin, as they might end the year.   1020
Such feats in former times had wrought the falls
Of crowing Chanticleers in Cloyster'd Walls.

Expell'd for this, and for their Lands they fled; ⎫
And Sister Partlet with her hooded head   ⎬
Was hooted hence, because she would not pray a Bed. ⎭ 1025
The way to win the restiff World to God,
Was to lay by the Disciplining Rod,
Unnatural Fasts, and Foreign Forms of Pray'r;
Religion frights us with a meen severe.
'Tis Prudence to reform her into Ease,   1030
And put Her in undress to make Her pleas:
A lively Faith will bear aloft the Mind,
And leave the Luggage of Good Works behind.

   Such Doctrines in the Pigeon-house were taught,
You need not ask how wondrously they wrought;   1035
But sure the common Cry was all for these
Whose Life, and Precept both encourag'd Ease.
Yet fearing those alluring Baits might fail,
And Holy Deeds o're all their Arts prevail:
(For Vice, tho' frontless, and of harden'd Face   1040
Is daunted at the sight of awfull Grace)
An hideous Figure of their Foes they drew,   ⎫
Nor Lines, nor Looks, nor Shades, nor Colours true; ⎬
And this Grotesque design, expos'd to Publick view. ⎭
One would have thought it some *Ægyptian* Piece, ⎫ 1045
With Garden-Gods, and barking Deities,   ⎬
More thick than *Ptolemy* has stuck the Skies.   ⎭
All so perverse a Draught, so far unlike,
It'was no Libell where it meant to strike:
Yet still the daubing pleas'd, and Great and Small   1050

1045 some *B C*: an *A D E*

To view the Monster crowded Pigeon-hall.
There Chanticleer was drawn upon his knees
Adoring Shrines, and Stocks of Sainted Trees,
And by him, a mishapen, ugly Race;
The Curse of God was seen on ev'ry Face: 1055
No *Holland* Emblem could that Malice mend,
But still the worse the look the fitter for a Fiend.

    The Master of the Farm displeas'd to find
So much of Rancour in so mild a kind,
Enquir'd into the Cause, and came to know,   1060
The Passive Church had struck the foremost blow:
With groundless Fears, and Jealousies possest,
As if this troublesome intruding Guest
Would drive the Birds of *Venus*, from their Nest.
A Deed his inborn Equity abhorr'd,   1065
But Int'rest will not trust, tho God should plight his Word.

    A Law, the Source of many Future harms,
Had banish'd all the Poultry from the Farms;
With loss of Life, if any should be found
To crow or peck on this forbidden Ground.   1070
That Bloody Statute chiefly was design'd
For *Chanticleer* the white, of Clergy kind;
But after-malice did not long forget
The Lay that wore the Robe, and Coronet;
For them, for their Inferiours and Allyes,   1075
Their Foes a deadly *Shibboleth* devise:
By which unrighteously it was decreed,
That none to Trust, or Profit should succeed,
Who would not swallow first a poysonous wicked Weed:
Or that, to which old *Socrates* was curs't,   1080
Or Henbane-Juice to swell 'em till they burst.
The Patron (as in reason) thought it hard
To see this Inquisition in his Yard,
By which the Soveraign was of Subjects use debarr'd.

    All gentle means he try'd, which might withdraw   1085
Th' Effects of so unnatural a Law:
But still the Dove-house obstinately stood
Deaf to their own, and to their Neighbours good:
And which was worse, (if any worse could be)
Repented of their boasted Loyalty: 1090

Now made the Champions of a cruel Cause,
And drunk with Fumes of Popular Applause;
For those whom God to ruine has design'd,
He fits for Fate, and first destroys their Mind.
New Doubts indeed they daily strove to raise,   1095
Suggested Dangers, interpos'd Delays,
And Emissary Pigeons had in store,
Such as the *Meccan* Prophet us'd of yore,
To whisper Counsels in their Patrons Ear,
And veil'd their false Advice with Zealous Fear.   1100
The Master smiled to see 'em work in vain,
To wear him out, and make an idle reign:
He saw, but suffer'd their Protractive Arts,
And strove by mildness to reduce their Hearts;
But they abus'd that Grace to make Allyes,   1105
And fondly clos'd with former Enemies;
For Fools are double Fools endeav'ring to be wise.
After a grave Consult what course were best,
One more mature in Folly than the rest,
Stood up, and told 'em, with his head aside,   1110
That desp'rate Cures must be to desp'rate Ills apply'd:
And therefore since their main impending fear
Was from th' encreasing race of *Chanticleer*:
Some Potent Bird of Prey they ought to find,
A Foe profess'd to him, and all his kind: 1115
Some haggar'd *Hawk*, who had her eyry nigh,
Well pounc'd to fasten, and well wing'd to fly;
One they might trust, their common wrongs to wreak:
The *Musquet*, and the *Coystrel* were too weak,
Too fierce the *Falcon*, but above the rest,   1120
The noble *Buzzard* ever pleas'd me best;
Of small Renown, 'tis true, for not to lye,
We call him but a *Hawk* by courtesie.
I know he haunts the *Pigeon*-House and Farm,
And more, in time of War, has done us harm;   1125
But all his hate on trivial Points depends,
Give up our Forms, and we shall soon be friends.
For *Pigeons* flesh he seems not much to care,
Cram'd *Chickens* are a more delicious fare;
On this high Potentate, without delay,   1130

I wish you would conferr the Sovereign sway:
Petition him t' accept the Government,
And let a splendid Embassy be sent.

This pithy speech prevail'd, and all agreed,
Old Enmity's forgot, the *Buzzard* should succeed.   1135

Their welcom Suit was granted soon as heard,
His Lodgings furnish'd, and a Train prepar'd,
With *B's* upon their Breast, appointed for his Guard.
He came, and Crown'd with great Solemnity,
God save King *Buzzard*, was the gen'rall cry.   1140

A Portly Prince, and goodly to the sight,
He seem'd a Son of *Anach* for his height:
Like those whom stature did to Crowns prefer;
Black-brow'd, and bluff, like *Homer's Jupiter*:
Broad-back'd, and Brawny built for Loves delight,   1145
A Prophet form'd, to make a female Proselyte.
A Theologue more by need than genial bent,
By Breeding sharp, by Nature confident.
Int'rest in all his Actions was discern'd;
More learn'd than Honest, more a Wit than learn'd.   1150
Or forc'd by Fear, or by his Profit led,
Or both conjoyn'd, his Native clime he fled:
But brought the Vertues of his Heav'n along;
A fair Behaviour, and a fluent Tongue.
And yet with all his Arts he could not thrive;   1155
The most unlucky Parasite alive.
Loud Praises to prepare his Paths he sent,
And then himself pursu'd his Compliment:
But, by reverse of Fortune chac'd away,
His Gifts no longer than their Author stay: 1160
He shakes the Dust against th' ungrateful race,
And leaves the stench of Ordures in the place.
Oft has he flatter'd, and blasphem'd the same,
For in his Rage, he spares no Sov'rains name:
The Hero, and the Tyrant change their style   1165
By the same measure that they frown or smile;

1147 genial *A* (*some copies*) *B C*: nat'ral *A* (*some copies*)   1148 Nature *A* (*some copies*) *B C*: Nation *A* (*some copies*)   1151 his Profit *A* (*some copies*) *B C*: Ambition *A* (*some copies*)   1152 both conjoyn'd, his Native *A* (*some copies*) *B C*: both, his own unhappy *A* (*some copies*)   1154 fluent *A* (*some copies*) *B C*: flatt'ring *A* (*some copies*)

When well receiv'd by hospitable Foes,
The kindness he returns, is to expose:
For Courtesies, tho' undeserv'd and great,
No gratitude in Fellon-minds beget,   1170
As tribute to his Wit, the churl receives the treat.

His praise of Foes is venemously Nice,
So touch'd, it turns a Vertue to a Vice:
A Greek, and bountiful forewarns us twice.

Sev'n Sacraments he wisely do's disown,   1175
Because he knows Confession stands for one;
Where Sins to sacred silence are convey'd,
And not for Fear, or Love, to be betray'd:
But he, uncall'd, his Patron to controul,
Divulg'd the secret whispers of his Soul: 1180
Stood forth th' accusing *Sathan* of his Crimes,
And offer'd to the *Moloch* of the Times.
Prompt to assayle, and careless of defence,
Invulnerable in his Impudence;
He dares the World, and eager of a name,   1185
He thrusts about, and justles into fame.
Frontless, and Satyr-proof he scow'rs the streets,
And runs an *Indian* muck at all he meets.
So fond of loud Report, that not to miss
Of being known (his last and utmost bliss)   1190
He rather would be known, for what he is.

   Such was, and is the Captain of the test,
Tho' half his Vertues are not here express't;
The modesty of Fame conceals the rest.

The spleenful *Pigeons* never could create   1195
A Prince more proper to revenge their hate:
Indeed, more proper to revenge, than save;
A King, whom in his wrath, th' Almighty gave:
For all the Grace the Landlord had allow'd,
But made the *Buzzard* and the *Pigeons* proud;   1200
Gave time to fix their Friends, and to seduce the crowd.
They long their Fellow-Subjects to inthrall,
Their Patrons promise into question call,
And vainly think he meant to make 'em Lords of all.

   False Fears their Leaders fail'd not to suggest,   1205
As if the *Doves* were to be dispossess't;

Nor Sighs, nor Groans, nor gogling Eyes did want;
For now the *Pigeons* too had learn'd to Cant.
The House of Pray'r is stock'd with large encrease;
Nor Doors, nor Windows can contain the Press: 1210
For Birds of ev'ry feather fill th' abode;
Ev'n Atheists out of envy own a God:
And reeking from the Stews, Adult'rers come,
Like *Goths* and *Vandals* to demolish *Rome.*
That Conscience which to all their Crimes was mute,   1215
Now calls aloud, and cryes to Persecute.
No rigour of the Laws to be releas'd,
And much the less, because it was their Lords request:
They thought it great their Sov'rain to controul,
And nam'd their Pride, Nobility of Soul.   1220
   'Tis true, the *Pigeons,* and their Prince Elect
Were short of Pow'r their purpose to effect:
But with their Quills, did all the hurt they cou'd,
And cuff'd the tender *Chickens* from their food:
And much the *Buzzard* in their Cause did stir,   1225
Tho' naming not the Patron, to infer
With all respect, He was a gross Idolater.
   But when th' Imperial owner did espy
That thus they turn'd his Grace to villany,
Not suff'ring wrath to discompose his mind,   1230
He strove a temper for th' extreams to find,
So to be just, as he might still be kind.
Then, all Maturely weigh'd, pronounc'd a Doom
Of Sacred Strength for ev'ry Age to come.
By this the Doves their Wealth and State possess,   1235
No Rights infring'd, but Licence to oppress:
Such Pow'r have they as Factious Lawyers long
To Crowns ascrib'd, that Kings can do no wrong.
But, since His own Domestick Birds have try'd
The dire Effects of their destructive Pride,   1240
He deems that Proof a Measure to the rest,
Concluding well within his Kingly Breast,
His Fowl of Nature too unjustly were opprest.
He therefore makes all Birds of ev'ry Sect
Free of his Farm, with promise to respect   1245
Their sev'ral Kinds alike, and equally protect.

His Gracious Edict the same Franchise yields
To all the wild Encrease of Woods and Fields,
And who in Rocks aloof, and who in Steeples builds.
To *Crows* the like Impartial Grace affords,   1250
And *Choughs* and *Daws*, and such Republick Birds:
Secur'd with ample Priviledge to feed,
Each has his District, and his Bounds decreed:
Combin'd in common Int'rest with his own,
But not to pass the Pigeons *Rubicon*.   1255

    Here ends the Reign of this pretended Dove;
All Prophecies accomplish'd from above,
For *Shiloh* comes the Scepter to Remove.
Reduc'd from Her Imperial High Abode,
Like *Dyonysius* to a private Rod: 1260
The Passive Church, that with pretended Grace
Did Her distinctive Mark in Duty place,
Now Touch'd, Reviles Her Maker to his Face.

    What after happen'd is not hard to guess;
The small Beginnings had a large Encrease,   1265
And Arts and Wealth succeed (the secret spoils of Peace.)
'Tis said the Doves repented, tho' too late,
Become the Smiths of their own Foolish Fate:
Nor did their Owner hasten their ill hour:
But, sunk in Credit, they decreas'd in Pow'r: 1270
Like Snows in warmth that mildly pass away,
Dissolving in the Silence of Decay.

    The *Buzzard* not content with equal place,
Invites the feather'd *Nimrods* of his Race,
To hide the thinness of their Flock from Sight,   1275
And all together make a seeming, goodly Flight:
But each have sep'rate Int'rests of their own,
Two *Czars*, are one too many for a Throne.
Nor can th' Usurper long abstain from Food,
Already he has tasted Pigeons Blood: 1280
And may be tempted to his former fare,
When this Indulgent Lord shall late to Heav'n repair.
Bare benting times, and moulting Months may come,
When lagging late, they cannot reach their home:
Or Rent in Schism, (for so their Fate decrees,)   1285
Like the Tumultuous Colledge of the Bees;

They fight their Quarrel, by themselves opprest,
The Tyrant smiles below, and waits the falling feast.
  Thus did the gentle *Hind* her fable end,
Nor would the *Panther* blame it, nor commend;   1290
But, with affected Yawnings at the close,
Seem'd to require her natural repose.
For now the streaky light began to peep;
And setting stars admonish'd both to sleep.
The Dame withdrew, and, wishing to her Guest   1295
The peace of Heav'n, betook her self to rest.
Ten thousand Angels on her slumbers waite
With glorious Visions of her future state.

A Song for St CECILIA's Day, 1687

I

From Harmony, from heav'nly Harmony
  This universal Frame began.
   When Nature underneath a heap
    Of jarring Atomes lay,
    And cou'd not heave her Head,   5
  The tuneful Voice was heard from high,
    Arise ye more than dead.
  Then cold, and hot, and moist, and dry,
  In order to their stations leap,
    And Musick's pow'r obey.   10
From Harmony, from heav'nly Harmony
   This universal Frame began:
    From Harmony to Harmony
  Through all the compass of the Notes it ran,
  The Diapason closing full in Man.   15

II

What Passion cannot Musick raise and quell!
   When *Jubal* struck the corded Shell,
  His list'ning Brethren stood around
  And wond'ring, on their Faces fell
  To worship that Celestial Sound.   20
Less than a God they thought there cou'd not dwell
   Within the hollow of that Shell
   That spoke so sweetly and so well.
What Passion cannot Musick raise and quell!

III

  The Trumpets loud Clangor   25
    Excites us to Arms
  With shrill Notes of Anger
    And mortal Alarms.
  The double double double beat
    Of the thundring Drum   30
  Cryes, heark the Foes come;
Charge, Charge, 'tis too late to retreat.

A Song. Text from the first edition, 1687.

IV

The soft complaining FLUTE
In dying Notes discovers
The Woes of hopeless Lovers,
Whose Dirge is whisper'd by the warbling LUTE.   35

V

Sharp VIOLINS proclaim
Their jealous Pangs, and Desperation,
Fury, frantick Indignation,
Depth of Pains, and height of Passion,   40
For the fair, disdainful Dame.

VI

But oh! what Art can teach
What human Voice can reach
The sacred ORGANS praise?
Notes inspiring holy Love,   45
Notes that wing their heav'nly ways
To mend the Choires above.

VII

Orpheus cou'd lead the savage race;
And Trees unrooted left their place;
Sequacious of the Lyre: 50
But bright *CECILIA* rais'd the wonder high'r;
When to her ORGAN, vocal Breath was giv'n
An Angel heard, and straight appear'd
Mistaking Earth for Heaven.

Grand CHORUS

As from the pow'r of sacred Lays   55
    The Spheres began to move,
And sung the great Creator's praise
    To all the bless'd above;
So when the last and dreadful hour
This crumbling Pageant shall devour,   60
The TRUMPET *shall be heard on high,*
The Dead shall live, the Living die,
And MUSICK *shall untune the Sky.*

[*Lines on* Milton]

THREE *Poets*, in three distant *Ages* born,
 Greece, *Italy*, and *England* did adorn.
The *First* in loftiness of thought Surpass'd;
The *Next* in Majesty; in both the *Last*.
The force of *Nature* cou'd no farther goe: 5
To make a *Third* she joynd the former two.

Lines on Milton. Text from Paradise Lost. A Poem in Twelve Books. . . . The Fourth
Edition, *1688*

BRITANNIA REDIVIVA

A POEM ON THE
BIRTH OF THE PRINCE

Dii Patrii Indigetes, & Romule, Vestaque Mater,
Quæ Tuscum Tiberim, & Romana Palatia servas,
Hunc saltem everso Puerum succurrere sæclo
Ne probibete: satis jampridem sanguine nostro
Laomedonteæ luimus Perjuria Trojæ.

VIRG. Georg. I.

BRITANNIA REDIVIVA

A POEM ON THE PRINCE
Born on the 10*th* of *June*, 1688

OUR Vows are heard betimes! and Heaven takes care
To grant, before we can conclude the Pray'r:
Preventing Angels met it half the way,
And sent us back to Praise, who came to Pray.

Just on the Day, when the high mounted Sun   5
Did farthest in his Northern Progress run,
He bended forward and ev'n stretch'd the Sphere
Beyond the limits of the lengthen'd year;
To view a Brighter Sun in *Britaine* Born;
That was the Bus'ness of his longest Morn,   10
The Glorious Object seen t'was time to turn.

Departing Spring cou'd only stay to shed
Her bloomy beauties on the Genial Bed,
But left the manly Summer in her sted,
With timely Fruit the longing Land to chear,   15
And to fulfill the promise of the year.
Betwixt two Seasons comes th' Auspicious Heir,
This Age to blossom, and the next to bear.

(*a*) Last solemn Sabbath saw the Church attend;
The Paraclete in fiery Pomp descend;   20
But when his Wondrous (*b*) Octave rowl'd again,
He brought a Royal Infant in his Train.

(*a*) *Whit-Sunday.*   (*b*) *Trinity-Sunday.*

Britannia Rediviva. Text from the first edition, 1688

So great a Blessing to so good a King
None but th' Eternal Comforter cou'd bring.

    Or did the Mighty Trinity conspire,   25
As once, in Council to Create our Sire?
It seems as if they sent the New-Born Guest
To wait on the Procession of their Feast;
And on their Sacred Anniverse decree'd
To stamp their Image on the promis'd Seed.   30
Three Realms united, and on One bestow'd,
An Emblem of their Mystick Union show'd:
The Mighty Trine the Triple Empire shar'd,
As every Person wou'd have One to guard.

    Hail Son of Pray'rs! by holy Violence   35
Drawn down from Heav'n; but long be banish'd thence,
And late to thy Paternal Skyes retire:
To mend our Crimes whole Ages wou'd require:
To change th' inveterate habit of our Sins,
And finish what thy Godlike Sire begins.   40
Kind Heav'n, to make us *English-Men* again,
No less can give us than a Patriarchs Reign.

    The Sacred Cradle to your Charge receive
Ye Seraphs, and by turns the Guard relieve;
Thy Father's Angel and Thy Father joyn   45
To keep Possession, and secure the Line,
But long defer the Honours of thy Fate,
Great may they be like his, like his be late.
That *James* this running Century may view,
And give his Son an Auspice to the New.   50

    Our wants exact at least that moderate stay:
For see the (*c*) Dragon winged on his way,
To watch the (*d*) Travail, and devour the Prey.
Or, if Allusions may not rise so high,
Thus, when *Alcides* rais'd his Infant Cry,   55
The Snakes besieg'd his Young Divinity:
But vainly with their forked Tongues they threat;
For Opposition makes a Heroe Great.
To needful Succour all the Good will run;
And *Jove* assert the Godhead of his Son.   60

(*c*) *Alluding only to the Common-wealth Party, here and in other places of the Poem.*
(*d*) Rev. 12. v. 4.

O still repining at your present state,
Grudging your selves the Benefits of Fate,
Look up, and read in Characters of Light
A Blessing sent you in your own Despight.
The Manna falls, yet that Cœlestial Bread   65
Like *Jews* you munch, and murmure while you feed.
May not your Fortune be like theirs, Exil'd,
Yet forty Years to wander in the Wild:
Or if it be, may *Moses* live at least
To lead you to the Verge of promis'd Rest.   70
　　Tho' Poets are not Prophets, to foreknow
What Plants will take the Blite, and what will grow,
By tracing Heav'n his Footsteps may be found:
Behold! how awfully He walks the round!
God is abroad, and wondrous in his ways,   75
The Rise of Empires, and their Fall surveys;
More (might I say) than with an usual Eye,　　　　　⎫
He sees his bleeding Church in Ruine lye,　　　　　　⎬
And hears the Souls of Saints beneath his Altar cry.　⎭
Already has he lifted high, the (*e*) Sign   80
Which Crown'd the Conquering Arms of *Constantine*:
The (*f*) Moon grows pale at that presaging sight,
And half her Train of Stars have lost their Light.
　　Behold another (*g*) *Sylvester*, to bless
The Sacred Standard and secure Success;   85
Large of his Treasures, of a Soul so great,
As fills and crowds his Universal Seat.
　　Now view at home a (*h*) second *Constantine*;
(The former too, was of the *Brittish* Line)
Has not his healing Balm your Breaches clos'd,   90
Whose Exile many sought, and few oppos'd?
Or, did not Heav'n by its Eternal Doom
Permit those Evils, that this Good might come?
So manifest, that ev'n the Moon-ey'd Sects
See *Whom* and *What* this Providence protects.   95
Methinks, had we within our Minds no more
Than that One Shipwrack on the Fatal (*i*) Ore,

(*e*) *The Cross.*　　(*f*) *The Crescent, which the* Turks *bear for their Arms.*　　(*g*) *The Pope in the time of* Constantine *the Great, alluding to the present Pope.*　　(*h*) K. James *the Second.*　　(*i*) *The Lemmon Ore.*

That only thought may make us think again,
What Wonders God reserves for such a Reign.
To dream that Chance his Preservation wrought,   100
Were to think *Noah* was preserv'd for nought;
Or the Surviving Eight were not design'd
To people Earth, and to restore their Kind.

    When humbly on the Royal Babe we gaze,
The Manly Lines of a Majestick face   105
Give awful joy: 'Tis Paradise to look
On the fair Frontispiece of Nature's Book;
If the first opening Page so charms the sight,
Think how th' unfolded Volume will delight!

    See how the Venerable Infant lyes   110
In early Pomp; how through the Mother's Eyes
The Father's Soul, with an undaunted view
Looks out, and takes our Homage as his due.
See on his future Subjects how He smiles,
Nor meanly flatters, nor with craft beguiles;   115
But with an open face, as on his Throne,
Assures our Birthrights, and assumes his own.

    Born in broad Day-light, that th' ungrateful Rout
May find no room for a remaining doubt:
Truth, which it self is light, does darkness shun,   120
And the true Eaglet safely dares the Sun.

    (*k*) Fain wou'd the Fiends have made a dubious birth,
Loth to confess the Godhead cloath'd in Earth.
But sickned after all their baffled lyes,
To find an Heir apparent of the Skyes: 125
Abandon'd to despair, still may they grudge,
And owning not the Saviour, prove the Judge.

    Not Great (*l*) *Æneas* stood in plainer Day,
When, the dark mantling Mist dissolv'd away,
He to the *Tyrians* shew'd his sudden face,   130
Shining with all his Goddess Mother's Grace:
For She her self had made his Count'nance bright,
Breath'd honour on his eyes, and her own Purple Light.

    If our Victorious (*m*) *Edward*, as they say,
Gave *Wales* a Prince on that Propitious Day,   135

(*k*) *Alluding to the Temptations in the Wilderness.*   (*l*) Virg. *Æneid.* **I.**
(*m*) *Edw. the black Prince, Born on Trinity-Sunday.*

Why may not Years revolving with his Fate
Produce his Like, but with a longer Date?
One who may carry to a distant shore
The Terrour that his Fam'd Forefather bore.
But why shou'd *James* or his Young Hero stay   140
For slight Presages of a Name or Day?
We need no *Edward*'s Fortune to adorn
That happy moment when our Prince was born:
Our Prince adorns his Day, and Ages hence
Shall wish his Birth-day for some future Prince.   145

(*n*) Great *Michael*, Prince of all th' Ætherial Hosts,
And what e're In-born Saints our *Britain* boasts;
And thou, th' (*o*) adopted Patron of our Isle,
With chearful Aspects on this Infant smile:
The Pledge of Heav'n, which dropping from above,   150
Secures our Bliss, and reconciles his Love.

Enough of Ills our dire Rebellion wrought,
When, to the Dregs, we drank the bitter draught;
Then airy Atoms did in Plagues conspire,
Nor did th' avenging Angel yet retire,   155
But purg'd our still encreasing Crimes with Fire.
Then perjur'd Plots, the still impending Test,
And worse; but Charity conceals the Rest:
Here stop the Current of the sanguine flood,
Require not, Gracious God, thy Martyrs Blood;   160
But let their dying pangs, their living toyl,
Spread a Rich Harvest through their Native Soil:
A Harvest ripening for another Reign,
Of which this Royal Babe may reap the Grain.

Enough of Early Saints one Womb has giv'n;   165
Enough encreas'd the Family of Heav'n:
Let them for his, and our Attonement go;
And Reigning blest above, leave him to Rule below.

Enough already has the Year foreslow'd
His wonted Course, the Seas have overflow'd,   170
The Meads were floated with a weeping Spring,
And frighten'd birds in Woods forgot to sing;
The Strong-limb'd Steed beneath his harness faints,
And the same shiv'ring sweat his Lord attaints.

(*n*) *The Motto of the Poem explain'd.*   (*o*) *St.* George.

When will the Minister of Wrath give o're?   175
Behold him; at (*p*) *Araunah*'s threshing-floor.
He stops, and seems to sheath his flaming brand;
Pleas'd with burnt Incense, from our *David*'s hand.
David has bought the *Jebusites* abode,
And rais'd an Altar to the Living God.   180

   Heav'n, to reward him, make his Joys sincere;
No future Ills, nor Accidents appear
To sully and pollute the Sacred Infant's Year.
Five Months to Discord and Debate were giv'n:
He sanctifies the yet remaining Sev'n.   185
Sabbath of Months! henceforth in Him be blest,
And prelude to the Realms perpetual Rest!

   Let his Baptismal Drops for us attone;
Lustrations for (*q*) Offences not his own.
Let Conscience, which is Int'rest ill disguis'd,   190
In the same Font be cleans'd, and all the Land Baptiz'd.

   (*r*) Un-nam'd as yet; at least unknown to Fame:
Is there a strife in Heav'n about his Name?
Where every Famous Predecessour vies,
And makes a Faction for it in the Skies?   195
Or must it be reserv'd to thought alone?
Such was the Sacred (*s*) *Tetragrammaton*.
Things worthy silence must not be reveal'd:
Thus the true Name of (*t*) *Rome* was kept conceal'd,
To shun the Spells, and Sorceries of those   200
Who durst her Infant Majesty oppose.
But when his tender strength in time shall rise
To dare ill Tongues, and fascinating Eyes;
This Isle, which hides the little Thund'rer's Fame,
Shall be too narrow to contain his Name: 205
Th' Artillery of Heav'n shall make him known;
(*u*) *Crete* cou'd not hold the God, when *Jove* was grown.

   As *Joves* (*x*) Increase, who from his Brain was born,
Whom Arms and Arts did equally adorn,

(*p*) *Alluding to the passage in the* I. *Book of Kings, Ch.* 24. *v.* 20th.   (*q*) *Original*
Sin.   (*r*) *The Prince Christen'd, but not nam'd.*   (*s*) *Jehovah, or the name of God*
unlawful to be pronounc'd by the Jews.   (*t*) *Some Authors say, That the true name of*
Rome *was kept a secret;* ne hostes incantamentis Deos elicerent.   (*u*) *Candie where*
Jupiter *was born and bred secretly.*   (*x*) *Pallas, or Minerva; said by the Poets,*
to have been bred up by Hand.

Free of the Breast was bred, whose milky taste   210
Minerva's Name to *Venus* had debas'd;
So this Imperial Babe rejects the Food
That mixes Monarchs with *Plebeian* blood:
Food that his inborn Courage might controul,
Extinguish all the Father in his Soul,   215
And, for his *Estian* Race, and *Saxon* Strain,
Might re-produce some second *Richard*'s Reign.
Mildness he shares from both his Parents blood,
But Kings too tame are despicably good:
Be this the Mixture of this Regal Child,   220
By Nature Manly, but by Virtue Mild.
    Thus far the Furious Transport of the News,
Had to Prophetick Madness fir'd the Muse;
Madness ungovernable, uninspir'd,
Swift to foretel whatever she desir'd;   225
Was it for me the dark Abyss to tread,
And read the Book which Angels cannot read?
How was I punish'd when the (*y*) sudden blast,
The Face of Heav'n, and our young Sun o'recast!
Fame, the swift Ill, encreasing as she rowl'd,   230
Disease, Despair, and Death, at three reprises told:
At three insulting strides she stalk'd the Town,
And, like Contagion, struck the Loyal down.
Down fell the winnow'd Wheat; but mounted high,
The Whirl-wind bore the Chaff, and hid the Sky.   235
Here black Rebellion shooting from below
(As Earth's (*z*) Gigantick brood by moments grow)
And here the Sons of God are petrify'd with Woe:
An *Appoplex* of Grief! so low were driv'n
The Saints, as hardly to defend their Heav'n.   240
    As, when pent Vapours run their hollow round,
Earth-quakes, which are Convulsions of the ground,
Break bellowing forth, and no Confinement brook,
Till the Third settles, what the Former shook;
Such heavings had our Souls; till slow and late,   245
Our life with his return'd, and Faith prevail'd on Fate.
By Prayers the mighty *Blessing* was implor'd,

(*y*) *The sudden false Report of the Prince's Death.*   (*z*) *Those Gyants are feign'd to have grown 15 Ells every day.*

To Pray'rs was granted, and by Pray'rs restor'd.

So e're the (*a*) *Shunamite* a Son conceiv'd,
The Prophet promis'd, and the Wife believ'd,　　　　250
A Son was sent, the Son so much desir'd,
But soon upon the Mother's Knees expir'd.
The troubled Seer approach'd the mournful Door,
Ran, pray'd, and sent his Past'ral-Staff before,
Then stretch'd his Limbs upon the Child, and mourn'd,　　255
Till Warmth, and breath, and a new Soul return'd.

Thus Mercy stretches out her hand, and saves
Desponding *Peter* sinking in the Waves.

As when a sudden Storm of Hail and Rain
Beats to the ground the yet unbearded Grain,　　　　260
Think not the hopes of Harvest are destroy'd
On the flat Field, and on the naked void;
The light, unloaded stem, from tempest free'd,
Will raise the youthful honours of his head;
And, soon restor'd by native vigour, bear　　　　265
The timely product of the bounteous Year.

Nor yet conclude all fiery *Trials* past,
For Heav'n will exercise us to the last;
Sometimes will check us in our full carreer,
With doubtful blessings, and with mingled fear;　　　270
That, still depending on his daily Grace,
His every mercy for an alms may pass.
With sparing hands will Dyet us to good;
Preventing Surfeits of our pamper'd blood.
So feeds the Mother-bird her craving young,　　　　275
With little Morsels, and delays 'em long.

True, this last blessing was a Royal Feast,
But, where's the Wedding Garment on the Guest?
Our Manners, as Religion were a Dream,
Are such as teach the Nations to *Blaspheme*.　　　　280
In Lusts we wallow, and with Pride we swell,
And Injuries, with Injuries repell;
Prompt to Revenge, not daring to forgive,
Our Lives unteach the Doctrine we believe;
Thus *Israel* Sin'd, impenitently hard,　　　　285
And vainly thought the (*b*) present Ark their Guard;

(*a*) *In the second Book of* Kings, *Chap. 4th.*　　(*b*) Sam. *4th.* v. 10*th.*

But when the haughty *Philistims* appear,
They fled abandon'd, to their Foes, and fear;
Their God was absent, though his Ark was there.
Ah! lest our Crimes shou'd snatch this Pledge away,   290
And make our Joys the blessing of a day!
For we have sin'd him hence, and that he lives,
God to his promise, not our practice gives.
Our Crimes wou'd soon weigh down the guilty Scale,
But *James*, and *Mary*, and the Church prevail.   295
Nor (*c*) *Amaleck* can rout the *Chosen Bands*,
While *Hur* and *Aaron* hold up *Moses* hands.

By living well, let us secure his days,
Mod'rate in hopes, and humble in our ways.
No force the Free-born Spirit can constrain,   300
But Charity, and great Examples gain.
Forgiveness is our thanks, for such a day;
'Tis Godlike, God in his own Coyn to pay.

But you, Propitious Queen, translated here,
From your mild Heav'n, to rule our rugged Sphere,   305
Beyond the Sunny walks, and circling Year:
You, who your Native Clymate have bereft
Of all the Virtues, and the Vices left;
Whom Piety, and Beauty make their boast,
Though Beautiful is well in Pious lost;   310
So lost, as Star-light is dissolv'd away,
And melts into the brightness of the day;
Or Gold about the Regal Diadem,
Lost to improve the lustre of the Gem:
What can we add to your Triumphant Day?   315
Let the Great Gift the beauteous Giver pay.
For shou'd our thanks awake the rising Sun,
And lengthen, as his latest shaddows run,
That, tho' the longest day, wou'd soon, too soon be done.

Let Angels voices, with their harps conspire,   320
But keep th' auspicious Infant from the Quire;
Late let him sing above, and let us know
No sweeter Musick, than his Cryes below.
  Nor can I wish to you, Great Monarch, more

(*c*) Exod. 17. v. 8*th*.

Than such an annual Income to your store;   325
The Day, which gave this *Unit*, did not shine
For a less Omen, than to fill the *Trine*.
After a *Prince*, an *Admiral* beget,
The *Royal Sov'raign* wants an Anchor yet.
Our Isle has younger Titles still in store,   330
And when th' exhausted Land can yield no more,
Your Line can force them from a Foreign shore.

   The Name of Great, your Martial mind will sute,
But Justice, is your Darling Attribute:
Of all the *Greeks*, 'twas but (*d*) one *Hero's* due,   335
And, in him, *Plutarch* Prophecy'd of you.
A Prince's favours but on few can fall,
But Justice is a Virtue shar'd by all.

   Some Kings the name of Conq'rours have assum'd,
Some to be Great, some to be Gods presum'd;   340
But boundless pow'r, and arbitrary Lust
Made Tyrants still abhor the Name of Just;
They shun'd the praise this Godlike Virtue gives,
And fear'd a Title, that reproach'd their Lives.

   The Pow'r from which all Kings derive their state,   345
Whom they pretend, at least, to imitate,
Is equal both to punish and reward;
For few wou'd love their God, unless they fear'd.

   Resistless Force and Immortality
Make but a Lame, Imperfect Deity: 350
Tempests have force unbounded to destroy,
And Deathless Being ev'n the Damn'd enjoy,
And yet Heav'ns Attributes, both last and first,
One without life, and one with life accurst;
But Justice is Heav'ns self, so strictly He,   355
That cou'd it fail, the God-head cou'd not be.
This Virtue is your own; but Life and State
Are One to Fortune subject, One to Fate:
Equal to all, you justly frown or smile,
Nor Hopes, nor Fears your steady Hand beguile;   360
Your self our Ballance hold, the Worlds, our Isle.

   (*d*)   Aristides, *see his Life in* Plutarch.

THE PROLOGUE and EPILOGUE
to the *HISTORY OF BACON*
IN VIRGINIA

PROLOGUE

Spoken by a Woman

PLAYS you will have; and to supply your Store,
  Our Poets trade to ev'ry Foreign Shore:
This is the Product of *Virginian* Ground,
And to the Port of *Covent-Garden* bound.
Our Cargo is, or should at least, be Wit: 5
Bless us from you damn'd Pyrates of the Pit:
And Vizard-Masks, those dreadful Apparitions;
She-Privateers, of Venomous Conditions,
That clap us oft aboard with *French* Commissions.
You Sparks, we hope, will wish us happy Trading;   10
For you have Ventures in our Vessel's Lading;
And tho you touch at this or t'other Nation;
Yet sure *Virginia* is your dear Plantation.
Expect no polish'd Scenes of Love shou'd rise
From the rude Growth of *Indian* Colonies.   15
Instead of Courtship, and a tedious pother,
They only tip the Wink at one another;
Nay often the whole Nation, pig together.
You Civil *Beaus*, when you pursue the Game,
With manners mince the meaning of—that same: 20
But ev'ry part has there its proper Name.
Good Heav'ns defend me, who am yet unbroken
From living there, where such Bug-words are spoken:
Yet surely, Sirs, it does good Stomachs show,
To talk so savour'ly of what they do.   25
But were I Bound to that broad speaking land,
What e're they said, I would not understand,
But innocently, with a Ladies Grace,

The Prologue and Epilogue. Text from the separate edition of 1689

Wou'd learn to whisk my Fan about my Face.
However, to secure you, let me swear,   30
That no such base *Mundungus* Stuff is here.
We bring you of the best the Soyl affords:
Buy it for once, and take it on our Words.
You wou'd not think a Countrey-Girl the worse,
If clean and wholsome, tho her Linnen's course.   35
Such are our Scenes; and I dare boldly say,
You may laugh less at a far better Play.
The Story's true; the Fact not long a-go;
The *Hero* of our Stage was *English* too:
And bate him one small frailty of Rebelling,   40
As brave as e're was born at *Iniskelling*.

EPILOGUE

Spoken by a Woman

BY this time you have lik'd, or damn'd our Plot;
Which tho I know, my Epilogue knows not:
For if it cou'd foretel, I shou'd not fail,
In decent wise, to thank you, or to rail.
But he who sent me here, is positive,   5
This Farce of Government is sure to thrive;
Farce is a Food as proper for your lips,
As for *Green-Sickness*, crumpt Tobacco-pipes.
Besides, the Author's dead, and here you sit,
Like the Infernal Judges of the Pit: 10
Be merciful; for 'tis in you this day,
To save or damn her Soul; and that's her Play.
She who so well cou'd Love's kind Passion paint,
We piously believe, must be a Saint:
Men are but Bunglers, when they wou'd express   15
The sweets of Love, the dying tenderness;
But Women, by their own abundance, measure,
And when they write, have deeper sense of Pleasure.
Yet tho her Pen did to the Mark arrive,
'Twas common Praise, to please you, when alive;   20
But of no other Woman, you have read,

Except this one, to please you, now she's dead.
'Tis like the Fate of Bees, whose golden pains,
Themselves extinguish'd, in their Hive remains.
Or in plain terms to speak, before we go,   25
What you young Gallants, by experience, know,
This is an Orphan Child; a bouncing Boy,
'Tis late to lay him out, or to destroy.
Leave your Dog-tricks, to lie and to forswear,
Pay *you* for Nursing, and we'll keep him here.   30

PROLOGUE and EPILOGUE
to *DON SEBASTIAN*

PROLOGUE
To DON SEBASTIAN King of *Portugal*

Spoken by a Woman

THE Judge remov'd, tho he's no more My Lord,
    May plead at Bar, or at the Council-Board:
So may cast Poets write; there's no Pretension,
To argue loss of Wit from loss of Pension.
Your looks are cheerful; and in all this place   5
I see not one, that wears a damning face.
The *British* Nation, is too brave to show,
Ignoble vengeance, on a vanquish'd foe.
At least be civil to the Wretch imploring;
And lay your Paws upon him, without roaring: 10
Suppose our Poet was your foe before;
Yet now, the bus'ness of the Field is o'er;
'Tis time to let your Civil Wars alone,
When Troops are into Winter-quarters gone.
Jove was alike to *Latian* and to *Phrygian*;   15
And you well know, a Play's of no Religion.
Take good advice, and please your selves this day;
No matter from what hands you have the Play.

Prologue and Epilogue. Text from Don Sebastian, King of Portugal: A Tragedy, *1690*

Among good Fellows ev'ry health will pass,
That serves to carry round another glass: 20
When, with full bowls of *Burgundy* you dine,
Tho at the Mighty Monarch you repine,
You grant him still most Christian, in his Wine.
    Thus far the Poet, but his brains grow Addle;
And all the rest is purely from this Noddle.   25
You've seen young Ladies at the Senate door,
Prefer Petitions, and your grace implore;
How ever grave the Legislators were,
Their Cause went ne'er the worse for being fair.
Reasons as weak as theirs, perhaps I bring;   30
But I cou'd bribe you, with as good a thing.
I heard him make advances of good Nature;
That he for once, wou'd sheath his cutting Satyr:
Sign but his Peace, he vows he'll ne'er again
The sacred Names of Fops and Beau's profane.   35
Strike up the Bargain quickly; for I swear,
As Times go now, he offers very fair.
Be not too hard on him, with Statutes neither,
Be kind; and do not set your Teeth together,
To stretch the Laws, as Coblers do their Leather.   40
Horses, by Papists are not to be ridden;
But sure the Muses Horse was ne'er forbidden.
For in no Rate-Book, it was ever found
That *Pegasus* was valued at Five-pound:
Fine him to daily Drudging and Inditing;   45
And let him pay his Taxes out, in Writing.

EPILOGUE
To Don Sebastian, King of Portugall

Spoken betwixt Antonio *and* Morayma

Mor. I QUAK'D at heart for fear the Royal Fashion
     Shou'd have seduc'd Us two to Separation:
To be drawn in, against our own desire,
Poor I to be a Nun, poor You a Fryar.

Ant.   I trembled when the Old Mans hand was in,

He would have prov'd we were too near of kin:
Discovering old Intrigues of Love, like t'other,
Betwixt my Father and thy sinfull Mother;
To make Us Sister Turk and Christian Brother.

Mor.   Excuse me there; that League shou'd have been rather   10
Betwixt your Mother and my *Mufti*-Father;
'Tis for my own and my Relations Credit
Your Friends shou'd bear the Bastard, mine shou'd get it.

Ant.   Suppose us two *Almeyda* and *Sebastian*
With Incest prov'd upon us:—

Mor.   Without question   15
Their Conscience was too queazy of digestion.

Ant.   Thou woud'st have kept the Councell of thy Brother
And sinn'd till we repented of each other.

Mor.   Beast as you are on Natures Laws to trample;
'Twere fitter that we follow'd their Example   20
And since all Marriage in Repentance ends,
'Tis good for us to part while we are Friends.
To save a Maids remorses and Confusions
E'en leave me now before We try Conclusions.

Ant.   To copy their Example first make certain   25
Of one good hour like theirs before our parting;
Make a debauch o're Night of Love and Madness;
And marry when we wake in sober sadness.

Mor.   I'le follow no new Sects of your inventing,
One Night might cost me nine long months repenting: 30
First wed, and if you find that life a fetter,
Dye when you please, the sooner Sir the better:
My wealth wou'd get me love e're I cou'd ask it:
Oh there's a strange Temptation in the Casket:
All these Young Sharpers wou'd my grace importune,   35
And make me thundring Votes of lives and fortune.

PROLOGUE TO *THE PROPHETESS*

Spoken by Mr. BETTERTON

WHAT *Nostradame*, with all his Art can guess
    The Fate of our approaching *Prophetess*?
A Play which like a Prospective set right,

Presents our vast Expences close to sight;
But turn the Tube, and there we sadly view   5
Our distant gains; and those uncertain too.
A sweeping Tax, which on our selves we raise;
And all like you, in hopes of better days.
When will our Losses warn us to be wise!
Our Wealth decreases, and our Charges rise: 10
Money the sweet Allurer of our hopes,
Ebbs out in Oceans, and comes in by Drops.
We raise new Objects to provoke delight;
But you grow sated e're the second sight.
False Men, even so, you serve your Mistresses;   15
They rise three Storys, in their towring dress;
And after all, you love not long enough,
To pay the Rigging, e're you leave 'em off.
Never content, with what you had before;
But true to Change, and *English* Men all ore.   20
New Honour calls you hence; and all your Care
Is to provide the horrid pomp of War:
In Plume and Scarf, Jack-boots and Bilbo Blade
Your Silver goes, that should support our Trade,
[But we shall flourish, sure, when you are paid.]   25
Go unkind Hero's, leave our Stage to mourn,
Till rich from vanquish'd Rebels you return;
And the fat Spoyls of *Teague* in Tryumph draw,
His Firkin-Butter, and his Usquebaugh.
Go Conquerors of your Male and Female Foes;   30
Men without Hearts, and Women without Hose.
Each bring his Love, a *Bogland* Captive home,
Such proper Pages, will long Trayns become:
With Copper-Collars, and with brawny Backs,
Quite to put down the Fashion of our Blacks.   35
Then shall the pious Muses pay their Vows,
And furnish all their Lawrels for your brows;
Their tuneful Voice shall rise for your delights;
We want not Poets fit to sing your fights.
But you bright Beauties, for whose only sake,   40
These doughty Knights such dangers undertake,

Prologue. Text from The Prophetess: or, The History of Dioclesian, *1690, collated with*
Poems on Affairs of State. Part III, *1698*   25 But . . . paid. *added in* 98

When they with happy Gales are gone away,
With your propitious Presence grace our Play;
And with a sigh, their empty seats survey.
Then think on that bare Bench my Servant sate; 45
I see him Ogle still, and hear him Chat:
Selling facetious Bargains, and propounding
That witty Recreation, call'd Dum-founding.
Their Loss with patience, we will try to bear;
And wou'd do more to see you often here. 50
That our Dead Stage, Reviv'd by your fair eyes,
Under a Female Regency may rise.

49 strive 98

PROLOGUE, EPILOGUE and SONGS
from *AMPHITRYON*

PROLOGUE
To *Amphitryon*; or, *The Two Sosia's*

Spoken by Mrs. *Bracegirdle*

THE lab'ring Bee, when his sharp Sting is gone,
   Forgets his Golden Work, and turns a Drone:
Such is a Satyr, when you take away
That Rage, in which his Noble Vigour lay.
What gain you, by not suffering him to teize ye? 5
He neither can offend you, now, nor please ye.
The Honey-bag, and Venome, lay so near,
That both, together, you resolv'd to tear;
And lost your Pleasure, to secure your Fear.
How can he show his Manhood, if you bind him 10
To box, like Boys, with one Hand ty'd behind him?
This is plain levelling of Wit; in which
The Poor has all th' advantage, not the Rich.
The Blockhead stands excus'd, for wanting Sense;
And Wits turn Blockheads in their own defence. 15
Yet, though the Stages Traffick is undone,
Still *Julian's* interloping Trade goes on:
Though Satyr on the Theatre you smother,
Yet in Lampoons, you Libel one another.
The first produces still, a second Jig; 20
You whip 'em out, like School-boys, till they gig:
And, with the same success, we Readers guess;
For, ev'ry one, still dwindles to a less.
And much good Malice, is so meanly drest,
That we wou'd laugh, but cannot find the Jest. 25
If no advice your Rhiming Rage can stay,
Let not the Ladies suffer in the Fray.
Their tender Sex, is priviledg'd from War;
'Tis not like Knights, to draw upon the Fair.

Prologue, Epilogue and Songs. Text from Amphitryon; or, The Two Socia's. A Comedy, 1690

What Fame expect you from so mean a Prize?   30
We wear no murd'ring Weapons, but our Eyes.
Our Sex, you know, was after yours design'd; ⎫
The last Perfection of the Makers mind: ⎬
Heav'n drew out all the Gold for us, and left your Dross behind. ⎭
Beauty, for Valours best Reward, He chose;   35
Peace, after War; and after Toil, Repose.
Hence ye Prophane; excluded from our sights; ⎫
And charm'd by Day, with Honour's vain delights, ⎬
Go, make your best of solitary Nights.   ⎭
Recant betimes, 'tis prudence to submit: 40
Our Sex, is still your Overmatch, in Wit:
We never fail, with new, successful Arts,
To make fine Fools of you; and all your Parts.

EPILOGUE

Spoken by *Phædra*. Mrs. *Mountfort*

I'M thinking, (and it almost makes me mad,)
How sweet a time, those Heathen Ladies had.
Idolatry, was ev'n their Gods own trade;
They Worshipt the fine Creatures they had made.
Cupid, was chief of all the Deities;   5
And Love was all the fashion, in the Skies.
When the sweet Nymph, held up the Lilly hand,
Jove, was her humble Servant, at Command.
The Treasury of Heav'n was ne're so bare,
But still there was a Pension for the Fair.   10
In all his Reign, Adultry was no Sin;
For *Jove*, the good Example did begin.
Mark, too, when he usurp'd the Husband's name,
How civilly he sav'd the Ladies fame.
The secret Joys of Love, he wisely hid;   15
But you, Sirs, boast of more, than e'er you did.
You teize your Cuckolds; to their face torment 'em;
But *Jove* gave his, new Honours to content 'em.
And, in the kind remembrance of the Fair,
On each exalted Son, bestow'd a Star.   20

For those good deeds, as by the date appears,
His Godship, flourish'd full Two thousand Years.
At last, when He and all his Priests grew old,
The Ladies grew in their devotion cold;
And, that false Worship wou'd no longer hold.   } 25
  Severity of Life did next begin;
(And always does, when we no more can Sin.)
That Doctrine, too, so hard, in Practice, lyes,
That, the next Age may see another rise.
Then, Pagan Gods, may, once again, succeed;   } 30
And *Jove*, or *Mars*, be ready, at our need,
To get young Godlings; and, so, mend our breed.   }

SONGS

I

SONG

I

CELIA, that I once was blest
Is now the Torment of my Brest;
  Since to curse me, you bereave me
  Of the Pleasures I possest:
Cruel Creature, to deceive me!   5
First to love, and then to leave me!

II

Had you the Bliss refus'd to grant,
Then I had never known the want:
  But possessing once the Blessing,
  Is the Cause of my Complaint: 10
Once possessing is but tasting;
'Tis no Bliss that is not lasting.

III

Celia now is mine no more;
But I am hers; and must adore:

Song. 4 Pleasures] Pleasure *Songs in Amphitryon, with the Musick* (*S*)   8 Then I] I
then *S*

Nor to leave her will endeavour;   15
Charms, that captiv'd me before,
No unkindness can dissever;
Love that's true, is Love for ever.

II

Mercury's SONG to *Phædra*

I

FAIR *Iris* I love, and hourly I dye,
    But not for a Lip, nor a languishing Eye:
She's fickle and false, and there we agree;
For I am as false, and as fickle as she:
We neither believe what either can say;   5
And, neither believing, we neither betray.

II

'Tis civil to swear, and say things of course;
We mean not the taking for better for worse.
When present, we love; when absent, agree:
I think not of *Iris*, nor *Iris* of me: 10
The Legend of Love no Couple can find
So easie to part, or so equally join'd.

III

A Pastoral Dialogue betwixt Thyrsis *and* Iris

I

Thyrsis. FAIR *Iris* and her Swain
            Were in a shady Bow'r;
        Where *Thyrsis* long in vain
            Had sought the Shepherd's hour:
    At length his Hand advancing upon her snowy Breast;   5
        He said, O kiss me longer,
        And longer yet and longer,
            If you will make me Blest.

Mercury's Song. 1 Fair . . . love] For . . . sigh *S*   4 For . . . she] O these are the
Virtues that Captivate me *S*   12 equally] easily *S*
A Pastoral Dialogue. 4 Shepherd's] happy *S*

II

Iris.   An easie yielding Maid,
               By trusting is undone;   10
         Our Sex is oft betray'd,
               By granting Love too soon.
         If you desire to gain me, your Suff'rings to redress;
               Prepare to love me longer,
               And longer yet, and longer,   15
                    Before you shall possess.

III

Thyrsis. The little Care you show,
               Of all my Sorrows past;
          Makes Death appear too slow,
               And Life too long to last.   20
          Fair *Iris* kiss me kindly, in pity of my Fate;
               And kindly still, and kindly,
                    Before it be too late.

IV

Iris.   You fondly Court your Bliss,
               And no Advances make;   25
          'Tis not for Maids to kiss,
               But 'tis for Men to take.
          So you may Kiss me kindly, and I will not rebell;
               And kindly still, and kindly,
                    But Kiss me not and tell.   30

V

A RONDEAU

Chorus.   Thus at the height we love and live,
               And fear not to be poor:
          We give, and give, and give, and give,
               Till we can give no more:
          But what to day will take away,   35
               To morrow will restore.
          Thus at the heighth we love and live,
               And fear not to be poor.

26 kiss] give *S*   30 Kiss me not] doe not kiss *S*

PROLOGUE to *THE MISTAKES*

Enter Mr. *Bright*.

GENTLEMEN, *we must beg your pardon; here's no Prologue to be had to day; Our New Play is like to come on, without a Frontispiece; as bald as one of you young Beaux, without your Perriwig. I left our young Poet, sniveling and sobbing behind the Scenes, and cursing some body that has deceiv'd him.*

Enter Mr. *Bowen*.

Hold your prating to the Audience: Here's honest Mr. Williams, *just come in, half mellow, from the* Rose-Tavern. *He swears he is inspir'd with Claret, and will come on, and that* Extempore *too, either with a Prologue of his own or something like one: O here he comes to his Tryal, at all Adventures; for my part I wish him a good Deliverance.*

Exeunt Mr. *Bright*, and Mr. *Bowen*.

Enter Mr. Williams.

Save ye Sirs, save ye! I am in a hopefull way.
I shou'd speak something, in Rhyme, now, for the Play:
But the duce take me, if I know what to say.
I'le stick to my Friend the Authour, that I can tell ye,
To the last drop of Claret, in my belly.   5
So far I'me sure 'tis Rhyme—that needs no granting:
And, if my verses feet stumble—you see my own are wanting.
Our young Poet, has brought a piece of work,
In which, though much of Art there does not lurk,
It may hold out three days—And that's as long as *Cork*.   10
But, for this Play—(which till I have done, we show not,)
What may be its fortune—By the Lord—I know not.
This I dare swear, no malice here is writ:
'Tis Innocent of all things—ev'n of wit.
He's no high Flyer—he makes no sky Rockets,   15
His Squibbs are only levell'd at your Pockets.
And if his Crackers light among your pelf
You are blown-up: if not, then he's blown-up himself.
By this time, I'me something recover'd of my fluster'd madness:
And, now, a word or two in sober sadness.   20

Prologue. Text from Harris's The Mistakes, or, The False Report: A Tragicomedy, 1691

Ours is a Common Play: and you pay down
A Common Harlots price—just half a Crown.
You'le say, I play the Pimp, on my Friends score;
But since 'tis for a Friend your gibes give o're:
For many a Mother has done that before.   } 25
How's this, you cry? an Actor write?—we know it;
But *Shakspear* was an Actor, and a Poet.
Has not Great *Johnsons* learning, often fail'd?
But *Shakspear*'s greater Genius, still prevail'd.
Have not some writing Actors, in this Age   30
Deserv'd and found Success upon the Stage?
To tell the truth, when our old Wits are tir'd,
Not one of us, but means to be inspir'd.
Let your kind presence grace our homely cheer;
Peace and the Butt, is all our bus'ness here: } 35
So much for that;—and the Devil take small beer..

PROLOGUE, EPILOGUE and SONGS
from *KING ARTHUR*

Prologue to the OPERA

Spoken by Mr. *Betterton*

SURE there's a Dearth of Wit in this dull Town,
When silly Plays so savourly go down:
As when Clipp'd Money passes, 'tis a sign
A Nation is not over-stock'd with Coin.
Happy is he, who, in his own Defence,   5
Can Write just level,to your humble Sence;
Who higher than your Pitch can never go;
And doubtless, he must creep, who Writes below.
So have I seen in Hall of Knight, or Lord,
A weak Arm, throw on a long Shovel-Board,   10
He barely lays his Piece, bar Rubs and Knocks,
Secur'd by Weakness not to reach the Box.

Prologue, Epilogue and Songs. Text from King Arthur: or, The British Worthy. A Dramatick Opera, *1691, collated with the edition of 1695*

A Feeble Poet will his Bus'ness do;
Who straining all he can, comes up to you:
For if you like your Selves, you like him too.   15
An Ape his own Dear Image will embrace;
An ugly *Beau* adores a Hatchet Face:
So some of you, on pure instinct of Nature,
Are led, by Kind, t' admire your fellow Creature.
In fear of which, our House has sent this Day,   20
T' insure our New-Built-Vessel, call'd a Play.
No sooner Nam'd, than one crys out, These Stagers
Come in good time, to make more Work for Wagers.
The Town divides, if it will take, or no;
The Courtiers Bet, the Cits, the Merchants too;   25
A sign they have but little else to do.
Betts, at the first, were Fool-Traps; where the Wise
Like Spiders, lay in Ambush for the Flies:
But now they're grown a common Trade for all,
And Actions, by the News-Book, Rise and Fall.   30
Wits, Cheats, and Fops, are free of Wager-Hall.
One Policy, as far as *Lyons* carries;
Another, nearer home sets up for *Paris*.
Our Betts, at last, wou'd ev'n to *Rome* extend,
But that the Pope has prov'd our Trusty Friend.   35
Indeed, it were a Bargain, worth our Money,
Cou'd we insure another *Ottobuoni*.
Among the rest, there are a sharping Sett,
That Pray for us, and yet against us Bett:
Sure Heav'n it self, is at a loss to know,   40
If these wou'd have their Pray'rs be heard, or no:
For in great Stakes, we piously suppose,
Men Pray but very faintly they may lose.
Leave off these Wagers; for in Conscience Speaking,
The City needs not your new Tricks for Breaking: 45
And if you Gallants lose, to all appearing
You'll want an Equipage for Volunteering;
While thus, no Spark of Honour left within ye,
When you shou'd draw the Sword, you draw the Guinea.

The *EPILOGUE*

Spoken by Mrs. BRACEGIRDLE

I'VE had to Day a Dozen *Billet-Doux*
From *Fops*, and *Wits*, and *Cits*, and *Bowstreet-Beaux*;
Some from *Whitehal*, but from the *Temple* more;
A *Covent-Garden* Porter brought me four.
I have not yet read all: But, without feigning,   5
We *Maids* can make shrewd Ghesses at your Meaning.
What if, to shew your Styles, I read 'em here?
Me thinks I hear one cry, *Oh Lord, forbear:*
No, Madam, no; by Heav'n, that's too severe.
Well then, be safe—   10
But swear henceforwards to renounce all Writing,
And take this Solemn Oath of my Inditing,
As you love Ease, and hate Campagnes and Fighting.
Yet, 'Faith, 'tis just to make some few Examples:
What if I shew'd you one or two for Samples?   15
Pulls one out. Here's one desires my Ladiship to meet
At the kind Couch above in *Bridges-Street.*
Oh Sharping Knave! That wou'd have you know what,
For a Poor Sneaking Treat of *Chocolat.*
Pulls out another. Now, in the Name of Luck, I'll break this open, 20
Because I Dreamt last Night I had a Token;
The Superscription is exceeding pretty,
To the Desire of all the Town and City.
Now, *Gallants*, you must know, this pretious *Fop*,
Is Foreman of a Haberdashers-Shop: 25
One who devoutly Cheats; demure in Carriage;
And Courts me to the Holy Bands of Marriage.
But with a *Civil Inuendo* too,
My Overplus of Love shall be for you.
Reads.—Madam, I swear your Looks are so Divine,   30
When I set up, your Face shall be my Sign:
Tho Times are hard; to shew how I Adore you,
Here's my whole Heart, and half a Guinea for you.
But have a care of Beaux; *They're false, my Honey;*
And which is worse, have not one Rag of Money.   35
See how Maliciously the Rogue would wrong ye;

But I know better Things of some among ye.
My wisest way will be to keep the Stage,
And trust to the Good Nature of the Age;
And he that likes the *Musick* and the *Play*,   40
Shall be my Favourite Gallant to Day.

SONGS

I

WODEN, first to thee,
    A Milk white Steed, in Battle won,
We have Sacrific'd.
Chor.   We have Sacrific'd.
Vers. Let our next Oblation be,   5
    To *Thor*, thy thundring Son,
    Of such another.
Chor.   We have Sacrific'd.
Vers. A third; (of *Friezeland* breed was he,)
    To *Woden*'s Wife, and to *Thor*'s Mother: 10
    And now we have atton'd all three:
    We have Sacrific'd.
Chor.   We have Sacrific'd.
2 Voc. The White Horse Neigh'd aloud.
    To *Woden* thanks we render.   15
    To *Woden*, we have vow'd.
Chor. To *Woden*, our Defender.
                [*The four last Lines in* CHORUS.
Vers. The Lot is Cast, and *Tanfan* pleas'd:
Chor. Of Mortal Cares you shall be eas'd,
    Brave Souls to be renown'd in Story.   20
    Honour prizing,
    Death despising,
    Fame acquiring
    By Expiring,
    Dye, and reap the fruit of Glory.   25
    Brave Souls to be renown'd in Story.

Vers. I call ye all,
  To *Woden*'s Hall;
  Your Temples round
  With Ivy bound,
  In Goblets Crown'd,   30
And plenteous Bowls of burnish'd Gold;
  Where you shall Laugh,
  And dance and quaff,
  The Juice, that makes the *Britons* bold.   35

II

A Battle supposed to be given behind the Scenes, with Drums, Trumpets, and Military Shouts and Excursions: After which, the Britons, *expressing their Joy for the Victory, sing this Song of Triumph.*

COME if you dare, our Trumpets sound;
Come if you dare, the Foes rebound:
We come, we come, we come, we come,
Says the double, double, double Beat of the Thundring Drum.

  Now they charge on amain,   5
  Now they rally again:
The Gods from above the Mad Labour behold,
And pity Mankind that will perish for Gold.

The Fainting *Saxons* quit their Ground,
Their Trumpets Languish in the Sound;   10
They fly, they fly, they fly, they fly;
Victoria, Victoria, the Bold *Britons* cry.

  Now the Victory's won,
  To the Plunder we run:
We return to our Lasses like Fortunate Traders,   15
Triumphant with Spoils of the Vanquish'd Invaders.

III

Phil.⎱ HITHER this way, this way bend,
sings.⎰ Trust not that Malicious Fiend:
  Those are false deluding Lights,
  Wafted far and near by Sprights.
Trust 'em not, for they'll deceive ye;
And in Bogs and Marshes leave ye.   5

Chor. of Phil. Spirits.   Hither this way, this way bend.

Chor. of Grimb. Spirits. This way, this way bend.

Phil. ⎫ If you step, no Danger thinking,

sings. ⎭ Down you fall, a Furlong sinking: 10

'Tis a Fiend who has annoy'd ye;

Name but Heav'n, and he'll avoid ye.

Chor. of Phil. Spirits.   Hither this way, this way bend.

Chor. of Grimb. Spirits. This way, this way bend.

Philidels Spirits.   Trust not that Malicious Fiend.   15

Grimbalds Spirits.   Trust me, I am no Malicious Fiend.

Philidels Spirits.   Hither this way, *&c.*

.   .   .   .

[*Grimbald*] *sings.* Let not a Moon-born Elf mislead ye,

From your Prey, and from your Glory.

Too far, Alas, he has betray'd ye: 20

Follow the Flames, that wave before ye:

Sometimes sev'n, and sometimes one;

Hurry, hurry, hurry, hurry on.

2

See, see, the Footsteps plain appearing,

That way *Oswald* chose for flying: 25

Firm is the Turff, and fit for bearing,

Where yonder Pearly Dews are lying.

Far he cannot hence be gone;

Hurry, hurry, hurry, hurry on.

.   .   .   .

Philidel sings.   Hither this way . . .   30

IV

Enter Shepherds and Shepherdesses.

1 *Shepherd* ⎫ How blest are Shepherds, how happy their Lasses,

sings. ⎭ While Drums and Trumpets are sounding Alarms!

Over our Lowly Sheds all the Storm passes;

And when we die, 'tis in each others Arms.

All the Day on our Herds, and Flocks employing;   5

All the Night on our Flutes, and in enjoying.

Chor. All the Day, *&c.*

2

Bright Nymphs of *Britain*, with Graces attended,
Let not your Days without Pleasure expire;
Honour's but empty, and when Youth is ended,   10
All Men will praise you, but none will desire.
Let not Youth fly away without Contenting;
Age will come time enough, for your Repenting.
   Chor. Let not Youth, *&c.*
Here the Men offer their Flutes to the Women, which they refuse.

2 Shepherdess. Shepherd, Shepherd, leave Decoying,   15
       Pipes are sweet, a Summers Day;
    But a little after Toying,
       Women have the Shot to Pay.

    Here are Marriage-Vows for signing,
       Set their Marks that cannot write: 20
    After that, without Repining,
       Play and Welcom, Day and Night.
Here the Women give the Men Contracts, which they accept.

   Chor. ⎫ Come, Shepherds, lead up, a lively Measure;
   of all. ⎭ The Cares of Wedlock, are Cares of Pleasure:
    But whether Marriage bring Joy, or Sorrow,   25
    Make sure of this Day, and hang to Morrow.

--

V

   Phil. WE must work, we must haste;
    Noon-Tyde Hour, is almost past:
    Sprights, that glimmer in the Sun,
    Into Shades already run.
    Osmond will be here, anon.   5

. . . .

Philidel approaches Emmeline, *sprinkling some of the Water over her Eyes,
out of the Vial.*
     Phil.   Thus, thus I infuse
       These Soveraign Dews.

Fly back, ye Films, that Cloud her sight,
And you, ye Chrystal Humours bright,
Your Noxious Vapours purg'd away,   10
Recover, and admit the Day.
Now cast your Eyes abroad, and see
    All but me.

VI

Airy Spirits appear in the Shapes of Men and Women.

Man sings.   OH Sight, the Mother of Desires,
              What Charming Objects dost thou yield!
                'Tis sweet, when tedious Night expires,
              To see the Rosie Morning guild
                The Mountain-Tops, and paint the Field!   5
              But, when *Clorinda* comes in sight,
              She makes the Summers Day more bright;
              And when she goes away, 'tis Night.
Chor.   When Fair *Clorinda* comes in sight, *&c.*

Wom. sings.   'Tis sweet the Blushing Morn to view;   10
              And Plains adorn'd with Pearly Dew:
              But such cheap Delights to see,
                Heaven and Nature,
                Give each Creature;
              They have Eyes, as well as we.   15
                This is the Joy, all Joys above,
                  To see, to see,
                  That only she,
                That only she we love!
Chor.   This is the Joy, all Joys above, *&c.*   20

Man sings.   And, if we may discover,
              What Charms both Nymph and Lover,
                'Tis, when the Fair at Mercy lies,
              With Kind and Amorous Anguish,
              To Sigh, to Look, to Languish,   25
                On each others Eyes!
Chor. of all ⎱ And if we may discover, *&c.*
Men & Wom.⎰

VII

Osmond strikes the Ground with his Wand: The Scene changes to a Prospect of Winter in Frozen Countries.

Cupid *Descends.*

Cup. sings.   WHAT ho, thou *Genius* of the Clime, what ho!
              Ly'st thou asleep beneath those Hills of Snow?
              Stretch out thy Lazy Limbs; Awake, awake,
              And Winter from thy Furry Mantle shake.

Genius *Arises.*

Genius.   What Power art thou, who from below,   5
            Hast made me Rise, unwillingly, and slow,
            From Beds of Everlasting Snow!
            See'st thou not how stiff, and wondrous old,
            Far unfit to bear the bitter Cold,
            I can scarcely move, or draw my Breath;   10
            Let me, let me, Freeze again to Death.

Cupid.   Thou Doting Fool, forbear, forbear;
            What, Dost thou Dream of Freezing here?
            At Loves appearing, all the Skie clearing,
              The Stormy Winds their Fury spare: 15
            Winter subduing, and Spring renewing,
              My Beams create a more Glorious Year.
            Thou Doting Fool, forbear, forbear;
            What, Dost thou Dream of Freezing here?

Genius.   Great Love, I know thee now;   20
            Eldest of the Gods art Thou:
            Heav'n and Earth, by Thee were made.
              Humane Nature,
              Is thy Creature,
            Every where Thou art obey'd.   25

Cupid.   No part of my Dominion shall be waste,
              To spread my Sway, and sing my Praise,
              Ev'n here I will a People raise,
            Of kind embracing Lovers, and embrac'd.

Cupid waves his Wand, upon which the Scene opens, and discovers a Prospect of Ice and Snow to the end of the Stage.

Singers and Dancers, Men and Women, appear.

Man.	See, see, we assemble,	30
	Thy Revels to hold:	
	Though quiv'ring with Cold,	
	We Chatter and Tremble.	
Cupid.	'Tis I, 'tis I, 'tis I, that have warm'd ye;	
	In spight of Cold Weather,	35
	I've brought ye together:	
	'Tis I, 'tis I, 'tis I, that have arm'd ye.	
Chor.	'Tis Love, 'tis Love, 'tis Love that has warm'd us;	
	In spight of Cold Weather,	
	He brought us together:	40
	'Tis Love, 'tis Love, 'tis Love that has arm'd us.	

Cupid.	Sound a Parley, ye Fair, and surrender;	
	Set your selves, and your Lovers at ease;	
	He's a Grateful Offender	
	Who Pleasure dare seize:	45
	But the Whining Pretender	
	Is sure to displease.	

2

Since the Fruit of Desire is possessing,
    'Tis Unmanly to Sigh and Complain;
When we Kneel for Redressing,   50
    We move your Disdain:
Love was made for a Blessing,
    And not for a Pain.

A Dance; after which the Singers and Dancers depart.

VIII

As [Arthur] is going to the Bridge, two Syrens arise from the Water; They shew themselves to the Waste, and Sing.

1 Syren.	O PASS not on, but stay,	
	And waste the Joyous Day	
	With us in gentle Play:	
	Unbend to Love, unbend thee:	
	O lay thy Sword aside,	
	And other Arms provide;	5

                    For other Wars attend thee,
                       And sweeter to be try'd.
   Chor.   For other Wars, &c.
   Both sing. Two Daughters of this Aged Stream are we;   10
                    And both our Sea-green Locks have comb'd for thee;
                    Come Bathe with us an Hour or two,
                    Come Naked in, for we are so;
                    What Danger from a Naked Foe?
                    Come Bathe with us, come Bathe, and share,   15
                    What Pleasures in the Floods appear;
                    We'll beat the Waters till they bound,
                    And Circle round, around, around,
                    And Circle round, around.

                              IX

   . . . Nymphs *and* Sylvans *come out from behind the Trees. Base and two*
   Trebles sing the following Song to a Minuet.
          Dance with the Song, all with Branches in their Hands.

              Song. HOW happy the Lover,
                        How easie his Chain,
                        How pleasing his Pain?
                     How sweet to discover!
                        He sighs not in vain.   5
                     For Love every Creature
                     Is form'd by his Nature;
                        No Joys are above
                        The Pleasures of Love.

   The Dance continues with the same Measure play'd alone.

                              2

                     In vain are our Graces,   10
                        In vain are your Eyes,
                        If Love you despise;
                     When Age furrows Faces,
                        'Tis time to be wise.
                     Then use the short Blessing,   15
                     That Flies in Possessing:
                        No Joys are above
                        The Pleasures of Love.

X

Merlin waves his Wand; the Scene changes, and discovers the British Ocean in a Storm. Æolus in a Cloud above: Four Winds hanging, &c.

Æolus ⎫   YE Blust'ring Brethren of the Skies,
singing. ⎭   Whose Breath has ruffl'd all the Watry Plain,
       Retire, and let *Britannia* Rise,
    In Triumph o'er the Main.
      Serene and Calm, and void of fear,   5
      The Queen of Islands must appear:
      Serene and Calm, as when the Spring
      The New-Created World began,
      And Birds on Boughs did softly sing,
      Their Peaceful Homage paid to Man,   10
      While *Eurus* did his Blasts forbear,
      In favour of the Tender Year.
    Retreat, Rude Winds, Retreat,
    To Hollow Rocks, your Stormy Seat;
    There swell your Lungs, and vainly, vainly threat.   15

Æolus ascends, and the four Winds fly off. The Scene opens, and discovers a calm Sea, to the end of the House. An Island *arises, to a soft Tune;* Britannia *seated in the Island, with Fishermen at her Feet, &c. The Tune changes; the Fishermen come ashore, and Dance a while; After which,* Pan *and a* Nereide *come on the Stage, and sing.*

Pan *and* Nereide *Sing.*

    Round thy Coasts, Fair Nymph of *Britain,*
      For thy Guard our Waters flow:
    Proteus all his Herd admitting,
      On thy Greens to Graze below.
    Foreign Lands thy Fishes Tasting,   20
    Learn from thee Luxurious Fasting.

Song of three Parts.

    For Folded Flocks, on Fruitful Plains,
    The Shepherds and the Farmers Gains,
      Fair *Britain* all the World outvyes;
    And *Pan,* as in *Arcadia* Reigns,   25
      Where Pleasure mixt with Profit lyes.

2

Though *Jasons* Office was Fam'd of old,
The *British* Wool is growing Gold;
　　No Mines can more of Wealth supply:
It keeps the Peasant from the Cold,　　　　　　30
　　And takes for Kings the *Tyrian* Dye.

*The last Stanza sung over again betwixt Pan and the Nereide. After which
the former Dance is varied, and goes on.*
Enter Comus with three Peasants, who sing the following Song in Parts.

Com.　　　Your Hay it is Mow'd, and your Corn is Reap'd;
　　　　　Your Barns will be full, and your Hovels heap'd:
　　　　　　　Come, my Boys, come;
　　　　　　　Come, my Boys, come;　　　　　　35
　　　　　And merrily Roar out Harvest Home;
　　　　　　　Harvest Home,
　　　　　　　Harvest Home;
　　　　　And merrily Roar out Harvest Home.
Chorus.　　Come, my Boys, come, &c.　　　　　　40
1 Man.　　We ha' cheated the Parson, we'll cheat him agen;
　　　　　For why shou'd a Blockhead ha' One in Ten?
　　　　　　　One in Ten,
　　　　　　　One in Ten,
　　　　　For why shou'd a Blockhead ha' One in Ten?　　45
Chorus.　　　One in Ten,
　　　　　　　One in Ten;
　　　　　For why shou'd a Blockhead ha' One in Ten?
2 [*Man*].　For Prating so long like a Book-learn'd Sot,
　　　　　Till Pudding and Dumplin burn to Pot;　　50
　　　　　　　Burn to Pot,
　　　　　　　Burn to Pot;
　　　　　Till Pudding and Dumplin burn to Pot.
Chorus.　　　Burn to Pot, &c.
3 [*Man*].　We'll toss off our Ale till we canno' stand,　　55
　　　　　And Hoigh for the Honour of Old *England*:
　　　　　　　Old *England*,
　　　　　　　Old *England*;
　　　　　And Hoigh for the Honour of Old *England*.
Chorus.　　　Old *England*, &c.　　　　　　60

　　　　　The Dance vary'd into a round Country-Dance.

Enter Venus.

Venus.   Fairest Isle, all Isles Excelling,
     Seat of Pleasures, and of Loves;
    Venus here, will chuse her Dwelling,
     And forsake her *Cyprian* Groves.

2

    Cupid, from his Fav'rite Nation,   65
     Care and Envy will Remove;
    Jealousie, that poysons Passion,
     And Despair that dies for Love.

3

    Gentle Murmurs, sweet Complaining,
     Sighs that blow the Fire of Love;   70
    Soft Repulses, kind Disdaining,
     Shall be all the Pains you prove.

4

    Every Swain shall pay his Duty,
     Grateful every Nymph shall prove;
    And as these Excel in Beauty,   75
     Those shall be Renown'd for Love.

XI

The Scene opens above, and discovers the Order of the Garter.

(*Honour sings.*)

1

Hon.   ST. *GEORGE*, the Patron of our Isle,
     A Soldier, and a Saint,
    On that Auspicious Order smile,
     Which Love and Arms will plant.

2

    Our Natives not alone appear   5
     To Court this Martiall Prize;
    But Foreign Kings, Adopted here,
     Their Crowns at Home despise.

3

Our Soveraign High, in Aweful State,
His Honours shall bestow;   10
And see his Sceptr'd Subjects wait
On his Commands below.

A full Chorus of the whole Song: After which the Grand Dance.

TO SIR GEORGE ETHEREGE
Mr. D.—— *Answer*

To you who live in chill Degree,
  (As Map informs) of Fifty three;
And do not much for Cold attone
By bringing thither Fifty one:
(Methinks) all Climes shou'd be alike,   5
From Tropick, e'en to Pole Artick;
Since you have such a Constitution,
As cannot suffer Diminution;
You can be old in grave Debate,
And young in Loves Affairs of State,   10
And both to Wives and Husbands show
The vigour of a Plenipo——
Like mighty Missioner you come,
Ad partes infidelium;
A work of wondrous Merit sure,   15
So far to go, so much endure,
And all to preach to German Dame,
Where sound of *Cupid* never came.
Less had you done, had you been sent,
As far as *Drake*, or *Pinto* went,   20
For Cloves and Nutmegs to the Line-a,
Or even for Oranges to *China*;
That had indeed been Charity
Where Love-sick Ladies helpless lye
Chop'd, and for want of Liquor dry;   25
But you have made your Zeal appear,
Within the Circle of the Bear;

To Sir George Etherege. Text from The History of Adolphus . . . With a Collection of Songs and Love-Verses. By several Hands, *1691*   11 Husbands] Husband *91*

What Region of the World so dull,
That is not of your Labours full.
Triptolemus, (so Sing the Nine)   30
Strew'd plenty from his Cart Divine;
But (spight of all those Fable-makers)
He never sow'd on Almaine Acres;
No, that was left by fates Decree,
To be perform'd and sung by thee.   35
Thou break'st thro' Forms, with as much Ease
As the French King thro' Articles;
In grand Affairs thy days are spent
In waging weighty Complement,
With such as Monarchs represent;   40
They whom such vast Fatigues attend,
Want some soft minutes to unbend,
To shew the World, that now and then
Great Ministers are mortal Men.
Then Rhenish Rummers walk the Round,   45
In Bumpers every King is Crown'd;
Besides Three holy Miter'd Hectors,
And the whole Colledge of Electors;
No health of Potentate is sunk,
That pays to make his Envoy Drunk.   50
These Dutch delights I mention'd last
Suit not, I know, your English Tast,
For Wine, to leave a Whore, or Play,
Was ne'er your Excellencies way;
Nor need the Title give offence,   55
For here you were his Excellence;
For Gaming, Writing, Speaking, Keeping,
His Excellence for all but sleeping.
Now if you tope in Form, and Treat,
'Tis the sour Sawce, to the sweet Meat,   60
The Fine you pay for being Great.
Nay, there's a harder Imposition,
Which is (indeed) the Court Petition,
That setting Worldly Pomp aside,
(Which Poet has at Font defi'd.)   65
You wou'd be pleas'd in humble way,
To write a trifle call'd a Play:

This truly is, a Degradation,
But wou'd oblige the Crown and Nation,
Next to your Wise Negotiation: 70
If you pretend, as well you may,
Your high Degree, your Friends will say,
The Duke St. *Aignan* made a Play;
If *Gallick* Peer affect you scarce,
His Grace of B.—— has made a Farce,   75
'And you whose comick Wit is Terseal,
Can hardly fall below Rehearsal.
Then finish what you once began,
But scrible faster if you can;
For yet no George, to our discerning,   80
E'er Writ without a Ten years warning.

TO Mr. Southern; ON HIS COMEDY,
called the WIVES EXCUSE

SURE there's a Fate in Plays; and 'tis in vain
    To write, while these malignant Planets Reign:
Some very foolish Influence rules the Pit,
Not always kind to Sence, or just to Wit.
And whilst it lasts, let Buffoonry succeed,   5
To make us laugh; for never was more need.
Farce, in it self, is of a nasty scent;
But the gain smells not of the Excrement.
The *Spanish* Nymph, a Wit and Beauty too,
With all her Charms bore but a single show: 10
But, let a Monster *Muscovite* appear,
He draws a crowded Audience round the Year.
May be thou hast not pleas'd the Box and Pit,
Yet those who blame thy Tale, commend thy Wit;
So *Terence* Plotted; but so *Terence* Writ.   15
Like his thy Thoughts are true, thy Language clean,
Ev'n Lewdness is made Moral, in thy Scene.
The Hearers may for want of *Nokes* repine,
But rest secure, the Readers will be thine.

To Mr. Southern. Text from The Wives Excuse: or, Cuckolds make Themselves.
A Comedy, *1692*

Nor was thy Labour'd *Drama*, damn'd or hiss'd, 20
But with a kind Civility, dismiss'd:
With such good manners as the *Wife did use,   *The Wife
Who, not accepting, did but just refuse.   in the
There was a glance at parting; such a look   Play, Mrs.
As bids thee not give o're, for one rebuke. 25 Friendall.
But if thou wou'dst be seen, as well as read;
Copy one living Author, and one dead;
The Standard of thy Style, let *Etherege* be:
For Wit, th' Immortal Spring of *Wycherly*.
Learn after both, to draw some just Design, 30
And the next Age will learn to Copy thine.

ELEONORA:

A PANEGYRICAL POEM
Dedicated to the MEMORY of the Late
COUNTESS OF ABINGDON

—Superas evadere ad auras,
Hoc opus, hic labor est. Pauci, quos æquus amavit
Juppiter, aut ardens evexit ad æthera virtus;
Diis geniti potuere. Virgil Æneid. l. 6.

TO THE RIGHT HONOURABLE
THE Earl of *Abingdon &c.*

MY LORD,

*T*HE *Commands, with which You honour'd me some Months ago, are now
perform'd: They had been sooner; but betwixt ill health, some business,
and many troubles, I was forc'd to deferr them till this time.* Ovid, *going to his
Banishment, and Writing from on Shipbord to his Friends, excus'd the Faults
of his Poetry by his Misfortunes; and told them, that good Verses never flow, but* 5
from a serene and compos'd Spirit. Wit, which is a kind of Mercury, *with
Wings fasten'd to his Head and Heels, can flye but slowly, in a damp air. I therefore chose rather to Obey You late, than ill: if at least I am capable of writing
any thing, at any time, which is worthy Your Perusal and Your Patronage. I
cannot say that I have escap'd from a Shipwreck; but have only gain'd a Rock* 10
*by hard swimming; where I may pant a while and gather breath: For the
Doctors give me a sad assurance, that my Disease never took its leave of any man,
but with a purpose·to return. However, my Lord, I have laid hold on the Interval,
and menag'd the small Stock which Age has left me, to the best advantage, in
performing this inconsiderable service to my Ladies Memory. We, who are* 15
Priests of Apollo, *have not the Inspiration when we please; but must wait till the
God comes rushing on us, and invades us with a fury, which we are not able to
resist: which gives us double strength while the Fit continues, and leaves us
languishing and spent, at its departure. Let me not seem to boast, my Lord; for
I have really felt it on this Occasion; and prophecy'd beyond my natural power.* 20
*Let me add, and hope to be believ'd, that the Excellency of the Subject contributed
much to the Happiness of the Execution: And that the weight of thirty Years was
taken off me, while I was writing. I swom with the Tyde, and the Water under
me was buoyant. The Reader will easily observe, that I was transported, by the*

multitude and variety of my Similitudes; which are generally the product of a 25
luxuriant Fancy; and the wantonness of Wit. Had I call'd in my Judgment to
my assistance, I had certainly retrench'd many of them. But I defend them not;
let them pass for beautiful faults amongst the better sort of Critiques: For the
whole Poem, though written in that which they call Heroique Verse, is of the
Pindarique nature, as well in the Thought as the Expression; and as such, 30
requires the same grains of allowance for it. It was intended, as Your Lordship
sees in the Title, not for an Elegie; but a Panegyrique. A kind of Apotheosis,
indeed; if a Heathen Word may be applyed to a Christian use. And on all Occa-
sions of Praise, if we take the Ancients for our Patterns, we are bound by
Prescription to employ the magnificence of Words, and the force of Figures, to 35
adorn the sublimity of Thoughts. Isocrates *amongst the* Grecian *Orators; and*
Cicero, *and the younger* Pliny, *amongst the* Romans, *have left us their Pre-*
cedents for our security: For I think I need not mention the inimitable Pindar,
who stretches on these Pinnions out of sight, and is carried upward, as it were,
into another World. 40

This at least, my Lord, I may justly plead, that if I have not perform'd so
well as I think I have, yet I have us'd my best endeavours to excel my self. One
Disadvantage I have had, which is, never to have known, or seen my Lady: And
to draw the Lineaments of her Mind, from the Description which I have receiv'd
from others, is for a Painter to set himself at work without the living Original 45
before him. Which the more beautiful it is, will be so much the more difficult for
him to conceive; when he has only a relation given him, of such and such Features
by an Acquaintance or a Friend; without the Nice Touches which give the best
Resemblance, and make the Graces of the Picture. Every Artist is apt enough to
flatter himself, (and I amongst the rest) that their own ocular Observations, 50
would have discover'd more perfections, at least others, than have been deliver'd
to them: Though I have receiv'd mine from the best hands, that is, from Persons
who neither want a just Understanding of my Lady's Worth, nor a due Venera-
tion for her Memory.

Doctor Donn *the greatest Wit, though not the best Poet of our Nation,* 55
acknowledges, that he had never seen Mrs. Drury, *whom he has made immortal*
in his admirable Anniversaries; I have had the same fortune; though I have not
succeeded to the same Genius. However, I have follow'd his footsteps in the Design
of his Panegyrick, which was to raise an Emulation in the living, to Copy out the
Example of the dead. And therefore it was, that I once intended to have call'd 60
this Poem, the Pattern: And though on a second consideration, I chang'd the
Title into the Name of that Illustrious Person, yet the Design continues, and,
Eleonora *is still the Pattern of Charity, Devotion, and Humility; of the best*
Wife, the best Mother, and the best of Friends.

And now, my Lord, though I have endeavour'd to answer Your Commands, yet 65
I cou'd not answer it to the World, nor to my Conscience, if I gave not Your
Lordship my Testimony of being the best Husband now living: I say my Testi-
mony only: For the praise of it, is given You by Your self. They who despise the
Rules of Virtue both in their Practice and their Morals, will think this a very
trivial Commendation. But I think it the peculiar happiness of the Countess of 70
Abingdon, to have been so truly lov'd by you, while she was living, and so grate-
fully honour'd, after she was dead. Few there are who have either had, or cou'd
have such a loss; and yet fewer who carried their Love and Constancy beyond the
Grave. The exteriours of Mourning, a decent Funeral, and black Habits, are the
usual stints of Common Husbands: and perhaps their Wives deserve no better than 75
to be mourn'd with Hypocrisie, and forgot with ease. But You have distinguish'd
Your self from ordinary Lovers, by a real, and lasting grief for the Deceas'd.
And by endeavouring to raise for her, the most durable Monument, which is
that of Verse. And so it wou'd have prov'd if the Workman had been equal to
the Work; and Your Choice of the Artificer, as happy as Your Design. Yet, as 80
Phidias when he had made the Statue of Minerva, *cou'd not forbear to ingrave*
his own Name, as Author of the Piece; so give me leave to hope, that by sub-
scribing mine to this Poem, I may live by the Goddess, and transmit my Name to
Posterity by the memory of Hers. 'Tis no flattery, to assure Your Lordship, that
she is remember'd in the present Age, by all who have had the Honour of her 85
Conversation and Acquaintance. And that I have never been in any Company
since the news of her death was first brought me, where they have not extoll'd her
Virtues; and even spoken the same things of her in Prose, which I have done in
Verse.

I therefore think my self oblig'd to thank Your Lordship for the Commission 90
which You have given me: How I have acquitted my self of it, must be left to the
Opinion of the World, in spight of any Protestation, which I can enter against
the present Age, as Incompetent, or Corrupt Judges. For my Comfort they are
but Englishmen, *and as such, if they Think Ill of me to Day, they are inconstant*
enough, to Think Well of me to Morrow. And, after all, I have not much to 95
thank my Fortune that I was born amongst them. The Good of both Sexes are so
few, in England, *that they stand like Exceptions against General Rules: And*
though one of them has deserv'd a greater Commendation, than I cou'd give her,
they have taken care, that I shou'd not tire my Pen, with frequent exercise on the
like Subjects; that Praises, like Taxes, shou'd be appropriated; and left almost as 100
Individual as the Person. They say my Talent is Satyre; if it be so, 'tis a Fruitful
Age; and there is an extraordinary Crop to gather. But a single hand is in-
sufficient for such a Harvest: They have sown the Dragons Teeth themselves; and
'tis but just they shou'd reap each other in Lampoons. You, my Lord, who have

the Character of Honour, though 'tis not my Happiness to know You, may stand 105
aside, with the small Remainders of the English Nobility, truly such, and unhurt
your selves, behold the mad Combat. If I have pleas'd You, and some few others,
I have obtain'd my end. You see, I have disabled my self, like an Elected Speaker
of the House; yet like him I have undertaken the Charge; and find the Burden
sufficiently recompenc'd by the Honour. Be pleas'd to accept of these my Unworthy 110
Labours; this Paper Monument; and let her Pious Memory, which I am sure
is Sacred to You, not only plead the Pardon of my many Faults, but gain me
Your Protection, which is ambitiously sought by,

MY LORD,

Your Lordship's

Most Obedient Servant,

John Dryden.

ELEONORA:

A PANEGYRICAL POEM
Dedicated to the MEMORY OF THE
Late Countess of *ABINGDON*

As, when some Great and Gracious Monarch dies,   *The Intro-*
  Soft whispers, first, and mournful Murmurs rise   *duction.*
Among the sad Attendants; then, the sound
Soon gathers voice, and spreads the news around,
Through Town and Country, till the dreadful blast   5
Is blown to distant Colonies at last;
Who, then perhaps, were off'ring Vows in vain,
For his long life, and for his happy Reign:
So slowly, by degrees, unwilling Fame
Did Matchless *Eleonora*'s fate proclaim,   10
Till publick as the loss, the news became.
  The Nation felt it, in th' extremest parts;
With eyes o'reflowing, and with bleeding hearts;   *Of her*
But most the Poor, whom daily she supply'd;   *Charity.*
Beginning to be such, but when she dy'd.   15
For, while she liv'd, they slept in peace, by night;

Secure of bread, as of returning light;
And, with such firm dependence on the Day,
That need grew pamper'd; and forgot to pray:
So sure the Dole, so ready at their call,　　　　20
They stood prepar'd to see the Manna fall.

　Such Multitudes she fed, she cloath'd, she nurst,
That she, her self, might fear her wanting first.
Of her Five Talents, other five she made;
Heav'n, that had largely giv'n, was largely pay'd:　　25
And, in few lives, in wondrous few, we find
A Fortune, better fitted to the Mind.
Nor did her Alms from Ostentation fall,
Or proud desire of Praise; the Soul gave all:
Unbrib'd it gave; or, if a bribe appear,　　　　30
No less than Heav'n; to heap huge treasures, there.

　Want pass'd for Merit, at her open door,
Heav'n saw, he safely might increase his Poor.
And trust their Sustenance with her so well,
As not to be at charge of Miracle.　　　　35
None cou'd be needy, whom she saw, or knew;
All, in the Compass of her Sphear, she drew:
He who cou'd touch her Garment, was as sure,
As the first Christians of th' Apostles cure.
The distant heard, by Fame, her pious deeds;　　40
And laid her up, for their extremest needs;
A future Cordial, for a fainting Mind;
For, what was ne're refus'd, all hop'd to find;
Each in his turn: The Rich might freely come,
As to a Friend; but to the Poor, 'twas Home.　　45
As to some Holy House th' Afflicted came;
The Hunger-starv'd, the Naked, and the Lame;
Want and Diseases fled before her Name.
For zeal like hers, her Servants were too slow;
She was the first where need requir'd, to go;　　50
Her self the Foundress, and Attendant too.

　Sure she had Guests sometimes to entertain,
Guests in disguise, of her Great Master's Train:
Her Lord himself might come, for ought we know;
Since in a Servant's form he liv'd below:　　　　55
Beneath her Roof, he might be pleas'd to stay:

Or some benighted Angel, in his way
Might ease his Wings; and seeing Heav'n appear
In its best work of Mercy, think it there,
Where all the deeds of Charity and Love   60
Were in as constant Method, as above:
All carry'd on; all of a piece with theirs;
As free her Alms, as diligent her cares;
As loud her Praises, and as warm her Pray'rs.   } 64

*Of her pru-
dent Man-
agement.*

    Yet was she not profuse; but fear'd to wast,
And wisely manag'd, that the stock might last;
That all might be supply'd; and she not grieve
When Crouds appear'd, she had not to relieve.
Which to prevent, she still increas'd her store;
Laid up, and spar'd, that she might give the more: 70
So *Pharaoh*, or some Greater King than he,
Provided for the sev'nth Necessity:
Taught from above, his Magazines to frame;
That Famine was prevented e're it came.
Thus Heav'n, though All-sufficient, shows a thrift   75
In his Oeconomy, and bounds his gift:
Creating for our Day, one single Light;
And his Reflection too supplies the Night:
Perhaps a thousand other Worlds, that lye
Remote from us, and latent in the Sky,   80
Are lighten'd by his Beams, and kindly nurst;
Of which our Earthly Dunghil is the worst.

    Now, as all Vertues keep the middle line,
Yet somewhat more to one extreme incline,
Such was her Soul; abhorring Avarice,   85
Bounteous, but, almost bounteous to a Vice:
Had she giv'n more, it had Profusion been,
And turn'd th' exccss of Goodness, into Sin.

*Of her
Humility.*

    These Vertues rais'd her Fabrick to the Sky;
For that which is next Heav'n, is Charity.   90
But, as high Turrets, for their Ay'ry steep
Require Foundations, in proportion deep:
And lofty Cedars, as far, upward shoot,
As to the neather Heav'ns they drive the root;
So low did her secure Foundation lye,   95
She was not Humble, but Humility.

Scarcely she knew that she was great, or fair,
Or wise, beyond what other Women are,
Or, which is better, knew; but never durst compare.
For to be consc'ious of what all admire,   100
And not be vain, advances Vertue high'r:
But still she found, or rather thought she found,
Her own worth wanting, others to abound:
Ascrib'd above their due to ev'ry one,
Unjust and scanty to her self alone.   105

Of her
Piety.
    Such her Devotion was, as might give rules
Of Speculation, to disputing Schools;
And teach us equally the Scales to hold
Betwixt the two Extremes of hot and cold;
That pious heat may mod'rately prevail,   110
And we be warm'd, but not be scorch'd with zeal.
Business might shorten, not disturb her Pray'r;
Heav'n had the best, if not the greater share.
An Active life, long Oraisons forbids;
Yet still she pray'd, for still she pray'd by deeds.   115
    Her ev'ry day was Sabbath: Only free
From hours of Pray'r, for hours of Charity.
Such as the *Jews* from servile toil releast;
Where works of Mercy were a part of rest:
Such as blest Angels exercise above,   120
Vary'd with Sacred Hymns, and Acts of Love;
Such Sabbaths as that one she now enjoys;
Ev'n that perpetual one, which she employs,
(For such vicissitudes in Heav'n there are)
In Praise alternate, and alternate Pray'r.   125
All this she practis'd here; that when she sprung
Amidst the Quires, at the first sight she sung.
Sung, and was sung her self, in Angels Lays;
For praising her, they did her Maker praise.
All Offices of Heav'n so well she knew,   130
Before she came, that nothing there was new.
And she was so familiarly receiv'd,
As one returning, not as one arriv'd.

Of her
various
Vertues.
    Muse, down again precipitate thy flight;
For how can Mortal Eyes sustain Immortal Light!   135
But as the Sun in Water we can bear,

Yet not the Sun, but his Reflection there,
So let us view her here, in what she was;
And take her Image, in this watry Glass:
Yet look not ev'ry Lineament to see; } 140
Some will be cast in shades; and some will be
So lamely drawn, you scarcely know, 'tis she.
For where such various Vertues we recite,
'Tis like the Milky-Way, all over bright, }
But sown so thick with Stars, 'tis undistinguish'd Light. } 145
    Her Vertue, not her Vertues let us call,
For one Heroick comprehends 'em all:
One, as a Constellation is but one; }
Though 'tis a Train of Stars, that, rolling on, }
Rise in their turn, and in the Zodiack run. } 150
Ever in Motion; now 'tis Faith ascends, }
Now Hope, now Charity, that upward tends, }
And downwards with diffusive Good, descends. }
    As in Perfumes compos'd with Art and Cost,
'Tis hard to say what Scent is uppermost; 155
Nor this part Musk or Civet can we call,
Or Amber, but a rich Result of all;
So, she was all a Sweet; whose ev'ry part,
In due proportion mix'd, proclaim'd the Maker's Art.
No single Virtue we cou'd most commend; 160
Whether the Wife, the Mother, or the Friend;
For she was all, in that supreme degree,
That, as no one prevail'd, so all was she.
The sev'ral parts lay hidden in the Piece;
Th' Occasion but exerted that, or this. 165
    A Wife as tender, and as true withall,
As the first Woman was, before her fall:
Made for the Man, of whom she was a part;
Made, to attract his Eyes, and keep his Heart.
A second *Eve*, but by no Crime accurst; 170
As beauteous, not as brittle as the first.
Had she been first, still Paradise had bin,
And Death had found no entrance by her sin.
So she not only had preserv'd from ill
Her Sex and ours, but liv'd their Pattern still. 175
    Love and Obedience to her Lord she bore,

Of her Conjugal Virtues.

She much obey'd him, but she lov'd him more.
Not aw'd to Duty by superior sway;
But taught by his Indulgence to obey.
Thus we love God as Author of our good;   180
So Subjects love just Kings, or so they shou'd.
Nor was it with Ingratitude return'd;   ⎞
In equal Fires the blissful Couple burn'd: ⎬
One Joy possess'd 'em both, and in one Grief they mourn'd. ⎠
His Passion still improv'd: he lov'd so fast   185
As if he fear'd each day wou'd be her last.
Too true a Prophet to foresee the Fate
That shou'd so soon divide their happy State:
When he to Heav'n entirely must restore
That Love, that Heart, where he went halves before.   190
Yet as the Soul is all in ev'ry part,
So God and He, might each have all her Heart.

Of her love   So had her Children too; for Charity
to her Chil-   Was not more fruitful, or more kind than she:
dren.   Each under other by degrees they grew;   195
A goodly Perspective of distant view:
Anchises look'd not with so pleas'd a Face
In numb'ring o'er his future *Roman* Race,
And Marshalling the Heroes of his name
As, in their Order, next to light they came;   200
Nor *Cybele* with half so kind an Eye,
Survey'd her Sons and Daughters of the Skie.
Proud, shall I say, of her immortal Fruit,
As far as Pride with Heav'nly Minds may suit.

Her care of   Her pious love excell'd to all she bore;   205
their Edu-   New Objects only multiply'd it more.
cation.   And as the Chosen found the perly Grain
As much as ev'ry Vessel cou'd contain;
As in the Blissfull Vision each shall share,   ⎞
As much of Glory, as his Soul can bear;   ⎬   210
So did she love, and so dispence her Care.   ⎠
Her eldest thus, by consequence, was best;
As longer cultivated than the rest:
The Babe had all that Infant care beguiles,
And early knew his Mother in her smiles: 215
But when dilated Organs let in day

To the young Soul, and gave it room to play,
At his first aptness, the Maternal Love
Those Rudiments of Reason did improve:
The tender Age was pliant to command;   220
Like Wax it yielded to the forming hand:
True to th' Artificer, the labour'd Mind
With ease was pious, generous, just and kind;
Soft for Impression from the first, prepar'd,
Till Vertue, with long exercise, grew hard;   225
With ev'ry Act confirm'd; and made, at last
So durable, as not to be effac'd,
It turn'd to Habit; and, from Vices free,
Goodness resolv'd into Necessity.

    Thus fix'd she Vertue's Image, that's her own,   230
Till the whole Mother in the Children shone;
For that was their Perfection: she was such,
They never cou'd express her Mind too much.
So unexhausted her Perfections were,
That, for more Children, she had more to spare: 235
For Souls unborn, whom her untimely death
Depriv'd of Bodies, and of mortal breath:
And (cou'd they take th' Impressions of her Mind)
Enough still left to sanctifie her Kind.   239

    Then wonder not to see this Soul extend   *Of her*
The bounds, and seek some other self, a Friend: *Friendship.*
As swelling Seas to gentle Rivers glide,
To seek repose, and empty out the Tyde;
So this full Soul, in narrow limits pent,
Unable to contain her, sought a vent,   245
To issue out, and in some friendly breast
Discharge her Treasures, and securely rest.
T' unbosom all the secrets of her Heart,
Take good advice, but better to impart.
For 'tis the bliss of Friendship's holy state   ⎫   250
To mix their Minds, and to communicate;   ⎬
Though Bodies cannot, Souls can penetrate.   ⎭
Fixt to her choice; inviolably true;
And wisely chusing, for she chose but few.
Some she must have; but in no one cou'd find   255
A Tally fitted for so large a Mind.

The Souls of Friends, like Kings in Progress are;
Still in their own, though from the Pallace far:
Thus her Friend's Heart her Country Dwelling was,
A sweet Retirement to a courser place: 260
Where Pomp and Ceremonies enter'd not;
Where Greatness was shut out, and Buis'ness well forgot.

    This is th' imperfect draught; but short as far
As the true height and bigness of a Star
Exceeds the Measures of th' Astronomer.   265
She shines above we know, but in what place,
How near the Throne, and Heav'ns Imperial Face,
By our weak Opticks is but vainly ghest;
Distance and Altitude conceal the rest.

Reflections
on the
shortness of
her life.

    Tho all these rare Endowments of the Mind   270
Were in a narrow space of life confin'd;
The Figure was with full Perfection crown'd;
Though not so large an Orb, as truly round.

    As when in glory, through the publick place,
The Spoils of conquer'd Nations were to pass,   275
And but one Day for Triumph was allow'd,
The Consul was constrain'd his Pomp to crowd;
And so the swift Procession hurry'd on,
That all, though not distinctly, might be shown;
So, in the straiten'd bounds of life confin'd,   280
She gave but glimpses of her glorious Mind:
And multitudes of Vertues pass'd along;
Each pressing foremost in the mighty throng;
Ambitious to be seen, and then make room,
For greater Multitudes that were to come.   285

    Yet unemploy'd no Minute slipt away;
Moments were precious in so short a stay.
The haste of Heav'n to have her was so great,
That some were single Acts, though each compleat;
But ev'ry Act stood ready to repeat.   290

    Her fellow Saints with busie care, will look
For her blest Name, in Fate's eternal Book;
And, pleas'd to be outdone, with joy will see
Numberless Vertues, endless Charity;
But more will wonder at so short an Age;   295
To find a Blank beyond the thirti'th Page;

And with a pious fear begin to doubt
The Piece imperfect, and the rest torn out.
But 'twas her Saviour's time; and, cou'd there be
A Copy near th' Original, 'twas she.   *She dy'd in her thirty third year.* 300

    As precious Gums are not for lasting fire,
They but perfume the Temple, and expire,
So was she soon exhal'd; and vanish'd hence;
A short sweet Odour, of a vast expence.
She vanish'd, we can scarcely say she dy'd;   305
For but a Now, did Heav'n and Earth divide:
She pass'd serenely with a single breath,
This Moment perfect health, the next was death.   *The manner of her death.*
One sigh, did her eternal Bliss assure;
So little Penance needs, when Souls are almost pure.   310
As gentle Dreams our waking Thoughts pursue;
Or, one Dream pass'd, we slide into a new;
(So close they follow, such wild Order keep,
We think our selves awake, and are asleep:)
So softly death succeeded life, in her;   315
She did but dream of Heav'n, and she was there.

    No Pains she suffer'd, nor expir'd with Noise;
Her Soul was whisper'd out, with God's still Voice:
As an old Friend is beckon'd to a Feast,
And treated like a long familiar Guest;   320
He took her as he found; but found her so,
As one in hourly readiness to go.   *Her pre-paredness to dye.*
Ev'n on that day, in all her Trim prepar'd;
As early notice she from Heav'n had heard,
And some descending Courtier, from above   325
Had giv'n her timely warning to remove:
Or counsell'd her to dress the nuptial Room;
For on that Night the Bridegroom was to come.
He kept his hour, and found her where she lay   329
Cloath'd all in white, the Liv'ry of the Day: *She dy'd on Whitsun-day night.*
Scarce had she sinn'd, in thought, or word, or act;
Unless Omissions were to pass for fact:
That hardly Death a Consequence cou'd draw,
To make her liable to Nature's Law.
And that she dy'd, we only have to show,   335
The mortal part of her she left below:

The rest (so smooth, so suddenly she went)
Look'd like Translation, through the Firmament;
Or like the fiery Carr, on the third Errand sent.

Apostrophe to her Soul.

   O happy Soul! If thou canst view from high,   340
Where thou art all Intelligence, all Eye,
If looking up to God, or down to us,
Thou find'st, that any way be pervious,
Survey the ruines of thy House, and see
Thy widow'd, and thy Orphan Family;   345
Look on thy tender Pledges left behind:
And, if thou canst a vacant Minute find
From Heav'nly Joys, that Interval afford
To thy sad Children, and thy mourning Lord.
See how they grieve, mistaken in their love,   350
And shed a beam of Comfort from above;
Give 'em, as much as mortal Eyes can bear,
A transient view of thy full glories there;
That they with mod'rate sorrow may sustain
And mollifie their Losses, in thy Gain.   355
Or else divide the grief, for such thou wert,
That shou'd not all Relations bear a part,
It were enough to break a single heart.

Epipho-nema: or close of the Poem.

   Let this suffice: Nor thou, great Saint, refuse
This humble Tribute of no vulgar Muse: 360
Who, not by Cares, or Wants, or Age deprest,
Stems a wild Deluge with a dauntless brest:
And dares to sing thy Praises, in a Clime
Where Vice triumphs, and Vertue is a Crime:
Where ev'n to draw the Picture of thy Mind,   365
Is Satyr on the most of Humane Kind:
Take it, while yet 'tis Praise; before my rage
Unsafely just, break loose on this bad Age;
So bad, that thou thy self had'st no defence,
From Vice, but barely by departing hence.   370

   Be what, and where thou art; To wish thy place,
Were in the best, Presumption, more than grace.
Thy Reliques (such thy Works of Mercy are)
Have, in this Poem, been my holy care.

As Earth thy Body keeps, thy Soul the Sky, 375
So shall this Verse preserve thy Memory;
For thou shalt make it live, because it sings of thee.

PROLOGUE, EPILOGUE and SONG
from *CLEOMENES*

PROLOGUE

Spoke by Mr. MOUNTFORT

I THINK or hope, at least, the Coast is clear,
That none but Men of Wit and Sence are here:
That our Bear-Garden Friends are all away,
Who bounce with Hands and Feet, and cry Play, Play.
Who to save Coach-hire, trudge along the Street, 5
Then print our Matted Seats with dirty Feet;
Who, while we speak, make Love to Orange-Wenches,
And between Acts stand strutting on the Benches:
Where got a Cock-horse, making vile Grimaces,
They to the Boxes show their Booby Faces. 10
A Merry-Andrew, such a Mob will serve,
And treat 'em with such Wit as they deserve:
Let 'em go People *Ireland*, where there's need
Of such new Planters to repair the Breed;
Or to *Virginia* or *Jamaica* Steer, 15
But have a care of some *French* Privateer;
For if they should become the Prize of Battle,
They'll take 'em Black and White for *Irish* Cattle.
Arise true Judges in your own Defence,
Controul those Foplings, and declare for Sence: 20
For should the Fools prevail, they stop not there,
But make their next Descent upon the Fair.
Then rise ye Fair; for it concerns you most,
That Fools no longer should your Favours boast;
'Tis time you should renounce 'em, for we find 25

Prologue, Epilogue and Song. Text from Cleomenes, the Spartan Heroe. A Tragedy, 1692

They plead a senseless Claim to Woman kind:
Such Squires are only fit for Country Towns,
To stink of Ale; and dust a Stand with Clownes:
Who, to be chosen for the Lands Protectors,
Tope and get Drunk before their Wise Electors.   30
Let not Farce Lovers your weak Choice upbraid,
But turn 'em over to the Chamber-maid.
Or if they come to see our Tragick Scenes,
Instruct them what a *Spartan* Hero means:
Teach 'em how manly Passions ought to move,   35
For such as cannot Think can never Love:
And since they needs will judge the Poets Art,
Point 'em with Fescu's to each shining Part.
Our Author hopes in you, but still in pain,
He fears your Charms will be employ'd in vain;   40
You can make Fools of Wits, we find each Hour,
But to make Wits of Fools, is past your Power.

EPILOGUE

Spoke by Mrs. BRACEGIRDLE

THIS Day, the Poet bloodily inclin'd,
    Has made me die, full sore against my Mind!
Some of you naughty Men, I fear, will cry,
Poor Rogue! would I might teach thee how to die!
Thanks for your Love; but I sincerely say,   5
I never mean to die, your wicked way.
Well, since it is Decreed all Flesh must go,
(And I am Flesh, at least for ought you know;)
I first declare, I die with pious Mind,
In perfect Charity with all Mankind.   10
Next for my Will:——— I have, in my dispose,
Some certain Moveables would please you Beaux;
As, first, my Youth; for as I have been told,
Some of you, modish Sparks, are dev'lish old.
My Chastity I need not leave among yee: 15
For to suspect old Fops, were much to wrong ye.
You swear y'are Sinners; but for all your haste,
Your Misses shake their Heads, and find you chaste.

I give my Courage to those bold Commanders
That stay with us, and dare not go for *Flanders*.   20
I leave my Truth, (to make his Plot more clear,)
To Mr. *Fuller*, when he next shall swear.
I give my Judgment, craving all your Mercyes,
To those that leave good Plays, for damn'd dull Farces.
My small Devotion let the Gallants share   25
That come to ogle us at Evening Pray'r.
I give my Person—let me well consider,
Faith e'en to him that is the fairest Bidder.
To some rich Hunks, if any be so bold
To say those dreadful Words, *To have and hold*.   30
But stay—to give, and be bequeathing still,
When I'm so poor, is just like *Wickham*'s Will:
Like that notorious Cheat, vast Sums I give,
Only that you may keep me while I live.
Buy a good Bargain, Gallants, while you may,   35
I'll cost you but your Half-a-Crown a day.

SONG

No no, poor suff'ring Heart no Change endeavour,
Choose to sustain the smart, rather than leave her;
My ravish'd Eyes behold such Charms about her,
I can dye with her, but not live without her.
One tender Sigh of hers to see me Languish,   5
Will more than pay the price of my past Anguish:
Beware O cruel Fair, how you smile on me,
'Twas a kind Look of yours that has undone me.

2

Love has in store for me one happy Minute,
And She will end my pain who did begin it;   10
Then no day void of Bliss, or Pleasure leaving,
Ages shall slide away without perceiving:
Cupid shall guard the Door the more to please us,
And keep out Time and Death when they would seize us:
Time and Death shall depart, and say in flying,   15
Love has found out a way to Live by Dying.

EPILOGUE to *HENRY THE SECOND*

Spoke by Mrs. *Bracegirdle*

THUS you the sad Catastrophe have seen,
Occasion'd by a Mistress and a Queen.
Queen *Eleanor* the Proud was *French*, they say;
But *English* Manufacture got the Day:
Jane Clifford was her Name, as Books aver, 5
Fair Rosamond was but her *Nom de Guerre*.
Now tell me, Gallants, wou'd you lead your Life
With such a Mistress, or with such a Wife?
If One must be your Choice, which d'ye approve,
The Curtain-Lecture, or the Curtain-Love? 10
Wou'd ye be Godly with perpetual Strife,
Still drudging on with homely *Joan* your Wife;
Or take your Pleasure in a wicked way,
Like honest Whoring *Harry* in the Play?
I guess your minds: The Mistress wou'd be taking, 15
And nauseous Matrimony sent a packing.
The Devil's in ye all; Mankind's a Rogue,
You love the Bride, but you detest the Clog:
After a Year, poor Spouse is left i'th' lurch;
And you, like *Haynes*, return to Mother-Church. 20
Or, if the name of Church comes cross your mind,
Chappels of Ease behind our Scenes you find:
The Play-house is a kind of Market-place;
One chaffers for a Voice, another for a Face.
Nay, some of you, I dare not say how many, 25
Would buy of me a Pen'worth for your Peny.
Ev'n this poor Face (which with my Fan I hide)
Would make a shift my Portion to provide,
With some small Perquisites I have beside.
Though for your Love, perhaps, I should not care, 30
I could not hate a Man that bids me fair.
What might ensue, 'tis hard for me to tell;
But I was drench'd to day for loving well,
And fear the Poyson that would make me swell.

Epilogue. Text from Henry the Second, King of England; with the Death of Rosamond. A Tragedy, *1693*

POEMS FROM
EXAMEN POETICUM

BEING THE THIRD PART OF Miscellany Poems.
SONG TO A Fair, Young LADY,
Going out of the TOWN In the SPRING

1

ASK not the Cause, why sullen *Spring*
   So long delays her Flow'rs to bear;
Why warbling Birds forget to sing,
   And Winter Storms invert the Year?
Chloris is gone; and Fate provides   5
To make it *Spring*, where she resides.

2

Chloris is gone, the Cruel Fair;
   She cast not back a pitying Eye:
But left her Lover in Despair;
   To sigh, to languish, and to die: 10
Ah, how can those fair Eyes endure
To give the Wounds they will not cure!

3

Great God of Love, why hast thou made
   A Face that can all Hearts command,
That all Religions can invade,   15
   And change the Laws of ev'ry Land?
Where thou hadst plac'd such Pow'r before,
Thou shou'dst have made her Mercy more.

4

When *Chloris* to the Temple comes,
   Adoring Crowds before her fall;   20
She can restore the Dead from Tombs,
   And ev'ry Life but mine recall.
I only am by Love design'd
To be the Victim for Mankind.

Poems. Text from the first edition, 1693

PROLOGUE TO THE UNIVERSITY
OF *OXFORD*, 1681

THE fam'd *Italian* Muse, whose Rhymes advance
  Orlando, and the *Paladins* of *France*,
Records, that when our Wit and Sense is flown,
'Tis lodg'd within the Circle of the Moon
In Earthen Jars, which one, who thither soar'd,   5
Set to his Nose, snufft up, and was restor'd.
What e're the Story be, the Moral's true,
The Wit we lost in Town, we find in you.
Our Poets their fled Parts may draw from hence,
And fill their windy Heads with sober Sense.   10
When *London* Votes with *Southwark*'s disagree,
Here they may find their long lost Loyalty.
Here busie Senates, to th' old Cause inclin'd,
May snuff the Votes their Fellows left behind:
Your Country Neighbours, when their Grain grows dear,   15
May come and find their *last Provision* here:
Whereas we cannot much lament our loss,
Who neither carry'd back, nor brought one Cross;
We look'd what Representatives wou'd bring,
But they help'd us, just as they did the King.   20
Yet we despair not, for we now lay forth
The *Sybill*'s Books, to those who know their worth:
And tho the first was Sacrific'd before,
These Volumes doubly will the price restore.
Our Poet bade us hope this Grace to find,   25
To whom by long Prescription you are kind.
He, whose undaunted Muse, with Loyal Rage,
Has never spar'd the Vices of the Age,
Here finding nothing that his Spleen can raise,
Is forc'd to turn his Satire into Praise.   30

PROLOGUE

GALLANTS, a bashful Poet bids me say
  He's come to lose his Maidenhead to day.
Be not too fierce, for he's but green of *Age*;

And ne're, till now, debauch'd upon the Stage.
He wants the suff'ring part of Resolution;   5
And comes with blushes to his Execution.
E're you deflow'r his Muse, he hopes the Pit
Will make some Settlement upon his Wit.
Promise him well, before the Play begin;
For he wou'd fain be cozen'd into Sin.   10
'Tis not but that he knows you mean to fail;
But, if you leave him after being frail,
He'll have, at least, a fair pretence to rail;
To call you base, and swear you us'd him ill,
And put you in the new Deserters Bill: 15
Lord, what a Troop of perjur'd Men we see;
Enow to fill another Mercury!
But this the Ladies may with patience brook:
Their's are not the first Colours you forsook!
He wou'd be loath the *Beauties* to offend;   20
But, if he shou'd, he's not too old to mend.
He's a young Plant, in his first Year of bearing,
But his Friend swears, he will be worth the reering.
His gloss is still upon him: tho 'tis true
He's yet unripe, yet take him for the blue.   25
You think an *Apricot* half green is best;
There's sweet and sour: and one side good at least.
Mango's and Limes, whose nourishment is little,
Tho' not for Food, are yet preserv'd for Pickle.
So this green Writer, may pretend, at least,   30
To whet your Stomachs for a better Feast.
He makes this difference in the Sexes too,
He sells to Men, he gives himself to you.
To both, he wou'd contribute some delight;
A mere Poetical Hermaphrodite.   35
Thus he's equipped, both to be woo'd, and woo;
With *Arms* offensive, and defensive too;
'Tis hard, he thinks, if neither part will do.

Veni Creator Spiritus,
Translated in PARAPHRASE

CREATOR Spirit, by whose aid
The World's Foundations first were laid,
Come visit ev'ry pious Mind;
Come pour thy Joys on Human Kind:
From Sin, and Sorrow set us free;   5
And make thy Temples worthy Thee.

O, Source of uncreated Light,
The Father's promis'd *Paraclite*!
Thrice Holy Fount, thrice Holy Fire,
Our Hearts with Heav'nly Love inspire;   10
Come, and thy Sacred Unction bring
To Sanctifie us, while we sing!

Plenteous of Grace, descend from high,
Rich in thy sev'n-fold Energy!
Thou strength of his Almighty Hand,   15
Whose Pow'r does Heav'n and Earth command:
Proceeding Spirit, our Defence,
Who do'st the Gift of Tongues dispence,
And crown'st thy Gift, with Eloquence!

Refine and purge our Earthy Parts;   20
But, oh, inflame and fire our Hearts!
Our Frailties help, our Vice controul;
Submit the Senses to the Soul;
And when Rebellious they are grown,
Then, lay thy hand, and hold 'em down.   25

Chace from our Minds th' Infernal Foe;
And Peace, the fruit of Love, bestow:
And, lest our Feet shou'd step astray,
Protect, and guide us in the way.

Make us Eternal Truths receive,   30
And practise, all that we believe:
Give us thy self, that we may see
The Father and the Son, by thee.

Immortal Honour, endless Fame
Attend th' Almighty Father's Name: 35
The Saviour Son, be glorify'd,
Who for lost Man's Redemption dy'd:
And equal Adoration be
Eternal *Paraclete*, to thee.

RONDELAY

1

CHLOE found *Amyntas* lying
   All in Tears, upon the Plain;
Sighing to himself, and crying,
   Wretched I, to love in vain!
Kiss me, Dear, before my dying;   5
   Kiss me once, and ease my pain!

2

Sighing to himself, and crying
   Wretched I, to love in vain:
Ever scorning and denying
   To reward your faithful Swain: 10
Kiss me, Dear, before my dying;
   Kiss me once, and ease my pain!

3

Ever scorning, and denying
   To reward your faithful Swain;
Chloe, laughing at his crying,   15
   Told him that he lov'd in vain:
Kiss me, Dear, before my dying;
   Kiss me once, and ease my pain!

4

Chloe, laughing at his crying,
   Told him that he lov'd in vain: 20
But repenting, and complying,
   When he kiss'd, she kiss'd again:
Kiss'd him up, before his dying;
   Kiss'd him up, and eas'd his pain.

An EPITAPH ON THE Lady *WHITMORE*

FAIR, Kind, and True, a Treasure each alone;
    A Wife, a Mistress, and a Friend in one;
Rest in this Tomb, rais'd at thy Husband's cost,
Here sadly summing, what he had, and lost.
    Come Virgins, e're in equal Bands you join,   5
    Come first and offer at her Sacred Shrine;
Pray but for half the Vertues of this Wife,
Compound for all the rest, with longer Life,
And wish your Vows like hers may be return'd,
So Lov'd when Living, and when Dead so Mourn'd.   10

AN EPITAPH, ON Sir *Palmes Fairborne*'s TOMB
IN *Westminster*-Abby

Sacred

To the Immortal Memory of Sir Palmes Fairborne, *Knight, Governor of*
Tangier; *in execution of which Command he was mortally wounded by a Shot*
from the Moors, *then Besieging the Town, in the* 46th. *year of his Age.*
October 24th. *1680.*

YE Sacred Relicks which your Marble keep,
    Here undisturb'd by Wars in quiet sleep:
Discharge the trust which when it was below
Fairborne's undaunted Soul did undergo,
And be the Towns Palladium from the Foe.   5
Alive and dead these Walls he will defend,
Great Actions great Examples must attend.
The *Candian* Siege his early Valour knew,
Where *Turkish* Blood did his young hands imbrew.
From thence returning with deserv'd Applause,   10
Against the *Moors* his well-flesh'd Sword he draws;
The same the Courage, and the same the Cause.

His Youth and Age, his Life and Death combine,
As in some great and regular design,
All of a Piece throughout, and all Divine.   15

Still nearer Heaven his Vertues shone more bright,
Like rising flames expanding in their height,
The *Martyr*'s Glory Crown'd the Soldiers Fight.
More bravely *Brittish* General never fell,
Nor General's Death was e're reveng'd so well,   20
Which his pleas'd Eyes beheld before their close,
Follow'd by thousand Victims of his Foes.
To his lamented loss for time to come,
His pious Widow Consecrates this Tomb.

To my Dear Friend Mr. Congreve,
On His COMEDY, call'd The Double-Dealer

WELL then; the promis'd hour is come at last;
    The present Age of Wit obscures the past:
Strong were our Syres; and as they Fought they Writ,
Conqu'ring with force of Arms, and dint of Wit;
Theirs was the Gyant Race, before the Flood;   5
And thus, when *Charles* Return'd, our Empire stood.
Like *Janus* he the stubborn Soil manur'd,
With Rules of Husbandry the rankness cur'd:
Tam'd us to manners, when the Stage was rude;
And boistrous *English* Wit, with Art indu'd.   10
Our Age was cultivated thus at length;
But what we gain'd in skill we lost in strength.
Our Builders were, with want of Genius, curst;
The second Temple was not like the first:
Till You, the best *Vitruvius*, come at length;   15
Our Beauties equal; but excel our strength.
Firm *Dorique* Pillars found Your solid Base:
The Fair *Corinthian* Crowns the higher Space;
Thus all below is Strength, and all above is Grace.
In easie Dialogue is *Fletcher*'s Praise: 20
He mov'd the mind, but had not power to raise.
Great *Johnson* did by strength of Judgment please:
Yet doubling *Fletcher*'s Force, he wants his Ease.

To . . . Mr. Congreve. Text from The Double-Dealer, A Comedy, *1694*
32 Nor] Now *94*

In differing Tallents both adorn'd their Age;
One for the Study, t'other for the Stage.   25
But both to *Congreve* justly shall submit,
One match'd in Judgment, both o'er-match'd in Wit.
In Him all Beauties of this Age we see;
Etherege his Courtship, *Southern*'s Purity;
The Satire, Wit, and Strength of Manly *Witcherly*.   30
All this in blooming Youth you have Atchiev'd;
Nor are your foil'd Contemporaries griev'd;
So much the sweetness of your manners move,
We cannot envy you because we Love.

Fabius might joy in *Scipio*, when he saw   35
A Beardless Consul made against the Law,
And joyn his Suffrage to the Votes of *Rome*;
Though He with *Hannibal* was overcome.
Thus old *Romano* bow'd to *Raphel*'s Fame;
And Scholar to the Youth he taught, became.   40
    Oh that your Brows my Lawrel had sustain'd,
Well had I been Depos'd, if You had reign'd!
The Father had descended for the Son;
For only You are lineal to the Throne.
Thus when the State one *Edward* did depose;   45
A Greater *Edward* in his room arose.
But now, not I, but Poetry is curs'd;
For *Tom* the Second reigns like *Tom* the first.
But let 'em not mistake my Patron's part;
Nor call his Charity their own desert.   50
Yet this I Prophesy; Thou shalt be seen,
(Tho' with some short Parenthesis between:)
High on the Throne of Wit; and seated there,
Not mine (that's little) but thy Lawrel wear.
Thy first attempt an early promise made;   55
That early promise this has more than paid.
So bold, yet so judiciously you dare,
That Your least Praise, is to be Regular.
Time, Place, and Action, may with pains be wrought,
But Genius must be born; and never can be taught.   60
This is Your Portion; this Your Native Store;
Heav'n that but once was Prodigal before,
To *Shakespeare* gave as much; she cou'd not give him more.

Maintain Your Post: That's all the Fame You need;
For 'tis impossible you shou'd proceed.   65
Already I am worn with Cares and Age;
And just abandoning th' Ungrateful Stage:
Unprofitably kept at Heav'ns expence,
I live a Rent-charge on his Providence:
But You, whom ev'ry Muse and Grace adorn,   70
Whom I foresee to better Fortune born,
Be kind to my Remains; and oh defend,
Against Your Judgment, Your departed Friend!

Let not the Insulting Foe my Fame pursue;
But shade those Lawrels which descend to You: 75
And take for Tribute what these Lines express:
You merit more; nor cou'd my Love do less.

PROLOGUE, EPILOGUE and SONGS
from *LOVE TRIUMPHANT*

PROLOGUE

Spoken by Mr. *Betterton*

As when some Treasurer lays down the Stick;
Warrants are Sign'd for ready Mony thick:
And many desperate Debentures paid;
Which never had been, had his Lordship staid:
So now, this Poet, who forsakes the Stage,   5
Intends to gratifie the present Age.
One Warrant shall be Sign'd for every Man;
All shall be Wits that will; and *Beaux* that can:
Provided still, this Warrant be not shown,
And you be Wits, but to your selves alone.   10
Provided too; you rail at one another:
For there's no one Wit, will allow a Brother.
Provided also; that you spare this Story,
Damn all the Plays that e're shall come before ye.

Prologue, Epilogue and Songs. Text from Love Triumphant; or, Nature will Prevail.
A Tragi-Comedy, *1694*

If one by chance prove good in half a score,   15
Let that one pay for all; and Damn it more.
For if a good one scape among the Crew,
And you continue Judging as you do;
Every bad Play will hope for Damning too.
You might Damn this, if it were worth your pains,   20
Here's nothing you will like; no fustian Scenes,
And nothing too of——you know what he means.
No double *Entendrès*, which you Sparks allow;
To make the Ladies look they know not how;
Simply as 'twere; and knowing both together,   25
Seeming to fan their Faces in cold Weather.
But here's a Story which no Books relate;
Coin'd from our own Old Poet's Addle-pate.
The Fable has a Moral too, if sought:
But let that go; for upon second Thought,   30
He fears but few come hither to be Taught.
Yet if you will be profited, you may;
And he would Bribe you too, to like his Play.
He Dies, at least to us, and to the Stage,
And what he has, he leaves this Noble Age.   35
He leaves you first, all Plays of his Inditing,
The whole Estate, which he has got by Writing.
The Beaux may think this nothing but vain Praise,
They'l find it something; the Testator says:
For half their Love, is made from scraps of Plays.   40
To his worst Foes, he leaves his Honesty;
That they may thrive upon't as much as he.
He leaves his Manners to the Roaring Boys,
Who come in Drunk, and fill the House with noise.
He leaves to the dire Critiques of his Wit,   45
His Silence and Contempt of all they Writ.
To *Shakespear*'s Critique, he bequeaths the Curse,
To find his faults; and yet himself make worse:
A precious Reader in Poetique Schools,
Who by his own Examples damns his Rules.   50
Last for the Fair, he wishes you may be,
From your dull Critiques, the Lampooners free.
Tho' he pretends no Legacy to leave you,
An Old Man may at least good wishes give you.

Your Beauty names the Play; and may it prove,   55
To each, an Omen of Triumphant Love.

EPILOGUE

Now, in Good Manners, nothing shou'd be sed
   Against this Play, because the Poet's dead.
The Prologue told us of a Moral here:
Wou'd I çou'd find it, but the Devil knows where.
If in my Part it lyes, I fear he means   5
To warn us of the Sparks behind our Scenes:
For if you'l take it on *Dalinda*'s Word,
'Tis a hard Chapter to refuse a Lord.
The Poet might pretend this Moral too,
That when a Wit and Fool together woo;   10
The Damsel (not to break an Ancient Rule,)
Shou'd leave the Wit, and take the Wealthy Fool.
This he might mean, but there's a Truth behind,
And since it touches none of all our Kind,
But Masks and Misses; faith, I'le speak my Mind.   15
What, if he Taught our Sex more cautious Carriage,
And not to be too Coming before Marriage:
For fear of my Misfortune in the Play,
A Kid brought home upon the Wedding day:
I fear there are few *Sancho's* in the Pit,   20
So good as to forgive, and to forget;
That will, like him, restore us into Favour,
And take us after on our good Behaviour.
Few, when they find the Mony Bag is rent,
Will take it for good Payment on content.   25
But in the Telling, there the difference is,
Sometimes they find it more than they cou'd wish.
Therefore be warn'd, you Misses and you Masks,
Look to your hits, nor give the first that asks.
Tears, Sighs, and Oaths, no truth of Passion prove,   30
True Settlement alone, declares true Love.
For him that Weds a Puss, who kept her first,
I say but little, but I doubt the worst:

The Wife that was a Cat may mind her house,
And prove an Honest, and a Careful Spouse;
But faith I wou'd not trust her with a Mouse.   } 35

Song of *Jealousie*

1

WHAT State of Life can be so blest
      As Love, that warms a Lover's Breast?
Two Souls in one, the same desire   •
To grant the Bliss, and to require!
But if in Heav'n a Hell we find,   5
'Tis all from thee,
O Jealousie!
'Tis all from thee,
O Jealousie!
Thou Tyrant, Tyrant Jealousie,   10
Thou Tyrant of the Mind!

2

All other ills, tho sharp they prove,
Serve to refine, and perfect Love:
In absence, or unkind disdain,
Sweet Hope relieves the Lover's pain: 15
But ah, no Cure but Death we find,
To set us free
From Jealousie:
O Jealousie!
Thou Tyrant, Tyrant Jealousie,   20
Thou Tyrant of the Mind.

3

False, in thy Glass all Objects are,
Some set too near, and some too far:
Thou art the Fire of endless Night,
The Fire that burns, and gives no Light.   25
All Torments of the Damn'd we find
In only thee
O Jealousie!

Thou Tyrant, Tyrant Jealousie,
Thou Tyrant of the Mind!   30

Song for a GIRL

1

YOUNG I am, and yet unskill'd
    How to make a Lover yield:
How to keep, or how to gain,
When to Love; and when to feign:

2

Take me, take me, some of you,   5
While I yet am Young and True;
E're I can my Soul disguise;
Heave my Breasts, and roul my Eyes.

3

Stay not till I learn the way,
How to Lye, and to Betray: 10
He that has me first, is blest,
For I may deceive the rest.

4

Cou'd I find a blooming Youth;
Full of Love, and full of Truth,
Brisk, and of a janty meen,   15
I shou'd long to be Fifteen.

To Sir *Godfrey Kneller*

ONCE I beheld the fairest of her Kind;
    (And still the sweet Idea charms my Mind:)
True she was dumb; for Nature gaz'd so long,
Pleas'd with her work, that she forgot her Tongue:
But, smiling, said, She still shall gain the Prize;   5

To Sir Godfrey Kneller. Text from The Annual Miscellany, *1694, collated with* Poems
on Various Occasions, *1701, where it is headed* To Sir Godfrey Kneller, Principal
Painter to His Majesty

I only have transferr'd it to her Eyes.
Such are thy Pictures, *Kneller*. Such thy Skill,
That Nature seems obedient to thy Will:
Comes out, and meets thy Pencil in the draught:
Lives there, and wants but words to speak her thought.   10
At least thy Pictures look a Voice; and we
Imagine sounds, deceiv'd to that degree,
We think 'tis somewhat more than just to see.
   Shadows are but privations of the Light,
Yet when we walk, they shoot before the Sight;   15
With us approach, retire, arise and fall;
Nothing themselves, and yet expressing all.

Such are thy Pieces; imitating Life
So near, they almost conquer'd in the strife;
And from their animated Canvass came,   20
Demanding Souls; and loosen'd from the Frame.
   Prometheus, were he here, wou'd cast away
His *Adam*, and refuse a Soul to Clay:
And either wou'd thy Noble Work Inspire;
Or think it warm enough, without his Fire.   25
   But vulgar Hands, may vulgar Likeness raise,
This is the least Attendant on thy Praise:
From hence the Rudiments of Art began;
A Coal, or Chalk, first imitated Man:
Perhaps, the Shadow taken on a Wall,   30
Gave out-lines to the rude Original:
E're Canvass yet was strain'd: before the Grace
Of blended Colours found their use and place:
Or Cypress Tablets, first receiv'd a Face.
   By slow degrees, the Godlike Art advanc'd;   35
As Man grew polish'd, Picture was inhanc'd;
Greece added posture, shade, and perspective;
And then the Mimick Piece began to Live.
Yet perspective was lame; no distance true;
But all came forward in one common view: 40
No point of Light was known, no bounds of Art;
When Light was there, it knew not to depart:
But glaring on remoter Objects play'd;
Not languish'd, and insensibly decay'd.

Rome rais'd not Art, but barely kept alive;   45
And with Old *Greece,* unequally did strive:
Till *Goths* and *Vandals,* a rude *Northern* Race,
Did all the matchless Monuments deface.
Then all the Muses in one ruine lye;
And Rhyme began t' enervate Poetry.   50
Thus in a stupid Military State,
The Pen and Pencil find an equal Fate.
Flat Faces, such as wou'd disgrace a Skreen,
Such as in *Bantam*'s Embassy were seen,
Unrais'd, unrounded, were the rude delight   55
Of Brutal Nations, only born to Fight.
   Long time the Sister Arts, in Iron sleep,

A heavy Sabbath did supinely keep;
At length, in *Raphael*'s Age, at once they rise;
Stretch all their Limbs, and open all their Eyes.   60
   Thence rose the *Roman,* and the *Lombard* Line:
One colour'd best, and one did best design.
Raphael's like *Homer*'s, was the Nobler part;
But *Titian*'s Painting, look'd like *Virgil*'s Art.
   Thy Genius gives thee both; where true design,   65
Postures unforc'd, and lively Colours joyn.
Likeness is ever there; but still the best,
Like proper Thoughts in lofty Language drest.
Where Light to Shades descending, plays, not strives;
Dyes by degrees, and by degrees revives.   70
Of various parts a perfect whole is wrought:
Thy Pictures think, and we Divine their Thought.
   *Shakespear thy Gift, I place before my sight;
With awe, I ask his Blessing e're I write;
With Reverence look on his Majestick Face;
Proud to be less; but of his Godlike Race.
His Soul Inspires me, while thy Praise I write,
And I like *Teucer,* under *Ajax* Fight;
Bids thee through me, be bold; with dauntless breast
Contemn the bad, and Emulate the best.   80
Like his, thy Criticks in th' attempt are lost;
When most they rail, know then, they envy most.
In vain they snarl a-loof; a noisy Crow'd,
Like Womens Anger, impotent and loud.

* Shake-
spear's *Picture
drawn by Sir*
Godfrey Knel-
ler, *and given
to the Author.*

While they their barren Industry deplore,   85
Pass on secure; and mind the Goal before:
Old as she is, my Muse shall march behind;
Bear off the blast, and intercept the wind.
Our Arts are Sisters; though not Twins in Birth:
For Hymns were sung in *Edens* happy Earth,   90
By the first Pair; while *Eve* was yet a Saint;
Before she fell with Pride, and learn'd to paint.
Forgive th' allusion; 'twas not meant to bite;
But Satire will have room, where e're I write.
For oh, the Painter Muse; though last in place,   95
Has seiz'd the Blessing first, like *Jacob*'s Race.
Apelles Art, an *Alexander* found;   ⎫
And *Raphael* did with *Leo*'s Gold abound;   ⎬
But *Homer*, was with barren Lawrel Crown'd.   ⎭
Thou hadst thy *Charles* a while, and so had I;   100
But pass we that unpleasing Image by.
Rich in thy self; and of thy self Divine,
All Pilgrims come and offer at thy Shrine.
A graceful truth thy Pencil can Command;
The fair themselves go mended from thy hand: 105
Likeness appears in every Lineament;
But Likeness in thy Work is Eloquent:
Though Nature, there, her true resemblance bears,
A nobler Beauty in thy Piece appears.
So warm thy Work, so glows the gen'rous frame,   110
Flesh looks less living in the Lovely Dame.
   Thou paint'st as we describe, improving still,   ⎫
When on wild Nature we ingraft our skill: ⎬
But not creating Beauties at our Will.   ⎭
   Some other Hand perhaps may reach a Face;   115
But none like thee, a finish'd Figure place:
None of this Age; for that's enough for thee,   ⎫
The first of these Inferiour Times to be: ⎬
Not to contend with Heroes Memory.   ⎭
   Due Honours to those mighty Names we grant,   120
But Shrubs may live beneath the lofty Plant:
Sons may succeed their greater Parents gone;
Such is thy Lott; and such I wish my own.

But Poets are confin'd in Narr'wer space;
To speak the Language of their Native Place:　　　125
The Painter widely stretches his command:
Thy Pencil speaks the Tongue of ev'ry Land.
From hence, my Friend, all Climates are your own;
Nor can you forfeit, for you hold of none.
All Nations all Immunities will give　　　130
To make you theirs; where e're you please to live;
And not seven Cities; but the World wou'd strive.

Sure some propitious Planet then did Smile,
When first you were conducted to this Isle:
(Our Genius brought you here, t' inlarge our Fame)　　　135
(For your good Stars are ev'ry where the same)
Thy matchless hand, of ev'ry Region free,
Adopts our Climate; not our Climate thee.

　*Great *Rome* and *Venice* early did impart　　　*He travel'd
To thee th' Examples of their wondrous Art.　　　*very young*
Those Masters then but seen, not understood,　　　*into* Italy.
With generous Emulation fir'd thy Blood:
For what in Nature's Dawn the Child admir'd,
The Youth endeavour'd, and the Man acquir'd.

　That yet thou hast not reach'd their high Degree　　　145
Seems only wanting to this Age, not thee:
Thy Genius bounded by the Times like mine,
Drudges on petty Draughts, nor dare design
A more Exalted Work, and more Divine.
For what a Song, or senceless Opera　　　150
Is to the Living Labour of a Play;
Or, what a Play to *Virgil*'s Work wou'd be,
Such is a single Piece to History.

　But we who Life bestow, our selves must live;
Kings cannot Reign, unless their Subjects give.　　　155
And they who pay the Taxes, bear the Rule:
Thus thou sometimes art forc'd to draw a Fool:
But so his Follies in thy Posture sink,
The senceless Ideot seems at least to think.

　Good Heav'n! that Sots and Knaves shou'd be so vain,　　　160
To wish their vile Resemblance may remain!
And stand recorded, at their own request,
To future Days, a Libel or a Jeast.

Mean time, while just Incouragement you want,
You only Paint to Live, not Live to Paint.   165
 Else shou'd we see, your Noble Pencil trace
Our Unities of Action, Time, and Place.
A whole compos'd of parts; and those the best;
With ev'ry various Character exprest.
Heroes at large; and at a nearer view;   170
Less, and at distance, an Ignobler Crew.
While all the Figures in one Action joyn,
As tending to Compleat the main Design.
 More cannot be by Mortal Art exprest;
But venerable Age shall add the rest.   175
For Time shall with his ready Pencil stand;
Retouch your Figures, with his ripening hand.
Mellow your Colours, and imbrown the Teint;
Add every Grace, which Time alone can grant:
To future Ages shall your Fame convey;   180
And give more Beauties, than he takes away.

AN ODE,
ON THE DEATH OF Mr. Henry Purcell;
Late Servant to his Majesty,
and Organist of the Chapel Royal,
and of St. *Peter*'s *Westminster*

The ODE

I

MARK how the Lark and Linnet Sing,
   With rival Notes
They strain their warbling Throats,
   To welcome in the Spring.
   But in the close of Night,   5
When *Philomel* begins her Heav'nly lay,
   They cease their mutual spight,

164–5 *om.* 1701

An Ode. Text from the first edition, 1696. The text accompanying the music has 12, 13 *the matchless Man* 21 *turn'd the jarring Spheres*

Drink in her Musick with delight,
And list'ning and silent, and silent and list'ning,
  and list'ning and silent obey.

II

So ceas'd the rival Crew when *Purcell* came,   10
They Sung no more, or only Sung his Fame.
Struck dumb they all admir'd the God-like Man,
  The God-like Man,
   Alas, too soon retir'd,
   As He too late began.   15
We beg not Hell, our *Orpheus* to restore,
   Had He been there,
   Their Sovereigns fear
  Had sent Him back before.
The pow'r of Harmony too well they know,   20
He long e'er this had Tun'd their jarring Sphere,
  And left no Hell below.

III

The Heav'nly Quire, who heard his Notes from high,
Let down the Scale of Musick from the Sky:
  They handed him along,   25
And all the way He taught, and all the way they Sung.
Ye Brethren of the *Lyre*, and tunefull Voice,
Lament his lott: but at your own rejoyce.
Now live secure and linger out your days,
The Gods are pleas'd alone with *Purcell*'s *Layes*,   30
  Nor know to mend their Choice.

EPILOGUE to *The Husband His own Cuckold*

THE PREFACE OF
Mr. *Dryden*, to his Son's Play

*. . . For what remains, both my Son and I are extreamly oblig'd to my dear
Friend Mr.* Congreve, *whose Excellent Prologue was one of the greatest Ornaments of the Play. Neither is my Epilogue the worst which I have written;*

Epilogue. Text from The Husband His own Cuckold. A Comedy, 1696

though it seems at the first sight to expose our young Clergy with too much free-
dom. It was on that Consideration that I had once begun it otherwise, and deliver'd
the Copy of it to be spoken, in case the first part of it had given offence. This I will
give you partly in my own justification, and partly too, because I think it not
unworthy of your sight. Only remembering you that the last line connects the
sense to the ensuing part of it. Farewell, Reader, if you are a Father you will for-
give me, if not, you will when you are a Father.

T IME was when none cou'd Preach without Degrees,
    And seven years toil at Universities:
But when the Canting Saints came once in play,
The Spirit did their bus'ness in a day:
A Zealous Cobler with the gift of Tongue,   5
If he cou'd Pray six hours, might Preach as long:
Thus, in the Primitive Times of Poetry,
The Stage to none but Men of sense was free.
But thanks to your judicious tast, my Masters,
It lies in common now to Poetasters.   10
You set them up, and 'till you dare Condemn,
The Satire lies on you, and not on them.
When Mountebanks their Drugs at Market cry,
Is it their fault to sell, or yours to buye?
'Tis true, they write with ease, and well they may,   } 15
Fly-blows are gotten every Summers day,
The Poet does but buz, and there's a Play.

Wit's not his business, *&c.*

EPILOGUE

Spoken by Mrs. *Bracegirdle*

L IKE some raw Sophister that mounts the Pulpit,
   So trembles a young Poet at a full Pit.
Unus'd to Crowds, the Parson quakes for fear,
And wonders how the Devil he durst come there;
Wanting three Talents needful for the Place,   5
Some Beard, some Learning, and some little Grace:
Nor is the Puny Poet void of Care;   }
For Authors, such as our new Authors are,
Have not much Learning, nor much Wit to spare:

And as for Grace, to tell the truth, there's scarce one,   10
But has as little as the very Parson:
Both say, they Preach and Write for your Instruction:
But 'tis for a Third Day, and for Induction.
The difference is, that tho' you like the Play,
The Poet's gain is ne'er beyond his Day.   15
But with the Parson 'tis another Case,
He, without Holiness, may rise to Grace;
The Poet has one disadvantage more,
That if his Play be dull, he's Damn'd all o'er,   ⎞
Not only a damn'd Blockhead, but damn'd Poor.   ⎠ 20

But Dullness well becomes the Sable Garment;
I warrant that ne'er spoil'd a Priest's Preferment:
Wit's not his Business, and as Wit now goes,   ⎞
Sirs, 'tis not so much yours as you suppose,   ⎬
For you like nothing now but nauseous Beaux.   ⎠ 25
You laugh not, Gallants, as by proof appears,   ⎞
At what his Beauship says, but what he wears;   ⎬
So 'tis your Eyes are tickled, not your Ears: ⎠
The Taylor and the Furrier find the Stuff,
The Wit lies in the Dress, and monstrous Muff.   30
The Truth on't is, the Payment of the Pit
Is like for like, Clipt Money for Clipt Wit.
You cannot from our absent Author hope
He should equip the Stage with such a Fop:
Fools Change in *England*, and new Fools arise,   ⎞ 35
For tho' th' Immortal Species never dies,   ⎬
Yet ev'ry Year new Maggots make new Flies.   ⎠
But where he lives abroad, he scarce can find
One Fool, for Million that he left behind.

Alexander's Feast;
OR THE POWER OF MUSIQUE.
AN ODE,
In HONOUR of St. CECILIA's Day

I

'TWAS at the Royal Feast, for *Persia* won,
   By *Philip*'s Warlike Son:
  Aloft in awful State
  The God-like Heroe sate
    On his Imperial Throne: 5
 His valiant Peers were plac'd around;
Their Brows with Roses and with Myrtles bound.
 (So shou'd Desert in Arms be Crown'd:)
 The Lovely *Thais* by his side,
 Sate like a blooming *Eastern* Bride   10
 In Flow'r of Youth and Beauty's Pride.
  Happy, happy, happy Pair!
  None but the Brave
  None but the Brave
  None but the Brave deserves the Fair.   15

CHORUS

* Happy, happy, happy Pair!*
* None but the Brave*
* None but the Brave*
* None but the Brave deserves the Fair.*

II

Timotheus plac'd on high   20
 Amid the tuneful Quire,
 With flying Fingers touch'd the Lyre:
The trembling Notes ascend the Sky,
    And Heav'nly Joys inspire.

Alexander's Feast. Text from the first edition, 1697

The Song began from *Jove*;   25
Who left his blissful Seats above,
(Such is the Pow'r of mighty Love.)
A Dragon's fiery Form bely'd the God:
Sublime on Radiant Spires He rode,
    When He to fair *Olympia* press'd: 30
    And while He sought her snowy Breast:
Then, round her slender Waste he curl'd,
And stamp'd an Image of himself, a Sov'raign of the World.
The list'ning Crowd admire the lofty Sound,
A present Deity, they shout around: 35
A present Deity the vaulted Roofs rebound.
        With ravish'd Ears
        The Monarch hears,
        Assumes the God,
        Affects to nod,   40
    And seems to shake the Spheres.

CHORUS

      With ravish'd Ears
      The Monarch hears,
      Assumes the God,
      Affects to Nod,   45
    And seems to shake the Spheres.

III

The Praise of *Bacchus* then, the sweet Musician sung;
    Of *Bacchus* ever Fair, and ever Young:
      The jolly God in Triumph comes;
      Sound the Trumpets; beat the Drums: 50
        Flush'd with a purple Grace
        He shews his honest Face,
Now give the Hautboys breath; He comes, He comes.
      Bacchus ever Fair and Young,
        Drinking Joys did first ordain: 55
      Bacchus Blessings are a Treasure;
      Drinking is the Soldiers Pleasure;
        Rich the Treasure,
        Sweet the Pleasure;
        Sweet is Pleasure after Pain.   60

CHORUS

Bacchus Blessings are a Treasure;
Drinking is the Soldier's Pleasure;
Rich the Treasure,
Sweet the Pleasure;
Sweet is Pleasure after Pain. 65

IV

Sooth'd with the Sound the King grew vain;
Fought all his Battails o'er again;
And thrice He routed all his Foes; and thrice He slew the slain.
The Master saw the Madness rise;
His glowing Cheeks, his ardent Eyes; 70
And while He Heav'n and Earth defy'd,
Chang'd his hand, and check'd his Pride.
He chose a Mournful Muse
Soft Pity to infuse:
He sung *Darius* Great and Good, 75
By too severe a Fate,
Fallen, fallen, fallen, fallen,
Fallen from his high Estate
And weltring in his Blood:
Deserted at his utmost Need, 80
By those his former Bounty fed:
On the bare Earth expos'd He lyes,
With not a Friend to close his Eyes.

With down-cast Looks the joyless Victor sate,
Revolveing in his alter'd Soul 85
The various Turns of Chance below;
And, now and then, a Sigh he stole;
And Tears began to flow.

CHORUS

Revolveing in his alter'd Soul
The various Turns of Chance below; 90
And, now and then, a Sigh he stole;
And Tears began to flow.

V

The Mighty Master smil'd to see
That Love was in the next Degree:
'Twas but a Kindred-Sound to move;   95
For Pity melts the Mind to Love.
    Softly sweet, in *Lydian* Measures,
    Soon He sooth'd his Soul to Pleasures.
    War, he sung, is Toil and Trouble;
    Honour but an empty Bubble.   100
        Never ending, still beginning,
    Fighting still, and still destroying,
        If the World be worth thy Winning,
    Think, O think, it worth Enjoying.
        Lovely *Thais* sits beside thee,   105
        Take the Good the Gods provide thee.

The Many rend the Skies, with loud Applause;
So Love was Crown'd, but Musique won the Cause.
    The Prince, unable to conceal his Pain,
        Gaz'd on the Fair   110
        Who caus'd his Care,
    And sigh'd and look'd, sigh'd and look'd,
    Sigh'd and look'd, and sigh'd again:
At length, with Love and Wine at once oppress'd,
The vanquish'd Victor sunk upon her Breast.   115

CHORUS

    The Prince, unable to conceal his Pain,
        Gaz'd on the Fair
        Who caus'd his Care,
      And sigh'd and look'd, sigh'd and look'd,
    Sigh'd and look'd, and sigh'd again: 120
At length, with Love and Wine at once oppress'd,
The vanquish'd Victor sunk upon her Breast.

VI

Now strike the Golden Lyre again:
A lowder yet, and yet a lowder Strain.

Break his Bands of Sleep asunder, 125
And rouze him, like a rattling Peal of Thunder.
Hark, hark, the horrid Sound
Has rais'd up his Head,
As awak'd from the Dead,
And amaz'd, he stares around. 130
Revenge, Revenge, *Timotheus* cries,
See the Furies arise!
See the Snakes that they rear,
How they hiss in their Hair,
And the Sparkles that flash from their Eyes! 135
Behold a ghastly Band,
Each a Torch in his Hand!
Those are *Grecian* Ghosts, that in Battail were slayn,
And unbury'd remain
Inglorious on the Plain. 140
Give the Vengeance due
To the Valiant Crew.
Behold how they toss their Torches on high,
How they point to the *Persian* Abodes,
And glitt'ring Temples of their Hostile Gods! 145
The Princes applaud, with a furious Joy;
And the King seyz'd a Flambeau, with Zeal to destroy;
Thais led the Way,
To light him to his Prey,
And, like another *Hellen*, fir'd another *Troy*. 150

CHORUS

And the King seyz'd a Flambeau, with Zeal to destroy;
Thais *led the Way,*
To light him to his Prey,
And, like another Hellen, *fir'd another* Troy.

VII

Thus, long ago 155
'Ere heaving Bellows learn'd to blow,
While Organs yet were mute;
Timotheus, to his breathing Flute,
And sounding Lyre,

Cou'd swell the Soul to rage, or kindle soft Desire.   160
    At last Divine *Cecilia* came,
    Inventress of the Vocal Frame;
The sweet Enthusiast, from her Sacred Store,
        Enlarg'd the former narrow Bounds,
        And added Length to solemn Sounds,   165
With Nature's Mother-Wit, and Arts unknown before.
    Let old *Timotheus* yield the Prize,
      Or both divide the Crown;
    He rais'd a Mortal to the Skies;
      She drew an Angel down.   170

Grand CHORUS

  At last Divine Cecilia *came,*
  Inventress of the Vocal Frame;
The sweet Enthusiast, from her Sacred Store,
      Enlarg'd the former narrow Bounds,
      And added Length to solemn Sounds,   175
With Nature's Mother-Wit, and Arts unknown before.
  Let old Timotheus *yield the Prize,*
    Or both divide the Crown;
  He rais'd a Mortal to the Skies;
    She drew an Angel down.   180

To Mr. *GRANVILLE*, on his Excellent Tragedy,
call'd *HEROICK LOVE*

AUSPICIOUS Poet, wert thou not my Friend,
  How could I envy, what I must commend!
But since 'tis Natures Law in Love and Wit
That Youth shou'd Reign, and with'ring Age submit,
With less regret, those Lawrels I resign,   5
Which dying on my Brows, revive on thine.
With better Grace an Ancient Chief may yield
The long contended Honours of the Field,
Than venture all his Fortune at a Cast,
And Fight, like *Hannibal*, to lose at last.   10

To Mr. Granville. Text from Heroick Love: A Tragedy, *1698*

Young Princes Obstinate to win the Prize,
Thô Yearly beaten, Yearly yet they rise:
Old Monarchs though Successful, still in Doubt,
Catch at a Peace; and wisely turn Devout.
Thine be the Lawrel then; thy blooming Age   15
Can best, if any can, support the Stage:
Which so declines, that shortly we may see,
Players and Plays reduc'd to second Infancy.
Sharp to the World, but thoughtless of Renown,
They Plot not on the Stage, but on the Town,   20
And in Despair their Empty Pit to fill,
Set up some Foreign Monster in a Bill:
Thus they jog on; still tricking, never thriving;
And Murd'ring Plays, which they miscal Reviving.
Our Sense is Nonsense, through their Pipes convey'd;   25
Scarce can a Poet know the Play He made;
'Tis so disguis'd in Death: Nor thinks 'tis He
That suffers in the Mangled Tragedy.
Thus *Itys* first was kill'd, and after dress'd
For his own Sire the Chief Invited Guest.   30
I say not this of thy successful Scenes;
Where thine was all the Glory, theirs the Gains;
With length of Time, much Judgment, and more Toil,
Not ill they Acted, what they cou'd not spoil:
Their Setting-Sun still shoots a Glim'ring Ray,   35
Like Ancient *Rome*, Majestick in decay:
And better gleanings, their worn Soil can boast,
Then the Crab-Vintage of the Neighb'ring Coast.
This difference, yet the judging World will see;
Thou Copiest *Homer*, and they Copy thee.   40

To my Friend, *the A U T H O R*
[PETER MOTTEUX]

'TIS hard, my Friend, to write in such an Age,
    As damns not only Poets, but the Stage.
That sacred Art, by Heav'n it self infus'd,

To Peter Motteux. Text from Motteux's Beauty in Distress. A Tragedy, *1698*

Which *Moses*, *David*, *Salomon* have us'd,
Is now to be no more: The Muses Foes   5
Wou'd sink their Maker's Praises into Prose.
Were they content to prune the lavish Vine
Of straggling Branches, and improve the Wine,
Who but a mad Man wou'd his Faults defend?
All wou'd submit; for all but Fools will mend.   10
But, when to common sense they give the Lie,
And turn distorted Words to Blasphemy,
They give the Scandal; and the Wise discern,
Their Glosses teach an Age too apt to learn.
What I have loosly, or profanely writ,   15
Let them to Fires (their due desert) commit.
Nor, when accus'd by me, let *them* complain:
Their Faults and not their Function I arraign.
Rebellion, worse than Witchcraft, they pursu'd:
The Pulpit preach'd the Crime; the People ru'd.   20
The Stage was silenc'd: for the Saints wou'd see
In fields perform'd their plotted Tragedy.
But let us first reform: and then so live,
That we may teach our Teachers to forgive.
Our Desk be plac'd below their lofty Chairs,   25
Ours be the Practice, as the Precept theirs.
The moral part at least we may divide,
Humility reward, and punish Pride:
Ambition, Int'rest, Avarice accuse:
These are the Province of the Tragic Muse.   30
These hast thou chosen; and the public Voice
Has equal'd thy performance, with thy choice.
Time, Action, Place, are so preserv'd by thee
That ev'n *Corneille*, might with envy see
Th' Alliance of his tripled Unity.   35
Thy Incidents, perhaps, too thick are sown;
But too much Plenty is thy fault alone:
At least but two, can that good Crime commit;
Thou in Design, and *Wycherley* in Wit.
Let thy own *Gauls* condemn thee if they dare;   40
Contented to be thinly regular.
Born there, but not for them, our fruitful Soil
With more Increase rewards thy happy Toil.

Their Tongue infeebled, is refin'd so much,
That, like pure Gold, it bends at ev'ry touch: 45
Our sturdy *Teuton*, yet will Art obey,
More fit for manly thought, and strengthen'd with Allay.
But whence art thou inspir'd, and Thou alone
To flourish in an Idiom, not thine own?
It moves our wonder, that a foreign Guest   50
Shou'd over-match the most, and match the best.
In underpraising, thy Deserts I wrong:
Here, find the first deficience of our Tongue:
Words, once my stock, are wanting to commend
So Great a Poet, and so Good a Friend.   55

FABLES

Ancient and *Modern*;

Translated into Verse,

from

Homer, Ovid, Boccace and Chaucer:

with Original Poems.

Nunc ultrò ad Cineres ipsius & ossa parentis
(Haud equidem sine mente, reor, sine numine divum)
Adsumus.   Virg. Æn. lib. 5.

Fables. Text from the first edition, 1700 (F)

S

TO HIS GRACE
The Duke of Ormond

My LORD,

SOME Estates are held in *England*, by paying a Fine at the change of
every Lord: I have enjoy'd the Patronage of your Family, from the
time of your excellent Grandfather to this present Day. I have dedicated
the Lives of *Plutarch* to the first Duke; and have celebrated the Memory
of your Heroick Father. Tho' I am very short of the Age of *Nestor*, yet 5
I have liv'd to a third Generation of your House; and by your Grace's
Favour am admitted still to hold from you by the same Tenure.

I am not vain enough to boast that I have deserv'd the value of so
Illustrious a Line; but my Fortune is the greater, that for three Descents
they have been pleas'd to distinguish my Poems from those of other 10
Men; and have accordingly made me their peculiar Care. May it be
permitted me to say, That as your Grandfather and Father were
cherish'd and adorn'd with Honours by two successive Monarchs, so
I have been esteem'd, and patronis'd, by the Grandfather, the Father,
and the Son, descended from one of the most Ancient, most Con- 15
spicuous, and most Deserving Families in *Europe*.

'Tis true, that by delaying the Payment of my last Fine, when it was
due by your Grace's Accession to the Titles, and Patrimonies of your
House, I may seem in rigour of Law to have made a forfeiture of my
Claim, yet my Heart has always been devoted to your Service: And 20
since you have been graciously pleas'd, by your permission of this
Address, to accept the tender of my Duty, 'tis not yet too late to lay
these Poems at your Feet.

The World is sensible that you worthily succeed, not only to the
Honours of your Ancestors, but also to their Virtues. The long Chain 25
of Magnanimity, Courage, easiness of Access, and desire of doing Good,
even to the Prejudice of your Fortune, is so far from being broken in
your Grace, that the precious Metal yet runs pure to the newest Link
of it: Which I will not call the last, because I hope and pray, it may
descend to late Posterity: And your flourishing Youth, and that of your 30
excellent Dutchess, are happy Omens of my Wish.

'Tis observ'd by *Livy* and by others, That some of the noblest *Roman*
Families retain'd a resemblance of their Ancestry, not only in their
Shapes and Features, but also in their Manners, their Qualities, and the

distinguishing Characters of their Minds: Some Lines were noted for 35
a stern, rigid Virtue, salvage, haughty, parcimonious and unpopular:
Others were more sweet, and affable; made of a more pliant Past,
humble, courteous, and obliging; studious of doing charitable Offices,
and diffusive of the Goods which they enjoy'd. The last of these is the
proper and indelible Character of your Grace's Family. God Almighty 40
has endu'd you with a Softness, a Beneficence, an attractive Behaviour
winning on the Hearts of others; and so sensible of their Misery, that
the Wounds of Fortune, seem not inflicted on them but on your self.
You are so ready to redress, that you almost prevent their Wishes, and
always exceed their Expectations: As if what was yours, was not your 45
own, and not given you to possess, but to bestow on wanting Merit.
But this is a Topick which I must cast in Shades, lest I offend your
Modesty, which is so far from being ostentatious of the Good you do,
that it blushes even to have it known: And therefore I must leave you
to the Satisfaction and Testimony of your own Conscience, which 50
though it be a silent Panegyrick, is yet the best.

You are so easy of Access, that *Poplicola* was not more, whose Doors
were open'd on the Outside to save the People even the common
Civility of asking entrance; where all were equally admitted; where
nothing that was reasonable was deny'd; where Misfortune was a 55
powerful Recommendation, and where (I can scarce forbear saying) that
Want it self was a powerful Mediator, and was next to Merit.

The History of *Peru* assures us, That their *Inca's* above all their Titles,
esteem'd that the highest, which call'd them Lovers of the Poor: A
Name more glorious, than the *Felix, Pius,* and *Augustus* of the *Roman* 60
Emperors; which were Epithets of Flattery, deserv'd by few of them;
and not running in a Blood like the perpetual Gentleness, and inherent
Goodness of the *ORMOND* Family.

Gold, as it is the purest, so it is the softest, and most ductile of all
Metals: Iron, which is the hardest, gathers Rust, corrodes its self; and 65
is therefore subject to Corruption: It was never intended for Coins and
Medals, or to bear the Faces and Inscriptions of the Great. Indeed 'tis
fit for Armour, to bear off Insults, and preserve the Wearer in the Day
of Battle: But the Danger once repell'd, 'tis laid aside by the Brave, as
a Garment too rough for civil Conversation; a necessary Guard in War, 70
but too harsh and cumbersome in Peace, and which keeps off the embraces of a more human Life.

For this Reason, my Lord, though you have Courage in a heroical
Degree, yet I ascribe it to you, but as your second Attribute: Mercy,

Beneficence, and Compassion, claim Precedence, as they are first in the 75 divine Nature. An intrepid Courage, which is inherent in your Grace, is at best but a Holiday-kind of Virtue, to be seldom exercis'd, and never but in Cases of Necessity: Affability, Mildness, Tenderness, and a Word, which I would fain bring back to its original Signification of Virtue, I mean good Nature, are of daily use: They are the Bread of 80 Mankind, and Staff of Life: Neither Sighs, nor Tears, nor Groans, nor Curses of the vanquish'd, follow Acts of Compassion, and of Charity: But a sincere Pleasure, and Serenity of Mind, in him who performs an Action of Mercy, which cannot suffer the Misfortunes of another, without redress; least they should bring a kind of Contagion along with 85 them, and pollute the Happiness which he enjoys.

Yet since the perverse Tempers of Mankind, since Oppression on one side, and Ambition on the other, are sometimes the unavoidable Occasions of War; that Courage, that Magnanimity, and Resolution, which is born with you, cannot be too much commended: And here it grieves 90 me that I am scanted in the pleasure of dwelling on many of your Actions: But αιδέομαι Τρῶας is an Expression which *Tully* often uses, when he would do what he dares not, and fears the Censure of the *Romans.*

I have sometimes been forc'd to amplify on others; but here, where 95 the Subject is so fruitful, that the Harvest overcomes the Reaper, I am shorten'd by my Chain, and can only see what is forbidden me to reach: Since it is not permitted me to commend you, according to the extent of my Wishes, and much less is it in my Power to make my Commendations equal to your Merits. 100

Yet in this Frugality of your Praises, there are some Things which I cannot omit, without detracting from your Character. You have so form'd your own Education, as enables you to pay the Debt you owe your Country; or more properly speaking, both your Countries: Because you were born, I may almost say in Purple at the Castle of *Dublin,* 105 when your Grandfather was Lord-Lieutenant, and have since been bred in the Court of *England.*

If this Address had been in Verse, I might have call'd you as *Claudian* calls *Mercury, Numen commune, Gemino faciens commercia mundo.* The better to satisfy this double Obligation you have early cultivated the Genius 110 you have to Arms, that when the Service of *Britain* or *Ireland* shall require your Courage, and your Conduct, you may exert them both to the Benefit of either Country. You began in the Cabinet what you afterwards practis'd in the Camp; and thus both *Lucullus* and *Cæsar* (to omit

a crowd of shining *Romans*) form'd themselves to the War by the Study 115
of History; and by the Examples of the greatest Captains, both of *Greece*
and *Italy*, before their time. I name those two Commanders in particular, because they were better read in Chronicle than any of the
Roman Leaders; and that *Lucullus* in particular, having only the Theory
of War from Books, was thought fit, without Practice, to be sent into 120
the Field, against the most formidable Enemy of *Rome*. *Tully* indeed was
call'd the learn'd Consul in derision; but then he was not born a Soldier:
His Head was turn'd another way: When he read the Tacticks he was
thinking on the Bar, which was his Field of Battle. The Knowledge of
Warfare is thrown away on a General who dares not make use of what 125
he knows. I commend it only in a Man of Courage and of Resolution;
in him it will direct his Martial Spirit; and teach him the way to the
best Victories, which are those that are least bloody, and which tho'
atchiev'd by the Hand, are manag'd by the Head. Science distinguishes
a Man of Honour from one of those Athletick Brutes whom undeservedly 130
we call Heroes. Curs'd be the Poet, who first honour'd with that Name
a meer *Ajax*, a Man-killing Ideot. The *Ulysses* of *Ovid* upbraids his Ignorance, that he understood not the Shield for which he pleaded: There
was engraven on it, Plans of Cities, and Maps of Countries, which *Ajax*
could not comprehend, but look'd on them as stupidly as his Fellow- 135
Beast the Lion. But on the other side, your Grace has given your self the
Education of his Rival; you have studied every Spot of Ground in
Flanders, which for these ten Years past has been the Scene of Battles and
of Sieges. No wonder if you perform'd your Part with such Applause
on a Theater which you understood so well.   140

If I design'd this for a Poetical Encomium, it were easy to enlarge on
so copious a Subject; but confining my self to the Severity of Truth,
and to what is becoming me to say, I must not only pass over many
Instances of your Military Skill, but also those of your assiduous Diligence in the War; and of your Personal Bravery, attended with an 145
ardent Thirst of Honour; a long Train of Generosity; Profuseness of
doing Good; a Soul unsatisfy'd with all it has done; and an unextinguish'd Desire of doing more. But all this is Matter for your own Historians; I am, as *Virgil* says, *Spatiis exclusus iniquis*.

Yet not to be wholly silent of all your Charities I must stay a little 150
on one Action, which preferr'd the Relief of Others, to the Consideration of your Self. When, in the Battle of *Landen*, your Heat of Courage
(a Fault only pardonable to your Youth) had transported you so far
before your Friends, that they were unable to follow, much less to

succour you; when you were not only dangerously, but in all appear- 155
ance mortally wounded; when in that desperate Condition you were
made Prisoner, and carried to *Namur* at that time in Possession of the
French; then it was, my Lord, that you took a considerable Part of what
was remitted to you of your own Revenues, and as a memorable Instance of your Heroick Charity, put it into the Hands of Count *Guiscard*, 160
who was Governor of the Place, to be distributed among your Fellow-
Prisoners. The *French* Commander, charm'd with the greatness of your
Soul, accordingly consign'd it to the Use for which it was intended by
the Donor: By which means the Lives of so many miserable Men were
sav'd, and a comfortable Provision made for their Subsistance, who had 165
otherwise perish'd, had not you been the Companion of their Misfortune: or rather sent by Providence, like another *Joseph*, to keep out
Famine from invading those, whom in Humility you call'd your Brethren. How happy was it for those poor Creatures, that your Grace was
made their Fellow-Sufferer? And how glorious for You, that you chose 170
to want rather than not relieve the Wants of others? The Heathen Poet,
in commending the Charity of *Dido* to the *Trojans*, spoke like a Christian: *Non ignara mali miseris, succurrere disco.* All Men, even those of a
different Interest, and contrary Principles, must praise this Action,
as the most eminent for Piety, not only in this degenerate Age, but 175
almost in any of the former; when Men were made *de meliore luto*;
when Examples of Charity were frequent, and when there were in
being, *Teucri pulcherrima proles, Magnanimi Heroes nati melioribus annis.*
No Envy can detract from this; it will shine in History; and like
Swans, grow whiter the longer it endures: And the Name of 180
ORMOND will be more celebrated in his Captivity, than in his
greatest Triumphs.

But all Actions of your Grace are of a piece; as Waters keep the
Tenour of their Fountains: your Compassion is general, and has the
same Effect as well on Enemies as Friends. 'Tis so much in your
Nature to do Good, that your Life is but one continued Act of placing 185
Benefits on many; as the Sun is always carrying his Light to some Part
or other of the World: And were it not that your Reason guides you
where to give, I might almost say that you could not help bestowing
more, than is consisting with the Fortune of a private Man, or with the
Will of any but an *Alexander*. 190

What Wonder is it then, that being born for a Blessing to Mankind,
your suppos'd Death in that Engagement, was so generally lamented
through the Nation? The Concernment for it was as universal as the

Loss: And though the Gratitude might be counterfeit in some, yet the Tears of all were real: Where every Man deplor'd his private Part in 195 that Calamity, and even those who had not tasted of your Favours, yet built so much on the Fame of your Beneficence, that they bemoan'd the Loss of their Expectations.

This brought the untimely Death of your Great Father into fresh remembrance; as if the same Decree had pass'd on two short successive 200 Generations of the Virtuous; and I repeated to my self the same Verses, which I had formerly apply'd to him: *Ostendunt terris hunc tantum fata, nec ultra, esse sinunt.* But to the Joy not only of all good Men, but of Mankind in general, the unhappy Omen took not place. You are still living to enjoy the Blessings and Applause of all the Good you have 205 perform'd, the Prayers of Multitudes whom you have oblig'd, for your long Prosperity; and that your Power of doing generous and charitable Actions, may be as extended as your Will; which is by none more zealously desir'd than by

Your GRACE's most humble,
most oblig'd, and most
obedient Servant,
John Dryden.

PREFACE

'TIS with a Poet, as with a Man who designs to build, and is very exact, as he supposes, in casting up the Cost beforehand: But, generally speaking, he is mistaken in his Account, and reckons short of the Expence he first intended: He alters his Mind as the Work proceeds, and will have this or that Convenience more, of which he had not 5 thought when he began. So has it hapned to me; I have built a House, where I intended but a Lodge: Yet with better Success than a certain Nobleman, who beginning with a Dog-kennil, never liv'd to finish the Palace he had contriv'd.

From translating the First of *Homer's Iliads,* (which I intended as an 10 Essay to the whole Work) I proceeded to the Translation of the Twelfth Book of *Ovid's Metamorphoses,* because it contains, among other Things, the Causes, the Beginning, and Ending, of the *Trojan* War: Here I ought in reason to have stopp'd; but the Speeches of *Ajax* and *Ulysses* lying next in my way, I could not balk 'em. When I had compass'd them, I 15 was so taken with the former Part of the Fifteenth Book, (which is the Master-piece of the whole *Metamorphoses*) that I enjoyn'd my self the pleasing Task of rendring it into *English*. And now I found, by the Number of my Verses, that they began to swell into a little Volume; which gave me an Occasion of looking backward on some Beauties of 20 my Author, in his former Books: There occur'd to me the Hunting of the Boar, *Cinyras* and *Myrrha*, the good-natur'd Story of *Baucis* and *Philemon*, with the rest, which I hope I have translated closely enough, and given them the same Turn of Verse, which they had in the Original; and this, I may say without vanity, is not the Talent of every Poet: 25 He who has arriv'd the nearest to it, is the Ingenious and Learned *Sandys*, the best Versifier of the former Age; if I may properly call it by that Name, which was the former Part of this concluding Century. For *Spencer* and *Fairfax* both flourish'd in the Reign of Queen *Elizabeth*: Great Masters in our Language; and who saw much farther into the 30 Beauties of our Numbers, than those who immediately followed them. *Milton* was the Poetical Son of *Spencer*, and Mr. *Waller* of *Fairfax*; for we have our Lineal Descents and Clans, as well as other Families: *Spencer* more than once insinuates, that the Soul of *Chaucer* was transfus'd into his Body; and that he was begotten by him Two hundred years after 35 his Decease. *Milton* has acknowledg'd to me, that *Spencer* was his Original; and many besides my self have heard our famous *Waller* own, that he deriv'd the Harmony of his Numbers from the *Godfrey of Bulloign*, which was turn'd into *English* by Mr. *Fairfax*. But to return: Having done with *Ovid* for this time, it came into my mind, that our old *English* 40 Poet *Chaucer* in many Things resembled him, and that with no disadvantage on the Side of the Modern Author, as I shall endeavour to prove when I compare them: And as I am, and always have been studious to promote the Honour of my Native Country, so I soon resolv'd to put their Merits to the Trial, by turning some of the *Canterbury* Tales 45 into our Language, as it is now refin'd: For by this Means both the Poets being set in the same Light, and dress'd in the same *English* Habit, Story to be compar'd with Story, a certain Judgment may be made betwixt them, by the Reader, without obtruding my Opinion on him: Or if I seem partial to my Country-man, and Predecessor in the Laurel, 50 the Friends of Antiquity are not few: And besides many of the Learn'd, *Ovid* has almost all the *Beaux*, and the whole Fair Sex, his declar'd Patrons. Perhaps I have assum'd somewhat more to my self than they allow me; because I have adventur'd to sum up the Evidence: But the Readers are the Jury; and their Privilege remains entire to decide 55

according to the Merits of the Cause: Or, if they please to bring it to
another Hearing, before some other Court. In the mean time, to follow
the Thrid of my Discourse, (as Thoughts, according to Mr. *Hobbs*, have
always some Connexion) so from *Chaucer* I was led to think on *Boccace*,
who was not only his Contemporary, but also pursu'd the same Studies; 60
wrote Novels in Prose, and many Works in Verse; particularly is said
to have invented the Octave Rhyme, or *Stanza* of Eight Lines, which
ever since has been maintain'd by the Practice of all *Italian* Writers, who
are, or at least assume the Title of *Heroick Poets*: He and *Chaucer*, among
other Things, had this in common, that they refin'd their Mother- 65
Tongues; but with this difference, that *Dante* had begun to file their
Language, at least in Verse, before the time of *Boccace*, who likewise
receiv'd no little Help from his Master *Petrarch*: But the Reformation
of their Prose was wholly owing to *Boccace* himself; who is yet the
Standard of Purity in the *Italian* Tongue; though many of his Phrases 70
are become obsolete, as in process of Time it must needs happen.
Chaucer (as you have formerly been told by our learn'd Mr. *Rhymer*)
first adorn'd and amplified our barren Tongue from the *Provencall*,
which was then the most polish'd of all the Modern Languages: But
this Subject has been copiously treated by that great Critick, who 75
deserves no little Commendation from us his Countrymen. For these
Reasons of Time, and Resemblance of Genius, in *Chaucer* and *Boccace*,
I resolv'd to join them in my present Work; to which I have added
some Original Papers of my own; which whether they are equal or
inferiour to my other Poems, an Author is the most improper Judge; 80
and therefore I leave them wholly to the Mercy of the Reader: I will
hope the best, that they will not be condemn'd; but if they should, I
have the Excuse of an old Gentleman, who mounting on Horseback
before some Ladies, when I was present, got up somewhat heavily, but
desir'd of the Fair Spectators, that they would count Fourscore and 85
eight before they judg'd him. By the Mercy of God, I am already come
within Twenty Years of his Number, a Cripple in my Limbs, but what
Decays are in my Mind, the Reader must determine. I think my self
as vigorous as ever in the Faculties of my Soul, excepting only my
Memory, which is not impair'd to any great degree; and if I lose not 90
more of it, I have no great reason to complain. What Judgment I had,
increases rather than diminishes; and Thoughts, such as they are, come
crowding in so fast upon me, that my only Difficulty is to chuse or to
reject; to run them into Verse, or to give them the other Harmony of
Prose. I have so long studied and practis'd both, that they are grown 95

into a Habit, and become familiar to me. In short, though I may lawfully plead some part of the old Gentleman's Excuse; yet I will reserve
it till I think I have greater need, and ask no Grains of Allowance for
the Faults of this my present Work, but those which are given of course
to Humane Frailty. I will not trouble my Reader with the shortness of 100
Time in which I writ it; or the several Intervals of Sickness: They who
think too well of their own Performances, are apt to boast in their
Prefaces how little Time their Works have cost them; and what other
Business of more importance interfer'd: But the Reader will be as apt
to ask the Question, Why they allow'd not a longer Time to make their 105
Works more perfect? and why they had so despicable an Opinion of
their Judges, as to thrust their indigested Stuff upon them, as if they
deserv'd no better?

With this Account of my present Undertaking, I conclude the first
Part of this Discourse: In the second Part, as at a second Sitting, though 110
I alter not the Draught, I must touch the same Features over again, and
change the Dead-colouring of the Whole. In general I will only say, that
I have written nothing which savours of Immorality or Profaneness; at
least, I am not conscious to my self of any such Intention. If there
happen to be found an irreverent Expression, or a Thought too wanton, 115
they are crept into my Verses through my Inadvertency: If the Searchers
find any in the Cargo, let them be stav'd or forfeited, like Counter-
banded Goods; at least, let their Authors be answerable for them, as
being but imported Merchandise, and not of my own Manufacture. On
the other Side, I have endeavour'd to chuse such Fables, both Ancient 120
and Modern, as contain in each of them some instructive Moral, which
I could prove by Induction, but the Way is tedious; and they leap foremost into sight, without the Reader's Trouble of looking after them.
I wish I could affirm with a safe Conscience, that I had taken the same
Care in all my former Writings; for it must be own'd, that supposing 125
Verses are never so beautiful or pleasing, yet if they contain any thing
which shocks Religion, or Good Manners, they are at best, what *Horace*
says of good Numbers without good Sense, *Versus inopes rerum, nugæque
canoræ:* Thus far, I hope, I am Right in Court, without renouncing to
my other Right of Self-defence, where I have been wrongfully accus'd, 130
and my Sense wire-drawn into Blasphemy or Bawdry, as it has often
been by a Religious Lawyer, in a late Pleading against the Stage; in
which he mixes Truth with Falshood, and has not forgotten the old
Rule, of calumniating strongly, that something may remain.

I resume the Thrid of my Discourse with the first of my Translations, 135

which was the First *Iliad* of *Homer*. If it shall please God to give me
longer Life, and moderate Health, my Intentions are to translate the
whole *Ilias*; provided still, that I meet with those Encouragements from
the Publick, which may enable me to proceed in my Undertaking with
some Chearfulness. And this I dare assure the World before-hand, that 140
I have found by Trial, *Homer* a more pleasing Task than *Virgil*, (though
I say not the Translation will be less laborious.) For the *Grecian* is more
according to my Genius, than the *Latin* Poet. In the Works of the two
Authors we may read their Manners, and natural Inclinations, which
are wholly different. *Virgil* was of a quiet, sedate Temper; *Homer* was 145
violent, impetuous, and full of Fire. The chief Talent of *Virgil* was
Propriety of Thoughts, and Ornament of Words: *Homer* was rapid in
his Thoughts, and took all the Liberties both of Numbers, and of Expressions, which his Language, and the Age in which he liv'd allow'd
him: *Homer*'s Invention was more copious, *Virgil*'s more confin'd: So 150
that if *Homer* had not led the Way, it was not in *Virgil* to have begun
Heroick Poetry: For, nothing can be more evident, than that the
Roman Poem is but the Second Part of the *Ilias*; a Continuation of the
same Story: And the Persons already form'd: The Manners of *Æneas*,
are those of *Hector* superadded to those which *Homer* gave him. The 155
Adventures of *Ulysses* in the *Odysseis*, are imitated in the first Six Books
of *Virgil*'s *Æneis*: And though the Accidents are not the same, (which
would have argu'd him of a servile, copying, and total Barrenness of
Invention) yet the Seas were the same, in which both the *Heroes* wander'd; and *Dido* cannot be deny'd to be the Poetical Daughter of *Calypso*. 160
The Six latter Books of *Virgil*'s Poem, are the Four and twenty *Iliads*
contracted: A Quarrel occasion'd by a Lady, a Single Combate, Battels
fought, and a Town besieg'd. I say not this in derogation to *Virgil*,
neither do I contradict any thing which I have formerly said in his just
Praise: For his *Episodes* are almost wholly of his own Invention; and the 165
Form which he has given to the Telling, makes the Tale his own, even
though the Original Story had been the same. But this proves, however,
that *Homer* taught *Virgil* to design: And if Invention be the first Vertue
of an Epick Poet, then the *Latin* Poem can only be allow'd the second
Place. Mr. *Hobbs*, in the Preface to his own bald Translation of the *Ilias*, 170
(studying Poetry as he did Mathematicks, when it was too late) Mr.
Hobbs, I say, begins the Praise of *Homer* where he should have ended it.
He tells us, that the first Beauty of an Epick Poem consists in Diction,
that is, in the Choice of Words, and Harmony of Numbers: Now, the
Words are the Colouring of the Work, which in the Order of Nature 175

is last to be consider'd. The Design, the Disposition, the Manners, and the Thoughts, are all before it: Where any of those are wanting or imperfect, so much wants or is imperfect in the Imitation of Humane Life; which is in the very Definition of a Poem. Words indeed, like glaring Colours, are the first Beauties that arise, and strike the Sight; 180 but if the Draught be false or lame, the Figures ill dispos'd, the Manners obscure or inconsistent, or the Thoughts unnatural, then the finest Colours are but Dawbing, and the Piece is a beautiful Monster at the best. Neither *Virgil* nor *Homer* were deficient in any of the former Beauties; but in this last, which is Expression, the *Roman* Poet is at least 185 equal to the *Grecian*, as I have said elsewhere; supplying the Poverty of his Language, by his Musical Ear, and by his Diligence. But to return: Our two Great Poets, being so different in their Tempers, one Cholerick and Sanguin, the other Phlegmatick and Melancholick; that which makes them excel in their several Ways, is, that each of them has fol- 190 low'd his own natural Inclination, as well in Forming the Design, as in the Execution of it. The very *Heroes* shew their Authors: *Achilles* is hot, impatient, revengeful, *Impiger, iracundus, inexorabilis, acer,* &c. *Æneas* patient, considerate, careful of his People, and merciful to his Enemies; ever submissive to the Will of Heaven, *quo fata trahunt retrahuntque,* 195 *sequamur.* I could please my self with enlarging on this Subject, but am forc'd to defer it to a fitter Time. From all I have said, I will only draw this Inference, That the Action of *Homer* being more full of Vigour than that of *Virgil*, according to the Temper of the Writer, is of consequence more pleasing to the Reader. One warms you by Degrees; the other 200 sets you on fire all at once, and never intermits his Heat. 'Tis the same Difference which *Longinus* makes betwixt the Effects of Eloquence in *Demosthenes*, and *Tully*. One persuades; the other commands. You never cool while you read *Homer*, even not in the Second Book, (a graceful Flattery to his Countrymen;) but he hastens from the Ships, and con- 205 cludes not that Book till he has made you an Amends by the violent playing of a new Machine. From thence he hurries on his Action with Variety of Events, and ends it in less Compass than Two Months. This Vehemence of his, I confess, is more suitable to my Temper: and there-fore I have translated his First Book with greater Pleasure than any 210 Part of *Virgil*: But it was not a Pleasure without Pains: The continual Agitations of the Spirits, must needs be a Weakning of any Constitu-tion, especially in Age: and many Pauses are required for Refreshment betwixt the Heats; the *Iliad* of its self being a third part longer than all *Virgil*'s Works together. 215

This is what I thought needful in this Place to say of *Homer*. I proceed to *Ovid*, and *Chaucer*; considering the former only in relation to the latter. With *Ovid* ended the Golden Age of the *Roman* Tongue: From *Chaucer* the Purity of the *English* Tongue began. The Manners of the Poets were not unlike: Both of them were well-bred, well-natur'd, 220 amorous, and Libertine, at least in their Writings, it may be also in their Lives. Their Studies were the same, Philosophy, and Philology. Both of them were knowing in Astronomy, of which *Ovid*'s Books of the *Roman* Feasts, and *Chaucer*'s Treatise of the *Astrolabe*, are sufficient Witnesses. But *Chaucer* was likewise an Astrologer, as were *Virgil, Horace,* 225 *Persius,* and *Manilius*. Both writ with wonderful Facility and Clearness; neither were great Inventors: For *Ovid* only copied the *Grecian* Fables; and most of *Chaucer*'s Stories were taken from his *Italian* Contemporaries, or their Predecessors: *Boccace* his *Decameron* was first publish'd; and from thence our *Englishman* has borrow'd many of his *Canterbury* Tales: 230 Yet that of *Palamon* and *Arcite* was written in all probability by some *Italian* Wit, in a former Age; as I shall prove hereafter: The Tale of *Grizild* was the Invention of *Petrarch*; by him sent to *Boccace*; from whom it came to *Chaucer*: *Troilus* and *Cressida* was also written by a *Lombard* Author; but much amplified by our *English* Translatour, as 235 well as beautified; the Genius of our Countrymen in general being rather to improve an Invention, than to invent themselves; as is evident not only in our Poetry, but in many of our Manufactures. I find I have anticipated already, and taken up from *Boccace* before I come to him: But there is so much less behind; and I am of the Temper of most 240 Kings, *who love to be in Debt,* are all for present Money, no matter how they pay it afterwards: Besides, the Nature of a Preface is rambling; never wholly out of the Way, nor in it. This I have learn'd from the Practice of honest *Montaign*, and return at my pleasure to *Ovid* and *Chaucer*, of whom I have little more to say. Both of them built on the 245 Inventions of other Men; yet since *Chaucer* had something of his own, as *The Wife of Baths Tale, The Cock and the Fox,* which I have translated, and some others, I may justly give our Countryman the Precedence in that Part; since I can remember nothing of *Ovid* which was wholly his. Both of them understood the Manners; under which Name I compre- 250 hend the Passions, and, in a larger Sense, the Descriptions of Persons, and their very Habits: For an Example, I see *Baucis* and *Philemon* as perfectly before me, as if some ancient Painter had drawn them; and all the Pilgrims in the *Canterbury* Tales, their Humours, their Features, and the very Dress, as distinctly as if I had supp'd with them at the *Tabard* in 255

Southwark: Yet even there too the Figures of *Chaucer* are much more lively, and set in a better Light: Which though I have not time to prove; yet I appeal to the Reader, and am sure he will clear me from Partiality. The Thoughts and Words remain to be consider'd, in the Comparison of the two Poets; and I have sav'd my self one half of that Labour, by owning that *Ovid* liv'd when the *Roman* Tongue was in its Meridian; *Chaucer*, in the Dawning of our Language: Therefore that Part of the Comparison stands not on an equal Foot, any more than the Diction of *Ennius* and *Ovid*; or of *Chaucer*, and our present *English*. The Words are given up as a Post not to be defended in our Poet, because he wanted the Modern Art of Fortifying. The Thoughts remain to be consider'd: And they are to be measur'd only by their Propriety; that is, as they flow more or less naturally from the Persons describ'd, on such and such Occasions. The Vulgar Judges, which are Nine Parts in Ten of all Nations, who call Conceits and Jingles Wit, who see *Ovid* full of them, and *Chaucer* altogether without them, will think me little less than mad, for preferring the *Englishman* to the *Roman*: Yet, with their leave, I must presume to say, that the Things they admire are only glittering Trifles, and so far from being Witty, that in a serious Poem they are nauseous, because they are unnatural. Wou'd any Man who is ready to die for Love, describe his Passion like *Narcissus*? Wou'd he think of *inopem me copia fecit*, and a Dozen more of such Expressions, pour'd on the Neck of one another, and signifying all the same Thing? If this were Wit, was this a Time to be witty, when the poor Wretch was in the Agony of Death? This is just *John Littlewit* in *Bartholomew Fair*, who had a Conceit (as he tells you) left him in his Misery; a miserable Conceit. On these Occasions the Poet shou'd endeavour to raise Pity: But instead of this, *Ovid* is tickling you to laugh. *Virgil* never made use of such Machines, when he was moving you to commiserate the Death of *Dido*: He would not destroy what he was building. *Chaucer* makes *Arcite* violent in his Love, and unjust in the Pursuit of it: Yet when he came to die, he made him think more reasonably: He repents not of his Love, for that had alter'd his Character; but acknowledges the Injustice of his Proceedings, and resigns *Emilia* to *Palamon*. What would *Ovid* have done on this Occasion? He would certainly have made *Arcite* witty on his Death-bed. He had complain'd he was farther off from Possession, by being so near, and a thousand such Boyisms, which *Chaucer* rejected as below the Dignity of the Subject. They who think otherwise, would by the same Reason prefer *Lucan* and *Ovid* to *Homer* and *Virgil*, and *Martial* to all Four of them. As for the Turn of Words, in which *Ovid* particularly excels all Poets; they are sometimes a Fault, and sometimes a Beauty, as they are us'd properly or improperly; but in strong Passions always to be shunn'd, because Passions are serious, and will admit no Playing. The *French* have a high Value for them; and I confess, they are often what they call Delicate, when they are introduc'd with Judgment; but *Chaucer* writ with more Simplicity, and follow'd Nature more closely, than to use them. I have thus far, to the best of my Knowledge, been an upright Judge betwixt the Parties in Competition, not medling with the Design nor the Disposition of it; because the Design was not their own; and in the disposing of it they were equal. It remains that I say somewhat of *Chaucer* in particular.

In the first place, As he is the Father of *English* Poetry, so I hold him in the same Degree of Veneration as the *Grecians* held *Homer*, or the *Romans Virgil*: He is a perpetual Fountain of good Sense; learn'd in all Sciences; and therefore speaks properly on all Subjects: As he knew what to say, so he knows also when to leave off; a Continence which is practis'd by few Writers, and scarcely by any of the Ancients, excepting *Virgil* and *Horace*. One of our late great Poets is sunk in his Reputation, because he cou'd never forgive any Conceit which came in his way; but swept like a Drag-net, great and small. There was plenty enough, but the Dishes were ill sorted; whole Pyramids of Sweet-meats, for Boys and Women; but little of solid Meat, for Men: All this proceeded not from any want of Knowledge, but of Judgment; neither did he want that in discerning the Beauties and Faults of other Poets; but only indulg'd himself in the Luxury of Writing; and perhaps knew it was a Fault, but hop'd the Reader would not find it. For this Reason, though he must always be thought a great Poet, he is no longer esteem'd a good Writer: And for Ten Impressions, which his Works have had in so many successive Years, yet at present a hundred Books are scarcely purchas'd once a Twelvemonth: For, as my last Lord *Rochester* said, though somewhat profanely, *Not being of God, he could not stand.*

Chaucer follow'd Nature every where; but was never so bold to go beyond her: And there is a great Difference of being *Poeta* and *nimis Poeta*, if we may believe *Catullus*, as much as betwixt a modest Behaviour and Affectation. The Verse of *Chaucer*, I confess, is not Harmonious to us; but 'tis like the Eloquence of one whom *Tacitus* commends, it was *auribus istius temporis accommodata:* They who liv'd with him, and some time after him, thought it Musical; and it continues so even in our Judgment, if compar'd with the Numbers of *Lidgate* and *Gower* his Contemporaries: There is the rude Sweetness of a *Scotch* Tune in it, which is natural and pleasing, though not perfect. 'Tis true, I cannot go so far as he who publish'd the last Edition of him; for he would make us believe the Fault is in our Ears, and that there were really Ten Syllables in a Verse where we find but Nine: But this Opinion is not worth con- 340 futing; 'tis so gross and obvious an Errour, that common Sense (which is a Rule in every thing but Matters of Faith and Revelation) must convince the Reader, that Equality of Numbers in every Verse which we call *Heroick*, was either not known, or not always practis'd in *Chaucer*'s Age. It were an easie Matter to produce some thousands of 345 his Verses, which are lame for want of half a Foot, and sometimes a whole one, and which no Pronunciation can make otherwise. We can only say, that he liv'd in the Infancy of our Poetry, and that nothing is brought to Perfection at the first. We must be Children before we grow Men. There was an *Ennius*, and in process of Time a *Lucilius*, and 350 a *Lucretius*, before *Virgil* and *Horace*; even after *Chaucer* there was a *Spencer*, a *Harrington*, a *Fairfax*, before *Waller* and *Denham* were in being: And our Numbers were in their Nonage till these last appear'd. I need say little of his Parentage, Life, and Fortunes: They are to be found at large in all the Editions of his Works. He was employ'd abroad, and 355 favour'd by *Edward* the Third, *Richard* the Second, and *Henry* the Fourth, and was Poet, as I suppose, to all Three of them. In *Richard*'s Time, I doubt, he was a little dipt in the Rebellion of the Commons; and being Brother-in-Law to *John of Ghant*, it was no wonder if he follow'd the Fortunes of that Family; and was well with *Henry* the Fourth when he 360 had depos'd his Predecessor. Neither is it to be admir'd, that *Henry*, who was a wise as well as a valiant Prince, who claim'd by Succession, and was sensible that his Title was not sound, but was rightfully in *Morti-mer*, who had married the Heir of *York*; it was not to be admir'd, I say, if that great Politician should be pleas'd to have the greatest Wit of 365 those Times in his Interests, and to be the Trumpet of his Praises. *Augustus* had given him the Example, by the Advice of *Mæcenas*, who re-commended *Virgil* and *Horace* to him; whose Praises help'd to make him Popular while he was alive, and after his Death have made him Precious to Posterity. As for the Religion of our Poet, he seems to have some 370 little Byas towards the Opinions of *Wickliff*, after *John of Ghant* his Patron; somewhat of which appears in the Tale of *Piers Plowman*: Yet I cannot blame him for inveighing so sharply against the Vices of the Clergy in his Age: Their Pride, their Ambition, their Pomp, their Avarice, their Worldly Interest, deserv'd the Lashes which he gave 375

them, both in that, and in most of his *Canterbury Tales*: Neither has his
Contemporary *Boccace*, spar'd them. Yet both those Poets liv'd in much
esteem, with good and holy Men in Orders: For the Scandal which
is given by particular Priests, reflects not on the Sacred Function.
Chaucer's Monk, his *Chanon*, and his *Fryar*, took not from the Character 380
of his *Good Parson*. A Satyrical Poet is the Check of the Laymen, on bad
Priests. We are only to take care, that we involve not the Innocent with
the Guilty in the same Condemnation. The Good cannot be too much
honour'd, nor the Bad too coursly us'd: For the Corruption of the Best,
becomes the Worst. When a Clergy-man is whipp'd, his Gown is first 385
taken off, by which the Dignity of his Order is secur'd: If he be wrongfully accus'd, he has his Action of Slander; and 'tis at the Poet's Peril,
if he transgress the Law. But they will tell us, that all kind of Satire,
though never so well deserv'd by particular Priests, yet brings the
whole Order into Contempt. Is then the Peerage of *England* any thing 390
dishonour'd, when a Peer suffers for his Treason? If he be libell'd, or
any way defam'd, he has his *Scandalum Magnatum* to punish the Offendor.
They who use this kind of Argument, seem to be conscious to themselves of somewhat which has deserv'd the Poet's Lash; and are less
concern'd for their Publick Capacity, than for their Private: At least, 395
there is Pride at the bottom of their Reasoning. If the Faults of Men
in Orders are only to be judg'd among themselves, they are all in some
sort Parties: For, since they say the Honour of their Order is concern'd
in every Member of it, how can we be sure, that they will be impartial
Judges? How far I may be allow'd to speak my Opinion in this Case, 400
I know not: But I am sure a Dispute of this Nature caus'd Mischief in
abundance betwixt a King of *England* and an Archbishop of *Canterbury*;
one standing up for the Laws of his Land, and the other for the Honour
(as he call'd it) of God's Church; which ended in the Murther of the
Prelate, and in the whipping of his Majesty from Post to Pillar for his 405
Penance. The Learn'd and Ingenious Dr. *Drake* has sav'd me the Labour
of inquiring into the Esteem and Reverence which the Priests have had
of old; and I would rather extend than diminish any part of it: Yet I
must needs say, that when a Priest provokes me without any Occasion
given him, I have no Reason, unless it be the Charity of a *Christian*, to 410
forgive him: *Prior læsit* is Justification sufficient in the Civil Law. If I
answer him in his own Language, Self-defence, I am sure, must be
allow'd me; and if I carry it farther, even to a sharp Recrimination,
somewhat may be indulg'd to Humane Frailty. Yet my Resentment
has not wrought so far, but that I have follow'd *Chaucer* in his Character 415

of a Holy Man, and have enlarg'd on that Subject with some Pleasure, reserving to my self the Right, if I shall think fit hereafter, to describe another sort of Priests, such as are more easily to be found than the Good Parson; such as have given the last Blow to Christianity in this Age, by a Practice so contrary to their Doctrine. But this will keep cold 420 till another time. In the mean while, I take up *Chaucer* where I left him. He must have been a Man of a most wonderful comprehensive Nature, because, as it has been truly observ'd of him, he has taken into the Compass of his *Canterbury Tales* the various Manners and Humours (as we now call them) of the whole *English* Nation, in his Age. Not a single 425 Character has escap'd him. All his Pilgrims are severally distinguish'd from each other; and not only in their Inclinations, but in their very Phisiognomies and Persons. *Baptista Porta* could not have describ'd their Natures better, than by the Marks which the Poet gives them. The Matter and Manner of their Tales, and of their Telling, are so suited 430 to their different Educations, Humours, and Callings, that each of them would be improper in any other Mouth. Even the grave and serious Characters are distinguish'd by their several sorts of Gravity: Their Discourses are such as belong to their Age, their Calling, and their Breeding; such as are becoming of them, and of them only. Some of his 435 Persons are Vicious, and some Vertuous; some are unlearn'd, or (as *Chaucer* calls them) Lewd, and some are Learn'd. Even the Ribaldry of the Low Characters is different: The *Reeve*, the *Miller*, and the *Cook*, are several Men, and distinguish'd from each other, as much as the mincing Lady Prioress, and the broad-speaking gap-tooth'd Wife of *Bathe*. But 440 enough of this: There is such a Variety of Game springing up before me, that I am distracted in my Choice, and know not which to follow. 'Tis sufficient to say according to the Proverb, that here is God's Plenty. We have our Fore-fathers and Great Grand-dames all before us, as they were in *Chaucer*'s Days; their general Characters are still remain- 445 ing in Mankind, and even in *England*, though they are call'd by other Names than those of *Moncks*, and *Fryars*, and *Chanons*, and *Lady Abbesses*, and *Nuns*: For Mankind is ever the same, and nothing lost out of Nature, though every thing is alter'd. May I have leave to do my self the Justice, (since my Enemies will do me none, and are so far from granting 450 me to be a good Poet, that they will not allow me so much as to be a Christian, or a Moral Man) may I have leave, I say, to inform my Reader, that I have confin'd my Choice to such Tales of *Chaucer*, as savour nothing of Immodesty. If I had desir'd more to please than to instruct, the *Reve*, the *Miller*, the *Shipman*, the *Merchant*, the *Sumner*, and 455

above all, the *Wife of Bathe*, in the Prologue to her Tale, would have
procur'd me as many Friends and Readers, as there are *Beaux* and Ladies
of Pleasure in the Town. But I will no more offend against Good
Manners: I am sensible as I ought to be of the Scandal I have given
by my loose Writings; and make what Reparation I am able, by this 460
Publick Acknowledgment. If any thing of this Nature, or of Profaneness,
be crept into these Poems, I am so far from defending it, that I disown it.
Totum hoc indictum volo. Chaucer makes another manner of Apologie for
his broad-speaking, and *Boccace* makes the like; but I will follow neither
of them. Our Country-man, in the end of his Characters, before the 465
Canterbury Tales, thus excuses the Ribaldry, which is very gross, in
many of his Novels.

> *But first, I pray you, of your courtesy,*
> *That ye ne arrete it nought my villany,*
> *Though that I plainly speak in this mattere*   470
> *To tellen you her words, and eke her chere:*
> *Ne though I speak her words properly,*
> *For this ye knowen as well as I,*
> *Who shall tellen a tale after a man*
> *He mote rehearse as nye, as ever He can:*   475
> *Everich word of it been in his charge,*
> All speke he, never so rudely, ne large.
> *Or else he mote tellen his tale untrue,*
> *Or feine things, or find words new:*
> *He may not spare, altho he were his brother,*   480
> *He mote as well say o word as another.*
> Christ *spake himself full broad in holy Writ,*
> *And well I wote no Villany is it.*
> *Eke* Plato *saith, who so can him rede,*
> *The words mote been Cousin to the dede.*   485

Yet if a Man should have enquir'd of *Boccace* or of *Chaucer*, what need
they had of introducing such Characters, where obscene Words were
proper in their Mouths, but very undecent to be heard; I know not
what Answer they could have made: For that Reason, such Tales shall
be left untold by me. You have here a *Specimen* of *Chaucer*'s Language, 490
which is so obsolete, that his Sense is scarce to be understood; and
you have likewise more than one Example of his unequal Numbers,
which were mention'd before. Yet many of his Verses consist of Ten

Syllables, and the Words not much behind our present *English*: As
for Example, these two Lines, in the Description of the Carpenter's 495
Young Wife:

> *Wincing she was, as is a jolly Colt,*
> *Long as a Mast, and upright as a Bolt.*

I have almost done with *Chaucer*, when I have answer'd some Objections relating to my present Work. I find some People are offended that 500
I have turn'd these Tales into modern *English*; because they think them
unworthy of my Pains, and look on *Chaucer* as a dry, old-fashion'd Wit,
not worth receiving. I have often heard the late Earl of *Leicester* say,
that Mr. *Cowley* himself was of that opinion; who having read him over
at my Lord's Request, declar'd he had no Taste of him. I dare not 505
advance my Opinion against the Judgment of so great an Author: But
I think it fair, however, to leave the Decision to the Publick: Mr. *Cowley*
was too modest to set up for a Dictatour; and being shock'd perhaps
with his old Style, never examin'd into the depth of his good Sense.
Chaucer, I confess, is a rough Diamond, and must first be polish'd e'er 510
he shines. I deny not likewise, that living in our early Days of Poetry,
he writes not always of a piece; but sometimes mingles trivial Things,
with those of greater Moment. Sometimes also, though not often, he
runs riot, like *Ovid*, and knows not when he has said enough. But there
are more great Wits, beside *Chaucer*, whose Fault is their Excess of 515
Conceits, and those ill sorted. An Author is not to write all he can, but
only all he ought. Having observ'd this Redundancy in *Chaucer*, (as it
is an easie Matter for a Man of ordinary Parts to find a Fault in one of
greater) I have not ty'd my self to a Literal Translation; but have often
omitted what I judg'd unnecessary, or not of Dignity enough to appear 520
in the Company of better Thoughts. I have presum'd farther in some
Places, and added somewhat of my own where I thought my Author
was deficient, and had not given his Thoughts their true Lustre, for
want of Words in the Beginning of our Language. And to this I was the
more embolden'd, because (if I may be permitted to say it of my self) 525
I found I had a Soul congenial to his, and that I had been conversant in
the same Studies. Another Poet, in another Age, may take the same
Liberty with my Writings; if at least they live long enough to deserve
Correction. It was also necessary sometimes to restore the Sense of
Chaucer, which was lost or mangled in the Errors of the Press: Let this 530
Example suffice at present; in the Story of *Palamon* and *Arcite*, where

the Temple of *Diana* is describ'd, you find these Verses, in all the
Editions of our Author:

> There saw I Danè *turned unto a Tree,*
> I *mean not the Goddess* Diane,
> But Venus *Daughter, which that hight* Danè.

535

Which after a little Consideration I knew was to be reform'd into this
Sense, that *Daphne* the Daughter of *Peneus* was turn'd into a Tree. I durst
not make thus bold with *Ovid,* lest some future *Milbourn* should arise,
and say, I varied from my Author, because I understood him not.   540

But there are other Judges who think I ought not to have translated
Chaucer into *English,* out of a quite contrary Notion: They suppose there
is a certain Veneration due to his old Language; and that it is little less
than Profanation and Sacrilege to alter it. They are farther of opinion,
that somewhat of his good Sense will suffer in this Transfusion, and 545
much of the Beauty of his Thoughts will infallibly be lost, which appear
with more Grace in their old Habit. Of this Opinion was that excellent Person, whom I mention'd, the late Earl of *Leicester,* who valu'd
Chaucer as much as Mr. *Cowley* despis'd him. My Lord dissuaded me
from this Attempt, (for I was thinking of it some Years before his 550
Death) and his Authority prevail'd so far with me, as to defer my
Undertaking while he liv'd, in deference to him: Yet my Reason was
not convinc'd with what he urg'd against it. If the first End of a Writer
be to be understood, then as his Language grows obsolete, his Thoughts
must grow obscure, *multa renascentur quæ nunc cecidere; cadentque quæ nunc* 555
sunt in honore vocabula, si volet usus, quem penes arbitrium est & jus & norma
loquendi. When an ancient Word for its Sound and Significancy deserves
to be reviv'd, I have that reasonable Veneration for Antiquity, to
restore it. All beyond this is Superstition. Words are not like Land-
marks, so sacred as never to be remov'd: Customs are chang'd, and even 560
Statutes are silently repeal'd, when the Reason ceases for which they
were enacted. As for the other Part of the Argument, that his Thoughts
will lose of their original Beauty, by the innovation of Words; in the
first place, not only their Beauty, but their Being is lost, where they
are no longer understood, which is the present Case. I grant, that some- 565
thing must be lost in all Transfusion, that is, in all Translations; but
the Sense will remain, which would otherwise be lost, or at least be
maim'd, when it is scarce intelligible; and that but to a few. How few
are there who can read *Chaucer,* so as to understand him perfectly? And
if imperfectly, then with less Profit, and no Pleasure. 'Tis not for the 570

Use of some old *Saxon* Friends, that I have taken these Pains with him:
Let them neglect my Version, because they have no need of it. I made it
for their sakes who understand Sense and Poetry, as well as they; when
that Poetry and Sense is put into Words which they understand. I will
go farther, and dare to add, that what Beauties I lose in some Places, I 575
give to others which had them not originally: But in this I may be
partial to my self; let the Reader judge, and I submit to his Decision.
Yet I think I have just Occasion to complain of them, who because they
understand *Chaucer*, would deprive the greater part of their Countrymen of the same Advantage, and hoord him up, as Misers do their 580
Grandam Gold, only to look on it themselves, and hinder others from
making use of it. In sum, I seriously protest, that no Man ever had, or
can have, a greater Veneration for *Chaucer*, than my self. I have translated some part of his Works, only that I might perpetuate his Memory,
or at least refresh it, amongst my Countrymen. If I have alter'd him any 585
where for the better, I must at the same time acknowledge, that I could
have done nothing without him: *Facile est inventis addere*, is no great
Commendation; and I am not so vain to think I have deserv'd a greater.
I will conclude what I have to say of him singly, with this one Remark:
A Lady of my Acquaintance, who keeps a kind of Correspondence with 590
some Authors of the Fair Sex in *France*, has been inform'd by them, that
Mademoiselle de Scudery, who is as old as *Sibyl*, and inspir'd like her by the
same God of Poetry, is at this time translating *Chaucer* into modern
French. From which I gather, that he has been formerly translated into
the old *Provencall*, (for, how she should come to understand Old *English*, 595
I know not.) But the Matter of Fact being true, it makes me think, that
there is something in it like Fatality; that after certain Periods of Time,
the Fame and Memory of Great Wits should be renew'd, as *Chaucer* is
both in *France* and *England*. If this be wholly Chance, 'tis extraordinary;
and I dare not call it more, for fear of being tax'd with Superstition. 600

    Boccace comes last to be consider'd, who living in the same Age with
Chaucer, had the same Genius, and follow'd the same Studies: Both writ
Novels, and each of them cultivated his Mother-Tongue: But the greatest Resemblance of our two Modern Authors being in their familiar
Style, and pleasing way of relating Comical Adventures, I may pass it 605
over, because I have translated nothing from *Boccace* of that Nature.
In the serious Part of Poetry, the Advantage is wholly on *Chaucer*'s Side;
for though the *Englishman* has borrow'd many Tales from the *Italian*, yet
it appears, that those of *Boccace* were not generally of his own making,
but taken from Authors of former Ages, and by him only modell'd: So 610

that what there was of Invention in either of them, may be judg'd equal.
But *Chaucer* has refin'd on *Boccace*, and has mended the Stories which he
has borrow'd, in his way of telling; though Prose allows more Liberty
of Thought, and the Expression is more easie, when unconfin'd by
Numbers. Our Countryman carries Weight, and yet wins the Race at 615
disadvantage. I desire not the Reader should take my Word; and therefore I will set two of their Discourses on the same Subject, in the same
Light, for every Man to judge betwixt them. I translated *Chaucer* first,
and amongst the rest, pitch'd on the Wife of *Bath*'s Tale; not daring,
as I have said, to adventure on her Prologue; because 'tis too licentious: 620
There *Chaucer* introduces an old Woman of mean Parentage, whom a
youthful Knight of Noble Blood was forc'd to marry, and consequently
loath'd her: The Crone being in bed with him on the wedding Night,
and finding his Aversion, endeavours to win his Affection by Reason,
and speaks a good Word for her self, (as who could blame her?) in hope 625
to mollifie the sullen Bridegroom. She takes her Topiques from the
Benefits of Poverty, the Advantages of old Age and Ugliness, the Vanity
of Youth, and the silly Pride of Ancestry and Titles without inherent
Vertue, which is the true Nobility. When I had clos'd *Chaucer*, I return'd
to *Ovid*, and translated some more of his Fables; and by this time had 630
so far forgotten the Wife of *Bath*'s Tale, that when I took up *Boccace*,
unawares I fell on the same Argument of preferring Virtue to Nobility
of Blood, and Titles, in the Story of *Sigismonda*; which I had certainly
avoided for the Resemblance of the two Discourses, if my Memory had
not fail'd me. Let the Reader weigh them both; and if he thinks me 635
partial to *Chaucer*, 'tis in him to right *Boccace*.

   I prefer in our Countryman, far above all his other Stories, the Noble
Poem of *Palamon* and *Arcite*, which is of the *Epique* kind, and perhaps not
much inferiour to the *Ilias* or the *Æneis*: the Story is more pleasing than
either of them, the Manners as perfect, the Diction as poetical, the 640
Learning as deep and various; and the Disposition full as artful: only it
includes a greater length of time; as taking up seven years at least; but
Aristotle has left undecided the Duration of the Action; which yet is
easily reduc'd into the Compass of a year, by a Narration of what pre-
ceded the Return of *Palamon* to *Athens*. I had thought for the Honour of 645
our Nation, and more particularly for his, whose Laurel, tho' unworthy,
I have worn after him, that this Story was of *English* Growth, and
Chaucer's own: But I was undeceiv'd by *Boccace*; for casually looking on
the End of his seventh *Giornata*, I found *Dioneo* (under which name he
shadows himself) and *Fiametta* (who represents his Mistress, the natural 650

Daughter of *Robert* King of *Naples*) of whom these Words are spoken. *Dioneo e Fiametta gran pezza cantarono insieme d'Arcita, e di Palamone:* by which it appears that this Story was written before the time of *Boccace*; but the Name of its Author being wholly lost, *Chaucer* is now become an Original; and I question not but the Poem has receiv'd many Beauties 655 by passing through his Noble Hands. Besides this Tale, there is another of his own Invention, after the manner of the *Provencalls*, call'd *The Flower and the Leaf*; with which I was so particularly pleas'd, both for the Invention and the Moral; that I cannot hinder my self from recommending it to the Reader. 660

As a Corollary to this Preface, in which I have done Justice to others, I owe somewhat to my self: not that I think it worth my time to enter the Lists with one *M——*, or one *B——*, but barely to take notice, that such Men there are who have written scurrilously against me without any Provocation. *M——*, who is in Orders, pretends amongst the rest 665 this Quarrel to me, that I have fallen foul on Priesthood; If I have, I am only to ask Pardon of good Priests, and am afraid his part of the Reparation will come to little. Let him be satisfied that he shall not be able to force himself upon me for an Adversary. I contemn him too much to enter into Competition with him. His own Translations of *Virgil* have 670 answer'd his Criticisms on mine. If (as they say, he has declar'd in Print) he prefers the Version of *Ogilby* to mine, the World has made him the same Compliment: For 'tis agreed on all hands, that he writes even below *Ogilby*: That, you will say, is not easily to be done; but what cannot *M——* bring about? I am satisfy'd however, that while he and 675 I live together, I shall not be thought the worst Poet of the Age. It looks as if I had desir'd him underhand to write so ill against me: But upon my honest Word I have not brib'd him to do me this Service, and am wholly guiltless of his Pamphlet. 'Tis true I should be glad, if I could persuade him to continue his good Offices, and write such another 680 Critique on any thing of mine: For I find by Experience he has a great Stroke with the Reader, when he condemns any of my Poems to make the World have a better Opinion of them. He has taken some Pains with my Poetry; but no body will be persuaded to take the same with his. If I had taken to the Church (as he affirms, but which was never in my 685 Thoughts) I should have had more Sense, if not more Grace, than to have turn'd my self out of my Benefice by writing Libels on my Parishioners. But his Account of my Manners and my Principles, are of a Piece with his Cavils and his Poetry: And so I have done with him for ever. 690

As for the City Bard, or Knight Physician, I hear his Quarrel to me is, that I was the Author of *Absalom and Achitophel,* which he thinks is a little hard on his Fanatique Patrons in *London.*

But I will deal the more civilly with his two Poems, because nothing ill is to be spoken of the Dead: And therefore Peace be to the *Manes* of 695 his *Arthurs.* I will only say that it was not for this Noble Knight that I drew the Plan of an Epick Poem on King *Arthur* in my Preface to the Translation of *Juvenal.* The Guardian Angels of Kingdoms were Machines too ponderous for him to manage; and therefore he rejected them as *Dares* did the Whirl-bats of *Eryx* when they were thrown before 700 him by *Entellus*: Yet from that Preface he plainly took his Hint: For he began immediately upon the Story; though he had the Baseness not to acknowledge his Benefactor; but in stead of it, to traduce me in a Libel.

I shall say the less of Mr. *Collier,* because in many Things he has tax'd me justly; and I have pleaded Guilty to all Thoughts and Expressions 705 of mine, which can be truly argu'd of Obscenity, Profaneness, or Immorality; and retract them. If he be my Enemy, let him triumph; if he be my Friend, as I have given him no Personal Occasion to be otherwise, he will be glad of my Repentance. It becomes me not to draw my Pen in the Defence of a bad Cause, when I have so often drawn it for a good 710 one. Yet it were not difficult to prove, that in many Places he has perverted my Meaning by his Glosses; and interpreted my Words into Blasphemy and Baudry, of which they were not guilty. Besides that, he is too much given to Horse-play in his Raillery; and comes to Battel, like a Dictatour from the Plough. I will not say, *The Zeal of God's House* 715 *has eaten him up;* but I am sure it has devour'd some Part of his Good Manners and Civility. It might also be doubted, whether it were altogether Zeal, which prompted him to this rough manner of Proceeding; perhaps it became not one of his Function to rake into the Rubbish of Ancient and Modern Plays; a Divine might have employ'd 720 his Pains to better purpose, than in the Nastiness of *Plautus* and *Aristophanes*; whose Examples, as they excuse not me, so it might be possibly suppos'd, that he read them not without some Pleasure. They who have written Commentaries on those Poets, or on *Horace, Juvenal,* and *Martial,* have explain'd some Vices, which without their Inter- 725 pretation had been unknown to Modern Times. Neither has he judg'd impartially betwixt the former Age and us.

There is more Baudry in one Play of *Fletcher's,* call'd *The Custom of the Country,* than in all ours together. Yet this has been often acted on the Stage in my remembrance. Are the Times so much more reform'd now, 730

than they were Five and twenty Years ago? If they are, I congratulate
the Amendment of our Morals. But I am not to prejudice the Cause of
my Fellow-Poets, though I abandon my own Defence: They have some
of them answer'd for themselves, and neither they nor I can think
Mr. *Collier* so formidable an Enemy, that we should shun him. He has 735
lost Ground at the latter end of the Day, by pursuing his Point too far,
like the Prince of *Condé* at the Battel of *Senneph*: From Immoral Plays, to
No Plays; *ab abusu ad usum, non valet consequentia.* But being a Party, I am
not to erect my self into a Judge. As for the rest of those who have
written against me, they are such Scoundrels, that they deserve not the 740
least Notice to be taken of them. *B——* and *M——* are only distinguish'd from the Crowd, by being remember'd to their Infamy.

————*Demetri, Teque Tigelli*
Discipularum inter jubeo plorare cathedras.

TO HER GRACE
THE DUTCHESS OF ORMOND,
With the following POEM of
Palamon and Arcite, from CHAUCER

MADAM,

THE Bard who first adorn'd our Native Tongue
Tun'd to his *British* Lyre this ancient Song:
Which *Homer* might without a Blush reherse,
And leaves a doubtful Palm in *Virgil*'s Verse:
He match'd their Beauties, where they most excell; 5
Of Love sung better, and of Arms as well.
Vouchsafe, Illustrious *Ormond*, to behold
What Pow'r the Charms of Beauty had of old;
Nor wonder if such Deeds of Arms were done,
Inspir'd by two fair Eyes, that sparkled like your own. 10
If *Chaucer* by the best Idea wrought,
And Poets can divine each others Thought,
The fairest Nymph before his Eyes he set;
And then the fairest was *Plantagenet*;
Who three contending Princes made her Prize, 15
And rul'd the Rival-Nations with her Eyes:

Who left Immortal Trophies of her Fame,
And to the Noblest Order gave the Name.
   Like Her, of equal Kindred to the Throne,
You keep her Conquests, and extend your own: 20
As when the Stars, in their Etherial Race,
At length have roll'd around the Liquid Space,
At certain Periods they resume their Place,
From the same Point of Heav'n their Course advance,
And move in Measures of their former Dance;   25
Thus, after length of Ages, she returns,
Restor'd in you, and the same Place adorns;
Or you perform her Office in the Sphere,
Born of her Blood, and make a new Platonick Year.
   O true *Plantagenet*, O Race Divine,   30
(For Beauty still is fatal to the Line,)
Had *Chaucer* liv'd that Angel-Face to view,
Sure he had drawn his *Emily* from You:
Or had You liv'd, to judge the doubtful Right,
Your Noble *Palamon* had been the Knight: 35
And Conqu'ring *Theseus* from his Side had sent
Your Gen'rous Lord, to guide the *Theban* Government.
   Time shall accomplish that; and I shall see
A *Palamon* in Him, in You an *Emily*.
   Already have the Fates your Path prepar'd,   40·
And sure Presage your future Sway declar'd:
When Westward, like the Sun, you took your Way,
And from benighted *Britain* bore the Day,
Blue *Triton* gave the Signal from the Shore,
The ready *Nereids* heard, and swam before   45
To smooth the Seas; a soft *Etesian* Gale
But just inspir'd, and gently swell'd the Sail;
Portunus took his Turn, whose ample Hand
Heav'd up the lighten'd Keel, and sunk the Sand,
And steer'd the sacred Vessel safe to Land.   50
The Land, if not restrain'd, had met Your Way,
Projected out a Neck, and jutted to the Sea.
Hibernia, prostrate at Your Feet, ador'd,
In You, the Pledge of her expected Lord;
Due to her Isle; a venerable Name;   55
His Father and his Grandsire known to Fame:

Aw'd by that House, accustom'd to command,
The sturdy *Kerns* in due Subjection stand;
Nor hear the Reins in any Foreign Hand.

At Your Approach, they crowded to the Port;   60
And scarcely Landed, You create a Court:
As *Ormond*'s Harbinger, to You they run;
For *Venus* is the Promise of the *Sun*.

The Waste of Civil Wars, their Towns destroy'd,
Pales unhonour'd, *Ceres* unemploy'd,   65
Were all forgot; and one Triumphant Day
Wip'd all the Tears of three Campaigns away.
Blood, Rapines, Massacres, were cheaply bought,
So mighty Recompence Your Beauty brought.

As when the Dove returning, bore the Mark   70
Of Earth restor'd to the long-lab'ring Ark,
The Relicks of Mankind, secure of Rest,
Op'd ev'ry Window to receive the Guest,
And the fair Bearer of the Message bless'd;
So, when You came, with loud repeated Cries,   75
The Nation took an Omen from your Eyes,
And God advanc'd his Rainbow in the Skies,
To sign inviolable Peace restor'd;
The Saints with solemn Shouts proclaim'd the new accord.

When at Your second Coming You appear,   80
(For I foretell that Millenary Year)
The sharpen'd Share shall vex the Soil no more,
But Earth unbidden shall produce her Store:
The Land shall laugh, the circling Ocean smile,
And Heav'ns Indulgence bless the Holy Isle.   85

Heav'n from all Ages has reserv'd for You
That happy Clyme, which Venom never knew;
Or if it had been there, Your Eyes alone
Have Pow'r to chase all Poyson, but their own.

Now in this Interval, which Fate has cast   90
Betwixt Your Future Glories, and Your Past,
This Pause of Pow'r, 'tis *Irelands* Hour to mourn;
While *England* celebrates Your safe Return,
By which You seem the Seasons to command,
And bring our Summers back to their forsaken Land.   95

The Vanquish'd Isle our Leisure must attend,
Till the Fair Blessing we vouchsafe to send;
Nor can we spare You long, though often we may lend.
The Dove was twice employ'd abroad, before
The World was dry'd; and she return'd no more.   100

Nor dare we trust so soft a Messenger,
New from her Sickness, to that Northern Air;
Rest here a while, Your Lustre to restore,
That they may see You as You shone before:
For yet, th' Eclipse not wholly past, You wade   105
Thro' some Remains, and Dimness of a Shade.

A Subject in his Prince may claim a Right,
Nor suffer him with Strength impair'd to fight;
Till Force returns, his Ardour we restrain,
And curb his Warlike Wish to cross the Main.   110

Now past the Danger, let the Learn'd begin
Th' Enquiry, where Disease could enter in;
How those malignant Atoms forc'd their Way,
What in the faultless Frame they found to make their Prey?
Where ev'ry Element was weigh'd so well,   115
That Heav'n alone, who mix'd the Mass, could tell
Which of the Four Ingredients could rebel;
And where, imprison'd in so sweet a Cage,
A Soul might well be pleas'd to pass an Age.

And yet the fine Materials made it weak;   120
Porcelain by being Pure, is apt to break:
Ev'n to Your Breast the Sickness durst aspire;
And forc'd from that fair Temple to retire,
Profanely set the Holy Place on Fire.
In vain Your Lord like young *Vespasian* mourn'd,   125
When the fierce Flames the Sanctuary burn'd:
And I prepar'd to pay in Verses rude
A most detested Act of Gratitude:
Ev'n this had been Your Elegy, which now
Is offer'd for Your Health, the Table of my Vow.   130

Your Angel sure our *Morley*'s Mind inspir'd,
To find the Remedy Your Ill requir'd;
As once the *Macedon*, by *Jove*'s Decree,
Was taught to dream an Herb for *Ptolomee*:
Or Heav'n, which had such Over-cost bestow'd,   135

As scarce it could afford to Flesh and Blood,
So lik'd the Frame, he would not work anew,
To save the Charges of another You.
Or by his middle Science did he steer,
And saw some great contingent Good appear,   140
Well worth a Miracle to keep You here:
And for that End, preserv'd the precious Mould,
Which all the future *Ormonds* was to hold;
And meditated in his better Mind
An Heir from You, who may redeem the failing Kind. 145
 Bless'd be the Pow'r which has at once restor'd
The Hopes of lost Succession to Your Lord,
Joy to the first, and last of each Degree,
Vertue to Courts, and what I long'd to see,
To You the Graces, and the Muse to me.   150
 O Daughter of the Rose, whose Cheeks unite
The diff'ring Titles of the Red and White;
Who Heav'ns alternate Beauty well display,
The Blush of Morning, and the Milky Way;
Whose Face is Paradise, but fenc'd from Sin: 155
For God in either Eye has plac'd a Cherubin.
 All is Your Lord's alone; ev'n absent, He
Employs the Care of Chast *Penelope*.
For him You waste in Tears Your Widow'd Hours,
For him Your curious Needle paints the Flow'rs: 160
Such Works of Old Imperial Dames were taught;
Such for *Ascanius*, fair *Elisa* wrought.
 The soft Recesses of Your Hours improve
The Three fair Pledges of Your Happy Love:
All other Parts of Pious Duty done,   165
You owe Your *Ormond* nothing but a Son:
To fill in future Times his Father's Place,
And wear the Garter of his Mother's Race.

PALAMON AND ARCITE:

Or, The Knight's Tale, from CHAUCER.
In Three Books.

BOOK I

IN Days of old, there liv'd, of mighty Fame
A valiant Prince; and *Theseus* was his Name:
A Chief, who more in Feats of Arms excell'd
The Rising nor the Setting Sun beheld.
Of *Athens* he was Lord; much Land he won,   5
And added Foreign Countrys to his Crown:
In *Scythia* with the Warriour Queen he strove,
Whom first by Force he conquer'd, then by Love;
He brought in Triumph back the beauteous Dame,
With whom her Sister, fair *Emilia*, came.   10
With Honour to his Home let *Theseus* ride,
With Love to Friend, and Fortune for his Guide,
And his victorious Army at his Side.
I pass their warlike Pomp, their proud Array,
Their Shouts, their Songs, their Welcome on the Way: 15
But, were it not too long, I would recite
The Feats of *Amazons*, the fatal Fight
Betwixt the hardy Queen, and *Heroe* Knight.
The Town besieg'd, and how much Blood it cost
The Female Army, and th' *Athenian* Host;   20
The Spousals of *Hippolita* the Queen;
What Tilts, and Turneys at the Feast were seen;
The Storm at their Return, the Ladies Fear:
But these and other Things I must forbear.
The Field is spacious I design to sow,   25
With Oxen far unfit to draw the Plow:
The Remnant of my Tale is of a length
To tire your Patience, and to waste my Strength;
And trivial Accidents shall be forborn,
That others may have time to take their Turn;   30
As was at first enjoin'd us by mine Host:
That he whose Tale is best, and pleases most,
Should win his Supper at our common Cost.

And therefore where I left, I will pursue
This ancient Story, whether false or true, $\Big\}$ 35
In hope it may be mended with a new.
The Prince I mention'd, full of high Renown,
In this Array drew near th' *Athenian* Town;
When in his Pomp and utmost of his Pride,
Marching, he chanc'd to cast his Eye aside,   40
And saw a Quire of mourning Dames, who lay
By Two and Two across the common Way:
At his Approach they rais'd a rueful Cry,
And beat their Breasts, and held their Hands on high,
Creeping and crying, till they seiz'd at last   45
His Coursers Bridle, and his Feet embrac'd.

    Tell me, said *Theseus*, what and whence you are,
And why this Funeral Pageant you prepare?
Is this the Welcome of my worthy Deeds,
To meet my Triumph in Ill-omen'd Weeds?   50
Or envy you my Praise, and would destroy
With Grief my Pleasures, and pollute my Joy?
Or are you injur'd, and demand Relief?
Name your Request, and I will ease your Grief.

    The most in Years of all the Mourning Train   55
Began; (but sounded first away for Pain)
Then scarce recover'd, spoke: Nor envy we
Thy great Renown, nor grudge thy Victory;
'Tis thine, O King, th' Afflicted to redress,
And Fame has fill'd the World with thy Success: 60
We wretched Women sue for that alone,
Which of thy Goodness is refus'd to none:
Let fall some Drops of Pity on our Grief,
If what we beg be just, and we deserve Relief:
For none of us, who now thy Grace implore,   65
But held the Rank of Sovereign Queen before;
Till, thanks to giddy Chance, which never bears
That Mortal Bliss should last for length of Years,
She cast us headlong from our high Estate,
And here in hope of thy Return we wait: 70
And long have waited in the Temple nigh,
Built to the gracious Goddess *Clemency*.
But rev'rence thou the Pow'r whose Name it bears,

Relieve th' Oppress'd, and wipe the Widows Tears.
I, wretched I, have other Fortune seen,   75
The Wife of *Capaneus*, and once a Queen:
At *Thebes* he fell; curs'd be the fatal Day!
And all the rest thou seest in this Array,
To make their moan, their Lords in Battel lost
Before that Town besieg'd by our Confed'rate Host: 80
But *Creon*, old and impious, who commands
The *Theban* City, and usurps the Lands,
Denies the Rites of Fun'ral Fires to those
Whose breathless Bodies yet he calls his Foes.
Unburn'd, unbury'd, on a Heap they lie;   85
Such is their Fate, and such his Tyranny;
No Friend has leave to bear away the Dead,
But with their Lifeless Limbs his Hounds are fed:
At this she skriek'd aloud, the mournful Train
Echo'd her Grief, and grov'ling on the Plain,   90
With Groans, and Hands upheld, to move his Mind,
Besought his Pity to their helpless Kind!
   The Prince was touch'd, his Tears began to flow,
And, as his tender Heart would break in two,
He sigh'd; and could not but their Fate deplore,   95
So wretched now, so fortunate before.
Then lightly from his lofty Steed he flew,
And raising one by one the suppliant Crew,
To comfort each, full solemnly he swore,
That by the Faith which Knights to Knighthood bore,   100
And what e'er else to Chivalry belongs,
He would not cease, till he reveng'd their Wrongs:
That *Greece* shou'd see perform'd what he declar'd,
And cruel *Creon* find his just Reward.
He said no more, but shunning all Delay,   105
Rode on; nor enter'd *Athens* on his Way:
But left his Sister and his Queen behind,
And wav'd his Royal Banner in the Wind:
Where in an *Argent* Field the God of War
Was drawn triumphant on his Iron Carr;   110
Red was his Sword, and Shield, and whole Attire,
And all the Godhead seem'd to glow with Fire;
Ev'n the Ground glitter'd where the Standard flew,

And the green Grass was dy'd to sanguin Hue.
High on his pointed Lance his Pennon bore   115
His *Cretan* Fight, the conquer'd *Minotaure*:
The Soldiers shout around with generous Rage,
And in that Victory, their own presage.
He prais'd their Ardour: inly pleas'd to see
His Host the Flow'r of *Grecian* Chivalry.   120
All Day he march'd; and all th' ensuing Night;
And saw the City with returning Light.
The Process of the War I need not tell,
How *Theseus* conquer'd, and how *Creon* fell:
Or after, how by Storm the Walls were won,   125
Or how the Victor sack'd and burn'd the Town:
How to the Ladies he restor'd again
The Bodies of their Lords in Battel slain:
And with what ancient Rites they were interr'd;
All these to fitter time shall be deferr'd: 130
I spare the Widows Tears, their woful Cries
And Howling at their Husbands Obsequies;
How *Theseus* at these Fun'rals did assist,
And with what Gifts the mourning Dames dismiss'd.
      Thus when the Victor Chief had *Creon* slain,   135
And conquer'd *Thebes*, he pitch'd upon the Plain
His mighty Camp, and when the Day return'd,
The Country wasted, and the Hamlets burn'd;
And left the Pillagers, to Rapine bred,
Without Controul to strip and spoil the Dead: 140
      There, in a Heap of Slain, among the rest
Two youthful Knights they found beneath a Load oppress'd
Of slaughter'd Foes, whom first to Death they sent,
The Trophies of their Strength, a bloody Monument.
Both fair, and both of Royal Blood they seem'd,   145
Whom Kinsmen to the Crown the Heralds deem'd;
That Day in equal Arms they fought for Fame;
Their Swords, their Shields, their Surcoats were the same.
Close by each other laid they press'd the Ground,
Their manly Bosoms pierc'd with many a griesly Wound;   150
Nor well alive, nor wholly dead they were,
But some faint Signs of feeble Life appear:
The wandring Breath was on the Wing to part,

Weak was the Pulse, and hardly heav'd the Heart.
These two were Sisters Sons; and *Arcite* one,   155
Much fam'd in Fields, with valiant *Palamon*.
From These their costly Arms the Spoilers rent,
And softly both convey'd to *Theseus* Tent;
Whom known of *Creon*'s Line, and cur'd with care,
He to his City sent as Pris'ners of the War,   160
Hopeless of Ransom, and condemn'd to lie
In Durance, doom'd a lingring Death to die.

   This done, he march'd away with warlike Sound,
And to his *Athens* turn'd with Laurels crown'd,
Where happy long he liv'd, much lov'd, and more renown'd.   } 165
But in a Tow'r, and never to be loos'd,
The woful captive Kinsmen are enclos'd;
   Thus Year by Year they pass, and Day by Day,
Till once ('twas on the Morn of chearful *May*)
The young *Emilia*, fairer to be seen   170
Than the fair Lilly on the Flow'ry Green,
More fresh than *May* her self in Blossoms new
(For with the Rosie Colour strove her Hue)
Wak'd as her Custom was before the Day,
To do th' Observance due to sprightly *May*:   175
For sprightly *May* commands our Youth to keep
The Vigils of her Night, and breaks their sluggard Sleep:
Each gentle Breast with kindly Warmth she moves;
Inspires new Flames, revives extinguish'd Loves.
In this Remembrance *Emily* e'er Day   180
Arose, and dress'd her self in rich Array;
Fresh as the Month, and as the Morning fair:
Adown her Shoulders fell her length of Hair:
A Ribband did the braided Tresses bind,
The rest was loose, and wanton'd in the Wind: 185
Aurora had but newly chas'd the Night,
And purpl'd o'er the Sky with blushing Light,
When to the Garden-walk she took her way,
To sport and trip along in Cool of Day,   }
And offer Maiden Vows in honour of the *May*.   } 190
   At ev'ry Turn, she made a little Stand,
And thrust among the Thorns her Lilly Hand
To draw the Rose, and ev'ry Rose she drew

She shook the Stalk, and brush'd away the Dew:
Then party-colour'd Flow'rs of white and red   195
She wove, to make a Garland for her Head:
This done, she sung and caroll'd out so clear,
That Men and Angels might rejoice to hear.
Ev'n wondring *Philomel* forgot to sing;
And learn'd from Her to welcome in the Spring.   200
The Tow'r, of which before was mention made,
Within whose Keep the captive Knights were laid,
Built of a large Extent, and strong withal,
Was one Partition of the Palace Wall:
The Garden was enclos'd within the Square   205
Where young *Emilia* took the Morning-Air.
    It happen'd *Palamon* the Pris'ner Knight,
Restless for Woe, arose before the Light,
And with his Jaylor's leave desir'd to breathe
An Air more wholesom than the Damps beneath.   210
This granted, to the Tow'r he took his way,
Cheer'd with the Promise of a glorious Day:
Then cast a languishing Regard around,
And saw with hateful Eyes the Temples crown'd
With golden Spires, and all the Hostile Ground.   } 215
He sigh'd, and turn'd his Eyes, because he knew
'Twas but a larger Jayl he had in view:
Then look'd below, and from the Castles height
Beheld a nearer and more pleasing Sight:
The Garden, which before he had not seen,   220
In Springs new Livery clad of White and Green,
Fresh Flow'rs in wide *Parterres*, and shady Walks between. }
This view'd, but not enjoy'd, with Arms across
He stood, reflecting on his Country's Loss;
Himself an Object of the Publick Scorn,   225
And often wish'd he never had been born.
At last (for so his Destiny requir'd)
With walking giddy, and with thinking tir'd,
He thro' a little Window cast his Sight,
Tho' thick of Bars, that gave a scanty Light: 230
But ev'n that Glimmering serv'd him to descry
Th' inevitable Charms of *Emily*.
    Scarce had he seen, but seiz'd with sudden Smart,

Stung to the Quick, he felt it at his Heart;
Struck blind with overpowering Light he stood,   235
Then started back amaz'd, and cry'd aloud.

    Young *Arcite* heard; and up he ran with haste,
To help his Friend, and in his Arms embrac'd;
And ask'd him why he look'd so deadly wan,
And whence, and how his change of Cheer began?   240
Or who had done th' Offence? But if, said he,
Your Grief alone is hard Captivity;
For Love of Heav'n, with Patience undergo
A cureless Ill, since Fate will have it so:
So stood our *Horoscope* in Chains to lie,   245
And *Saturn* in the Dungeon of the Sky,
Or other baleful Aspect, rul'd our Birth,
When all the friendly Stars were under Earth:
Whate'er betides, by Destiny 'tis done;
And better bear like Men, than vainly seek to shun.   250
Nor of my Bonds, said *Palamon* again,
Nor of unhappy Planets I complain;
But when my mortal Anguish caus'd my Cry,
That Moment I was hurt thro' either Eye;
Pierc'd with a Random-shaft, I faint away   255
And perish with insensible Decay:
A Glance of some new Goddess gave the Wound,
Whom, like *Acteon*, unaware I found.
Look how she walks along yon shady Space,
Not *Juno* moves with more Majestick Grace;   260
And all the *Cyprian* Queen is in her Face.
If thou art *Venus*, (for thy Charms confess
That Face was form'd in Heav'n) nor art thou less;
Disguis'd in Habit, undisguis'd in Shape,
O help us Captives from our Chains to scape;   265
But if our Doom be past in Bonds to lie
For Life, and in a loathsom Dungeon die;
Then be thy Wrath appeas'd with our Disgrace,
And shew Compassion to the *Theban* Race,
Oppress'd by Tyrant Pow'r! While yet he spoke,   270
Arcite on *Emily* had fix'd his Look;
The fatal Dart a ready Passage found,
And deep within his Heart infix'd the Wound:

So that if *Palamon* were wounded sore,
Arcite was hurt as much as he, or more: 275
Then from his inmost Soul he sigh'd, and said,
The Beauty I behold has struck me dead:
Unknowingly she strikes; and kills by chance;
Poyson is in her Eyes, and Death in ev'ry Glance.
O, I must ask; nor ask alone, but move   280
Her Mind to Mercy, or must die for Love.
    Thus *Arcite*: And thus *Palamon* replies,
(Eager his Tone, and ardent were his Eyes.)
Speak'st thou in earnest, or in jesting Vein?
Jesting, said *Arcite*, suits but ill with Pain.   285
It suits far worse (said *Palamon* again,
And bent his Brows) with Men who Honour weigh,
Their Faith to break, their Friendship to betray;
But worst with Thee, of Noble Lineage born,
My Kinsman, and in Arms my Brother sworn.   290
Have we not plighted each our holy Oath,
That one shou'd be the Common Good of both?
One Soul shou'd both inspire, and neither prove
His Fellows Hindrance in pursuit of Love?
To this before the Gods we gave our Hands,   295
And nothing but our Death can break the Bands.
This binds thee, then, to farther my Design;
As I am bound by Vow to farther thine:
Nor canst, nor dar'st thou, Traytor, on the Plain
Appeach my Honour, or thy own maintain,   300
Since thou art of my Council, and the Friend
Whose Faith I trust, and on whose Care depend:
And would'st thou court my Ladies Love, which I
Much rather than release, would chuse to die?
But thou false *Arcite* never shalt obtain   305
Thy bad Pretence; I told thee first my Pain:
For first my Love began e'er thine was born;
Thou, as my Council, and my Brother sworn,
Art bound t' assist my Eldership of Right,
Or justly to be deem'd a perjur'd Knight.   310
    Thus *Palamon*: But *Arcite* with disdain
In haughty Language thus reply'd again:
Forsworn thy self: The Traytor's odious Name

I first return, and then disprove thy Claim.
If Love be Passion, and that Passion nurst   315
With strong Desires, I lov'd the Lady first.
Canst thou pretend Desire, whom Zeal inflam'd
To worship, and a Pow'r Cœlestial nam'd?
Thine was Devotion to the Blest above,
I saw the Woman, and desir'd her Love;   320
First own'd my Passion, and to thee commend
Th' important Secret, as my chosen Friend.
Suppose (which yet I grant not) thy Desire
A Moment elder than my Rival Fire;
Can Chance of seeing first thy Title prove?   325
And know'st thou not, no Law is made for Love?
Law is to Things which to free Choice relate;
Love is not in our Choice, but in our Fate:
Laws are but positive: Loves Pow'r we see
Is Natures Sanction, and her first Decree.   330
Each Day we break the Bond of Humane Laws
For Love, and vindicate the Common Cause.
Laws for Defence of Civil Rights are plac'd,
Love throws the Fences down, and makes a general Waste:
Maids, Widows, Wives, without distinction fall;   335
The sweeping Deluge, Love, comes on, and covers all.
If then the Laws of Friendship I transgress,
I keep the Greater, while I break the Less;
And both are mad alike, since neither can possess.
Both hopeless to be ransom'd, never more   340
To see the Sun, but as he passes o'er.
Like *Esop*'s Hounds contending for the Bone,
Each pleaded Right, and wou'd be Lord alone:
The fruitless Fight continu'd all the Day;
A Cur came by, and snatch'd the Prize away.   345
As Courtiers therefore justle for a Grant,
And when they break their Friendship, plead their Want,
So thou, if Fortune will thy Suit advance,
Love on; nor envy me my equal Chance:
For I must love, and am resolv'd to try   350
My Fate, or failing in th' Adventure die.
    Great was their Strife, which hourly was renew'd,
Till each with mortal Hate his Rival view'd:

Now Friends no more, nor walking Hand in Hand;
But when they met, they made a surly Stand;   355
And glar'd like angry Lions as they pass'd,
And wish'd that ev'ry Look might be their last.

It chanc'd at length, *Perithous* came, t' attend
This worthy *Theseus*, his familiar Friend:
Their Love in early Infancy began,   360
And rose as Childhood ripen'd into Man.
Companions of the War; and lov'd so well,
That when one dy'd, as ancient Stories tell,
His Fellow to redeem him went to Hell.

But to pursue my Tale; to welcome home   365
His Warlike Brother, is *Perithous* come:
Arcite of *Thebes* was known in Arms long since,
And honour'd by this young *Thessalian* Prince.
Theseus, to gratifie his Friend and Guest,
Who made our *Arcite*'s Freedom his Request,   370
Restor'd to Liberty the Captive Knight,
But on these hard Conditions I recite:
That if hereafter *Arcite* shou'd be found
Within the Compass of *Athenian* Ground,
By Day or Night, or on whate'er Pretence,   375
His Head shou'd pay the Forfeit of th' Offence.
To this, *Perithous* for his Friend, agreed,
And on his Promise was the Pris'ner freed.

Unpleas'd and pensive hence he takes his way,
At his own Peril; for his Life must pay.   380
Who now but *Arcite* mourns his bitter Fate,
Finds his dear Purchase, and repents too late?
What have I gain'd, he said, in Prison pent,
If I but change my Bonds for Banishment?
And banish'd from her Sight, I suffer more   385
In Freedom, than I felt in Bonds before;
Forc'd from her Presence, and condemn'd to live:
Unwelcom Freedom, and unthank'd Reprieve:
Heav'n is not but where *Emily* abides,
And where she's absent, all is Hell besides.   390
Next to my Day of Birth, was that accurst
Which bound my Friendship to *Perithous* first:
Had I not known that Prince, I still had been

In Bondage, and had still *Emilia* seen:
For tho' I never can her Grace deserve,   395
'Tis Recompence enough to see and serve.
O *Palamon*, my Kinsman and my Friend,
How much more happy Fates thy Love attend!
Thine is th' Adventure; thine the Victory:
Well has thy Fortune turn'd the Dice for thee: 400
Thou on that Angels Face maist feed thy Eyes,
In Prison, no; but blissful Paradise!
Thou daily seest that Sun of Beauty shine,
And lov'st at least in Loves extreamest Line.
I mourn in Absence, Loves Eternal Night,   405
And who can tell but since thou hast her Sight,
And art a comely, young, and valiant Knight,
Fortune (a various Pow'r) may cease to frown,
And by some Ways unknown thy Wishes crown:
But I, the most forlorn of Humane Kind,   410
Nor Help can hope, nor Remedy can find;
But doom'd to drag my loathsom Life in Care,
For my Reward, must end it in Despair.
Fire, Water, Air, and Earth, and Force of Fates
That governs all, and Heav'n that all creates,   415
Nor Art, nor Natures Hand can ease my Grief,
Nothing but Death, the Wretches last Relief:
Then farewel Youth, and all the Joys that dwell
With Youth and Life, and Life it self farewell.

     But why, alas! do mortal Men in vain   420
Of Fortune, Fate, or Providence complain?
God gives us what he knows our Wants require,
And better Things than those which we desire:
Some pray for Riches; Riches they obtain;
But watch'd by Robbers, for their Wealth are slain: 425
Some pray from Prison to be freed; and come
When guilty of their Vows, to fall at home;
Murder'd by those they trusted with their Life,
A favour'd Servant, or a Bosom Wife.
Such dear-bought Blessings happen ev'ry Day,   430
Because we know not for what Things to pray.
Like drunken Sots about the Streets we roam;
Well knows the Sot he has a certain Home;

Yet knows not how to find th' uncertain Place,
And blunders on, and staggers ev'ry Pace.   435
Thus all seek Happiness; but few can find,
For far the greater Part of Men are blind.
This is my Case, who thought our utmost Good
Was in one Word of Freedom understood:
The fatal Blessing came: From Prison free,   440
I starve abroad, and lose the Sight of *Emily*.
    Thus *Arcite*; but if *Arcite* thus deplore
His Suff'rings, *Palamon* yet suffers more.
For when he knew his Rival freed and gone,
He swells with Wrath; he makes outrageous Moan: 445
He frets, he fumes, he stares, he stamps the Ground;
The hollow Tow'r with Clamours rings around:
With briny Tears he bath'd his fetter'd Feet,
And dropp'd all o'er with Agony of Sweat.
Alas! he cry'd, I Wretch in Prison pine,   450
Too happy Rival, while the Fruit is thine:
Thou liv'st at large, thou draw'st thy Native Air,
Pleas'd with thy Freedom, proud of my Despair:
Thou may'st, since thou hast Youth and Courage join'd,
A sweet Behaviour, and a solid Mind,   455
Assemble ours, and all the *Theban* Race,
To vindicate on *Athens* thy Disgrace.
And after (by some Treaty made) possess
Fair *Emily*, the Pledge of lasting Peace.
So thine shall be the beauteous Prize, while I   460
Must languish in Despair, in Prison die.
Thus all th' Advantage of the Strife is thine,
Thy Portion double Joys, and double Sorrows mine.
    The Rage of Jealousie then fir'd his Soul,
And his Face kindl'd like a burning Coal: 465
Now cold Despair, succeeding in her stead,
To livid Paleness turns the glowing Red.
His Blood scarce Liquid, creeps within his Veins,
Like Water, which the freezing Wind constrains.
Then thus he said; Eternal Deities,   470
Who rule the World with absolute Decrees,
And write whatever Time shall bring to pass
With Pens of Adamant, on Plates of Brass;

What is the Race of Humane Kind your Care
Beyond what all his Fellow-Creatures are?   475
He with the rest is liable to Pain,
And like the Sheep, his Brother-Beast, is slain.
Cold, Hunger, Prisons, Ills without a Cure,
All these he must, and guiltless oft, endure:
Or does your Justice, Pow'r, or Prescience fail,   480
When the Good suffer, and the Bad prevail?
What worse to wretched Vertue could befall,
If Fate, or giddy Fortune govern'd all?
Nay, worse than other Beasts is our Estate;
Them, to pursue their Pleasures you create;   485
We, bound by harder Laws, must curb our Will,
And your Commands, not our Desires fulfil:
Then when the Creature is unjustly slain,
Yet after Death at least he feels no Pain;
But Man in Life surcharg'd with Woe before,   490
Not freed when dead, is doom'd to suffer more.
A Serpent shoots his Sting at unaware;
An ambush'd Thief forelays a Traveller;
The Man lies murder'd, while the Thief and Snake,
One gains the Thickets, and one thrids the Brake.   495
This let Divines decide; but well I know,
Just, or unjust, I have my Share of Woe:
Through *Saturn* seated in a luckless Place,
And *Juno*'s Wrath, that persecutes my Race;
Or *Mars* and *Venus* in a Quartil, move   500
My Pangs of Jealousie for *Arcite*'s Love.

     Let *Palamon* oppress'd in Bondage mourn,
While to his exil'd Rival we return.
By this the Sun declining from his Height,
The Day had shortned to prolong the Night: 505
The lengthen'd Night gave length of Misery
Both to the Captive Lover, and the Free.
For *Palamon* in endless Prison mourns,
And *Arcite* forfeits Life if he returns.
The Banish'd never hopes his Love to see,   510
Nor hopes the Captive Lord his Liberty:

'Tis hard to say who suffers greater Pains,
One sees his Love, but cannot break his Chains:

One free, and all his Motions uncontroul'd,
Beholds whate'er he wou'd, but what he wou'd behold.   515
Judge as you please, for I will haste to tell
What Fortune to the banish'd Knight befel.
When *Arcite* was to *Thebes* return'd again,
The Loss of her he lov'd renew'd his Pain;
What could be worse, than never more to see   520
His Life, his Soul, his charming *Emily*?
He rav'd with all the Madness of Despair,
He roar'd, he beat his Breast, he tore his Hair.
Dry Sorrow in his stupid Eyes appears,
For wanting Nourishment, he wanted Tears: 525
His Eye-balls in their hollow Sockets sink,
Bereft of Sleep; he loaths his Meat and Drink.
He withers at his Heart, and looks as wan
As the pale Spectre of a murder'd Man:
That Pale turns Yellow, and his Face receives   530
The faded Hue of sapless Boxen Leaves:
In solitary Groves he makes his Moan,
Walks early out, and ever is alone.
Nor mix'd in Mirth, in youthful Pleasure shares,
But sighs when Songs and Instruments he hears: 535
His Spirits are so low, his Voice is drown'd,
He hears as from afar, or in a Swound,
Like the deaf Murmurs of a distant Sound:
Uncomb'd his Locks, and squalid his Attire,
Unlike the Trim of Love and gay Desire;   540
But full of museful Mopings, which presage
The loss of Reason, and conclude in Rage.

  This when he had endur'd a Year and more,
Now wholly chang'd from what he was before,
It happen'd once, that slumbring as he lay,   545
He dreamt (his Dream began at Break of Day)
That *Hermes* o'er his Head in Air appear'd,
And with soft Words his drooping Spirits cheer'd:
His Hat, adorn'd with Wings, disclos'd the God,
And in his Hand he bore the Sleep-compelling Rod: 550
Such as he seem'd, when at his Sire's Command
On *Argus* Head he laid the Snaky Wand:
Arise, he said, to conqu'ring *Athens* go,

There Fate appoints an End of all thy Woe.
The Fright awaken'd *Arcite* with a Start,   555
Against his Bosom bounc'd his heaving Heart;
But soon he said, with scarce-recover'd Breath,
And thither will I go, to meet my Death,
Sure to be slain; but Death is my Desire,
Since in *Emilia*'s Sight I shall expire.   560
By chance he spy'd a Mirrour while he spoke,
And gazing there beheld his alter'd Look;
Wondring, he saw his Features and his Hue
So much were chang'd, that scarce himself he knew.
A sudden Thought then starting in his Mind,   565
Since I in *Arcite* cannot *Arcite* find,
The World may search in vain with all their Eyes,
But never penetrate through this Disguise.
Thanks to the Change which Grief and Sickness give,
In low Estate I may securely live,   570
And see unknown my Mistress Day by Day:
He said; and cloth'd himself in course Array;
A lab'ring Hind in shew: Then forth he went,
And to th' *Athenian* Tow'rs his Journey bent:
One Squire attended in the same Disguise,   575
Made conscious of his Master's Enterprize.
Arriv'd at *Athens*, soon he came to Court,
Unknown, unquestion'd in that thick Resort;
Proff'ring for Hire his Service at the Gate,
To drudge, draw Water, and to run or wait.   580
   So fair befel him, that for little Gain
He serv'd at first *Emilia*'s Chamberlain;
And watchful all Advantages to spy,
Was still at Hand, and in his Master's Eye;
And as his Bones were big, and Sinews strong,   585
Refus'd no Toil that could to Slaves belong;
But from deep Wells with Engines Water drew,
And us'd his Noble Hands the Wood to hew.
He pass'd a Year at least attending thus
On *Emily*, and call'd *Philostratus*.   590
   But never was there Man of his Degree
So much esteem'd, so well belov'd as he.
So gentle of Condition was he known,

That through the Court his Courtesie was blown:
All think him worthy of a greater Place,   595
And recommend him to the Royal Grace;
That exercis'd within a higher Sphere,
His Vertues more conspicuous might appear.
Thus by the general Voice was *Arcite* prais'd,
And by Great *Theseus* to high Favour rais'd;   600
Among his Menial Servants first enroll'd,
And largely entertain'd with Sums of Gold:
Besides what secretly from *Thebes* was sent,
Of his own Income, and his Annual Rent.
This well employ'd, he purchas'd Friends and Fame,   605
But cautiously conceal'd from whence it came.
Thus for three Years he liv'd with large Increase,
In Arms of Honour, and Esteem in Peace;
To *Theseus* Person he was ever near,
And *Theseus* for his Vertues held him dear.   610

PALAMON AND ARCITE:
Or, The Knight's Tale.

BOOK II

WHILE *Arcite* lives in Bliss, the Story turns
Where hopeless *Palamon* in Prison mourns.
For six long Years immur'd, the captive Knight
Had dragg'd his Chains, and scarcely seen the Light:
Lost Liberty, and Love at once he bore;   5
His Prison pain'd him much, his Passion more:
Nor dares he hope his Fetters to remove,
Nor ever wishes to be free from Love.
But when the sixth revolving Year was run,
And *May* within the *Twins* receiv'd the Sun,   10
Were it by Chance, or forceful Destiny,
Which forms in Causes first whate'er shall be,
Assisted by a Friend one Moonless Night,

This *Palamon* from Prison took his Flight:
A pleasant Beverage he prepar'd before   15
Of Wine and Honey mix'd, with added Store
Of *Opium*; to his Keeper this he brought,
Who swallow'd unaware the sleepy Draught,
And snor'd secure till Morn, his Senses bound
In Slumber, and in long Oblivion drown'd.   20
Short was the Night, and careful *Palamon*
Sought the next Covert e'er the Rising Sun.
A thick spread Forest near the City lay,
To this with lengthen'd Strides he took his way,
(For far he cou'd not fly, and fear'd the Day:)   25
Safe from Pursuit, he meant to shun the Light,
Till the brown Shadows of the friendly Night
To *Thebes* might favour his intended Flight.
When to his Country come, his next Design
Was all the *Theban* Race in Arms to join,   30
And war on *Theseus*, till he lost his Life,
Or won the Beauteous *Emily* to Wife.
Thus while his Thoughts the lingring Day beguile,
To gentle *Arcite* let us turn our Style;
Who little dreamt how nigh he was to Care,   35
Till treacherous Fortune caught him in the Snare.
The Morning-Lark, the Messenger of Day,
Saluted in her Song the Morning gray;
And soon the Sun arose with Beams so bright,
That all th' Horizon laugh'd to see the joyous Sight;   40
He with his tepid Rays the Rose renews,
And licks the dropping Leaves, and dries the Dews;
When *Arcite* left his Bed, resolv'd to pay
Observance to the Month of merry *May*:
Forth on his fiery Steed betimes he rode,   45
That scarcely prints the Turf on which he trod:
At ease he seem'd, and pransing o'er the Plains,
Turn'd only to the Grove his Horses Reins,
The Grove I nam'd before; and lighting there,
A Woodbind Garland sought to crown his Hair;   50
Then turn'd his Face against the rising Day,
And rais'd his Voice to welcom in the *May*.
    For thee, sweet Month, the Groves green Liv'ries wear:

If not the first, the fairest of the Year:
For thee the Graces lead the dancing Hours,   55
And Nature's ready Pencil paints the Flow'rs:
When thy short Reign is past, the Fev'rish Sun
The sultry Tropick fears, and moves more slowly on.
So may thy tender Blossoms fear no Blite,
Nor Goats with venom'd Teeth thy Tendrils bite,   60
As thou shalt guide my wandring Feet to find
The fragrant Greens I seek, my Brows to bind.

   His Vows address'd, within the Grove he stray'd,
Till Fate, or Fortune, near the Place convey'd
His Steps where secret *Palamon* was laid.   65
Full little thought of him the gentle Knight,
Who flying Death had there conceal'd his Flight,
In Brakes and Brambles hid, and shunning Mortal Sight.
And less he knew him for his hated Foe,
But fear'd him as a Man he did not know.   70
But as it has been said of ancient Years,
That Fields are full of Eyes, and Woods have Ears;
For this the Wise are ever on their Guard,
For, Unforeseen, they say, is unprepar'd.
Uncautious *Arcite* thought himself alone,   75
And less than all suspected *Palamon*,
Who listning heard him, while he search'd the Grove,
And loudly sung his Roundelay of Love.
But on the sudden stopp'd, and silent stood,
(As Lovers often muse, and change their Mood;)   80
Now high as Heav'n, and then as low as Hell;
Now up, now down, as Buckets in a Well:
For *Venus*, like her Day, will change her Cheer,
And seldom shall we see a *Friday* clear.
Thus *Arcite* having sung, with alter'd Hue   85
Sunk on the Ground, and from his Bosom drew
A desp'rate Sigh, accusing Heav'n and Fate,
And angry *Juno*'s unrelenting Hate.
Curs'd be the Day when first I did appear;
Let it be blotted from the Calendar,   90
Lest it pollute the Month, and poison all the Year.
Still will the jealous Queen pursue our Race?
Cadmus is dead, the *Theban* City *was*:

Yet ceases not her Hate: For all who come
From *Cadmus* are involv'd in *Cadmus* Doom.   95
I suffer for my Blood: Unjust Decree!
That punishes another's Crime on me.
In mean Estate I serve my mortal Foe,
The Man who caus'd my Countrys Overthrow.
This is not all; for *Juno*, to my shame,   100
Has forc'd me to forsake my former Name;
Arcite I was, *Philostratus* I am.
That Side of Heav'n is all my Enemy:
Mars ruin'd *Thebes*; his Mother ruin'd me.
Of all the Royal Race remains but one   105
Beside my self, th' unhappy *Palamon*,
Whom *Theseus* holds in Bonds, and will not free;
Without a Crime, except his Kin to me.
Yet these, and all the rest I cou'd endure;
But Love's a Malady without a Cure: 110
Fierce Love has pierc'd me with his fiery Dart,
He fries within, and hisses at my Heart.
Your Eyes, fair *Emily*, my Fate pursue;
I suffer for the rest, I die for you.
Of such a Goddess no Time leaves Record,   115
Who burn'd the Temple where she was ador'd:
And let it burn, I never will complain,
Pleas'd with my Suff'rings, if you knew my Pain.
    At this a sickly Qualm his Heart assail'd,
His Ears ring inward, and his Senses fail'd.   120
No Word miss'd *Palamon* of all he spoke,
But soon to deadly Pale he chang'd his Look:
He trembl'd ev'ry Limb, and felt a Smart,
As if cold Steel had glided through his Heart;
Nor longer staid, but starting from his Place,   125
Discover'd stood, and shew'd his hostile Face:
False Traytor *Arcite*, Traytor to thy Blood,
Bound by thy sacred Oath to seek my Good,
Now art thou found forsworn, for *Emily*;
And dar'st attempt her Love, for whom I die.   130
So hast thou cheated *Theseus* with a Wile,
Against thy Vow, returning to beguile
Under a borrow'd Name: As false to me,

So false thou art to him who set thee free:
But rest assur'd, that either thou shalt die,   135
Or else renounce thy Claim in *Emily*:
For though unarm'd I am, and (freed by Chance)
Am here without my Sword, or pointed Lance;
Hope not, base Man, unquestion'd hence to go,
For I am *Palamon* thy mortal Foe.   140

   Arcite, who heard his Tale, and knew the Man,
His Sword unsheath'd, and fiercely thus began:
Now by the Gods, who govern Heav'n above,
Wert thou not weak with Hunger, mad with Love,
That Word had been thy last, or in this Grove   145
This Hand should force thee to renounce thy Love.
The Surety which I gave thee, I defie;
Fool, not to know that Love endures no Tie,
And *Jove* but laughs at Lovers Perjury.
Know I will serve the Fair in thy despight;   150
But since thou art my Kinsman, and a Knight,
Here, have my Faith, to morrow in this Grove
Our Arms shall plead the Titles of our Love:
And Heav'n so help my Right, as I alone
Will come, and keep the Cause and Quarrel both unknown;   155
With Arms of Proof both for my self and thee;
Chuse thou the best, and leave the worst to me.
And, that at better ease, thou maist abide,
Bedding and Clothes I will this Night provide,
And needful Sustenance, that thou maist be   160
A Conquest better won, and worthy me.
His Promise *Palamon* accepts; but pray'd,
To keep it better than the first he made.
Thus fair they parted till the Morrows Dawn,
For each had laid his plighted Faith to pawn.   165
Oh Love! Thou sternly dost thy Pow'r maintain,
And wilt not bear a Rival in thy Reign,
Tyrants and thou all Fellowship disdain.
This was in *Arcite* prov'd, and *Palamon*,
Both in Despair, yet each would love alone.   170
Arcite return'd, and, as in Honour ty'd,
His Foe with Bedding, and with Food supply'd;
Then, e'er the Day, two Suits of Armour sought,

Which born before him on his Steed he brought:
Both were of shining Steel, and wrought so pure,   175
As might the Strokes of two such Arms endure.
Now, at the Time, and in th' appointed Place,
The Challenger, and Challeng'd, Face to Face,
Approach; each other from afar they knew,
And from afar their Hatred chang'd their Hue.   180
So stands the *Thracian* Heardsman with his Spear,
Full in the Gap, and hopes the hunted Bear,
And hears him rustling in the Wood, and sees
His Course at Distance by the bending Trees;
And thinks, Here comes my mortal Enemy,   185
And either he must fall in Fight, or I:
This while he thinks, he lifts aloft his Dart; ⎫
A gen'rous Chilness seizes ev'ry Part;   ⎬
The Veins pour back the Blood, and fortifie the Heart. ⎭

  Thus pale they meet; their Eyes with Fury burn;   190
None greets; for none the Greeting will return:
But in dumb Surliness, each arm'd with Care
His Foe profest, as Brother of the War:
Then both, no Moment lost, at once advance
Against each other, arm'd with Sword and Lance: 195
They lash, they foin, they pass, they strive to bore
Their Corslets, and the thinnest Parts explore.
Thus two long Hours in equal Arms they stood,
And wounded, wound; till both were bath'd in Blood;
And not a Foot of Ground had either got,   200
As if the World depended on the Spot.
Fell *Arcite* like an angry Tyger far'd,
And like a Lion *Palamon* appear'd:
Or as two Boars whom Love to Battel draws,
With rising Bristles, and with froathy Jaws,   205
Their adverse Breasts with Tusks oblique they wound;
With Grunts and Groans the Forest rings around.
So fought the Knights, and fighting must abide,
Till Fate an Umpire sends their Diff'rence to decide.
The Pow'r that ministers to God's Decrees,   210
And executes on Earth what Heav'n foresees,
Call'd Providence, or Chance, or fatal Sway,
Comes with resistless Force, and finds or makes her Way.

Nor Kings, nor Nations, nor united Pow'r
One Moment can retard th' appointed Hour.   215
And some one Day, some wondrous Chance appears,
Which happen'd not in Centuries of Years:
For sure, whate'er we Mortals hate or love,
Or hope, or fear, depends on Pow'rs above;
They move our Appetites to Good or Ill,   220
And by Foresight necessitate the Will.
In *Theseus* this appears; whose youthful Joy
Was Beasts of Chase in Forests to destroy;
This gentle Knight, inspir'd by jolly *May*,
Forsook his easie Couch at early Day,   225
And to the Wood and Wilds pursu'd his Way.
Beside him rode *Hippolita* the Queen,
And *Emily* attir'd in lively Green:
With Horns, and Hounds, and all the tuneful Cry,
To hunt a Royal Hart within the Covert nigh: 230
And as he follow'd *Mars* before, so now
He serves the Goddess of the Silver Bow.
The Way that *Theseus* took was to the Wood
Where the two Knights in cruel Battel stood:
The Laund on which they fought, th' appointed Place   235
In which th' uncoupl'd Hounds began the Chace.
Thither forth-right he rode to rowse the Prey,
That shaded by the Fern in Harbour lay;
And thence dislodg'd, was wont to leave the Wood,
For open Fields, and cross the Crystal Flood.   240
Approach'd, and looking underneath the Sun,
He saw proud *Arcite*, and fierce *Palamon*,
In mortal Battel doubling Blow on Blow,
Like Lightning flam'd their Fauchions to and fro,
And shot a dreadful Gleam; so strong they strook,   245
There seem'd less Force requir'd to fell an Oak:
He gaz'd with Wonder on their equal Might,
Look'd eager on, but knew not either Knight:
Resolv'd to learn, he spurr'd his fiery Steed
With goring Rowels, to provoke his Speed.   250
The Minute ended that began the Race,
So soon he was betwixt 'em on the Place;
And with his Sword unsheath'd, on pain of Life

Commands both Combatants to cease their Strife:
Then with imperious Tone pursues his Threat;   25*
What are you? Why in Arms together met?
How dares your Pride presume against my Laws,
As in a listed Field to fight your Cause?
Unask'd the Royal Grant; no Marshal by,
As Knightly Rites require; nor Judge to try?   26c
Then *Palamon*, with scarce recover'd Breath,
Thus hasty spoke; We both deserve the Death,
And both wou'd die; for look the World around,
A Pair so wretched is not to be found.
Our Life's a Load; encumber'd with the Charge,   265
We long to set th' imprison'd Soul at large.
Now as thou art a Sovereign Judge, decree
The rightful Doom of Death to him and me,
Let neither find thy Grace; for Grace is Cruelty.
Me first, O kill me first; and cure my Woe: 270
Then sheath the Sword of Justice on my Foe:
Or kill him first; for when his Name is heard,
He foremost will receive his due Reward.
Arcite of *Thebes* is he; thy mortal Foe,
On whom thy Grace did Liberty bestow,   275
But first contracted, that if ever found
By Day or Night upon th' *Athenian* Ground,
His Head should pay the Forfeit: See return'd
The perjur'd Knight, his Oath and Honour scorn'd.
For this is he, who with a borrow'd Name   280
And profer'd Service, to thy Palace came,
Now call'd *Philostratus*: retain'd by thee,
A Traytor trusted, and in high Degree,
Aspiring to the Bed of beauteous *Emily*.
My Part remains: From *Thebes* my Birth I own,   285
And call my self th' unhappy *Palamon*.
Think me not like that Man; since no Disgrace
Can force me to renounce the Honour of my Race.
Know me for what I am: I broke thy Chain,
Nor promis'd I thy Pris'ner to remain: 290
The Love of Liberty with Life is giv'n,
And Life it self th' inferiour Gift of Heaven.
Thus without Crime I fled; but farther know,

I with this *Arcite* am thy mortal Foe:
Then give me Death, since I thy Life pursue,   295
For Safeguard of thy self, Death is my Due.
More would'st thou know? I love bright *Emily*,
And for her Sake, and in her Sight will die:
But kill my Rival too; for he no less
Deserves; and I thy righteous Doom will bless,   300
Assur'd that what I lose, he never shall possess.
To this reply'd the stern *Athenian* Prince,
And sow'rly smild, In owning your Offence
You judge your self; and I but keep Record
In place of Law, while you pronounce the Word.   305
Take your Desert, the Death you have decreed;
I seal your Doom, and ratifie the Deed.
By *Mars*, the Patron of my Arms, you die.
     He said; dumb Sorrow seiz'd the Standers by.
The Queen above the rest, by Nature Good,   310
(The Pattern form'd of perfect Womanhood)
For tender Pity wept: When she began,
Through the bright Quire th' infectious Vertue ran.
All dropp'd their Tears, ev'n the contended Maid;
And thus among themselves they softly said: 315
What Eyes can suffer this unworthy Sight!
Two Youths of Royal Blood, renown'd in Fight,
The Mastership of Heav'n in Face and Mind,
And Lovers, far beyond their faithless Kind;
See their wide streaming Wounds; they neither came   320
From Pride of Empire, nor desire of Fame:
Kings fight for Kingdoms, Madmen for Applause;
But Love for Love alone; that crowns the Lover's Cause.
This Thought, which ever bribes the beauteous Kind,
Such Pity wrought in ev'ry Ladies Mind,   325
They left their Steeds, and prostrate on the Place,
From the fierce King, implor'd th' Offenders Grace.
     He paus'd a while, stood silent in his Mood,
(For yet, his Rage was boiling in his Blood)
But soon his tender Mind th' Impression felt,   330
(As softest Metals are not slow to melt
And Pity soonest runs in gentle Minds:)
Then reasons with himself; and first he finds

His Passion cast a Mist before his Sense,
And either made, or magnifi'd th' Offence.   335
Offence! of what? to whom? Who judg'd the Cause?
The Pris'ner freed himself by Natures Laws:
Born free, he sought his Right: The Man he freed
Was perjur'd, but his Love excus'd the Deed:
Thus pond'ring, he look'd under with his Eyes,   340
And saw the Womens Tears, and heard their Cries;
Which mov'd Compassion more: He shook his Head,
And softly sighing to himself, he said,
   Curse on th' unpard'ning Prince, whom Tears can draw
To no Remorse; who rules by Lions Law;   345
And deaf to Pray'rs, by no Submission bow'd,
Rends all alike; the Penitent, and Proud:
At this, with Look serene, he rais'd his Head,
Reason resum'd her Place, and Passion fled:
Then thus aloud he spoke: The Pow'r of Love,   350
In Earth, and Seas, and Air, and Heav'n above,
Rules, unresisted, with an awful Nod;
By daily Miracles declar'd a God:
He blinds the Wise, gives Eye-sight to the Blind;
And moulds and stamps anew the Lover's Mind.   355
Behold that *Arcite*, and this *Palamon*,
Freed from my Fetters, and in Safety gone,
What hinder'd either in their Native Soil
At ease to reap the Harvest of their Toil?
But Love, their Lord, did otherwise ordain,   360
And brought 'em in their own despite again,
To suffer Death deserv'd; for well they know,
'Tis in my Pow'r, and I their deadly Foe;
The Proverb holds, That to be wise and love,
Is hardly granted to the Gods above.   365
See how the Madmen bleed: Behold the Gains
With which their Master, Love, rewards their Pains:
For sev'n long Years, on Duty ev'ry Day,
Lo their Obedience, and their Monarch's Pay:
Yet, as in Duty bound, they serve him on,   370
And ask the Fools, they think it wisely done:
Nor Ease, nor Wealth, nor Life it self regard,
For 'tis their Maxim, Love is Love's Reward.

This is not all; the Fair for whom they strove
Nor knew before, nor could suspect their Love,   375
Nor thought, when she beheld the Fight from far,
Her Beauty was th' Occasion of the War.
But sure a gen'ral Doom on Man is past,
And all are Fools and Lovers, first or last:
This both by others and my self I know,   380
For I have serv'd their Sovereign, long ago.
Oft have been caught within the winding Train
Of Female Snares, and felt the Lovers Pain,
And learn'd how far the God can Humane Hearts constrain.
To this Remembrance, and the Pray'rs of those   385
Who for th' offending Warriors interpose,
I give their forfeit Lives; on this accord,
To do me Homage as their Sov'reign Lord;
And as my Vassals, to their utmost Might,
Assist my Person, and assert my Right.   390
This, freely sworn, the Knights their Grace obtain'd;
Then thus the King his secret Thoughts explain'd:
If Wealth, or Honour, or a Royal Race,
Or each, or all, may win a Ladies Grace,
Then either of you Knights may well deserve   395
A Princess born; and such is she you serve:
For *Emily* is Sister to the Crown,
And but too well to both her Beauty known:
But shou'd you combate till you both were dead,
Two Lovers cannot share a single Bed: 400
As therefore both are equal in Degree,
The Lot of both be left to Destiny.
Now hear th' Award, and happy may it prove
To her, and him who best deserves her Love.
Depart from hence in Peace, and free as Air,   405
Search the wide World, and where you please repair;
But on the Day when this returning Sun
To the same Point through ev'ry Sign has run,
Then each of you his Hundred Knights shall bring,
In Royal Lists, to fight before the King;   410
And then, the Knight whom Fate or happy Chance
Shall with his Friends to Victory advance,
And grace his Arms so far in equal Fight,

From out the Bars to force his Opposite,
Or kill, or make him Recreant on the Plain,   415
The Prize of Valour and of Love shall gain;
The vanquish'd Party shall their Claim release,
And the long Jars conclude in lasting Peace.
The Charge be mine t' adorn the chosen Ground,
The Theatre of War, for Champions so renown'd;   420
And take the Patrons Place of either Knight,
With Eyes impartial to behold the Fight;
And Heav'n of me so judge, as I shall judge aright.
If both are satisfi'd with this Accord,
Swear by the Laws of Knighthood on my Sword.   425
    Who now but *Palamon* exults with Joy?
And ravish'd *Arcite* seems to touch the Sky:
The whole assembl'd Troop was pleas'd as well,
Extol'd th' Award, and on their Knees they fell
To bless the gracious King. The Knights with Leave   430
Departing from the Place, his last Commands receive;
On *Emily* with equal Ardour look,
And from her Eyes their Inspiration took.
From thence to *Thebes* old Walls pursue their Way,
Each to provide his Champions for the Day.   435
    It might be deem'd on our Historian's Part,
Or too much Negligence, or want of Art,
If he forgot the vast Magnificence
Of Royal *Theseus*, and his large Expence.
He first enclos'd for Lists a level Ground,   440
The whole Circumference a Mile around:
The Form was Circular; and all without
A Trench was sunk, to Moat the Place about.
Within, an Amphitheatre appear'd,
Rais'd in Degrees; to sixty Paces rear'd: 445
That when a Man was plac'd in one Degree,
Height was allow'd for him above to see.
    Eastward was built a Gate of Marble white;
The like adorn'd the Western opposite.
A nobler Object than this Fabrick was,   450
Rome never saw; nor of so vast a Space.
For, rich with Spoils of many a conquer'd Land,
All Arts and Artists *Theseus* could command;

Who sold for Hire, or wrought for better Fame:
The Master-Painters, and the Carvers came.   455
So rose within the Compass of the Year
An Ages Work, a glorious Theatre.
Then, o'er its Eastern Gate was rais'd above
A Temple, sacred to the Queen of Love;
An Altar stood below: On either Hand   460
A Priest with Roses crown'd, who held a Myrtle Wand.
   The Dome of *Mars* was on the Gate oppos'd,
And on the North a Turret was enclos'd,
Within the Wall, of Alabaster white,
And crimson Coral, for the Queen of Night,   }   465
Who takes in Sylvan Sports her chaste Delight.
   Within these Oratories might you see
Rich Carvings, Pourtraitures, and Imagery:
Where ev'ry Figure to the Life express'd
The Godhead's Pow'r to whom it was address'd.   470
In *Venus* Temple, on the Sides were seen
The broken Slumbers of inamour'd Men:
Pray'rs that ev'n spoke, and Pity seem'd to call,
And issuing Sighs that smoak'd along the Wall.
Complaints, and hot Desires, the Lover's Hell,   475
And scalding Tears, that wore a Channel where they fell:
And all around were Nuptial Bonds, the Ties   }
Of Loves Assurance, and a Train of Lies,   }
That, made in Lust, conclude in Perjuries.   }
Beauty, and Youth, and Wealth, and Luxury,   480
And spritely Hope, and short-enduring Joy;
And Sorceries to raise th' Infernal Pow'rs,
And Sigils fram'd in Planetary Hours:
Expence, and After-thought, and idle Care,
And Doubts of motley Hue, and dark Despair: 485
Suspicions, and fantastical Surmise,
And Jealousie suffus'd, with Jaundice in her Eyes;
Discolouring all she view'd, in Tawney dress'd;
Down-look'd, and with a Cuckow on her Fist.
Oppos'd to her, on t'other side, advance   490
The costly Feast, the Carol, and the Dance,
Minstrels, and Musick, Poetry, and Play,
And Balls by Night, and Turnaments by Day.

All these were painted on the Wall, and more;
With Acts, and Monuments of Times before: 495
And others added by Prophetick Doom,
And Lovers yet unborn, and Loves to come:
For there, th' *Idalian* Mount, and *Citheron*,
The Court of *Venus*, was in Colours drawn:
Before the Palace-gate, in careless Dress,   500
And loose Array, sat Portress Idleness:
There, by the Fount, *Narcissus* pin'd alone;
There *Samson* was; with wiser *Solomon*,
And all the mighty Names by Love undone:
Medea's Charms were there, *Circean* Feasts,   505
With Bowls that turn'd inamour'd Youth to Beasts.
Here might be seen, that Beauty, Wealth, and Wit,
And Prowess, to the Pow'r of Love submit:
The spreading Snare for all Mankind is laid;
And Lovers all betray, and are betray'd.   510
The Goddess self, some noble Hand had wrought;
Smiling she seem'd, and full of pleasing Thought:
From Ocean as she first began to rise,
And smooth'd the ruffl'd Seas, and clear'd the Skies;
She trode the Brine all bare below the Breast,   515
And the green Waves, but ill conceal'd the rest;
A Lute she held; and on her Head was seen
A Wreath of Roses red, and Myrtles green:
Her Turtles fann'd the buxom Air above;
And, by his Mother, stood an Infant-Love: 520
With Wings unfledg'd; his Eyes were banded o'er;
His Hands a Bow, his Back a Quiver bore,
Supply'd with Arrows bright and keen, a deadly Store.

But in the Dome of mighty *Mars* the Red,
With diff 'rent Figures all the Sides were spread: 525
This Temple, less in Form, with equal Grace
Was imitative of the first in *Thrace*:
For that cold Region was the lov'd Abode,
And Sov'reign Mansion of the Warriour-God.
The Landscape was a Forest wide and bare;   530
Where neither Beast, nor Humane Kind repair;
The Fowl, that scent afar, the Borders fly,

And shun the bitter Blast, and wheel about the Sky.
A Cake of Scurf lies baking on the Ground,
And prickly Stubs, instead of Trees, are found; 535
Or Woods with Knots and Knares, deform'd and old;
Headless the most, and hideous to behold:
A ratling Tempest through the Branches went,
That stripp'd 'em bare, and one sole way they bent.
Heav'n froze above, severe, the Clouds congeal, 540
And through the Crystal Vault appear'd the standing Hail.
Such was the Face without, a Mountain stood
Threatning from high, and overlook'd the Wood:
Beneath the lowring Brow, and on a Bent,
The Temple stood of *Mars* Armipotent: 545
The Frame of burnish'd Steel, that cast a Glare
From far, and seem'd to thaw the freezing Air.
A streight, long Entry, to the Temple led,
Blind with high Walls; and Horrour over Head:
Thence issu'd such a Blast, and hollow Rore, 550
As threaten'd from the Hinge, to heave the Door;
In, through that Door, a Northern Light there shone;
'Twas all it had, for Windows there were none.
The Gate was Adamant; Eternal Frame!
Which hew'd by *Mars* himself, from *Indian* Quarries came, 555
The Labour of a God; and all along
Tough Iron Plates were clench'd to make it strong.
A Tun about, was ev'ry Pillar there;
A polish'd Mirrour shone not half so clear.
There saw I how the secret Fellon wrought, ⎫ 560
And Treason lab'ring in the Traytor's Thought; ⎬
And Midwife Time the ripen'd Plot to Murder brought. ⎭
There, the Red Anger dar'd the Pallid Fear;
Next stood Hypocrisie, with holy Lear:
Soft, smiling, and demurely looking down, 565
But hid the Dagger underneath the Gown:
Th' assassinating Wife, the Houshold Fiend;
And far the blackest there, the Traytor-Friend.
On t'other Side there stood Destruction bare;
Unpunish'd Rapine, and a Waste of War. 570
Contest, with sharpen'd Knives in Cloysters drawn,

And all with Blood bespread the holy Lawn.
Loud Menaces were heard, and foul Disgrace,
And bawling Infamy, in Language base;
Till Sense was lost in Sound, and Silence fled the Place.   575
The Slayer of Himself yet saw I there,
The Gore congeal'd was clotter'd in his Hair:
With Eyes half clos'd, and gaping Mouth he lay,
And grim, as when he breath'd his sullen Soul away.
In midst of all the Dome, Misfortune sat,   580
And gloomy Discontent, and fell Debate:
And Madness laughing in his ireful Mood;
And arm'd Complaint on Theft; and Cries of Blood.
There was the murder'd Corps, in Covert laid,
And Violent Death in thousand Shapes display'd: 585
The City to the Soldier's Rage resign'd:
Successless Wars, and Poverty behind:
Ships burnt in Fight, or forc'd on Rocky Shores,
And the rash Hunter strangled by the Boars:
The new-born Babe by Nurses overlaid;   590
And the Cook caught within the raging Fire he made.
All Ills of *Mars* his Nature, Flame and Steel:
The gasping Charioteer, beneath the Wheel
Of his own Car; the ruin'd House that falls
And intercepts her Lord betwixt the Walls: 595
The whole Division that to *Mars* pertains,
All Trades of Death that deal in Steel for Gains,
Were there: The Butcher, Armourer, and Smith,
Who forges sharpen'd Fauchions, or the Scythe.
The scarlet Conquest on a Tow'r was plac'd,   600
With Shouts, and Soldiers Acclamations grac'd:
A pointed Sword hung threatning o'er his Head,
Sustain'd but by a slender Twine of Thred.
There saw I *Mars* his *Ides*, the *Capitol*,
The Seer in vain foretelling *Cæsar*'s Fall,   605
The last *Triumvirs*, and the Wars they move,
And *Antony*, who lost the World for Love.
These, and a thousand more, the Fane adorn;
Their Fates were painted e'er the Men were born,
All copied from the Heav'ns, and ruling Force   610
Of the Red Star, in his revolving Course.

The Form of *Mars* high on a Chariot stood,
All sheath'd in Arms, and gruffly look'd the God:
Two Geomantick Figures were display'd
Above his Head, a *Warriour and a Maid,   **Rubeus, &* 615
One when Direct, and one when Retrograde.   *Puella.*

   Tir'd with Deformities of Death, I haste
To the third Temple of *Diana* chaste;
A Sylvan Scene with various Greens was drawn,
Shades on the Sides, and on the midst a Lawn: 620
The Silver *Cynthia*, with her Nymphs around,
Pursu'd the flying Deer, the Woods with Horns resound:
Calistho there stood manifest of Shame,
And turn'd a Bear, the Northern Star became:
Her Son was next, and by peculiar Grace   625
In the cold Circle held the second Place:
The Stag *Acteon* in the Stream had spy'd
The naked Huntress, and, for seeing, dy'd:
His Hounds, unknowing of his Change, pursue
The Chace, and their mistaken Master slew.   630
Peneian Daphne too was there to see
Apollo's Love before, and now his Tree:
Th' adjoining Fane th' assembl'd *Greeks* express'd,
And hunting of the *Caledonian* Beast.
Oenides Valour, and his envy'd Prize;   635
The fatal Pow'r of *Atalanta*'s Eyes;
Diana's Vengeance on the Victor shown,
The Murdress Mother, and consuming Son.
The *Volscian* Queen extended on the Plain;
The Treason punish'd, and the Traytor slain.   640
The rest were various Huntings, well design'd,
And Salvage Beasts destroy'd, of ev'ry Kind:
The graceful Goddess was array'd in Green;
About her Feet were little Beagles seen,
That watch'd with upward Eyes the Motions of their Queen. 645
Her Legs were Buskin'd, and the Left before,
In act to shoot, a Silver Bow she bore,
And at her Back a painted Quiver wore.
She trod a wexing Moon, that soon wou'd wane,
And drinking borrow'd Light, be fill'd again: 650
With down-cast Eyes, as seeming to survey

The dark Dominions, her alternate Sway.
Before her stood a Woman in her Throws,
And call'd *Lucina*'s Aid, her Burden to disclose.
All these the Painter drew with such Command,   655
That Nature snatch'd the Pencil from his Hand,
Asham'd and angry that his Art could feign
And mend the Tortures of a Mothers Pain.
Theseus beheld the Fanes of ev'ry God,
And thought his mighty Cost was well bestow'd: 660
So Princes now their Poets should regard;
But few can write, and fewer can reward.

The Theater thus rais'd, the Lists enclos'd,
And all with vast Magnificence dispos'd,
We leave the Monarch pleas'd, and haste to bring   665
The Knights to combate; and their Arms to sing.

PALAMON AND ARCITE:
Or, The Knight's Tale.

BOOK III

THE Day approach'd when Fortune shou'd decide
    Th' important Enterprize, and give the Bride;
For now, the Rivals round the World had sought,
And each his Number, well appointed, brought.
The Nations far and near, contend in Choice,   5
And send the Flow'r of War by Publick Voice;
That after, or before, were never known
Such Chiefs; as each an Army seem'd alone:
Beside the Champions; all of high Degree,
Who Knighthood lov'd, and Deeds of Chivalry,   10
Throng'd to the Lists, and envy'd to behold
The Names of others, not their own inroll'd.
Nor seems it strange; for ev'ry Noble Knight,
Who loves the Fair, and is endu'd with Might,
In such a Quarrel wou'd be proud to fight.   15
There breaths not scarce a Man on *British* Ground
(An Isle for Love, and Arms of old renown'd)

But would have sold his Life to purchase Fame,
To *Palamon* or *Arcite* sent his Name:
And had the Land selected of the best,   20
Half had come hence, and let the World provide the rest.
A hundred Knights with *Palamon* there came,
Approv'd in Fight, and Men of mighty Name;
Their Arms were sev'ral, as their Nations were,
But furnish'd all alike with Sword and Spear.   25
Some wore Coat-armour, imitating Scale;
And next their Skins were stubborn Shirts of Mail.
Some wore a Breastplate and a light Juppon,
Their Horses cloth'd with rich Caparison:
Some for Defence would Leathern Bucklers use,   30
Of folded Hides; and others Shields of Pruce.
One hung a Poleax at his Saddle-bow,
And one a heavy Mace, to stun the Foe:
One for his Legs and Knees provided well,
With *Jambeux* arm'd, and double Plates of Steel: 35
This on his Helmet wore a Ladies Glove,
And that a Sleeve embroider'd by his Love.

   With *Palamon*, above the rest in Place,
Lycurgus came, the surly King of *Thrace*;
Black was his Beard, and manly was his Face: 40
The Balls of his broad Eyes roll'd in his Head,
And glar'd betwixt a Yellow and a Red:
He look'd a Lion with a gloomy Stare,
And o'er his Eye-brows hung his matted Hair:
Big-bon'd, and large of Limbs, with Sinews strong,   45
Broad-shoulder'd, and his Arms were round and long.
Four Milk-white Bulls (the *Thracian* Use of old)
Were yok'd to draw his Car of burnish'd Gold.
Upright he stood, and bore aloft his Shield,
Conspicuous from afar, and over-look'd the Field.   50
His Surcoat was a Bear-skin on his Back;
His Hair hung long behind, and glossy Raven-black.
His ample Forehead bore a Coronet
With sparkling Diamonds, and with Rubies set:
Ten Brace, and more, of Greyhounds, snowy fair,   55
And tall as Stags, ran loose, and cours'd around his Chair,
A Match for Pards in flight, in grappling, for the Bear:

With Golden Muzzles all their Mouths were bound,
And Collars of the same their Necks surround.
Thus thro' the Fields *Lycurgus* took his way;   60
His hundred Knights attend in Pomp and proud Array.
    To match this Monarch, with strong *Arcite* came
Emetrius King of *Inde*, a mighty Name,
On a Bay Courser, goodly to behold,
The Trappings of his Horse emboss'd with barb'rous Gold.   65
Not *Mars* bestrode a Steed with greater Grace;
His Surcoat o'er his Arms was Cloth of *Thrace*,
Adorn'd with Pearls, all Orient, round, and great;
His Saddle was of Gold, with Emeralds set.
His Shoulders large, a Mantle did attire,   70
With Rubies thick, and sparkling as the Fire:
His Amber-colour'd Locks in Ringlets run,
With graceful Negligence, and shone against the Sun.
His Nose was Aquiline, his Eyes were blue,
Ruddy his Lips, and fresh and fair his Hue: 75
Some sprinkled Freckles on his Face were seen,
Whose Dusk set off the Whiteness of the Skin:
His awful Presence did the Crowd surprize,
Nor durst the rash Spectator meet his Eyes,
Eyes that confess'd him born for Kingly Sway,   80
So fierce, they flash'd intolerable Day.
His Age in Nature's youthful Prime appear'd,
And just began to bloom his yellow Beard.
Whene'er he spoke, his Voice was heard around,
Loud as a Trumpet, with a Silver Sound.   85
A Laurel wreath'd his Temples, fresh, and green;
And Myrtle-sprigs, the Marks of Love, were mix'd between.
Upon his Fist he bore, for his Delight,
An Eagle well reclaim'd, and Lilly-white.
    His hundred Knights attend him to the War,   90
All arm'd for Battel; save their Heads were bare.
Words, and Devices blaz'd on ev'ry Shield,
And pleasing was the Terrour of the Field.
For Kings, and Dukes, and Barons you might see,
Like sparkling Stars, though diff 'rent in Degree,   }   95
All for th' Increase of Arms, and Love of Chivalry.
Before the King, tame Leopards led the way,

And Troops of Lions innocently play.
So *Bacchus* through the conquer'd *Indies* rode,
And Beasts in Gambols frisk'd before their honest God.   100
   In this Array the War of either Side
Through *Athens* pass'd with Military Pride.
At Prime, they enter'd on the *Sunday* Morn;
Rich Tap'stry spread the Streets, and Flow'rs the Posts adorn.
The Town was all a Jubilee of Feasts;   105
So *Theseus* will'd, in Honour of his Guests:
Himself with open Arms the Kings embrac'd,
Then all the rest in their Degrees were grac'd.
No Harbinger was needful for the Night,
For ev'ry House was proud to lodge a Knight.   110
   I pass the Royal Treat, nor must relate
The Gifts bestow'd, nor how the Champions sate;
Who first, who last, or how the Knights address'd
Their Vows, or who was fairest at the Feast;
Whose Voice, whose graceful Dance did most surprise,   115
Soft am'rous Sighs, and silent Love of Eyes.
The Rivals call my Muse another way,
To sing their Vigils for th' ensuing Day.
   'Twas ebbing Darkness, past the Noon of Night;
And *Phospher* on the Confines of the Light,   120
Promis'd the Sun; e'er Day began to spring
The tuneful Lark already stretch'd her Wing,
And flick'ring on her Nest, made short Essays to sing:
When wakeful *Palamon*, preventing Day,
Took, to the Royal Lists, his early way,   125
To *Venus* at her Fane, in her own House to pray.
There, falling on his Knees before her Shrine,
He thus implor'd with Pray'rs her Pow'r Divine.
Creator *Venus*, Genial Pow'r of Love,
The Bliss of Men below, and Gods above,   130
Beneath the sliding Sun thou runn'st thy Race,
Dost fairest shine, and best become thy Place.
For thee the Winds their Eastern Blasts forbear,
Thy Month reveals the Spring, and opens all the Year.

Book III. 104 Posts] Pots F

Thee, Goddess, thee the Storms of Winter fly,   135
Earth smiles with Flow'rs renewing; laughs the Sky,
And Birds to Lays of Love their tuneful Notes apply.
For thee the Lion loaths the Taste of Blood,
And roaring hunts his Female through the Wood:
For thee the Bulls rebellow through the Groves,   140
And tempt the Stream, and snuff their absent Loves.
'Tis thine, whate'er is pleasant, good, or fair:
All Nature is thy Province, Life thy Care;
Thou mad'st the World, and dost the World repair.
Thou Gladder of the Mount of *Cytheron*,   145
Increase of *Jove*, Companion of the Sun;
If e'er *Adonis* touch'd thy tender Heart,
Have pity, Goddess, for thou know'st the Smart:
Alas! I have not Words to tell my Grief;
To vent my Sorrow wou'd be some Relief: 150
Light Suff'rings give us leisure to complain;
We groan, but cannot speak, in greater Pain.
O Goddess, tell thy self what I would say,
Thou know'st it, and I feel too much to pray.
So grant my Suit, as I enforce my Might,   155
In Love to be thy Champion, and thy Knight;
A Servant to thy Sex, a Slave to thee,
A Foe profest to barren Chastity.
Nor ask I Fame or Honour of the Field,
Nor chuse I more to vanquish, than to yield: 160
In my Divine *Emilia* make me blest,
Let Fate, or partial Chance, dispose the rest:
Find thou the Manner, and the Means prepare;
Possession, more than Conquest, is my Care.
Mars is the Warriour's God; in him it lies,   165
On whom he favours, to confer the Prize;
With smiling Aspect you serenely move
In your fifth Orb, and rule the Realm of Love.
The Fates but only spin the courser Clue,
The finest of the Wooll is left for you.   170
Spare me but one small Portion of the Twine,
And let the Sisters cut below your Line:
The rest among the Rubbish may they sweep,
Or add it to the Yarn of some old Miser's Heap.

But if you this ambitious Pray'r deny,   175
(A Wish, I grant, beyond Mortality)
Then let me sink beneath proud *Arcite*'s Arms,
And I once dead, let him possess her Charms.

    Thus ended he; then, with Observance due,
The sacred Incense on her Altar threw: 180
The curling Smoke mounts heavy from the Fires;
At length it catches Flame, and in a Blaze expires;
At once the gracious Goddess gave the Sign,
Her Statue shook, and trembl'd all the Shrine:
Pleas'd *Palamon* the tardy *Omen* took: 185
For, since the Flames pursu'd the trailing Smoke,
He knew his Boon was granted; but the Day
To distance driv'n, and Joy adjourn'd with long Delay.

    Now Morn with Rosie Light had streak'd the Sky,
Up rose the Sun, and up rose *Emily*;   190
Address'd her early Steps to *Cynthia*'s Fane,
In State attended by her Maiden Train,
Who bore the Vests that Holy Rites require,
Incence, and od'rous Gums, and cover'd Fire.
The plenteous Horns with pleasant Mead they crown,   195
Nor wanted ought besides in honour of the Moon.
Now while the Temple smoak'd with hallow'd Steam,
They wash the Virgin in a living Stream;
The secret Ceremonies I conceal:
Uncouth; perhaps unlawful to reveal: 200
But such they were as Pagan Use requir'd,
Perform'd by Women when the Men retir'd,
Whose Eyes profane, their chast mysterious Rites
Might turn to Scandal, or obscene Delights.
Well-meaners think no Harm; but for the rest,   205
Things Sacred they pervert, and Silence is the best.
Her shining Hair, uncomb'd, was loosly spread,
A Crown of Mastless Oak adorn'd her Head:
When to the Shrine approach'd, the spotless Maid
Had kindling Fires on either Altar laid: 210
(The Rites were such as were observ'd of old,
By *Statius* in his *Theban* Story told.)
Then kneeling with her Hands across her Breast,
Thus lowly she preferr'd her chast Request.

O Goddess, Haunter of the Woodland Green,   215
To whom both Heav'n and Earth and Seas are seen;
Queen of the nether Skies, where half the Year
Thy Silver Beams descend, and light the gloomy Sphere;
Goddess of Maids, and conscious of our Hearts,
So keep me from the Vengeance of thy Darts,   220
Which *Niobe*'s devoted Issue felt,
When hissing through the Skies the feather'd Deaths were dealt:
As I desire to live a Virgin-life,
Nor know the Name of Mother or of Wife.
Thy Votress from my tender Years I am,   225
And love, like thee, the Woods and Sylvan Game.
Like Death, thou know'st, I loath the Nuptial State, ⎫
And Man, the Tyrant of our Sex, I hate,   ⎬
A lowly Servant, but a lofty Mate.   ⎭
Where Love is Duty, on the Female Side;   230
On theirs meer sensual Gust, and sought with surly Pride.
Now by thy triple Shape, as thou art seen
In Heav'n, Earth, Hell, and ev'ry where a Queen,
Grant this my first Desire; let Discord cease,
And make betwixt the Rivals lasting Peace: 235
Quench their hot Fire, or far from me remove
The Flame, and turn it on some other Love.
Or if my frowning Stars have so decreed,
That one must be rejected, one succeed,
Make him my Lord within whose faithful Breast   240
Is fix'd my Image, and who loves me best.
But, oh! ev'n that avert! I chuse it not,
But take it as the least unhappy Lot.
A Maid I am, and of thy Virgin-Train;
Oh, let me still that spotless Name retain!   245
Frequent the Forests, thy chast Will obey,
And only make the Beasts of Chace my Prey!
    The Flames ascend on either Altar clear,
While thus the blameless Maid address'd her Pray'r.
When lo! the burning Fire that shone so bright,   250
Flew off, all sudden, with extinguish'd Light,
And left one Altar dark, a little space;
Which turn'd self-kindl'd, and renew'd the Blaze:
That other Victour-Flame a Moment stood,

Then fell, and lifeless left th' extinguish'd Wood;   255
For ever lost, th' irrevocable Light
Forsook the blackning Coals, and sunk to Night:
At either End it whistled as it flew,
And as the Brands were green, so dropp'd the Dew;
Infected as it fell with Sweat of Sanguin Hue.   260

  The Maid from that ill *Omen* turn'd her Eyes,
And with loud Shrieks and Clamours rent the Skies,
Nor knew what signifi'd the boding Sign,
But found the Pow'rs displeas'd, and fear'd the Wrath Divine.

  Then shook the Sacred Shrine, and sudden Light   265
Sprung through the vaulted Roof, and made the Temple bright.
The Pow'r, behold! the Pow'r in Glory shone,
By her bent Bow, and her keen Arrows known:
The rest, a Huntress issuing from the Wood,
Reclining on her Cornel Spear she stood.   270
Then gracious thus began; Dismiss thy Fear,
And Heav'ns unchang'd Decrees attentive hear:
More pow'rful Gods have torn thee from my Side,
Unwilling to resign, and doom'd a Bride:
The two contending Knights are weigh'd above;   275
One *Mars* protects, and one the Queen of Love:
But which the Man, is in the Thund'rer's Breast,
This he pronounc'd, 'tis he who loves thee best.
The Fire that once extinct, reviv'd again,
Foreshews the Love allotted to remain.   280
Farewell, she said, and vanish'd from the Place;
The Sheaf of Arrows shook, and rattl'd in the Case.
Agast at this, the Royal Virgin stood,
Disclaim'd, and now no more a Sister of the Wood:
But to the parting Goddess thus she pray'd;   285
Propitious still be present to my Aid,
Nor quite abandon your once favour'd Maid.
Then sighing she return'd; but smil'd betwixt,
With Hopes, and Fears, and Joys with Sorrows mixt.

  The next returning Planetary Hour   290
Of *Mars*, who shar'd the Heptarchy of Pow'r,
His Steps bold *Arcite* to the Temple bent,
T' adore with Pagan Rites the Pow'r Armipotent:
Then prostrate, low before his Altar lay,

And rais'd his manly Voice, and thus began to pray.   295
Strong God of Arms, whose Iron Scepter sways
The freezing North, and *Hyperborean* Seas,
And *Scythian* Colds, and *Thracia*'s Wintry Coast,
Where stand thy Steeds, and thou art honour'd most:
There most; but ev'ry where thy Pow'r is known,   300
The Fortune of the Fight is all thy own:
Terrour is thine, and wild Amazement flung
From out thy Chariot, withers ev'n the Strong:
And Disarray and shameful Rout ensue,
And Force is added to the fainting Crew.   305
Acknowledg'd as thou art, accept my Pray'r,
If ought I have atchiev'd deserve thy Care:
If to my utmost Pow'r with Sword and Shield
I dar'd the Death, unknowing how to yield,
And falling in my Rank, still kept the Field: 310
Then let my Arms prevail, by thee sustain'd,
That *Emily* by Conquest may be gain'd.
Have pity on my Pains; nor those unknown
To *Mars*, which when a Lover, were his own.
Venus, the Publick Care of all above,   315
Thy stubborn Heart has softned into Love:
Now by her Blandishments and pow'rful Charms
When yielded, she lay curling in thy Arms,
Ev'n by thy Shame, if Shame it may be call'd,
When *Vulcan* had thee in his Net inthrall'd;   320
O envy'd Ignominy, sweet Disgrace,
When ev'ry God that saw thee, wish'd thy Place!
By those dear Pleasures, aid my Arms in Fight,
And make me conquer in my Patron's Right:
For I am young, a Novice in the Trade,   325
The Fool of Love, unpractis'd to persuade;
And want the soothing Arts that catch the Fair,
But caught my self, lie strugling in the Snare:
And she I love, or laughs at all my Pain,
Or knows her Worth too well; and pays me with Disdain.   330
For sure I am, unless I win in Arms,
To stand excluded from *Emilia*'s Charms:
Nor can my Strength avail, unless by thee
Endu'd with Force, I gain the Victory:

Then for the Fire which warm'd thy gen'rous Heart,   335
Pity thy Subject's Pains, and equal Smart.
So be the Morrows Sweat and Labour mine,
The Palm and Honour of the Conquest thine:
Then shall the War, and stern Debate, and Strife
Immortal, be the Bus'ness of my Life;   340
And in thy Fane, the dusty Spoils among,
High on the burnish'd Roof, my Banner shall be hung;
Rank'd with my Champions Bucklers, and below
With Arms revers'd, th' Atchievements of my Foe:
And while these Limbs the Vital Spirit feeds,   345
While Day to Night, and Night to Day succeeds,
Thy smoaking Altar shall be fat with Food
Of Incence, and the grateful Steam of Blood;
Burnt Off'rings Morn and Ev'ning shall be thine;
And Fires eternal in thy Temple shine.   350
This Bush of yellow Beard, this Length of Hair,
Which from my Birth inviolate I bear,
Guiltless of Steel, and from the Razour free,
Shall fall a plenteous Crop, reserv'd for thee.
So may my Arms with Victory be blest,   355
I ask no more; let Fate dispose the rest.
    The Champion ceas'd; there follow'd in the Close
A hollow Groan, a murm'ring Wind arose,
The Rings of Ir'n, that on the Doors were hung,
Sent out a jarring Sound, and harshly rung: 360
The bolted Gates flew open at the Blast,
The Storm rush'd in; and *Arcite* stood agast:
The Flames were blown aside, yet shone they bright,
Fann'd by the Wind, and gave a ruffl'd Light:
    Then from the Ground a Scent began to rise,   365
Sweet-smelling, as accepted Sacrifice:
This *Omen* pleas'd, and as the Flames aspire
With od'rous Incence *Arcite* heaps the Fire:
Nor wanted Hymns to *Mars*, or Heathen Charms:
At length the nodding Statue clash'd his Arms,   370
And with a sullen Sound, and feeble Cry,
Half sunk, and half pronounc'd the Word of Victory.
For this, with Soul devout, he thank'd the God,
And of Success secure, return'd to his Abode.

These Vows thus granted, rais'd a Strife above,   375
Betwixt the God of War, and Queen of Love.
She granting first, had Right of Time to plead;
But he had granted too, nor would recede.
Jove was for *Venus*; but he fear'd his Wife,
And seem'd unwilling to decide the Strife;   380
Till *Saturn* from his Leaden Throne arose,
And found a Way the Diff'rence to compose:
Though sparing of his Grace, to Mischief bent,
He seldom does a Good with good Intent.
Wayward, but wise; by long Experience taught   385
To please both Parties, for ill Ends, he sought:
For this Advantage Age from Youth has won,
As not to be outridden, though outrun.
By Fortune he was now to *Venus* Trin'd,
And with stern *Mars* in *Capricorn* was join'd: 390
Of him disposing in his own Abode,
He sooth'd the Goddess, while he gull'd the God:
Cease, Daughter, to complain; and stint the Strife;
Thy *Palamon* shall have his promis'd Wife:
And *Mars*, the Lord of Conquest, in the Fight   395
With Palm and Laurel shall adorn his Knight.
Wide is my Course, nor turn I to my Place
Till length of Time, and move with tardy Pace.
Man feels me, when I press th' Etherial Plains,
My Hand is heavy, and the Wound remains.   400
Mine is the Shipwreck, in a Watry Sign;
And in an Earthy, the dark Dungeon mine.
Cold shivering Agues, melancholy Care,
And bitter blasting Winds, and poison'd Air,
Are mine, and wilful Death, resulting from Despair.   405
The throtling Quinsey 'tis my Star appoints,
And Rheumatisms I send to rack the Joints:
When Churls rebel against their Native Prince,
I arm their Hands, and furnish the Pretence;
And housing in the Lion's hateful Sign,   410
Bought Senates, and deserting Troops are mine.
Mine is the privy Pois'ning, I command
Unkindly Seasons, and ungrateful Land.
By me Kings Palaces are push'd to Ground,

And Miners, crush'd beneath their Mines are found. 415
'Twas I slew *Samson*, when the Pillar'd Hall
Fell down, and crush'd the Many with the Fall.
My Looking is the Sire of Pestilence,
That sweeps at once the People and the Prince.
Now weep no more, but trust thy Grandsire's Art; 420
Mars shall be pleas'd, and thou perform thy Part.
'Tis ill, though diff'rent your Complexions are,
The Family of Heav'n for Men should war.
Th' Expedient pleas'd, where neither lost his Right:
Mars had the Day, and *Venus* had the Night. 425
The Management they left to *Chronos* Care;
Now turn we to th' Effect, and sing the War.

   In *Athens*, all was Pleasure, Mirth, and Play,
All proper to the Spring, and spritely *May*:
Which ev'ry Soul inspir'd with such Delight, 430
'Twas Justing all the Day, and Love at Night.
Heav'n smil'd, and gladded was the Heart of Man;
And *Venus* had the World, as when it first began.
At length in Sleep their Bodies they compose,
And dreamt the future Fight, and early rose. 435

   Now scarce the dawning Day began to spring,
As at a Signal giv'n, the Streets with Clamours ring:
At once the Crowd arose; confus'd and high
Ev'n from the Heav'n was heard a shouting Cry;
For *Mars* was early up, and rowz'd the Sky. 440
The Gods came downward to behold the Wars,
Sharpning their Sights, and leaning from their Stars.
The Neighing of the gen'rous Horse was heard,
For Battel by the busie Groom prepar'd:
Rustling of Harness, ratling of the Shield, 445
Clatt'ring of Armour, furbish'd for the Field.
Crowds to the Castle mounted up the Street,
Batt'ring the Pavement with their Coursers Feet:
The greedy Sight might there devour the Gold
Of glittring Arms, too dazling to behold; 450
And polish'd Steel that cast the View aside,
And Crested Morions, with their Plumy Pride.
Knights, with a long Retinue of their Squires,
In gawdy Liv'ries march, and quaint Attires.

One lac'd the Helm, another held the Lance: 455
A third the shining Buckler did advance.
The Courser paw'd the Ground with restless Feet,
And snorting foam'd, and champ'd the Golden Bit.
The Smiths and Armourers on Palfreys ride,
Files in their Hands, and Hammers at their Side,   } 460
And Nails for loosen'd Spears, and Thongs for Shields provide.
The Yeomen guard the Streets, in seemly Bands;
And Clowns come crowding on, with Cudgels in their Hands.
    The Trumpets, next the Gate, in order plac'd,
Attend the Sign to sound the Martial Blast: 465
The Palace-yard is fill'd with floating Tides,
And the last Comers bear the former to the Sides.
The Throng is in the midst: The common Crew
Shut out, the Hall admits the better Few.
In Knots they stand, or in a Rank they walk,   470
Serious in Aspect, earnest in their Talk:
Factious, and fav'ring this or t'other Side,
As their strong Fancies, and weak Reason, guide:
Their Wagers back their Wishes: Numbers hold
With the fair freckl'd King, and Beard of Gold: 475
So vig'rous are his Eyes, such Rays they cast,
So prominent his Eagles Beak is plac'd.
But most their Looks on the black Monarch bend,
His rising Muscles, and his Brawn commend;
His double-biting Ax, and beamy Spear,   480
Each asking a Gygantick Force to rear.
All spoke as partial Favour mov'd the Mind;
And safe themselves, at others Cost divin'd.
    Wak'd by the Cries, th' *Athenian* Chief arose,
The Knightly Forms of Combate to dispose;   485
And passing through th' obsequious Guards, he sate
Conspicuous on a Throne, sublime in State;
There, for the two contending Knights he sent:
Arm'd *Cap-a-pe*, with Rev'rence low they bent;
He smil'd on both, and with superiour Look   490
Alike their offer'd Adoration took.
The People press on ev'ry Side to see
Their awful Prince, and hear his high Decree.
Then signing to the Heralds with his Hand,

They gave his Orders from their lofty Stand.   495
Silence is thrice enjoin'd; then thus aloud
The King at Arms bespeaks the Knights and listning Crowd.
    Our Sovereign Lord has ponder'd in his Mind
The Means to spare the Blood of gentle Kind;
And of his Grace, and in-born Clemency,   500
He modifies his first severe Decree;
The keener Edge of Battel to rebate,
The Troops for Honour fighting, not for Hate.
He wills, not Death shou'd terminate their Strife;
And Wounds, if Wounds ensue, be short of Life.   505
But issues, e'er the Fight, his dread Command,
That Slings afar, and Ponyards Hand to Hand,
Be banish'd from the Field; that none shall dare
With shortned Sword to stab in closer War;
But in fair Combate fight with manly Strength,   510
Nor push with biting Point, but strike at length.
The Turney is allow'd but one Career,
Of the tough Ash, with the sharp-grinded Spear.
But Knights unhors'd may rise from off the Plain,
And fight on Foot, their Honour to regain.   515
Nor, if at Mischief taken, on the Ground
Be slain, but Pris'ners to the Pillar bound,
At either Barrier plac'd; nor (Captives made,)
Be freed, or arm'd anew the Fight invade.
The Chief of either Side, bereft of Life,   520
Or yielded to his Foe, concludes the Strife.
Thus dooms the Lord: Now valiant Knights and young,
Fight each his fill with Swords and Maces long.
    The Herald ends: The vaulted Firmament
With loud Acclaims, and vast Applause is rent: 525
Heav'n guard a Prince so gracious and so good,
So just, and yet so provident of Blood!
This was the gen'ral Cry. The Trumpets sound,
And Warlike Symphony is heard around.
The marching Troops through *Athens* take their way,   530
The great Earl-Marshal orders their Array.
The Fair from high the passing Pomp behold;
A Rain of Flow'rs is from the Windows roll'd.
The Casements are with Golden Tissue spread,

And Horses Hoofs, for Earth, on Silken Tap'stry tread.   535
The King goes midmost, and the Rivals ride
In equal Rank, and close his either Side.
Next after these, there rode the Royal Wife,
With *Emily*, the Cause, and the Reward of Strife.
The following Cavalcade, by Three and Three,   540
Proceed by Titles marshall'd in Degree.
Thus through the Southern Gate they take their Way,
And at the Lists arriv'd e'er Prime of Day.
There, parting from the King, the Chiefs divide,
And wheeling East and West, before their Many ride.   545
Th' *Athenian* Monarch mounts his Throne on high,
And after him the Queen, and *Emily*:
Next these, the Kindred of the Crown are grac'd
With nearer Seats, and Lords by Ladies plac'd.
Scarce were they seated, when with Clamours loud   550
In rush'd at once a rude promiscuous Crowd:
The Guards, and then each other overbare,
And in a Moment throng the spacious Theatre.
Now chang'd the jarring Noise to Whispers low,
As Winds forsaking Seas more softly blow;   555
When at the Western Gate, on which the Car
Is plac'd aloft, that bears the God of War,
Proud *Arcite* entring arm'd before his Train,
Stops at the Barrier, and divides the Plain.
Red was his Banner, and display'd abroad   560
The bloody Colours of his Patron God.
    At that self-moment enters *Palamon*
The Gate of *Venus*, and the Rising Sun;
Wav'd by the wanton Winds, his Banner flies,
All Maiden White, and shares the Peoples Eyes.   565
From East to West, look all the World around,
Two Troops so match'd were never to be found:
Such Bodies built for Strength, of equal Age,
In Stature siz'd; so proud an Equipage:
The nicest Eye cou'd no Distinction make,   570
Where lay th' Advantage, or what Side to take.
    Thus rang'd, the Herald for the last proclaims
A Silence, while they answer'd to their Names:
For so the King decreed, to shun with Care

The Fraud of Musters false, the common Bane of War.   575
The Tale was just, and then the Gates were clos'd;
And Chief to Chief, and Troop to Troop oppos'd.
The Heralds last retir'd, and loudly cry'd,
The Fortune of the Field be fairly try'd.

  At this, the Challenger with fierce Defie   580
His Trumpet sounds; the Challeng'd makes Reply:
With Clangour rings the Field, resounds the vaulted Sky.
Their Vizors clos'd, their Lances in the Rest,
Or at the Helmet pointed, or the Crest;
They vanish from the Barrier, speed the Race,   585
And spurring see decrease the middle Space.
A Cloud of Smoke envellops either Host,
And all at once the Combatants are lost:
Darkling they join adverse, and shock unseen,
Coursers with Coursers justling, Men with Men: 590
As lab'ring in Eclipse, a while they stay,
Till the next Blast of Wind restores the Day.
They look anew: The beauteous Form of Fight
Is chang'd, and War appears a grizly Sight.
Two Troops in fair Array one Moment show'd,   595
The next, a Field with fallen Bodies strow'd:
Not half the Number in their Seats are found,
But Men and Steeds lie grov'ling on the Ground.
The Points of Spears are stuck within the Shield,
The Steeds without their Riders scour the Field.   600
The Knights unhors'd, on Foot renew the Fight;
The glitt'ring Fauchions cast a gleaming Light:
Hauberks and Helms are hew'd with many a Wound;
Out spins the streaming Blood, and dies the Ground.
The mighty Maces with such haste descend,   605
They break the Bones, and make the solid Armour bend.
This thrusts amid the Throng with furious Force;
Down goes, at once, the Horseman and the Horse:
That Courser stumbles on the fallen Steed,
And floundring, throws the Rider o'er his Head.   610
One rolls along, a Foot-ball to his Foes;
One with a broken Truncheon deals his Blows.
This halting, this disabl'd with his Wound,
In Triumph led, is to the Pillar bound,

Where by the King's Award he must abide: 615
There goes a Captive led on t'other Side.
By Fits they cease; and leaning on the Lance,
Take Breath a while, and to new Fight advance.

    Full oft the Rivals met, and neither spar'd
His utmost Force, and each forgot to ward.   620
The Head of this was to the Saddle bent,
That other backward to the Crupper sent:
Both were by Turns unhors'd; the jealous Blows
Fall thick and heavy, when on Foot they close.
So deep their Fauchions bite, that ev'ry Stroke   625
Pierc'd to the Quick; and equal Wounds they gave and took.
Born far asunder by the Tides of Men,
Like Adamant and Steel they meet agen.

    So when a Tyger sucks the Bullock's Blood,
A famish'd Lion issuing from the Wood   630
Roars Lordly fierce, and challenges the Food.
Each claims Possession, neither will obey,
But both their Paws are fasten'd on the Prey:
They bite, they tear; and while in vain they strive,
The Swains come arm'd between, and both to distance drive.   635

    At length, as Fate foredoom'd, and all things tend
By Course of Time to their appointed End;
So when the Sun to West was far declin'd,
And both afresh in mortal Battel join'd,
The strong *Emetrius* came in *Arcite*'s Aid,   640
And *Palamon* with Odds was overlaid:
For turning short, he struck with all his Might
Full on the Helmet of th' unwary Knight.
Deep was the Wound; he stagger'd with the Blow,
And turn'd him to his unexpected Foe;   645
Whom with such Force he struck, he fell'd him down,
And cleft the Circle of his Golden Crown.
But *Arcite*'s Men, who now prevail'd in Fight,
Twice Ten at once surround the single Knight:
O'erpowr'd at length, they force him to the Ground,   650
Unyielded as he was, and to the Pillar bound;
And King *Lycurgus*, while he fought in vain
His Friend to free, was tumbl'd on the Plain.

    Who now laments but *Palamon*, compell'd

No more to try the Fortune of the Field!   655
And worse than Death, to view with hateful Eyes
His Rival's Conquest, and renounce the Prize!
   The Royal Judge on his Tribunal plac'd,
Who had beheld the Fight from first to last,
Bad cease the War; pronouncing from on high   660
Arcite of *Thebes* had won the beauteous *Emily*.
The Sound of Trumpets to the Voice reply'd,
And round the Royal Lists the Heralds cry'd,
Arcite of *Thebes* has won the beauteous Bride.
   The People rend the Skies with vast Applause;   665
All own the Chief, when Fortune owns the Cause.
Arcite is own'd ev'n by the Gods above,
And conqu'ring *Mars* insults the Queen of Love.
So laugh'd he, when the rightful *Titan* fail'd,
And *Jove*'s usurping Arms in Heav'n prevail'd.   670
Laugh'd all the Pow'rs who favour Tyranny;
And all the Standing Army of the Sky.
But *Venus* with dejected Eyes appears,
And weeping, on the Lists, distill'd her Tears;
Her Will refus'd, which grieves a Woman most,   675
And in her Champion foil'd, the Cause of Love is lost.
Till *Saturn* said, Fair Daughter, now be still,
The blustring Fool has satisfi'd his Will:
His Boon is giv'n; his Knight has gain'd the Day,
But lost the Prize, th' Arrears are yet to pay.   680
Thy Hour is come, and mine the Care shall be
To please thy Knight, and set thy Promise free.
   Now while the Heralds run the Lists around,
And *Arcite*, *Arcite*, Heav'n and Earth resound;
A Miracle (nor less it could be call'd)   685
Their Joy with unexpected Sorrow pall'd.
The Victor Knight had laid his Helm aside,
Part for his Ease, the greater part for Pride:
Bare-headed, popularly low he bow'd,
And paid the Salutations of the Crowd.   690
Then spurring at full speed, ran endlong on
Where *Theseus* sat on his Imperial Throne;
Furious he drove, and upward cast his Eye,
Where next the Queen was plac'd his *Emily*;

Then passing, to the Saddle-bow he bent,   695
A sweet Regard the gracious Virgin lent:
(For Women, to the Brave an easie Prey,
Still follow Fortune, where she leads the Way:)
Just then, from Earth sprung out a flashing Fire,
By *Pluto* sent, at *Saturn*'s bad Desire;   700
The startling Steed was seiz'd with sudden Fright,
And, bounding, o'er the Pummel cast the Knight:
Forward he flew, and pitching on his Head,
He quiver'd with his Feet, and lay for Dead.
Black was his Count'nance in a little space,   705
For all the Blood was gather'd in his Face.
Help was at Hand; they rear'd him from the Ground,
And from his cumbrous Arms his Limbs unbound;
Then lanc'd a Vein, and watch'd returning Breath;
It came, but clogg'd with Symptoms of his Death.   710
The Saddle-bow the Noble Parts had prest,
All bruis'd and mortifi'd his Manly Breast.
Him still entranc'd, and in a Litter laid,
They bore from Field, and to his Bed convey'd.
At length he wak'd, and with a feeble Cry,   715
The Word he first pronounc'd was *Emily*.

    Mean time the King, though inwardly he mourn'd,
In Pomp triumphant to the Town return'd,
Attended by the Chiefs, who fought the Field;
(Now friendly mix'd, and in one Troop compell'd.)   720
Compos'd his Looks to counterfeited Cheer,
And bade them not for *Arcite*'s Life to fear.
But that which gladded all the Warriour Train,
Though most were sorely wounded, none were slain.
The Surgeons soon despoil'd 'em of their Arms,   725
And some with Salves they cure, and some with Charms.
Foment the Bruises, and the Pains asswage,
And heal their inward Hurts with Sov'reign Draughts of Sage.
The King in Person visits all around,
Comforts the Sick, congratulates the Sound;   730
Honours the Princely Chiefs, rewards the rest,
And holds for thrice three Days a Royal Feast.
None was disgrac'd; for Falling is no Shame;
And Cowardice alone is Loss of Fame.

The vent'rous Knight is from the Saddle thrown;   735
But 'tis the Fault of Fortune, not his own.
If Crowns and Palms the conqu'ring Side adorn,
The Victor under better Stars was born:
The brave Man seeks not popular Applause,
Now overpow'r'd with Arms, deserts his Cause;   740
Unsham'd, though foil'd, he does the best he can;
Force is of Brutes, but Honour is of Man.

    Thus *Theseus* smil'd on all with equal Grace;
And each was set according to his Place.
With ease were reconcil'd the diff'ring Parts,   745
For Envy never dwells in Noble Hearts.
At length they took their Leave, the Time expir'd;
Well pleas'd; and to their sev'ral Homes retir'd.

    Mean while the Health of *Arcite* still impairs;
From Bad proceeds to Worse, and mocks the Leaches Cares: 750
Swoln is his Breast, his inward Pains increase,
All Means are us'd, and all without Success.
The clotted Blood lies heavy on his Heart,
Corrupts, and there remains in spite of Art:
Nor breathing Veins, nor Cupping will prevail;   755
All outward Remedies and inward fail:
The Mold of Natures Fabrick is destroy'd,
Her Vessels discompos'd, her Vertue void:
The Bellows of his Lungs begins to swell:
All out of frame is ev'ry secret Cell,   760
Nor can the Good receive, nor Bad expel.
Those breathing Organs thus within opprest,
With Venom soon distend the Sinews of his Breast.
Nought profits him to save abandon'd Life,
Nor Vomits upward aid, nor downward Laxatife.   765
The midmost Region batter'd, and destroy'd,
When Nature cannot work, th' Effect of Art is void.
For Physick can but mend our crazie State,
Patch an old Building, not a new create.
Arcite is doom'd to die in all his Pride,   770
Must leave his Youth, and yield his beauteous Bride,
Gain'd hardly, against Right, and unenjoy'd.

When 'twas declar'd, all Hope of Life was past,
Conscience, that of all Physick works the last,
Caus'd him to send for *Emily* in haste.   775
With her, at his desire, came *Palamon*;
Then on his Pillow rais'd, he thus begun.
No Language can express the smallest part
Of what I feel, and suffer in my Heart,
For you, whom best I love and value most;   780
But to your Service I bequeath my Ghost;
Which from this mortal Body when unty'd,
Unseen, unheard, shall hover at your Side;
Nor fright you waking, nor your Sleep offend,
But wait officious, and your Steps attend: 785
How I have lov'd, excuse my faltring Tongue,
My Spirit's feeble, and my Pains are strong:
This I may say, I only grieve to die
Because I lose my charming *Emily*:
To die, when Heav'n had put you in my Pow'r,   790
Fate could not chuse a more malicious Hour!
What greater Curse cou'd envious Fortune give,
Than just to die, when I began to live!
Vain Men, how vanishing a Bliss we crave,
Now warm in Love, now with'ring in the Grave!   795
Never, O never more to see the Sun!
Still dark, in a damp Vault, and still alone!
This Fate is common; but I lose my Breath
Near Bliss, and yet not bless'd before my Death.
Farewell; but take me dying in your Arms,   800
'Tis all I can enjoy of all your Charms:
This Hand I cannot but in Death resign;
Ah, could I live! But while I live 'tis mine.
I feel my End approach, and thus embrac'd,
Am pleas'd to die; but hear me speak my last.   805
Ah! my sweet Foe, for you, and you alone,
I broke my Faith with injur'd *Palamon*.
But Love the Sense of Right and Wrong confounds,
Strong Love and proud Ambition have no Bounds.
And much I doubt, shou'd Heav'n my Life prolong,   810
I shou'd return to justifie my Wrong:
For while my former Flames remain within,

Repentance is but want of Pow'r to sin.
With mortal Hatred I pursu'd his Life,
Nor he, nor you, were guilty of the Strife;   815
Nor I, but as I lov'd: Yet all combin'd,
Your Beauty, and my Impotence of Mind;
And his concurrent Flame, that blew my Fire;
For still our Kindred Souls had one Desire.
He had a Moments Right in point of Time;   820
Had I seen first, then his had been the Crime.
Fate made in mine, and justified his Right;
Nor holds this Earth a more deserving Knight,
For Vertue, Valour, and for Noble Blood,
Truth, Honour, all that is compriz'd in Good;   825
So help me Heav'n, in all the World is none
So worthy to be lov'd as *Palamon.*
He loves you too; with such a holy Fire,
As will not, cannot but with Life expire:
Our vow'd Affections both have often try'd,   830
Nor any Love but yours cou'd ours divide.
Then by my Loves inviolable Band,
By my long Suff'ring, and my short Command,
If e'er you plight your Vows when I am gone,
Have pity on the faithful *Palamon.*   835
    This was his last; for Death came on amain,
And exercis'd below, his Iron Reign;
Then upward, to the Seat of Life he goes;
Sense fled before him, what he touch'd he froze:
Yet cou'd he not his closing Eyes withdraw,   840
Though less and less of *Emily* he saw:
So, speechless, for a little space he lay;
Then grasp'd the Hand he held, and sigh'd his Soul away.
    But whither went his Soul, let such relate
Who search the Secrets of the future State: 845
Divines can say but what themselves believe;
Strong Proofs they have, but not demonstrative:
For, were all plain, then all Sides must agree,
And Faith it self be lost in Certainty.
To live uprightly then is sure the best,   850
To save our selves, and not to damn the rest.
The Soul of *Arcite* went, where Heathens go,

Who better live than we, though less they know.
   In *Palamon* a manly Grief appears;
Silent, he wept, asham'd to shew his Tears: 855
Emilia shriek'd but once, and then oppress'd
With Sorrow, sunk upon her Lovers Breast:
Till *Theseus* in his Arms convey'd with Care,
Far from so sad a Sight, the swooning Fair.
'Twere loss of Time her Sorrow to relate;   860
Ill bears the Sex a youthful Lover's Fate,
When just approaching to the Nuptial State.
But like a low-hung Cloud, it rains so fast,
That all at once it falls, and cannot last.
The Face of Things is chang'd, and *Athens* now,   865
That laugh'd so late, becomes the Scene of Woe:
Matrons and Maids, both Sexes, ev'ry State,
With Tears lament the Knight's untimely Fate.
Not greater Grief in falling *Troy* was seen
For *Hector*'s Death; but *Hector* was not then.   870
Old Men with Dust deform'd their hoary Hair,
The Women beat their Breasts, their Cheeks they tear.
Why would'st thou go, with one Consent they cry,
When thou hadst Gold enough, and *Emily*!
   Theseus himself, who shou'd have cheer'd the Grief   875
Of others, wanted now the same Relief.
Old *Egeus* only could revive his Son,
Who various Changes of the World had known;
And strange Vicissitudes of Humane Fate,
Still alt'ring, never in a steady State: 880
Good after Ill, and after Pain, Delight;
Alternate, like the Scenes of Day and Night:
Since ev'ry Man who lives, is born to die,
And none can boast sincere Felicity.
With equal Mind, what happens, let us bear,   885
Nor joy, nor grieve too much for Things beyond our Care.
Like Pilgrims, to th' appointed Place we tend;
The World's an Inn, and Death the Journeys End.

Ev'n Kings but play; and when their Part is done,
Some other, worse or better, mount the Throne.   890
With Words like these the Crowd was satisfi'd,
And so they would have been, had *Theseus* dy'd.

But he, their King, was lab'ring in his Mind,
A fitting Place for Fun'ral Pomps to find,
Which were in Honour of the Dead design'd.   895
And after long Debate, at last he found
(As Love it self had mark'd the Spot of Ground)
That Grove for ever green, that conscious Lawnd,
Where he with *Palamon* fought Hand to Hand:
That where he fed his amorous Desires   900
With soft Complaints, and felt his hottest Fires,
There other Flames might waste his Earthly Part,
And burn his Limbs, where Love had burn'd his Heart.
     This once resolv'd, the Peasants were enjoin'd
Sere Wood, and Firs, and dodder'd Oaks to find.   905
With sounding Axes to the Grove they go,
Fell, split, and lay the Fewel on a Row,
Vulcanian Food: A Bier is next prepar'd,
On which the lifeless Body should be rear'd,
Cover'd with Cloth of Gold, on which was laid   910
The Corps of *Arcite*, in like Robes array'd.
White Gloves were on his Hands, and on his Head
A Wreath of Laurel, mix'd with Myrtle, spread.
A Sword keen-edg'd within his Right he held,
The warlike Emblem of the conquer'd Field: 915
Bare was his manly Visage on the Bier;
Menac'd his Count'nance; ev'n in Death severe.
Then to the Palace-Hall they bore the Knight,
To lie in solemn State, a Publick Sight.
Groans, Cries, and Howlings fill the crowded Place,   920
And unaffected Sorrow sat on ev'ry Face.
Sad *Palamon* above the rest appears,
In Sable Garments, dew'd with gushing Tears:
His Aubourn Locks on either Shoulder flow'd,
Which to the Fun'ral of his Friend he vow'd: 925
But *Emily*, as Chief, was next his Side,
A Virgin-Widow, and a *Mourning Bride*.
     And that the Princely Obsequies might be
Perform'd according to his high Degree,
The Steed that bore him living to the Fight,   930
Was trapp'd with polish'd Steel, all shining bright,
And cover'd with th' Atchievements of the Knight.

The Riders rode abreast, and one his Shield,
His Lance of Cornel-wood another held;
The third his Bow, and, glorious to behold,   935
The costly Quiver, all of burnish'd Gold.
The Noblest of the *Grecians* next appear,
And weeping, on their Shoulders bore the Bier;
With sober Pace they march'd, and often staid,
And through the Master-Street the Corps convey'd.   940
The Houses to their Tops with Black were spread,
And ev'n the Pavements were with Mourning hid.
The Right-side of the Pall old *Egeus* kept,
And on the Left the Royal *Theseus* wept:
Each bore a Golden Bowl of Work Divine,   945
With Honey fill'd, and Milk, and mix'd with ruddy Wine.
Then *Palamon* the Kinsman of the Slain,
And after him appear'd th' Illustrious Train:
To grace the Pomp, came *Emily* the Bright,
With cover'd Fire, the Fun'ral Pile to light.   950
With high Devotion was the Service made,
And all the Rites of Pagan-Honour paid:
So lofty was the Pile, a *Parthian* Bow,
With Vigour drawn, must send the Shaft below.
The Bottom was full twenty Fathom broad,   955
With crackling Straw beneath in due Proportion strow'd.
The Fabrick seem'd a Wood of rising Green,
With Sulphur and Bitumen cast between,
To feed the Flames: The Trees were unctuous Fir,   ⎫
And Mountain-Ash, the Mother of the Spear;   ⎬   960
The Mourner Eugh, and Builder Oak were there: ⎭
The Beech, the swimming Alder, and the Plane,   ⎫
Hard Box, and Linden of a softer Grain,   ⎬
And Laurels, which the Gods for Conqu'ring Chiefs ordain. ⎭
How they were rank'd, shall rest untold by me,   965
With nameless Nymphs that liv'd in ev'ry Tree;
Nor how the Dryads, and the Woodland Train,
Disherited, ran howling o'er the Plain:
Nor how the Birds to Foreign Seats repair'd,
Or Beasts, that bolted out, and saw the Forest bar'd: 970
Nor how the Ground, now clear'd, with gastly Fright
Beheld the sudden Sun, a Stranger to the Light.

The Straw, as first I said, was laid below;
Of Chips and Sere-wood was the second Row;
The third of Greens, and Timber newly fell'd;   975
The fourth high Stage the fragrant Odours held,
And Pearls, and Precious Stones, and rich Array;
In midst of which, embalm'd, the Body lay.
The Service sung, the Maid with mourning Eyes
The Stubble fir'd; the smouldring Flames arise: 980
This Office done, she sunk upon the Ground;
But what she spoke, recover'd from her Swoond,
I want the Wit in moving Words to dress;
But by themselves the tender Sex may guess.
While the devouring Fire was burning fast,   985
Rich Jewels in the Flame the Wealthy cast;
And some their Shields, and some their Lances threw,
And gave the Warriour's Ghost a Warriour's Due.
Full Bowls of Wine, of Honey, Milk, and Blood,
Were pour'd upon the Pile of burning Wood,   990
And hissing Flames receive, and hungry lick the Food.
Then thrice the mounted Squadrons ride around
The Fire, and *Arcite*'s Name they thrice resound:
Hail, and Farewell, they shouted thrice amain,
Thrice facing to the Left, and thrice they turn'd again: 995
Still as they turn'd, they beat their clatt'ring Shields;
The Women mix their Cries; and Clamour fills the Fields.
The warlike Wakes continu'd all the Night,
And Fun'ral Games were plaid at new-returning Light:
Who naked wrestl'd best, besmear'd with Oil,   1000
Or who with Gantlets gave or took the Foil,
I will not tell you, nor wou'd you attend;
But briefly haste to my long Stories End.
    I pass the rest; the Year was fully mourn'd,
And *Palamon* long since to *Thebes* return'd,   1005
When, by the *Grecians* general Consent,
At *Athens Theseus* held his Parliament:
Among the Laws that pass'd, it was decreed,
That conquer'd *Thebes* from Bondage shou'd be freed;
Reserving Homage to th' *Athenian* Throne,   1010
To which the Sov'reign summon'd *Palamon*.
Unknowing of the Cause, he took his Way,

Mournful in Mind, and still in Black Array.
    The Monarch mounts the Throne, and plac'd on high,
Commands into the Court the beauteous *Emily*:   1015
So call'd, she came; the Senate rose, and paid
Becoming Rev'rence to the Royal Maid.
And first soft Whispers through th' Assembly went:
With silent Wonder then they watch'd th' Event:
All hush'd, the King arose with awful Grace,   1020
Deep Thought was in his Breast, and Counsel in his Face.
At length he sigh'd; and having first prepar'd
Th' attentive Audience, thus his Will declar'd.
    The Cause and Spring of Motion, from above
Hung down on Earth the Golden Chain of Love: 1025
Great was th' Effect, and high was his Intent,
When Peace among the jarring Seeds he sent.
Fire, Flood, and Earth, and Air by this were bound,
And Love, the common Link, the new Creation crown'd.
The Chain still holds; for though the Forms decay,   1030
Eternal Matter never wears away:
The same First Mover certain Bounds has plac'd,
How long those perishable Forms shall last;
Nor can they last beyond the Time assign'd
By that All-seeing, and All-making Mind: 1035
Shorten their Hours they may; for Will is free;
But never pass th' appointed Destiny.
So Men oppress'd, when weary of their Breath,
Throw off the Burden, and subborn their Death.
Then since those Forms begin, and have their End,   1040
On some unalter'd Cause they sure depend:
Parts of the Whole are we; but God the Whole;
Who gives us Life, and animating Soul.
For Nature cannot from a Part derive
That Being, which the Whole can only give: 1045
He perfect, stable; but imperfect We,
Subject to Change, and diff'rent in Degree.
Plants, Beasts, and Man; and as our Organs are,
We more or less of his Perfection share.
But by a long Descent, th' Etherial Fire   1050
Corrupts; and Forms, the mortal Part, expire:
As he withdraws his Vertue, so they pass,

And the same Matter makes another Mass:
This Law th' Omniscient Pow'r was pleas'd to give,
That ev'ry Kind should by Succession live;   1055
That Individuals die, his Will ordains;
The propagated Species still remains.
The Monarch Oak, the Patriarch of the Trees,
Shoots rising up, and spreads by slow Degrees:
Three Centuries he grows, and three he stays,   1060
Supreme in State; and in three more decays:
So wears the paving Pebble in the Street,
And Towns and Tow'rs their fatal Periods meet.
So Rivers, rapid once, now naked lie,
Forsaken of their Springs; and leave their Channels dry.   1065
So Man, at first a Drop, dilates with Heat,
Then form'd, the little Heart begins to beat;
Secret he feeds, unknowing in the Cell;
At length, for Hatching ripe, he breaks the Shell,
And struggles into Breath, and cries for Aid;   1070
Then, helpless, in his Mothers Lap is laid.
He creeps, he walks, and issuing into Man,
Grudges their Life, from whence his own began.
Retchless of Laws, affects to rule alone,
Anxious to reign, and restless on the Throne: 1075
First vegetive, then feels, and reasons last;
Rich of Three Souls, and lives all three to waste.
Some thus; but thousands more in Flow'r of Age:
For few arrive to run the latter Stage.
Sunk in the first, in Battel some are slain,   1080
And others whelm'd beneath the stormy Main.
What makes all this, but *Jupiter* the King,
At whose Command we perish, and we spring?
Then 'tis our best, since thus ordain'd to die,
To make a Vertue of Necessity.   1085
Take what he gives, since to rebel is vain;
The Bad grows better, which we well sustain:
And cou'd we chuse the Time, and chuse aright,
'Tis best to die, our Honour at the height.
When we have done our Ancestors no Shame,   1090
But serv'd our Friends, and well secur'd our Fame;
Then should we wish our happy Life to close,

And leave no more for Fortune to dispose:
So should we make our Death a glad Relief,
From future Shame, from Sickness, and from Grief: 1095
Enjoying while we live the present Hour,
And dying in our Excellence, and Flow'r.
Then round our Death-bed ev'ry Friend shou'd run,
And joy us of our Conquest, early won:
While the malicious World with envious Tears   1100
Shou'd grudge our happy End, and wish it Theirs.
Since then our *Arcite* is with Honour dead,
Why shou'd we mourn, that he so soon is freed,
Or call untimely, what the Gods decreed?
With Grief as just, a Friend may be deplor'd,   1105
From a foul Prison to free Air restor'd.
Ought he to thank his Kinsman, or his Wife,
Cou'd Tears recall him into wretched Life!
Their Sorrow hurts themselves; on him is lost;
And worse than both, offends his happy Ghost.   1110
What then remains, but after past Annoy,
To take the good Vicissitude of Joy?
To thank the gracious Gods for what they give,
Possess our Souls, and while we live, to live?
Ordain we then two Sorrows to combine,   1115
And in one Point th' Extremes of Grief to join;
That thence resulting Joy may be renew'd,
As jarring Notes in Harmony conclude.
Then I propose, that *Palamon* shall be
In Marriage join'd with beauteous *Emily*;   1120
For which already I have gain'd th' Assent
Of my free People in full Parliament.
Long Love to her has born the faithful Knight,
And well deserv'd, had Fortune done him Right:
'Tis time to mend her Fault; since *Emily*   1125
By *Arcite*'s Death from former Vows is free:
If you, Fair Sister, ratifie th' Accord,
And take him for your Husband, and your Lord.
'Tis no Dishonour to confer your Grace
On one descended from a Royal Race: 1130
And were he less, yet Years of Service past
From grateful Souls exact Reward at last:

Pity is Heav'ns and yours: Nor can she find
A Throne so soft as in a Womans Mind.

He said; she blush'd; and as o'eraw'd by Might,   1135
Seem'd to give *Theseus*, what she gave the Knight.
Then turning to the *Theban*, thus he said;
Small Arguments are needful to persuade
Your Temper to comply with my Command;
And speaking thus, he gave *Emilia*'s Hand.   1140
Smil'd *Venus*, to behold her own true Knight
Obtain the Conquest, though he lost the Fight,
And bless'd with Nuptial Bliss the sweet laborious Night. }
Eros, and *Anteros*, on either Side,
One fir'd the Bridegroom, and one warm'd the Bride;   1145
And long-attending *Hymen* from above
Showr'd on the Bed the whole *Idalian* Grove.
All of a Tenour was their After-Life,
No Day discolour'd with Domestick Strife;
No Jealousie, but mutual Truth believ'd,   1150
Secure Repose, and Kindness undeceiv'd.
Thus Heav'n, beyond the Compass of his Thought,
Sent him the Blessing he so dearly bought.

So may the Queen of Love long Duty bless,
And all true Lovers find the same Success.   1155

To my Honour'd Kinsman, JOHN DRIDEN, OF CHESTERTON IN THE COUNTY OF HUNTINGDON, ESQUIRE

How Bless'd is He, who leads a Country Life,
Unvex'd with anxious Cares, and void of Strife!
Who studying Peace, and shunning Civil Rage,
Enjoy'd his Youth, and now enjoys his Age:
All who deserve his Love, he makes his own;   5
And, to be lov'd himself, needs only to be known.

Just, Good, and Wise, contending Neighbours come,
From your Award, to wait their final Doom; }
And, Foes before, return in Friendship home.

Without their Cost, you terminate the Cause;   10
And save th' Expence of long Litigious Laws:
Where Suits are travers'd; and so little won,
That he who conquers, is but last undone:
Such are not your Decrees; but so design'd,
The Sanction leaves a lasting Peace behind;   } 15
Like your own Soul, Serene; a Pattern of your Mind.

   Promoting Concord, and composing Strife,
Lord of your self, uncumber'd with a Wife;
Where, for a Year, a Month, perhaps a Night,
Long Penitence succeeds a short Delight: 20
Minds are so hardly match'd, that ev'n the first,
Though pair'd by Heav'n, in Paradise, were curs'd.
For Man and Woman, though in one they grow,
Yet, first or last, return again to Two.
He to God's Image, She to His was made;   25
So, farther from the Fount, the Stream at random stray'd.

   How cou'd He stand, when put to double Pain,
He must a Weaker than himself sustain!
Each might have stood perhaps; but each alone;
Two Wrestlers help to pull each other down.   30

   Not that my Verse wou'd blemish all the Fair;
But yet, if *some* be Bad, 'tis Wisdom to beware;   }
And better shun the Bait, than struggle in the Snare.
Thus have you shunn'd, and shun the married State,
Trusting as little as you can to Fate.   35

   No Porter guards the Passage of your Door;
T' admit the Wealthy, and exclude the Poor:
For God, who gave the Riches, gave the Heart
To sanctifie the Whole, by giving Part:
Heav'n, who foresaw the Will, the Means has wrought,   40
And to the Second Son, a Blessing brought:
The First-begotten had his Father's Share;
But you, like *Jacob*, are *Rebecca*'s Heir.

   So may your Stores, and fruitful Fields increase;
And ever be you bless'd, who live to bless.   45
As *Ceres* sow'd, where e'er her Chariot flew;
As Heav'n in Desarts rain'd the Bread of Dew,
So free to Many, to Relations most,
You feed with Manna your own *Israel*-Host.

With Crowds attended of your ancient Race, 50
You seek the Champian-Sports, or Sylvan-Chace:
With well-breath'd Beagles, you surround the Wood;
Ev'n then, industrious of the Common Good:
And often have you brought the wily Fox
To suffer for the Firstlings of the Flocks; 55
Chas'd ev'n amid the Folds; and made to bleed,
Like Felons, where they did the murd'rous Deed.
This fiery Game, your active Youth maintain'd;
Not yet, by Years extinguish'd, though restrain'd:
You season still with Sports your serious Hours; 60
For Age but tastes of Pleasures, Youth devours.
The Hare, in Pastures or in Plains is found,
Emblem of Humane Life, who runs the Round;
And, after all his wand'ring Ways are done,
His Circle fills, and ends where he begun, 65
Just as the Setting meets the Rising Sun.

Thus Princes ease their Cares: But happier he,
Who seeks not Pleasure thro' Necessity,
Than such as once on slipp'ry Thrones were plac'd;
And chasing, sigh to think themselves are chas'd. 70

So liv'd our Sires, e'er Doctors learn'd to kill,
And multiply'd with theirs, the Weekly Bill:
The first Physicians by Debauch were made:
Excess began, and Sloth sustains the Trade.
Pity the gen'rous Kind their Cares bestow 75
To search forbidden Truths; (a Sin to know:)
To which, if Humane Science cou'd attain,
The Doom of Death, pronounc'd by God, were vain.
In vain the Leech wou'd interpose Delay;
Fate fastens first, and vindicates the Prey. 80
What Help from Arts Endeavours can we have!
Guibbons but guesses, nor is sure to save:
But *Maurus* sweeps whole Parishes, and Peoples ev'ry Grave.

And no more Mercy to Mankind will use,
Than when he robb'd and murder'd *Maro*'s Muse. 85
Wou'dst thou be soon dispatch'd, and perish whole?
Trust *Maurus* with thy Life, and *M-lb—rn* with thy Soul.

By Chace our long-liv'd Fathers earn'd their Food;
Toil strung the Nerves, and purifi'd the Blood:

But we, their Sons, a pamper'd Race of Men,   90
Are dwindl'd down to threescore Years and ten.
Better to hunt in Fields, for Health unbought,
Than fee the Doctor for a nauseous Draught.
The Wise, for Cure, on Exercise depend;
God never made his Work, for Man to mend.   95
    The Tree of Knowledge, once in *Eden* plac'd,
Was easie found, but was forbid the Taste:
O, had our Grandsire walk'd without his Wife,
He first had sought the better Plant of Life!
Now, both are lost: Yet, wandring in the dark,   100
Physicians for the Tree, have found the Bark:
They, lab'ring for Relief of Humane Kind,
With sharpen'd Sight some Remedies may find;
Th' Apothecary-Train is wholly blind.
From Files, a Random-*Recipe* they take,   105
And Many Deaths of One Prescription make.
Garth, gen'rous as his Muse, prescribes and gives;
The Shop-man sells; and by Destruction lives:
Ungrateful Tribe! who, like the Viper's Brood,
From Med'cine issuing, suck their Mother's Blood!   110
Let These obey; and let the Learn'd prescribe;
That Men may die, without a double Bribe:
Let Them, but under their Superiours kill;
When Doctors first have sign'd the bloody Bill:
He scapes the best, who Nature to repair,   115
Draws Phisick from the Fields, in Draughts of Vital Air.
    You hoard not Health, for your own private Use;
But on the Publick spend the rich Produce:
When, often urg'd, unwilling to be Great,
Your Country calls you from your lov'd Retreat,   120
And sends to Senates, charg'd with Common Care,
Which none more shuns; and none can better bear.
Where cou'd they find another form'd so fit,
To poise, with solid Sense, a spritely Wit!
Were these both wanting, (as they both abound)   125
Where cou'd so firm Integrity be found?
    Well-born, and Wealthy; wanting no Support,
You steer betwixt the Country and the Court:
Nor gratifie whate'er the Great desire,

Nor grudging give, what Publick Needs require.   130
Part must be left, a Fund when Foes invade;
And Part employ'd to roll the Watry Trade:
Ev'n *Canaans* happy Land, when worn with Toil,
Requir'd a Sabbath-Year, to mend the meagre Soil.

    Good Senators, (and such are you,) so give,   135
That Kings may be supply'd, the People thrive.
And He, when Want requires, is truly Wise,
Who slights not Foreign Aids, nor over-buys;
But, on our Native Strength, in time of need, relies.
Munster was bought, we boast not the Success;   140
Who fights for Gain, for greater, makes his Peace.

    Our Foes, compell'd by Need, have Peace embrac'd:
The Peace both Parties want, is like to last:
Which, if secure, securely we may trade;
Or, not secure, shou'd never have been made.   145
Safe in our selves, while on our selves we stand,
The Sea is ours, and that defends the Land.
Be, then, the Naval Stores the Nations Care,
New Ships to build, and batter'd to repair.

    Observe the War, in ev'ry Annual Course;   150
What has been done, was done with *British* Force:
Namur Subdu'd, is *England*'s Palm alone;
The Rest Besieg'd; but we Constrain'd the Town:
We saw th' Event that follow'd our Success;
France, though pretending Arms, pursu'd the Peace;   155
Oblig'd, by one sole Treaty, to restore
What Twenty Years of War had won before.
Enough for *Europe* has our *Albion* fought:
Let us enjoy the Peace our Blood has bought.
When once the *Persian* King was put to Flight,   160
The weary *Macedons* refus'd to fight:
Themselves their own Mortality confess'd;
And left the Son of *Jove*, to quarrel for the rest.

    Ev'n Victors are by Victories undone;
Thus *Hannibal*, with Foreign Laurels won,   165
To *Carthage* was recall'd, too late to keep his own.
While sore of Battel, while our Wounds are green,
Why shou'd we tempt the doubtful Dye agen?
In Wars renew'd, uncertain of Success,

Sure of a Share, as Umpires of the Peace. 170
    A Patriot, both the King and Country serves;
Prerogative, and Privilege preserves:
Of Each, our Laws the certain Limit show;
One must not ebb, nor t'other overflow:
Betwixt the Prince and Parliament we stand; 175
The Barriers of the State on either Hand:
May neither overflow, for then they drown the Land.
When both are full, they feed our bless'd Abode;
Like those, that water'd once, the Paradise of God.
    Some Overpoise of Sway, by Turns they share; 180
In Peace the People, and the Prince in War:
Consuls of mod'rate Pow'r in Calms were made;
When the *Gauls* came, one sole Dictator sway'd.
    Patriots, in Peace, assert the Peoples Right;
With noble Stubbornness resisting Might: 185
No Lawless Mandates from the Court receive,
Nor lend by Force; but in a Body give.
Such was your gen'rous Grandsire; free to grant
In Parliaments, that weigh'd their Prince's Want:
But so tenacious of the Common Cause, 190
As not to lend the King against his Laws.
And, in a lothsom Dungeon doom'd to lie,
In Bonds retain'd his Birthright Liberty,
And sham'd Oppression, till it set him free.
    O true Descendent of a Patriot Line, 195
Who, while thou shar'st their Lustre, lend'st 'em thine,
Vouchsafe this Picture of thy Soul to see;
'Tis so far Good, as it resembles thee:
The Beauties to th' Original I owe;
Which, when I miss, my own Defects I show: 200
Nor think the Kindred-Muses thy Disgrace;
A Poet is not born in ev'ry Race.
Two of a House, few Ages can afford;
One to perform, another to record.
Praise-worthy Actions are by thee embrac'd; 205
And 'tis my Praise, to make thy Praises last.
For ev'n when Death dissolves our Humane Frame,
The Soul returns to Heav'n, from whence it came;
Earth keeps the Body, Verse preserves the Fame.

MELEAGER AND ATALANTA,
Out of the Eighth Book of
OVID'S Metamorphosis

CONNEXION to the Former STORY

Ovid, *having told how* Theseus *had freed* Athens *from the Tribute of Chil-dren,* (*which was impos'd on them by* Minos *King of* Creta) *by killing the* Minotaur, *here makes a Digression to the Story of* Meleager *and* Atalanta, *which is one of the most inartificial Connexions in all the* Metamorphoses: *For he only says, that* Theseus *obtain'd such Honour from that Combate, that* 5 *all* Greece *had recourse to him in their Necessities; and, amongst others,* Calydon, *though the* Heroe *of that Country, Prince* Meleager, *was then living.*

FROM him, the *Caledonians* sought Relief;
Tho' valiant *Meleagrus* was their Chief.
The Cause, a Boar, who ravag'd far and near:
Of *Cynthia*'s Wrath, th' avenging Minister.
For *Oeneus* with Autumnal Plenty bless'd,   5
By Gifts to Heav'n his Gratitude express'd:
Cull'd Sheafs, to *Ceres;* to *Lyæus,* Wine;   ⎫
To *Pan,* and *Pales,* offer'd Sheep and Kine;   ⎬
And Fat of Olives, to *Minerva*'s Shrine.   ⎭
Beginning from the Rural Gods, his Hand   10
Was lib'ral to the Pow'rs of high Command:
Each Deity in ev'ry Kind was bless'd,
Till at *Diana*'s Fane th' invidious Honour ceas'd.
   Wrath touches ev'n the Gods; the Queen of Night
Fir'd with Disdain, and jealous of her Right,   15
Unhonour'd though I am, at least, said she,
Not unreveng'd that impious Act shall be.
Swift as the Word, she sped the Boar away,
With Charge on those devoted Fields to prey.
No larger Bulls th' *Ægyptian* Pastures feed,   20
And none so large *Sicilian* Meadows breed:
His Eye-balls glare with Fire suffus'd with Blood;
His Neck shoots up a thick-set thorny Wood;
His bristled Back a Trench impal'd appears,

And stands erected, like a Field of Spears.   25
Froth fills his Chaps, he sends a grunting Sound,
And part he churns, and part befoams the Ground.
For Tusks with *Indian* Elephants he strove,
And *Jove*'s own Thunder from his Mouth he drove.
He burns the Leaves; the scorching Blast invades   30
The tender Corn, and shrivels up the Blades:
Or suff'ring not their yellow Beards to rear,
He tramples down the Spikes, and intercepts the Year.
In vain the Barns expect their promis'd Load,
Nor Barns at home, nor Reeks are heap'd abroad: 35
In vain the Hinds the Threshing-Floor prepare,
And exercise their Flails in empty Air.
With Olives ever-green the Ground is strow'd,
And Grapes ungather'd shed their gen'rous Blood.
Amid the Fold he rages, nor the Sheep   40
Their Shepherds, nor the Grooms their Bulls can keep.
    From Fields to Walls the frighted Rabble run,
Nor think themselves secure within the Town:
Till *Meleagros*, and his chosen Crew,
Contemn the Danger, and the Praise pursue.   45
Fair *Leda*'s Twins (in time to Stars decreed)
One fought on Foot, one curb'd the fiery Steed;
Then issu'd forth fam'd *Jason* after These,
Who mann'd the foremost Ship that sail'd the Seas;
Then *Theseus* join'd with bold *Perithous* came;   50
A single Concord in a double Name:
The *Thestian* Sons, *Idas* who swiftly ran,
And *Ceneus*, once a Woman, now a Man.
Lynceus, with Eagles Eyes, and Lions Heart;
Leucippus, with his never-erring Dart;   55
Acastus, Phileus, Phœnix, Telamon,   ⎫
Echion, Lelex, and *Eurytion,*   ⎬
Achilles Father, and Great *Phocus* Son; ⎭
Dryas the Fierce, and *Hippasus* the Strong;
With twice old *Iolas*, and *Nestor* then but young.   60
Laertes active, and *Ancæus* bold;   ⎫
Mopsus the Sage, who future Things foretold;   ⎬
And t'other Seer, yet by his Wife* unsold.   **Amphiaraus.*⎭
A thousand others of immortal Fame;

Among the rest, fair *Atalanta* came,   65
Grace of the Woods: A Diamond Buckle bound
Her Vest behind, that else had flow'd upon the Ground,
And shew'd her buskin'd Legs; her Head was bare,
But for her Native Ornament of Hair;
Which in a simple Knot was ty'd above,   70
Sweet Negligence! unheeded Bait of Love!
Her sounding Quiver, on her Shoulder ty'd,
One Hand a Dart, and one a Bow supply'd.
Such was her Face, as in a Nymph display'd
A fair fierce Boy, or in a Boy betray'd   } 75
The blushing Beauties of a modest Maid.
The *Caledonian* Chief at once the Dame
Beheld, at once his Heart receiv'd the Flame,
With Heav'ns averse. O happy Youth, he cry'd,
For whom thy Fates reserve so fair a Bride!   80
He sigh'd, and had no leisure more to say;
His Honour call'd his Eyes another way,   }
And forc'd him to pursue the now neglected Prey.

    There stood a Forest on a Mountains Brow,
Which over-look'd the shaded Plains below.   85
No sounding Ax presum'd those Trees to bite;
Coeval with the World, a venerable Sight.
The *Heroes* there arriv'd, some spread around
The Toils; some search the Footsteps on the Ground: }
Some from the Chains the faithful Dogs unbound.   90
Of Action eager, and intent in Thought,
The Chiefs their honourable Danger sought:
A Valley stood below; the common Drain
Of Waters from above, and falling Rain:
The Bottom was a moist and marshy Ground,   95
Whose Edges were with bending Oziers crown'd:
The knotty Bulrush next in Order stood,
And all within of Reeds a trembling Wood.
    From hence the Boar was rows'd, and sprung amain
Like Lightning sudden, on the Warriour-Train;   100
Beats down the Trees before him, shakes the Ground,   }
The Forest echoes to the crackling Sound;
Shout the fierce Youth, and Clamours ring around.   }
All stood with their protended Spears prepar'd,

With broad Steel Heads, and brandish'd Weapons glar'd.   10

The Beast impetuous with his Tusks aside
Deals glancing Wounds; the fearful Dogs divide:
All spend their Mouth aloof, but none abide.

Echion threw the first, but miss'd his Mark,
And stuck his Boar-spear on a Maples Bark.   11
Then *Jason*: and his Javelin seem'd to take,
But fail'd with over-force, and whiz'd above his Back.
Mopsus was next; but e'er he threw, address'd
To *Phœbus*, thus: O Patron, help thy Priest:
If I adore, and ever have ador'd   11
Thy Pow'r Divine, thy present Aid afford;
That I may reach the Beast. The God allow'd
His Pray'r, and smiling, gave him what he cou'd:
He reach'd the Savage, but no Blood he drew,
Dian, unarm'd the Javelin as it flew.   12

   This chaf'd the Boar, his Nostrils Flames expire,
And his red Eye-balls roll with living Fire.
Whirl'd from a Sling, or from an Engine thrown,
Amid the Foes, so flies a mighty Stone,
As flew the Beast: The Left Wing put to flight,   12
The Chiefs o'er-born, he rushes on the Right.
Empalamos and *Pelagon* he laid
In Dust, and next to Death, but for their Fellows Aid.
Onesimus far'd worse, prepar'd to fly,
The fatal Fang drove deep within his Thigh,   13
And cut the Nerves: The Nerves no more sustain
The Bulk; the Bulk unprop'd, falls headlong on the Plain.

   Nestor had fail'd the Fall of *Troy* to see,
But leaning on his Lance, he vaulted on a Tree;
Then gath'ring up his Feet, look'd down with Fear,   13
And thought his monstrous Foe was still too near.
Against a Stump his Tusk the Monster grinds,
And in the sharpen'd Edge new Vigour finds;
Then, trusting to his Arms, young *Othrys* found,
And ranch'd his Hips with one continu'd Wound.   14
Now *Leda*'s Twins, the future Stars, appear;
White were their Habits, white their Horses were:
Conspicuous both, and both in act to throw,
Their trembling Lances brandish'd at the Foe:

Nor had they miss'd; but he to Thickets fled,   145
Conceal'd from aiming Spears, not pervious to the Steed.
But *Telamon* rush'd in, and happ'd to meet
A rising Root, that held his fastned Feet;
So down he fell; whom, sprawling on the Ground,
His Brother from the Wooden Gyves unbound.   150
  Mean time the Virgin-Huntress was not slow
T' expel the Shaft from her contracted Bow:
Beneath his Ear the fastned Arrow stood,
And from the Wound appear'd the trickling Blood.
She blush'd for Joy: But *Meleagros* rais'd   155
His voice with loud Applause, and the fair Archer prais'd.
He was the first to see, and first to show
His Friends the Marks of the successful Blow.
Nor shall thy Valour want the Praises due,
He said; a vertuous Envy seiz'd the Crew.   160
They shout; the Shouting animates their Hearts,
And all at once employ their thronging Darts:
But out of Order thrown, in Air they joyn;
And Multitude makes frustrate the Design.
With both his Hands the proud *Anceus* takes,   165
And flourishes his double-biting Ax:
Then forward to his Fate, he took a Stride
Before the rest, and to his Fellows cry'd,
Give place, and mark the diff'rence, if you can,
Between a Woman Warriour, and a Man;   170
The Boar is doom'd; nor though *Diana* lend
Her Aid, *Diana* can her Beast defend.
Thus boasted he; then stretch'd, on Tiptoe stood,
Secure to make his empty Promise good.
But the more wary Beast prevents the Blow,   175
And upward rips the Groin of his audacious Foe.
Anceus falls; his Bowels from the Wound
Rush out, and clotter'd Blood distains the Ground.
  Perithous, no small Portion of the War
Press'd on, and shook his Lance: To whom from far   180
Thus *Theseus* cry'd; O stay, my better Part,
My more than Mistress; of my Heart, the Heart.
The Strong may fight aloof; *Anceus* try'd
His Force too near, and by presuming dy'd:

He said, and while he spake his Javelin threw,   185
Hissing in Air th' unerring Weapon flew;
But on an Arm of Oak, that stood betwixt
The Marks-man and the Mark, his Lance he fixt.
    Once more bold *Jason* threw, but fail'd to wound
The Boar, and slew an undeserving Hound;   } 190
And through the Dog the Dart was nail'd to Ground.
    Two Spears from *Meleager*'s Hand were sent,
With equal Force, but various in th' Event:
The first was fix'd in Earth, the second stood
On the Boars bristled Back, and deeply drank his Blood.   195
Now while the tortur'd Salvage turns around,
And flings about his Foam, impatient of the Wound,
The Wounds great Author close at Hand, provokes
His Rage, and plyes him with redoubled Strokes;
Wheels as he wheels; and with his pointed Dart   200
Explores the nearest Passage to his Heart.
Quick, and more quick he spins in giddy Gires,
Then falls, and in much Foam his Soul expires.
This Act with Shouts Heav'n high the friendly Band
Applaud, and strain in theirs the Victour Hand.   205
Then all approach the Slain with vast Surprize,
Admire on what a Breadth of Earth he lies,
And scarce secure, reach out their Spears afar,
And blood their Points, to prove their Partnership of War.
    But he, the conqu'ring Chief, his Foot impress'd   210
On the strong Neck of that destructive Beast;
And gazing on the Nymph with ardent Eyes,
Accept, said he, fair *Nonacrine*, my Prize,
And, though inferiour, suffer me to join

My Labours, and my Part of Praise with thine: 215
At this presents her with the Tusky Head
And Chine, with rising Bristles roughly spread.
Glad, she receiv'd the Gift; and seem'd to take
With double Pleasure, for the Giver's sake.
The rest were seiz'd with sullen Discontent,   220
And a deaf Murmur through the Squadron went:
All envy'd; but the *Thestyan* Brethren show'd
The least Respect, and thus they vent their Spleen aloud:

Lay down those honour'd Spoils, nor think to share,
Weak Woman as thou art, the Prize of War: 225
Ours is the Title, thine a foreign Claim,
Since *Meleagros* from our Lineage came.
Trust not thy Beauty; but restore the Prize,
Which he, besotted on that Face and Eyes,
Would rend from us: At this, inflam'd with Spite,   230
From her they snatch the Gift, from him the Givers Right.

But soon th' impatient Prince his Fauchion drew,
And cry'd, Ye Robbers of another's Due,
Now learn the Diff'rence, at your proper Cost,
Betwixt true Valour, and an empty Boast.   235
At this advanc'd, and sudden as the Word,
In proud *Plexippus* Bosom plung'd the Sword:
Toxeus amaz'd, and with Amazement slow,
Or to revenge, or ward the coming Blow,
Stood doubting; and, while doubting thus he stood,   240
Receiv'd the Steel bath'd in his Brother's Blood.

Pleas'd with the first, unknown the second News,
Althea, to the Temples, pays their Dues,
For her Son's Conquest; when at length appear
Her griesly Brethren stretch'd upon the Bier: } 245
Pale at the sudden Sight, she chang'd her Cheer,
And with her Cheer her Robes; but hearing tell
The Cause, the Manner, and by whom they fell,
'Twas Grief no more, or Grief and Rage were one
Within her Soul; at last 'twas Rage alone;   250
Which burning upwards in succession dries
The Tears that stood consid'ring in her Eyes.

There lay a Log unlighted on the Hearth,
When she was lab'ring in the Throws of Birth
For th' unborn Chief; the Fatal Sisters came,   255
And rais'd it up, and toss'd it on the Flame:
Then on the Rock a scanty Measure place
Of Vital Flax, and turn'd the Wheel apace;
And turning sung, To this red Brand and thee,
O new-born Babe, we give an equal Destiny: 260
So vanish'd out of View. The frighted Dame
Sprung hasty from her Bed, and quench'd the Flame:

The Log in secret lock'd, she kept with Care,
And that, while thus preserv'd, preserv'd her Heir.
This Brand she now produc'd; and first she strows   265
The Hearth with Heaps of Chips, and after blows,
Thrice heav'd her Hand, and heav'd, she thrice repress'd: ⎫
The Sister and the Mother long contest   ⎬
Two doubtful Titles in one tender Breast: ⎭
And now her Eyes and Cheeks with Fury glow,   270
Now pale her Cheeks, her Eyes with Pity flow:
Now lowring Looks presage approaching Storms,
And now prevailing Love her Face reforms:
Resolv'd, she doubts again; the Tears she dry'd
With burning Rage, are by new Tears supply'd;   275
And as a Ship, which Winds and Waves assail,   ⎫
Now with the Current drives, now with the Gale,   ⎬
Both opposite, and neither long prevail: ⎭
She feels a double Force, by Turns obeys
Th' imperious Tempest, and th' impetuous Seas: 280
So fares *Althæa*'s Mind; she first relents
With Pity, of that Pity then repents:
Sister and Mother long the Scales divide,
But the Beam nodded on the Sisters side.
Sometimes she softly sigh'd, then roar'd aloud;   285
But Sighs were stifl'd in the Cries of Blood.

The pious, impious Wretch at length decreed,
To please her Brother's Ghost, her Son shou'd bleed:
And when the Fun'ral Flames began to rise,
Receive, she said, a Sisters Sacrifice;   290
A Mothers Bowels burn: High in her Hand
Thus while she spoke, she held the fatal Brand;
Then thrice before the kindled Pyle she bow'd,
And the three Furies thrice invok'd aloud:
Come, come, revenging Sisters, come and view   295
A Sister paying her dead Brothers Due:
A Crime I punish, and a Crime commit;
But Blood for Blood, and Death for Death is fit:
Great Crimes must be with greater Crimes repaid,
And second Funerals on the former laid.   300
Let the whole Houshold in one Ruine fall,
And may *Diana*'s Curse o'ertake us all.

Shall Fate to happy *Oeneus* still allow
One Son, while *Thestius* stands depriv'd of two?
Better three lost, than one unpunish'd go.   305
Take then, dear Ghosts, (while yet admitted new
In Hell you wait my Duty) take your Due:
A costly Off'ring on your Tomb is laid,
When with my Blood the Price of yours is paid.

    Ah! Whither am I hurried? Ah! forgive,   310
Ye Shades, and let your Sisters Issue live:
A Mother cannot give him Death, though he
Deserves it, he deserves it not from me.

    Then shall th' unpunish'd Wretch insult the Slain,
Triumphant live, nor only live, but reign?   315
While you, thin Shades, the Sport of Winds, are toss'd
O'er dreery Plains, or tread the burning Coast.
I cannot, cannot bear; 'tis past, 'tis done;
Perish this impious, this detested Son:
Perish his Sire, and perish I withal;   320
And let the Houses Heir, and the hop'd Kingdom fall.

    Where is the Mother fled, her pious Love,
And where the Pains with which ten Months I strove!
Ah! hadst thou dy'd, my Son, in Infant-years,
Thy little Herse had been bedew'd with Tears.   325

    Thou liv'st by me; to me thy Breath resign;
Mine is the Merit, the Demerit thine.
Thy Life by double Title I require;
Once giv'n at Birth, and once preserv'd from Fire:
One Murder pay, or add one Murder more,   330
And me to them who fell by thee restore.

    I wou'd, but cannot: My Son's Image stands
Before my Sight; and now their angry Hands
My Brothers hold, and Vengeance these exact,
This pleads Compassion, and repents the Fact.   335

    He pleads in vain, and I pronounce his Doom:
My Brothers, though unjustly, shall o'ercome.
But having paid their injur'd Ghosts their Due,
My Son requires my Death, and mine shall his pursue.

    At this, for the last time she lifts her Hand,   340
Averts her Eyes, and, half unwilling, drops the Brand.
The Brand, amid the flaming Fewel thrown,

Or drew, or seem'd to draw a dying Groan:
The Fires themselves but faintly lick'd their Prey,
Then loath'd their impious Food, and wou'd have shrunk away.   345
    Just then the *Heroe* cast a doleful Cry,
And in those absent Flames began to fry:
The blind Contagion rag'd within his Veins;
But he with manly Patience bore his Pains:
He fear'd not Fate, but only griev'd to die   350
Without an honest Wound, and by a Death so dry.
Happy *Ancæus*, thrice aloud he cry'd,
With what becoming Fate in Arms he dy'd!
Then call'd his Brothers, Sisters, Sire, around,
And her to whom his Nuptial Vows were bound;   355
Perhaps his Mother; a long Sigh he drew,
And his Voice failing, took his last Adieu:
For as the Flames augment, and as they stay
At their full Height, then languish to decay,
They rise, and sink by Fits; at last they soar   360
In one bright Blaze, and then descend no more:
Just so his inward Heats at height, impair,
Till the last burning Breath shoots out the Soul in Air.
    Now lofty *Calidon* in Ruines lies;
All Ages, all Degrees unsluice their Eyes;   365
And Heav'n and Earth resound with Murmurs, Groans, and Cries.
Matrons and Maidens beat their Breasts, and tear
Their Habits, and root up their scatter'd Hair:
The wretched Father, Father now no more,
With Sorrow sunk, lies prostrate on the Floor,   370
Deforms his hoary Locks with Dust obscene,
And curses Age, and loaths a Life prolong'd with Pain.
By Steel her stubborn Soul his Mother freed,
And punish'd on her self her impious Deed.
    Had I a hundred Tongues, a Wit so large   375
As cou'd their hundred Offices discharge;
Had *Phœbus* all his *Helicon* bestow'd
In all the Streams inspiring all the God;
Those Tongues, that Wit, those Streams, that God, in vain
Wou'd offer to describe his Sisters pain: 380
They beat their Breasts with many a bruizing Blow,
Till they turn'd livid, and corrupt the Snow.

The Corps they cherish, while the Corps remains,
And exercise and rub with fruitless Pains;
And when to Fun'ral Flames 'tis born away,   385
They kiss the Bed on which the Body lay:
And when those Fun'ral Flames no longer burn,
(The Dust compos'd within a pious Urn)
Ev'n in that Urn their Brother they confess,
And hug it in their Arms, and to their Bosoms press.   390

   His Tomb is rais'd; then, stretch'd along the Ground,
Those living Monuments his Tomb surround:
Ev'n to his Name, inscrib'd, their Tears they pay,
Till Tears and Kisses wear his Name away.

   But *Cynthia* now had all her Fury spent,   395
Not with less Ruine than a Race, content:
Excepting *Gorge*, perish'd all the Seed,
And *Her whom Heav'n for *Hercules* decreed.   *Dejanira*.
Satiate at last, no longer she pursu'd
The weeping Sisters; but with Wings endu'd,   400
And Horny Beaks, and sent to flit in Air;
Who yearly round the Tomb in Feather'd Flocks repair.

SIGISMONDA AND GUISCARDO,
FROM BOCCACE

WHILE *Norman Tancred* in *Salerno* reign'd,
  The Title of a Gracious Prince he gain'd;
Till turn'd a Tyrant in his latter Days,
He lost the Lustre of his former Praise;
And from the bright Meridian where he stood,   5
Descending, dipp'd his Hands in Lovers Blood.

   This Prince, of Fortunes Favour long possess'd,
Yet was with one fair Daughter only bless'd;
And bless'd he might have been with her alone:
But oh! how much more happy, had he none!   10
She was his Care, his Hope, and his Delight,
Most in his Thought, and ever in his Sight:
Next, nay beyond his Life, he held her dear;

She liv'd by him, and now he liv'd in her.
For this, when ripe for Marriage, he delay'd   15
Her Nuptial Bands, and kept her long a Maid,
As envying any else should share a Part
Of what was his, and claiming all her Heart.
At length, as Publick Decency requir'd,
And all his Vassals eagerly desir'd,   20
With Mind averse, he rather underwent
His Peoples Will, than gave his own Consent:
So was she torn, as from a Lover's Side,
And made almost in his despite a Bride.

    Short were her Marriage-Joys; for in the Prime   25
Of Youth, her Lord expir'd before his time:
And to her Father's Court, in little space   ⎫
Restor'd anew, she held a higher Place;   ⎬
More lov'd, and more exalted into Grace.   ⎭
This Princess fresh and young, and fair, and wise,   30
The worshipp'd Idol of her Father's Eyes,
Did all her Sex in ev'ry Grace exceed,
And had more Wit beside than Women need.

    Youth, Health, and Ease, and most an amorous Mind, ⎫
To second Nuptials had her Thoughts inclin'd: ⎬ 35
And former Joys had left a secret Sting behind.   ⎭
But prodigal in ev'ry other Grant,
Her Sire left unsupply'd her only Want;
And she, betwixt her Modesty and Pride,
Her Wishes, which she could not help, would hide.   40

    Resolv'd at last to lose no longer Time,
And yet to please her self without a Crime,
She cast her Eyes around the Court, to find
A worthy Subject suiting to her Mind,
To him in holy Nuptials to be ty'd,   45
A seeming Widow, and a secret Bride.
Among the Train of Courtiers, one she found
With all the Gifts of bounteous Nature crown'd,
Of gentle Blood; but one whose niggard Fate
Had set him far below her high Estate;   50
Guiscard his Name was call'd, of blooming Age,
Now Squire to *Tancred*, and before his Page:
To him, the Choice of all the shining Crowd,

Her Heart the noble *Sigismonda* vow'd.

    Yet hitherto she kept her Love conceal'd, 55
And with close Glances ev'ry Day beheld
The graceful Youth; and ev'ry Day increas'd
The raging Fire that burn'd within her Breast:
Some secret Charm did all his Acts attend,
And what his Fortune wanted, hers could mend: 60
Till, as the Fire will force its outward way,
Or, in the Prison pent, consume the Prey;
So long her earnest Eyes on his were set,
At length their twisted Rays together met;
And he, surpriz'd with humble Joy, survey'd 65
One sweet Regard, shot by the Royal Maid:
Not well assur'd, while doubtful Hopes he nurs'd,
A second Glance came gliding like the first;
And he who saw the Sharpness of the Dart,
Without Defence receiv'd it in his Heart. 70
In Publick though their Passion wanted Speech,
Yet mutual Looks interpreted for each:
Time, Ways, and Means of Meeting were deny'd;
But all those Wants ingenious Love supply'd.
Th' inventive God, who never fails his Part, 75
Inspires the Wit, when once he warms the Heart.

    When *Guiscard* next was in the Circle seen,
Where *Sigismonda* held the Place of Queen,
A hollow Cane within her Hand she brought,
But in the Concave had enclos'd a Note: 80
With this she seem'd to play, and, as in sport,
Toss'd to her Love, in presence of the Court;
Take it, she said; and when your Needs require,
This little Brand will serve to light your Fire.

He took it with a Bow, and soon divin'd 85
The seeming Toy was not for nought design'd:
But when retir'd, so long with curious Eyes
He view'd the Present, that he found the Prize.
Much was in little writ; and all convey'd
With cautious Care, for fear to be betray'd   } 90
By some false Confident, or Fav'rite Maid.
The Time, the Place, the Manner how to meet,
Were all in punctual Order plainly writ:

But since a Trust must be, she thought it best
To put it out of Laymens Pow'r at least,   95
And for their solemn Vows prepar'd a Priest.
   Guiscard (her secret Purpose understood)
With Joy prepar'd to meet the coming Good;
Nor Pains nor Danger was resolv'd to spare,
But use the Means appointed by the Fair.   100
   Near the proud Palace of *Salerno* stood
A Mount of rough Ascent, and thick with Wood;
Through this a Cave was dug with vast Expence,
The Work it seem'd of some suspicious Prince,
Who, when abusing Pow'r with lawless Might,   105
From Publick Justice would secure his Flight.
The Passage made by many a winding Way,
Reach'd ev'n the Room in which the Tyrant lay.
Fit for his Purpose, on a lower Floor
He lodg'd, whose Issue was an Iron Door,   110
From whence, by Stairs descending to the Ground,
In the blind Grot a safe Retreat he found.
Its Outlet ended in a Brake o'ergrown
With Brambles, choak'd by Time, and now unknown.
A Rift there was, which from the Mountains Height   115
Convey'd a glimm'ring and malignant Light,
A Breathing-place to draw the Damps away,
A Twilight of an intercepted Day.
The Tyrants Den, whose Use though lost to Fame,
Was now th' Apartment of the Royal Dame;   120
The Cavern only to her Father known,
By him was to his Darling-Daughter shown.
   Neglected long she let the Secret rest,
Till Love recall'd it to her lab'ring Breast,
And hinted as the Way by Heav'n design'd   125
The Teacher, by the Means he taught, to blind.
What will not Women do, when Need inspires
Their Wit, or Love their Inclination fires!
Though Jealousie of State th' Invention found,
Yet Love refin'd upon the former Ground.   130
That Way, the Tyrant had reserv'd, to fly
Pursuing Hate, now serv'd to bring two Lovers nigh.
   The Dame, who long in vain had kept the Key,

Bold by Desire, explor'd the secret Way;
Now try'd the Stairs, and wading through the Night,   135
Search'd all the deep Recess, and issu'd into Light.
All this her Letter had so well explain'd,
Th' instructed Youth might compass what remain'd:
The Cavern-mouth alone was hard to find,
Because the Path disus'd, was out of mind: 140
But in what Quarter of the Cops it lay,
His Eye by certain Level could survey:
Yet (for the Wood perplex'd with Thorns he knew)
A Frock of Leather o'er his Limbs he drew:
And thus provided, search'd the Brake around,   145
Till the choak'd Entry of the Cave he found.

    Thus, all prepar'd, the promis'd Hour arriv'd,
So long expected, and so well contriv'd:
With Love to Friend, th' impatient Lover went,
Fenc'd from the Thorns, and trod the deep Descent.   150
The conscious Priest, who was suborn'd before,
Stood ready posted at the Postern-door;
The Maids in distant Rooms were sent to rest,
And nothing wanted but th' invited Guest.
He came, and knocking thrice, without delay,   155
The longing Lady heard, and turn'd the Key;
At once invaded him with all her Charms,
And the first Step he made, was in her Arms:
The Leathern Out-side, boistrous as it was,
Gave way, and bent beneath her strict Embrace: 160
On either Side the Kisses flew so thick,
That neither he nor she had Breath to speak.
The holy Man amaz'd at what he saw,
Made haste to sanctifie the Bliss by Law;
And mutter'd fast the Matrimony o're,   165
For fear committed Sin should get before.
His Work perform'd, he left the Pair alone,
Because he knew he could not go too soon;
His Presence odious, when his Task was done.
What Thoughts he had, beseems not me to say;   170
Though some surmise he went to fast and pray,
And needed both, to drive the tempting Thoughts away.
    The Foe once gone, they took their full Delight;

'Twas restless Rage, and Tempest all the Night:
For greedy Love each Moment would employ,   175
And grudg'd the shortest Pauses of their Joy.

Thus were their Loves auspiciously begun,
And thus with secret Care were carried on.
The Stealth it self did Appetite restore,
And look'd so like a Sin, it pleas'd the more.   180

The Cave was now become a common Way,
The Wicket often open'd, knew the Key:
Love rioted secure, and long enjoy'd,
Was ever eager, and was never cloy'd.

But as Extremes are short, of Ill and Good,   185
And Tides at highest Mark regorge the Flood;
So Fate, that could no more improve their Joy,
Took a malicious Pleasure to destroy.

Tancred, who fondly lov'd, and whose Delight
Was plac'd in his fair Daughters daily Sight,   190
Of Custom, when his State-Affairs were done,
Would pass his pleasing Hours with her alone:
And, as a Father's Privilege allow'd,
Without Attendance of th' officious Crowd.

It happen'd once, that when in Heat of Day   195
He try'd to sleep, as was his usual Way,
The balmy Slumber fled his wakeful Eyes,
And forc'd him, in his own despite, to rise:
Of Sleep forsaken, to relieve his Care,
He sought the Conversation of the Fair: 200
But with her Train of Damsels she was gone,
In shady Walks the scorching Heat to shun:
He would not violate that sweet Recess,
And found besides a welcome Heaviness
That seiz'd his Eyes; and Slumber, which forgot   205
When call'd before to come, now came unsought.
From Light retir'd, behind his Daughters Bed,
He for approaching Sleep compos'd his Head;
A Chair was ready, for that Use design'd,
So quilted, that he lay at ease reclin'd;   210
The Curtains closely drawn, the Light to skreen,
As if he had contriv'd to lie unseen:

Thus cover'd with an artificial Night,
Sleep did his Office soon, and seal'd his Sight.

    With Heav'n averse, in this ill-omen'd Hour   215
Was *Guiscard* summon'd to the secret Bow'r,
And the fair Nymph, with Expectation fir'd,
From her attending Damsels was retir'd:
For, true to Love, she measur'd Time so right,
As not to miss one Moment of Delight.   220
The Garden, seated on the level Floor,
She left behind, and locking ev'ry Door,
Thought all secure; but little did she know,
Blind to her Fate, she had inclos'd her Foe.
Attending *Guiscard*, in his Leathern Frock,   225
Stood ready, with his thrice-repeated Knock:
Thrice with a doleful Sound the jarring Grate
Rung deaf, and hollow, and presag'd their Fate.
The Door unlock'd, to known Delight they haste,
And panting in each others Arms, embrac'd;   230
Rush to the conscious Bed, a mutual Freight,
And heedless press it with their wonted Weight.

    The sudden Bound awak'd the sleeping Sire,
And shew'd a Sight no Parent can desire:
His opening Eyes at once with odious View   235
The Love discover'd, and the Lover knew:
He would have cry'd; but hoping that he dreamt,
Amazement ty'd his Tongue, and stopp'd th' Attempt.
Th' ensuing Moment all the Truth declar'd,
But now he stood collected, and prepar'd;   240
For Malice and Revenge had put him on his Guard.

    So, like a Lion that unheeded lay,
Dissembling Sleep, and watchful to betray,
With inward Rage he meditates his Prey.
The thoughtless Pair, indulging their Desires,   245
Alternate, kindl'd, and then quench'd their Fires;
Nor thinking in the Shades of Death they play'd,
Full of themselves, themselves alone survey'd,
And, too secure, were by themselves betray'd.
Long time dissolv'd in Pleasure thus they lay,   250

Till Nature could no more suffice their Play;
Then rose the Youth, and through the Cave again
Return'd; the Princess mingl'd with her Train.
    Resolv'd his unripe Vengeance to defer,
The Royal Spy, when now the Coast was clear,   255
Sought not the Garden, but retir'd unseen,
To brood in secret on his gather'd Spleen,
And methodize Revenge: To Death he griev'd;
And, but he saw the Crime, had scarce believ'd.
Th' Appointment for th' ensuing Night he heard;   260
And therefore in the Cavern had prepar'd
Two brawny Yeomen of his trusty Guard.
    Scarce had unwary *Guiscard* set his Foot
Within the farmost Entrance of the Grot,
When these in secret Ambush ready lay,   265
And rushing on the sudden seiz'd the Prey:
Encumber'd with his Frock, without Defence,
An easie Prize, they led the Pris'ner thence,
And, as commanded, brought before the Prince.
The gloomy Sire, too sensible of Wrong   270
To vent his Rage in Words, restrain'd his Tongue;
And only said, Thus Servants are preferr'd,
And trusted, thus their Sov'reigns they reward.
Had I not seen, had not these Eyes receiv'd
Too clear a Proof, I could not have believ'd.   275
    He paus'd, and choak'd the rest. The Youth, who saw
His forfeit Life abandon'd to the Law,
The Judge th' Accuser, and th' Offence to him
Who had both Pow'r and Will t' avenge the Crime,
No vain Defence prepar'd; but thus reply'd,   280
The Faults of Love by Love are justifi'd:
With unresisted Might the Monarch reigns,
He levels Mountains, and he raises Plains;
And not regarding Diff'rence of Degree,
Abas'd your Daughter, and exalted me.   285
    This bold Return with seeming Patience heard,
The Pris'ner was remitted to the Guard.
The sullen Tyrant slept not all the Night,
But lonely walking by a winking Light,
Sobb'd, wept, and groan'd, and beat his wither'd Breast,   290

But would not violate his Daughters Rest;
Who long expecting lay, for Bliss prepar'd,
Listning for Noise, and griev'd that none she heard;
Oft rose, and oft in vain employ'd the Key,
And oft accus'd her Lover of Delay;   295
And pass'd the tedious Hours in anxious Thoughts away.

   The Morrow came; and at his usual Hour
Old *Tancred* visited his Daughters Bow'r;
Her Cheek (for such his Custom was) he kiss'd,
Then bless'd her kneeling, and her Maids dismiss'd.   300
The Royal Dignity thus far maintain'd,
Now left in private, he no longer feign'd;
But all at once his Grief and Rage appear'd,
And Floods of Tears ran trickling down his Beard.

   O *Sigismonda*, he began to say: 305
Thrice he began, and thrice was forc'd to stay,
Till Words with often trying found their Way:
I thought, O *Sigismonda*, (But how blind
Are Parents Eyes, their Childrens Faults to find!)
Thy Vertue, Birth, and Breeding were above   310
A mean Desire, and vulgar Sense of Love:
Nor less than Sight and Hearing could convince
So fond a Father, and so just a Prince,
Of such an unforeseen, and unbeliev'd Offence.
Then what indignant Sorrow must I have,   315
To see thee lie subjected to my Slave!
A Man so smelling of the Peoples Lee,
The Court receiv'd him first for Charity;
And since with no Degree of Honour grac'd,
But only suffer'd, where he first was plac'd: 320
A grov'ling Insect still; and so design'd
By Natures Hand, nor born of Noble Kind:
A Thing, by neither Man nor Woman priz'd,
And scarcely known enough, to be despis'd.
To what has Heav'n reserv'd my Age? Ah! why   325
Should Man, when Nature calls, not chuse to die,
Rather than stretch the Span of Life, to find
Such Ills as Fate has wisely cast behind,
For those to feel, whom fond Desire to live
Makes covetous of more than Life can give!   330

Each has his Share of Good; and when 'tis gone,
The Guest, though hungry, cannot rise too soon.
But I, expecting more, in my own wrong
Protracting Life, have liv'd a Day too long.
If Yesterday cou'd be recall'd again,   335
Ev'n now would I conclude my happy Reign:
But 'tis too late, my glorious Race is run,
And a dark Cloud o'ertakes my setting Sun.
Hadst thou not lov'd, or loving sav'd the Shame,
If not the Sin, by some Illustrious Name,   340
This little Comfort had reliev'd my Mind,
'Twas frailty, not unusual to thy Kind:
But thy low Fall beneath thy Royal Blood,
Shews downward Appetite to mix with Mud:
Thus not the least Excuse is left for thee,   345
Nor the least Refuge for unhappy me.
    For him I have resolv'd: whom by Surprize
I took, and scarce can call it, in Disguise:
For such was his Attire, as with Intent
Of Nature, suited to his mean Descent: 350
The harder Question yet remains behind,
What Pains a Parent and a Prince can find
To punish an Offence of this degenerate Kind.
    As I have lov'd, and yet I love thee more
Than ever Father lov'd a Child before;   355
So, that Indulgence draws me to forgive:
Nature, that gave thee Life, would have thee live.
But, as a Publick Parent of the State,
My Justice, and thy Crime, requires thy Fate.
Fain would I chuse a middle Course to steer;   360
Nature's too kind, and Justice too severe:
Speak for us both, and to the Balance bring
On either side, the Father, and the King.
Heav'n knows, my Heart is bent to favour thee;
Make it but scanty weight, and leave the rest to me.   365
    Here stopping with a Sigh, he pour'd a Flood
Of Tears, to make his last Expression good.
    She, who had heard him speak, nor saw alone
The secret Conduct of her Love was known;
But he was taken who her Soul possess'd,   370

Felt all the Pangs of Sorrow in her Breast:
And little wanted, but a Womans Heart
With Cries, and Tears, had testifi'd her Smart:
But in-born Worth, that Fortune can controul,
New strung, and stiffer bent her softer Soul;   375
The *Heroine* assum'd the Womans Place,
Confirm'd her Mind, and fortifi'd her Face:
Why should she beg, or what cou'd she pretend,
When her stern Father had condemn'd her Friend!
Her Life she might have had; but her Despair   380
Of saving his, had put it past her Care:
Resolv'd on Fate, she would not lose her Breath
But rather than not die, sollicit Death.
Fix'd on this Thought, she not as Women use,
Her Fault by common Frailty would excuse;   385
But boldly justifi'd her Innocence,
And while the Fact was own'd, deny'd th' Offence:
Then with dry Eyes, and with an open Look,
She met his Glance mid-way, and thus undaunted spoke.

   Tancred, I neither am dispos'd to make   390
Request for Life, nor offer'd Life to take:
Much less deny the Deed; but least of all
Beneath pretended Justice weakly fall.
My Words to sacred Truth shall be confin'd,
My Deeds shall shew the Greatness of my Mind.   395
That I have lov'd, I own; that still I love,
I call to Witness all the Pow'rs above:
Yet more I own: To *Guiscard*'s Love I give
The small remaining Time I have to live;
And if beyond this Life Desire can be,   400
Not Fate it self shall set my Passion free.

   This first avow'd; nor Folly warp'd my Mind,
Nor the frail Texture of the Female Kind
Betray'd my Vertue: For, too well I knew
What Honour was, and Honour had his Due: 405
Before the Holy Priest my Vows were ty'd,
So came I not a Strumpet, but a Bride;
This for my Fame: and for the Publick Voice:
Yet more, his Merits justifi'd my Choice;
Which had they not, the first Election thine,   410

That Bond dissolv'd, the next is freely mine:
Or grant I err'd, (which yet I must deny,)
Had Parents pow'r ev'n second Vows to tie,
Thy little Care to mend my Widow'd Nights
Has forc'd me to recourse of Marriage-Rites,   } 415
To fill an empty Side, and follow known Delights.
What have I done in this, deserving Blame?
State-Laws may alter: Nature's are the same;
Those are usurp'd on helpless Woman-kind,
Made without our Consent, and wanting Pow'r to bind.   420
    Thou, *Tancred*, better should'st have understood,
That as thy Father gave thee Flesh and Blood,
So gav'st thou me: Not from the Quarry hew'd,
But of a softer Mould, with Sense endu'd;
Ev'n softer than thy own, of suppler Kind,   425
More exquisite of Taste, and more than Man refin'd.
Nor need'st thou by thy Daughter to be told,
Though now thy spritely Blood with Age be cold,
Thou hast been young; and canst remember still,
That when thou hadst the Pow'r, thou hadst the Will;   430
And from the past Experience of thy Fires,   )
Canst tell with what a Tide our strong Desires   }
Come rushing on in Youth, and what their Rage requires.)
    And grant thy Youth was exercis'd in Arms,
When Love no leisure found for softer Charms;   435
My tender Age in Luxury was train'd,   )
With idle Ease and Pageants entertain'd;   }
My Hours my own, my Pleasures unrestrain'd.   )
So bred, no wonder if I took the Bent
That seem'd ev'n warranted by thy Consent;   440
For, when the Father is too fondly kind,
Such Seed he sows, such Harvest shall he find.
Blame then thy self, as Reason's Law requires,
(Since Nature gave, and thou foment'st my Fires;)
If still those Appetites continue strong,   445
Thou maist consider, I am yet but young:
Consider too, that having been a Wife,
I must have tasted of a better Life,
And am not to be blam'd, if I renew,
By lawful Means, the Joys which then I knew.   450

Where was the Crime, if Pleasure I procur'd,
Young, and a Woman, and to Bliss inur'd?
That was my Case, and this is my Defence;
I pleas'd my self, I shunn'd Incontinence,
And, urg'd by strong Desires, indulg'd my Sense. } 455

   Left to my self, I must avow, I strove
From publick Shame to screen my secret Love,
And, well acquainted with thy Native Pride,
Endeavour'd, what I could not help, to hide; } 460
For which, a Womans Wit an easie Way supply'd.
How this, so well contriv'd, so closely laid,
Was known to thee, or by what Chance betray'd,
Is not my Care: To please thy Pride alone,
I could have wish'd it had been still unknown.

   Nor took I *Guiscard* by blind Fancy led, 465
Or hasty Choice, as many Women wed;
But with delib'rate Care, and ripen'd Thought,
At leisure first design'd, before I wrought:
On him I rested, after long Debate,
And not without consid'ring, fix'd my Fate: 470
His Flame was equal, though by mine inspir'd;
(For so the Diff'rence of our Birth requir'd:)
Had he been born like me, like me his Love
Had first begun, what mine was forc'd to move:
But thus beginning, thus we persevere; } 475
Our Passions yet continue what they were,
Nor length of Trial makes our Joys the less sincere. }

   At this my Choice, though not by thine allow'd,
(Thy Judgment herding with the common Crowd)
Thou tak'st unjust Offence; and, led by them, 480
Dost less the Merit, than the Man esteem.
Too sharply, *Tancred*, by thy Pride betray'd,
Hast thou against the Laws of Kind inveigh'd;
For all th' Offence is in Opinion plac'd,
Which deems high Birth by lowly Choice debas'd: 485
This Thought alone with Fury fires thy Breast,
(For Holy Marriage justifies the rest)
That I have sunk the Glories of the State,
And mix'd my Blood with a Plebeian Mate:

In which I wonder thou shouldst oversee   490
Superiour Causes, or impute to me
The Fault of Fortune, or the Fates Decree.
Or call it Heav'ns Imperial Pow'r alone,
Which moves on Springs of Justice, though unknown;
Yet this we see, though order'd for the best,   495
The Bad exalted, and the Good oppress'd;
Permitted Laurels grace the Lawless Brow,
Th' Unworthy rais'd, the Worthy cast below.

    But leaving that: Search we the secret Springs,
And backward trace the Principles of Things;   500
There shall we find, that when the World began,
One common Mass compos'd the Mould of Man;
One Paste of Flesh on all Degrees bestow'd,
And kneaded up alike with moistning Blood.
The same Almighty Pow'r inspir'd the Frame   505
With kindl'd Life, and form'd the Souls the same:
The Faculties of Intellect, and Will,
Dispens'd with equal Hand, dispos'd with equal Skill,
Like Liberty indulg'd with Choice of Good or Ill.
Thus born alike, from Vertue first began   510
The Diff'rence that distinguish'd Man from Man:
He claim'd no Title from Descent of Blood,
But that which made him Noble, made him Good:
Warm'd with more Particles of Heav'nly Flame,
He wing'd his upward Flight, and soar'd to Fame;   515
The rest remain'd below, a Tribe without a Name.

    This Law, though Custom now diverts the Course,
As Natures Institute, is yet in force;
Uncancell'd, tho disus'd: And he whose Mind
Is Vertuous, is alone of Noble Kind.   520
Though poor in Fortune, of Celestial Race;
And he commits the Crime, who calls him Base.

    Now lay the Line; and measure all thy Court,
By inward Vertue, not external Port,
And find whom justly to prefer above   525
The Man on whom my Judgment plac'd my Love:
So shalt thou see his Parts, and Person shine;
And thus compar'd, the rest a base degen'rate Line.
Nor took I, when I first survey'd thy Court,

His Valour, or his Vertues on Report;   530
But trusted what I ought to trust alone,
Relying on thy Eyes, and not my own;
Thy Praise (and Thine was then the Publick Voice)
First recommended *Guiscard* to my Choice:
Directed thus by thee, I look'd, and found   535
A Man, I thought, deserving to be crown'd;
First by my Father pointed to my Sight,
Nor less conspicuous by his Native Light:
His Mind, his Meen, the Features of his Face,
Excelling all the rest of Humane Race: 540
These were thy Thoughts, and thou could'st judge aright,
Till Int'rest made a Jaundice in thy Sight.
   Or shou'd I grant, thou didst not rightly see;
Then thou wert first deceiv'd, and I deceiv'd by thee.
But if thou shalt alledge, through Pride of Mind,   545
Thy Blood with one of base Condition join'd,
'Tis false; for 'tis not Baseness to be Poor;
His Poverty augments thy Crime the more;
Upbraids thy Justice with the scant Regard
Of Worth: Whom Princes praise, they shou'd reward.   550
Are these the Kings intrusted by the Crowd
With Wealth, to be dispens'd for Common Good?
The People sweat not for their King's Delight,
T' enrich a Pimp, or raise a Parasite;
Theirs is the Toil; and he who well has serv'd   555
His Country, has his Countrys Wealth deserv'd.
   Ev'n mighty Monarchs oft are meanly born,
And Kings by Birth, to lowest Rank return;
All subject to the Pow'r of giddy Chance,
For Fortune can depress, or can advance: 560
But true Nobility, is of the Mind,
Not giv'n by Chance, and not to Chance resign'd.
   For the remaining Doubt of thy Decree,
What to resolve, and how dispose of me,
Be warn'd to cast that useless Care aside,   565
My self alone, will for my self provide:
If in thy doting, and decrepit Age,
Thy Soul, a Stranger in thy Youth to Rage,
Begins in cruel Deeds to take Delight,

Gorge with my Blood thy barb'rous Appetite;   570
For I so little am dispos'd to pray
For Life, I would not cast a Wish away.
Such as it is, th' Offence is all my own;
And what to *Guiscard* is already done,
Or to be done, is doom'd by thy Decree,   575
That, if not executed first by thee,
Shall on my Person be perform'd by me.

    Away, with Women weep, and leave me here,
Fix'd, like a Man to die, without a Tear;
Or save, or slay us both this present Hour,   580
'Tis all that Fate has left within thy Pow'r.

    She said: Nor did her Father fail to find,
In all she spoke, the Greatness of her Mind;
Yet thought she was not obstinate to die,
Nor deem'd the Death she promis'd was so nigh: 585
Secure in this Belief, he left the Dame,
Resolv'd to spare her Life, and save her Shame;
But that detested Object to remove,
To wreak his Vengeance, and to cure her Love.

    Intent on this, a secret Order sign'd,   590
The Death of *Guiscard* to his Guards enjoin'd;
Strangling was chosen, and the Night the Time,
A mute Revenge, and blind as was the Crime:
His faithful Heart, a bloody Sacrifice,
Torn from his Breast, to glut the Tyrant's Eyes,   595
Clos'd the severe Command: For, (Slaves to Pay)
What Kings decree, the Soldier must obey:
Wag'd against Foes; and, when the Wars are o'er,
Fit only to maintain Despotick Pow'r:
Dang'rous to Freedom, and desir'd alone   600

By Kings, who seek an Arbitrary Throne:
Such were these Guards; as ready to have slain
The Prince himself, allur'd with greater gain:
So was the Charge perform'd with better Will,
By Men inur'd to Blood, and exercis'd in Ill.   605

    Now, though the sullen Sire had eas'd his Mind,
The Pomp of his Revenge was yet behind,
A Pomp prepar'd to grace the Present he design'd.
A Goblet rich with Gems, and rough with Gold,

Of Depth, and Breadth, the precious Pledge to hold,   610
With cruel Care he chose: The hollow Part
Inclos'd; the Lid conceal'd the Lover's Heart:
Then of his trusted Mischiefs, one he sent,
And bad him with these Words the Gift present;
Thy Father sends thee this, to cheer thy Breast,   615
And glad thy Sight with what thou lov'st the best;
As thou hast pleas'd his Eyes, and joy'd his Mind,
With what he lov'd the most of Humane Kind.

E'er this the Royal Dame, who well had weigh'd
The Consequence of what her Sire had said,   620
Fix'd on her Fate, against th' expected Hour,
Procur'd the Means to have it in her Pow'r:
For this, she had distill'd, with early Care,
The Juice of Simples, friendly to Despair,
A Magazine of Death; and thus prepar'd,   625
Secure to die, the fatal Message heard:
Then smil'd severe; nor with a troubl'd Look,
Or trembling Hand, the Fun'ral Present took;
Ev'n kept her Count'nance, when the Lid remov'd,
Disclos'd the Heart, unfortunately lov'd: 630
She needed not be told within whose Breast
It lodg'd; the Message had explain'd the rest.
Or not amaz'd, or hiding her Surprize,
She sternly on the Bearer fix'd her Eyes:
Then thus; Tell *Tancred*, on his Daughters part,   635
The Gold, though precious, equals not the Heart:
But he did well to give his best; and I,
Who wish'd a worthier Urn, forgive his Poverty.

At this, she curb'd a Groan, that else had come,
And pausing, view'd the Present in the Tomb: 640
Then, to the Heart ador'd, devoutly glew'd
Her Lips, and raising it, her Speech renew'd;
Ev'n from my Day of Birth, to this, the Bound
Of my unhappy Being, I have found
My Father's Care, and Tenderness express'd: 645
But this last Act of Love excels the rest:
For this so dear a Present, bear him back
The best Return that I can live to make.

The Messenger dispatch'd, again she view'd

The lov'd Remains, and sighing, thus pursu'd;   650
Source of my Life, and Lord of my Desires,
In whom I liv'd, with whom my Soul expires;
Poor Heart, no more the Spring of Vital Heat,
Curs'd be the Hands that tore thee from thy Seat!
The Course is finish'd, which thy Fates decreed,   655
And thou, from thy Corporeal Prison freed:
Soon hast thou reach'd the Goal with mended Pace,
A World of Woes dispatch'd in little space:
Forc'd by thy Worth, thy Foe in Death become
Thy Friend, has lodg'd thee in a costly Tomb;   660
There yet remain'd thy Fun'ral Exequies,
The weeping Tribute of thy Widows Eyes,
And those, indulgent Heav'n has found the way
That I, before my Death, have leave to pay.
My Father ev'n in Cruelty is kind,   ⎞
Or Heav'n has turn'd the Malice of his Mind   ⎬ 665
To better Uses than his Hate design'd;   ⎠
And made th' Insult which in his Gift appears,
The Means to mourn thee with my pious Tears;
Which I will pay thee down, before I go,   670
And save my self the Pains to weep below,
If Souls can weep; though once I meant to meet
My Fate with Face unmov'd, and Eyes unwet,
Yet since I have thee here in narrow Room,
My Tears shall set thee first afloat within thy Tomb: 675
Then (as I know thy Spirit hovers nigh)
Under thy friendly Conduct will I fly
To Regions unexplor'd, secure to share   ⎞
Thy State; nor Hell shall Punishment appear;   ⎬
And Heav'n is double Heav'n, if thou art there.   ⎠ 680
     She said: Her brim-full Eyes, that ready stood,
And only wanted Will to weep a Flood,
Releas'd their watry Store, and pour'd amain,
Like Clouds low hung, a sober Show'r of Rain;
Mute solemn Sorrow, free from Female Noise,   685
Such as the Majesty of Grief destroys:
For, bending o'er the Cup, the Tears she shed
Seem'd by the Posture to discharge her Head,
O'er-fill'd before; and oft (her Mouth apply'd

To the cold Heart) she kiss'd at once, and cry'd.   690
Her Maids, who stood amaz'd, nor knew the Cause
Of her Complaining, nor whose Heart it was;
Yet all due Measures of her Mourning kept,
Did Office at the Dirge, and by Infection wept;
And oft enquir'd th' Occasion of her Grief,   695
(Unanswer'd but by Sighs) and offer'd vain Relief.
At length, her Stock of Tears already shed,
She wip'd her Eyes, she rais'd her drooping Head,
And thus pursu'd: O ever faithful Heart,
I have perform'd the Ceremonial Part,   700
The Decencies of Grief: It rests behind,
That as our Bodies were, our Souls be join'd:
To thy whate'er abode, my Shade convey,
And as an elder Ghost, direct the way.
She said; and bad the Vial to be brought,   705
Where she before had brew'd the deadly Draught,
First pouring out the med'cinable Bane,
The Heart, her Tears had rins'd, she bath'd again;
Then down her Throat the Death securely throws,
And quaffs a long Oblivion of her Woes.   710
    This done, she mounts the Genial Bed, and there,
(Her Body first compos'd with honest Care,)
Attends the welcom Rest: Her Hands yet hold
Close to her Heart, the Monumental Gold;
Nor farther Word she spoke, but clos'd her Sight,   715
And quiet, sought the Covert of the Night.
    The Damsels, who the while in Silence mourn'd,
Not knowing, nor suspecting Death suborn'd,
Yet, as their Duty was, to *Tancred* sent,
Who, conscious of th' Occasion, fear'd th' Event.   720
Alarm'd, and with presaging Heart he came,
And drew the Curtains, and expos'd the Dame
To loathsom Light: then with a late Relief
Made vain Efforts, to mitigate her Grief.
She, what she could, excluding Day, her Eyes   725
Kept firmly seal'd, and sternly thus replies:
    Tancred, restrain thy Tears, unsought by me,
And Sorrow, unavailing now to thee:
Did ever Man before, afflict his Mind,

To see th' Effect of what himself design'd?   730
Yet if thou hast remaining in thy Heart
Some Sense of Love, some unextinguish'd Part
Of former Kindness, largely once profess'd,
Let me by that adjure thy harden'd Breast,
Not to deny thy Daughters last Request: 735
The secret Love, which I so long enjoy'd,
And still conceal'd, to gratifie thy Pride,
Thou hast disjoin'd; but, with my dying Breath,
Seek not, I beg thee, to disjoin our Death:
Where-e'er his Corps by thy Command is laid,   740
Thither let mine in publick be convey'd;
Expos'd in open View, and Side by Side,
Acknowledg'd as a Bridegroom and a Bride.

    The Prince's Anguish hinder'd his Reply:
And she, who felt her Fate approaching nigh,   745
Seiz'd the cold Heart, and heaving to her Breast,
Here, precious Pledge, she said, securely rest:
These Accents were her last; the creeping Death
Benum'd her Senses first, then stopp'd her Breath.

    Thus she for Disobedience justly dy'd;   750
The Sire was justly punish'd for his Pride:
The Youth, least guilty, suffer'd for th' Offence
Of Duty violated to his Prince;
Who late repenting of his cruel Deed,
One common Sepulcher for both decreed;   755
Intomb'd the wretched Pair in Royal State,
And on their Monument inscrib'd their Fate.

BAUCIS AND PHILEMON,
Out of the Eighth Book of
OVID'S Metamorphoses

The Author pursuing the Deeds of Theseus; *relates how He, with his Friend*
Perithous, *were invited by* Achelous, *the River-God, to stay with him, till*
his Waters were abated. Achelous *entertains them with a Relation of his*
own Love to Perimele, *who was chang'd into an Island by* Neptune, *at his*
Request. Perithous, *being an Atheist, derides the Legend, and denies the* 5
Power of the Gods, to work that Miracle. Lelex, *another Companion of*
Theseus, *to confirm the Story of* Achelous, *relates another Metamorphosis*
of Baucis *and* Philemon, *into Trees; of which he was partly an Eye-witness.*

T HUS *Achelous* ends: His Audience hear,
 With admiration, and admiring, fear
The Pow'rs of Heav'n; except *Ixion*'s Son,
Who laugh'd at all the Gods, believ'd in none:
He shook his impious Head, and thus replies,   5
These Legends are no more than pious Lies:
You attribute too much to Heavenly Sway,
To think they give us Forms, and take away.
  The rest of better Minds, their Sense declar'd
Against this Doctrine, and with Horrour heard.   10
Then *Lelex* rose, an old experienc'd Man,
And thus with sober Gravity began:
Heav'ns Pow'r is Infinite: Earth, Air, and Sea,
The Manufacture Mass, the making Pow'r obey:
By Proof to clear your Doubt; In *Phrygian* Ground   15
Two neighb'ring Trees, with Walls encompass'd round,
Stand on a mod'rate Rise, with wonder shown,
One a hard Oak, a softer Linden one:
I saw the Place and them, by *Pittheus* sent
To *Phrygian* Realms, my Grandsire's Government.   20
Not far from thence is seen a Lake, the Haunt
Of Coots, and of the fishing Cormorant:
Here *Jove* with *Hermes* came; but in Disguise
Of mortal Men conceal'd their Deities;
One laid aside his Thunder, one his Rod;   25
And many toilsom Steps together trod:

For Harbour at a thousand Doors they knock'd,
Not one of all the thousand but was lock'd.
At last an hospitable House they found,
A homely Shed; the Roof, not far from Ground,   } 30
Was thatch'd with Reeds, and Straw together bound.
There *Baucis* and *Philemon* liv'd, and there
Had liv'd long marry'd, and a happy Pair:
Now old in Love, though little was their Store,
Inur'd to Want, their Poverty they bore,   } 35
Nor aim'd at Wealth, professing to be poor.
For Master or for Servant here to call,
Was all alike, where only Two were All.
Command was none, where equal Love was paid,
Or rather both commanded, both obey'd.   40
    From lofty Roofs the Gods repuls'd before,
Now stooping, enter'd through the little Door:
The Man (their hearty Welcome first express'd)
A common Settle drew for either Guest,   }
Inviting each his weary Limbs to rest.   } 45
But e'er they sat, officious *Baucis* lays
Two Cushions stuff'd with Straw, the Seat to raise;
Course, but the best she had; then rakes the Load
Of Ashes from the Hearth, and spreads abroad
The living Coals; and, lest they shou'd expire,   50
With Leaves and Barks she feeds her Infant-fire:
It smoaks; and then with trembling Breath she blows,
Till in a chearful Blaze the Flames arose.
With Brush-wood and with Chips she strengthens these,
And adds at last the Boughs of rotten Trees.   55
The Fire thus form'd, she sets the Kettle on,
(Like burnish'd Gold the little Seether shone)
Next took the Coleworts which her Husband got
From his own Ground, (a small well-water'd Spot;)
She stripp'd the Stalks of all their Leaves; the best   60
She cull'd, and then with handy-care she dress'd.
High o'er the Hearth a Chine of Bacon hung;
Good old *Philemon* seiz'd it with a Prong,
And from the sooty Rafter drew it down,
Then cut a Slice, but scarce enough for one;   65
Yet a large Portion of a little Store,

Which for their Sakes alone he wish'd were more.
This in the Pot he plung'd without delay,
To tame the Flesh, and drain the Salt away.
The Time between, before the Fire they sat,   70
And shorten'd the Delay by pleasing Chat.

A Beam there was, on which a Beechen Pail
Hung by the Handle, on a driven Nail:
This fill'd with Water, gently warm'd, they set
Before their Guests; in this they bath'd their Feet,   75
And after with clean Towels dry'd their Sweat:
This done, the Host produc'd the genial Bed,
Sallow the Feet, the Borders, and the Sted,
Which with no costly Coverlet they spread;
But course old Garments, yet such Robes as these   80
They laid alone, at Feasts, on Holydays.
The good old Huswife tucking up her Gown,
The Table sets; th' invited Gods lie down.
The Trivet-Table of a Foot was lame,
A Blot which prudent *Baucis* overcame,   85
Who thrusts beneath the limping Leg, a Sherd,
So was the mended Board exactly rear'd:
Then rubb'd it o'er with newly-gather'd Mint,
A wholesom Herb, that breath'd a grateful Scent.
Pallas began the Feast, where first was seen   90
The party-colour'd Olive, Black, and Green:
Autumnal Cornels next in order serv'd,
In Lees of Wine well pickl'd, and preserv'd.
A Garden-Sallad was the third Supply,
Of Endive, Radishes, and Succory: 95
Then Curds and Cream, the Flow'r of Country-Fare,
And new-laid Eggs, which *Baucis* busie Care
Turn'd by a gentle Fire, and roasted rear.
All these in Earthen Ware were serv'd to Board;
And next in place, an Earthen Pitcher stor'd   100
With Liquor of the best the Cottage cou'd afford.
This was the Tables Ornament, and Pride,
With Figures wrought: Like Pages at his Side
Stood Beechen Bowls; and these were shining clean,
Vernish'd with Wax without, and lin'd within.   105
By this the boiling Kettle had prepar'd,

And to the Table sent the smoaking Lard;
On which with eager Appetite they dine,
A sav'ry Bit, that serv'd to rellish Wine:
The Wine it self was suiting to the rest,   110
Still working in the Must, and lately press'd.
The Second Course succeeds like that before,
Plums, Apples, Nuts, and of their Wintry Store,
Dry Figs, and Grapes, and wrinkl'd Dates were set
In Canisters, t' enlarge the little Treat: 115
All these a Milk-white Honey-comb surround,
Which in the midst the Country-Banquet crown'd:
But the kind Hosts their Entertainment grace
With hearty Welcom, and an open Face:
In all they did, you might discern with ease,   120
A willing Mind, and a Desire to please.

  Mean time the Beechen Bowls went round, and still
Though often empty'd, were observ'd to fill;
Fill'd without Hands, and of their own accord
Ran without Feet, and danc'd about the Board.   125
Devotion seiz'd the Pair, to see the Feast
With Wine, and of no common Grape, increas'd;
And up they held their Hands, and fell to Pray'r,
Excusing as they cou'd, their Country Fare.

  One Goose they had, ('twas all they cou'd allow)   130
A wakeful Cent'ry, and on Duty now,
Whom to the Gods for Sacrifice they vow:
Her, with malicious Zeal, the Couple view'd;
She ran for Life, and limping they pursu'd:
Full well the Fowl perceiv'd their bad intent,   135
And wou'd not make her Masters Compliment;
But persecuted, to the Pow'rs she flies,
And close between the Legs of *Jove* she lies:
He with a gracious Ear the Suppliant heard,
And sav'd her Life; then what he was declar'd,   140
And own'd the God. The Neighbourhood, said he,
Shall justly perish for Impiety:
You stand alone exempted; but obey
With speed, and follow where we lead the way:

  Leave these accurs'd; and to the Mountains Height   145
Ascend; nor once look backward in your Flight.

They haste, and what their tardy Feet deny'd,
The trusty Staff (their better Leg) supply'd.
An Arrows Flight they wanted to the Top,
And there secure, but spent with Travel, stop;   150
Then turn their now no more forbidden Eyes;
Lost in a Lake the floated Level lies:
A Watry Desart covers all the Plains,
Their Cot alone, as in an Isle, remains:
Wondring with weeping Eyes, while they deplore   155
Their Neighbours Fate, and Country now no more,
Their little Shed, scarce large enough for Two,
Seems, from the Ground increas'd, in Height and Bulk to grow.
A stately Temple shoots within the Skies,
The Crotches of their Cot in Columns rise: 160
The Pavement polish'd Marble they behold,
The Gates with Sculpture grac'd, the Spires and Tiles of Gold.
     Then thus the Sire of Gods, with Look serene,
Speak thy Desire, thou only Just of Men;
And thou, O Woman, only worthy found   165
To be with such a Man in Marriage bound.
     A while they whisper; then to *Jove* address'd,
Philemon thus prefers their joint Request.
We crave to serve before your sacred Shrine,
And offer at your Altars Rites Divine: 170
And since not any Action of our Life
Has been polluted with Domestick Strife,
We beg one Hour of Death; that neither she
With Widows Tears may live to bury me,
Nor weeping I, with wither'd Arms may bear   175
My breathless *Baucis* to the Sepulcher.
     The Godheads sign their Suit. They run their Race
In the same Tenor all th' appointed Space:
Then, when their Hour was come, while they relate
These past Adventures at the Temple-gate,   180
Old *Baucis* is by old *Philemon* seen
Sprouting with sudden Leaves of spritely Green:
Old *Baucis* look'd where old *Philemon* stood,
And saw his lengthen'd Arms a sprouting Wood:
New Roots their fasten'd Feet begin to bind,   185
Their Bodies stiffen in a rising Rind:

Then e'er the Bark above their Shoulders grew,
They give and take at once their last Adieu:
At once, Farewell, O faithful Spouse, they said;
At once th' incroaching Rinds their closing Lips invade.   190
Ev'n yet, an ancient *Tyanæan* shows
A spreading Oak, that near a Linden grows;
The Neighbourhood confirm the Prodigie,
Grave Men, not vain of Tongue, or like to lie.
I saw my self the Garlands on their Boughs,   195
And Tablets hung for Gifts of granted Vows;
And off'ring fresher up, with pious Pray'r,
The Good, said I, are God's peculiar Care,
And such as honour Heav'n, shall heav'nly Honour share.

PYGMALION AND THE STATUE,
Out of the Tenth Book of
OVID'S Metamorphoses

The Propætides, *for their impudent Behaviour, being turn'd into Stone by*
Venus, Pygmalion, *Prince of* Cyprus, *detested all Women for their Sake,*
and resolv'd never to marry: He falls in love with a Statue of his own making,
which is chang'd into a Maid, whom he marries. One of his Descendants is
Cinyras, *the Father of* Myrrha; *the Daughter incestuously loves her own* 5
Father; for which she is chang'd into the Tree which bears her Name. These
two Stories immediately follow each other, and are admirably well connected.

*P*YGMALION loathing their lascivious Life,
Abhorr'd all Womankind, but most a Wife:
So single chose to live, and shunn'd to wed,
Well pleas'd to want a Consort of his Bed.
Yet fearing Idleness, the Nurse of Ill,   5
In Sculpture exercis'd his happy Skill;
And carv'd in Iv'ry such a Maid, so fair,
As Nature could not with his Art compare,
Were she to work; but in her own Defence
Must take her Pattern here, and copy hence.   10

Pleas'd with his Idol, he commends, admires,
Adores; and last, the Thing ador'd, desires.
A very Virgin in her Face was seen,
And had she mov'd, a living Maid had been:
One wou'd have thought she cou'd have stirr'd; but strove   15
With Modesty, and was asham'd to move.
Art hid with Art, so well perform'd the Cheat,
It caught the Carver with his own Deceit:
He knows 'tis Madness, yet he must adore,
And still the more he knows it, loves the more: 20
The Flesh, or what so seems, he touches oft,
Which feels so smooth, that he believes it soft.
Fir'd with this Thought, at once he strain'd the Breast,
And on the Lips a burning Kiss impress'd.
'Tis true, the harden'd Breast resists the Gripe,   25
And the cold Lips return a Kiss unripe:
But when, retiring back, he look'd agen,
To think it Iv'ry, was a Thought too mean:
So wou'd believe she kiss'd, and courting more,
Again embrac'd her naked Body o'er;   30
And straining hard the Statue, was afraid
His Hands had made a Dint, and hurt his Maid:
Explor'd her, Limb by Limb, and fear'd to find
So rude a Gripe had left a livid Mark behind:
With Flatt'ry now, he seeks her Mind to move,   35
And now with Gifts, (the pow'rful Bribes of Love:)
He furnishes her Closet first; and fills
The crowded Shelves with Rarities of Shells;
Adds Orient Pearls, which from the Conchs he drew,
And all the sparkling Stones of various Hue: 40
And Parrots, imitating Humane Tongue,
And Singing-birds in Silver Cages hung;
And ev'ry fragrant Flow'r, and od'rous Green,
Were sorted well, with Lumps of Amber laid between:
Rich, fashionable Robes her Person deck,   45
Pendants her Ears, and Pearls adorn her Neck:
Her taper'd Fingers too with Rings are grac'd,
And an embroider'd Zone surrounds her slender Waste.
Thus like a Queen array'd, so richly dress'd,
Beauteous she shew'd, but naked shew'd the best.   50

Then, from the Floor, he rais'd a Royal Bed,
With Cov'rings of *Sydonian* Purple spread:
The Solemn Rites perform'd, he calls her Bride,
With Blandishments invites her to his Side,
And as she were with Vital Sense possess'd,   55
Her Head did on a plumy Pillow rest.

    The Feast of *Venus* came, a Solemn Day,
To which the *Cypriots* due Devotion pay;
With gilded Horns, the Milk-white Heifers led,
Slaughter'd before the sacred Altars, bled: 60
Pygmalion off 'ring, first, approach'd the Shrine,
And then with Pray'rs implor'd the Pow'rs Divine,
Almighty Gods, if all we Mortals want,
If all we can require, be yours to grant;
Make this fair Statue mine, he wou'd have said,   65
But chang'd his Words, for shame; and only pray'd,
Give me the Likeness of my Iv'ry Maid.

    The Golden Goddess, present at the Pray'r,
Well knew he meant th' inanimated Fair,
And gave the Sign of granting his Desire;   70
For thrice in chearful Flames ascends the Fire.
The Youth, returning to his Mistress, hies,
And impudent in Hope, with ardent Eyes,
And beating Breast, by the dear Statue lies.
He kisses her white Lips, renews the Bliss,   75
And looks, and thinks they redden at the Kiss;
He thought them warm before: Nor longer stays,
But next his Hand on her hard Bosom lays:
Hard as it was, beginning to relent,
It seem'd, the Breast beneath his Fingers bent;   80
He felt again, his Fingers made a Print,
'Twas Flesh, but Flesh so firm, it rose against the Dint:
The pleasing Task he fails not to renew;
Soft, and more soft at ev'ry Touch it grew;
Like pliant Wax, when chafing Hands reduce   85
The former Mass to Form, and frame for Use.
He would believe, but yet is still in pain,
And tries his Argument of Sense again,
Presses the Pulse, and feels the leaping Vein.
Convinc'd, o'erjoy'd, his studied Thanks and Praise,   90

To her who made the Miracle, he pays:
Then Lips to Lips he join'd; now freed from Fear,
He found the Savour of the Kiss sincere:
At this the waken'd Image op'd her Eyes,
And view'd at once the Light and Lover, with surprize.   95
The Goddess present at the Match she made,
So bless'd the Bed, such Fruitfulness convey'd,
That e'er ten Moons had sharpen'd either Horn,
To crown their Bliss, a lovely Boy was born;
Paphos his Name, who grown to Manhood, wall'd   100
The City *Paphos*, from the Founder call'd.

CINYRAS AND MYRRHA,
Out of the Tenth Book of
OVID'S Metamorphoses

There needs no Connection of this Story with the Former; for the Beginning of This immediately follows the End of the Last: The Reader is only to take notice, that Orpheus, *who relates both, was by Birth a* Thracian; *and his Country far distant from* Cyprus *where* Myrrha *was born, and from* Arabia *whither she fled. You will see the Reason of this Note, soon after the first Lines* 5 *of this Fable.*

NOR him alone produc'd the fruitful Queen;
   But *Cinyras*, who like his Sire had been
A happy Prince, had he not been a Sire.
Daughters and Fathers from my Song retire;
I sing of Horrour; and could I prevail,   5
You shou'd not hear, or not believe my Tale.
Yet if the Pleasure of my Song be such,
That you will hear, and credit me too much,
Attentive listen to the last Event,
And with the Sin believe the Punishment: 10
Since Nature cou'd behold so dire a Crime,
I gratulate at least my Native Clime,
That such a Land, which such a Monster bore,
So far is distant from our *Thracian* Shore.
Let *Araby* extol her happy Coast,   15
Her Cinamon, and sweet *Amomum* boast,

Her fragrant Flow'rs, her Trees with precious Tears, }
Her second Harvests, and her double Years;
How can the Land be call'd so bless'd that *Myrrha* bears?
Nor all her od'rous Tears can cleanse her Crime,   20
Her Plant alone deforms the happy Clime:
Cupid denies to have inflam'd thy Heart,
Disowns thy Love, and vindicates his Dart:
Some Fury gave thee those infernal Pains,
And shot her venom'd Vipers in thy Veins.   25
To hate thy Sire, had meritted a Curse;
But such an impious Love deserv'd a worse.
The Neighb'ring Monarchs, by thy Beauty led,
Contend in Crowds, ambitious of thy Bed:
The World is at thy Choice; except but one,   30
Except but him thou canst not chuse alone.
She knew it too, the miserable Maid, }
E'er impious Love her better Thoughts betray'd,
And thus within her secret Soul she said:
Ah *Myrrha*! whither wou'd thy Wishes tend?   35
Ye Gods, ye sacred Laws, my Soul defend
From such a Crime, as all Mankind detest,
And never lodg'd before in Humane Breast!
But is it Sin? Or makes my Mind alone
Th' imagin'd Sin? For Nature makes it none.   40
What Tyrant then these envious Laws began,
Made not for any other Beast, but Man!
The Father-Bull his Daughter may bestride,
The Horse may make his Mother-Mare a Bride;
What Piety forbids the lusty Ram   45
Or more salacious Goat, to rut their Dam?
The Hen is free to wed the Chick she bore,
And make a Husband, whom she hatch'd before.
All Creatures else are of a happier Kind, }
Whom nor ill-natur'd Laws from Pleasure bind,   50
Nor Thoughts of Sin disturb their Peace of mind.
But Man, a Slave of his own making lives;
The Fool denies himself what Nature gives:
Too busie Senates, with an over-care
To make us better than our Kind can bear,   55
Have dash'd a Spice of Envy in the Laws,

And straining up too high, have spoil'd the Cause.
Yet some wise Nations break their cruel Chains,
And own no Laws, but those which Love ordains:
Where happy Daughters with their Sires are join'd,   60
And Piety is doubly paid in Kind.
O that I had been born in such a Clime,
Not here, where 'tis the Country makes the Crime!
But whither wou'd my impious Fancy stray?
Hence Hopes, and ye forbidden Thoughts away!   65
His Worth deserves to kindle my Desires,
But with the Love, that Daughters bear to Sires.
Then had not *Cinyras* my Father been,
What hinder'd *Myrrha*'s Hopes to be his Queen?
But the Perverseness of my Fate is such,   70
That he's not mine, because he's mine too much:
Our Kindred-Blood debars a better Tie;
He might be nearer, were he not so nigh.
Eyes and their Objects never must unite,
Some Distance is requir'd to help the Sight: 75
Fain wou'd I travel to some Foreign Shore,
Never to see my Native Country more,
So might I to my self my self restore;
So might my Mind these impious Thoughts remove,
And ceasing to behold, might cease to love.   80
But stay I must, to feed my famish'd Sight,
To talk, to kiss; and more, if more I might:
More, impious Maid! What more canst thou design,
To make a monstrous Mixture in thy Line,
And break all Statutes Humane and Divine?   85
Canst thou be call'd (to save thy wretched Life)
Thy Mother's Rival, and thy Father's Wife?
Confound so many sacred Names in one,
Thy Brother's Mother, Sister to thy Son!
And fear'st thou not to see th' Infernal Bands,   90
Their Heads with Snakes, with Torches arm'd their Hands;
Full at thy Face, th' avenging Brands to bear,
And shake the Serpents from their hissing Hair?
But thou in time th' increasing Ill controul,
Nor first debauch the Body by the Soul;   95
Secure the sacred Quiet of thy Mind,

And keep the Sanctions Nature has design'd.
Suppose I shou'd attempt, th' Attempt were vain,
No Thoughts like mine his sinless Soul profane:
Observant of the Right; and O, that he   100
Cou'd cure my Madness, or be mad like me!
Thus she: But *Cinyras* who daily sees
A Crowd of Noble Suitors at his Knees,
Among so many, knew not whom to chuse,
Irresolute to grant, or to refuse.   105
But having told their Names, enquir'd of her,
Who pleas'd her best, and whom she would prefer?
The blushing Maid stood silent with Surprize,
And on her Father fix'd her ardent Eyes,
And looking sigh'd, and as she sigh'd, began   110
Round Tears to shed, that scalded as they ran.
The tender Sire, who saw her blush, and cry,
Ascrib'd it all to Maiden-modesty,
And dry'd the falling Drops, and yet more kind,
He stroak'd her Cheeks, and holy Kisses join'd.   115
She felt a secret Venom fire her Blood,
And found more Pleasure than a Daughter shou'd;
And, ask'd again, what Lover of the Crew
She lik'd the best, she answer'd, One like you.
Mistaking what she meant, her pious Will   120
He prais'd, and bad her so continue still:
The Word of Pious heard, she blush'd with shame
Of secret Guilt, and cou'd not bear the Name.

      'Twas now the mid of Night, when Slumbers close
Our Eyes, and sooth our Cares with soft Repose;   125
But no Repose cou'd wretched *Myrrha* find,
Her Body rouling, as she rould her Mind:
Mad with Desire, she ruminates her Sin,
And wishes all her Wishes o'er again:
Now she despairs, and now resolves to try;   130
Wou'd not, and wou'd again, she knows not why;
Stops, and returns, makes and retracts the Vow;
Fain wou'd begin, but understands not how.
As when a Pine is hew'd upon the Plains,
And the last mortal Stroke alone remains,   135
Lab'ring in Pangs of Death, and threatning all,

This way, and that she nods, consid'ring where to fall:
So *Myrrha*'s Mind, impell'd on either Side,
Takes ev'ry Bent, but cannot long abide:
Irresolute on which she shou'd relie,   140
At last unfix'd in all, is only fix'd to die;
On that sad Thought she rests, resolv'd on Death,
She rises, and prepares to choak her Breath:
Then while about the Beam her Zone she ties,
Dear *Cinyras*, farewell, she softly cries;   145
For thee I die, and only wish to be
Not hated, when thou know'st I die for thee:
Pardon the Crime, in pity to the Cause:
This said, about her Neck the Noose she draws.
The Nurse, who lay without, her faithful Guard,   150
Though not the Words, the Murmurs overheard,
And Sighs, and hollow Sounds: Surpriz'd with Fright,
She starts, and leaves her Bed, and springs a Light;
Unlocks the Door, and entring out of Breath,
The Dying saw, and Instruments of Death;   155
She shrieks, she cuts the Zone, with trembling haste,
And in her Arms, her fainting Charge embrac'd:
Next, (for she now had leisure for her Tears)
She weeping ask'd, in these her blooming Years,
What unforeseen Misfortune caus'd her Care,   160
To loath her Life, and languish in Despair!
The Maid, with down-cast Eyes, and mute with Grief
For Death unfinish'd, and ill-tim'd Relief,
Stood sullen to her Suit: The Beldame press'd
The more to know, and bar'd her wither'd Breast,   165
Adjur'd her by the kindly Food she drew
From those dry Founts, her secret Ill to shew.
Sad *Myrrha* sigh'd, and turn'd her Eyes aside;
The Nurse still urg'd, and wou'd not be deny'd:
Nor only promis'd Secresie; but pray'd   170
She might have leave to give her offer'd Aid.
Good-will, she said, my want of Strength supplies,
And Diligence shall give, what Age denies:
If strong Desires thy Mind to Fury move,
With Charms, and Med'cines, I can cure thy Love: 175
If envious Eyes their hurtful Rays have cast,

More pow'rful Verse shall free thee from the Blast:
If Heav'n offended sends thee this Disease,
Offended Heav'n with Pray'rs we can appease.
What then remains, that can these Cares procure?   180
Thy House is flourishing, thy Fortune sure:
Thy careful Mother yet in Health survives,
And, to thy Comfort, thy kind Father lives.
The Virgin started at her Father's Name,
And sigh'd profoundly, conscious of the Shame: 185
Nor yet the Nurse her impious Love divin'd;
But yet surmis'd, that Love disturb'd her Mind:
Thus thinking, she pursu'd her Point, and laid
And lull'd within her Lap the mourning Maid;
Then softly soothed her thus, I guess your Grief: 190
You love, my Child; your Love shall find Relief.
My long-experienc'd Age shall be your Guide;
Relie on that, and lay Distrust aside:
No Breath of Air shall on the Secret blow,
Nor shall (what most you fear) your Father know.   195
Struck once again, as with a Thunder-clap,
The guilty Virgin bounded from her Lap,
And threw her Body prostrate on the Bed,
And, to conceal her Blushes, hid her Head:
There silent lay, and warn'd her with her Hand   200
To go: But she receiv'd not the Command;
Remaining still importunate to know:
Then *Myrrha* thus; Or ask no more, or go:
I prethee go, or staying spare my Shame;
What thou wou'dst hear, is impious ev'n to name.   205
At this, on high the Beldame holds her Hands,
And trembling, both with Age, and Terrour, stands;
Adjures, and falling at her Feet intreats,
Sooths her with Blandishments, and frights with Threats,
To tell the Crime intended, or disclose   210
What Part of it she knew, if she no farther knows.
And last; if conscious to her Counsel made,
Confirms anew the Promise of her Aid.
Now *Myrrha* rais'd her Head; but soon oppress'd
With Shame, reclin'd it on her Nurses Breast;   215
Bath'd it with Tears, and strove to have confess'd:

Twice she began, and stopp'd; again she try'd;
The falt'ring Tongue its Office still deny'd.
At last her Veil before her Face she spread, ⎫
And drew a long preluding Sigh, and said, ⎬ 220
O happy Mother, in thy Marriage-bed! ⎭
Then groan'd, and ceas'd; the good Old Woman shook,
Stiff were her Eyes, and ghastly was her Look:
Her hoary Hair upright with Horrour stood,
Made (to her Grief) more knowing than she wou'd: 225
Much she reproach'd, and many Things she said,
To cure the Madness of th' unhappy Maid:
In vain: For *Myrrha* stood convict of Ill;
Her Reason vanquish'd, but unchang'd her Will:
Perverse of Mind, unable to reply; 230
She stood resolv'd or to possess, or die.
At length the Fondness of a Nurse prevail'd
Against her better Sense, and Vertue fail'd:
Enjoy, my Child, since such is thy Desire,
Thy Love, she said; she durst not say, thy Sire. 235
Live, though unhappy, live on any Terms:
Then with a second Oath her Faith confirms.

The Solemn Feast of *Ceres* now was near,
When long white Linen Stoles the Matrons wear;
Rank'd in Procession walk the pious Train, 240
Off'ring First-fruits, and Spikes of yellow Grain:
For nine long Nights the Nuptial-Bed they shun,
And sanctifying Harvest, lie alone.

Mix'd with the Crowd, the Queen forsook her Lord,
And *Ceres* Pow'r with secret Rites ador'd: 245
The Royal Couch now vacant for a time,
The crafty Crone, officious in her Crime,
The curst Occasion took: The King she found
Easie with Wine, and deep in Pleasures drown'd,
Prepar'd for Love: The Beldame blew the Flame, 250
Confess'd the Passion, but conceal'd the Name.
Her Form she prais'd; the Monarch ask'd her Years,
And she reply'd, The same thy *Myrrha* bears.
Wine and commended Beauty fir'd his Thought;
Impatient, he commands her to be brought. 255
Pleas'd with her Charge perform'd, she hies her home,

And gratulates the Nymph, the Task was overcome.
Myrrha was joy'd the welcom News to hear;
But clogg'd with Guilt, the Joy was unsincere:
So various, so discordant is the Mind,   260
That in our Will, a diff'rent Will we find.
Ill she presag'd, and yet pursu'd her Lust;
For guilty Pleasures give a double Gust.
'Twas Depth of Night: *Arctophylax* had driv'n
His lazy Wain half round the Northern Heav'n;   265
When *Myrrha* hasten'd to the Crime desir'd,
The Moon beheld her first, and first retir'd:
The Stars amaz'd, ran backward from the Sight,
And (shrunk within their Sockets) lost their Light.
Icarius first withdraws his holy Flame: 270
The Virgin Sign, in Heav'n the second Name,
Slides down the Belt, and from her Station flies,
And Night with Sable Clouds involves the Skies.
Bold *Myrrha* still pursues her black Intent;
She stumbl'd thrice, (an Omen of th' Event;)   275
Thrice shriek'd the Fun'ral Owl, yet on she went,
Secure of Shame, because secure of Sight;
Ev'n bashful Sins are impudent by Night.
Link'd Hand in Hand, th' Accomplice, and the Dame,
Their Way exploring, to the Chamber came: 280
The Door was ope, they blindly grope their Way,
Where dark in Bed th' expecting Monarch lay:
Thus far her Courage held, but here forsakes;
Her faint Knees knock at ev'ry Step she makes.
The nearer to her Crime, the more within   285
She feels Remorse, and Horrour of her Sin;
Repents too late her criminal Desire,
And wishes, that unknown she cou'd retire.
Her, lingring thus, the Nurse (who fear'd Delay
The fatal Secret might at length betray)   290
Pull'd forward, to compleat the Work begun,
And said to *Cinyras*, Receive thy own:
Thus saying, she deliver'd Kind to Kind,
Accurs'd, and their devoted Bodies join'd.
The Sire, unknowing of the Crime, admits   295
His Bowels, and profanes the hallow'd Sheets;

He found she trembl'd, but believ'd she strove
With Maiden-Modesty, against her Love,
And sought with flatt'ring Words vain Fancies to remove.
Perhaps he said, My Daughter, cease thy Fears,   300
(Because the Title suited with her Years;)
And Father, she might whisper him agen,
That Names might not be wanting to the Sin.
Full of her Sire, she left th' incestuous Bed,
And carry'd in her Womb the Crime she bred: 305
Another, and another Night she came;
For frequent Sin had left no Sense of Shame:
Till *Cinyras* desir'd to see her Face,
Whose Body he had held in close Embrace,
And brought a Taper; the Revealer, Light,   310
Expos'd both Crime, and Criminal to Sight:
Grief, Rage, Amazement, cou'd no Speech afford,
But from the Sheath he drew th' avenging Sword;
The Guilty fled: The Benefit of Night,
That favour'd first the Sin, secur'd the Flight.   315
Long wandring through the spacious Fields, she bent
Her Voyage to th' *Arabian* Continent;
Then pass'd the Region which *Panchæa* join'd,
And flying left the Palmy Plains behind.
Nine times the Moon had mew'd her Horns; at length   320
With Travel weary, unsupply'd with Strength,
And with the Burden of her Womb oppress'd,
Sabæan Fields afford her needful Rest:
There, loathing Life, and yet of Death afraid,
In anguish of her Spirit, thus she pray'd.   325
Ye Pow'rs, if any so propitious are
T' accept my Penitence, and hear my Pray'r;
Your Judgments, I confess, are justly sent;
Great Sins deserve as great a Punishment:
Yet since my Life the Living will profane,   330
And since my Death the happy Dead will stain,
A middle State your Mercy may bestow,
Betwixt the Realms above, and those below:
Some other Form to wretched *Myrrha* give,
Nor let her wholly die, nor wholly live.   335
The Pray'rs of Penitents are never vain;

At least, she did her last Request obtain:
For while she spoke, the Ground began to rise,
And gather'd round her Feet, her Leggs, and Thighs;
Her Toes in Roots descend, and spreading wide,   340
A firm Foundation for the Trunk provide:
Her solid Bones convert to solid Wood,
To Pith her Marrow, and to Sap her Blood:
Her Arms are Boughs, her Fingers change their Kind,
Her tender Skin is harden'd into Rind.   345
And now the rising Tree her Womb invests,
Now, shooting upwards still, invades her Breasts,
And shades the Neck; when, weary with Delay,
She sunk her Head within, and met it half the Way.
And though with outward Shape she lost her Sense,   350
With bitter Tears she wept her last Offence;
And still she weeps, nor sheds her Tears in vain;
For still the precious Drops her Name retain.
Mean time the mis-begotten Infant grows,
And, ripe for Birth, distends with deadly Throws   355
The swelling Rind, with unavailing Strife,
To leave the wooden Womb, and pushes into Life.
The Mother-Tree, as if oppress'd with Pain,
Writhes here and there, to break the Bark, in vain;
And, like a Lab'ring Woman, wou'd have pray'd,   360
But wants a Voice to call *Lucina*'s Aid:
The bending Bole sends out a hollow Sound,
And trickling Tears fall thicker on the Ground.
The mild *Lucina* came uncall'd, and stood
Beside the struggling Boughs, and heard the groaning Wood: 365
Then reach'd her Midwife-Hand, to speed the Throws,
And spoke the pow'rful Spells that Babes to Birth disclose.
The Bark divides, the living Load to free,
And safe delivers the Convulsive Tree.
The ready Nymphs receive the crying Child,   370
And wash him in the Tears the Parent-Plant distill'd.
They swath'd him with their Scarfs; beneath him spread
The Ground with Herbs; with Roses rais'd his Head.
The lovely Babe was born with ev'ry Grace,
Ev'n Envy must have prais'd so fair a Face: 375
Such was his Form, as Painters when they show

Their utmost Art, on naked Loves bestow:
And that their Arms no Diff'rence might betray,
Give him a Bow, or his from *Cupid* take away.
Time glides along, with undiscover'd haste,   380
The Future but a Length behind the past;
So swift are Years: The Babe whom just before
His Grandsire got, and whom his Sister bore;
The Drop, the Thing which late the Tree inclos'd,
And late the yawning Bark to Life expos'd;   385
A Babe, a Boy, a beauteous Youth appears,
And lovelier than himself at riper Years.
Now to the Queen of Love he gave Desires,
And, with her Pains, reveng'd his Mother's Fires.

THE FIRST BOOK OF HOMER'S ILIAS

THE ARGUMENT

Chryses, *Priest of* Apollo, *brings Presents to the* Grecian *Princes, to ransom his Daughter* Chryseis, *who was Prisoner in the Fleet.* Agamemnon, *the General, whose Captive and Mistress the young Lady was, refuses to deliver her, threatens the Venerable Old Man, and dismisses him with Contumely. The Priest craves Vengeance of his God; who sends a Plague among the* Greeks: 5 *Which occasions* Achilles, *their Great Champion, to summon a Council of the Chief Officers: He encourages* Calchas, *the High Priest and Prophet, to tell the Reason, why the Gods were so much incens'd against them.* Calchas *is fearful of provoking* Agamemnon, *till* Achilles *engages to protect him: Then, embolden'd by the Heroe, he accuses the General as the Cause of all,* 10 *by detaining the Fair Captive, and refusing the Presents offer'd for her Ransom. By this Proceeding,* Agamemnon *is oblig'd, against his Will, to restore* Chryseis, *with Gifts, that he might appease the Wrath of* Phœbus; *but, at the same time, to revenge himself on* Achilles, *sends to seize his Slave* Briseis. Achilles, *thus affronted, complains to his Mother* Thetis; *and begs* 15 *her to revenge his Injury, not only on the General, but on all the Army, by giving Victory to the* Trojans, *till the ungrateful King became sensible of his Injustice. At the same time, he retires from the Camp to his Ships, and withdraws his Aid from his Country-men.* Thetis *prefers her Son's Petition to* Jupiter, *who grants her Sute.* Juno *suspects her Errand, and quarrels with* 20 *her Husband, for his Grant; till* Vulcan *reconciles his Parents with a Bowl of* Nectar, *and sends them peaceably to Bed.*

THE Wrath of *Peleus* Son, O Muse, resound;
 Whose dire Effects the *Grecian* Army found:
And many a Heroe, King, and hardy Knight,
Were sent, in early Youth, to Shades of Night:
Their Limbs a Prey to Dogs and Vulturs made;   5
So was the Sov'reign Will of *Jove* obey'd:
From that ill-omen'd Hour when Strife begun,
Betwixt *Atrides* Great, and *Thetis* God-like Son.

 What Pow'r provok'd, and for what Cause, relate,
Sow'd, in their Breasts, the Seeds of stern Debate: 10
Jove's and *Latona*'s Son his Wrath express'd,
In Vengeance of his violated Priest,
Against the King of Men; who swoln with Pride,
Refus'd his Presents, and his Pray'rs deny'd.
For this the God a swift Contagion spread   15
Amid the Camp; where Heaps on Heaps lay dead.

 For Venerable *Chryses* came to buy,
With Gold and Gifts of Price, his Daughters Liberty.
Suppliant before the *Grecian* Chiefs he stood;
Awful, and arm'd with Ensigns of his God: 20
Bare was his hoary Head; one holy Hand
Held forth his Laurel Crown, and one his Sceptre of Command.
His Suit was common; but above the rest,
To both the Brother-Princes thus address'd:

 Ye Sons of *Atreus*, and ye *Grecian* Pow'rs,   25
So may the Gods who dwell in Heav'nly Bow'rs
Succeed your Siege, accord the Vows you make,
And give you *Troys* Imperial Town to take;
So, by their happy Conduct, may you come
With Conquest back to your sweet Native Home;   30
As you receive the Ransom which I bring,
(Respecting *Jove*, and the far-shooting King,)
And break my Daughters Bonds, at my desire;
And glad with her Return her grieving Sire.

 With Shouts of loud Acclaim the *Greeks* decree   35
To take the Gifts, to set the Damsel free.
The King of Men alone with Fury burn'd;

And haughty, these opprobrious Words return'd:
Hence, Holy Dotard, and avoid my Sight,
E'er Evil intercept thy tardy Flight: 40
Nor dare to tread this interdicted Strand,
Lest not that idle Sceptre in thy Hand,
Nor thy God's Crown, my vow'd Revenge withstand.
Hence on thy Life: The Captive-Maid is mine;
Whom not for Price or Pray'rs I will resign: 45
Mine she shall be, till creeping Age and Time
Her Bloom have wither'd, and consum'd her Prime:
Till then my Royal Bed she shall attend;
And having first adorn'd it, late ascend:
This, for the Night; by Day, the Web and Loom   50
And homely Houshold-task, shall be her Doom,
Far from thy lov'd Embrace, and her sweet Native Home.
He said: The helpless Priest reply'd no more,
But sped his Steps along the hoarse-resounding Shore:
Silent he fled; secure at length he stood,   55
Devoutly curs'd his Foes, and thus invok'd his God.

O Source of Sacred Light, attend my Pray'r,
God with the Silver Bow, and Golden Hair;
Whom *Chrysa, Cilla, Tenedos* obeys,
And whose broad Eye their happy Soil surveys: 60
If, *Smintheus*, I have pour'd before thy Shrine
The Blood of Oxen, Goats, and ruddy Wine,
And Larded Thighs on loaded Altars laid,
Hear, and my just Revenge propitious aid.
Pierce the proud *Greeks*, and with thy Shafts attest   65
How much thy Pow'r is injur'd in thy Priest.

He pray'd, and *Phœbus* hearing, urg'd his Flight,
With Fury kindled, from *Olympus* Height;
His Quiver o'er his ample Shoulders threw;
His Bow twang'd, and his Arrows rattl'd as they flew.   70
Black as a stormy Night, he rang'd around
The Tents, and compass'd the devoted Ground.
Then with full Force his deadly Bowe he bent,
And Feather'd Fates among the Mules and Sumpters sent:
Th' Essay of Rage, on faithful Dogs the next;   75
And last, in Humane Hearts his Arrows fix'd.
The God nine Days the *Greeks* at Rovers kill'd,

Nine Days the Camp with Fun'ral Fires was fill'd;
The Tenth, *Achilles*, by the Queens Command,
Who bears Heav'ns awful Sceptre in her Hand,   80
A Council summon'd: for the Goddess griev'd
Her favour'd Hoast shou'd perish unreliev'd.

The Kings, assembl'd, soon their Chief inclose;
Then from his Seat the Goddess-born arose,
And thus undaunted spoke: What now remains,   85
But that once more we tempt the watry Plains,
And wandring homeward, seek our Safety hence,
In Flight at least if we can find Defence?
Such Woes at once encompass us about,
The Plague within the Camp, the Sword without.   90
Consult, O King, the Prophets of th' event: ⎫
And whence these Ills, and what the Gods intent,   ⎬
Let them by Dreams explore; for Dreams from *Jove* are sent. ⎭
What want of offer'd Victims, what Offence
In Fact committed cou'd the Sun incense,   95
To deal his deadly Shafts? What may remove
His settled Hate, and reconcile his Love?
That he may look propitious on our Toils;
And hungry Graves no more be glutted with our Spoils.

Thus to the King of Men the Hero spoke,   100
Then *Calchas* the desir'd Occasion took:
Calchas the sacred Seer, who had in view
Things present and the past; the Things to come foreknew.
Supream of Augurs, who by *Phœbus* taught
The *Grecian* Pow'rs to *Troy*'s Destruction brought. 105
Skill'd in the secret Causes of their Woes,
The Reverend Priest in graceful Act arose:
And thus bespoke *Pelides*: Care of *Jove*,
Favour'd of all th' Immortal Pow'rs above;
Wou'dst thou the Seeds deep sown of Mischief know,   110
And why, provok'd *Apollo* bends his Bow?
Plight first thy Faith, inviolably true,
To save me from those Ills, that may ensue.

For I shall tell ungrateful Truths, to those
Whose boundless Pow'r of Life and Death dispose.   115
And Sov'reigns ever jealous of their State,
Forgive not those whom once they mark for Hate;

Ev'n tho' th' Offence they seemingly digest,
Revenge, like Embers, rak'd within their Breast,
Bursts forth in Flames; whose unresisted Pow'r   120
Will seize th' unwary Wretch and soon devour.
Such, and no less is he, on whom depends
The sum of Things; and whom my Tongue of force offends.
Secure me then from his foreseen Intent,
That what his Wrath may doom, thy Valour may prevent.   125
  To this the stern *Achilles* made Reply:
Be bold; and on my plighted Faith rely,
To speak what *Phœbus* has inspir'd thy Soul
For common Good; and speak without controul.
His Godhead I invoke, by him I swear,   130
That while my Nostrils draw this vital Air,
None shall presume to violate those Bands;
Or touch thy Person with unhallow'd Hands:
Ev'n not the King of Men that all commands.
  At this, resuming Heart, the Prophet said: 135
Nor Hecatombs unslain, nor Vows unpaid,
On *Greeks*, accurs'd, this dire Contagion bring;
Or call for Vengeance from the Bowyer King;
But he the Tyrant, whom none dares resist,
Affronts the Godhead in his injur'd Priest: 140
He keeps the Damsel Captive in his Chain,
And Presents are refus'd, and Pray'rs preferr'd in vain.
For this th' avenging Pow'r employs his Darts;
And empties all his Quiver in our Hearts.
Thus will persist, relentless in his Ire,   145
Till the fair Slave be render'd to her Syre:
And Ransom-free restor'd to his Abode,
With Sacrifice to reconcile the God:
Then he, perhaps, atton'd by Pray'r, may cease
His Vengeance justly vow'd; and give the Peace.   150
  Thus having said he sate: Thus answer'd then
Upstarting from his Throne, the King of Men,
His Breast with Fury fill'd, his Eyes with Fire;
Which rowling round, he shot in Sparkles on the Sire:
Augur of Ill, whose Tongue was never found   155
Without a Priestly Curse or boding Sound;
For not one bless'd Event foretold to me

Pass'd through that Mouth, or pass'd unwillingly.
And now thou dost with Lies the Throne invade,
By Practice harden'd in thy sland'ring Trade.					160
Obtending Heav'n, for what e'er Ills befal;
And sputtring under specious Names thy Gall.
Now *Phœbus* is provok'd; his Rites and Laws
Are in his Priest profan'd, and I the Cause:
Since I detain a Slave, my Sov'reign Prize;					165
And sacred Gold, your Idol-God, despise.
I love her well: And well her Merits claim,
To stand preferr'd before my *Grecian* Dame:
Not *Clytemnestra's* self in Beauties Bloom
More charm'd, or better ply'd the various Loom:					170
Mine is the Maid; and brought in happy Hour
With every Houshold-grace adorn'd, to bless my Nuptial Bow'r.
Yet shall she be restor'd; since publick Good
For private Int'rest ought not be withstood,
To save th' Effusion of my People's Blood.					175
But Right requires, if I resign my own,
I shou'd not suffer for your sakes alone:
Alone excluded from the Prize I gain'd,
And by your common Suffrage have obtain'd.
The Slave without a Ransom shall be sent:					180
It rests for you to make th' Equivalent.
	To this the fierce *Thessalian* Prince reply'd:
O first in Pow'r, but passing all in Pride,
Griping, and still tenacious of thy Hold,
Would'st thou the *Grecian* Chiefs, though largely Sould,					185
Shou'd give the Prizes they had gain'd before;
And with their Loss thy Sacrilege restore?
Whate'er by force of Arms the Soldier got,
Is each his own, by dividend of Lot:
Which to resume, were both unjust, and base:					190
Not to be born but by a servile Race.
But this we can: If *Saturn's* Son bestows
The Sack of *Troy*, which he by Promise owes;
Then shall the conquering *Greeks* thy Loss restore,
And with large Int'rest, make th' advantage more.					195
	To this *Atrides* answer'd, Though thy Boast
Assumes the foremost Name of all our Host,

Pretend not, mighty Man, that what is mine
Controll'd by thee, I tamely shou'd resign.
Shall I release the Prize I gain'd by Right,   200
In taken Towns, and many a bloody Fight,
While thou detain'st *Briseis* in thy Bands,
By priestly glossing on the God's Commands?
Resolve on this, (a short Alternative)
Quit mine, or, in exchange, another give;   205
Else I, assure thy Soul, by Sov'reign Right
Will seize thy Captive in thy own Despight.
Or from stout *Ajax*, or *Ulysses*, bear
What other Prize my Fancy shall prefer:
Then softly murmur, or aloud complain,   210
Rage as you please, you shall resist in vain.
But more of this, in proper Time and Place,
To Things of greater moment let us pass.

A Ship to sail the sacred Seas prepare;
Proud in her Trim; and put on board the Fair,   215
With Sacrifice and Gifts, and all the pomp of Pray'r.
The Crew well chosen, the Command shall be
In *Ajax*; or if other I decree,
In *Creta*'s King, or *Ithacus*, or if I please in Thee:
Most fit thy self to see perform'd th' intent   220
For which my Pris'ner from my Sight is sent;
(Thanks to thy pious Care) that *Phœbus* may relent.

    At this, *Achilles* roul'd his furious Eyes,
Fix'd on the King askant; and thus replies.
O, Impudent, regardful of thy own,   225
Whose Thoughts are center'd on thy self alone,
Advanc'd to Sovereign Sway, for better Ends
Than thus like abject Slaves to treat thy Friends.
What *Greek* is he, that urg'd by thy Command,
Against the *Trojan* Troops will lift his Hand?   230
Not I: Nor such inforc'd Respect I owe;
Nor *Pergamus* I hate, nor *Priam* is my Foe.
What Wrong from *Troy* remote, cou'd I sustain,
To leave my fruitful Soil, and happy Reign,
And plough the Surges of the stormy Main?   235
Thee, frontless Man, we follow'd from afar;

Thy Instruments of Death, and Tools of War.
Thine is the Triumph; ours the Toil alone:
We bear thee on our Backs, and mount thee on the Throne.
For thee we fall in Fight; for thee redress   240
Thy baffled Brother; not the Wrongs of *Greece*.
And now thou threaten'st with unjust Decree,
To punish thy affronting Heav'n, on me.
To seize the Prize which I so dearly bought;
By common Suffrage giv'n, confirm'd by Lot.   245
Mean Match to thine: For still above the rest,
Thy hook'd rapacious Hands usurp the best.
Though mine are first in Fight, to force the Prey;
And last sustain the Labours of the Day.
Nor grudge I thee, the much the *Grecians* give;   250
Nor murm'ring take the little I receive.
Yet ev'n this little, thou, who woud'st ingross
The whole, Insatiate, envy'st as thy Loss.
Know, then, for *Phthya*, fix'd is my return:
Better at home my ill-paid Pains to mourn,   255
Than from an Equal here sustain the publick Scorn.

    The King, whose Brows with shining Gold were bound;
Who saw his Throne with scepter'd Slaves incompass'd round,
Thus answer'd stern! Go, at thy Pleasure, go:
We need not such a Friend, nor fear we such a Foe.   260
There will not want to follow me in Fight:
Jove will assist, and *Jove* assert my Right.
But thou of all the Kings (his Care below)
Art least at my Command, and most my Foe.
Debates, Dissentions, Uproars are thy Joy;   265
Provok'd without Offence, and practis'd to destroy.
Strength is of Brutes; and not thy Boast alone;
At least 'tis lent from Heav'n; and not thy own.
Fly then, ill-manner'd, to thy Native Land,
And there, thy Ant-born *Myrmidons* command.   270
But mark this Menace; since I must resign
My black-ey'd Maid, to please the Pow'rs divine:
(A well-rigg'd Vessel in the Port attends,
Man'd at my Charge! commanded by my Friends;)
The Ship shall waft her to her wish'd Abode,   275
Full fraught with holy Bribes to the far-shooting God.

This thus dispatch'd, I owe my self the Care,
My Fame and injur'd Honour to repair:
From thy own Tent, proud Man, in thy despight,
This Hand shall ravish thy pretended Right.   280
Briseis shall be mine, and thou shalt see,
What odds of awful Pow'r I have on thee:
That others at thy cost may learn the diff'rence of degree.

   At this th' Impatient Hero sowrly smil'd:
His Heart, impetuous in his Bosom boil'd,   285
And justled by two Tides of equal sway,
Stood, for a while, suspended in his way.
Betwixt his Reason, and his Rage untam'd;
One whisper'd soft, and one aloud reclaim'd:
That only counsell'd to the safer side;   290
This to the Sword, his ready Hand apply'd.
Unpunish'd to support th' Affront was hard:
Nor easy was th' Attempt to force the Guard.
But soon the thirst of Vengeance fir'd his Blood:
Half shone his Faulchion, and half sheath'd it stood.   295

   In that nice moment, *Pallas*, from above,
Commission'd by th' Imperial Wife of *Jove*,
Descended swift: (the white arm'd Queen was loath
The Fight shou'd follow; for she favour'd both:)
Just as in Act he stood, in Clouds inshrin'd,   300
Her Hand she fasten'd on his Hair behind;
Then backward by his yellow Curls she drew:
To him, and him alone confess'd in view.
Tam'd by superiour Force he turn'd his Eyes
Aghast at first, and stupid with Surprize: 305
But by her sparkling Eyes, and ardent Look,
The Virgin-Warrior known, he thus bespoke.

   Com'st thou, Celestial, to behold my Wrongs?
Then view the Vengeance which to Crimes belongs.

   Thus He. The blue-ey'd Goddess thus rejoin'd: 310
I come to calm thy turbulence of Mind,
If Reason will resume her soveraign Sway,
And sent by *Juno*, her Commands obey.
Equal she loves you both, and I protect:
Then give thy Guardian Gods their due respect;   315
And cease Contention; be thy Words severe,

Sharp as he merits: But the Sword forbear.
An Hour unhop'd already wings her way,
When he his dire Affront shall dearly pay:
When the proud King shall sue, with trebble Gain,   320
To quit thy Loss, and conquer thy Disdain.
But thou secure of my unfailing Word,
Compose thy swelling Soul; and sheath the Sword.

    The Youth thus answer'd mild; Auspicious Maid,
Heav'ns will be mine; and your Commands obey'd.   325
The Gods are just, and when subduing Sense,
We serve their Pow'rs, provide the Recompence.
He said; with surly Faith believ'd her Word,
And, in the Sheath, reluctant, plung'd the Sword.
Her Message done, she mounts the bless'd Abodes,   330
And mix'd among the Senate of the Gods.

    At her departure his Disdain return'd:
The Fire she fan'd, with greater Fury burn'd;
Rumbling within till thus it found a vent:
Dastard, and Drunkard, Mean and Insolent: 335
Tongue-valiant Hero, Vaunter of thy Might,
In Threats the foremost, but the lag in Fight;
When did'st thou thrust amid the mingled Preace,
Content to bid the War aloof in Peace?
Arms are the Trade of each *Plebeyan* Soul;   340
'Tis Death to fight; but Kingly to controul.
Lord-like at ease, with arbitrary Pow'r,
To peel the Chiefs, the People to devour.
These, Traitor, are thy Tallents; safer far
Than to contend in Fields, and Toils of War.   345
Nor coud'st thou thus have dar'd the common Hate,
Were not their Souls as abject as their State.
But, by this Scepter, solemnly I swear,
(Which never more green Leaf or growing Branch shall bear:
Torn from the Tree, and giv'n by *Jove* to those   350
Who Laws dispence and mighty Wrongs oppose)
That when the *Grecians* want my wonted Aid,
No Gift shall bribe it, and no Pray'r persuade.
When *Hector* comes, the Homicide, to wield
His conquering Arms, with Corps to strow the Field;   355
Then shalt thou mourn thy Pride; and late confess,

My Wrong repented when 'tis past redress:
He said: And with Disdain in open view,
Against the Ground his golden Scepter threw;
Then sate: with boiling Rage *Atrides* burn'd: 360
And Foam betwixt his gnashing Grinders churn'd.

But from his Seat the *Pylian* Prince arose,
With Reas'ning mild, their Madness to compose:
Words, sweet as Hony, from his Mouth distill'd;
Two Centuries already he fulfill'd;   365
And now began the third; unbroken yet:
Once fam'd for Courage; still in Council great.

What worse, he said, can *Argos* undergo,
What can more gratify the *Phrygian* Foe,
Than these distemper'd Heats? If both the Lights   370
Of *Greece* their private Int'rest disunites!
Believe a Friend, with thrice your Years increas'd,
And let these youthful Passions be repress'd:
I flourish'd long before your Birth; and then
Liv'd equal with a Race of braver Men,   } 375
Than these dim Eyes shall e'er behold agen.
Ceneus and *Dryas*, and, excelling them,
Great *Theseus*, and the force of greater *Polypheme*.
With these I went, a Brother of the War,
Their Dangers to divide; their Fame to share.   380
Nor idle stood with unassisting Hands,
When salvage Beasts, and Men's more salvage Bands,
Their virtuous Toil subdu'd: Yet those I sway'd,
With pow'rful Speech: I spoke and they obey'd.
If such as those, my Councils cou'd reclaim,   385
Think not, young Warriors, your diminish'd Name,
Shall lose of Lustre, by subjecting Rage
To the cool Dictates of experienc'd Age.
Thou, King of Men, stretch not thy sovereign Sway
Beyond, the Bounds free Subjects can obey: 390
But let *Pelides* in his Prize rejoice,
Atchiev'd in Arms, allow'd by publick Voice.
Nor Thou, brave Champion, with his Pow'r contend,
Before whose Throne, ev'n Kings their lower'd Scepters bend.
The Head of Action He, and Thou the Hand,   395
Matchless thy Force; but mightier his Command:

Thou first, O King, release the rights of Sway,
Pow'r, self-restrain'd, the People best obey.
Sanctions of Law from Thee derive their Source;
Command thy Self, whom no Commands can force.   400
The Son of *Thetis* Rampire of our Host,
Is worth our Care to keep; nor shall my Pray'rs be lost.
    Thus *Nestor* said, and ceas'd: *Atrides* broke
His Silence next; but ponder'd e'er he spoke.
Wise are thy Words, and glad I would obey,   405
But this proud Man affects Imperial Sway.
Controlling Kings, and trampling on our State
His Will is Law; and what he wills is Fate.
The Gods have giv'n him Strength: But whence the Style,
Of lawless Pow'r assum'd, or Licence to revile?   410
    Achilles, cut him short; and thus reply'd:
My Worth allow'd in Words, is in effect deny'd.
For who but a Poltron, possess'd with Fear,
Such haughty Insolence, can tamely bear?
Command thy Slaves: My freeborn Soul disdains   415
A Tyrant's Curb; and restiff breaks the Reins.
Take this along; that no Dispute shall rise
(Though mine the Woman) for my ravish'd Prize:
But she excepted, as unworthy Strife,
Dare not, I charge thee dare not, on thy Life,   420
Touch ought of mine beside, by Lot my due,
But stand aloof, and think profane to view:
This Fauchion, else, not hitherto withstood,
These hostile Fields shall fatten with thy Blood.
    He said; and rose the first; the Council broke;   425
And all their grave Consults dissolv'd in Smoke.
    The Royal Youth retir'd, on Vengeance bent,
Patroclus follow'd silent to his Tent.
    Mean time, the King with Gifts a Vessel stores;
Supplies the Banks with twenty chosen Oars: 430
And next, to reconcile the shooter God,
Within her hollow Sides the Sacrifice he stow'd:
Chryseis last was set on board; whose Hand
Ulysses took, intrusted with Command;
They plow the liquid Seas; and leave the less'ning Land.   435
    Atrides then his outward Zeal to boast,

Bade purify the Sin-polluted Host.
With perfect Hecatombs the God they grac'd;
Whose offer'd Entrails in the Main were cast.
Black Bulls, and bearded Goats on Altars lie;   440
And clouds of sav'ry stench, involve the Sky.
These Pomps the Royal Hypocrite design'd,
For Shew: But harbour'd Vengeance in his Mind:
Till holy Malice, longing for a vent,
At length, discover'd his conceal'd Intent.   445
Talthybius, and *Eurybates* the just,
Heralds of Arms, and Ministers of Trust,
He call'd; and thus bespoke: Haste hence your way;
And from the Goddess-born demand his Prey.
If yielded, bring the Captive: If deny'd,   450
The King (so tell him) shall chastise his Pride:
And with arm'd Multitudes in Person come
To vindicate his Pow'r, and justify his Doom.

This hard Command unwilling they obey,
And o'er the barren Shore pursue their way,   455
Where quarter'd in their Camp, the fierce *Thessalians* lay.
Their Sov'reign seated on his Chair, they find;
His pensive Cheek upon his Hand reclin'd,
And anxious Thoughts revolving in his Mind.
With gloomy Looks he saw them entring in   460
Without Salute: Nor durst they first begin,
Fearful of rash Offence and Death foreseen.
He soon the Cause divining, clear'd his Brow;
And thus did liberty of Speech allow.

Interpreters of Gods and Men, be bold: 465
Awful your Character, and uncontroll'd;
Howe'er unpleasing, be the News you bring,
I blame not you, but your Imperious King.
You come, I know, my Captive to demand;
Patroclus, give her, to the Herald's Hand.   470
But you, authentick Witnesses I bring,
Before the Gods, and your ungrateful King,
Of this my Manifest: That never more
This Hand shall combate on the crooked Shore:
No, let the *Grecian* Pow'rs oppress'd in Fight,   475
Unpity'd perish in their Tyrants sight.

Blind of the future and by Rage misled,
He pulls his Crimes upon his People's Head.
Forc'd from the Field in Trenches to contend,
And his Insulted Camp from Foes defend.						480
He said, and soon obeying his intent,
Patroclus brought *Briseis* from her Tent;
Then to th' intrusted Messengers resign'd:
She wept, and often cast her Eyes behind;
Forc'd from the Man she lov'd: They led her thence,		485
Along the Shore a Pris'ner to their Prince.

    Sole on the barren Sands the suff'ring Chief
Roar'd out for Anguish, and indulg'd his Grief.
Cast on his Kindred Seas a stormy Look,
And his upbraided Mother thus bespoke.					490

    Unhappy Parent, of a short-liv'd Son,
Since *Jove* in pity by thy Pray'rs was won
To grace my small Remains of Breath with Fame,
Why loads he this imbitter'd Life with Shame?
Suff'ring his King of Men to force my Slave,				495
Whom well deserv'd in War, the *Grecians* gave.

    Set by old Ocean's side the Goddess heard;
Then from the sacred Deep her Head she rear'd:
Rose like a Morning-mist; and thus begun
To sooth the Sorrows of her plaintive Son.				500
Why cry's my Care, and why conceals his Smart?
Let thy afflicted Parent, share her part.

    Then, sighing from the bottom of his Breast,
To the Sea-Goddess thus the Goddess-born address'd.
Thou know'st my Pain, which telling but recals:			505
By force of Arms we raz'd the *Theban* Walls;
The ransack'd City, taken by our Toils,
We left, and hither brought the golden Spoils:
Equal we shar'd them; but before the rest,
The proud Prerogative had seiz'd the best.				510
Chryseis was the greedy Tyrant's Prize,
Chryseis rosy Cheek'd with charming Eyes.
Her Syre, *Apollo*'s Priest, arriv'd to buy
With proffer'd Gifts of Price, his Daughter's liberty.
Suppliant before the *Grecians* Chiefs he stood,			515
Awful, and arm'd with Ensigns of his God:

Bare was his hoary Head, one holy Hand
Held forth his Lawrel-Crown, and one, his Scepter of Command.
His Suit was common, but above the rest
To both the Brother-Princes was address'd.   520
With Shouts of loud Acclaim the *Greeks* agree
To take the Gifts, to set the Pris'ner free.
Not so the Tyrant, who with scorn the Priest
Receiv'd, and with opprobrious Words dismiss'd.
The good old Man, forlorn of human Aid,   525
For Vengeance to his heav'nly Patron pray'd:
The Godhead gave a favourable Ear,
And granted all to him he held so dear;
In an ill hour his piercing Shafts he sped;
And heaps on heaps of slaughter'd *Greeks* lay dead,   530
While round the Camp he rang'd: At length arose
A Seer who well divin'd; and durst disclose
The Source of all our Ills: I took the Word;
And urg'd the sacred Slave to be restor'd,
The God appeas'd: The swelling Monarch storm'd;   535
And then, the Vengeance, vow'd; he since perform'd:
The *Greeks* 'tis true, their Ruin to prevent
Have to the Royal Priest, his Daughter sent;
But from their haughty King his Heralds came
And seiz'd by his Command, my Captive Dame,   540
By common Suffrage given; but, thou, be won,
If in thy Pow'r, t' avenge thy injur'd Son:
Ascend the Skies; and supplicating move
Thy just Complaint, to Cloud-compelling *Jove*.
If thou by either Word or Deed hast wrought   545
A kind remembrance in his grateful Thought,
Urge him by that: For often hast thou said
Thy Pow'r was once not useless in his Aid.
When He who high above the Highest reigns,
Surpriz'd by Traytor-Gods, was bound in Chains.   550
When *Juno*, *Pallas*, with Ambition fir'd,
And his blue Brother of the Seas conspir'd.
Thou freed'st the Soveraign from unworthy Bands,
Thou brought'st *Briareus* with his hundred Hands,
(So call'd in Heav'n, but mortal Men below   555
By his terrestrial Name, *Ægeon* know:

Twice stronger than his *Syre*, who sate above,
Assessor to the Throne of thundring *Jove*.)
The Gods, dismay'd at his approach, withdrew
Nor durst their unaccomplish'd Crime, pursue.   560
That Action to his grateful Mind recal;
Embrace his Knees, and at his Footstool fall:
That now if ever, he will aid our Foes;
Let *Troy*'s triumphant Troops the Camp inclose:
Ours beaten to the Shore, the Siege forsake;   565
And what their King deserves with him partake.
That the proud Tyrant at his proper cost,
May learn the value of the Man he lost.

To whom the Mother-Goddess thus reply'd,
Sigh'd e'er she spoke, and while she spoke she cry'd,   570
Ah wretched me! by Fates averse, decreed,
To bring thee forth with Pain, with care to breed!
Did envious Heav'n not otherwise ordain,
Safe in thy hollow Ships thou shou'd'st remain;
Nor ever tempt the fatal Field again.   575
But now thy Planet sheds his pois'nous Rays:
And short, and full of Sorrow are thy Days.
For what remains, to Heav'n I will ascend,
And at the Thund'rer's Throne thy Suit commend.
'Till then, secure in Ships, abstain from Fight;   580
Indulge thy Grief in Tears, and vent thy Spight.
For yesterday the Court of Heav'n with *Jove*,
Remov'd: 'Tis dead Vacation now above.
Twelve Days the Gods their solemn Revels keep,
And quaff with blameless *Ethiops* in the Deep.   585
Return'd from thence, to Heav'n my Flight I take,
Knock at the brazen Gates, and Providence awake.
Embrace his Knees, and suppliant to the Sire,
Doubt not I will obtain the grant of thy desire.

She said: And parting left him on the place,   590
Swoln with Disdain, resenting his Disgrace:
Revengeful Thoughts revolving in his Mind,
He wept for Anger and for Love he pin'd.

Mean time with prosperous Gales, *Ulysses* brought
The Slave, and Ship with Sacrifices fraught,   595
To *Chrysa*'s Port: Where entring with the Tide

He drop'd his Anchors, and his Oars he ply'd.
Furl'd every Sail, and drawing down the Mast,
His Vessel moor'd; and made with Haulsers fast.
Descending on the Plain, ashore they bring   600
The Hecatomb to please the shooter King.
The Dame before an Altars holy Fire,
Ulysses led; and thus bespoke her Sire.
    Reverenc'd be thou, and be thy God ador'd:
The King of Men thy Daughter has restor'd;   605
And sent by me with Presents and with Pray'r;
He recommends him to thy pious Care.
That *Phœbus* at thy Sute his Wrath may cease,
And give the penitent Offenders Peace.
    He said, and gave her to her Father's Hands,   610
Who glad receiv'd her, free from servile Bands.
This done, in Order they with sober Grace
Their Gifts around the well-built Altar place.
Then wash'd, and took the Cakes; while *Chryses* stood
With Hands upheld, and thus invok'd his God.   615
    God, of the Silver Bow, whose Eyes survey
The sacred *Cilla*, thou whose awful Sway
Chrysa the bless'd, and *Tenedos* obey:
Now hear, as thou before my Pray'r hast heard,
Against the *Grecians*, and their Prince, preferr'd: 620
Once thou hast honour'd, honour once again
Thy Priest; nor let his second Vows be vain.
But from th' afflicted Host and humbled Prince,
Avert thy Wrath, and cease thy Pestilence.
    Apollo heard, and conquering his Disdain,   625
Unbent his Bow and *Greece* respir'd again.
    Now when the solemn Rites of Pray'r were past,
Their salted Cakes on crackling Flames they cast.
Then, turning back, the Sacrifice they sped:
The fatted Oxen slew, and flea'd the Dead.   630
Chop'd off their nervous Thighs, and next prepar'd
T' involve the lean in Cauls, and mend with Lard.
Sweet-breads and Collops, were with Skewers prick'd
About the Sides; inbibing what they deck'd.
The Priest with holy Hands was seen to tine   635
The cloven Wood, and pour the ruddy Wine.

The Youth approach'd the Fire and as it burn'd
On five sharp Broachers rank'd, the Roast they turn'd:
These Morsels stay'd their Stomachs; then the rest
They cut in Legs and Fillets for the Feast;   64
Which drawn and serv'd, their Hunger they appease
With sav'ry Meat, and set their Minds at ease.

Now when the rage of Eating was repell'd,
The Boys with generous Wine the Goblets fill'd.
The first Libations to the Gods they pour: 64
And then with Songs indulge the Genial Hour.
Holy Debauch! Till Day to Night they bring,
With Hymns and *Pæans* to the Bowyer King.
At Sun-set to their Ship they make return,
And snore secure on Decks, till rosy Morn.   65

The Skies with dawning Day were purpled o'er;
Awak'd, with lab'ring Oars they leave the Shore:
The Pow'r appeas'd, with Winds suffic'd the Sail,
The bellying Canvass strutted with the Gale;
The Waves indignant roar with surly Pride,   65
And press against the Sides, and beaten off divide.
They cut the foamy way, with Force impell'd
Superiour, till the *Trojan* Port they held:
Then hauling on the Strand their Gally Moor,
And pitch their Tents along the crooked Shore.   66

Mean time the Goddess-born, in secret pin'd;
Nor visited the Camp, nor in the Council join'd,
But keeping close, his gnawing Heart he fed
With hopes of Vengeance on the Tyrant's Head:
And wish'd for bloody Wars and mortal Wounds,   66
And of the *Greeks* oppress'd in Fight, to hear the dying Sounds.

Now, when twelve Days compleat had run their Race,
The Gods bethought them of the Cares belonging to their place.
Jove at their Head ascending from the Sea,
A shoal of puny Pow'rs attend his way.   67
Then *Thetis* not unmindful of her Son
Emerging from the Deep, to beg her Boon,
Pursu'd their Track; and waken'd from his rest,
Before the Soveraign stood a Morning Guest.
Him in the Circle but apart, she found: 67
The rest at awful distance stood around.

She bow'd, and e'er she durst her Sute begin,
One Hand embrac'd his Knees, one prop'd his Chin.
Then thus. If I, Celestial Sire, in aught
Have serv'd thy Will, or gratify'd thy Thought,   680
One glimpse of Glory to my Issue give;
Grac'd for the little time he has to live.
Dishonour'd by the King of Men he stands:
His rightful Prize is ravish'd from his Hands.
But thou, O Father, in my Son's Defence,   685
Assume thy Pow'r, assert thy Providence.
Let *Troy* prevail, till *Greece* th' Affront has paid,
With doubled Honours; and redeem'd his Aid.

   She ceas'd, but the consid'ring God was mute:
'Till she resolv'd to win, renew'd her Sute: 690
Nor loos'd her Hold, but forc'd him to reply,
Or grant me my Petition, or deny:
Jove cannot fear: Then tell me to my Face
That I, of all the Gods am least in grace.
This I can bear: The Cloud-Compeller mourn'd,   695
And sighing, first, this Answer he return'd.

   Know'st thou what Clamors will disturb my Reign,
What my stun'd Ears from *Juno* must sustain?
In Council she gives Licence to her Tongue,
Loquacious, Brawling, ever in the wrong.   700
And now she will my partial Pow'r upbraid,
If alienate from *Greece*, I give the *Trojans* Aid.
But thou depart, and shun her jealous Sight,
The Care be mine, to do *Pelides* right.
Go then, and on the Faith of *Jove* rely;   705
When nodding to thy Sute, he bows the Sky.
This ratifies th' irrevocable Doom:
The Sign ordain'd, that what I will shall come:
The Stamp of Heav'n, and Seal of Fate: He said,
And shook the sacred Honours of his Head.   710
With Terror trembled Heav'ns subsiding Hill:
And from his shaken Curls Ambrosial Dews distil.
The Goddess goes exulting from his Sight,
And seeks the Seas profound; and leaves the Realms of Light.

   He moves into his Hall: The Pow'rs resort,   715
Each from his House to fill the Soveraign's Court.

Nor waiting Summons, nor expecting stood;
But met with Reverence, and receiv'd the God.
He mounts the Throne; and *Juno* took her place:
But sullen Discontent sate lowring on her Face.   720
With jealous Eyes, at distance she had seen,
Whisp'ring with *Jove* the Silver-footed Queen;
Then, impotent of Tongue (her Silence broke)
Thus turbulent in rattling Tone she spoke.

Author of Ills, and close Contriver *Jove*,   725
Which of thy Dames, what Prostitute of Love,
Has held thy Ear so long and begg'd so hard
For some old Service done, some new Reward?
Apart you talk'd, for that's your special care
The Consort never must the Council share.   730
One gracious Word is for a Wife too much:
Such is a Marriage-Vow, and *Jove*'s own Faith is such.

Then thus the Sire of Gods, and Men below,
What I have hidden, hope not thou to know.
Ev'n Goddesses are Women: And no Wife   735
Has Pow'r to regulate her Husband's Life:
Counsel she may; and I will give thy Ear
The Knowledge first, of what is fit to hear.
What I transact with others, or alone,
Beware to learn; nor press too near the Throne.   740

To whom the Goddess with the charming Eyes,
What hast thou said, O Tyrant of the Skies,
When did I search the Secrets of thy Reign,
Though priviledg'd to know, but priviledg'd in vain?
But well thou dost, to hide from common Sight   745
Thy close Intrigues, too bad to bear the Light.
Nor doubt I, but the Silver-footed Dame,
Tripping from Sea, on such an Errand came,
To grace her Issue, at the *Grecians* Cost,
And for one peevish Man destroy an Host.   750

To whom the Thund'rer made this stern Reply;
My Houshold Curse, my lawful Plague, the Spy
Of *Jove*'s Designs, his other squinting Eye;
Why this vain prying, and for what avail?
Jove will be Master still and *Juno* fail.   755
Shou'd thy suspicious Thoughts divine aright,

Thou but becom'st more odious to my Sight,
For this Attempt: uneasy Life to me
Still watch'd, and importun'd, but worse for thee.
Curb that impetuous Tongue, before too late   760
The Gods behold, and tremble at thy Fate.
Pitying, but daring not in thy Defence,
To lift a Hand against Omnipotence.

   This heard, the Imperious Queen sate mute with Fear;
Nor further durst incense the gloomy Thunderer.   765
Silence was in the Court at this Rebuke:
Nor cou'd the Gods abash'd, sustain their Sov'reigns Look.

   The Limping Smith, observ'd the sadden'd Feast;
And hopping here and there (himself a Jest)
Put in his Word, that neither might offend;   770
To *Jove* obsequious, yet his Mother's Friend.
What end in Heav'n will be of civil War,
If Gods of Pleasure will for Mortals jar?
Such Discord but disturbs our Jovial Feast;
One Grain of Bad, embitters all the best.   775
Mother, tho' wise your self, my Counsel weigh;
'Tis much unsafe my Sire to disobey.
Not only you provoke him to your Cost,
But Mirth is marr'd, and the good Chear is lost.
Tempt not his heavy Hand; for he has Pow'r   780
To throw you Headlong, from his Heav'nly Tow'r.
But one submissive Word, which you let fall,
Will make him in good Humour with us All.

   He said no more but crown'd a Bowl, unbid:
The laughing Nectar overlook'd the Lid: 785
Then put it to her Hand; and thus pursu'd,
This cursed Quarrel be no more renew'd.
Be, as becomes a Wife, obedient still;
Though griev'd, yet subject to her Husband's Will.
I wou'd not see you beaten; yet affraid   790
Of *Jove*'s superiour Force, I dare not aid.
Too well I know him, since that hapless Hour
When I, and all the Gods employ'd our Pow'r
To break your Bonds: Me by the Heel he drew;
And o'er Heav'n's Battlements with Fury threw.   795
All Day I fell; My Flight at Morn begun,

And ended not but with the setting Sun.
Pitch'd on my Head, at length the *Lemnian*-ground
Receiv'd my batter'd Skull, the *Sinthians* heal'd my Wound.
   At *Vulcan*'s homely Mirth his Mother smil'd,   800
And smiling took the Cup the Clown had fill'd.
The Reconciler Bowl, went round the Board,
Which empty'd, the rude Skinker still restor'd.
Loud Fits of Laughter seiz'd the Guests, to see
The limping God so deft at his new Ministry.   805
The Feast continu'd till declining Light:
They drank, they laugh'd, they lov'd, and then 'twas Night.
Nor wanted tuneful Harp, nor vocal Quire;
The Muses sung; *Apollo* touch'd the Lyre.
Drunken at last, and drowsy they depart,   810
Each to his House; Adorn'd with labour'd Art
Of the lame Architect: The thund'ring God
Ev'n he withdrew to rest, and had his Load.
His swimming Head to needful Sleep apply'd;
And *Juno* lay unheeded by his Side.   815

THE COCK and the FOX:
OR, THE TALE OF THE NUN'S PRIEST,
FROM CHAUCER

THERE liv'd, as Authors tell, in Days of Yore,
A Widow somewhat old, and very poor:
Deep in a Dell her Cottage lonely stood,
Well thatch'd, and under covert of a Wood.

This Dowager, on whom my Tale I found,   5
Since last she laid her Husband in the Ground,
A simple sober Life, in patience led,
And had but just enough to buy her Bread:
But Huswifing the little Heav'n had lent,
She duly paid a Groat for Quarter-Rent;   10
And pinch'd her Belly with her Daughters two,
To bring the Year about with much ado.

The Cattel in her Homestead were three Sows,
An Ewe call'd *Mally*; and three brinded Cows.
Her Parlor-Window stuck with Herbs around,   15
Of sav'ry Smell; and Rushes strew'd the Ground.
A Maple-Dresser, in her Hall she had,
On which full many a slender Meal she made:
For no delicious Morsel pass'd her Throat;
According to her Cloth she cut her Coat: 20
No paynant Sawce she knew, no costly Treat,
Her Hunger gave a Relish to her Meat:
A sparing Diet did her Health assure;
Or sick, a Pepper-Posset was her Cure.
Before the Day was done her Work she sped,   25
And never went by Candle-light to Bed:
With Exercise she sweat ill Humors out,
Her Dancing was not hinder'd by the Gout.
Her Poverty was glad; her Heart content,
Nor knew she what the Spleen or Vapors meant.   30

Of Wine she never tasted through the Year,
But White and Black was all her homely Chear;
Brown Bread, and Milk, (but first she skim'd her Bowls)

The Cock and the Fox. 3 Dell] Cell F   11 Daughters] Daughter F

And Rashers of sindg'd Bacon, on the Coals.
On Holy-Days, an Egg or two at most;   35
But her Ambition never reach'd to roast.
   A Yard she had with Pales enclos'd about,
Some high, some low, and a dry Ditch without.
Within this Homestead, liv'd without a Peer,
For crowing loud, the noble Chanticleer: 40
So hight her Cock, whose singing did surpass
The merry Notes of Organs at the Mass.
More certain was the crowing of a Cock
To number Hours, than is an Abbey-clock;
And sooner than the Mattin-Bell was rung,   45
He clap'd his Wings upon his Roost, and sung:
For when Degrees fifteen ascended right,
By sure Instinct he knew 'twas One at Night.
High was his Comb, and Coral-red withal,
In dents embattel'd like a Castle-Wall;   50
His Bill was Raven-black, and shon like Jet,
Blue were his Legs, and Orient were his Feet:
White were his Nails, like Silver to behold,
His Body glitt'ring like the burnish'd Gold.
   This gentle Cock for solace of his Life,   55
Six Misses had beside his lawful Wife;
Scandal that spares no King, tho' ne'er so good,
Says, they were all of his own Flesh and Blood:
His Sisters both by Sire, and Mother's side,
And sure their likeness show'd them near ally'd.   60
But make the worst, the Monarch did no more,
Than all the *Ptolomeys* had done before:
When Incest is for Int'rest of a Nation,
'Tis made no Sin by Holy Dispensation.
Some Lines have been maintain'd by this alone,   65
Which by their common Ugliness are known.
   But passing this as from our Tale apart,
Dame Partlet was the Soveraign of his Heart:
Ardent in Love, outragious in his Play,
He feather'd her a hundred times a Day: 70
And she that was not only passing fair,
But was withal discreet, and debonair,
Resolv'd the passive Doctrin to fulfil

Tho' loath: And let him work his wicked Will.
At Board and Bed was affable and kind,   75
According as their Marriage-Vow did bind,
And as the Churches Precept had enjoin'd.
Ev'n since she was a Sennight old, they say
Was chast, and humble to her dying Day,
Nor Chick nor Hen was known to disobey.   80
  By this her Husband's Heart she did obtain,
What cannot Beauty, join'd with Virtue, gain!
She was his only Joy, and he her Pride,
She, when he walk'd, went pecking by his side;
If spurning up the Ground, he sprung a Corn,   85
The Tribute in his Bill to her was born.
But oh! what Joy it was to hear him sing
In Summer, when the Day began to spring,
Stretching his Neck, and warbling in his Throat,
Solus cum Sola, then was all his Note.   90
For in the Days of Yore, the Birds of Parts
Were bred to Speak, and Sing, and learn the lib'ral Arts.
  It happ'd that perching on the Parlor-beam
Amidst his Wives he had a deadly Dream;
Just at the Dawn, and sigh'd, and groan'd so fast,   95
As ev'ry Breath he drew wou'd be his last.
Dame Partlet, ever nearest to his Side,
Heard all his piteous Moan, and how he cry'd
For Help from Gods and Men: And sore aghast
She peck'd and pull'd, and waken'd him at last.   100
Dear Heart, said she, for Love of Heav'n declare
Your Pain, and make me Partner of your Care.
You groan, Sir, ever since the Morning-light,
As something had disturb'd your noble Spright.
  And Madam, well I might, said Chanticleer,   105
Never was *Shrovetide*-Cock in such a fear.
Ev'n still I run all over in a Sweat,
My Princely Senses not recover'd yet.
For such a Dream I had of dire Portent,
That much I fear my Body will be shent: 110
It bodes I shall have Wars and woful Strife,
Or in a loathsom Dungeon end my Life.

Know Dame, I dreamt within my troubled Breast,
That in our Yard, I saw a murd'rous Beast,
That on my Body would have made Arrest.   115
With waking Eyes I ne'er beheld his Fellow,
His Colour was betwixt a Red and Yellow:
Tipp'd was his Tail, and both his pricking Ears
With black; and much unlike his other Hairs:
The rest, in shape a Beagle's Whelp throughout,   120
With broader Forehead, and a sharper Snout:
Deep in his Front were sunk his glowing Eyes,
That yet methinks I see him with Surprize.
Reach out your Hand, I drop with clammy Sweat,
And lay it to my Heart, and feel it beat.   125
  Now fy for Shame, quoth she, by Heav'n above,
Thou hast for ever lost thy Ladies Love;
No Woman can endure a Recreant Knight,
He must be bold by Day, and free by Night:
Our Sex desires a Husband or a Friend,   130
Who can our Honour and his own defend;
Wise, Hardy, Secret, lib'ral of his Purse:
A Fool is nauseous, but a Coward worse:
No bragging Coxcomb, yet no baffled Knight,
How dar'st thou talk of Love, and dar'st not Fight?   135
How dar'st thou tell thy Dame thou art affer'd,
Hast thou no manly Heart, and hast a Beard?
  If ought from fearful Dreams may be divin'd,
They signify a Cock of Dunghill-kind.
All Dreams, as in old *Gallen* I have read,   140
Are from Repletion and Complexion bred:
From rising Fumes of indigested Food,
And noxious Humors that infect the Blood:
And sure, my Lord, if I can read aright,
These foolish Fancies you have had to Night   145
Are certain Symptoms (in the canting Style)
Of boiling Choler, and abounding Bile:
This yellow Gaul that in your Stomach floats,
Ingenders all these visionary Thoughts.
When Choler overflows, then Dreams are bred   150
Of Flames and all the Family of Red;
Red Dragons, and red Beasts in sleep we view;

For Humors are distinguish'd by their Hue.
From hence we dream of Wars and Warlike Things,
And Wasps and Hornets with their double Wings. 155
    Choler adust congeals our Blood with Fear;
Then black Bulls toss us, and black Devils tear.
In sanguine airy Dreams aloft we bound,
With Rhumes oppress'd we sink in Rivers drown'd.
    More I could say, but thus conclude my Theme, 160
The dominating Humour makes the Dream.
Cato was in his time accounted Wise,
And he condemns them all for empty Lies.
Take my Advice, and when we fly to Ground
With Laxatives preserve your Body sound, 165
And purge the peccant Humors that abound.
I should be loath to lay you on a Bier;
And though there lives no 'Pothecary near,
I dare for once prescribe for your Disease,
And save long Bills, and a damn'd Doctor's Fees. 170
    Two Soveraign Herbs, which I by practise know,
And both at Hand, (for in our Yard they grow;)
On peril of my Soul shall rid you wholly
Of yellow Choler, and of Melancholy:
You must both Purge, and Vomit; but obey, 175
And for the love of Heav'n make no delay.
Since hot and dry in your Complexion join,
Beware the Sun when in a vernal Sign;
For when he mounts exalted in the Ram,
If then he finds your Body in a Flame, 180
Replete with Choler, I dare lay a Groat,
A Tertian Ague is at least your Lot.
Perhaps a Fever (which the Gods forefend)
May bring your Youth to some untimely end.
And therefore, Sir, as you desire to live, 185
A Day or two before your Laxative,
Take just three Worms, nor over nor above,
Because the Gods unequal Numbers love.
These Digestives prepare you for your Purge,
Of Fumetery, Centaury, and Spurge, 190
And of Ground-Ivy add a Leaf, or two,
All which within our Yard or Garden grow.

Eat these, and be, my Lord, of better Cheer,
Your Father's Son was never born to fear.

   Madam, quoth he, Grammercy for your Care,   195
But *Cato*, whom you quoted, you may spare:
'Tis true, a wise, and worthy Man he seems,
And (as you say) gave no belief to Dreams:
But other Men of more Authority,
And by th' Immortal Pow'rs as wise as He   200
Maintain, with sounder Sense, that Dreams forbode;
For *Homer* plainly says they come from God.
Nor *Cato* said it: But some modern Fool,
Impos'd in *Cato*'s Name on Boys at School.

   Believe me, Madam, Morning Dreams foreshow   205
Th' events of Things, and future Weal or Woe:
Some Truths are not by Reason to be try'd,
But we have sure Experience for our Guide.
An ancient Author, equal with the best,
Relates this Tale of Dreams among the rest.   210

   Two Friends, or Brothers, with devout Intent,
On some far Pilgrimage together went.
It happen'd so that when the Sun was down,
They just arriv'd by twilight at a Town;
That Day had been the baiting of a Bull,   215
'Twas at a Feast, and ev'ry Inn so full;
That no void Room in Chamber, or on Ground,
And but one sorry Bed was to be found:
And that so little it would hold but one,
Though till this Hour they never lay alone.   220

   So were they forc'd to part; one stay'd behind,
His Fellow sought what Lodging he could find:
At last he found a Stall where Oxen stood,
And that he rather chose than lie abroad.
'Twas in a farther Yard without a Door,   225
But for his ease, well litter'd was the Floor.

   His Fellow, who the narrow Bed had kept,
Was weary, and without a Rocker slept:
Supine he snor'd; but in the dead of Night,
He dreamt his Friend appear'd before his Sight,   230
Who with a ghastly Look and doleful Cry,
Said help me Brother, or this Night I die:

Arise, and help, before all Help be vain,
Or in an Oxes Stall I shall be slain.

Rowz'd from his Rest he waken'd in a start,   235
Shiv'ring with Horror, and with aking Heart;
At length to cure himself by Reason tries;
'Twas but a Dream, and what are Dreams but Lies?
So thinking chang'd his Side, and clos'd his Eyes.
His Dream returns; his Friend appears again,   240
The Murd'rers come; now help, or I am slain:
'Twas but a Vision still, and Visions are but vain.

He dreamt the third: But now his Friend appear'd
Pale, naked, pierc'd with Wounds, with Blood besmear'd:
Thrice warn'd awake, said he; Relief is late,   245
The Deed is done; but thou revenge my Fate:
Tardy of Aid, unseal thy heavy Eyes,
Awake, and with the dawning Day arise:
Take to the Western Gate thy ready way,
For by that Passage they my Corps convey: 250
My Corpse is in a Tumbril laid; among
The Filth, and Ordure, and enclos'd with Dung.
That Cart arrest, and raise a common Cry,
For sacred hunger of my Gold I die;
Then shew'd his grisly Wounds; and last he drew   255
A piteous Sigh; and took a long Adieu.

The frighted Friend arose by break of Day,
And found the Stall where late his Fellow lay.
Then of his impious Host enquiring more,
Was answer'd that his Guest was gone before: 260
Muttring he went, said he, by Morning-light,
And much complain'd of his ill Rest by Night.
This rais'd Suspicion in the Pilgrim's Mind;
Because all Hosts are of an evil Kind,
And oft, to share the Spoil, with Robbers join'd.   265
His Dream confirm'd his Thought: with troubled Look
Strait to the Western-Gate his way he took.
There, as his Dream foretold, a Cart he found,
That carry'd Composs forth to dung the Ground.
This, when the Pilgrim saw, he stretch'd his Throat,   270
And cry'd out Murther, with a yelling Note.
My murther'd Fellow in this Cart lies dead,

Vengeance and Justice on the Villain's Head.
You, Magistrates, who sacred Laws dispense,
On you I call to punish this Offence.   275
   The Word thus giv'n, within a little space,
The Mob came roaring out, and throng'd the Place.
All in a trice they cast the Cart to Ground,
And in the Dung the murther'd Body found;
Though breathless, warm, and reeking from the Wound.   280
Good Heav'n, whose darling Attribute we find
Is boundless Grace, and Mercy to Mankind,
Abhors the Cruel; and the Deeds of Night
By wond'rous Ways reveals in open Light:
Murther may pass unpunished for a time,   285
But tardy Justice will o'ertake the Crime.
And oft a speedier Pain the Guilty feels;
The Hue and Cry of Heav'n pursues him at the Heels,
Fresh from the Fact; as in the present Case;
The Criminals are seiz'd upon the Place: 290
Carter and Host confronted Face to Face.
Stiff in denial, as the Law appoints
On Engins they distend their tortur'd Joints:
So was Confession forc'd, th' Offence was known,
And publick Justice on th' Offenders done.   295
   Here may you see that Visions are to dread:
And in the Page that follows this; I read
Of two young Merchants, whom the hope of Gain
Induc'd in Partnership to cross the Main:
Waiting till willing Winds their Sails supply'd,   300
Within a Trading-Town they long abide,
Full fairly situate on a Haven's side.
   One Evening it befel that looking out,
The Wind they long had wish'd was come about:
Well pleas'd they went to Rest; and if the Gale   305
'Till Morn continu'd, both resolv'd to sail.
But as together in a Bed they lay,
The younger had a Dream at break of Day.
A Man, he thought, stood frowning at his side;
Who warn'd him for his Safety to provide,   310
Not put to Sea, but safe on Shore abide.

279 found] bound *F*

I come, thy Genius, to command thy stay;
Trust not the Winds, for fatal is the Day,
And Death unhop'd attends the watry way.

    The Vision said: And vanish'd from his sight,   315
The Dreamer waken'd in a mortal Fright:
Then pull'd his drowzy Neighbour, and declar'd
What in his Slumber he had seen, and heard.
His Friend smil'd scornful, and with proud contempt
Rejects as idle what his Fellow dreamt.   320
Stay, who will stay: For me no Fears restrain,
Who follow *Mercury* the God of Gain:
Let each Man do as to his Fancy seems,
I wait, not I, till you have better Dreams.
Dreams are but Interludes, which Fancy makes,   325
When Monarch-Reason sleeps, this Mimick wakes:
Compounds a Medley of disjointed Things,
A Mob of Coblers, and a Court of Kings:
Light Fumes are merry, grosser Fumes are sad;
Both are the reasonable Soul run mad: 330
And many monstrous Forms in sleep we see,
That neither were, nor are, nor e'er can be.
Sometimes, forgotten Things long cast behind
Rush forward in the Brain, and come to mind.
The Nurses Legends are for Truths receiv'd,   335
And the Man dreams but what the Boy believ'd.

    Sometimes we but rehearse a former Play,
The Night restores our Actions done by Day;
As Hounds in sleep will open for their Prey.
In short, the Farce of Dreams is of a piece,   340
Chimera's all; and more absurd, or less:
You, who believe in Tales, abide alone,
What e'er I get this Voyage is my own.

    Thus while he spoke he heard the shouting Crew
That call'd aboard, and took his last adieu.   345
The Vessel went before a merry Gale,
And for quick Passage put on ev'ry Sail:
But when least fear'd, and ev'n in open Day,
The Mischief overtook her in the way:
Whether she sprung a Leak, I cannot find,   350
Or whether she was overset with Wind;

Or that some Rock below, her bottom rent,
But down at once with all her Crew she went;
Her Fellow Ships from far her Loss descry'd;
But only she was sunk, and all were safe beside.   355

    By this Example you are taught again,
That Dreams and Visions are not always vain:
But if, dear Partlet, you are yet in doubt,
Another Tale shall make the former out.

    Kenelm the Son of *Kenulph*, *Mercia*'s King,   360
Whose holy Life the Legends loudly sing,
Warn'd, in a Dream, his Murther did foretel
From Point to Point as after it befel:
All Circumstances to his Nurse he told,
(A Wonder, from a Child of sev'n Years old:)   365
The Dream with Horror heard, the good old Wife
From Treason counsell'd him to guard his Life:
But close to keep the Secret in his Mind,
For a Boy's Vision small Belief would find.
The pious Child, by Promise bound, obey'd,   370
Nor was the fatal Murther long delay'd:
By *Quenda* slain he fell before his time,
Made a young Martyr by his Sister's Crime.
The Tale is told by venerable *Bede*,
Which, at your better leisure, you may read.   375

    Macrobius too relates the Vision sent
To the great *Scipio* with the fam'd event,
Objections makes, but after makes Replies,
And adds, that Dreams are often Prophecies.

    Of *Daniel*, you may read in Holy Writ,   380
Who, when the King his Vision did forget,
Cou'd Word for Word the wond'rous Dream repeat.
Nor less of Patriarch *Joseph* understand
Who by a Dream inslav'd th' *Egyptian* Land,
The Years of Plenty and of Dearth foretold,   385
When for their Bread, their Liberty they sold.
Nor must th' exalted Buttler be forgot,
Nor he whose Dream presag'd his hanging Lot.

    And did not *Crœsus* the same Death foresee,
Rais'd in his Vision on a lofty Tree?   390
The Wife of *Hector* in his utmost Pride,

Dreamt of his Death the Night before he dy'd:
Well was he warn'd from Battle to refrain,
But Men to Death decreed are warn'd in vain:
He dar'd the Dream, and by his fatal Foe was slain.   395

    Much more I know, which I forbear to speak,
For see the ruddy Day begins to break:
Let this suffice, that plainly I foresee
My Dream was bad, and bodes Adversity:
But neither Pills nor Laxatives I like,   400
They only serve to make a well-man sick:
Of these his Gain the sharp Phisician makes,
And often gives a Purge, but seldom takes:
They not correct, but poyson all the Blood,
And ne'er did any but the Doctors good.   405
Their Tribe, Trade, Trinkets, I defy them all,
With ev'ry Work of 'Pothecary's Hall.

    These melancholy Matters I forbear:
But let me tell Thee, Partlet mine, and swear,
That when I view the Beauties of thy Face,   410
I fear not Death, nor Dangers, nor Disgrace:
So may my Soul have Bliss, as when I spy
The Scarlet Red about thy Partridge Eye,
While thou art constant to thy own true Knight,
While thou art mine, and I am thy delight,   415
All Sorrows at thy Presence take their flight.
For true it is, as *in Principio*,
Mulier est hominis confusio.
Madam, the meaning of this Latin is,
That Woman is to Man his Soveraign Bliss.   420
For when by Night I feel your tender Side,
Though for the narrow Perch I cannot ride,
Yet I have such a Solace in my Mind,
That all my boding Cares are cast behind:
And ev'n already I forget my Dream;   425
He said, and downward flew from off the Beam.
For Day-light now began apace to spring,
The Thrush to whistle, and the Lark to sing.
Then crowing clap'd his Wings, th' appointed call
To chuck his Wives together in the Hall.   430

    By this the Widow had unbarr'd the Door,

And Chanticleer went strutting out before,
With Royal Courage, and with Heart so light,
As shew'd he scorn'd the Visions of the Night.
Now roaming in the Yard he spurn'd the Ground,   43
And gave to Partlet the first Grain he found.
Then often feather'd her with wanton Play,
And trod her twenty times e'er prime of Day;
And took by turns and gave so much delight,
Her Sisters pin'd with Envy at the sight.   44

He chuck'd again, when other Corns he found,
And scarcely deign'd to set a Foot to Ground.
But swagger'd like a Lord about his Hall,
And his sev'n Wives came running at his call.

'Twas now the Month in which the World began,   44
(If *March* beheld the first created Man:)
And since the vernal Equinox, the Sun,
In *Aries* twelve Degrees, or more had run,
When casting up his Eyes against the Light,
Both Month, and Day, and Hour he measur'd right;   4
And told more truly, than th' Ephemeris,
For Art may err, but Nature cannot miss.

Thus numb'ring Times, and Seasons in his Breast,
His second crowing the third Hour confess'd.
Then turning, said to Partlet, See, my Dear,   4
How lavish Nature has adorn'd the Year;
How the pale Primrose, and blue Violet spring,
And Birds essay their Throats disus'd to sing:
All these are ours; and I with pleasure see
Man strutting on two Legs, and aping me!   4
An unfledg'd Creature, of a lumpish frame,
Indew'd with fewer Particles of Flame:
Our Dame sits couring o'er a Kitchin-fire,
I draw fresh Air, and Nature's Works admire:
And ev'n this Day, in more delight abound,   4
Than since I was an Egg, I ever found.

The time shall come when Chanticleer shall wish
His Words unsaid, and hate his boasted Bliss:
The crested Bird shall by Experience know,
Jove made not him his Master-piece below;
And learn the latter end of Joy is Woe.

The Vessel of his Bliss to Dregs is run,
And Heav'n will have him tast his other Tun.

Ye Wise draw near, and hearken to my Tale,
Which proves that oft the Proud by Flatt'ry fall: 475
The Legend is as true I undertake
As *Tristram* is, and *Launcelot* of the Lake:
Which all our Ladies in such rev'rence hold,
As if in Book of Martyrs it were told.

A Fox full fraught with seeming Sanctity,   480
That fear'd an Oath, but like the Devil, would lie,
Who look'd like Lent, and had the holy Leer,
And durst not sin before he say'd his Pray'r:
This pious Cheat that never suck'd the Blood,
Nor chaw'd the Flesh of Lambs but when he cou'd,   } 485
Had pass'd three Summers in the neighb'ring Wood;
And musing long, whom next to circumvent,
On Chanticleer his wicked Fancy bent:
And in his high Imagination cast,
By Stratagem to gratify his Tast.   490

The Plot contriv'd, before the break of Day,
Saint *Reynard* through the Hedge had made his way;
The Pale was next, but proudly with a bound
He lept the Fence of the forbidden Ground:
Yet fearing to be seen, within a Bed   495
Of Colworts he conceal'd his wily Head;
There sculk'd till Afternoon, and watch'd his time,
(As Murd'rers use) to perpetrate his Crime.

O Hypocrite, ingenious to destroy,
O Traytor, worse than *Sinon* was to *Troy*;   500
O vile Subverter of the *Gallick* Reign,
More false than *Gano* was to *Charlemaign*!
O Chanticleer, in an unhappy Hour
Did'st thou forsake the Safety of thy Bow'r:
Better for Thee thou had'st believ'd thy Dream,   505
And not that Day descended from the Beam!

But here the Doctors eagerly dispute:
Some hold Predestination absolute:
Some Clerks maintain, that Heav'n at first foresees,
And in the virtue of Foresight decrees.   510
If this be so, then Prescience binds the Will,

And Mortals are not free to Good or Ill:
For what he first foresaw, he must ordain,
Or its eternal Prescience may be vain:
As bad for us as Prescience had not bin: 515
For first, or last, he's Author of the Sin.
And who says that, let the blaspheming Man
Say worse ev'n of the Devil, if he can.
For how can that Eternal Pow'r be just
To punish Man, who Sins because he must?   520
Or, how can He reward a vertuous Deed,
Which is not done by us; but first decreed?
  I cannot boult this Matter to the Bran,
As *Bradwardin* and holy *Austin* can:
If Prescience can determine Actions so   525
That we must do, because he did foreknow;
Or that foreknowing, yet our choice is free,
Not forc'd to Sin by strict necessity:
This strict necessity they simple call,
Another sort there is conditional.   530
The first so binds the Will, that Things foreknown
By Spontaneity, not Choice, are done.
Thus Galley-Slaves tug willing, at their Oar,
Consent to work, in prospect of the Shore;
But wou'd not work at all, if not constrain'd before.   535
That other does not Liberty constrain,
But Man may either act, or may refrain.
Heav'n made us Agents free to Good or Ill,
And forc'd it not, tho' he foresaw the Will.
Freedom was first bestow'd on human Race,   540
And Prescience only held the second place.
  If he could make such Agents wholly free,
I not dispute; the Point's too high for me;
For Heav'n's unfathom'd Pow'r what Man can sound,
Or put to his Omnipotence a Bound?   545
He made us to his Image all agree;
That Image is the Soul, and that must be,
Or not the Maker's Image, or be free.
  But whether it were better Man had been
By Nature bound to Good, not free to Sin,   550

I wave, for fear of splitting on a Rock,
The Tale I tell is only of a Cock;
Who had not run the hazard of his Life
Had he believ'd his Dream, and not his Wife:
For Women, with a mischief to their Kind,   555
Pervert, with bad Advice, our better Mind.
A Woman's Counsel brought us first to Woe,
And made her Man his Paradice forego,
Where at Heart's ease he liv'd; and might have bin
As free from Sorrow as he was from Sin.   560
For what the Devil had their Sex to do,
That, born to Folly, they presum'd to know,
And could not see the Serpent in the Grass?
But I my self presume, and let it pass.

    Silence in times of Suff'ring is the best,   565
'Tis dang'rous to disturb a Hornet's Nest.
In other Authors you may find enough,
But all they say of Dames is idle Stuff.
Legends of lying Wits together bound,
The Wife of *Bath* would throw 'em to the Ground: 570
These are the Words of Chanticleer, not mine,
I honour Dames, and think their Sex divine.

    Now to continue what my Tale begun.
Lay Madam Partlet basking in the Sun,
Breast-high in Sand: Her Sisters in a row,   575
Enjoy'd the Beams above, the Warmth below.
The Cock that of his Flesh was ever free,
Sung merrier than the Mermaid in the Sea:
And so befel, that as he cast his Eye,
Among the Colworts on a Butterfly,   580
He saw false *Reynard* where he lay full low,
I need not swear he had no list to Crow:
But cry'd Cock, Cock, and gave a suddain start,
As sore dismaid and frighted at his Heart.
For Birds and Beasts, inform'd by Nature, know   585
Kinds opposite to theirs, and fly their Foe.
So, Chanticleer, who never saw a Fox,
Yet shun'd him as a Sailor shuns the Rocks.

    But the false Loon who cou'd not work his Will
By open Force, employ'd his flatt'ring Skill;   590

I hope, my Lord, said he, I not offend,
Are you afraid of me, that am your Friend?
I were a Beast indeed to do you wrong,
I, who have lov'd and honour'd you so long:
Stay, gentle Sir, nor take a false Alarm,   595
For on my Soul I never meant you harm.
I come no Spy, nor as a Traytor press,
To learn the Secrets of your soft Recess:
Far be from *Reynard* so prophane a Thought,
But by the sweetness of your Voice was brought: 600
For, as I bid my Beads, by chance I heard,
The Song as of an Angel in the Yard:
A Song that wou'd have charm'd th' infernal Gods,
And banish'd Horror from the dark Abodes:
Had *Orpheus* sung it in the neather Sphere,   ⎞ 605
So much the Hymn had pleas'd the Tyrant's Ear,   ⎬
The Wife had been detain'd, to keep the Husband there. ⎠
     My Lord, your Sire familiarly I knew,
A Peer deserving such a Son, as you:
He, with your Lady-Mother (whom Heav'n rest)   610
Has often grac'd my House, and been my Guest:
To view his living Features does me good,
For I am your poor Neighbour in the Wood;
And in my Cottage shou'd be proud to see
The worthy Heir of my Friend's Family.   615
     But since I speak of Singing let me say,
As with an upright Heart I safely may,
That, save your self, there breaths not on the Ground,
One like your Father for a Silver sound.
So sweetly wou'd he wake the Winter-day,   ⎞ 620
That Matrons to the Church mistook their way,   ⎬
And thought they heard the merry Organ play.   ⎠
And he to raise his Voice with artful Care,
(What will not Beaux attempt to please the Fair?)
On Tiptoe stood to sing with greater Strength,   625
And stretch'd his comely Neck at all the length:
And while he pain'd his Voice to pierce the Skies,
As Saints in Raptures use, would shut his Eyes,
That the sound striving through the narrow Throat,

His winking might avail, to mend the Note.   630
By this, in Song, he never had his Peer,
From sweet *Cecilia* down to Chanticleer;
Not *Maro*'s Muse who sung the mighty Man,
Nor *Pindar*'s heav'nly Lyre, nor *Horace* when a Swan.
Your Ancestors proceed from Race divine,   635
From *Brennus* and *Belinus* is your Line:
Who gave to sov'raign *Rome* such loud Alarms,
That ev'n the Priests were not excus'd from Arms.
   Besides, a famous Monk of modern times,
Has left of Cocks recorded in his Rhimes,   640
That of a Parish-Priest the Son and Heir,
(When Sons of Priests were from the Proverb clear)
Affronted once a Cock of noble Kind,
And either lam'd his Legs, or struck him blind;
For which the Clerk his Father was disgrac'd,   645
And in his Benefice another plac'd.
Now sing, my Lord, if not for love of me,
Yet for the sake of sweet Saint Charity;
Make Hills, and Dales, and Earth and Heav'n rejoice,
And emulate your Father's Angel-voice.   650
   The Cock was pleas'd to hear him speak so fair,
And proud beside, as solar People are:
Nor cou'd the Treason from the Truth descry,
So was he ravish'd with this Flattery:
So much the more as from a little Elf,   655
He had a high Opinion of himself:
Though sickly, slender, and not large of Limb,
Concluding all the World was made for him.
   Ye Princes rais'd by Poets to the Gods,
And *Alexander'd* up in lying Odes,   660
Believe not ev'ry flatt'ring Knave's report,
There's many a *Reynard* lurking in the Court;
And he shall be receiv'd with more regard
And list'ned to, than modest Truth is heard.
   This Chanticleer of whom the Story sings,   665
Stood high upon his Toes, and clap'd his Wings;
Then stretch'd his Neck, and wink'd with both his Eyes;
Ambitious, as he sought, th' Olympick Prize.
But while he pain'd himself to raise his Note,

False *Reynard* rush'd, and caught him by the Throat.   670
Then on his Back he laid the precious Load,
And sought his wonted shelter of the Wood;
Swiftly he made his way, the Mischief done,
Of all unheeded, and pursu'd by none.

Alas, what stay is there in human State,   675
Or who can shun inevitable Fate?
The Doom was written, the Decree was past,
E'er the Foundations of the World were cast!
In *Aries* though the Sun exalted stood,
His Patron-Planet to procure his good;   680
Yet *Saturn* was his mortal Foe, and he
In *Libra* rais'd, oppos'd the same Degree:
The Rays both good and bad, of equal Pow'r,
Each thwarting other made a mingled Hour.

On *Friday*-morn he dreamt this direful Dream,   685
Cross to the worthy Native, in his Scheme!
Ah blissful *Venus*, Goddess of Delight,
How cou'd'st thou suffer thy devoted Knight,
On thy own Day to fall by Foe oppress'd,
The wight of all the World who serv'd thee best?   690
Who true to Love, was all for Recreation,
And minded not the Work of Propagation.
Gaufride, who could'st so well in Rhime complain,
The Death of *Richard* with an Arrow slain,
Why had not I thy Muse, or thou my Heart,   695
To sing this heavy Dirge with equal Art!
That I like thee on *Friday* might complain;
For on that Day was *Ceur de Lion* slain.

Not louder Cries when *Ilium* was in Flames,
Were sent to Heav'n by woful *Trojan* Dames,   700
When *Pyrrhus* toss'd on high his burnish'd Blade,
And offer'd *Priam* to his Father's Shade,
Than for the Cock the widow'd Poultry made.
Fair Partlet first, when he was born from sight,
With soveraign Shrieks bewail'd her Captive Knight.   705
Far lowder than the *Carthaginian* Wife,
When *Asdrubal* her Husband lost his Life,
When she beheld the smouldring Flames ascend,
And all the *Punick* Glories at an end:

Willing into the Fires she plung'd her Head, 710
With greater Ease than others seek their Bed.
Not more aghast the Matrons of Renown,
When Tyrant *Nero* burn'd th' Imperial Town,
Shriek'd for the downfal in a doleful Cry,
For which their guiltless Lords were doom'd to die. 715
  Now to my Story I return again.
The trembling Widow, and her Daughters twain,
This woful cackling Cry with Horror heard,
Of those distracted Damsels in the Yard;
And starting up beheld the heavy Sight, 720
How *Reynard* to the Forest took his Flight,
And cross his Back as in triumphant Scorn,
The Hope and Pillar of the House was born.
  The Fox, the wicked Fox, was all the Cry,
Out from his House ran ev'ry Neighbour nigh: 725
The Vicar first, and after him the Crew,
With Forks and Staves the Fellon to pursue.
Ran *Coll* our Dog, and *Talbot* with the Band,
And *Malkin*, with her Distaff in her Hand:
Ran Cow and Calf, and Family of Hogs, 730
In Panique Horror of pursuing Dogs,
With many a deadly Grunt and doleful Squeak
Poor Swine, as if their pretty Hearts would break.
The Shouts of Men, the Women in dismay,
With Shrieks augment the Terror of the Day. 735
The Ducks that heard the Proclamation cry'd,
And fear'd a Persecution might betide,
Full twenty Mile from Town their Voyage take,
Obscure in Rushes of the liquid Lake.
The Geese fly o'er the Barn; the Bees in Arms, 740
Drive headlong from their Waxen Cells in Swarms.
Jack Straw at *London*-stone with all his Rout
Struck not the City with so loud a Shout;
Not when with *English* Hate they did pursue
A *French* Man, or an unbelieving *Jew*: 745
Not when the Welkin rung with one and all;
And Echoes bounded back from *Fox*'s Hall;
Earth seem'd to sink beneath, and Heav'n above to fall.
With Might and Main they chas'd the murd'rous Fox,

With brazen Trumpets, and inflated Box,   750
To kindle *Mars* with military Sounds,
Nor wanted Horns t' inspire sagacious Hounds.

But see how Fortune can confound the Wise,
And when they least expect it, turn the Dice.
The Captive Cock, who scarce cou'd draw his Breath,   755
And lay within the very Jaws of Death;
Yet in this Agony his Fancy wrought
And Fear supply'd him with this happy Thought:
Yours is the Prize, victorious Prince, said he,
The Vicar my defeat, and all the Village see.   760
Enjoy your friendly Fortune while you may,
And bid the Churls that envy you the Prey,
Call back their mungril Curs, and cease their Cry,
See Fools, the shelter of the Wood is nigh,
And Chanticleer in your despight shall die.   765
He shall be pluck'd, and eaten to the Bone.

'Tis well advis'd, in Faith it shall be done;
This *Reynard* said: but as the Word he spoke,
The Pris'ner with a Spring from Prison broke:
Then stretch'd his feather'd Fans with all his might,   770
And to the neighb'ring Maple wing'd his flight.

Whom when the Traytor safe on Tree beheld,
He curs'd the Gods, with Shame and Sorrow fill'd;
Shame for his Folly; Sorrow out of time,
For Plotting an unprofitable Crime: 775
Yet mast'ring both, th' Artificer of Lies
Renews th' Assault, and his last Batt'ry tries.

Though I, said he, did ne'er in Thought offend,
How justly may my Lord suspect his Friend?
Th' appearance is against me, I confess,   780
Who seemingly have put you in Distress:
You, if your Goodness does not plead my Cause,
May think I broke all hospitable Laws,
To bear you from your Palace-yard by Might,
And put your noble Person in a Fright: 785
This, since you take it ill, I must repent,
Though Heav'n can witness with no bad intent,
I practis'd it, to make you taste your Cheer,
With double Pleasure first prepar'd by fear.

So loyal Subjects often seize their Prince,   ) 790
Forc'd (for his Good) to seeming Violence,   }
Yet mean his sacred Person not the least Offence.   )
Descend; so help me *Jove* as you shall find
That *Reynard* comes of no dissembling Kind.

Nay, quoth the Cock; but I beshrew us both,   795
If I believe a Saint upon his Oath:
An honest Man may take a Knave's Advice,
But Idiots only will be couzen'd twice:
Once warn'd is well bewar'd: No flatt'ring Lies   )
Shall sooth me more to sing with winking Eyes,   } 800
And open Mouth, for fear of catching Flies.   )
Who Blindfold walks upon a Rivers brim
When he should see, has he deserv'd to swim?
Better, Sir Cock, let all Contention cease,
Come down, said *Reynard*, let us treat of Peace.   805
A Peace with all my Soul, said Chanticleer;
But with your Favour, I will treat it here:
And least the Truce with Treason should be mixt,
'Tis my concern to have the Tree betwixt.

The MORAL

In this plain Fable you th' Effect may see   810
Of Negligence, and fond Credulity:
And learn besides of Flatt'rers to beware,
Then most pernicious when they speak too fair.
The Cock and Fox, the Fool and Knave imply;
The Truth is moral, though the Tale a Lie.   815
Who spoke in Parables, I dare not say;   )
But sure, he knew it was a pleasing way,   }
Sound Sense, by plain Example, to convey.   )
And in a Heathen Author we may find,   )
That Pleasure with Instruction should be join'd: } 820
So take the Corn, and leave the Chaff behind.   )

THEODORE AND HONORIA,
FROM BOCCACE

O F all the Cities in *Romanian* Lands,
The chief, and most renown'd *Ravenna* stands:
Adorn'd in ancient Times with Arms and Arts,
And rich Inhabitants, with generous Hearts.
But *Theodore* the Brave, above the rest,   5
With Gifts of Fortune, and of Nature bless'd,
The foremost Place, for Wealth and Honour held,
And all in Feats of Chivalry excell'd.

  This noble Youth to Madness lov'd a Dame,
Of high Degree, *Honoria* was her Name: 10
Fair as the Fairest, but of haughty Mind,
And fiercer than became so soft a kind;
Proud of her Birth; (for equal she had none;)
The rest she scorn'd; but hated him alone.
His Gifts, his constant Courtship, nothing gain'd;   15
For she, the more he lov'd, the more disdain'd:
He liv'd with all the Pomp he cou'd devise,
At Tilts and Turnaments obtain'd the Prize,
But found no favour in his Ladies Eyes:
Relentless as a Rock, the lofty Maid   20
Turn'd all to Poyson that he did, or said:
Nor Pray'rs, nor Tears, nor offer'd Vows could move;
The Work went backward; and the more he strove
T' advance his Sute, the farther from her Love.

  Weary'd at length, and wanting Remedy,   25
He doubted oft, and oft resolv'd to die.
But Pride stood ready to prevent the Blow,
For who would die to gratify a Foe?
His generous Mind disdain'd so mean a Fate;
That pass'd, his next Endeavour was to Hate.   30
But vainer that Relief than all the rest,
The less he hop'd with more Desire possess'd;
Love stood the Siege, and would not yield his Breast.
  Change was the next, but change deceiv'd his Care,
He sought a Fairer, but found none so Fair.   35

He would have worn her out by slow degrees,
As Men by Fasting starve th' untam'd Disease:
But present Love requir'd a present Ease.
Looking he feeds alone his famish'd Eyes,
Feeds lingring Death, but looking not he dies.   40
Yet still he chose the longest way to Fate,
Wasting at once his Life, and his Estate.

His Friends beheld, and pity'd him in vain,
For what Advice can ease a Lover's Pain!
Absence, the best Expedient they could find   45
Might save the Fortune, if not cure the Mind:
This Means they long propos'd, but little gain'd,
Yet after much pursuit, at length obtain'd.

Hard, you may think it was, to give consent,
But, struggling with his own Desires, he went: 50
With large Expence, and with a pompous Train,
Provided, as to visit *France* or *Spain*,
Or for some distant Voyage o'er the Main.
But Love had clipp'd his Wings, and cut him short,
Confin'd within the purlieus of his Court: 55
Three Miles he went, nor farther could retreat;
His Travels ended at his Country-Seat:
To *Chassis* pleasing Plains he took his way,
There pitch'd his Tents, and there resolv'd to stay.

The Spring was in the Prime; the neighb'ring Grove,   60
Supply'd with Birds, the Choristers of Love:
Musick unbought, that minister'd Delight
To Morning-walks, and lull'd his Cares by Night:
There he discharg'd his Friends; but not th' Expence
Of frequent Treats, and proud Magnificence.   65
He liv'd as Kings retire, though more at large,
From publick Business, yet with equal Charge;
With House, and Heart still open to receive;
As well content, as Love would give him leave:
He would have liv'd more free; but many a Guest,   70
Who could forsake the Friend, pursu'd the Feast.

It happ'd one Morning, as his Fancy led,
Before his usual Hour, he left his Bed;
To walk within a lonely Lawn, that stood
On ev'ry side surrounded by the Wood: 75

Alone he walk'd, to please his pensive Mind,
And sought the deepest Solitude to find:
'Twas in a Grove of spreading Pines he stray'd;
The Winds, within the quiv'ring Branches plaid,
And Dancing-Trees a mournful Musick made.   80
The Place it self was suiting to his Care,
Uncouth, and Salvage, as the cruel Fair.
He wander'd on, unknowing where he went,
Lost in the Wood, and all on Love intent:
The Day already half his Race had run,   85
And summon'd him to due Repast at Noon,
But Love could feel no Hunger but his own.
    While list'ning to the murm'ring Leaves he stood,
More than a Mile immers'd within the Wood,
At once the Wind was laid; the whisp'ring sound   90
Was dumb; a rising Earthquake rock'd the Ground:
With deeper Brown the Grove was overspred:
A suddain Horror seiz'd his giddy Head,
And his Ears tinckled, and his Colour fled.
Nature was in alarm; some Danger nigh   95
Seem'd threaten'd, though unseen to mortal Eye:
Unus'd to fear, he summon'd all his Soul
And stood collected in himself, and whole;
Not long: For soon a Whirlwind rose around,
And from afar he heard a screaming sound,   100
As of a Dame distress'd, who cry'd for Aid,
And fill'd with loud Laments the secret Shade.
    A Thicket close beside the Grove there stood
With Breers, and Brambles choak'd, and dwarfish Wood:
From thence the Noise: Which now approaching near   10
With more distinguish'd Notes invades his Ear:
He rais'd his Head, and saw a beauteous Maid,
With Hair dishevell'd, issuing through the Shade;
Stripp'd of her Cloaths, and e'en those Parts reveal'd,
Which modest Nature keeps from Sight conceal'd.   110
Her Face, her Hands, her naked Limbs were torn,
With passing through the Brakes, and prickly Thorn:
Two Mastiffs gaunt and grim, her Flight pursu'd,
And oft their fasten'd Fangs in Blood embru'd:
Oft they came up and pinch'd her tender Side,   11

Mercy, O Mercy, Heav'n, she ran, and cry'd;
When Heav'n was nam'd they loos'd their Hold again,
Then sprung she forth, they follow'd her amain.

   Not far behind, a Knight of swarthy Face,
High on a Coal-black Steed pursu'd the Chace;   120
With flashing Flames his ardent Eyes were fill'd,
And in his Hands a naked Sword he held:
He chear'd the Dogs to follow her who fled,
And vow'd Revenge on her devoted Head.

   As *Theodore* was born of noble Kind,   125
The brutal Action rowz'd his manly Mind:
Mov'd with unworthy Usage of the Maid,
He, though unarm'd, resolv'd to give her Aid.
A Saplin Pine he wrench'd from out the Ground,
The readiest Weapon that his Fury found.   130
Thus furnish'd for Offence, he cross'd the way
Betwixt the graceless Villain, and his Prey.

   The Knight came thund'ring on, but from afar
Thus in imperious Tone forbad the War:
Cease, *Theodore*, to proffer vain Relief,   135
Nor stop the vengeance of so just a Grief;
But give me leave to seize my destin'd Prey,
And let eternal Justice take the way:
I but revenge my Fate; disdain'd, betray'd,
And suff'ring Death for this ungrateful Maid.   140

   He say'd; at once dismounting from the Steed;
For now the Hell-hounds with superiour Speed
Had reach'd the Dame, and fast'ning on her Side,
The Ground with issuing Streams of Purple dy'd.
Stood *Theodore* surpriz'd in deadly Fright,   145
With chatt'ring Teeth and bristling Hair upright;
Yet arm'd with inborn Worth, What e'er, said he,
Thou art, who know'st me better than I thee;
Or prove thy rightful Cause, or be defy'd:
The Spectre, fiercely staring, thus reply'd.   150

   Know, *Theodore*, thy Ancestry I claim,
And *Guido Cavalcanti* was my Name.
One common Sire our Fathers did beget,
My Name and Story some remember yet:
Thee, then a Boy, within my Arms I laid,   155

When for my Sins I lov'd this haughty Maid;
Not less ador'd in Life, nor serv'd by Me,
Than proud *Honoria* now is lov'd by Thee.
What did I not her stubborn Heart to gain?
But all my Vows were answer'd with Disdain;   160
She scorn'd my Sorrows, and despis'd my Pain.
Long time I dragg'd my Days in fruitless Care,
Then loathing Life, and plung'd in deep Despair,
To finish my unhappy Life, I fell
On this sharp Sword, and now am damn'd in Hell.   165

    Short was her Joy; for soon th' insulting Maid
By Heav'n's Decree in the cold Grave was laid,
And as in unrepenting Sin she dy'd,
Doom'd to the same bad Place, is punish'd for her Pride;
Because she deem'd I well deserv'd to die,   170
And made a Merit of her Cruelty.
There, then, we met; both try'd and both were cast,
And this irrevocable Sentence pass'd;
That she whom I so long pursu'd in vain,
Should suffer from my Hands a lingring Pain: 175
Renew'd to Life, that she might daily die,
I daily doom'd to follow, she to fly;
No more a Lover but a mortal Foe,
I seek her Life (for Love is none below:)
As often as my Dogs with better speed   180
Arrest her Flight, is she to Death decreed.
Then with this fatal Sword on which I dy'd,
I pierce her open'd Back or tender Side,
And tear that harden'd Heart from out her Breast,
Which, with her Entrails, makes my hungry Hounds a Feast. 185
Nor lies she long, but as her Fates ordain,
Springs up to Life, and fresh to second Pain,
Is sav'd to Day, to Morrow to be slain.

    This, vers'd in Death, th' infernal Knight relates,
And then for Proof fulfill'd their common Fates;   190
Her Heart and Bowels through her Back he drew,
And fed the Hounds that help'd him to pursue.
Stern look'd the Fiend, as frustrate of his Will
Not half suffic'd, and greedy yet to kill.

And now the Soul expiring through the Wound,   195
Had left the Body breathless on the Ground,
When thus the grisly Spectre spoke again:
Behold the Fruit of ill-rewarded Pain:
As many Months as I sustain'd her Hate,
So many Years is she condemn'd by Fate   200
To daily Death; and ev'ry several Place,
Conscious of her Disdain, and my Disgrace,
Must witness her just Punishment; and be
A Scene of Triumph and Revenge to me.
As in this Grove I took my last Farewel,   205
As on this very spot of Earth I fell,
As *Friday* saw me die, so she my Prey
Becomes ev'n here, on this revolving Day.

    Thus while he spoke, the Virgin from the Ground
Upstarted fresh, already clos'd the Wound,   210
And unconcern'd for all she felt before
Precipitates her Flight along the Shore:
The Hell-hounds, as ungorg'd with Flesh and Blood
Pursue their Prey, and seek their wonted Food:
The Fiend remounts his Courser; mends his Pace,   215
And all the Vision vanish'd from the Place.

    Long stood the noble Youth oppress'd with Awe,
And stupid at the wond'rous Things he saw
Surpassing common Faith; transgressing Nature's Law.
He would have been asleep, and wish'd to wake,   220
But Dreams, he knew, no long Impression make,
Though strong at first: If Vision, to what end,
But such as must his future State portend?
His Love the Damsel, and himself the Fiend.
But yet reflecting that it could not be   225
From Heav'n, which cannot impious Acts decree,
Resolv'd within himself to shun the Snare
Which Hell for his Distruction did prepare;
And as his better Genius should direct
From an ill Cause to draw a good effect.   230

    Inspir'd from Heav'n he homeward took his way,
Nor pall'd his new Design with long delay:
But of his Train a trusty Servant sent;

To call his Friends together at his Tent.
They came, and usual Salutations paid,   23?
With Words premeditated thus he said:
What you have often counsell'd, to remove
My vain pursuit of unregarded Love;
By Thrift my sinking Fortune to repair,
Tho' late, yet is at last become my Care: 24?
My Heart shall be my own; my vast Expence
Reduc'd to bounds, by timely Providence:
This only I require; invite for me
Honoria, with her Father's Family,
Her Friends, and mine; the Cause I shall display,   24?
On *Friday* next, for that's th' appointed Day.

    Well pleas'd were all his Friends, the Task was light;
The Father, Mother, Daughter, they invite;
Hardly the Dame was drawn to this repast;
But yet resolv'd, because it was the last.   25?
The Day was come; the Guests invited came,
And, with the rest, th' inexorable Dame:
A Feast prepar'd with riotous Expence,
Much Cost, more Care, and most Magnificence.
The Place ordain'd was in that haunted Grove,   25?
Where the revenging Ghost pursu'd his Love:
The Tables in a proud Pavilion spred,
With Flow'rs below, and Tissue overhead:
The rest in rank; *Honoria* chief in place,
Was artfully contriv'd to set her Face   26?
To front the Thicket, and behold the Chace.
The Feast was serv'd; the time so well forecast,
That just when the Dessert, and Fruits were plac'd,
The Fiend's Alarm began; the hollow sound
Sung in the Leaves, the Forest shook around,   26?
Air blacken'd; rowl'd the Thunder; groan'd the Ground.

    Nor long before the loud Laments arise,
Of one distress'd, and Mastiffs mingled Cries;
And first the Dame came rushing through the Wood,
And next the famish'd Hounds that sought their Food   27?
And grip'd her Flanks, and oft essay'd their Jaws in Blood.
Last came the Fellon on the Sable Steed,
Arm'd with his naked Sword, and urg'd his Dogs to speed:

She ran, and cry'd; her Flight directly bent,
(A Guest unbidden) to the fatal Tent, 275
The Scene of Death, and Place ordain'd for Punishment.
Loud was the Noise, aghast was every Guest,
The Women shriek'd, the Men forsook the Feast;
The Hounds at nearer distance hoarsly bay'd;
The Hunter close pursu'd the visionary Maid, 280
She rent the Heav'n with loud Laments, imploring Aid.

The Gallants to protect the Ladies right,
Their Fauchions brandish'd at the grisly Spright;
High on his Stirrups, he provok'd the Fight.
Then on the Crowd he cast a furious Look, 285
And wither'd all their Strength before he strook:
Back on your Lives; let be, said he, my Prey,
And let my Vengeance take the destin'd way.
Vain are your Arms, and vainer your Defence,
Against th' eternal Doom of Providence: 290
Mine is th' ungrateful Maid by Heav'n design'd:
Mercy she would not give, nor Mercy shall she find.
At this the former Tale again he told
With thund'ring Tone, and dreadful to behold:
Sunk were their Hearts with Horror of the Crime, 295
Nor needed to be warn'd a second time,
But bore each other back; some knew the Face,
And all had heard the much lamented Case,
Of him who fell for Love, and this the fatal Place.

And now th' infernal Minister advanc'd, 300
Seiz'd the due Victim, and with Fury lanch'd
Her Back, and piercing through her inmost Heart,
Drew backward, as before, th' offending part.
The reeking Entrails next he tore away,
And to his meagre Mastiffs made a Prey: 305
The pale Assistants, on each other star'd
With gaping Mouths for issuing Words prepar'd;
The still-born sounds upon the Palate hung,
And dy'd imperfect on the faltring Tongue.
The Fright was general; but the Female Band 310
(A helpless Train) in more Confusion stand;

280 close] clos'd F

With Horror shuddring, on a heap they run,
Sick at the sight of hateful Justice done;
For Conscience rung th' Alarm, and made the Case their own.
　　So spread upon a Lake with upward Eye   315
A plump of Fowl behold their Foe on high,
They close their trembling Troop; and all attend
On whom the sowsing Eagle will descend.
　　But most the proud *Honoria* fear'd th' event,
And thought to her alone the Vision sent.   320
Her Guilt presents to her distracted Mind
Heav'ns Justice, *Theodore*'s revengeful Kind,
And the same Fate to the same Sin assign'd;
Already sees her self the Monster's Prey,
And feels her Heart, and Entrails torn away.   325
'Twas a mute Scene of Sorrow, mix'd with fear,
Still on the Table lay th' unfinish'd Cheer;
The Knight, and hungry Mastiffs stood around,
The mangled Dame lay breathless on the Ground:
When on a suddain reinspired with Breath,   330
Again she rose, again to suffer Death;
Nor stay'd the Hell-hounds, nor the Hunter stay'd,
But follow'd, as before, the flying Maid:
Th' Avenger took from Earth th' avenging Sword,
And mounting light as Air, his Sable Steed he spurr'd: 335
The Clouds dispell'd, the Sky resum'd her Light,
And Nature stood recover'd of her Fright.
　　But Fear, the last of Ills, remain'd behind,
And Horror heavy sat on ev'ry Mind.
Nor *Theodore* incourag'd more his Feast,   340
But sternly look'd, as hatching in his Breast
Some deep Design, which when *Honoria* view'd,
The fresh Impulse her former Fright renew'd:
She thought her self the trembling Dame who fled,
And him the grisly Ghost that spurr'd th' infernal Steed: 345
The more dismay'd, for when the Guests withdrew,
Their courteous Host saluting all the Crew
Regardless pass'd her o'er; nor grac'd with kind adieu.
That Sting infix'd within her haughty Mind,
The downfal of her Empire she divin'd;   350
And her proud Heart with secret Sorrow pin'd.

Home as they went, the sad Discourse renew'd
Of the relentless Dame to Death pursu'd,
And of the Sight obscene so lately view'd.
None durst arraign the righteous Doom she bore,   355
Ev'n they who pity'd most yet blam'd her more:
The Parallel they needed not to name,
But in the Dead they damn'd the living Dame.

   At ev'ry little Noise she look'd behind,
For still the Knight was present to her Mind: 360
And anxious oft she started on the way,
And thought the Horseman-Ghost came thundring for his Prey.
Return'd, she took her Bed, with little Rest,
But in short Slumbers dreamt the Funeral Feast:
Awak'd, she turn'd her Side, and slept again;   365
The same black Vapors mounted in her Brain,
And the same Dreams return'd with double Pain.

   Now forc'd to wake because afraid to sleep
Her Blood all Fever'd, with a furious Leap
She sprung from Bed, distracted in her Mind,   370
And fear'd, at ev'ry Step, a twitching Spright behind.
Darkling and desp'rate with a stagg'ring pace,
Of Death afraid, and conscious of Disgrace;
Fear, Pride, Remorse, at once her Heart assail'd,
Pride put Remorse to flight, but Fear prevail'd.   375
Friday, the fatal Day, when next it came,
Her Soul forethought the Fiend would change his Game,
And her pursue, or *Theodore* be slain,
And two Ghosts join their Packs to hunt her o'er the Plain.

   This dreadful Image so possess'd her Mind,   380
That desp'rate any Succour else to find,
She ceas'd all farther hope; and now began
To make reflection on th' unhappy Man.
Rich, Brave, and Young, who past expression lov'd,
Proof to Disdain; and not to be remov'd: 385
Of all the Men respected, and admir'd,
Of all the Dames, except her self, desir'd.
Why not of her? Preferr'd above the rest
By him with Knightly Deeds, and open Love profess'd?
So had another been; where he his Vows address'd.   390
This quell'd her Pride, yet other Doubts remain'd,

That once disdaining she might be disdain'd:
The Fear was just, but greater Fear prevail'd,
Fear of her Life by hellish Hounds assail'd:
He took a low'ring leave; but who can tell,   395
What outward Hate, might inward Love conceal?
Her Sexes Arts she knew, and why not then,
Might deep dissembling have a place in Men?
Here Hope began to dawn; resolv'd to try,
She fix'd on this her utmost Remedy;   400
Death was behind, but hard it was to die.
'Twas time enough at last on Death to call,
The Precipice in sight: A Shrub was all,
That kindly stood betwixt to break the fatal fall.

    One Maid she had, belov'd above the rest,   405
Secure of her, the Secret she confess'd:
And now the chearful Light her Fears dispell'd,
She with no winding turns the Truth conceal'd,
But put the Woman off, and stood reveal'd:
With Faults confess'd commission'd her to go,   410
If Pity yet had place, and reconcile her Foe:
The welcom Message made, was soon receiv'd;
'Twas what he wish'd, and hop'd, but scarce believ'd;
Fate seem'd a fair occasion to present,
He knew the Sex, and fear'd she might repent,   415
Should he delay the moment of Consent.
There yet remain'd to gain her Friends (a Care
The modesty of Maidens well might spare;)
But she with such a Zeal the Cause embrac'd,
(As Women where they will, are all in hast)   420
That Father, Mother, and the Kin beside,
Were overborn by fury of the Tide:
With full consent of all, she chang'd her State,
Resistless in her Love, as in her Hate.

    By her Example warn'd, the rest beware;   425
More Easy, less Imperious, were the Fair;
And that one Hunting which the Devil design'd,
For one fair Female, lost him half the Kind.

CEYX AND ALCYONE

CONNECTION OF THIS FABLE WITH THE FORMER

Ceyx, *the Son of* Lucifer, (*the Morning Star*) *and King of* Trachin *in* Thessaly, *was married to* Alcyone *Daughter to* Æolus *God of the Winds. Both the Husband and the Wife lov'd each other with an entire Affection.* Dædalion, *the Elder Brother of* Ceyx (*whom he succeeded*) *having been turn'd into a Falcon by* Apollo, *and* Chione, Dædalion's *Daughter, slain* by Diana; Ceyx *prepares a Ship to sail to* Claros *there to consult the Oracle of* Apollo, *and (as* Ovid *seems to intimate) to enquire how the Anger of the Gods might be atton'd.*

THESE Prodigies afflict the pious Prince,
But more perplex'd with those that happen'd since,
He purposes to seek the *Clarian* God,
Avoiding *Delphos*, his more fam'd Abode;
Since *Phlegyan* Robbers made unsafe the Road.   5
Yet cou'd he not from her he lov'd so well
The fatal Voyage, he resolv'd, conceal;
But when she saw her Lord prepar'd to part,
A deadly Cold ran shiv'ring to her Heart:
Her faded Cheeks are chang'd to Boxen Hue,   10
And in her Eyes the Tears are ever new:
She thrice assay'd to Speak; her Accents hung
And faltring dy'd unfinish'd on her Tongue,
Or vanish'd into Sighs: With long delay
Her Voice return'd; and found the wonted way.   15

Tell me, my Lord, she said, what Fault unknown
Thy once belov'd *Alcyone* has done?
Whether, ah whether is thy Kindness gone!
Can *Ceyx* then sustain to leave his Wife,
And unconcern'd forsake the Sweets of Life?   20
What can thy Mind to this long Journey move,
Or need'st thou absence to renew thy Love?
Yet, if thou go'st by Land, tho' Grief possess
My Soul ev'n then, my Fears will be the less.
But ah! be warn'd to shun the Watry Way,   25
The Face is frightful of the stormy Sea.
For late I saw a-drift disjointed Planks,

And empty Tombs erected on the Banks.
Nor let false Hopes to trust betray thy Mind,
Because my Sire in Caves constrains the Wind,   30
Can with a Breath their clam'rous Rage appease,
They fear his Whistle, and forsake the Seas;
Not so, for once indulg'd, they sweep the Main;
Deaf to the Call, or hearing hear in vain;
But bent on Mischief bear the Waves before,   35
And not content with Seas insult the Shoar,
When Ocean, Air, and Earth, at once ingage
And rooted Forrests fly before their Rage:
At once the clashing Clouds to Battle move,
And Lightnings run across the Fields above: 40
I know them well, and mark'd their rude Comport,
While yet a Child, within my Father's Court:
In times of Tempest they command alone,
And he but sits precarious on the Throne:
The more I know, the more my Fears augment,   45
And Fears are oft prophetick of th' event.
But if not Fears, or Reasons will prevail,
If Fate has fix'd thee obstinate to sail,
Go not without thy Wife, but let me bear
My part of Danger with an equal share,   } 50
And present, what I suffer only fear:
Then o'er the bounding Billows shall we fly,
Secure to live together, or to die.

These Reasons mov'd her starlike Husband's Heart,
But still he held his Purpose to depart: 55
For as he lov'd her equal to his Life,
He wou'd not to the Seas expose his Wife;
Nor cou'd be wrought his Voyage to refrain,
But sought by Arguments to sooth her Pain:
Nor these avail'd; at length he lights on one,   60
With which, so difficult a Cause he won:
My Love, so short an absence cease to fear,
For by my Father's holy Flame, I swear,
Before two Moons their Orb with Light adorn,
If Heav'n allow me Life, I will return.   65

This Promise of so short a stay prevails;
He soon equips the Ship, supplies the Sails,

And gives the Word to launch; she trembling views
This pomp of Death, and parting Tears renews:
Last with a Kiss, she took a long farewel,   70
Sigh'd, with a sad Presage, and swooning fell:
While *Ceyx* seeks Delays, the lusty Crew
Rais'd on their Banks their Oars in order drew
To their broad Breasts; the Ship with fury flew.

    The Queen recover'd rears her humid Eyes,   75
And first her Husband on the Poop espies
Shaking his Hand at distance on the Main;
She took the Sign; and shook her Hand again.
Still as the Ground recedes, contracts her View
With sharpen'd Sight, till she no longer knew   80
The much-lov'd Face; that Comfort lost supplies
With less, and with the Galley feeds her Eyes;
The Galley born from view by rising Gales
She follow'd with her Sight the flying Sails:
When ev'n the flying Sails were seen no more   85
Forsaken of all Sight, she left the Shoar.

    Then on her Bridal-Bed her Body throws,
And sought in sleep her weary'd Eyes to close:
Her Husband's Pillow, and the Widow'd part
Which once he press'd, renew'd the former Smart.   90

    And now a Breeze from Shoar began to blow,
The Sailors ship their Oars, and cease to row;
Then hoist their Yards a-trip, and all their Sails
Let fall, to court the Wind, and catch the Gales:
By this the Vessel half her Course had run,   95
And as much rested till the rising Sun;
Both Shores were lost to Sight, when at the close
Of Day, a stiffer Gale at East arose:
The Sea grew White, the rowling Waves from far
Like Heralds first denounce, the Wat'ry War.   100

    This seen, the Master soon began to cry,
Strike, strike the Top-sail; let the Main-sheet fly,
And furl your Sails: The Winds repel the sound,
And in the Speaker's Mouth the Speech is drown'd.
Yet of their own accord, as Danger taught   105
Each in his way, officiously they wrought;
Some stow their Oars, or stop the leaky Sides,

Another bolder yet the Yard bestrides,
And folds the Sails; a fourth with Labour, laves
Th' intruding Seas, and Waves ejects on Waves.   110
    In this Confusion while their Work they ply,
The Winds augment the Winter of the Sky,
And wage intestine Wars; the suff'ring Seas
Are toss'd, and mingled as their Tyrants please.
The Master wou'd command, but in despair   115
Of Safety, stands amaz'd with stupid Care,
Nor what to bid, or what forbid he knows,
Th' ungovern'd Tempest to such Fury grows:
Vain is his Force, and vainer is his Skill;
With such a Concourse comes the Flood of Ill: 120
The Cries of Men are mix'd with rattling Shrowds;
Seas dash on Seas, and Clouds encounter Clouds:
At once from East to West, from Pole to Pole,
The forky Lightnings flash, the roaring Thunders roul.
    Now Waves on Waves ascending scale the Skies,   125
And in the Fires above, the Water fries:
When yellow Sands are sifted from below,
The glitt'ring Billows give a golden Show:
And when the fouler bottom spews the Black,
The *Stygian* Dye the tainted Waters take: 130
Then frothy White appear the flatted Seas,
And change their Colour, changing their Disease.
Like various Fits the *Trachin* Vessel finds,
And now sublime, she rides upon the Winds;
As from a lofty Summet looks from high,   135
And from the Clouds beholds the neather Sky;
Now from the depth of Hell they lift their Sight,
And at a distance see superiour Light:
The lashing Billows make a loud report
And beat her Sides, as batt'ring Rams, a Fort: 140
Or as a Lyon, bounding in his way
With Force augmented bears against his Prey;
Sidelong to seize; or unappal'd with fear
Springs on the Toils, and rushes on the Spear:
So Seas impell'd by Winds with added Pow'r   145
Assault the Sides, and o'er the Hatches tow'r.
    The Planks (their pitchy Cov'ring wash'd away)

Now yield; and now a yawning Breach display:
The roaring Waters with a hostile Tide
Rush through the Ruins of her gaping Side.   150
Mean time in Sheets of Rain the Sky descends,
And Ocean swell'd with Waters upwards tends,
One rising, falling one, the Heav'ns, and Sea
Meet at their Confines, in the middle Way:
The Sails are drunk with Show'rs, and drop with Rain,   155
Sweet Waters mingle with the briny Main.
No Star appears to lend his friendly Light:
Darkness and Tempest make a double Night.
But flashing Fires disclose the Deep by turns,
And while the Light'nings blaze, the Water burns.   160

   Now all the Waves, their scatter'd Force unite,
And as a Soldier, foremost in the Fight
Makes way for others: And an Host alone
Still presses on, and urging gains the Town;
So while th' invading Billows come a-brest,   165
The Hero tenth advanc'd before the rest,
Sweeps all before him with impetuous Sway,
And from the Walls descends upon the Prey;
Part following enter, part remain without,
With Envy hear their Fellows conqu'ring Shout: 170
And mount on others Backs, in hope to share
The City, thus become the Seat of War.

   An universal Cry resounds aloud,
The Sailors run in heaps, a helpless Crowd;
Art fails, and Courage falls, no Succour near;   175
As many Waves, as many Deaths appear.
One weeps, and yet despairs of late Relief;
One cannot weep, his Fears congeal his Grief,
But stupid, with dry Eyes expects his Fate: ⎫
One with loud Shrieks laments his lost Estate,   ⎬ 180
And calls those happy whom their Funerals wait. ⎭
This Wretch with Pray'rs, and Vows the Gods implores,
And ev'n the Sky's he cannot see, adores.
That other on his Friends his Thoughts bestows,
His careful Father, and his faithful Spouse.   185
The covetous Worldling in his anxious Mind

Thinks only on the Wealth he left behind.

   All *Ceyx* his *Alcyone* employs,
For her he grieves, yet in her absence joys:
His Wife he wishes, and wou'd still be near,   190
Not her with him, but wishes him with her:
Now with last Looks he seeks his Native Shoar,
Which Fate has destin'd him to see no more,
He sought, but in the dark tempestuous Night
He knew not whether to direct his Sight.   195
So whirl the Seas, such Darkness blinds the Sky,
That the black Night receives a deeper Dye.

   The giddy Ship ran round; the Tempest tore
Her Mast, and over-board the Rudder bore.
One Billow mounts; and with a scornful Brow   200
Proud of her Conquest gain'd insults the Waves below;
Nor lighter falls, than if some Gyant tore
Pyndus and *Athos*, with the Freight they bore,
And toss'd on Seas; press'd with the pondrous Blow
Down sinks the Ship within th' Abyss below: 205
Down with the Vessel sink into the Main
The many, never more to rise again.
Some few on scatter'd Planks with fruitless Care
Lay hold, and swim, but while they swim, despair.

   Ev'n he who late a Scepter did command   210
Now grasps a floating Fragment in his Hand,
And while he struggles on the stormy Main,
Invokes his Father, and his Wife's, in vain;
But yet his Consort is his greatest Care;
Alcyone he names amidst his Pray'r,   215
Names as a Charm against the Waves, and Wind;
Most in his Mouth, and ever in his Mind:
Tir'd with his Toyl, all hopes of Safety past,
From Pray'rs to Wishes he descends at last:
That his dead Body wafted to the Sands,   220
Might have its Burial from her Friendly Hands.
As oft as he can catch a gulp of Air,
And peep above the Seas, he names the Fair,
And ev'n when plung'd beneath, on her he raves,
Murm'ring *Alcyone* below the Waves: 225
At last a falling Billow stops his Breath,

Breaks o'er his Head, and whelms him underneath.
Bright *Lucifer* unlike himself appears
That Night, his heav'nly Form obscur'd with Tears,
And since he was forbid to leave the Skies,   230
He muffled with a Cloud his mournful Eyes.

  Mean time *Alcyone* (his Fate unknown)
Computes how many Nights he had been gone,
Observes the waning Moon with hourly view,
Numbers her Age, and wishes for a new;   235
Against the promis'd Time provides with care,
And hastens in the Woof the Robes he was to wear:
And for her Self employs another Loom,
New-dress'd to meet her Lord returning home,
Flatt'ring her Heart with Joys that never were to come: 240
She fum'd the Temples with an odrous Flame,
And oft before the sacred Altars came,
To pray for him, who was an empty Name.
All Pow'rs implor'd, but far above the rest
To *Juno* she her pious Vows address'd,   245
Her much-lov'd Lord from Perils to protect
And safe o'er Seas his Voyage to direct:
Then pray'd that she might still possess his Heart,
And no pretending Rival share a part;
This last Petition heard of all her Pray'r,   250
The rest dispers'd by Winds were lost in Air.

  But she, the Goddess of the Nuptial-Bed,
Tir'd with her vain Devotions for the Dead,
Resolv'd the tainted Hand should be repell'd
Which Incense offer'd, and her Altar held: 255
Then *Iris* thus bespoke; Thou faithful Maid
By whom thy Queen's Commands are well convey'd,
Hast to the House of Sleep, and bid the God
Who rules the Night by Visions with a Nod,
Prepare a Dream, in Figure and in Form   260
Resembling him who perish'd in the Storm;
This Form before *Alcyone* present,
To make her certain of the sad Event.

  Indu'd with Robes of various Hew she flies,
And flying draws an Arch, (a segment of the Skies:)   265
Then leaves her bending Bow, and from the steep

Descends to search the silent House of Sleep.
   Near the *Cymmerians*, in his dark Abode
Deep in a Cavern, dwells the drowzy God;
Whose gloomy Mansion nor the rising Sun   270
Nor setting, visits, nor the lightsome Noon:
But lazy Vapors round the Region fly,
Perpetual Twilight, and a doubtful Sky;
No crowing Cock does there his Wings display
Nor with his horny Bill provoke the Day: 275
Nor watchful Dogs, nor the more wakeful Geese,
Disturb with nightly Noise the sacred Peace:
Nor Beast of Nature, nor the Tame are nigh,
Nor Trees with Tempests rock'd, nor human Cry,
But safe Repose without an air of Breath   280
Dwells here, and a dumb Quiet next to Death.
   An Arm of *Lethe* with a gentle flow
Arising upwards from the Rock below,
The Palace moats, and o'er the Pebbles creeps
And with soft Murmers calls the coming Sleeps: 285
Around its Entry nodding Poppies grow,
And all cool Simples that sweet Rest bestow;
Night from the Plants their sleepy Virtue drains,
And passing sheds it on the silent Plains:
No Door there was th' unguarded House to keep,   290
On creaking Hinges turn'd, to break his Sleep.
   But in the gloomy Court was rais'd a Bed
Stuff'd with black Plumes, and on an Ebon-sted:
Black was the Cov'ring too, where lay the God
And slept supine, his Limbs display'd abroad: 295
About his Head fantastick Visions fly,
Which various Images of Things supply,
And mock their Forms, the Leaves on Trees not more;
Nor bearded Ears in Fields, nor Sands upon the Shore.
   The Virgin entring bright indulg'd the Day   300
To the brown Cave, and brush'd the Dreams away:
The God disturb'd with this new glare of Light
Cast sudden on his Face, unseal'd his Sight,
And rais'd his tardy Head, which sunk agen,
And sinking on his Bosom knock'd his Chin;   305
At length shook off himself; and ask'd the Dame,

(And asking yawn'd) for what intent she came?

　To whom the Goddess thus: O sacred Rest,
Sweet pleasing Sleep, of all the Pow'rs the best!
O Peace of Mind, repairer of Decay,　　　　　　　　　　310
Whose Balm renews the Limbs to Labours of the Day,
Care shuns thy soft approach, and sullen flies away!
Adorn a Dream, expressing human Form,
The Shape of him who suffer'd in the Storm,
And send it flitting to the *Trachin* Court,　　　　　　315
The Wreck of wretched *Ceyx* to report:
Before his Queen bid the pale Spectre stand,
Who begs a vain Relief at *Juno*'s Hand.
She said, and scarce awake her Eyes cou'd keep,
Unable to support the fumes of Sleep:　　　　　　　　320
But fled returning by the way she went,
And swerv'd along her Bow with swift ascent.

　The God uneasy till he slept again
Resolv'd at once to rid himself of Pain;
And tho' against his Custom, call'd aloud,　　　　　　325
Exciting *Morpheus* from the sleepy Crowd:
Morpheus of all his numerous Train express'd
The Shape of Man, and imitated best;
The Walk, the Words, the Gesture cou'd supply,
The Habit mimick, and the Mien bely;　　　　　　　330
Plays well, but all his Action is confin'd,
Extending not beyond our human kind.

Another Birds, and Beasts, and Dragons apes,
And dreadful Images, and Monster shapes:
This Demon, *Icelos*, in Heav'ns high Hall　　　　　335
The Gods have nam'd; but Men *Phobetor* call:
A third is *Phantasus*, whose Actions roul
On meaner Thoughts, and Things devoid of Soul;
Earth, Fruits and Flow'rs, he represents in Dreams,
And solid Rocks unmov'd, and running Streams:　　　340
These three to Kings, and Chiefs their Scenes display,
The rest before th' ignoble Commons play:
Of these the chosen *Morpheus* is dispatch'd,
Which done, the lazy Monarch overwatch'd
Down from his propping Elbow drops his Head,　　　345

311 Balm] Balms F

Dissolv'd in Sleep, and shrinks within his Bed.
 Darkling the Demon glides for Flight prepar'd,
So soft that scarce his fanning Wings are heard.
To *Trachin*, swift as Thought, the flitting Shade
Through Air his momentary Journey made: 350
Then lays aside the steerage of his Wings,
Forsakes his proper Form, assumes the Kings;
And pale as Death despoil'd of his Array
Into the Queen's Apartment takes his way,
And stands before the Bed at dawn of Day: 355
Unmov'd his Eyes, and wet his Beard appears;
And shedding vain, but seeming real Tears;
The briny Water dropping from his Hairs;
Then staring on her with a ghastly Look
And hollow Voice, he thus the Queen bespoke.   360
 Know'st thou not me? Not yet unhappy Wife?
Or are my Features perish'd with my Life?
Look once again, and for thy Husband lost,
Lo all that's left of him, thy Husband's Ghost!
Thy Vows for my return were all in vain;   365
The stormy South o'ertook us in the Main;
And never shalt thou see thy living Lord again.
Bear witness Heav'n I call'd on Thee in Death,
And while I call'd, a Billow stop'd my Breath:
Think not that flying Fame reports my Fate;   370
I present, I appear, and my own Wreck relate.
Rise wretched Widow, rise, nor undeplor'd
Permit my Ghost to pass the *Stygian* Ford:
But rise, prepar'd in Black, to mourn thy perish'd Lord.
 Thus said the Player-God; and adding Art   375
Of Voice and Gesture, so perform'd his part,
She thought (so like her Love the Shade appears)
That *Ceyx* spake the Words, and *Ceyx* shed the Tears:
She groan'd, her inward Soul with Grief opprest,
She sigh'd, she wept; and sleeping beat her Breast: 380
Then stretch'd her Arms t' embrace his Body bare,
Her clasping Arms inclose but empty Air:
At this not yet awake she cry'd, O stay,
One is our Fate, and common is our way!
So dreadful was the Dream, so loud she spoke,   385

That starting sudden up, the Slumber broke:
Then cast her Eyes around in hope to view
Her vanish'd Lord, and find the Vision true:
For now the Maids, who waited her Commands,
Ran in with lighted Tapers in their Hands. 390
Tir'd with the Search, not finding what she seeks,
With cruel Blows she pounds her blubber'd Cheeks:
Then from her beaten Breast the Linnen tare,
And cut the golden Caull that bound her Hair.
Her Nurse demands the Cause; with louder Cries, 395
She prosecutes her Griefs, and thus replies.
    No more *Alcyone*; she suffer'd Death
With her lov'd Lord, when *Ceyx* lost his Breath:
No Flatt'ry, no false Comfort, give me none,
My Shipwreck'd *Ceyx* is for ever gone: 400
I saw, I saw him manifest in view,
His Voice, his Figure, and his Gestures knew:
His Lustre lost, and ev'ry living Grace,
Yet I retain'd the Features of his Face;
Tho' with pale Cheeks, wet Beard, and dropping Hair, 405
None but my *Ceyx* cou'd appear so fair:
I would have strain'd him with a strict Embrace,
But through my Arms he slip'd, and vanish'd from the Place:
There, ev'n just there he stood; and as she spoke
Where last the Spectre was, she cast her Look: 410
Fain wou'd she hope, and gaz'd upon the Ground
If any printed Footsteps might be found.
    Then sigh'd and said; This I too well foreknew,
And, my prophetick Fear presag'd too true:
'Twas what I beg'd when with a bleeding Heart 415
I took my leave, and suffer'd Thee to part;
Or I to go along, or Thou to stay,
Never, ah never to divide our way!
Happier for me, that all our Hours assign'd
Together we had liv'd; e'en not in Death disjoin'd! 420
So had my *Ceyx* still been living here,
Or with my *Ceyx* I had perish'd there:
Now I die absent, in the vast profound;
And Me without my Self the Seas have drown'd:
The Storms were not so cruel; should I strive 425

To lengthen Life, and such a Grief survive;
But neither will I strive, nor wretched Thee
In Death forsake, but keep thee Company.
If not one common Sepulcher contains
Our Bodies, or one Urn, our last Remains,   430
Yet *Ceyx* and *Alcyone* shall join,
Their Names remember'd in one common Line.

No farther Voice her mighty Grief affords,
For Sighs come rushing in betwixt her Words,
And stop'd her Tongue, but what her Tongue deny'd   435
Soft Tears, and Groans, and dumb Complaints supply'd.

'Twas Morning; to the Port she takes her way,
And stands upon the Margin of the Sea:
That Place, that very Spot of Ground she sought,
Or thither by her Destiny was brought;   440
Where last he stood: And while she sadly said
'Twas here he left me, lingring here delay'd
His parting Kiss; and there his Anchors weigh'd:

Thus speaking, while her Thoughts past Actions trace,
And call to mind admonish'd by the Place,   445
Sharp at her utmost Ken she cast her Eyes,
And somewhat floating from afar descries:
It seem'd a Corps adrift, to distant Sight,
But at a distance who could judge aright?

It wafted nearer yet, and then she knew   450
That what before she but surmis'd, was true.
A Corps it was, but whose it was, unknown,
Yet mov'd, howe'er, she made the Case her own:
Took the bad Omen of a shipwreck'd Man,
As for a Stranger wept, and thus began.   455

Poor Wretch, on stormy Seas to lose thy Life,
Unhappy thou, but more thy widdow'd Wife!
At this she paus'd; for now the flowing Tide
Had brought the Body nearer to the side:
The more she looks, the more her Fears increase,   460
At nearer Sight; and she's her self the less:
Now driv'n ashore, and at her Feet it lies,
She knows too much, in knowing whom she sees:
Her Husband's Corps; at this she loudly shrieks,
'Tis he, 'tis he, she cries, and tears her Cheeks,   465

Her Hair, her Vest, and stooping to the Sands
About his Neck she cast her trembling Hands.
   And is it thus, O dearer than my Life,
Thus, thus return'st Thou to thy longing Wife!
She said, and to the neighb'ring Mole she strode,   470
(Rais'd there to break th' Incursions of the Flood;)
   Headlong from hence to plunge her self she springs,
But shoots along supported on her Wings,
A Bird new-made about the Banks she plies,
Not far from Shore; and short Excursions tries;   475
Nor seeks in Air her humble Flight to raise,
Content to skim the Surface of the Seas:
Her Bill, tho' slender, sends a creaking Noise,
And imitates a lamentable Voice:
Now lighting where the bloodless Body lies,   480
She with a Funeral Note renews her Cries.
At all her stretch her little Wings she spread,
And with her feather'd Arms embrac'd the Dead:
Then flick'ring to his palid Lips, she strove
To print a Kiss, the last essay of Love: 485
Whether the vital Touch reviv'd the Dead,
Or that the moving Waters rais'd his Head
To meet the Kiss, the Vulgar doubt alone;
For sure a present Miracle was shown.
   The Gods their Shapes to Winter-Birds translate,   490
But both obnoxious to their former Fate.
Their conjugal Affection still is ty'd,
And still the mournful Race is multiply'd:
They bill, they tread; *Alcyone* compress'd
Sev'n Days sits brooding on her floating Nest: 495
A wintry Queen: Her Sire at length is kind,
Calms ev'ry Storm, and hushes ev'ry Wind;
Prepares his Empire for his Daughter's Ease,
And for his hatching Nephews smooths the Seas.

THE FLOWER AND THE LEAF:
OR, THE LADY IN THE ARBOUR.
A VISION

Now turning from the wintry Signs, the Sun
  His Course exalted through the Ram had run:
And whirling up the Skies, his Chariot drove
Through *Taurus*, and the lightsome Realms of Love;
Where *Venus* from her Orb descends in Show'rs   5
To glad the Ground, and paint the Fields with Flow'rs:
When first the tender Blades of Grass appear,
And Buds that yet the blast of *Eurus* fear,
Stand at the door of Life; and doubt to cloath the Year;
Till gentle Heat, and soft repeated Rains,   10
Make the green Blood to dance within their Veins:
Then, at their Call, embolden'd out they come,
And swell the Gems, and burst the narrow Room;
Broader and broader yet, their Blooms display,
Salute the welcome Sun, and entertain the Day.   15
Then from their breathing Souls the Sweets repair
To scent the Skies, and purge th' unwholsome Air:
Joy spreads the Heart, and with a general Song,
Spring issues out, and leads the jolly Months along.
  In that sweet Season, as in Bed I lay,   20
And sought in Sleep to pass the Night away,
I turn'd my weary Side, but still in vain,
Tho' full of youthful Health, and void of Pain:

Cares I had none, to keep me from my Rest,
For Love had never enter'd in my Breast;   25
I wanted nothing Fortune could supply,
Nor did she Slumber till that hour deny:
I wonder'd then, but after found it true,
Much Joy had dry'd away the balmy Dew:
Sea's wou'd be Pools, without the brushing Air,   30
To curl the Waves; and sure some little Care
Shou'd weary Nature so, to make her want repair.
  When Chaunticleer the second Watch had sung,
Scorning the Scorner Sleep from Bed I sprung.

And dressing, by the Moon, in loose Array,   35
Pass'd out in open Air, preventing Day,
And sought a goodly Grove as Fancy led my way.
Strait as a Line in beauteous Order stood
Of Oaks unshorn a venerable Wood;
Fresh was the Grass beneath, and ev'ry Tree   40
At distance planted in a due degree,
Their branching Arms in Air with equal space
Stretch'd to their Neighbours with a long Embrace:
And the new Leaves on ev'ry Bough were seen,
Some ruddy-colour'd, some of lighter green.   45
The painted Birds, Companions of the Spring,
Hopping from Spray to Spray, were heard to sing;
Both Eyes and Ears receiv'd a like Delight,
Enchanting Musick, and a charming Sight.
On *Philomel* I fix'd my whole Desire;   50
And list'n'd for the Queen of all the Quire;
Fain would I hear her heav'nly Voice to sing;
And wanted yet an Omen to the Spring.
    Attending long in vain; I took the way,
Which through a Path, but scarcely printed, lay;   55
In narrow Mazes oft it seem'd to meet,
And look'd, as lightly press'd, by Fairy Feet.
Wandring I walk'd alone, for still methought
To some strange End so strange a Path was wrought:
At last it led me where an Arbour stood,   60
The sacred Receptacle of the Wood:
This Place unmark'd though oft I walk'd the Green,
In all my Progress I had never seen:

And seiz'd at once with Wonder and Delight,
Gaz'd all arround me, new to the transporting Sight.   65
'Twas bench'd with Turf, and goodly to be seen,
The thick young Grass arose in fresher Green:
The Mound was newly made, no Sight cou'd pass
Betwixt the nice Partitions of the Grass;
The well-united Sods so closely lay;   70
And all arround the Shades defended it from Day.
For Sycamours with Eglantine were spread,
A Hedge about the Sides, a Covering over Head.
And so the fragrant Brier was wove between,

The Sycamour and Flow'rs were mix'd with Green,   75
That Nature seem'd to vary the Delight;
And satisfy'd at once the Smell and Sight.
The Master Work-man of the Bow'r was known
Through Fairy-Lands, and built for *Oberon*;
Who twining Leaves with such Proportion drew,   80
They rose by Measure, and by Rule they grew:
No mortal Tongue can half the Beauty tell;
For none but Hands divine could work so well.
Both Roof and Sides were like a Parlour made,
A soft Recess, and a cool Summer shade;   85
The Hedge was set so thick, no Foreign Eye
The Persons plac'd within it could espy:
But all that pass'd without with Ease was seen,
As if nor Fence nor Tree was plac'd between.
'Twas border'd with a Field; and some was plain   90
With Grass; and some was sow'd with rising Grain.
That (now the Dew with Spangles deck'd the Ground:)
A sweeter spot of Earth was never found.
I look'd, and look'd, and still with new Delight;
Such Joy my Soul, such Pleasures fill'd my Sight: 95
And the fresh Eglantine exhal'd a Breath;
Whose Odours were of Pow'r to raise from Death:
Nor sullen Discontent, nor anxious Care,
Ev'n tho' brought thither, could inhabit there:
But thence they fled as from their mortal Foe;   100
For this sweet Place cou'd only Pleasure know.
    Thus, as I mus'd, I cast aside my Eye

And saw a Medlar-Tree was planted nigh;
The spreading Branches made a goodly Show,
And full of opening Blooms was ev'ry Bough: 105
A Goldfinch there I saw with gawdy Pride
Of painted Plumes, that hopp'd from side to side,
Still pecking as she pass'd; and still she drew
The Sweets from ev'ry Flow'r, and suck'd the Dew:
Suffic'd at length, she warbled in her Throat,   110
And tun'd her Voice to many a merry Note,
But indistinct, and neither Sweet nor Clear,
Yet such as sooth'd my Soul, and pleas'd my Ear.
    Her short Performance was no sooner try'd,

When she I sought, the Nightingale reply'd: 　　　　115
So sweet, so shrill, so variously she sung,
That the Grove eccho'd, and the Valleys rung:
And I so ravish'd with her heav'nly Note
I stood intranc'd, and had no room for Thought.
But all o'er-pou'r'd with Extasy of Bliss, 　　　　120
Was in a pleasing Dream of Paradice;
At length I wak'd; and looking round the Bow'r
Search'd ev'ry Tree, and pry'd on ev'ry Flow'r,
If any where by chance I might espy
The rural Poet of the Melody: 　　　　125
For still methought she sung not far away;
At last I found her on a Lawrel Spray,
Close by my Side she sate, and fair in Sight,
Full in a Line, against her opposite;
Where stood with Eglantine the Lawrel twin'd: 　　　130
And both their native Sweets were well conjoin'd.

　　On the green Bank I sat, and listen'd long;
(Sitting was more convenient for the Song!)
Nor till her Lay was ended could I move,
But wish'd to dwell for ever in the Grove. 　　　　135
Only methought the time too swiftly pass'd,
And ev'ry Note I fear'd wou'd be the last.
My Sight, and Smell, and Hearing were employ'd,
And all three Senses in full Gust enjoy'd.
And what alone did all the rest surpass, 　　　　140
The sweet Possession of the Fairy Place;
Single, and conscious to my Self alone,
Of Pleasures to th' excluded World unknown.
Pleasures which no where else, were to be found,
And all *Elysium* in a spot of Ground. 　　　　145

　　Thus while I sat intent to see and hear,
And drew Perfumes of more than vital Air,
All suddenly I heard th' approaching sound
Of vocal Musick, on th' enchanted Ground:
An Host of Saints it seem'd, so full the Quire; 　　　150
As if the Bless'd above did all conspire,
To join their Voices, and neglect the Lyre.
At length there issu'd from the Grove behind
A fair Assembly of the Female Kind:

A Train less fair, as ancient Fathers tell,   155
Seduc'd the Sons of Heaven to rebel.
I pass their Forms, and ev'ry charming Grace,
Less than an Angel wou'd their Worth debase:
But their Attire like Liveries of a kind,
All rich and rare, is fresh within my Mind.   160
In Velvet white as Snow the Troop was gown'd,
The Seams with sparkling Emeralds, set around;
Their Hoods and Sleeves the same: And purfled o'er
With Diamonds, Pearls, and all the shining store
Of Eastern Pomp: Their long descending Train   165
With Rubies edg'd, and Saphires, swept the Plain:
High on their Heads, with Jewels richly set
Each Lady wore a radiant Coronet.
Beneath the Circles, all the Quire was grac'd
With Chaplets green on their fair Foreheads plac'd.   170
Of Lawrel some, of Woodbine many more;
And Wreaths of *Agnus castus*, others bore:
These last who with those Virgin Crowns were dress'd,
Appear'd in higher Honour than the rest.
They danc'd around, but in the midst was seen   ⎫   175
A Lady of a more majestique Mien;   ⎬
By Stature, and by Beauty mark'd their Sovereign Queen. ⎭
   She in the midst began with sober Grace;
Her Servants Eyes were fix'd upon her Face:
And as she mov'd or turn'd her Motions view'd,   180
Her Measures kept, and Step by Step pursu'd.

Methought she trod the Ground with greater Grace,
With more of Godhead shining in her Face;
And as in Beauty she surpass'd the Quire,
So, nobler than the rest, was her Attire.   185
A Crown of ruddy Gold inclos'd her Brow,
Plain without Pomp, and Rich without a Show:
A Branch of *Agnus castus* in her Hand,
She bore aloft (her Scepter of Command;)
Admir'd, ador'd by all the circling Crowd,   190
For wheresoe'er she turn'd her Face, they bow'd:
And as she danc'd, a Roundelay she sung,
In honour of the Lawrel, ever young:

She rais'd her Voice on high, and sung so clear, ⎫
The Fawns came scudding from the Groves to hear: ⎬ 195
And all the bending Forest lent an Ear. ⎭
At ev'ry Close she made, th' attending Throng
Reply'd, and bore the Burden of the Song:
So just, so small, yet in so sweet a Note,
It seem'd the Musick melted in the Throat.   200

   Thus dancing on, and singing as they danc'd,
They to the middle of the Mead advanc'd:
Till round my Arbour, a new Ring they made,
And footed it about the secret Shade:
O'erjoy'd to see the jolly Troop so near,   205
But somewhat aw'd I shook with holy Fear;
Yet not so much, but that I noted well
Who did the most in Song, or Dance excel.

   Not long I had observ'd, when from afar
I heard a suddain Symphony of War;   210
The neighing Coursers, and the Soldiers cry,
And sounding Trumps that seem'd to tear the Sky:
I saw soon after this, behind the Grove
From whence the Ladies did in order move,
Come issuing out in Arms a Warrior-Train,   215
That like a Deluge pour'd upon the Plain:
On barbed Steeds they rode in proud Array,
Thick as the College of the Bees in *May*,
When swarming o'er the dusky Fields they fly,
New to the Flow'rs, and intercept the Sky.   220
So fierce they drove, their Coursers were so fleet,
That the Turf trembled underneath their Feet.

   To tell their costly Furniture were long,
The Summers Day wou'd end before the Song:
To purchase but the Tenth of all their Store,   225
Would make the mighty *Persian* Monarch poor.
Yet what I can, I will; before the rest
The Trumpets issu'd in white Mantles dress'd:
A numerous Troop, and all their Heads around ⎫
With Chaplets green of Cerrial-Oak were crown'd, ⎬ 230
And at each Trumpet was a Banner bound; ⎭
Which waving in the Wind display'd at large
Their Master's Coat of Arms, and Knightly Charge.

Broad were the Banners, and of snowy Hue,
A purer Web the Silk-worm never drew.   235
The chief about their Necks, the Scutcheons wore,
With Orient Pearls and Jewels pouder'd o'er:
Broad were their Collars too, and ev'ry one
Was set about with many a costly Stone.
Next these of Kings at Arms a goodly Train,   240
In proud Array came prancing o'er the Plain:
Their Cloaks were Cloth of Silver mix'd with Gold,
And Garlands green arround their Temples roll'd:
Rich Crowns were on their royal Scutcheons plac'd
With Saphires, Diamonds, and with Rubies grac'd.   245
And as the Trumpets their appearance made,
So these in Habits were alike array'd;
But with a Pace more sober, and more slow:
And twenty, Rank in Rank, they rode a-row.
The Pursevants came next in number more;   250
And like the Heralds each his Scutcheon bore:
Clad in white Velvet all their Troop they led,
With each an Oaken Chaplet on his Head.
    Nine royal Knights in equal Rank succeed,
Each Warrior mounted on a fiery Steed: 255
In golden Armour glorious to behold;
The Rivets of their Arms were nail'd with Gold.
Their Surcoats of white Ermin-Fur were made;
With Cloth of Gold between that cast a glitt'ring Shade.
The Trappings of their Steeds were of the same;   260
The golden Fringe ev'n set the Ground on flame;
And drew a precious Trail: A Crown divine
Of Lawrel did about their Temples twine.
    Three Henchmen were for ev'ry Knight assign'd,
All in rich Livery clad, and of a kind: 265
White Velvet, but unshorn, for Cloaks they wore,
And each within his Hand a Truncheon bore:
The foremost held a Helm of rare Device;
A Prince's Ransom wou'd not pay the Price.
The second bore the Buckler of his Knight,   ⎫ 270
The third of Cornel-Wood a Spear upright,   ⎬
Headed with piercing Steel, and polish'd bright.   ⎭
Like to their Lords their Equipage was seen,

And all their Foreheads crown'd with Garlands green.
   And after these came arm'd with Spear and Shield   275
An Host so great, as cover'd all the Field:
And all their Foreheads, like the Knights before,
With Lawrels ever green were shaded o'er,
Or Oak, or other Leaves of lasting kind,
Tenacious of the Stem and firm against the Wind.   280
Some in their Hands besides the Lance and Shield,
The Boughs of Woodbind or of Hauthorn held,
Or Branches for their mistique Emblems took,
Of Palm, of Lawrel, or of Cerrial Oak.
   Thus marching to the Trumpets lofty sound   285
Drawn in two Lines adverse they wheel'd around,
And in the middle Meadow took their Ground.
Among themselves the Turney they divide,
In equal Squadrons, rang'd on either side.
Then turn'd their Horses Heads, and Man to Man,   290
And Steed to Steed oppos'd, the Justs began.
They lightly set their Lances in the rest,
And, at the Sign, against each other press'd:
They met, I sitting at my Ease beheld
The mix'd Events, and Fortunes of the Field.   295
Some broke their Spears, some tumbled Horse and Man,
And round the Fields the lighten'd Coursers ran.
An Hour and more like Tides, in equal sway
They rush'd, and won by turns, and lost the Day:
At length the Nine (who still together held)   300
Their fainting Foes to shameful Flight compell'd,
And with resistless Force, o'er-ran the Field.
Thus, to their Fame, when finish'd was the Fight,
The Victors from their lofty Steeds alight:
Like them dismounted all the Warlike Train,   305
And two by two proceeded o'er the Plain:
Till to the fair Assembly they advanc'd,
Who near the secret Arbour sung and danc'd.
   The Ladies left their Measures at the Sight,
To meet the Chiefs returning from the Fight,   310
And each with open Arms embrac'd her chosen Knight.

The Flower and the Leaf. 301 Flight] Fight F

Amid the Plain a spreading Lawrel stood,
The Grace and Ornament of all the Wood:
That pleasing Shade they sought, a soft retreat
From suddain *April* Show'rs, a Shelter from the Heat.   315
Her leavy Arms with such extent were spread,
So near the Clouds was her aspiring Head,
That Hosts of Birds, that wing the liquid Air,
Perch'd in the Boughs, had nightly Lodging there.
And Flocks of Sheep beneath the Shade from far   320
Might hear the ratling Hail, and wintry War;
From Heav'ns Inclemency here found retreat,
Enjoy'd the cool, and shun'd the scorching Heat:
A hundred Knights might there at Ease abide;
And ev'ry Knight a Lady by his side: 325
The Trunk it self such Odours did bequeath,
That a Moluccan Breeze to these was common Breath.
The Lords, and Ladies here approaching, paid
Their Homage, with a low Obeisance made:
And seem'd to venerate the sacred Shade.   330
These Rites perform'd, their Pleasures they pursue,
With Songs of Love, and mix with Measures new;
Around the holy Tree their Dance they frame,
And ev'ry Champion leads his chosen Dame.
  I cast my Sight upon the farther Field,   335
And a fresh Object of Delight beheld:
For from the Region of the West I heard
New Musick sound, and a new Troop appear'd;
Of Knights, and Ladies mix'd a jolly Band,
But all on Foot they march'd, and Hand in Hand.   340
  The Ladies dress'd in rich Symarrs were seen
Of *Florence* Satten, flow'r'd with White and Green,
And for a Shade betwixt the bloomy Gridelin.
The Borders of their Petticoats below
Were guarded thick with Rubies on a-row;   345
And ev'ry Damsel wore upon her Head
Of Flow'rs a Garland blended White and Red.
Attir'd in Mantles all the Knights were seen,
That gratify'd the View with chearful Green:
Their Chaplets of their Ladies Colours were   350
Compos'd of White and Red to shade their shining Hair.

Before the merry Troop the Minstrels play'd,
All in their Masters Liveries were array'd:
And clad in Green, and on their Temples wore
The Chaplets White and Red their Ladies bore. 355

Their Instruments were various in their kind,
Some for the Bow, and some for breathing Wind:
The Sawtry, Pipe, and Hautbois noisy band,
And the soft Lute trembling beneath the touching Hand.

A Tuft of Daisies on a flow'ry Lay 360
They saw, and thitherward they bent their way:
To this both Knights and Dames their Homage made,
And due Obeisance to the Daisy paid.

And then the Band of Flutes began to play,
To which a Lady sung a Virelay; 365
And still at ev'ry close she wou'd repeat
The Burden of the Song, *The Daisy is so sweet.*

The Daisy is so sweet when she begun,
The Troop of Knights and Dames continu'd on.
The Concert and the Voice so charm'd my Ear, 370
And sooth'd my Soul, that it was Heav'n to hear.

But soon their Pleasure pass'd: At Noon of Day,
The Sun with sultry Beams began to play:
Not *Syrius* shoots a fiercer Flame from high,
When with his pois'nous Breath he blasts the Sky: 375
Then droop'd the fading Flow'rs (their Beauty fled)
And clos'd their sickly Eyes, and hung the Head;
And, rivell'd up with Heat, lay dying in their Bed.
The Ladies gasp'd, and scarcely could respire;
The Breath they drew, no longer Air, but Fire; 380
The fainty Knights were scorch'd; and knew not where
To run for Shelter, for no Shade was near.
And after this the gath'ring Clouds amain,
Pour'd down a Storm of rattling Hail and Rain.
And Lightning flash'd betwixt: The Field, and Flow'rs 385
Burnt up before, were bury'd in the Show'rs.
The Ladies, and the Knights no Shelter nigh,
Bare to the Weather, and the wintry Sky,
Were dropping wet, disconsolate and wan,
And through their thin Array receiv'd the Rain. 390

While those in White protected by the Tree

Saw pass the vain Assault, and stood from Danger free.
But as Compassion mov'd their gentle Minds,
When ceas'd the Storm, and silent were the Winds,
Displeas'd at what, not suff'ring they had seen,   395
They went to chear the Faction of the Green:
The Queen in white Array before her Band,
Saluting, took her Rival by the Hand;
So did the Knights and Dames, with courtly Grace
And with Behaviour sweet their Foes embrace.   400
Then thus the Queen with Lawrel on her Brow,
Fair Sister I have suffer'd in your Woe:
Nor shall be wanting ought within my Pow'r
For your Relief in my refreshing Bow'r.
That other answer'd with a lowly Look,   405
And soon the gracious Invitation took:
For ill at ease both she and all her Train
The scorching Sun had born, and beating Rain.
Like Courtesy was us'd by all in White,
Each Dame a Dame receiv'd, and ev'ry Knight a Knight.   410
The Lawrel-Champions with their Swords invade
The neighb'ring Forests where the Justs were made,
And Serewood from the rotten Hedges took,
And Seeds of Latent-Fire from Flints provoke:
A chearful Blaze arose, and by the Fire,   415
They warm'd their frozen Feet, and dry'd their wet Attire.
Refresh'd with Heat the Ladies sought around
For virtuous Herbs which gather'd from the Ground
They squeez'd the Juice; and cooling Ointment made,
Which on their Sun-burnt Cheeks, and their chapt Skins they laid: 420
Then sought green Salads which they bad 'em eat,
A Soveraign Remedy for inward Heat.
　　The Lady of the Leaf ordain'd a Feast,
And made the Lady of the Flow'r her Guest:
When lo, a Bow'r ascended on the Plain,   425
With suddain Seats adorn'd, and large for either Train.
This Bow'r was near my pleasant Arbour plac'd,
That I could hear and see whatever pass'd:
The Ladies sat, with each a Knight between
Distinguish'd by their Colours White and Green: 430
The vanquish'd Party with the Victors join'd,

Nor wanted sweet Discourse, the Banquet of the Mind.
Mean time the Minstrels play'd on either side
Vain of their Art, and for the Mast'ry vy'd:
The sweet Contention lasted for an Hour, 435
And reach'd my secret Arbour from the Bow'r.

The Sun was set; and *Vesper* to supply
His absent Beams, had lighted up the Sky:
When *Philomel*, officious all the Day
To sing the Service of th' ensuing *May*, 440
Fled from her Lawrel Shade, and wing'd her Flight
Directly to the Queen array'd in White:
And hopping sate familiar on her Hand,
A new Musitian, and increas'd the Band.

The Goldfinch, who to shun the scalding Heat, 445
Had chang'd the Medlar for a safer Seat,
And hid in Bushes scap'd the bitter Show'r,
Now perch'd upon the Lady of the Flow'r;
And either Songster holding out their Throats,
And folding up their Wings renew'd their Notes: 450
As if all Day, preluding to the Fight,
They only had rehears'd, to sing by Night.
The Banquet ended, and the Battle done,
They danc'd by Star-light and the friendly Moon:

And when they were to part, the Laureat Queen, 455
Supply'd with Steeds the Lady of the Green.
Her, and her Train conducting on the way
The Moon to follow, and avoid the Day.

This when I saw, inquisitive to know
The secret Moral of the Mystique Show, 460
I started from my Shade in hopes to find
Some Nymph to satisfy my longing Mind:
And as my fair Adventure fell, I found
A Lady all in White with Lawrel crown'd
Who clos'd the Rear, and softly pac'd along, 465
Repeating to her self the former Song.
With due respect my Body I inclin'd,
As to some Being of Superiour Kind,
And made my Court, according to the Day,
Wishing her Queen and Her a happy *May*. 470
Great Thanks my Daughter, with a gracious Bow
She said; and I who much desir'd to know

Of whence she was, yet fearful how to break
My Mind, adventur'd humbly thus to speak.
Madam, Might I presume and not offend,   475
So may the Stars and shining Moon attend
Your Nightly Sports, as you vouchsafe to tell,
What Nymphs they were who mortal Forms excel,
And what the Knights who fought in listed Fields so well.

   To this the Dame reply'd, Fair Daughter know   480
That what you saw, was all a Fairy Show:
And all those airy Shapes you now behold
Were humane Bodies once, and cloath'd with earthly Mold:
Our Souls not yet prepar'd for upper Light,
Till Doomsday wander in the Shades of Night;   485
This only Holiday of all the Year,
We priviledg'd in Sun-shine may appear:
With Songs and Dance we celebrate the Day,
And with due Honours usher in the *May*.
At other Times we reign by Night alone,   490
And posting through the Skies pursue the Moon:
But when the Morn arises, none are found;
For cruel *Demogorgon* walks the round,
And if he finds a Fairy lag in Light,
He drives the Wretch before; and lashes into Night.   495

   All Courteous are by Kind; and ever proud
With friendly Offices to help the Good.
In every Land we have a larger Space
Than what is known to you of mortal Race:
Where we with Green adorn our Fairy Bow'rs,   500
And ev'n this Grove unseen before, is ours.
Know farther; Ev'ry Lady cloath'd in White,
And, crown'd with Oak and Lawrel ev'ry Knight,
Are Servants to the Leaf, by Liveries known
Of Innocence; and I my self am one.   505
Saw you not Her so graceful to behold
In white Attire, and crown'd with Radiant Gold:
The Soveraign Lady of our Land is She,
Diana call'd, the Queen of Chastity:
And, for the spotless Name of Maid she bears,   510
That *Agnus castus* in her Hand appears:

And all her Train with leavy Chaplets crown'd
Were for unblam'd Virginity renown'd:
But those the chief and highest in Command
Who bear those holy Branches in their Hand: 515
The Knights adorn'd with Lawrel-Crowns, are they ⎫
Whom Death nor Danger ever cou'd dismay,   ⎬
Victorious Names, who made the World obey: ⎭
Who while they liv'd, in Deeds of Arms excell'd,
And after Death for Deities were held.   520
But those who wear the Woodbine on their Brow
Were Knights of Love, who never broke their Vow:
Firm to their plighted Faith, and ever free
From Fears and fickle Chance, and Jealousy.
The Lords and Ladies, who the Woodbine bear,   525
As true as *Tristram*, and *Isotta* were.

    But what are those said I, th' unconquer'd Nine
Who crown'd with Lawrel-Wreaths in golden Armour shine?
And who the Knights in Green, and what the Train
Of Ladies dress'd with Daisies on the Plain?   530
Why both the Bands in Worship disagree,
And some adore the Flow'r, and some the Tree?

    Just is your Suit, fair Daughter, said the Dame,
Those lawrell'd Chiefs were Men of mighty Fame;
Nine Worthies were they call'd of diff'rent Rites,   535
Three Jews, three Pagans, and three Christian Knights.
These, as you see, ride foremost in the Field, ⎫
As they the foremost Rank of Honour held,   ⎬
And all in Deeds of Chivalry excell'd.   ⎭
Their Temples wreath'd with Leafs, that still renew; 540
For deathless Lawrel is the Victor's due:
Who bear the Bows were Knights in *Arthur*'s Reign,
Twelve they, and twelve the Peers of *Charlemain*:
For Bows the Strength of brawny Arms imply,
Emblems of Valour, and of Victory.   545
Behold an Order yet of newer Date
Doubling their Number, equal in their State;
Our *England*'s Ornament, the Crown's Defence,
In Battle brave, Protectors of their Prince.
Unchang'd by Fortune, to their Soveraign true,   550

For which their manly Legs are bound with Blue.
These, of the Garter call'd, of Faith unstain'd,
In fighting Fields the Lawrel have obtain'd,
And well repaid those Honours which they gain'd.
The Lawrel-Wreaths were first by *Cæsar* worn,   555
And still they *Cæsar*'s Successors adorn:
One Leaf of this is Immortality,
And more of Worth, than all the World can buy.

   One Doubt remains, said I, the Dames in Green,
What were their Qualities, and who their Queen?   560
Flora commands, said she, those Nymphs and Knights,
Who liv'd in slothful Ease, and loose Delights:
Who never Acts of Honour durst pursue,
The Men inglorious Knights, the Ladies all untrue:
Who nurs'd in Idleness, and train'd in Courts,   565
Pass'd all their precious Hours in Plays, and Sports,
Till Death behind came stalking on, unseen,
And wither'd (like the Storm) the freshness of their Green.
These, and their Mates, enjoy the present Hour,
And therefore pay their Homage to the Flow'r.   570
But Knights in Knightly Deeds should persevere,
And still continue what at first they were;
Continue, and proceed in Honours fair Career.
No room for Cowardise, or dull delay;
From Good to Better they should urge their way.   575
For this with golden Spurs the Chiefs are grac'd,
With pointed Rowels arm'd to mend their haste;
For this with lasting Leaves their Brows are bound;
For Lawrel is the Sign of Labour crown'd;
Which bears the bitter Blast, nor shaken falls to Ground: 580
From Winter-Winds it suffers no decay,
For ever fresh and fair, and ev'ry Month is *May.*
Ev'n when the vital Sap retreats below,
Ev'n when the hoary Head is hid in Snow;
The Life is in the Leaf, and still between   585
The Fits of falling Snows, appears the streaky Green.
Not so the Flow'r which lasts for little space
A short-liv'd Good, and an uncertain Grace;
This way and that the feeble Stem is driv'n,
Weak to sustain the Storms, and Injuries of Heav'n.   590

Prop'd by the Spring, it lifts aloft, the Head,
But of a sickly Beauty, soon to shed;
In Summer living, and in Winter dead.
For Things of tender Kind for Pleasure made
Shoot up with swift Increase, and suddain are decay'd.   595

   With humble Words, the wisest I could frame,
And profer'd Service I repaid the Dame:
That of her Grace she gave her Maid to know
The secret meaning of this moral Show.
And she to prove what Profit I had made,   600
Of mystique Truth, in Fables first convey'd,
Demanded, till the next returning *May*,
Whether the Leaf or Flow'r I would obey?
I chose the Leaf; she smil'd with sober Chear,
And wish'd me fair Adventure for the Year.   605
And gave me Charms and Sigils, for Defence
Against ill Tongues that scandal Innocence:
But I, said she, my Fellows must pursue,
Already past the Plain, and out of view.

   We parted thus; I homeward sped my way,   610
Bewilder'd in the Wood till Dawn of Day:
And met the merry Crew who danc'd about the *May*.
Then late refresh'd with Sleep I rose to write
The visionary Vigils of the Night:
Blush, as thou may'st, my little Book for Shame,   615
Nor hope with homely Verse to purchase Fame;
For such thy Maker chose; and so design'd
Thy simple Style to sute thy lowly Kind.

THE TWELFTH BOOK OF OVID
HIS METAMORPHOSES, Wholly Translated

CONNECTION TO THE END OF THE
ELEVENTH BOOK

Æsacus, *the Son of* Priam, *loving a Country-Life, forsakes the Court: Living
obscurely, he falls in Love with a Nymph; who flying from him, was kill'd by a
Serpent; for Grief of this, he wou'd have drown'd himself; but by the pity of
the Gods, is turn'd into a Cormorant.* Priam, *not hearing of* Æsacus, *believes*

him to be dead, and raises a Tomb to preserve his Memory. By this Transition, 5
which is one of the finest in all Ovid, *the Poet naturally falls into the Story
of the* Trojan War, *which is summ'd up, in the present Book, but so very
briefly, in many Places, that* Ovid *seems more short than* Virgil, *contrary to
his usual Style. Yet the House of Fame, which is here describ'd, is one of the
most beautiful Pieces in the whole* Metamorphoses. *The Fight of* Achilles 10
and Cygnus, *and the Fray betwixt the* Lapythæ *and* Centaurs, *yield to no
other part of this Poet: And particularly the Loves and Death of* Cyllarus
and Hylonome, *the Male and Female* Centaur, *are wonderfully moving.*

P*RIAM*, to whom the Story was unknown,
      As dead, deplor'd his Metamorphos'd Son:
A Cenotaph his Name and Title kept,
And *Hector* round the Tomb, with all his Brothers wept.
      This pious Office *Paris* did not share,   5
Absent alone; and Author of the War,
Which, for the *Spartan* Queen, the *Grecians* drew
T' avenge the Rape; and *Asia* to subdue.
      A thousand Ships were man'd, to sail the Sea:
Nor had their just Resentments found delay,   10
Had not the Winds and Waves, oppos'd their way.
At *Aulis*, with United Pow'rs they meet,
But there, Cross-winds or Calms, detain'd the Fleet.
      Now, while they raise an Altar on the Shore,
And *Jove* with solemn Sacrifice adore;   15
A boding Sign the Priests and People see:
A Snake of size immense, ascends a Tree.
And in the leavy Summet, spy'd a Neast,
Which, o'er her Callow young, a Sparrow press'd.
Eight were the Birds unfledg'd; their Mother flew;   20
And hover'd round her Care; but still in view:
Till the fierce Reptile first devour'd the Brood;
Then siez'd the flutt'ring Dam, and drunk her Blood.
This dire Ostent, the fearful People view;
Calchas alone, by *Phœbus* taught, foreknew   25
What Heav'n decreed; and with a smiling Glance,
Thus gratulates to *Greece* her happy Chance.
O *Argives* we shall Conquer: *Troy* is ours,
But long Delays shall first afflict our Pow'rs:
Nine Years of Labour, the nine Birds portend;   30

The Tenth shall in the Town's Destruction end.
   The Serpent, who his Maw obscene had fill'd,
The Branches in his curl'd Embraces held:
But, as in Spires he stood, he turn'd to Stone:
The stony Snake retain'd the Figure still his own.   35
   Yet, not for this, the Wind-bound Navy weigh'd,
Slack were their Sails; and *Neptune* disobey'd.
Some thought him loath the Town shou'd be destroy'd,
Whose Building had his Hands divine employ'd:
Not so the Seer; who knew, and known foreshow'd,   40
The Virgin *Phœbe*, with a Virgin's Blood
Must first be reconcil'd; the common Cause
Prevail'd; and Pity yielding to the Laws,
Fair *Iphigenia* the devoted Maid
Was, by the weeping Priests, in Linnen-Robes array'd;   45
All mourn her Fate; but no Relief appear'd:
The Royal Victim bound, the Knife already rear'd:
When that offended Pow'r, who caus'd their Woe,
Relenting ceas'd her Wrath; and stop'd the coming Blow.
A Mist before the Ministers she cast;   50
And, in the Virgin's room, a Hind she plac'd.
Th' Oblation slain, and *Phœbe* reconcil'd,
The Storm was hush'd, and dimpled Ocean smil'd:

A favourable Gale arose from Shore,
Which to the Port desir'd, the *Grecian* Gallies bore.   55
   Full in the midst of this Created Space,
Betwixt Heav'n, Earth and Skies, there stands a Place,
Confining on all three; with triple Bound;
Whence all Things, though remote, are view'd around;
And thither bring their Undulating Sound.   60
The Palace of loud Fame; her Seat of Pow'r;
Plac'd on the Summet of a lofty Tow'r;
A thousand winding Entries long and wide,
Receive of fresh Reports a flowing Tide.
A thousand Crannies in the Walls are made;   65
Nor Gate nor Bars exclude the busy Trade.
'Tis built of Brass the better to diffuse
The spreading Sounds, and multiply the News:
Where Eccho's, in repeated Eccho's play:
A Mart for ever full; and open Night and Day.   70

Nor Silence is within, nor Voice express,
But a deaf Noise of Sounds that never cease.
Confus'd, and Chiding, like the hollow Roar
Of Tides, receding from th' insulted Shore.
Or like the broken Thunder, heard from far,   75
When *Jove* to distance drives the rowling War.
The Courts are fill'd with a tumultuous Din
Of Crowds, or issuing forth, or entring in:
A thorough fare of News: Where some devise
Things never heard; some mingle Truth with Lies: 80
The troubled Air with empty Sounds they beat:
Intent to hear; and eager to repeat.
Error sits brooding there; with added Train
Of vain Credulity; and Joys as vain:
Suspicion, with Sedition join'd, are near;   85
And Rumors rais'd, and Murmurs mix'd, and Panique Fear.
Fame sits aloft; and sees the subject Ground;
And Seas about, and Skies above; enquiring all around.
    The Goddess gives th' Alarm; and soon is known
The *Grecian* Fleet, descending on the Town.   90
Fix'd on Defence the *Trojans* are not slow
To guard their Shore, from an expected Foe.

They meet in Fight: By *Hector*'s fatal Hand
Protesilaus falls; and bites the Strand;
Which with expence of Blood the *Grecians* won;   95
And prov'd the Strength unknown of *Priam*'s Son.
And to their Cost the *Trojan* Leaders felt
The *Grecian* Heroes; and what Deaths they dealt.
    From these first Onsets, the *Sigæan* Shore
Was strew'd with Carcasses; and stain'd with Gore: 100
Neptunian Cygnus, Troops of *Greeks* had slain;
Achilles in his Carr had scow'r'd the Plain;
And clear'd the *Trojan* Ranks: Where e'er he fought,
Cygnus, or *Hector*, through the Fields he sought:
Cygnus he found; on him his Force essay'd: 105
For *Hector* was to the tenth Year delay'd.
His white man'd Steeds, that bow'd beneath the Yoke
He chear'd to Courage, with a gentle Stroke;
Then urg'd his fiery Chariot on the Foe;
And rising, shook his Lance; in act to throw.   110

But first, he cry'd, O Youth be proud to bear
Thy Death, enobled, by *Pelides* Spear.
The Lance pursu'd the Voice without delay;
Nor did th' whizzing Weapon miss the way:
But pierc'd his Cuirass, with such Fury sent;   115
And sign'd his Bosom with a Purple dint.
At this the Seed of *Neptune*; Goddess-born,
For Ornament, not Use, these Arms are worn;
This Helm, and heavy Buckler I can spare;
As only Decorations of the War: 120
So *Mars* is arm'd for Glory, not for Need.
'Tis somewhat more from *Neptune* to proceed,
Than from a Daughter of the Sea to spring:
Thy Sire is Mortal; mine is Ocean's King.
Secure of Death, I shou'd contemn thy Dart,   125
Tho' naked; and impassible depart:
He said, and threw: The trembling Weapon pass'd
Through nine Bull-hides, each under other plac'd,
On his broad Shield; and stuck within the last.
Achilles wrench'd it out; and sent again   130

The hostile Gift: The hostile Gift was vain.
He try'd a third, a tough well-chosen Spear,
Th' inviolable Body stood sincere;
Though *Cygnus* then did no Defence provide,
But scornful offer'd his unshielded Side.   135

  Not otherwise th' impatient Hero far'd,
Than as a Bull, incompass'd with a Guard
Amid the *Circus* roars: Provok'd from far
By sight of Scarlet, and a sanguine War:
They quit their Ground; his bended Horns elude;   140
In vain pursuing, and in vain pursu'd.

  Before to farther Fight he wou'd advance,
He stood considering, and survey'd his Lance.
Doubts if he wielded not a Wooden Spear
Without a Point: He look'd, the Point was there   145
This is my Hand, and this my Lance he se'd;
By which so many thousand Foes are dead.
O whether is their usual Virtue fled!
I had it once; and the *Lyrnessian* Wall,
And *Tenedos* confess'd it in their fall.   150

Thy Streams, *Caicus*, rowl'd a Crimson-Flood;
And *Thebes* ran Red with her own Natives Blood.
Twice *Telephus* employ'd this piercing Steel,
To wound him first, and afterward to heal.
The Vigour of this Arm, was never vain;   155
And that my wonted Prowess I retain,
Witness these heaps of Slaughter on the Plain.
He said; and doubtful of his former Deeds,
To some new trial of his Force proceeds.
He chose *Menœtes* from among the rest;   160
At him he lanch'd his Spear; and pierc'd his Breast:
On the hard Earth, the *Lycian* knock'd his Head;
And lay supine; and forth the Spirit fled.

Then thus the Hero; neither can I blame;
The Hand, or Javelin; both are still the same.   165
The same I will employ against this Foe;
And wish but with the same Success to throw.
So spoke the Chief; and while he spoke he threw;
The Weapon with unerring Fury flew!

At his left Shoulder aim'd: Nor entrance found;   170
But back, as from a Rock, with swift rebound
Harmless return'd: A bloody Mark appear'd,
Which with false Joy, the flatter'd Hero chear'd.
Wound there was none; the Blood that was in view,
The Lance before from slain *Menœtes* drew.   175

Headlong he leaps from off his lofty Car,
And in close Fight on foot renews the War.
Raging with high Disdain, repeats his Blows;
Nor Shield nor Armour can their Force oppose;
Huge Cantlets of his Buckler strew the Ground,   180
And no Defence in his bor'd Arms is found.
But on his Flesh, no Wound or Blood is seen;
The Sword it self, is blunted on the Skin.

This vain Attempt the Chief no longer bears;
But round his hollow Temples and his Ears   185
His Buckler beats: The Son of *Neptune*, stun'd
With these repeated Buffets, quits his Ground;
A sickly Sweat succeeds; and Shades of Night:
Inverted Nature swims before his Sight:
Th' insulting Victor presses on the more,   190

And treads the Steps the vanquish'd trod before.
Nor Rest, nor Respite gives: A Stone there lay,
Behind his trembling Foe; and stop'd his way.
Achilles took th' Advantage which he found,
O'er-turn'd, and push'd him backward on the Ground.   195
His Buckler held him under, while he press'd
With both his Knees above, his panting Breast.
Unlac'd his Helm: About his Chin the Twist
He ty'd; and soon the strangled Soul dismiss'd.

  With eager haste he went to strip the Dead: 200
The vanish'd Body from his Arms was fled.
His Sea-God Sire t' immortalize his Fame,
Had turn'd it to the Bird, that bears his Name.

  A Truce succeeds the Labours of this Day,
And Arms suspended with a long delay.   205
While *Trojan* Walls are kept with Watch and Ward,
The *Greeks* before their Trenches, mount the Guard;
The Feast approach'd; when to the blue-Ey'd Maid
His Vows for *Cygnus* slain the Victor paid,
And a white Heyfer, on her Altar laid.   210
The reeking Entrails on the Fire they threw;
And to the Gods the grateful Odour flew:
Heav'n had its part in Sacrifice: The rest
Was broil'd and roasted for the future Feast.
The chief invited Guests, were set around: 215
And Hunger first asswag'd, the Bowls were crown'd,
Which in deep Draughts, their Cares and Labours drown'd.
The mellow Harp did not their Ears employ:
And mute was all the Warlike Symphony:
Discourse, the Food of Souls, was their Delight,   220
And pleasing Chat, prolong'd the Summers-night.
The Subject, Deeds of Arms; and Valour shown
Or on the *Trojan* side, or on their own.
Of Dangers undertaken, Fame atchiev'd;
They talk'd by turns; the Talk by turns reliev'd.   225
What Things but these, cou'd fierce *Achilles* tell,
Or what cou'd fierce *Achilles* hear so well?
The last great Act perform'd, of *Cygnus* slain,
Did most the Martial Audience entertain:
Wondring to find a Body, free by Fate   230

From Steel; and which cou'd ev'n that Steel rebate:
Amaz'd, their Admiration they renew;
And scarce *Pelides* cou'd believe it true.

Then *Nestor*, thus: What once this Age has known,
In fated *Cygnus*, and in him alone,   235
Those Eyes have seen in *Cæneus* long before,
Whose Body, not a thousand Swords cou'd bore.
Cæneus, in Courage, and in Strength excell'd;
And still his *Othrys*, with his Fame is fill'd:
But what did most his Martial Deeds adorn,   240
(Though since he chang'd his Sex) a Woman born.

A Novelty so strange, and full of Fate,
His list'ning Audience ask'd him to relate.
Achilles, thus commends their common Sute;
O Father, first for Prudence in repute,   245
Tell, with that Eloquence, so much thy own,
What thou hast heard, or what of *Cæneus* known:
What was he, whence his change of Sex begun,
What Trophies, join'd in Wars with thee, he won?
Who conquer'd him, and in what fatal Strife   250
The Youth without a Wound, cou'd lose his Life?

Neleides then; though tardy Age, and Time
Have shrunk my Sinews, and decay'd my Prime:
Though much I have forgotten of my Store,
Yet not exhausted, I remember more.   255
Of all that Arms atchiev'd, or Peace design'd,
That Action still is fresher in my Mind
Than ought beside. If Reverend Age can give
To Faith a Sanction, in my third I live.

'Twas in my second Cent'ry, I survey'd   260
Young *Cænis*, then a fair *Thessalian* Maid:
Cænis the bright, was born to high Command;
A Princess; and a Native of thy Land,
Divine *Achilles*; every Tongue proclaim'd
Her Beauty; and her Eyes all Hearts inflam'd.   265
Peleus, thy Sire, perhaps had sought her Bed;
Among the rest; but he had either led
Thy Mother then; or was by Promise ty'd:
But she to him, and all alike her Love deny'd.

It was her Fortune once, to take her way   270

Along the sandy Margin of the Sea:
The Pow'r of Ocean view'd her as she pass'd,
And lov'd as soon as seen, by Force embrac'd.
So Fame reports. Her Virgin-Treasure seiz'd,
And his new Joys, the Ravisher so pleas'd,   275
That thus, transported, to the Nymph he cry'd;
Ask what thou wilt, no Pray'r shall be deny'd.
This also Fame relates: The haughty Fair
Who not the Rape, ev'n of a God cou'd bear,
This Answer, proud, return'd: To mighty Wrongs   280
A mighty Recompence, of right, belongs.
Give me no more to suffer such a Shame;
But change the Woman, for a better Name,
One Gift for all: She said; and while she spoke,
A stern, majestick, manly Tone she took.   285

A Man she was: And as the Godhead swore,
To *Cæneus* turn'd, who *Cænis* was before.
    To this the Lover adds without request:
No force of Steel shou'd violate his Breast.
Glad of the Gift, the new-made Warrior goes: 290
And Arms among the *Greeks*; and longs for equal Foes.
    Now brave *Perithous*, bold *Ixion*'s Son,
The Love of fair *Hippodame* had won.
The Cloud-begotten Race half Men, half Beast,
Invited, came to grace the Nuptial Feast: 295
In a cool Cave's recess, the Treat was made,
Whose entrance, Trees with spreading Boughs o'ershade.
They sate: And summon'd by the Bridegroom, came
To mix with those the *Lapythæan* Name:
Nor wanted I: The Roofs with Joy resound: 300
And *Hymen*, *Io Hymen*, rung around.
Rais'd Altars shone with holy Fires; the Bride,
Lovely her self (and lovely by her side
A bevy of bright Nimphs, with sober Grace,)
Came glitt'ring like a Star; and took her Place.   305
Her heav'nly Form beheld, all wish'd her Joy;
And little wanted, but in vain, their Wishes all employ.
    For One, most Brutal, of the Brutal Brood,
Or whether Wine or Beauty fir'd his Blood,
Or both at once; beheld with lustful Eyes   310

The Bride; at once resolv'd to make his Prize.
Down went the Board; and fastning on her Hair,
He seiz'd with sudden Force the frighted Fair.
'Twas *Eurytus* began: His bestial Kind
His Crime pursu'd; and each as pleas'd his Mind,   315
Or her, whom Chance presented, took: The Feast
An Image of a taken Town express'd.

   The Cave resounds with Female Shrieks; we rise,
Mad with Revenge, to make a swift Reprise:
And *Theseus* first; what Frenzy has possess'd   320
O *Eurytus*, he cry'd, thy brutal Breast,
To wrong *Perithous*, and not him alone,
But while I live, two Friends conjoyn'd in one?

   To justify his Threat, he thrusts aside
The Crowd of Centaurs; and redeems the Bride: 325
The Monster nought reply'd: For Words were vain;
And Deeds cou'd only Deeds unjust maintain:
But answers with his Hand; and forward press'd,
With Blows redoubled, on his Face and Breast.
An ample Goblet stood, of antick Mold,   330
And rough with Figures of the rising Gold;
The Hero snatch'd it up: And toss'd in Air,
Full at the Front of the foul Ravisher.
He falls; and falling vomits forth a Flood
Of Wine, and Foam and Brains, and mingled Blood.   335
Half roaring, and half neighing through the Hall,
Arms, Arms, the double form'd with Fury call;
To wreak their Brother's death: A Medley-Flight
Of Bowls and Jars, at first supply the Fight.
Once Instruments of Feasts; but now of Fate;   340
Wine animates their Rage, and arms their Hate.

   Bold *Amycus*, from the robb'd Vestry brings
The Chalices of Heav'n; and holy Things
Of precious Weight: A Sconce, that hung on high,
With Tapers fill'd, to light the Sacristy,   345
Torn from the Cord, with his unhallow'd Hand
He threw amid the *Lapythæan* Band.
On *Celadon* the Ruin fell; and left
His Face of Feature and of Form bereft:
So, when some brawny Sacrificer knocks   350

Before an Altar led, an offer'd Oxe,
His Eye-balls rooted out, are thrown to Ground;
Nis Nose dismantled, in his Mouth is found,
His Jaws, Cheeks, Front, one undistinguish'd Wound.

 This, *Belates*, th' Avenger, cou'd not brook;   355
But, by the Foot a Maple-board he took;
And hurl'd at *Amycus*; his Chin it bent
Against his Chest, and down the Centaur sent:
Whom sputtring bloody Teeth, the second Blow
Of his drawn Sword, dispatch'd to Shades below.   360

 Grineus was near; and cast a furious Look
On the side Altar, cens'd with sacred Smoke,
And bright with flaming Fires; the Gods, he cry'd,
Have with their holy Trade, our Hands supply'd:
Why use we not their Gifts? Then from the Floor   365
An Altar-Stone he heav'd, with all the Load it bore:
Altar and Altars freight together flew,
Where thickest throng'd the *Lapythæan* Crew:
And *Broteas*, and at once, *Oryus* slew.
Oryus Mother, *Mycale*, was known   370
Down from her Sphere, to draw the lab'ring Moon.

 Exadius cry'd, unpunish'd shall not go
This Fact, if Arms are found against the Foe.
He look'd about, where on a Pine were spred
The votive Horns of a Stags branching Head: 375
At *Grineus* these he throws; so just they fly,
That the sharp Antlers stuck in either Eye:
Breathless and Blind he fell; with Blood besmear'd;
His Eye-balls beaten out, hung dangling on his Beard.

Fierce *Rhœtus*, from the Hearth a burning Brand   380
Selects, and whirling waves; till, from his Hand
The Fire took Flame; then dash'd it from the right,
On fair *Charaxus* Temples; near the Sight:
The whistling Pest came on; and pierc'd the Bone,
And caught the yellow Hair, that shrievel'd while it shone.   385
Caught, like dry Stubble fir'd; or like Seerwood;
Yet from the Wound ensu'd no Purple Flood;
But look'd a bubbling Mass, of frying Blood.
His blazing Locks, sent forth a crackling Sound;
And hiss'd, like red hot Iron, within the Smithy drown'd.   390

The wounded Warrior shook his flaming Hair,
Then (what a Team of Horse cou'd hardly rear)
He heaves the Threshold-Stone; but cou'd not throw;
The Weight it self, forbad the threaten'd Blow,
Which dropping from his lifted Arms, came down,					395
Full on *Cometes* Head; and crush'd his Crown.
Nor *Rhœtus* then retain'd his Joy; but se'd;
So by their Fellows may our Foes be sped;
Then, with redoubled Strokes he plies his Head:
The burning Lever, not deludes his Pains;					400
But drives the batter'd Skull, within the Brains.
	Thus flush'd, the Conqueror, with Force renew'd,
Evagrus, Dryas, Corythus, pursu'd:
First, *Corythus,* with downy Cheeks, he slew;
Whose fall, when fierce *Evagrus* had in view,					405
He cry'd, what Palm is from a beardless Prey?
Rhœtus prevents what more he had to say;
And drove within his Mouth the fiery Death,
Which enter'd hissing in, and choak'd his Breath.
At *Dryas* next he flew: But weary Chance					410
No longer wou'd the same Success advance.
For while he whirl'd in fiery Circles round
The Brand, a sharpen'd Stake strong *Dryas* found;
And in the Shoulder's Joint inflicts the Wound.
The Weapon stuck; which roaring out with Pain,					415
He drew; nor longer durst the Fight maintain,
But turn'd his Back, for fear; and fled amain.
With him fled *Orneus,* with like Dread possess'd;
Thaumas, and *Medon* wounded in the Breast;
And *Mermeros* in the late Race renown'd,					420
Now limping ran, and tardy with his Wound.
Pholus and *Melaneus* from Fight withdrew,
And *Abas* maim'd, who Boars encountring slew:
And Augur *Astylos,* whose Art in vain
From Fight dissuaded the four-footed Train,
Now beat the Hoof with *Nessus* on the Plain;					425
But to his Fellow cry'd, be safely slow,
Thy Death deferr'd is due to great *Alcides* Bow.
	Mean time strong *Dryas* urg'd his Chance so well,
That *Lycidas, Areos, Imbreus* fell;					430

All, one by one, and fighting Face to Face:
Crenæus fled, to fall with more Disgrace:
For, fearful, while he look'd behind, he bore
Betwixt his Nose and Front, the Blow before.
Amid the Noise and Tumult of the Fray,   435
Snoring, and drunk with Wine, *Aphidas* lay.
Ev'n then the Bowl within his Hand he kept:
And on a Bear's rough Hide securely slept.
Him *Phorbas* with his flying Dart, transfix'd;
Take thy next Draught, with *Stygian* Waters mix'd,   440
And sleep thy fill, th' insulting Victor cry'd;
Surpris'd with Death unfelt, the Centaur dy'd;
The ruddy Vomit, as he breath'd his Soul,
Repass'd his Throat; and fill'd his empty Bowl.

I saw *Petræus* Arms, employ'd around   445
A well-grown Oak, to root it from the Ground.
This way, and that, he wrench'd the fibrous Bands;
The Trunk, was like a Sappling in his Hands
And still obey'd the Bent: While thus he stood,
Perithous Dart drove on; and nail'd him to the Wood.   450
Lycus, and *Chromys* fell by him oppress'd:
Helops and *Dictys* added to the rest
A nobler Palm: *Helops* through either Ear
Transfix'd, receiv'd the penetrating Spear.
This, *Dictys* saw; and seiz'd with suddain Fright   455
Leapt headlong from the Hill of steepy height;
And crush'd an Ash beneath, that cou'd not bear his weight.
The shatter'd Tree receives his fall; and strikes
Within his full-blown Paunch, the sharpen'd Spikes.
Strong *Aphareus* had heav'd a mighty Stone,   460
The Fragment of a Rock; and wou'd have thrown;
But *Theseus* with a Club of harden'd Oak,
The Cubit-bone of the bold Centaur broke;
And left him maim'd; nor seconded the Stroke.
Then leapt on tall *Bianor*'s Back: (Who bore   465
No mortal Burden but his own, before.)
Press'd with his Knees his Sides; the double Man
His speed with Spurs increas'd, unwilling ran.
One Hand the Hero fasten'd on his Locks;
His other ply'd him with repeated Strokes.   470

The Club rung round his Ears, and batter'd Brows;
He falls; and lashing up his Heels, his Rider throws.
   The same *Herculean* Arms, *Nedymnus* wound;
And lay by him *Lycotas* on the Ground.
And *Hippasus*, whose Beard his Breast invades;   475
And *Ripheus*, haunter of the Woodland Shades:
And *Tereus* us'd with Mountain-Bears to strive;
And from their Dens to draw th' indignant Beasts alive.
   Demoleon cou'd not bear this hateful Sight,
Or the long Fortune of th' *Athenian* Knight: 480
But pull'd with all his Force, to disengage
From Earth a Pine; the Product of an Age:
The Root stuck fast: The broken Trunk he sent
At *Theseus*: *Theseus* frustrates his Intent,
And leaps aside; by *Pallas* warn'd, the Blow   485
To shun: (for so he said; and we believ'd it so.)
Yet not in vain, th' enormous Weight was cast;
Which *Crantor*'s Body sunder'd at the Waist.
Thy Father's Squire, *Achilles*, and his Care;
Whom Conquer'd in the *Dolopeian* War,   490
Their King, his present Ruin to prevent,
A Pledge of Peace implor'd, to *Peleus* sent.
   Thy Sire, with grieving Eyes, beheld his Fate;
And cry'd, not long, lov'd *Crantor*, shalt thou wait
Thy vow'd Revenge. At once he said, and threw   495
His Ashen-Spear; which quiver'd as it flew;
With all his Force and all his Soul apply'd;
The sharp Point enter'd in the Centaur's Side:
Both Hands, to wrench it out, the Monster join'd;
And wrench'd it out; but left the Steel behind.   500
Stuck in his Lungs it stood: Inrag'd he rears
His Hoofs, and down to Ground thy Father bears.
Thus trampled under Foot, his Shield defends
His Head; his other Hand the Lance protends.
Ev'n while he lay extended on the Dust,   505
He sped the Centaur, with one single Thrust.
Two more, his Lance before transfix'd from far;
And two, his Sword had slain, in closer War.
To these was added *Dorylas*: Who spread

A Bull's two goring Horns around his Head.   510
With these he push'd; in Blood already dy'd:
Him, fearless, I approach'd; and thus defy'd:
Now Monster, now, by Proof it shall appear,
Whether thy Horns, are sharper or my Spear.
At this, I threw: For want of other Ward,   515
He lifted up his Hand, his Front to guard.
His Hand it pass'd: And fix'd it to his Brow:
Loud Shouts of ours, attend the lucky Blow.
Him *Peleus* finish'd, with a second Wound,
Which through the Navel pierc'd: He reel'd around;   } 520
And drag'd his dangling Bowels on the Ground.
Trod what he drag'd; and what he trod he crush'd:
And to his Mother-Earth, with empty Belly rush'd.

   Nor cou'd thy Form, O *Cyllarus*, foreslow
Thy Fate; (if Form to Monsters Men allow:)   525
Just bloom'd thy Beard: Thy Beard of golden Hew:
Thy Locks in golden Waves, about thy Shoulders flew.
Sprightly thy Look: Thy Shapes in ev'ry part
So clean, as might instruct the Sculptor's Art;
As far as Man extended: Where began   530
The Beast, the Beast was equal to the Man.
Add but a Horses Head and Neck; and he,
O *Castor*, was a Courser worthy thee.
So was his Back proportion'd for the Seat;
So rose his brawny Chest; so swiftly mov'd his Feet.   535
Coal-black his Colour, but like Jet it shone;
His Legs and flowing Tail, were White alone.
Belov'd by many Maidens of his Kind;
But fair *Hylonome*, possess'd his Mind:
Hylonome, for Features, and for Face   540
Excelling all the Nymphs of double Race:
Nor less her Blandishments, than Beauty move;
At once both loving, and confessing Love.
For him she dress'd: For him with Female Care
She comb'd, and set in Curls, her auborn Hair.   545
Of Roses, Violets, and Lillies mix'd
And Sprigs of flowing Rosemary betwixt
She form'd the Chaplet, that adorn'd her Front:

In Waters of the *Pagasæan* Fount,
And in the Streams that from the Fountain play,   550
She wash'd her Face; and bath'd her twice a Day.
The Scarf of Furs, that hung below her Side,
Was Ermin, or the Panther's spotted Pride;
Spoils of no common Beast: With equal Flame
They lov'd: Their *Sylvan* Pleasures were the same: 555
All Day they hunted: And when Day expir'd,

Together to some shady Cave retir'd:
Invited to the Nuptials, both repair:
And Side by Side, they both ingage in War.
    Uncertain from what Hand, a flying Dart   560
At *Cyllarus* was sent; which pierc'd his Heart.
The Javelin drawn from out the mortal Wound,
He faints with staggring Steps; and seeks the Ground:
The Fair, within her Arms receiv'd his fall,
And strove his wandring Spirits to recal: 565
And while her Hand the streaming Blood oppos'd,
Join'd Face to Face, his Lips with hers she clos'd.
Stiffled with Kisses, a sweet Death he dies;
She fills the Fields with undistinguish'd Cries:
At least her Words, were in her Clamour drown'd;   570
For my stun'd Ears receiv'd no vocal Sound.
In madness of her Grief, she seiz'd the Dart
New-drawn, and reeking from her Lover's Heart;
To her bare Bosom the sharp Point apply'd;
And wounded fell; and falling by his Side,   575
Embrac'd him in her Arms; and thus embracing, dy'd.
    Ev'n still methinks, I see *Phæocomes*;
Strange was his Habit; and as odd his Dress.
Six Lion's Hides, with Thongs together fast,
His upper part defended to his Waist: 580
And where Man ended, the continued Vest,
Spread on his Back, the Houss and Trappings of a Beast.
A Stump too heavy for a Team to draw,
(It seems a Fable, tho' the Fact I saw;)
He threw at *Pholon*; the descending Blow   585
Divides the Skull, and cleaves his Head in two.
The Brains, from Nose and Mouth, and either Ear
Came issuing out, as through a Colendar

The curdled Milk: or from the Press the Whey
Driv'n down by Weights above, is drain'd away.   590
    But him, while stooping down to spoil the Slain,
Pierc'd through the Paunch, I tumbled on the Plain.
Then *Chthonyus*, and *Teleboas* I slew:
A Fork the former arm'd; a Dart his Fellow threw.
The Javelin wounded me; (behold the Skar.)   595
Then was my time to seek the *Trojan* War;
Then I was *Hector*'s Match in open Field;
But he was then unborn; at least a Child:
Now, I am nothing. I forbear to tell
By *Periphantas* how *Pyretus* fell,   600
The Centaur by the Knight: Nor will I stay
On *Amphyx*, or what Deaths he dealt that Day:
What Honour, with a pointless Lance he won,
Stuck in the front of a four-footed Man.
What Fame young *Macareus* obtain'd in Fight: 605
Or dwell on *Nessus*, now return'd from Flight.
How Prophet *Mopsus*, not alone devin'd,
Whose Valour equall'd his foreseeing Mind.
    Already *Cæneus*, with his conquering Hand,
Had slaughter'd five the boldest of their Band.   610
Pyrachmus, *Helymus*, *Antimachus*,
Bromus the Brave, and stronger *Stiphelus*,
Their Names I number'd, and remember well,
No Trace remaining, by what Wounds they fell.
    Latreus, the bulkiest of the double Race,   615
Whom the spoil'd Arms of slain *Halesus* grace,
In Years retaining still his Youthful Might,
Though his black Hairs were interspers'd with White,
Betwixt th' imbattled Ranks, began to prance,
Proud of his Helm, and *Macedonian* Lance;   620
And rode the Ring around; that either Hoast
Might hear him, while he made this empty Boast.
And from a Strumpet shall we suffer Shame,
For *Cænis* still, not *Cæneus* is thy Name:
And still the Native Softness of thy Kind   625
Prevails; and leaves the Woman in thy Mind?
Remember what thou wert; what Price was paid
To change thy Sex: To make thee not a Maid;

And but a Man in shew: Go, Card and Spin;
And leave the Business of the War to Men.   630
  While thus the Boaster exercis'd his Pride
The fatal Spear of *Cæneus* reach'd his Side:
Just in the mixture of the Kinds it ran;
Betwixt the neather Beast, and upper Man:
The Monster mad with Rage, and stung with Smart,   635
His Lance directed at the Hero's Heart:
It strook: But bounded from his harden'd Breast,
Like Hail from Tiles, which the safe House invest.
Nor seem'd the Stroke with more effect to come,
Than a small Pebble falling on a Drum.   640
He next his Fauchion try'd, in closer Fight;
But the keen Fauchion, had no Pow'r to bite.
He thrust; the blunted Point return'd again:
Since downright Blows, he cry'd, and Thrusts are vain,
I'll prove his Side: In strong Embraces held   645
He prov'd his Side; his Side the Sword repell'd:
His hollow Belly eccho'd to the Stroke;   ⎫
Untouch'd his Body, as a solid Rock;   ⎬
Aim'd at his Neck at last, the Blade in Shivers broke.   ⎭
  Th' Impassive Knight stood Idle, to deride   ⎫ 650
His Rage, and offer'd oft his naked Side: ⎬
At length, Now Monster, in thy turn he cry'd   ⎭
Try thou the Strength of *Cæneus*: At the Word
He thrust; and in his Shoulder plung'd the Sword.
Then writh'd his Hand; and as he drove it down,   655
Deep in his Breast, made many Wounds in one.
  The Centaurs saw inrag'd, th' unhop'd Success;
And rushing on, in Crowds, together press;
At him, and him alone, their Darts they threw:
Repuls'd they from his fated Body flew.   660
Amaz'd they stood; till *Monychus* began,
O Shame, a Nation conquer'd by a Man!
A Woman-Man; yet more a Man is He,
Than all our Race; and what He was, are We.
Now, what avail our Nerves? The united Force,   665
Of two the strongest Creatures, Man and Horse:
Nor Goddess-born; nor of *Ixion's* Seed

We seem; (a Lover built for *Juno*'s Bed;)
Master'd by this half Man. Whole Mountains throw
With Woods at once, and bury him below.   670
This only way remains. Nor need we doubt
To choak the Soul within; though not to force it out.
Heap Weights, instead of Wounds: He chanc'd to see
Where Southern Storms had rooted up a Tree;
This, rais'd from Earth, against the Foe he threw;   675
Th' Example shewn, his Fellow-Brutes pursue.
With Forest-loads the Warrior they invade;
Othrys and *Pelion* soon were void of Shade;
And spreading Groves were naked Mountains made.
Press'd with the Burden, *Cæneus* pants for Breath;   680
And on his Shoulders bears the Wooden Death.
To heave th' intolerable Weight he tries;
At length it rose above his Mouth and Eyes:
Yet still he heaves: And strugling with Despair,
Shakes all aside; and gains a gulp of Air: 685
A short Relief, which but prolongs his Pain;
He faints by Fits; and then respires again:
At last, the Burden only nods above,
As when an Earthquake stirs th' *Idæan* Grove.
Doubtful his Death: He suffocated seem'd,   690
To most; but otherwise our *Mopsus* deem'd.
Who said he saw a yellow Bird arise
From out the Pile, and cleave the liquid Skies:
I saw it too: With golden Feathers bright;
Nor e're before, beheld so strange a Sight.   695
Whom *Mopsus* viewing, as it soar'd around
Our Troop, and heard the Pinions rattling Sound,
All hail he cry'd, thy Countries Grace and Love;
Once first of Men below; now first of Birds above.
Its Author to the Story gave Belief: 700
For us, our Courage was increas'd by Grief:
Asham'd to see a single Man, pursu'd
With Odds, to sink beneath a Multitude:
We push'd the Foe; and forc'd to shameful Flight;
Part fell; and part escap'd by favour of the Night.   705
   This Tale by *Nestor* told, did much displease
Tlepolemus, the Seed of *Hercules*:

For, often he had heard his Father say,
That he himself was present at the Fray;
And more than shar'd the Glories of the Day. ⎫ 710

    Old Chronicle, he said, among the rest,
You might have nam'd *Alcides* at the least:
Is he not worth your Praise? The *Pylian* Prince
Sigh'd e'er he spoke; then made this proud Defence.
My former Woes in long Oblivion drown'd, 715
I wou'd have lost; but you renew the Wound:
Better to pass him o'er, than to relate
The Cause I have your mighty Sire to hate.
His Fame has fill'd the World, and reach'd the Sky;
(Which, Oh, I wish with Truth, I cou'd deny!) 720
We praise not *Hector*; though his Name, we know
Is great in Arms; 'tis hard to praise a Foe.

    He, your Great Father, levell'd to the Ground
Messenia's Tow'rs: Nor better Fortune found
Elis, and *Pylos*; that a neighb'ring State 725
And this my own: Both guiltless of their Fate.

    To pass the rest, twelve wanting one, he slew;
My Brethren, who their Birth from *Neleus* drew.
All Youths of early Promise, had they liv'd;
By him they perish'd: I alone surviv'd. 730
The rest were easy Conquest: But the Fate
Of *Periclymenos*, is wondrous to relate.
To him, our common Grandsire of the Main
Had giv'n to change his Form; and chang'd, resume again.
Vary'd at Pleasure, every Shape he try'd; 735
And in all Beasts *Alcides* still defy'd:
Vanquish'd on Earth, at length he soar'd above;
Chang'd to the Bird, that bears the Bolt of *Jove*.
The new-dissembled Eagle, now endu'd
With Beak and Pounces, *Hercules* pursu'd: 740
And cuff'd his manly Cheeks, and tore his Face;
Then, safe retir'd, and tour'd in empty space.
Alcides bore not long his flying Foe;
But bending his inevitable Bow,
Reach'd him in Air, suspended as he stood; 745
And in his Pinion fix'd the feather'd Wood.
Light was the Wound; but in the Sinew hung

The Point; and his disabled Wing unstrung.
He wheel'd in Air, and stretch'd his Vans in vain;
His Vans no longer cou'd his Flight sustain: 750
For while one gather'd Wind, one unsupply'd
Hung drooping down; nor pois'd his other Side.

He fell: The Shaft that slightly was impress'd,
Now from his heavy Fall with weight increas'd,
Drove through his Neck, aslant; he spurns the Ground;   755
And the Soul issues through the Weazon's Wound.

　　Now, brave Commander of the *Rhodian* Seas,
What Praise is due from me, to *Hercules*?
Silence is all the Vengeance I decree
For my slain Brothers; but 'tis Peace with thee.   760

　　Thus with a flowing Tongue old *Nestor* spoke:
Then, to full Bowls each other they provoke:
At length, with Weariness, and Wine oppress'd,
They rise from Table; and withdraw to Rest.

　　The Sire of *Cygnus*, Monarch of the Main,   765
Mean time, laments his Son, in Battle slain:
And vows the Victor's Death; nor vows in vain.
For nine long Years the smoother'd Pain he bore;
(*Achilles* was not ripe for Fate, before:)
Then when he saw the promis'd Hour was near,   770
He thus bespoke the God, that guides the Year.
Immortal Offspring of my Brother *Jove*;
My brightest Nephew, and whom best I love,
Whose Hands were join'd with mine, to raise the Wall
Of tottring *Troy*, now nodding to her fall,   775
Dost thou not mourn our Pow'r employ'd in vain;
And the Defenders of our City slain?
To pass the rest, cou'd noble *Hector* lie
Unpity'd, drag'd around his Native *Troy*?
And yet the Murd'rer lives: Himself by far   780
A greater Plague, than all the wastful War:
He lives; the proud *Pelides* lives to boast
Our Town destroy'd, our common Labour lost!
O, cou'd I meet him! But I wish too late:
To prove my Trident is not in his Fate!   785
But let him try (for that's allow'd) thy Dart,
And pierce his only penetrable Part.

Apollo bows to the superiour Throne;
And to his Uncle's Anger, adds his own.
Then in a Cloud involv'd, he takes his Flight,   790
Where *Greeks* and *Trojans* mix'd in mortal Fight;
And found out *Paris*, lurking where he stood,
And stain'd his Arrows with *Plebeyan* Blood:
Phœbus to him alone the God confess'd,
Then to the recreant Knight, he thus address'd.   795
Dost thou not blush, to spend thy Shafts in vain
On a degenerate, and ignoble Train?
If Fame, or better Vengeance be thy Care,
There aim: And with one Arrow, end the War.

    He said; and shew'd from far the blazing Shield 800
And Sword, which but *Achilles* none cou'd weild;
And how he mov'd a God, and mow'd the standing Field.
The Deity himself directs aright
Th' invenom'd Shaft; and wings the fatal Flight.

    Thus fell the foremost of the *Grecian* Name;   805
And He, the base Adult'rer, boasts the Fame.
A Spectacle to glad the *Trojan* Train;
And please old *Priam*, after *Hector* slain.
If by a Female Hand he had foreseen
He was to die, his Wish had rather been   810
The Lance and double Axe of the fair Warriour Queen.

    And now the Terror of the *Trojan* Field,
The *Grecian* Honour, Ornament, and Shield,
High on a Pile, th' Unconquer'd Chief is plac'd,
The God that arm'd him first, consum'd at last.   815
Of all the Mighty Man, the small Remains
A little Urn, and scarcely fill'd, contains.
Yet great in *Homer*, still *Achilles* lives;
And equal to himself, himself survives.

    His Buckler owns its former Lord; and brings   820
New cause of Strife, betwixt contending Kings;
Who Worthiest after him, his Sword to weild,
Or wear his Armour, or sustain his Shield.
Ev'n *Diomede* sate Mute, with down-cast Eyes;
Conscious of wanted Worth to win the Prize: 825
Nor *Menelas* presum'd these Arms to claim,

811 Warriour] Warrious F

Nor He the King of Men, a greater Name.
Two Rivals only rose: *Laertes* Son,
And the vast Bulk of *Ajax Telamon*:
The King, who cherish'd each, with equal Love,   830
And, from himself all Envy wou'd remove,
Left both to be determin'd by the Laws;
And to the *Grecian* Chiefs, transferr'd the Cause.

THE SPEECHES OF AJAX AND ULYSSES
FROM Ovid's Metamorphoses Book XIII

THE Chiefs were set; the Soldiers crown'd the Field:
    To these the Master of the sevenfold Shield,
Upstarted fierce: And kindled with Disdain
Eager to speak, unable to contain
His boiling Rage, he rowl'd his Eyes around   5
The Shore, and *Grecian* Gallies hall'd a-ground.
Then stretching out his Hands, O *Jove*, he cry'd,
Must then our Cause before the Fleet be try'd?
And dares *Ulysses* for the Prize contend,
In sight of what he durst not once defend?   10
But basely fled that memorable Day,
When I from *Hector*'s Hands redeem'd the flaming Prey.
So much 'tis safer at the noisy Bar
With Words to flourish than ingage in War.
By different Methods we maintain our Right,   15
Nor am I made to Talk, nor he to Fight.
In bloody Fields I labour to be great;
His Arms are a smooth Tongue; and soft Deceit:
Nor need I speak my Deeds, for those you see,
The Sun and Day are Witnesses for me.   20
Let him who fights unseen relate his own,
And vouch the silent Stars, and conscious Moon;
Great is the Prize demanded, I confess,
But such an abject Rival makes it less;
That Gift, those Honours, he but hop'd to gain   25
Can leave no room for *Ajax* to be vain:
Losing he wins, because his Name will be
Enobled by Defeat, who durst contend with me.

Were my known Valour question'd, yet my Blood
Without that Plea wou'd make my Title good: 30
My Sire was *Telamon* whose Arms, employ'd
With *Hercules*, these *Trojan* Walls destroy'd;
And who before with *Jason*, sent from *Greece*
In the first Ship brought home the Golden Fleece:
Great *Telamon* from *Æacus* derives   35
His Birth (th' Inquisitor of guilty lives
In Shades below where *Sysiphus* whose Son
This Thief is thought rouls up the restless heavy Stone.)
Just *Æacus* the King of Gods, above
Begot: Thus *Ajax* is the third from *Jove*.   40
Nor shou'd I seek advantage from my Line,
Unless (*Achilles*) it were mix'd with thine:
As next of Kin *Achilles* Arms I claim,
This Fellow wou'd ingraft a Foreign Name
Upon our Stock, and the *Sysiphian* Seed   45
By Fraud and Theft asserts his Father's Breed:
Then must I lose these Arms, because I came
To fight uncall'd, a voluntary Name,
Nor shun'd the Cause, but offer'd you my Aid,
While he long lurking was to War betray'd: 50
Forc'd to the Field he came, but in the Reer;
And feign'd Distraction to conceal his Fear:
Till one more cunning caught him in the Snare;
(Ill for himself) and drag'd him into War.
Now let a Hero's Arms a Coward vest,   55
And he who shun'd all Honours, gain the best:
And let me stand excluded from my Right
Rob'd of my Kinsman's Arms, who first appear'd in Fight.
Better for us at home had he remain'd
Had it been true, the Madness which he feign'd,   60
Or so believ'd; the less had been our Shame,
The less his counsell'd Crime which brands the *Grecian* Name;
Nor *Philoctetes* had been left inclos'd
In a bare Isle to Wants and Pains expos'd,
Where to the Rocks, with solitary Groans   65
His Suff'rings and our Baseness he bemoans;
And wishes (so may Heav'n his Wish fulfill)
The due Reward to him who caus'd his Ill.

Now he with us to *Troy*'s Destruction sworn
Our Brother of the War, by whom are born   70
Alcides Arrows, pent in narrow Bounds
With Cold and Hunger pinch'd, and pain'd with Wounds,
To find him Food and Cloathing must employ
Against the Birds the Shafts due to the Fate of *Troy*.
Yet still he lives, and lives from Treason free,   75
Because he left *Ulysses* Company:
Poor *Palamede* might wish, so void of Aid,
Rather to have been left, than so to Death betray'd:
The Coward bore the Man immortal Spight,
Who sham'd him out of Madness into Fight: 80
Nor daring otherwise to vent his Hate
Accus'd him first of Treason to the State;
And then for proof produc'd the golden Store,
Himself had hidden in his Tent before:
Thus of two Champions he depriv'd our Hoast,   85
By Exile one, and one by Treason lost.
Thus fights *Ulysses*, thus his Fame extends,
A formidable Man, but to his Friends:
Great, for what Greatness is in Words and Sound,
Ev'n faithful *Nestor* less in both is found: 90
But that he might without a Rival reign,
He left this faithful *Nestor* on the Plain;
Forsook his Friend ev'n at his utmost Need,
Who tir'd, and tardy with his wounded Steed
Cry'd out for Aid, and call'd him by his Name;   95
But Cowardice has neither Ears nor Shame:
Thus fled the good old Man, bereft of Aid,
And for as much as lay in him, betray'd:
That this is not a Fable forg'd by me,
Like one of his, an *Ulyssean* Lie,   100
I vouch ev'n *Diomede*, who tho' his Friend
Cannot that Act excuse, much less defend:
He call'd him back aloud, and tax'd his Fear;
And sure enough he heard, but durst not hear.
    The Gods with equal Eyes on Mortals look,   105
He justly was forsaken, who forsook:
Wanted that Succour he refused to lend,
Found ev'ry Fellow such another Friend:

No wonder, if he roar'd that all might hear;
His Elocution was increas'd by fear: 110
I heard, I ran, I found him out of Breath,
Pale, trembling, and half dead, with fear of Death.
Though he had judg'd himself by his own Laws,
And stood condemn'd, I help'd the common Cause:
With my broad Buckler hid him from the Foe;   115
(Ev'n the Shield trembled as he lay below;)
And from impending Fate the Coward freed:
Good Heav'n forgive me for so bad a Deed!
If still he will persist, and urge the Strife,
First let him give me back his forfeit Life: 120
Let him return to that opprobrious Field;
Again creep under my protecting Shield:
Let him lie wounded, let the Foe be near,
And let his quiv'ring Heart confess his Fear;
There put him in the very Jaws of Fate;   125
And let him plead his Cause in that Estate:
And yet when snatch'd from Death, when from below
My lifted Shield I loos'd, and let him go:
Good Heav'ns how light he rose, with what a bound
He sprung from Earth, forgetful of his Wound;   130
How fresh, how eager then his Feet to ply,
Who had not Strength to stand, had Speed to fly!
    Hector came on, and brought the Gods along;
Fear seiz'd alike the Feeble and the Strong:
Each *Greek* was an *Ulysses*; such a Dread   135
Th' approach, and ev'n the sound of *Hector* bred:
Him, flesh'd with Slaughter, and with Conquest crown'd,
I met, and over-turn'd him to the Ground;
When after, matchless as he deem'd, in Might,
He challeng'd all our Hoast to single Fight;   140
All Eyes were fix'd on me: The Lots were thrown;
But for your Champion I was wish'd alone:
Your Vows were heard, we Fought, and neither yield;
Yet I return'd unvanquish'd from the Field.
With *Jove* to friend th' insulting *Trojan* came,   145
And menac'd us with Force, our Fleet with Flame:
Was it the Strength of this Tongue-valiant Lord,
In that black Hour, that sav'd you from the Sword?

Or was my Breast expos'd alone, to brave
A thousand Swords, a thousand Ships to save?   150
The hopes of your return! And can you yield,
For a sav'd Fleet, less than a single Shield?
Think it no Boast, O *Grecians*, if I deem
These Arms want *Ajax*, more than *Ajax* them;
Or, I with them an equal Honour share;   155
They honour'd to be worn, and I to wear.
Will he compare my Courage with his Slight?
As well he may compare the Day with Night.
Night is indeed the Province of his Reign:
Yet all his dark Exploits no more contain   160
Than a Spy taken, and a Sleeper slain,
A Priest made Pris'ner, *Pallas* made a Prey,
But none of all these Actions done by Day:
Nor ought of these was done, and *Diomed* away.
If on such petty Merits you confer   165
So vast a Prize, let each his Portion share;
Make a just Dividend; and if not all,
The greater part to *Diomed* will fall.
But why, for *Ithacus* such Arms as those,
Who naked and by Night invades his Foes?   170
The glitt'ring Helm by Moonlight will proclaim
The latent Robber, and prevent his Game:
Nor cou'd he hold his tott'ring Head upright
Beneath that Motion, or sustain the Weight;
Nor that right Arm cou'd toss the beamy Lance;   175
Much less the left that ampler Shield advance;
Pond'rous with precious Weight, and rough with Cost
Of the round World in rising Gold emboss'd.
That Orb would ill become his Hand to wield,
And look as for the Gold he stole the Shield;   180
Which, shou'd your error on the Wretch bestow,
It would not frighten, but allure the Foe:
Why asks he, what avails him not in Fight,
And wou'd but cumber and retard his Flight,
In which his only Excellence is plac'd?   185
You give him Death, that intercept his hast.
Add, that his own is yet a Maiden-Shield,
Nor the least Dint has suffer'd in the Field,

Guiltless of Fight: Mine batter'd, hew'd, and bor'd,
Worn out of Service, must forsake his Lord.　　　　　　190
What farther need of Words our Right to scan?
My Arguments are Deeds, let Action speak the Man.
Since from a Champion's Arms the Strife arose,
So cast the glorious Prize amid the Foes:
Then send us to redeem both Arms and Shield,　　　　　195
And let him wear who wins 'em in the Field.

He said: A Murmur from the Multitude,
Or somewhat like a stiffled Shout ensu'd!
Till from his Seat arose *Laertes* Son,
Look'd down awhile, and paus'd e'er he begun;　　　　200
Then to th' expecting Audience rais'd his Look,
And not without prepar'd Attention spoke:
Soft was his Tone, and sober was his Face;
Action his Words, and Words his Action grace.

If Heav'n, my Lords, had heard our common Pray'r,　　205
These Arms had caus'd no Quarrel for an Heir;
Still great *Achilles* had his own possess'd,
And we with great *Achilles* had been bless'd;
But since hard Fate, and Heav'ns severe Decree
Have ravish'd him away from you and me,　　　　　　210
(At this he sigh'd, and wip'd his Eyes, and drew
Or seem'd to draw some Drops of kindly Dew)
Who better can succeed *Achilles* lost,
Than He who gave *Achilles* to your Hoast?
This only I request, that neither He　　　　　　　　215
May gain, by being what he seems to be,
A stupid Thing, nor I may lose the Prize,
By having Sense, which Heav'n to him denies:
Since, great or small, the Talent I enjoy'd
Was ever in the common Cause employ'd:　　　　　　220
Nor let my Wit, and wonted Eloquence
Which often has been us'd in your Defence
And in my own, this only time be brought
To bear against my self, and deem'd a Fault.
Make not a Crime, where Nature made it none;　　　225
For ev'ry Man may freely use his own.
The Deeds of long descended Ancestors
Are but by grace of Imputation ours,

Theirs in effect; but since he draws his Line
From *Jove*, and seems to plead a Right Divine,   230
From *Jove*, like him, I claim my Pedigree;
And am descended in the same degree:
My Sire *Laertes* was *Arcesius* Heir,
Arcesius was the Son of *Jupiter*:
No Paricide, no banish'd Man is known,   235
In all my Line: Let him excuse his own.
Hermes ennobles too, my Mother's Side,
By both my Parents to the Gods ally'd;
But not because that on the Female Part
My Blood is better, dare I claim Desert,   240
Or that my Sire from Paricide is free;
But judge by Merit betwixt Him and Me:
The Prize be to the best; provided yet,
That *Ajax* for a while his Kin forget;
And his great Sire, and greater Uncles, Name,   245
To fortify by them his feeble Claim:
Be Kindred and Relation laid aside,
And Honours Cause by Laws of Honour try'd:
For if he plead Proximity of Blood;
That empty Title is with Ease withstood.   250
Peleus, the Hero's Sire, more nigh than he,
And *Pyrrhus*, his undoubted Progeny,
Inherit first these Trophies of the Field;
To *Scyros*, or to *Phthya*, send the Shield:
And *Teucer* has an Uncle's Right; yet he   255
Waves his Pretensions, nor contends with me.
   Then since the Cause on pure Desert is plac'd,
Whence shall I take my rise, what reckon last?
I not presume on ev'ry Act to dwell,
But take these few, in order as they fell.   260
   Thetis, who knew the Fates, apply'd her Care
To keep *Achilles* in disguise from War;
And till the threat'ning Influence were past,
A Woman's Habit on the Hero cast:
All Eyes were couzen'd by the borrow'd Vest,   265
And *Ajax* (never wiser than the rest)
Found no *Pelides* there: At length I came

With proffer'd Wares to this pretended Dame;
She not discover'd by her Mien or Voice,
Betray'd her Manhood by her manly Choice;   270
And while on Female Toys her Fellows look,
Grasp'd in her Warlike Hand, a Javelin shook,
Whom by this Act reveal'd I thus bespoke:
O Goddess born! resist not Heav'ns Decree,
The fall of *Ilium*, is reserv'd for Thee;   275
Then seiz'd him, and produc'd in open Light,
Sent blushing to the Field the fatal Knight.
Mine then are all his Actions of the War,
Great *Telephus* was conquer'd by my Spear
And after cur'd: To me the *Thebans* owe,   280
Lesbos, and *Tenedos*, their overthrow;
Syros and *Cylla*! Not on all to dwell,
By me *Lyrnesus*, and strong *Chrysa* fell:
And since I sent the Man who *Hector* slew,
To me the noble *Hector*'s Death is due: 285
Those Arms I put into his living Hand,
Those Arms, *Pelides* dead, I now demand.

When *Greece* was injur'd in the *Spartan* Prince,
And met at *Aulis* to revenge th' Offence,
'Twas a dead Calm, or adverse Blasts that reign'd,   290
And in the Port the Wind-bound Fleet detain'd:
Bad Signs were seen, and Oracles severe
Were daily thunder'd in our General's Ear;
That by his Daughter's Blood we must appease
Diana's kindled Wrath, and free the Seas.   295
Affection, Int'rest, Fame, his Heart assail'd;
But soon the Father o'er the King prevail'd:
Bold, on himself he took the pious Crime,
As angry with the Gods, as they with him.
No Subject cou'd sustain their Sov'raign's Look,   300
Till this hard Enterprize I undertook:
I only durst th' Imperial Pow'r controul,
And undermin'd the Parent in his Soul;
Forc'd him t' exert the King for common Good,
And pay our Ransom with his Daughters Blood.   305
Never was Cause more difficult to plead,

Than where the Judge against himself decreed:
Yet this I won by dint of Argument;
The Wrongs his injur'd Brother underwent;
And his own Office sham'd him to consent.   } 310

    'Twas harder yet to move the Mother's Mind,
And to this heavy Task was I design'd:
Reasons against her Love I knew were vain;
I circumvented whom I could not gain:
Had *Ajax* been employ'd, our slacken'd Sails   315
Had still at *Aulis* waited happy Gales.

    Arriv'd at *Troy*, your choice was fix'd on me
A fearless Envoy, fit for a bold Embassy:
Secure, I enter'd through the hostile Court,
Glitt'ring with Steel, and crowded with Resort: 320
There, in the midst of Arms, I plead our Cause,
Urge the foul Rape, and violated Laws;
Accuse the Foes, as Authors of the Strife,
Reproach the Ravisher, demand the Wife.
Priam, *Antenor*, and the wiser few   325
I mov'd; but *Paris* and his lawless Crew
Scarce held their Hands, and lifted Swords: But stood
In Act to quench their impious Thirst of Blood:
This *Menelaus* knows; expos'd to share
With me the rough Preludium of the War.   330

    Endless it were to tell what I have done,
In Arms, or Council, since the Siege begun:
The first Encounters past, the Foe repell'd,
They skulk'd within the Town, we kept the Field.
War seem'd asleep for nine long Years; at length   335
Both Sides resolv'd to push, we try'd our Strength.
Now what did *Ajax* while our Arms took Breath,
Vers'd only in the gross mechanick Trade of Death?
If you require my Deeds, with ambush'd Arms
I trap'd the Foe, or tir'd with false Alarms;   340
Secur'd the Ships, drew Lines along the Plain,
The Fainting chear'd, chastis'd the Rebel-train,
Provided Forage, our spent Arms renew'd,
Employ'd at home, or sent abroad, the common Cause pursu'd.

    The King, deluded in a Dream by *Jove*,   345
Despair'd to take the Town, and order'd to remove.

What Subject durst arraign the Pow'r supreme,
Producing *Jove* to justify his Dream?
Ajax might wish the Soldiers to retain
From shameful Flight, but Wishes were in vain: 350
As wanting of effect had been his Words,
Such as of course his thundring Tongue affords.
But did this Boaster threaten, did he pray,
Or by his own Example urge their stay?
None, none of these, but ran himself away.   355
I saw him run, and was asham'd to see;
Who ply'd his Feet so fast to get aboard as He?
Then speeding through the Place, I made a stand,
And loudly cry'd, O base, degenerate Band,
To leave a Town already in your Hand!   360
After so long expence of Blood, for Fame,
To bring home nothing but perpetual Shame!
These Words, or what I have forgotten since,
(For Grief inspir'd me then with Eloquence)
Reduc'd their Minds; they leave the crowded Port,   365
And to their late forsaken Camp resort:
Dismay'd the Council met: This Man was there,
But mute, and not recover'd of his Fear.
Thersites tax'd the King, and loudly rail'd,
But his wide opening Mouth with Blows I seal'd.   370
Then rising I excite their Souls to Fame,
And kindle sleeping Virtue into Flame.
From thence, whatever he perform'd in Fight
Is justly mine, who drew him back from Flight.
    Which of the *Grecian* Chiefs consorts with Thee?   375
But *Diomede*, desires my Company,
And still communicates his Praise with me.
As guided by a God, secure he goes,
Arm'd with my Fellowship amid the Foes;
And sure no little Merit I may boast,   380
Whom such a Man selects from such an Hoast;
Unforc'd by Lots I went without affright,
To dare with him the Dangers of the Night:
On the same Errand sent, we met the Spy,
Of *Hector*, double-tongu'd, and us'd to lie;   385
Him I dispatch'd, but not till undermin'd,

I drew him first to tell what treacherous *Troy* design'd:
My Task perform'd, with Praise I had retir'd,
But not content with this, to greater Praise aspir'd.
Invaded *Rhœsus*, and his *Thracian* Crew,   390
And him, and his, in their own Strength I slew:
Return'd a Victor all my Vows compleat,
With the King's Chariot, in his Royal Seat:
Refuse me now his Arms, whose fiery Steeds
Were promis'd to the Spy for his Nocturnal Deeds: 395
And let dull *Ajax* bear away my Right,
When all his Days out-ballance this one Night.
  Nor fought I Darkling still: The Sun beheld
With slaughter'd *Lycians* when I strew'd the Field:
You saw, and counted as I pass'd along,   400
Alastor, *Cromyus*, *Ceranos* the Strong,
Alcander, *Prytanis*, and *Halius*,
Noemon, *Charopes*, and *Ennomus*;
Choon, *Chersidamas*; and five beside
Men of obscure Descent, but Courage try'd: 405
All these this Hand laid breathless on the Ground;
Nor want I Proofs of many a manly Wound:
All honest, all before: Believe not me,
Words may deceive, but credit what you see.
  At this he bar'd his Breast, and show'd his Scars,   410
As of a furrow'd Field, well plough'd with Wars;
Nor is this Part unexercis'd, said he;
That Gyant-bulk of his from Wounds is free:
Safe in his Shield he fears no Foe to try,
And better manages his Blood than I: 415
But this avails me not; our Boaster strove
Not with our Foes alone, but partial *Jove*,
To save the Fleet: This I confess is true,
(Nor will I take from any Man his due:)
But thus assuming all, he robs from you.   420
Some part of Honour to your share will fall,
He did the best indeed, but did not all.
Patroclus in *Achilles* Arms, and thought
The Chief he seem'd, with equal Ardour fought;
Preserv'd the Fleet, repell'd the raging Fire,   425
And forc'd the fearful *Trojans* to retire.

But *Ajax* boasts, that he was only thought
A Match for *Hector*, who the Combat sought:
Sure he forgets the King, the Chiefs, and Me:
All were as eager for the Fight as He: 430
He but the ninth, and not by publick Voice,
Or ours preferr'd, was only Fortunes choice:
They fought; nor can our Hero boast the Event,
For *Hector* from the Field, unwounded went.

Why am I forc'd to name that fatal Day,   435
That snatch'd the Prop and Pride of *Greece* away?
I saw *Pelides* sink, with pious Grief,
And ran in vain, alas, to his Relief;
For the brave Soul was fled: Full of my Friend
I rush'd amid the War his Relicks to defend: 440
Nor ceas'd my Toil till I redeem'd the Prey,
And loaded with *Achilles*, march'd away:
Those Arms, which on these Shoulders then I bore,
'Tis just you to these Shoulders should restore.
You see I want not Nerves, who cou'd sustain   445
The pond'rous Ruins of so great a Man:
Or if in others equal Force you find,
None is endu'd with a more grateful Mind.

Did *Thetis* then, ambitious in her Care,
These Arms thus labour'd for her Son prepare;   450
That *Ajax* after him the heav'nly Gift shou'd wear.
For that dull Soul to stare with stupid Eyes,
On the learn'd unintelligible Prize!
What are to him the Sculptures of the Shield,
Heav'ns Planets, Earth, and Oceans watry Field?   455
The *Pleiads*, *Hyads*; less, and greater Bear,
Undipp'd in Seas; *Orion*'s angry Star;
Two diff'ring Cities, grav'd on either Hand;
Would he wear Arms he cannot understand?

Beside, what wise Objections he prepares   460
Against my late accession to the Wars?
Does not the Fool perceive his Argument
Is with more force against *Achilles* bent?

For if Dissembling be so great a Crime,
The Fault is common, and the same in him: 465
And if he taxes both of long delay,

My Guilt is less who sooner came away.
His pious Mother anxious for his Life,
Detain'd her Son, and me, my pious Wife.
To them the Blossoms of our Youth were due,   470
Our riper Manhood we reserv'd for you.
But grant me guilty, 'tis not much my care,
When with so great a Man my Guilt I share:
My Wit to War the matchless Hero brought,
But by this Fool I never had been caught.   475

    Nor need I wonder, that on me he threw
Such foul Aspersions, when he spares not you:
If *Palamede* unjustly fell by me,
Your Honour suffer'd in th' unjust Decree:
I but accus'd, you doom'd: And yet he dy'd,   480
Convinc'd of Treason, and was fairly try'd:
You heard not he was false; your Eyes beheld
The Traytor manifest; the Bribe reveal'd.

    That *Philoctetes* is on *Lemnos* left
Wounded, forlorn, of human Aid bereft,   485
Is not my Crime, or not my Crime alone,
Defend your Justice, for the Fact's your own:
'Tis true, th' Advice was mine; that staying there ⎫
He might his weary Limbs with rest repair,   ⎬
From a long Voyage free, and from a longer War.   ⎭ 490
He took the Counsel, and he lives at least;
Th' event declares I counsell'd for the best:
Though Faith is all, in Ministers of State;
For who can promise to be fortunate?
Now since his Arrows are the Fate of *Troy*,   495
Do not my Wit, or weak Address employ;
Send *Ajax* there, with his persuasive Sense
To mollify the Man, and draw him thence:
But *Xanthus* shall run backward; *Ida* stand
A leafless Mountain; and the *Grecian* Band   500
Shall fight for *Troy*; if when my Counsel fail,
The Wit of heavy *Ajax* can prevail.

    Hard *Philoctetes*, exercise thy Spleen,
Against thy Fellows, and the King of Men;
Curse my devoted Head, above the rest,   505
And wish in Arms to meet me Breast to Breast:

Yet I the dang'rous Task will undertake
And either die my self, or bring thee back.

    Nor doubt the same Success, as when before
The *Phrygian* Prophet to these Tents I bore,   510
Surpriz'd by Night, and forc'd him to declare
In what was plac'd the fortune of the War,
Heav'ns dark Decrees, and Answers to display,
And how to take the Town, and where the Secret lay:
Yet this I compass'd, and from *Troy* convey'd   515
The fatal Image of their Guardian-Maid;
That Work was mine; for *Pallas*, though our Friend,
Yet while she was in *Troy* did *Troy* defend.
Now what has *Ajax* done, or what design'd,
A noisy Nothing, and an empty Wind?   520
If he be what he promises in Show,
Why was I sent, and why fear'd he to go?
Our boasting Champion thought the Task not light
To pass the Guards, commit himself to Night;
Not only through a hostile Town to pass,   525
But scale, with steep ascent, the sacred Place;
With wand'ring Steps to search the Cittadel,
And from the Priests their Patroness to steal:
Then through surrounding Foes to force my way,
And bear in Triumph home the heav'nly Prey;   530
Which had I not: *Ajax* in vain had held,
Before that monst'rous Bulk, his sev'nfold Shield.
That Night to conquer *Troy* I might be said,
When *Troy* was liable to Conquest made.

    Why point'st thou to my Partner of the War?   535
Tydides had indeed a worthy share
In all my Toil, and Praise; but when thy Might
Our Ships protected, did'st thou singly fight?
All join'd, and thou of many wert but one;
I ask'd no Friend, nor had, but him alone: 540
Who, had he not been well assur'd, that Art
And Conduct were of War the better part,
And more avail'd than Strength, my valiant Friend
Had urg'd a better Right, than *Ajax* can pretend:
As good at least *Euripylus* may claim,   545
And the more moderate *Ajax* of the Name:

The *Cretan* King, and his brave Charioteer,
And *Menelaus* bold with Sword and Spear:
All these had been my Rivals in the Shield,
And yet all these to my Pretensions yield.   550
Thy boist'rous Hands are then of use, when I
With this directing Head those Hands apply.
Brawn without Brain is thine: My prudent Care
Foresees, provides, administers the War:
Thy Province is to Fight; but when shall be   555
The time to Fight, the King consults with me:
No dram of Judgment with thy Force is join'd,
Thy Body is of Profit, and my Mind.
But how much more the Ship her Safety owes
To him who steers, than him that only rows,   560
By how much more the Captain merits Praise
Than he who Fights, and Fighting but obeys;
By so much greater is my Worth than thine,
Who can'st but execute what I design.
What gain'st thou brutal Man, if I confess   565
Thy Strength superiour when thy Wit is less?
Mind is the Man: I claim my whole Desert,
From the Mind's Vigour, and th' immortal part.
    But you, O *Grecian* Chiefs, reward my Care,
Be grateful to your Watchman of the War: 570
For all my Labours in so long a space,
Sure I may plead a Title to your Grace:
Enter the Town; I then unbarr'd the Gates,
When I remov'd their tutelary Fates.
By all our common hopes, if hopes they be   575
Which I have now reduc'd to Certainty;
By falling *Troy*, by yonder tott'ring Tow'rs,
And by their taken Gods, which now are ours;
Or if there yet a farther Task remains,
To be perform'd by Prudence or by Pains;   580
If yet some desperate Action rests behind
That asks high Conduct, and a dauntless Mind;
If ought be wanting to the *Trojan* Doom
Which none but I can manage and o'ercome,
Award, those Arms I ask, by your Decree: 585
Or give to this what you refuse to me.

He ceas'd: And ceasing with Respect he bow'd,
And with his Hand at once the fatal Statue show'd.
Heav'n, Air and Ocean rung, with loud Applause,
And by the general Vote he gain'd his Cause.   590
Thus Conduct won the Prize, when Courage fail'd,
And Eloquence o'er brutal Force prevail'd.

The Death of Ajax

He who cou'd often, and alone withstand
The Foe, the Fire, and *Jove*'s own partial Hand,
Now cannot his unmaster'd Grief sustain,   595
But yields to Rage, to Madness, and Disdain;
Then snatching out his Fauchion, Thou, said He,
Art mine; *Ulysses* lays no claim to Thee.
O often try'd, and ever trusty Sword,
Now do thy last kind Office to thy Lord: 600
'Tis *Ajax*, who requests thy Aid, to show
None but himself, himself cou'd overthrow:
He said, and with so good a Will to die
Did to his Breast the fatal Point apply,
It found his Heart, a way till then unknown,   605
Where never Weapon enter'd, but his own.
No Hands cou'd force it thence, so fix'd it stood
Till out it rush'd, expell'd by Streams of spouting Blood.
The fruitful Blood produc'd a Flow'r, which grew
On a green Stem; and of a Purple Hue: 610
Like his, whom unaware *Apollo* slew:
Inscrib'd in both, the Letters are the same,
But those express the Grief, and these the Name.

THE WIFE OF BATH HER TALE

IN Days of Old when *Arthur* fill'd the Throne,
Whose Acts and Fame to Foreign Lands were blown;
The King of Elfs and little Fairy Queen
Gamboll'd on Heaths, and danc'd on ev'ry Green.
And where the jolly Troop had led the round   5

The Grass unbidden rose, and mark'd the Ground:
Nor darkling did they dance, the Silver Light
Of *Phœbe* serv'd to guide their Steps aright,
And, with their Tripping pleas'd, prolong'd the Night.
Her Beams they follow'd, where at full she plaid,   10
Nor longer than she shed her Horns they staid,
From thence with airy Flight to Foreign Lands convey'd.
Above the rest our *Britain* held they dear,
More solemnly they kept their Sabbaths here,
And made more spacious Rings, and revell'd half the Year.   15
      I speak of ancient Times, for now the Swain
Returning late may pass the Woods in vain,
And never hope to see the nightly Train:
In vain the Dairy now with Mints is dress'd,
The Dairy-Maid expects no Fairy Guest,   20
To skim the Bowls and after pay the Feast.
She sighs and shakes her empty Shoes in vain,
No Silver Penny to reward her Pain:
For Priests with Pray'rs, and other godly Geer,
Have made the merry Goblins disappear;   25
And where they plaid their merry Pranks before,
Have sprinkled Holy Water on the Floor:
And Fry'rs that through the wealthy Regions run
Thick as the Motes, that twinkle in the Sun;
Resort to Farmers rich, and bless their Halls   30
And exorcise the Beds, and cross the Walls:
This makes the Fairy Quires forsake the Place,
When once 'tis hallow'd with the Rites of Grace:
But in the Walks where wicked Elves have been,
The Learning of the Parish now is seen,   35
The Midnight Parson posting o'er the Green,
With Gown tuck'd up to Wakes; for *Sunday* next,
With humming Ale encouraging his Text;
Nor wants the holy Leer to Country-Girl betwixt.
From Fiends and Imps he sets the Village free,   40
There haunts not any Incubus, but He.
The Maids and Women need no Danger fear
To walk by Night, and Sanctity so near:
For by some Haycock or some shady Thorn
He bids his Beads both Even-song and Morn.   45

It so befel in this King *Arthur*'s Reign,
A lusty Knight was pricking o'er the Plain;
A Batchelor he was, and of the courtly Train.
It happen'd as he rode, a Damsel gay
In Russet-Robes to Market took her way;   50
Soon on the Girl he cast an amorous Eye,
So strait she walk'd, and on her Pasterns high:
If seeing her behind he lik'd her Pace,
Now turning short he better lik'd her Face:
He lights in hast, and full of Youthful Fire,   55
By Force accomplish'd his obscene Desire:
This done away he rode, not unespy'd,
For swarming at his Back the Country cry'd;
And once in view they never lost the Sight,
But seiz'd, and pinion'd brought to court the Knight.   60
   Then Courts of Kings were held in high Renown,
E'er made the common Brothels of the Town:
There, Virgins honourable Vows receiv'd,
But chast as Maids in Monasteries liv'd:
The King himself to Nuptial Ties a Slave,   65
No bad Example to his Poets gave:
And they not bad, but in a vicious Age,
Had not to please the Prince debauch'd the Stage.
   Now what shou'd *Arthur* do? He lov'd the Knight,
But Soveraign Monarchs are the Source of Right: 70
Mov'd by the Damsels Tears and common Cry,
He doom'd the brutal Ravisher to die.
But fair *Geneura* rose in his Defence,
And pray'd so hard for Mercy from the Prince;
That to his Queen the King th' Offender gave,   75
And left it in her Pow'r to Kill or Save:
This gracious Act the Ladies all approve,
Who thought it much a Man should die for Love.
And with their Mistress join'd in close Debate,
(Covering their Kindness with dissembled Hate;)   80
If not to free him, to prolong his Fate.
At last agreed they call'd him by consent
Before the Queen and Female Parliament.
And the fair Speaker rising from her Chair,
Did thus the Judgment of the House declare.   85

Sir Knight, tho' I have ask'd thy Life, yet still
Thy Destiny depends upon my Will:
Nor hast thou other Surety than the Grace
Not due to thee from our offended Race.
But as our Kind is of a softer Mold,   90
And cannot Blood without a Sigh behold,
I grant thee Life; reserving still the Pow'r
To take the Forfeit when I see my Hour:
Unless thy Answer to my next Demand
Shall set Thee free from our avenging Hand;   95
The Question, whose Solution I require,
Is *what the Sex of Women most desire?*
In this Dispute thy Judges are at Strife;
Beware; for on thy Wit depends thy Life.
Yet (lest surpriz'd, unknowing what to say   100
Thou damn thy self) we give thee farther Day:
A Year is thine to wander at thy Will;
And learn from others if thou want'st the Skill.
But, our Proffer not to hold in Scorn,
Good Sureties will we have for thy return;   105
That at the time prefix'd thou shalt obey,
And at thy Pledges Peril keep thy Day.

Woe was the Knight at this severe Command!
But well he knew 'twas bootless to withstand:
The Terms accepted as the Fair ordain,   110
He put in Bail for his return again.
And promis'd Answer at the Day assign'd,
The best, with Heav'ns Assistance, he could find.

His Leave thus taken, on his Way he went
With heavy Heart, and full of Discontent,   } 115
Misdoubting much, and fearful of th' Event.
'Twas hard the Truth of such a Point to find,
As was not yet agreed among the Kind.
Thus on he went; still anxious more and more,
Ask'd all he met; and knock'd at ev'ry Door;   120
Enquir'd of Men; but made his chief Request
To learn from Women what they lov'd the best.
They answer'd each according to her Mind;

The Wife of Bath Her Tale. 104 our Proffer not to hold *Ed. conj.*: not to hold our Proffer F

To please her self, not all the Female Kind.
One was for Wealth, another was for Place: 125
Crones old and ugly, wish'd a better Face.
The Widow's Wish was oftentimes to Wed;
The wanton Maids were all for Sport a Bed.
Some said the Sex were pleas'd with handsom Lies,
And some gross Flatt'ry lov'd without disguise: 130
Truth is, says one, he seldom fails to win
Who Flatters well, for that's our darling Sin.
But long Attendance, and a duteous Mind,
Will work ev'n with the wisest of the Kind.
One thought the Sexes prime Felicity   135
Was from the Bonds of Wedlock to be free:
Their Pleasures, Hours, and Actions all their own,
And uncontroll'd to give Account to none.
Some wish a Husband-Fool; but such are curst,
For Fools perverse, of Husbands are the worst: 140
All Women wou'd be counted Chast and Wise,
Nor should our Spouses see, but with our Eyes;
For Fools will prate; and tho' they want the Wit
To find close Faults, yet open Blots will hit:
Tho' better for their Ease to hold their Tongue,   145
For Womankind was never in the Wrong.
So Noise ensues, and Quarrels last for Life;
The Wife abhors the Fool, the Fool the Wife.
And some Men say that great Delight have we,
To be for Truth extoll'd, and Secrecy: 150
And constant in one Purpose still to dwell;
And not our Husband's Counsels to reveal.
But that's a Fable; for our Sex is frail,
Inventing rather than not tell a Tale.
Like leaky Sives no Secrets we can hold: 155
Witness the famous Tale that *Ovid* told.

  Midas the King, as in his Book appears,
By *Phœbus* was endow'd with Asses Ears,
Which under his long Locks, he well conceal'd,
(As Monarch's Vices must not be reveal'd)   160
For fear the People have 'em in the Wind,
Who long ago were neither Dumb nor Blind;
Nor apt to think from Heav'n their Title springs,

Since *Jove* and *Mars* left off begetting Kings.
This *Midas* knew; and durst communicate   165
To none but to his Wife, his Ears of State:
One must be trusted, and he thought her fit,
As passing prudent; and a parlous Wit.
To this sagacious Confessor he went,
And told her what a Gift the Gods had sent: 170
But told it under Matrimonial Seal,
With strict Injunction never to reveal.
The Secret heard she plighted him her Troth,
(And sacred sure is every Woman's Oath)
The royal Malady should rest unknown   175
Both for her Husband's Honour and her own:
But ne'ertheless she pin'd with Discontent;
The Counsel rumbled till it found a vent.
The Thing she knew she was oblig'd to hide;
By Int'rest and by Oath the Wife was ty'd;   180
But if she told it not the Woman dy'd.
Loath to betray a Husband and a Prince,
But she must burst, or blab; and no pretence
Of Honour ty'd her Tongue from Self-defence.
A marshy Ground commodiously was near,   185
Thither she ran, and held her Breath for fear,
Lest if a Word she spoke of any Thing,
That Word might be the Secret of the King.
Thus full of Counsel to the Fen she went,
Grip'd all the way, and longing for a vent: 190
Arriv'd, by pure Necessity compell'd,
On her majestick mary-bones she kneel'd:
Then to the Waters-brink she laid her Head,
And, as a Bittour bumps within a Reed,
To thee alone, O Lake, she said, I tell   195
(And as thy Queen command thee to conceal)
Beneath his Locks the King my Husband wears
A goodly Royal pair of Asses Ears:
Now I have eas'd my Bosom of the Pain
Till the next longing Fit return again!   200
    Thus through a Woman was the Secret known;
Tell us, and in effect you tell the Town:
But to my Tale: The Knight with heavy Cheer,

Wandring in vain had now consum'd the Year:
One Day was only left to solve the Doubt,   205
Yet knew no more than when he first set out.
But home he must: And as th' Award had been,
Yield up his Body Captive to the Queen.
In this despairing State he hap'd to ride
As Fortune led him, by a Forest-side: 210
Lonely the Vale, and full of Horror stood
Brown with the shade of a religious Wood:
When full before him at the Noon of night,
(The Moon was up and shot a gleamy Light)
He saw a Quire of Ladies in a round,   215
That featly footing seem'd to skim the Ground:
Thus dancing Hand in Hand, so light they were,
He knew not where they trod, on Earth or Air.
At speed he drove, and came a suddain Guest,
In hope where many Women were, at least,   220
Some one by chance might answer his Request.
But faster than his Horse the Ladies flew,
And in a trice were vanish'd out of view.

  One only Hag remain'd: But fowler far
Than Grandame Apes in *Indian* Forests are: 225
Against a wither'd Oak she lean'd her weight,
Prop'd on her trusty Staff, not half upright,
And drop'd an awkard Court'sy to the Knight.
Then said, What make you Sir so late abroad
Without a Guide, and this no beaten Road?   230
Or want you ought that here you hope to find,
Or travel for some Trouble in your Mind?
The last I guess; and, if I read aright,
Those of our Sex are bound to serve a Knight:
Perhaps good Counsel may your Grief asswage,   235
Then tell your Pain: For Wisdom is in Age.

  To this the Knight: Good Mother, wou'd you know
The secret Cause and Spring of all my Woe?
My Life must with to Morrow's Light expire,
Unless I tell, what Women most desire: 240
Now cou'd you help me at this hard Essay,
Or for your inborn Goodness, or for Pay:
Yours is my Life, redeem'd by your Advice,

Ask what you please, and I will pay the Price:
The proudest Kerchief of the Court shall rest   245
Well satisfy'd of what they love the best.
Plight me thy Faith, quoth she: That what I ask,
Thy Danger over, and perform'd the Task;
That shalt thou give for Hire of thy Demand,
Here take thy Oath; and seal it on my Hand;   250
I warrant thee on Peril of my Life,
Thy Words shall please both Widow, Maid and Wife.

   More Words there needed not to move the Knight
To take her Offer, and his Truth to plight.
With that she spread her Mantle on the Ground,   255
And first enquiring whether he was bound,
Bade him not fear, tho' long and rough the Way,
At Court he should arrive e'er break of Day:
His Horse should find the way without a Guide,
She said: With Fury they began to ride,   260
He on the midst, the Beldam at his Side.
The Horse, what Devil drove I cannot tell,
But only this, they sped their Journey well:
And all the way the Crone inform'd the Knight,
How he should answer the Demand aright.   265

   To Court they came: The News was quickly spread
Of his returning to redeem his Head.
The Female Senate was assembled soon,
With all the Mob of Women in the Town:
The Queen sate Lord Chief Justice of the Hall,   270
And bad the Cryer cite the Criminal.
The Knight appear'd; and Silence they proclaim,
Then first the *Culprit* answer'd to his Name:
And after Forms of Laws, was last requir'd
To name the Thing that Women most desir'd.   275

   Th' Offender, taught his Lesson by the way,
And by his Counsel order'd what to say,
Thus bold began; My Lady Liege, said he,
What all your Sex desire is *Soveraignty*.
The Wife affects her Husband to command,   280
All must be hers, both Mony, House, and Land.
The Maids are Mistresses ev'n in their Name;
And of their Servants full Dominion claim.

This, at the Peril of my Head, I say
A blunt plain Truth, the Sex aspires to sway,   285
You to rule all; while we, like Slaves, obey.

    There was not one or Widow, Maid, or Wife,
But said the Knight had well deserv'd his Life.
Ev'n fair *Geneura*, with a Blush confess'd,
The Man had found what Women love the best.   290

    Upstarts the Beldam, who was there unseen,
And Reverence made, accosted thus the Queen.
My Liege, said she, before the Court arise,
May I poor Wretch find Favour in your Eyes;
To grant my just Request: 'Twas I who taught   295
The Knight this Answer, and inspir'd his Thought.
None but a Woman could a Man direct
To tell us Women, what we most affect.
But first I swore him on his Knightly Troth,
(And here demand performance of his Oath)   300
To grant the Boon that next I should desire;
He gave his Faith, and I expect my Hire:
My Promise is fulfill'd: I sav'd his Life,
And claim his Debt to take me for his Wife.
The Knight was ask'd, nor cou'd his Oath deny,   305
But hop'd they would not force him to comply.
The Women, who would rather wrest the Laws,
Than let a Sister-Plantiff lose the Cause,
(As Judges on the Bench more gracious are,
And more attent to Brothers of the Bar)   310
Cry'd one, and all, the Suppliant should have Right,
And to the Grandame-Hag adjudg'd the Knight.

    In vain he sigh'd, and oft with Tears desir'd,
Some reasonable Sute, might be requir'd.
But still the Crone was constant to her Note;·   315
The more he spoke, the more she stretch'd her Throat.

In vain he proffer'd all his Goods, to save
His Body, destin'd to that living Grave.
The liquorish Hag rejects the Pelf with scorn:
And nothing but the Man would serve her turn.   320
Not all the Wealth of Eastern Kings, said she,
Have Pow'r to part my plighted Love, and me:
And Old, and Ugly as I am, and Poor;

Yet never will I break the Faith I swore;
For mine thou art by Promise, during Life,   325
And I thy loving and obedient Wife.

    My Love! Nay rather my Damnation Thou,
Said he: Nor am I bound to keep my Vow:
The Fiend thy Sire has sent thee from below,
Else how cou'dst thou my secret Sorrows know?   330
Avaunt old Witch, for I renounce thy Bed:
The Queen may take the Forfeit of my Head,
E'er any of my Race so foul a Crone shall wed.

    Both heard, the Judge pronounc'd against the Knight;
So was he Marry'd in his own despight;   335
And all Day after hid him as an Owl,
Not able to sustain a Sight so foul.
Perhaps the Reader thinks I do him wrong
To pass the Marriage-Feast, and Nuptial Song:
Mirth there was none, the Man was *a-la-mort*:   340
And little Courage had to make his Court.
To Bed they went, the Bridegroom and the Bride:
Was never such an ill-pair'd Couple ty'd.
Restless he toss'd and tumbled to and fro,
And rowl'd, and wriggled further off; for Woe.   345
The good old Wife lay smiling by his Side,
And caught him in her quiv'ring Arms, and cry'd,
When you my ravish'd Predecessor saw,
You were not then become this Man of Straw;
Had you been such, you might have scap'd the Law.   350
Is this the Custom of King *Arthur*'s Court?
Are all Round-Table Knights of such a sort?
Remember I am she who sav'd your Life,
Your loving, lawful, and complying Wife:
Not thus you swore in your unhappy Hour,   355
Nor I for this return employ'd my Pow'r.
In time of Need I was your faithful Friend;
Nor did I since, nor ever will offend.
Believe me my lov'd Lord, 'tis much unkind;
What Fury has possess'd your alter'd Mind?   360
Thus on my Wedding-night—Without Pretence—
Come turn this way, or tell me my Offence.
If not your Wife, let Reasons Rule persuade,

Name but my Fault, amends shall soon be made.
   Amends! Nay that's impossible, said he,   365
What change of Age, or Ugliness can be!
Or, could *Medea*'s Magick mend thy Face,
Thou art descended from so mean a Race,
That never Knight was match'd with such Disgrace.
What wonder, Madam, if I move my Side,   370
When if I turn, I turn to such a Bride?
   And is this all that troubles you so sore!
   And what the Devil cou'dst thou wish me more?
Ah *Benedicite*, reply'd the Crone:
Then cause of just Complaining have you none.   375
The Remedy to this were soon apply'd,
Wou'd you be like the Bridegroom to the Bride.
But, for you say a long descended Race,
And Wealth, and Dignity, and Pow'r, and Place,
Make Gentlemen, and that your high Degree   380
Is much disparag'd to be match'd with me;
Know this, my Lord, Nobility of Blood
Is but a glitt'ring, and fallacious Good:
The Nobleman is he whose noble Mind
Is fill'd with inborn Worth, unborrow'd from his Kind.   385
The King of Heav'n was in a Manger laid;
And took his Earth but from an humble Maid:
Then what can Birth, or mortal Men bestow,
Since Floods no higher than their Fountains flow.
We who for Name, and empty Honour strive,   390
Our true Nobility from him derive.
Your Ancestors who puff your Mind with Pride,
And vast Estates to mighty Titles ty'd,
Did not your Honour, but their own advance,
For Virtue comes not by Inheritance.   395
If you tralineate from your Father's Mind,
What are you else but of a Bastard-kind?
Do, as your great Progenitors have done,
And by their Virtues prove your self their Son.
No Father can infuse, or Wit, or Grace,   400
A Mother comes across, and marrs the Race.
A Grandsire, or a Grandame taints the Blood;
And seldom three Descents continue Good.

Were Virtue by Descent, a noble Name
Cou'd never villanize his Father's Fame: 405
But as the first, the last of all the Line,
Wou'd like the Sun ev'n in Descending shine.
Take Fire; and bear it to the darkest House,
Betwixt King *Arthur*'s Court and *Caucasus*,
If you depart, the Flame shall still remain,   410
And the bright Blaze enlighten all the Plain:
Nor, till the Fewel perish, can decay,
By Nature form'd on Things combustible to prey.
Such is not Man, who mixing better Seed
With worse, begets a base, degenerate Breed: 415
The Bad corrupts the Good, and leaves behind
No trace of all the great Begetter's Mind.
The Father sinks within his Son, we see,
And often rises in the third Degree;
If better Luck, a better Mother give: 420
Chance gave us being, and by Chance we live.
Such as our Atoms were, ev'n such are we,   }
Or call it Chance, or strong Necessity.
Thus, loaded with dead weight, the Will is free.   }
And thus it needs must be: For Seed conjoin'd   425
Lets into Nature's Work th' imperfect Kind:
But Fire, th' enliv'ner of the general Frame
Is one, its Operation still the same.
Its Principle is in it self: While ours
Works as Confederates War, with mingled Pow'rs: 430
Or Man, or Woman, which soever fails:
And, oft, the Vigour of the Worse prevails.
Æther with Sulphur blended, alters hue,
And casts a dusky gleam of *Sodom* blue.
Thus in a Brute, their ancient Honour ends,   435
And the fair Mermaid in a Fish descends:
The Line is gone; no longer Duke or Earl;
But by himself degraded turns a Churl.
Nobility of Blood is but Renown
Of thy great Fathers by their Virtue known,   } 440
And a long trail of Light, to thee descending down.   }
If in thy Smoke it ends: Their Glories shine;
But Infamy and Villanage are thine.

Then what I said before, is plainly show'd,
That true Nobility proceeds from God: 445
Not left us by Inheritance, but giv'n
By Bounty of our Stars, and Grace of Heav'n.
Thus from a Captive *Servius Tullus* rose,
Whom for his Virtues, the first *Romans* chose:
Fabritius from their Walls repell'd the Foe,   450
Whose noble Hands had exercis'd the Plough.
From hence, my Lord, and Love, I thus conclude,
That tho' my homely Ancestors, were rude,
Mean as I am, yet I may have the Grace,
To make you Father of a generous Race: 455
And Noble then am I, when I begin
In Virtue cloath'd, to cast the Rags of Sin:
If Poverty be my upbraided Crime,
And you believe in Heav'n; there was a time,
When He, the great Controller of our Fate   460
Deign'd to be Man; and liv'd in low Estate:
Which he who had the World at his dispose,
If Poverty were Vice, wou'd never choose.
Philosophers have said, and Poets sing,
That a glad Poverty's an honest Thing.   465
Content is Wealth, the Riches of the Mind;
And happy He who can that Treasure find.
But the base Miser starves amidst his Store,
Broods on his Gold, and griping still at more
Sits sadly pining, and believes he's Poor.   470
The ragged Beggar, tho' he wants Relief,
Has not to lose, and sings before the Thief.
Want is a bitter, and a hateful Good,
Because its Virtues are not understood:
Yet many Things impossible to Thought   475
Have been by Need to full Perfection brought:
The daring of the Soul proceeds from thence,
Sharpness of Wit, and active Diligence:
Prudence at once, and Fortitude it gives,
And if in patience taken mends our Lives;   480
For ev'n that Indigence that brings me low
Makes me my self; and Him above to know.
A Good which none would challenge, few would choose,

A fair Possession, which Mankind refuse.

    If we from Wealth to Poverty descend,   485
Want gives to know the Flatt'rer from the Friend.
If I am Old, and Ugly, well for you,
No leud Adult'rer will my Love pursue.
Nor Jealousy the Bane of marry'd Life,
Shall haunt you, for a wither'd homely Wife: 490
For Age, and Ugliness, as all agree,
Are the best Guards of Female Chastity.

    Yet since I see your Mind is Worldly bent,
I'll do my best to further your Content.
And therefore of two Gifts in my dispose,   495
Think e'er you speak, I grant you leave to choose:
Wou'd you I should be still Deform'd, and Old,
Nauseous to Touch, and Loathsome to Behold;
On this Condition, to remain for Life
A careful, tender and obedient Wife,   500
In all I can contribute to your Ease,
And not in Deed or Word, or Thought displease?
Or would you rather have me Young and Fair,
And take the Chance that happens to your share?
Temptations are in Beauty, and in Youth,   505
And how can you depend upon my Truth?
Now weigh the Danger, with the doubtful Bliss,
And thank your self, if ought should fall amiss.

    Sore sigh'd the Knight, who this long Sermon heard,
At length considering all, his Heart he chear'd: 510
And thus reply'd, My Lady, and my Wife,
To your wise Conduct I resign my Life:
Choose you for me, for well you understand
The future Good and Ill, on either Hand:
But if an humble Husband may request,   515
Provide, and order all Things for the best;
Your's be the Care to profit, and to please:
And let your Subject-Servant take his Ease.

    Then thus in Peace, quoth she, concludes the Strife,
Since I am turn'd the Husband, you the Wife: 520
The Matrimonial Victory is mine,
Which having fairly gain'd, I will resign;
Forgive, if I have said, or done amiss,

And seal the Bargain with a Friendly Kiss:
I promis'd you but one Content to share,   525
But now I will become both Good, and Fair.
No Nuptial Quarrel shall disturb your Ease,
The Business of my Life shall be to please:
And for my Beauty that, as Time shall try;
But draw the Curtain first, and cast your Eye.   530
    He look'd, and saw a Creature heav'nly Fair,
In bloom of Youth, and of a charming Air.
With Joy he turn'd, and seiz'd her Iv'ry Arm;
And like *Pygmalion* found the Statue warm.
Small Arguments there needed to prevail,   535
A Storm of Kisses pour'd as thick as Hail.
    Thus long in mutual Bliss they lay embrac'd,
And their first Love continu'd to the last:
One Sun-shine was their Life; no Cloud between;
Nor ever was a kinder Couple seen.   540
    And so may all our Lives like their's be led;
Heav'n send the Maids young Husbands, fresh in Bed:
May Widows Wed as often as they can,
And ever for the better change their Man.
And some devouring Plague pursue their Lives,   545
Who will not well be govern'd by their Wives.

OF THE PYTHAGOREAN PHILOSOPHY
From Ovid's Metamorphoses Book XV

The Fourteenth Book concludes with the Death and Deification of Romulus*:*
The Fifteenth begins with the Election of Numa *to the Crown of* Rome*. On*
this Occasion, Ovid *following the Opinion of some Authors, makes* Numa *the*
Schollar of Pythagoras*; and to have begun his Acquaintance with that*
Philosopher at Crotona*, a Town in* Italy*; from thence he makes a Digression* 5
to the Moral and Natural Philosophy of Pythagoras*: On both which our*
Author enlarges; and which are, the most learned and beautiful Parts of the
whole Metamorphoses.

A KING is sought to guide the growing State,
    One able to support the Publick Weight,
And fill the Throne where *Romulus* had sat.

543 often as they] often they F

Renown, which oft bespeaks the Publick Voice,
Had recommended *Numa* to their choice: 5
A peaceful, pious Prince; who not content
To know the *Sabine* Rites, his Study bent
To cultivate his Mind: To learn the Laws
Of Nature, and explore their hidden Cause.
Urg'd by this Care, his Country he forsook,   10
And to *Crotona* thence, his Journey took.
Arriv'd, he first enquir'd the Founder's Name,
Of this new Colony; and whence he came.
Then thus a Senior of the Place replies,
(Well read, and curious of Antiquities)   15
'Tis said; *Alcides* hither took his way,
From *Spain*, and drove along his conquer'd Prey;
Then leaving in the Fields his grazing Cows,
He sought himself some hospitable House:
Good *Croton* entertain'd his Godlike Guest;   20
While he repair'd his weary Limbs with rest.
The Hero, thence departing, bless'd the Place;
And here, he said, in Times revolving Race
A rising Town shall take his Name from thee;
Revolving Time fulfill'd the Prophecy: 25
For *Myscelos*, the justest Man on Earth,
Alemon's Son, at *Argos* had his Birth:
Him *Hercules*, arm'd with his Club of Oak
O'ershadow'd in a Dream, and thus bespoke;
Go, leave thy Native Soil, and make Abode   30
Where *Æsaris* rowls down his rapid Flood;
He said; and Sleep forsook him, and the God.
Trembling he wak'd, and rose with anxious Heart;
His Country Laws, forbad him to depart;
What shou'd he do? 'Twas Death to go away,   35
And the God menac'd if he dar'd to stay:
All Day he doubted, and when Night came on,
Sleep, and the same forewarning Dream begun:
Once more the God stood threatning o'er his Head;
With added Curses if he disobey'd.   40
Twice warn'd, he study'd Flight; but wou'd convey
At once his Person, and his Wealth away:
Thus while he linger'd, his Design was heard;

A speedy Process form'd, and Death declar'd.
Witness there needed none of his Offence,   45
Against himself the Wretch was Evidence:
Condemn'd, and destitute of human Aid,
To him, for whom he suffer'd, thus he pray'd.

O Pow'r who hast deserv'd in Heav'n a Throne
Not giv'n, but by thy Labours made thy own,   50
Pity thy Suppliant, and protect his Cause,
Whom thou hast made obnoxious to the Laws.

A Custom was of old, and still remains;
Which Life or Death by Suffrages ordains;
White Stones and Black within an Urn are cast,   55
The first absolve, but Fate is in the last.
The Judges to the common Urn bequeath
Their Votes, and drop the Sable Signs of Death;
The Box receives all Black, but pour'd from thence
The Stones came candid forth: The Hue of Innocence.   60
Thus *Alemonides* his Safety won,
Preserv'd from Death by *Alcumena*'s Son:
Then to his Kinsman-God his Vows he pays,
And cuts with prosp'rous Gales th' *Ionian* Seas:
He leaves *Tarentum* favour'd by the Wind,   65
And *Thurine* Bays, and *Temises* behind;
Soft *Sybaris*, and all the Capes that stand
Along the Shore, he makes in sight of Land;
Still doubling, and still coasting, till he found
The Mouth of *Æsaris*, and promis'd Ground,   70
Then saw where on the Margin of the Flood
The Tomb, that held the Bones of *Croton* stood:
Here, by the God's Command, he built and wall'd
The Place predicted; and *Crotona* call'd:
Thus Fame from time to time delivers down   75
The sure Tradition of th' *Italian* Town.

Here dwelt the Man divine whom *Samos* bore,
But now Self-banish'd from his Native Shore,
Because he hated Tyrants, nor cou'd bear
The Chains which none but servile Souls will wear: 80
He, tho' from Heav'n remote, to Heav'n cou'd move,
With Strength of Mind, and tread th' Abyss above;
And penetrate with his interiour Light

Those upper Depths, which Nature hid from Sight:
And what he had observ'd, and learnt from thence,   85
Lov'd in familiar Language to dispence.
   The Crowd with silent Admiration stand
And heard him, as they heard their God's Command;
While he discours'd of Heav'ns mysterious Laws,
The World's Original, and Nature's Cause;   90
And what was God, and why the fleecy Snows
In silence fell, and rattling Winds arose;
What shook the stedfast Earth, and whence begun
The dance of Planets round the radiant Sun;
If Thunder was the Voice of angry *Jove*,   95
Or Clouds with Nitre pregnant burst above:
Of these, and Things beyond the common reach
He spoke, and charm'd his Audience with his Speech.
   He first the tast of Flesh from Tables drove,
And argu'd well, if Arguments cou'd move.   100
O Mortals! from your Fellow's Blood abstain,
Nor taint your Bodies with a Food profane:
While Corn and Pulse by Nature are bestow'd,
And planted Orchards bend their willing Load;
While labour'd Gardens wholsom Herbs produce,   105
And teeming Vines afford their generous Juice:
Nor tardier Fruits of cruder Kind are lost,
But tam'd with Fire, or mellow'd by the Frost:
While Kine to Pails distended Udders bring,
And Bees their Hony redolent of Spring: 110
While Earth not only can your Needs supply,
But lavish of her Store, provides for Luxury;
A guiltless Feast administers with Ease,
And without Blood is prodigal to please.
Wild Beasts their Maws with their slain Brethren fill;   115
And yet not all, for some refuse to kill:
Sheep, Goats, and Oxen, and the nobler Steed
On Browz and Corn, and flow'ry Meadows feed.
Bears, Tygers, Wolves, the Lion's angry Brood,
Whom Heav'n endu'd with Principles of Blood,   120
He wisely sundred from the rest, to yell
In Forests, and in lonely Caves to dwell,
Where stronger Beasts oppress the weak by Might,

And all in Prey, and Purple Feasts delight.

   O impious use! to Nature's Laws oppos'd,   125
Where Bowels are in other Bowels clos'd:
Where fatten'd by their Fellow's Fat they thrive;
Maintain'd by Murder, and by Death they live.
'Tis then for nought that Mother Earth provides
The Stores of all she shows, and all she hides,   130
If Men with fleshy Morsels must be fed,
And chaw with bloody Teeth the breathing Bread:
What else is this but to devour our Guests,
And barb'rously renew *Cyclopean* Feasts!
We, by destroying Life, our Life sustain;   135
And gorge th' ungodly Maw with Meats obscene.

   Not so the Golden Age, who fed on Fruit,
Nor durst with bloody Meals their Mouths pollute.
Then Birds in airy space might safely move,
And timerous Hares on Heaths securely rove: 140
Nor needed Fish the guileful Hooks to fear,
For all was peaceful; and that Peace sincere.
Whoever was the Wretch (and curs'd be He)
That envy'd first our Food's simplicity;
Th' essay of bloody Feasts on Brutes began,   145
And after forg'd the Sword to murther Man.
Had he the sharpen'd Steel alone employ'd,
On Beasts of Prey that other Beasts destroy'd,
Or Man invaded with their Fangs and Paws,
This had been justify'd by Nature's Laws,   150
And Self-defence: But who did Feasts begin
Of Flesh, he stretch'd Necessity to Sin.
To kill Man-killers, Man has lawful Pow'r,
But not th' extended Licence, to devour.

   Ill Habits gather by unseen degrees,   155
As Brooks make Rivers, Rivers run to Seas.
The Sow, with her broad Snout for rooting up
Th' intrusted Seed, was judg'd to spoil the Crop,
And intercept the sweating Farmer's hope:
The cov'tous Churl of unforgiving kind,   160
Th' Offender to the bloody Priest resign'd:
Her Hunger was no Plea: For that she dy'd.

   Of the Pythagorean Philosophy. 145 Brutes] Bruits *F*

The Goat came next in order, to be try'd:
The Goat had cropt the tendrills of the Vine:
In vengeance Laity, and Clergy join,   165
Where one had lost his Profit, one his Wine.
Here was at least, some shadow of Offence:
The Sheep was sacrific'd on no pretence,
But meek, and unresisting Innocence.
A patient, useful Creature, born to bear   170
The warm and woolly Fleece, that cloath'd her Murderer,
And daily to give down the Milk she bred,
A Tribute for the Grass on which she fed.
Living, both Food and Rayment she supplies,
And is of least advantage when she dies.   175
   How did the toiling Oxe his Death deserve,
A downright simple Drudge, and born to serve?
O Tyrant! with what Justice can'st thou hope
The promise of the Year, a plenteous Crop;
When thou destroy'st thy lab'ring Steer, who till'd,   180
And plough'd with Pains, thy else ungrateful Field?
From his yet reeking Neck to draw the Yoke,
That Neck, with which the surly Clods he broke;
And to the Hatchet yield thy Husband-Man,
Who finish'd Autumn and the Spring began!   185
   Nor this alone! but Heav'n it self to bribe,
We to the Gods our impious Acts ascribe:
First recompence with Death their Creatures Toil,
Then call the Bless'd above to share the Spoil:
The fairest Victim must the Pow'rs appease,   190
(So fatal 'tis sometimes too much to please!)
A purple Fillet his broad Brows adorns,
With flow'ry Garlands crown'd, and gilded Horns:
He hears the murd'rous Pray'r the Priest prefers,
But understands not, 'tis his Doom he hears: 195
Beholds the Meal betwixt his Temples cast,
(The Fruit and Product of his Labours past;)
And in the Water views perhaps the Knife
Uplifted, to deprive him of his Life;
Then broken up alive his Entrails sees,   200
Torn out for Priests t' inspect the God's Decrees.
   From whence, O mortal Men, this gust of Blood

Have you deriv'd, and interdicted Food?
Be taught by me this dire Delight to shun,
Warn'd by my Precepts, by my Practice won:　　　　　205
And when you eat the well deserving Beast,
Think, on the Lab'rer of your Field, you feast!
　　Now since the God inspires me to proceed,
Be that, whate'er inspiring Pow'r, obey'd.
For I will sing of mighty Mysteries,　　　　　210
Of Truths conceal'd before, from human Eyes,
Dark Oracles unveil, and open all the Skies.
Pleas'd as I am to walk along the Sphere
Of shining Stars, and travel with the Year,
To leave the heavy Earth, and scale the height　　　　　215
Of *Atlas*, who supports the heav'nly weight;
To look from upper Light, and thence survey
Mistaken Mortals wandring from the way,
And wanting Wisdom, fearful for the state
Of future Things, and trembling at their Fate!　　　　　220
　　Those I would teach; and by right Reason bring
To think of Death, as but an idle Thing.
Why thus affrighted at an empty Name,
A Dream of Darkness, and fictitious Flame?
Vain Themes of Wit, which but in Poems pass,　　　　　225
And Fables of a World, that never was!
What feels the Body when the Soul expires,
By time corrupted, or consum'd by Fires?
Nor dies the Spirit, but new Life repeats
In other Forms, and only changes Seats.　　　　　230
　　Ev'n I, who these mysterious Truths declare,
Was once *Euphorbus* in the *Trojan* War;
My Name and Lineage I remember well,
And how in Fight by *Sparta*'s King I fell.
In *Argive Juno*'s Fane I late beheld　　　　　235
My Buckler hung on high, and own'd my former Shield.
　　Then, Death, so call'd, is but old Matter dress'd
In some new Figure, and a vary'd Vest:
Thus all Things are but alter'd, nothing dies;
And here and there th' unbodied Spirit flies,　　　　　240
By Time, or Force, or Sickness dispossest,
And lodges, where it lights, in Man or Beast;

Or hunts without, till ready Limbs it find,
And actuates those according to their kind;
From Tenement to Tenement is toss'd;   245
The Soul is still the same, the Figure only lost:
And, as the soften'd Wax new Seals receives,
This Face assumes, and that Impression leaves;
Now call'd by one, now by another Name;
The Form is only chang'd, the Wax is still the same: 250
So Death, so call'd, can but the Form deface,
Th' immortal Soul flies out in empty space;
To seek her Fortune in some other Place.

    Then let not Piety be put to flight,
To please the tast of Glutton-Appetite;   255
But suffer inmate Souls secure to dwell,
Lest from their Seats your Parents you expel;
With rabid Hunger feed upon your kind,
Or from a Beast dislodge a Brother's Mind.

    And since, like *Tiphys* parting from the Shore,   260
In ample Seas I sail, and Depths untry'd before,
This let me further add, that Nature knows
No stedfast Station, but, or Ebbs, or Flows:
Ever in motion; she destroys her old,
And casts new Figures in another Mold.   265
Ev'n Times are in perpetual Flux; and run
Like Rivers from their Fountain rowling on;
For Time no more than Streams, is at a stay:
The flying Hour is ever on her way;
And as the Fountain still supplies her store,   270
The Wave behind impels the Wave before;
Thus in successive Course the Minutes run,
And urge their Predecessor Minutes on,
Still moving, ever new: For former Things
Are set aside, like abdicated Kings: 275
And every moment alters what is done,
And innovates some Act till then unknown.

    Darkness we see emerges into Light,
And shining Suns descend to Sable Night;
Ev'n Heav'n it self receives another die,   280
When weari'd Animals in Slumbers lie,
Of Midnight Ease: Another when the gray

Of Morn preludes the Splendor of the Day.
The disk of *Phœbus* when he climbs on high,
Appears at first but as a bloodshot Eye;   285
And when his Chariot downward drives to Bed,
His Ball is with the same Suffusion red;
But mounted high in his Meridian Race
All bright he shines, and with a better Face:
For there, pure Particles of *Æther* flow,   290
Far from th' Infection of the World below.

Nor equal Light th' unequal Moon adorns,
Or in her wexing or her waning Horns.
For ev'ry Day she wanes, her Face is less,
But gath'ring into Globe, she fattens at increase.   295

Perceiv'st thou not the process of the Year,
How the four Seasons in four Forms appear,
Resembling human Life in ev'ry Shape they wear?
Spring first, like Infancy, shoots out her Head,
With milky Juice requiring to be fed: 300
Helpless, tho' fresh, and wanting to be led.
The green Stem grows in Stature and in Size,
But only feeds with hope the Farmer's Eyes;
Then laughs the childish Year with Flourets crown'd,
And lavishly perfumes the Fields around,   305
But no substantial Nourishment receives,
Infirm the Stalks, unsolid are the Leaves.

Proceeding onward whence the Year began
The Summer grows adult, and ripens into Man.
This Season, as in Men, is most repleat,   310
With kindly Moisture, and prolifick Heat.
Autumn succeeds, a sober tepid Age,
Not froze with Fear, nor boiling into Rage;
More than mature, and tending to decay,
When our brown Locks repine to mix with odious Grey.   315

Last Winter creeps along with tardy pace,
Sour is his Front, and furrow'd is his Face;
His Scalp if not dishonour'd quite of Hair,
The ragged Fleece is thin, and thin is worse than bare.

Ev'n our own Bodies daily change receive,   320
Some part of what was theirs before, they leave;
Nor are to Day what Yesterday they were;

Nor the whole same to Morrow will appear.

    Time was, when we were sow'd, and just began
From some few fruitful Drops, the promise of a Man;   325
Then Nature's Hand (fermented as it was)
Moulded to Shape the soft, coagulated Mass;
And when the little Man was fully form'd,
The breathless Embryo with a Spirit warm'd;
But when the Mothers Throws begin to come,   330
The Creature, pent within the narrow Room,
Breaks his blind Prison, pushing to repair
His stiffled Breath, and draw the living Air;
Cast on the Margin of the World he lies,
A helpless Babe, but by Instinct he cries.   335
He next essays to walk, but downward press'd
On four Feet imitates his Brother Beast:
By slow degrees he gathers from the Ground
His Legs, and to the rowling Chair is bound;
Then walks alone; a Horseman now become   340
He rides a Stick, and travels round the Room:
In time he vaunts among his youthful Peers,
Strong-bon'd, and strung with Nerves, in pride of Years,
He runs with Mettle his first merry Stage,
Maintains the next abated of his Rage,   345
But manages his Strength, and spares his Age.
Heavy the third, and stiff, he sinks apace,
And tho' 'tis down-hill all, but creeps along the Race.
Now sapless on the verge of Death he stands,
Contemplating his former Feet, and Hands;   350
And *Milo*-like, his slacken'd Sinews sees,
And wither'd Arms, once fit to cope with *Hercules*,
Unable now to shake, much less to tear the Trees.

    So *Helen* wept when her too faithful Glass
Reflected to her Eyes the ruins of her Face: 355
Wondring what Charms her Ravishers cou'd spy,
To force her twice, or ev'n but once enjoy!

    Thy Teeth, devouring Time, thine, envious Age,
On Things below still exercise your Rage:
With venom'd Grinders you corrupt your Meat,   360
And then at lingring Meals, the Morsels eat.

Nor those, which Elements we call, abide,
Nor to this Figure, nor to that are ty'd:
For this eternal World is said of Old
But four prolifick Principles to hold,   365
Four different Bodies; two to Heaven ascend,
And other two down to the Center tend:
Fire first with Wings expanded mounts on high,
Pure, void of weight, and dwells in upper Sky;
Then Air, because unclogg'd in empty space   370
Flies after Fire, and claims the second Place:
But weighty Water as her Nature guides,
Lies on the lap of Earth; and Mother Earth subsides.

All Things are mix'd of these, which all contain,
And into these are all resolv'd again: 375
Earth rarifies to Dew; expanded more,
The subtil Dew in Air begins to soar;
Spreads as she flies, and weary of her Name
Extenuates still, and changes into Flame;
Thus having by degrees Perfection won,   380
Restless they soon untwist the Web they spun,
And Fire begins to lose her radiant Hue,
Mix'd with gross Air, and Air descends to Dew:
And Dew condensing, does her Form forego,
And sinks, a heavy lump of Earth below.   385

Thus are their Figures never at a stand,
But chang'd by Nature's innovating Hand;
All Things are alter'd, nothing is destroy'd,
The shifted Scene, for some new Show employ'd.

Then to be born, is to begin to be   390
Some other Thing we were not formerly:
And what we call to Die, is not t' appear,
Or be the Thing that formerly we were.
Those very Elements which we partake,
Alive, when Dead some other Bodies make: 395
Translated grow, have Sense, or can Discourse,
But Death on deathless Substance has no force.

That Forms are chang'd I grant; that nothing can
Continue in the Figure it began:
The Golden Age, to Silver was debas'd: 400
To Copper that; our Mettal came at last.

The Face of Places, and their Forms decay;
And that is solid Earth, that once was Sea:
Seas in their turn retreating from the Shore,
Make solid Land, what Ocean was before;   405
And far from Strands are Shells of Fishes found,
And rusty Anchors fix'd on Mountain-Ground:
And what were Fields before, now wash'd and worn
By falling Floods from high, to Valleys turn,
And crumbling still descend to level Lands;   410
And Lakes, and trembling Bogs are barren Sands:
And the parch'd Desart floats in Streams unknown;
Wondring to drink of Waters not her own.

   Here Nature living Fountains ope's; and there
Seals up the Wombs where living Fountains were;   415
Or Earthquakes stop their ancient Course, and bring
Diverted Streams to feed a distant Spring.
So *Lycus*, swallow'd up, is seen no more,
But far from thence knocks out another Door.
Thus *Erasinus* dives; and blind in Earth   420
Runs on, and gropes his way to second Birth,
Starts up in *Argos* Meads, and shakes his Locks,
Around the Fields, and fattens all the Flocks.
So *Mysus* by another way is led,
And, grown a River now disdains his Head: 425
Forgets his humble Birth, his Name forsakes,
And the proud Title of *Caicus* takes.
Large *Amenane*, impure with yellow Sands,
Runs rapid often, and as often stands,
And here he threats the drunken Fields to drown;   430
And there his Dugs deny to give their Liquor down.
   Anigros once did wholsome Draughts afford,
But now his deadly Waters are abhorr'd:
Since, hurt by *Hercules*, as Fame resounds,
The Centaurs, in his current wash'd their Wounds.   435
The Streams of *Hypanis* are sweet no more,
But brackish lose the tast they had before.
Antissa, *Pharos*, *Tyre*, in Seas were pent,
Once Isles, but now increase the Continent;
While the *Leucadian* Coast, main Land before,   440
By rushing Seas is sever'd from the Shore.

So *Zancle* to th' *Italian* Earth was ty'd,
And Men once walk'd where Ships at Anchor ride.
Till *Neptune* overlook'd the narrow way,
And in disdain pour'd in the conqu'ring Sea.   445
    Two Cities that adorn'd th' *Achaian* Ground,
Buris and *Helice*, no more are found,
But whelm'd beneath a Lake are sunk and drown'd;
And Boatsmen through the Chrystal Water show
To wond'ring Passengers the Walls below.   450
    Near *Trœzen* stands a Hill, expos'd in Air
To Winter-Winds; of leafy Shadows bare:
This once was level Ground: But (strange to tell)
Th' included Vapors, that in Caverns dwell,
Lab'ring with Cholick Pangs, and close confin'd,   455
In vain sought issue for the rumbling Wind:
Yet still they heav'd for vent, and heaving still
Inlarg'd the Concave, and shot up the Hill;
As Breath extends a Bladder, or the Skins
Of Goats are blown t' inclose the hoarded Wines: 460
The Mountain yet retains a Mountain's Face,
And gather'd Rubbish heals the hollow space.
    Of many Wonders, which I heard or knew,
Retrenching most, I will relate but few:
What, are not Springs with Qualities oppos'd,   465
Endu'd at Seasons, and at Seasons lost?
Thrice in a Day thine, *Ammon*, change their Form,
Cold at high Noon, at Morn and Evening warm:
Thine, *Athaman*, will kindle Wood, if thrown
On the pil'd Earth, and in the waning Moon.   470
The *Thracians* have a Stream, if any try
The tast, his harden'd Bowels petrify;
Whate'er it touches it converts to Stones,
And makes a Marble Pavement where it runs.
    Crathis, and *Sybaris* her Sister Flood,   475
That slide through our *Calabrian* Neighbour Wood,
With Gold and Amber die the shining Hair,
And thither Youth resort; (for who wou'd not be Fair?)
    But stranger Virtues yet in Streams we find,
Some change not only Bodies, but the Mind: 480
Who has not heard of *Salmacis* obscene,

Whose Waters into Women soften Men?
Or *Æthyopian* Lakes which turn the Brain
To Madness, or in heavy Sleep constrain?
Clytorian Streams the love of Wine expel,   485
(Such is the Virtue of th' abstemious Well;)
Whether the colder Nymph that rules the Flood
Extinguishes, and balks the drunken God;
Or that *Melampus* (so have some assur'd)
When the mad *Prætides* with Charms he cur'd;   490
And pow'rful Herbs, both Charms and Simples cast
Into th' sober Spring, where still their Virtues last.

    Unlike Effects *Lyncestis* will produce,
Who drinks his Waters, tho' with moderate use,
Reels as with Wine, and sees with double Sight: 495
His Heels too heavy, and his Head too light.
Ladon, once *Pheneos*, an *Arcadian* Stream,
(Ambiguous in th' Effects, as in the Name)
By Day is wholsom Bev'rage; but is thought
By Night infected, and a deadly Draught.   500

    Thus running Rivers, and the standing Lake
Now of these Virtues, now of those partake:
Time was (and all Things Time and Fate obey)
When fast *Ortygia* floated on the Sea:
Such were *Cyanean* Isles, when *Tiphys* steer'd   505
Betwixt their Streights and their Collision fear'd;
They swam where now they sit; and firmly join'd
Secure of rooting up, resist the Wind.
Nor *Ætna* vomiting sulphureous Fire
Will ever belch; for Sulphur will expire,   510
(The Veins exhausted of the liquid Store:)
Time was she cast no Flames; in time will cast no more.

    For whether Earth's an Animal, and Air
Imbibes, her Lungs with coolness to repair,
And what she sucks remits; she still requires   515
Inlets for Air, and Outlets for her Fires;
When tortur'd with convulsive Fits she shakes,
That motion choaks the vent till other vent she makes:
Or when the Winds in hollow Caves are clos'd,
And subtil Spirits find that way oppos'd,   520

They toss up Flints in Air; the Flints that hide
The Seeds of Fire, thus toss'd in Air, collide,
Kindling the Sulphur, till the Fewel spent
The Cave is cool'd, and the fierce Winds relent.
Or whether Sulphur, catching Fire, feeds on   525
Its unctuous Parts, till all the Matter gone
The Flames no more ascend; for Earth supplies
The Fat that feeds them; and when Earth denies
That Food, by length of Time consum'd, the Fire
Famish'd for want of Fewel must expire.   530
   A Race of Men there are, as Fame has told,
Who shiv'ring suffer *Hyperborean* Cold,
Till nine times bathing in *Minerva*'s Lake,
Soft Feathers, to defend their naked Sides, they take.
'Tis said, the *Scythian* Wives (believe who will)   535
Transform themselves to Birds by Magick Skill;
Smear'd over with an Oil of wond'rous Might,
That adds new Pinions to their airy Flight.
   But this by sure Experiment we know,
That living Creatures from Corruption grow: 540
Hide in a hollow Pit a slaughter'd Steer,
Bees from his putrid Bowels will appear;
Who like their Parents haunt the Fields, and bring
Their Hony-Harvest home, and hope another Spring.
The Warlike-Steed is multiply'd we find,   545
To Wasps and Hornets of the Warrior Kind.
Cut from a Crab his crooked Claws, and hide
The rest in Earth, a Scorpion thence will glide
And shoot his Sting, his Tail in Circles toss'd
Refers the Limbs his backward Father lost.   550
And Worms, that stretch on Leaves their filmy Loom,
Crawl from their Bags, and Butterflies become.
Ev'n Slime begets the Frog's loquacious Race:
Short of their Feet at first, in little space
With Arms and Legs endu'd, long leaps they take,   555
Rais'd on their hinder part, and swim the Lake,
And Waves repel: For Nature gives their Kind
To that intent, a length of Legs behind.
   The Cubs of Bears, a living lump appear,
When whelp'd, and no determin'd Figure wear.   560

Their Mother licks 'em into Shape, and gives
As much of Form, as she her self receives.
    The Grubs from their sexangular abode
Crawl out unfinish'd, like the Maggot's Brood:
Trunks without Limbs; till time at leisure brings   565
The Thighs they wanted, and their tardy Wings.
    The Bird who draws the Carr of *Juno*, vain
Of her crown'd Head, and of her Starry Train;
And he that bears th' Artillery of *Jove*,
The strong-pounc'd Eagle, and the billing Dove;   570
And all the feather'd Kind, who cou'd suppose   ⎫
(But that from sight the surest Sense he knows)   ⎬
They from th' included Yolk, not ambient White arose.   ⎭
    There are who think the Marrow of a Man,
Which in the Spine, while he was living ran;   575
When dead, the Pith corrupted will become
A Snake, and hiss within the hollow Tomb.
    All these receive their Birth from other Things;
But from himself the *Phœnix* only springs:
Self-born, begotten by the Parent Flame   580
In which he burn'd, another and the same;
Who not by Corn or Herbs his Life sustains,
But the sweet Essence of *Amomum* drains:
And watches the rich Gums *Arabia* bears,
While yet in tender Dew they drop their Tears.   585
He, (his five Cent'ries of Life fulfill'd)
His Nest on Oaken Boughs begins to build,
Or trembling tops of Palm, and first he draws
The Plan with his broad Bill, and crooked Claws,
Nature's Artificers; on this the Pile   590
Is form'd, and rises round, then with the Spoil
Of *Casia*, *Cynamon*, and Stems of *Nard*,
(For softness strew'd beneath,) his Fun'ral Bed is rear'd:
Fun'ral and Bridal both; and all around
The Borders with corruptless Myrrh are crown'd,   595
On this incumbent; till ætherial Flame
First catches, then consumes the costly Frame:
Consumes him too, as on the Pile he lies;
He liv'd on Odours, and in Odours dies.
    An Infant-*Phœnix* from the former springs   600

His Father's Heir, and from his tender Wings
Shakes off his Parent Dust, his Method he pursues,
And the same Lease of Life on the same Terms renews.
When grown to Manhood he begins his reign,
And with stiff Pinions can his Flight sustain,					605
He lightens of its Load, the Tree that bore
His Father's Royal Sepulcher before,
And his own Cradle: (This with pious Care
Plac'd on his Back) he cuts the buxome Air,
Seeks the Sun's City, and his sacred Church,					610
And decently lays down his Burden in the Porch.

 A Wonder more amazing wou'd we find?
Th' *Hyæna* shows it, of a double kind,
Varying the Sexes in alternate Years,
In one begets, and in another bears.					615
The thin *Camelion* fed with Air, receives
The colour of the Thing to which he cleaves.

 India when conquer'd, on the conqu'ring God
For planted Vines the sharp-ey'd *Lynx* bestow'd,
Whose Urine shed, before it touches Earth,					620
Congeals in Air, and gives to Gems their Birth.
So *Coral* soft, and white in Oceans Bed,
Comes harden'd up in Air, and glows with Red.

 All changing Species should my Song recite;
Before I ceas'd, wou'd change the Day to Night.					625
Nations and Empires flourish, and decay,
By turns command, and in their turns obey;
Time softens hardy People, Time again
Hardens to War a soft, unwarlike Train.
Thus *Troy* for ten long Years her Foes withstood,					630
And daily bleeding bore th' expence of Blood:
Now for thick Streets it shows an empty space,
Or only fill'd with Tombs of her own perish'd Race,
Her self becomes the Sepulcher of what she was.

 Mycene, *Sparta*, *Thebes* of mighty Fame,					635
Are vanish'd out of Substance into Name.
And *Dardan Rome* that just begins to rise,
On *Tiber*'s Banks, in time shall mate the Skies;
Widening her Bounds, and working on her way;
Ev'n now she meditates Imperial Sway:					640

Yet this is change, but she by changing thrives,
Like Moons new-born, and in her Cradle strives
To fill her Infant-Horns; an Hour shall come
When the round World shall be contain'd in *Rome*.

    For thus old Saws foretel, and *Helenus*   645
Anchises drooping Son enliven'd thus;
When *Ilium* now was in a sinking State;
And he was doubtful of his future Fate:
O Goddess born, with thy hard Fortune strive,
Troy never can be lost, and thou alive.   650
Thy Passage thou shalt free through Fire and Sword,
And *Troy* in Foreign Lands shall be restor'd.
In happier Fields a rising Town I see,
Greater than what e'er was, or is, or e'er shall be:
And Heav'n yet owes the World a Race deriv'd from Thee. } 655
Sages, and Chiefs of other Lineage born
The City shall extend, extended shall adorn:
But from *Julus* he must draw his Birth,
By whom thy *Rome* shall rule the conquer'd Earth:
Whom Heav'n will lend Mankind on Earth to reign,   660
And late require the precious Pledge again.
This *Helenus* to great *Æneas* told,
Which I retain, e'er since in other Mould
My Soul was cloath'd; and now rejoice to view
My Country Walls rebuilt, and *Troy* reviv'd anew,   665
Rais'd by the fall: Decreed by Loss to Gain;
Enslav'd but to be free, and conquer'd but to reign.

    'Tis time my hard mouth'd Coursers to controul,
Apt to run Riot, and transgress the Goal:
And therefore I conclude, whatever lies   670
In Earth, or flits in Air, or fills the Skies,
All suffer change, and we, that are of Soul
And Body mix'd, are Members of the whole.
Then, when our Sires, or Grandsires shall forsake
The Forms of Men, and brutal Figures take,   675
Thus hous'd, securely let their Spirits rest,
Nor violate thy Father in the Beast.
Thy Friend, thy Brother, any of thy Kin,
If none of these, yet there's a Man within:

O spare to make a *Thyestæan* Meal,   680
T' inclose his Body, and his Soul expel.
  Ill Customs by degrees to Habits rise,
Ill Habits soon become exalted Vice:
What more advance can Mortals make in Sin
So near Perfection, who with Blood begin?   685
Deaf to the Calf that lies beneath the Knife,
Looks up, and from her Butcher begs her Life:
Deaf to the harmless Kid, that e'er he dies
All Methods to procure thy Mercy tries,
And imitates in vain thy Children's Cries.   690
Where will he stop, who feeds with Houshold Bread,
Then eats the Poultry which before he fed?
Let plough thy Steers; that when they lose their Breath
To Nature, not to thee they may impute their Death.
Let Goats for Food their loaded Udders lend,   695
And Sheep from Winter-cold thy Sides defend;
But neither Sprindges, Nets, nor Snares employ,
And be no more Ingenious to destroy.
Free as in Air, let Birds on Earth remain,
Nor let insidious Glue their Wings constrain;   700
Nor opening Hounds the trembling Stag affright,
Nor purple Feathers intercept his Flight:
Nor Hooks conceal'd in Baits for Fish prepare,
Nor Lines to heave 'em twinkling up in Air.
  Take not away the Life you cannot give: 705
For all Things have an equal right to live.
Kill noxious Creatures, where 'tis Sin to save;
This only just Prerogative we have:
But nourish Life with vegetable Food,
And shun the sacrilegious tast of Blood.   710
  These Precepts by the *Samian* Sage were taught,
Which Godlike *Numa* to the *Sabines* brought,
And thence transferr'd to *Rome*, by Gift his own:
A willing People, and an offer'd Throne.
O happy Monarch, sent by Heav'n to bless   715
A Salvage Nation with soft Arts of Peace,
To teach Religion, Rapine to restrain,
Give Laws to Lust, and Sacrifice ordain:
Himself a Saint, a Goddess was his Bride,
And all the Muses o'er his Acts preside.   720

THE CHARACTER OF A GOOD PARSON;
Imitated from CHAUCER, And Inlarg'd

A PARISH-PRIEST, was of the Pilgrim-Train:
    An Awful, Reverend, and Religious Man.
His Eyes diffus'd a venerable Grace,
And Charity it self was in his Face.
Rich was his Soul, though his Attire was poor;   5
(As God had cloath'd his own Embassador;)
For such, on Earth, his bless'd Redeemer bore.
Of Sixty Years he seem'd; and well might last
To Sixty more, but that he liv'd too fast;
Refin'd himself to Soul, to curb the Sense;   10
And made almost a Sin of Abstinence.
Yet, had his Aspect nothing of severe,
But such a Face as promis'd him sincere.
Nothing reserv'd or sullen was to see:
But sweet Regards; and pleasing Sanctity: 15
Mild was his Accent, and his Action free.
With Eloquence innate his Tongue was arm'd;
Tho' harsh the Precept, yet the Preacher charm'd.
For, letting down the golden Chain from high,
He drew his Audience upward to the Sky: 20
And oft, with holy Hymns, he charm'd their Ears:
(A Musick more melodious than the Spheres.)
For *David* left him, when he went to rest,
His Lyre; and after him, he sung the best.
He bore his great Commission in his Look: 25
But sweetly temper'd Awe; and soften'd all he spoke.
He preach'd the Joys of Heav'n, and Pains of Hell;
And warn'd the Sinner with becoming Zeal;
But on Eternal Mercy lov'd to dwell.
He taught the Gospel rather than the Law: 30
And forc'd himself to drive; but lov'd to draw.
For Fear but freezes Minds; but Love, like Heat,
Exhales the Soul sublime, to seek her Native Seat.
    To Threats, the stubborn Sinner oft is hard:
Wrap'd in his Crimes, against the Storm prepar'd;   35
But, when the milder Beams of Mercy play,

He melts, and throws his cumb'rous Cloak away.
　Lightnings and Thunder (Heav'ns Artillery)
As Harbingers before th' Almighty fly:
Those, but proclaim his Stile, and disappear;   40
The stiller Sound succeeds; and God is there.
　The Tythes, his Parish freely paid, he took;
But never Su'd; or Curs'd with Bell and Book.
With Patience bearing wrong; but off'ring none:
Since every Man is free to lose his own.   45
The Country-Churles, according to their Kind,
(Who grudge their Dues, and love to be behind,)
The less he sought his Off'rings, pinch'd the more;
And prais'd a Priest, contented to be Poor.
　Yet, of his little, he had some to spare,   50
To feed the Famish'd, and to cloath the Bare:
For Mortify'd he was, to that degree,
A poorer than himself, he wou'd not see.
True Priests, he said, and Preachers of the Word,
Were only Stewards of their Soveraign Lord;   55
Nothing was theirs; but all the publick Store:
Intrusted Riches, to relieve the Poor.
Who, shou'd they steal, for want of his Relief,
He judg'd himself Accomplice with the Thief.
　Wide was his Parish; not contracted close   60
In Streets, but here and there a straggling House;
Yet still he was at Hand, without Request
To serve the Sick; to succour the Distress'd:
Tempting, on Foot, alone, without affright,
The Dangers of a dark, tempestuous Night.   65
　All this, the good old Man, perform'd alone,
Nor spar'd his Pains; for Curate he had none.
Nor durst he trust another with his Care;
Nor rode himself to *Pauls*, the publick Fair,
To chaffer for Preferment with his Gold,   70
Where Bishopricks, and *sine Cures* are sold.
But duly watch'd his Flock, by Night and Day;
And from the prowling Wolf, redeem'd the Prey;
And hungry sent the wily Fox away.
　The Proud he tam'd, the Penitent he chear'd: 75
Nor to rebuke the rich Offender fear'd.

His Preaching much, but more his Practice wrought;
(A living Sermon of the Truths he taught;)
For this by Rules severe his Life he squar'd:
That all might see the Doctrin which they heard.   80
For Priests, he said, are Patterns for the rest:
(The Gold of Heav'n, who bear the God Impress'd:)
But when the precious Coin is kept unclean,
The Soveraign's Image is no longer seen.
If they be foul, on whom the People trust,   85
Well may the baser Brass, contract a Rust.
    The Prelate, for his Holy Life he priz'd;
The worldly Pomp of Prelacy despis'd.
His Saviour came not with a gawdy Show;
Nor was his Kingdom of the World below.   90
Patience in Want, and Poverty of Mind,
These Marks of Church and Churchmen he design'd,
And living taught; and dying left behind.
The Crown he wore was of the pointed Thorn:
In Purple he was Crucify'd, not born.   95
They who contend for Place and high Degree,
Are not his Sons, but those of *Zebadee*.
    Not, but he knew the Signs of Earthly Pow'r
Might well become St. *Peter*'s Successor:
The Holy Father holds a double Reign,   100
The Prince may keep his Pomp; the Fisher must be plain.
    Such was the Saint; who shone with every Grace:
Reflecting, *Moses*-like, his Maker's Face.
God, saw his Image lively was express'd;
And his own Work, as in Creation bless'd.   105
    The Tempter saw him too, with envious Eye;
And, as on *Job*, demanded leave to try.
He took the time when *Richard* was depos'd:
And High and Low, with happy *Harry* clos'd.
This Prince, tho' great in Arms, the Priest withstood: 110
Near tho' he was, yet not the next of Blood.
Had *Richard* unconstrain'd, resign'd the Throne:
A King can give no more than is his own:
The Title stood entail'd, had *Richard* had a Son.
    Conquest, an odious Name, was laid aside,   115
Where all submitted; none the Battle try'd.

The senseless Plea of Right by Providence,
Was, by a flatt'ring Priest, invented since:
And lasts no longer than the present sway;
But justifies the next who comes in play.   120

　　The People's Right remains; let those who dare
Dispute their Pow'r, when they the Judges are.

　　He join'd not in their Choice; because he knew
Worse might, and often did from Change ensue.
Much to himself he thought; but little spoke: 125
And, Undepriv'd, his Benefice forsook.

　　Now, through the Land, his Cure of Souls he stretch'd:
And like a Primitive Apostle preach'd.
Still Chearful; ever Constant to his Call;
By many follow'd; Lov'd by most, Admir'd by All.   130
With what he beg'd, his Brethren he reliev'd;
And gave the Charities himself receiv'd.
Gave, while he Taught; and Edify'd the more,
Because he shew'd by Proof, 'twas easy to be Poor.

　　He went not, with the Crowd, to see a Shrine;   135
But fed us by the way, with Food divine.

　　In deference to his Virtues, I forbear
To shew you, what the rest in Orders were:
This Brillant, is so Spotless, and so Bright,
He needs no Foyl: But shines by his own proper Light.   140

THE MONUMENT OF A FAIR MAIDEN
LADY, Who dy'd at *Bath*, and is there Interr'd

BELOW this Marble Monument, is laid
　　All that Heav'n wants of this Celestial Maid.
Preserve, O sacred Tomb, thy Trust consign'd:
The Mold was made on purpose for the Mind:
And she wou'd lose, if at the latter Day   5
One Atom cou'd be mix'd, of other Clay.
Such were the Features of her heav'nly Face,
Her Limbs were form'd with such harmonious Grace,
So faultless was the Frame, as if the Whole
Had been an Emanation of the Soul;   10

Which her own inward Symmetry reveal'd;
And like a Picture shone, in Glass Anneal'd.
Or like the Sun eclips'd, with shaded Light:
Too piercing, else, to be sustain'd by Sight.
Each Thought was visible that rowl'd within: 15
As through a Crystal Case, the figur'd Hours are seen.
And Heav'n did this transparent Veil provide,
Because she had no guilty Thought to hide.
All white, a Virgin-Saint, she sought the Skies:
For Marriage, tho' it sullies not, it dies.   20
High tho' her Wit, yet Humble was her Mind;
As if she cou'd not, or she wou'd not find
How much her Worth transcended all her Kind.
Yet she had learn'd so much of Heav'n below,
That when arriv'd, she scarce had more to know: 25
But only to refresh the former Hint;
And read her Maker in a fairer Print.
So Pious, as she had no time to spare
For human Thoughts, but was confin'd to Pray'r.
Yet in such Charities she pass'd the Day,   30
'Twas wond'rous how she found an Hour to Pray.
A Soul so calm, it knew not Ebbs or Flows,
Which Passion cou'd but curl; not discompose.
A Female Softness, with a manly Mind:
A Daughter duteous, and a Sister kind: 35
In Sickness patient; and in Death resign'd.

CYMON AND IPHIGENIA,
FROM BOCCACE

Poeta loquitur,

OLD as I am, for Ladies Love unfit,
The Pow'r of Beauty I remember yet,
Which once inflam'd my Soul, and still inspires my Wit.
If Love be Folly, the severe Divine
Has felt that Folly, tho' he censures mine;   5
Pollutes the Pleasures of a chast Embrace,
Acts what I write, and propagates in Grace
With riotous Excess, a Priestly Race:

Suppose him free, and that I forge th' Offence,
He shew'd the way, perverting first my Sense: 10
In Malice witty, and with Venom fraught,
He makes me speak the Things I never thought.
Compute the Gains of his ungovern'd Zeal;
Ill sutes his Cloth the Praise of Railing well!
The World will think that what we loosly write,   15
Tho' now arraign'd, he read with some delight;
Because he seems to chew the Cud again,
When his broad Comment makes the Text too plain:
And teaches more in one explaining Page,
Than all the double Meanings of the Stage.   20
    What needs he Paraphrase on what we mean?
We were at worst but Wanton; he's Obscene.
I, nor my Fellows, nor my Self excuse;
But Love's the Subject of the Comick Muse:
Nor can we write without it, nor would you   25
A Tale of only dry Instruction view;
Nor Love is always of a vicious Kind,
But oft to virtuous Acts inflames the Mind.
Awakes the sleepy Vigour of the Soul,
And, brushing o'er, adds Motion to the Pool.   30
Love, studious how to please, improves our Parts,
With polish'd Manners, and adorns with Arts.
Love first invented Verse, and form'd the Rhime,
The Motion measur'd, harmoniz'd the Chime;
To lib'ral Acts inlarg'd the narrow-Soul'd: 35
Soften'd the Fierce, and made the Coward Bold:
The World when wast, he Peopled with increase,
And warring Nations reconcil'd in Peace.
Ormond, the first, and all the Fair may find ⎫
In this one Legend to their Fame design'd, ⎬ 40
When Beauty fires the Blood, how Love exalts the Mind. ⎭

IN that sweet Isle, where *Venus* keeps her Court,
And ev'ry Grace, and all the Loves resort;
Where either Sex is form'd of softer Earth,
And takes the bent of Pleasure from their Birth;   45
There liv'd a *Cyprian* Lord, above the rest,
Wise, Wealthy, with a num'rous Issue blest.

But as no Gift of Fortune is sincere,
Was only wanting in a worthy Heir:
His eldest Born a goodly Youth to view   50
Excell'd the rest in Shape, and outward Shew;
Fair, Tall, his Limbs with due Proportion join'd,
But of a heavy, dull, degenerate Mind.
His Soul bely'd the Features of his Face;
Beauty was there, but Beauty in disgrace.   55
A clownish Mien, a Voice with rustick sound,
And stupid Eyes, that ever lov'd the Ground.
He look'd like Nature's Error; as the Mind   ⎫
And Body were not of a Piece design'd,   ⎬
But made for two, and by mistake in one were join'd. ⎭ 60
    The ruling Rod, the Father's forming Care,
Were exercis'd in vain, on Wit's despair;
The more inform'd the less he understood,
And deeper sunk by flound'ring in the Mud.
Now scorn'd of all, and grown the publick Shame,   65
The People from *Galesus* chang'd his Name,
And *Cymon* call'd, which signifies a Brute;
So well his Name did with his Nature sute.
    His Father, when he found his Labour lost,
And Care employ'd, that answer'd not the Cost,   70
Chose an ungrateful Object to remove,
And loath'd to see what Nature made him love;
So to his Country-Farm the Fool confin'd:
Rude Work well suted with a rustick Mind.
Thus to the Wilds the sturdy *Cymon* went,   75
A Squire among the Swains, and pleas'd with Banishment.
His Corn, and Cattle, were his only Care,
And his supreme Delight a Country-Fair.
    It happen'd on a Summers Holiday,   ⎫
That to the Greenwood-shade he took his way;   ⎬ 80
For *Cymon* shun'd the Church, and us'd not much to Pray. ⎭
His Quarter-Staff, which he cou'd ne'er forsake,
Hung half before, and half behind his Back.
He trudg'd along unknowing what he sought,
And whistled as he went, for want of Thought.   85

By Chance conducted, or by Thirst constrain'd,
The deep Recesses of the Grove he gain'd;
Where in a Plain, defended by the Wood,
Crept through the matted Grass a Chrystal Flood,
By which an Alablaster Fountain stood: 90
And on the Margin of the Fount was laid
(Attended by her Slaves) a sleeping Maid.
Like *Dian*, and her Nymphs, when tir'd with Sport,
To rest by cool *Eurotas* they resort:
The Dame herself the Goddess well express'd,   95
Not more distinguish'd by her Purple Vest,
Than by the charming Features of her Face,
And ev'n in Slumber a superiour Grace:
Her comely Limbs compos'd with decent Care,
Her Body shaded with a slight Cymarr;   100
Her Bosom to the view was only bare:
Where two beginning Paps were scarcely spy'd,
For yet their Places were but signify'd:
The fanning Wind upon her Bosom blows,
To meet the fanning Wind the Bosom rose;   105
The fanning Wind, and purling Streams continue her repose.
    The Fool of Nature, stood with stupid Eyes
And gaping Mouth, that testify'd Surprize,
Fix'd on her Face, nor cou'd remove his Sight,
New as he was to Love, and Novice in Delight: 110
Long mute he stood, and leaning on his Staff,
His Wonder witness'd with an Ideot laugh;
Then would have spoke, but by his glimmering Sense
First found his want of Words, and fear'd Offence:
Doubted for what he was he should be known,   115
By his Clown-Accent, and his Country-Tone.
    Through the rude Chaos thus the running Light
Shot the first Ray that pierc'd the Native Night:
Then Day and Darkness in the Mass were mix'd,
Till gather'd in a Globe, the Beams were fix'd: 120
Last shon the Sun who radiant in his Sphere
Illumin'd Heav'n, and Earth, and rowl'd around the Year.
So Reason in this Brutal Soul began:
Love made him first suspect he was a Man;

Love made him doubt his broad barbarian Sound, 125
By Love his want of Words, and Wit he found:
That sense of want prepar'd the future way
To Knowledge, and disclos'd the promise of a Day.
  What not his Father's Care, nor Tutor's Art
Cou'd plant with Pains in his unpolish'd Heart, 130
The best Instructor Love at once inspir'd,
As barren Grounds to Fruitfulness are fir'd:
Love taught him Shame, and Shame with Love at Strife
Soon taught the sweet Civilities of Life;
His gross material Soul at once could find 135
Somewhat in her excelling all her Kind:
Exciting a Desire till then unknown,
Somewhat unfound, or found in her alone.
This made the first Impression in his Mind,
Above, but just above the Brutal Kind. 140
For Beasts can like, but not distinguish too,
Nor their own liking by reflection know;
Nor why they like or this, or t'other Face,
Or judge of this or that peculiar Grace,
But love in gross, and stupidly admire; 145
As Flies allur'd by Light, approach the Fire.
Thus our Man-Beast advancing by degrees
First likes the whole, then sep'rates what he sees;
On sev'ral Parts a sev'ral Praise bestows,
The ruby Lips, the well-proportion'd Nose, 150
The snowy Skin, the Raven-glossy Hair,
The dimpled Cheek, the Forehead rising fair,
And ev'n in Sleep it self a smiling Air.
From thence his Eyes descending view'd the rest,
Her plump round Arms, white Hands, and heaving Breast. 155
Long on the last he dwelt, though ev'ry part
A pointed Arrow sped to pierce his Heart.
  Thus in a trice a Judge of Beauty grown,
(A Judge erected from a Country-Clown)
He long'd to see her Eyes in Slumber hid; 160
And wish'd his own cou'd pierce within the Lid:
He wou'd have wak'd her, but restrain'd his Thought,
And Love new-born the first good Manners taught.
An awful Fear his ardent Wish withstood,

Nor durst disturb the Goddess of the Wood;   165
For such she seem'd by her celestial Face,
Excelling all the rest of human Race:
And Things divine by common Sense he knew,
Must be devoutly seen at distant view:
So checking his Desire, with trembling Heart   170
Gazing he stood, nor would, nor could depart;
Fix'd as a Pilgrim wilder'd in his way,
Who dares not stir by Night for fear to stray,
But stands with awful Eyes to watch the dawn of Day.

   At length awaking, *Iphigene* the Fair   175
(So was the Beauty call'd who caus'd his Care)
Unclos'd her Eyes, and double Day reveal'd,
While those of all her Slaves in Sleep were seal'd.

   The slavering Cudden prop'd upon his Staff,
Stood ready gaping with a grinning Laugh,   180
To welcome her awake, nor durst begin
To speak, but wisely kept the Fool within.
Then she; What make you *Cymon* here alone?
(For *Cymon*'s Name was round the Country known
Because descended of a noble Race,   185
And for a Soul ill sorted with his Face.)

   But still the Sot stood silent with Surprize,
With fix'd regard on her new open'd Eyes,
And in his Breast receiv'd th' invenom'd Dart,
A tickling Pain that pleas'd amid the Smart.   190
But conscious of her Form, with quick distrust
She saw his sparkling Eyes, and fear'd his brutal Lust:
This to prevent she wak'd her sleepy Crew,
And rising hasty took a short Adieu.

   Then *Cymon* first his rustick Voice essay'd,   195
With proffer'd Service to the parting Maid
To see her safe; his Hand she long deny'd,
But took at length, asham'd of such a Guide.
So *Cymon* led her home, and leaving there
No more wou'd to his Country Clowns repair,   200
But sought his Father's House with better Mind,
Refusing in the Farm to be confin'd.

   The Father wonder'd at the Son's return,
And knew not whether to rejoice or mourn;

But doubtfully receiv'd, expecting still   205
To learn the secret Causes of his alter'd Will.
Nor was he long delay'd; the first Request
He made, was, like his Brothers to be dress'd,
And, as his Birth requir'd, above the rest.

    With ease his Sute was granted by his Syre,   210
Distinguishing his Heir by rich Attire:
His Body thus adorn'd, he next design'd
With lib'ral Arts to cultivate his Mind:
He sought a Tutor of his own accord,
And study'd Lessons he before abhorr'd.   215

    Thus the Man-Child advanc'd, and learn'd so fast,
That in short time his Equals he surpass'd:
His brutal Manners from his Breast exil'd,
His Mien he fashion'd, and his Tongue he fil'd;
In ev'ry Exercise of all admir'd,   220
He seem'd, nor only seem'd, but was inspir'd:
Inspir'd by Love, whose Business is to please;
He Rode, he Fenc'd, he mov'd with graceful Ease,
More fam'd for Sense, for courtly Carriage more,
Than for his brutal Folly known before.   225

    What then of alter'd *Cymon* shall we say,
But that the Fire which choak'd in Ashes lay,
A Load too heavy for his Soul to move,
Was upward blown below, and brush'd away by Love?
Love made an active Progress through his Mind,   230
The dusky Parts he clear'd, the gross refin'd;
The drowsy wak'd; and as he went impress'd
The Maker's Image on the human Beast.
Thus was the Man amended by Desire,
And tho' he lov'd perhaps with too much Fire,   235
His Father all his Faults with Reason scan'd,
And lik'd an error of the better Hand;
Excus'd th' excess of Passion in his Mind,
By Flames too fierce, perhaps too much refin'd:
So *Cymon*, since his Sire indulg'd his Will,   240
Impetuous lov'd, and would be *Cymon* still;
Galesus he disown'd, and chose to bear
The Name of Fool confirm'd, and Bishop'd by the Fair.

    To *Cipseus* by his Friends his Sute he mov'd,

Cipseus the Father of the Fair he lov'd: 245
But he was pre-ingag'd by former Ties,
While *Cymon* was endeav'ring to be wise:
And *Iphigene* oblig'd by former Vows,
Had giv'n her Faith to wed a Foreign Spouse:
Her Sire and She to *Rhodian Pasimond,*   250
Tho' both repenting, were by Promise bound,
Nor could retract; and thus, as Fate decreed,
Tho' better lov'd, he spoke too late to speed.

    The Doom was past, the Ship already sent,
Did all his tardy Diligence prevent: 255
Sigh'd to herself the fair unhappy Maid,
While stormy *Cymon* thus in secret said:
The time is come for *Iphigene* to find
The Miracle she wrought upon my Mind:
Her Charms have made me Man, her ravish'd Love   260
In rank shall place me with the Bless'd above.
For mine by Love, by Force she shall be mine,
Or Death, if Force should fail, shall finish my Design.

    Resolv'd he said: And rigg'd with speedy Care
A Vessel strong, and well equipp'd for War.   265
The secret Ship with chosen Friends he stor'd;
And bent to die, or conquer, went aboard.
Ambush'd he lay behind the *Cyprian* Shore,
Waiting the Sail that all his Wishes bore;
Nor long expected, for the following Tide   270
Sent out the hostile Ship and beauteous Bride.

    To *Rhodes* the Rival Bark directly steer'd,
When *Cymon* sudden at her Back appear'd,
And stop'd her Flight: Then standing on his Prow
In haughty Terms he thus defy'd the Foe,   275
Or strike your Sails at Summons, or prepare
To prove the last Extremities of War.
Thus warn'd, the *Rhodians* for the Fight provide;
Already were the Vessels Side by Side,
These obstinate to save, and those to seize the Bride.   280
But *Cymon* soon his crooked Grapples cast,
Which with tenacious hold his Foes embrac'd,
And arm'd with Sword and Shield, amid the Press he pass'd.
Fierce was the Fight, but hast'ning to his Prey,

By force the furious Lover freed his way: 285
Himself alone dispers'd the *Rhodian* Crew,
The Weak disdain'd, the Valiant overthrew;
Cheap Conquest for his following Friends remain'd,
He reap'd the Field, and they but only glean'd.

   His Victory confess'd, the Foes retreat,   290
And cast their Weapons at the Victor's Feet.
Whom thus he chear'd: O *Rhodian* Youth, I fought
For Love alone, nor other Booty sought;
Your Lives are safe; your Vessel I resign,
Yours be your own, restoring what is mine: 295
In *Iphigene* I claim my rightful Due,
Rob'd by my Rival, and detain'd by you:
Your *Pasimond* a lawless Bargain drove,
The Parent could not sell the Daughters Love;
Or if he cou'd, my Love disdains the Laws,   300
And like a King by Conquest gains his Cause:
Where Arms take place, all other Pleas are vain,
Love taught me Force, and Force shall Love maintain.
You, what by Strength you could not keep, release,
And at an easy Ransom buy your Peace.   305

   Fear on the conquer'd Side soon sign'd th' Accord,
And *Iphigene* to *Cymon* was restor'd:
While to his Arms the blushing Bride he took,
To seeming Sadness she compos'd her Look;
As if by Force subjected to his Will,   310
Tho' pleas'd, dissembling, and a Woman still.
And, for she wept, he wip'd her falling Tears,
And pray'd her to dismiss her empty Fears;
For yours I am, he said, and have deserv'd
Your Love much better whom so long I serv'd,   315
Than he to whom your formal Father ty'd
Your Vows; and sold a Slave, not sent a Bride.
Thus while he spoke he seiz'd the willing Prey,
As *Paris* bore the *Spartan* Spouse away:
Faintly she scream'd, and ev'n her Eyes confess'd   320
She rather would be thought, than was Distress'd.

   Who now exults but *Cymon* in his Mind,
Vain hopes, and empty Joys of human Kind,
Proud of the present, to the future blind!

Secure of Fate while *Cymon* plows the Sea,   325
And steers to *Candy* with his conquer'd Prey,
Scarce the third Glass of measur'd Hours was run,
When like a fiery Meteor sunk the Sun;
The Promise of a Storm; the shifting Gales
Forsake by Fits, and fill the flagging Sails: 330
Hoarse Murmurs of the Main from far were heard,
And Night came on, not by degrees prepar'd,
But all at once; at once the Winds arise,
The Thunders roul, the forky Lightning flies:
In vain the Master issues out Commands,   335
In vain the trembling Sailors ply their Hands:
The Tempest unforeseen prevents their Care,
And from the first they labour in despair.
The giddy Ship betwixt the Winds and Tides
Forc'd back and forwards, in a Circle rides,   340
Stun'd with the diff'rent Blows; then shoots amain
Till counterbuff'd she stops, and sleeps again.
Not more aghast the proud Archangel fell,
Plung'd from the height of Heav'n to deepest Hell,
Than stood the Lover of his Love possess'd,   345
Now curs'd the more, the more he had been bless'd;
More anxious for her Danger than his own,
Death he defies; but would be lost alone.
    Sad *Iphigene* to Womanish Complaints
Adds pious Pray'rs, and wearies all the Saints;   350
Ev'n if she could, her Love she would repent,
But since she cannot, dreads the Punishment:
Her forfeit Faith, and *Pasimond* betray'd,
Are ever present, and her Crime upbraid.
She blames herself, nor blames her Lover less,   355
Augments her Anger as her Fears increase;
From her own Back the Burden would remove,
And lays the Load on his ungovern'd Love,
Which interposing durst in Heav'n's despight
Invade, and violate another's Right: 360
The Pow'rs incens'd awhile deferr'd his Pain,
And made him Master of his Vows in vain:
But soon they punish'd his presumptuous Pride;
That for his daring Enterprize she dy'd,
Who rather not resisted, than comply'd.   365

Then impotent of Mind, with alter'd Sense,
She hugg'd th' Offender, and forgave th' Offence,
Sex to the last: Mean time with Sails declin'd
The wand'ring Vessel drove before the Wind:
Toss'd, and retoss'd, aloft, and then alow;   370
Nor Port they seek, nor certain Course they know,
But ev'ry moment wait the coming Blow.
Thus blindly driv'n, by breaking Day they view'd
The Land before 'em, and their Fears renew'd;
The Land was welcome, but the Tempest bore   375
The threaten'd Ship against a rocky Shore.

A winding Bay was near; to this they bent,
And just escap'd; their Force already spent:
Secure from Storms and panting from the Sea,
The Land unknown at leisure they survey;   380
And saw (but soon their sickly Sight withdrew)
The rising Tow'rs of *Rhodes* at distant view;
And curs'd the hostile Shoar of *Pasimond*,
Sav'd from the Seas, and shipwreck'd on the Ground.

The frighted Sailors try'd their Strength in vain   385
To turn the Stern, and tempt the stormy Main;
But the stiff Wind withstood the lab'ring Oar,
And forc'd them forward on the fatal Shoar!
The crooked Keel now bites the *Rhodian* Strand,
And the Ship moor'd, constrains the Crew to land: 390
Yet still they might be safe because unknown,
But as ill Fortune seldom comes alone,
The Vessel they dismiss'd was driv'n before,
Already shelter'd on their Native Shoar;
Known each, they know: But each with change of Chear; 395
The vanquish'd side exults; the Victors fear,
Not them but theirs; made Pris'ners e'er they Fight,
Despairing Conquest, and depriv'd of Flight.

The Country rings around with loud Alarms,
And raw in Fields the rude Militia swarms;   400
Mouths without Hands; maintain'd at vast Expence,
In Peace a Charge, in War a weak Defence:
Stout once a Month they march a blust'ring Band,
And ever, but in times of Need, at hand:
This was the Morn when issuing on the Guard,   405

Drawn up in Rank and File they stood prepar'd
Of seeming Arms to make a short essay,
Then hasten to be Drunk, the Business of the Day.

    The Cowards would have fled, but that they knew
Themselves so many, and their Foes so few;   410
But crowding on, the last the first impel;
Till overborn with weight the *Cyprians* fell.
Cymon inslav'd, who first the War begun,
And *Iphigene* once more is lost and won.

    Deep in a Dungeon was the Captive cast,   415
Depriv'd of Day, and held in Fetters fast:
His Life was only spar'd at their Request,
Whom taken he so nobly had releas'd:
But *Iphigenia* was the Ladies Care,
Each in their turn address'd to treat the Fair;   420
While *Pasimond* and his, the Nuptial Feast prepare.

    Her secret Soul to *Cymon* was inclin'd,
But she must suffer what her Fates assign'd;
So passive is the Church of Womankind.
What worse to *Cymon* could his Fortune deal,   425
Rowl'd to the lowest Spoke of all her Wheel?
It rested to dismiss the downward weight,
Or raise him upward to his former height;
The latter pleas'd; and Love (concern'd the most)
Prepar'd th' amends, for what by Love he lost.   430

    The Sire of *Pasimond* had left a Son,
Though younger, yet for Courage early known,
Ormisda call'd; to whom by Promise ty'd,
A *Rhodian* Beauty was the destin'd Bride:
Cassandra was her Name, above the rest   435
Renown'd for Birth, with Fortune amply bless'd.
Lysymachus who rul'd the *Rhodian* State,
Was then by choice their annual Magistrate:
He lov'd *Cassandra* too with equal Fire,
But Fortune had not favour'd his Desire;   440
Cross'd by her Friends, by her not disapprov'd,
Nor yet preferr'd, or like *Ormisda* lov'd:
So stood th' Affair: Some little Hope remain'd,
That should his Rival chance to lose, he gain'd.

    Mean time young *Pasimond* his Marriage press'd,   445

Ordain'd the Nuptial Day, prepar'd the Feast;
And frugally resolv'd (the Charge to shun,
Which would be double should he wed alone)
To join his Brother's Bridal with his own.

   Lysymachus oppress'd with mortal Grief   450
Receiv'd the News, and study'd quick Relief:
The fatal Day approach'd: If Force were us'd,
The Magistrate his publick Trust abus'd;
To Justice, liable as Law requir'd;
For when his Office ceas'd, his Pow'r expir'd: 455
While Pow'r remain'd, the Means were in his Hand
By Force to seize, and then forsake the Land:
Betwixt Extreams he knew not how to move,
A Slave to Fame, but more a Slave to Love:
Restraining others, yet himself not free,   460
Made impotent by Pow'r, debas'd by Dignity!
Both Sides he weigh'd: But after much Debate,
The Man prevail'd above the Magistrate.

   Love never fails to master what he finds,
But works a diff'rent way in diff'rent Minds,   465
The Fool enlightens, and the Wise he blinds.
This Youth proposing to possess, and scape,
Began in Murder, to conclude in Rape:
Unprais'd by me, tho' Heav'n sometime may bless
An impious Act with undeserv'd Success: 470
The Great, it seems, are priviledg'd alone
To punish all Injustice but their own.
But here I stop, not daring to proceed,
Yet blush to flatter an unrighteous Deed:
For Crimes are but permitted, not decreed.   475

   Resolv'd on Force, his Wit the Pretor bent,
To find the Means that might secure th' event;
Not long he labour'd, for his lucky Thought
In Captive *Cymon* found the Friend he sought;
Th' Example pleas'd: The Cause and Crime the same;   480
An injur'd Lover, and a ravish'd Dame.
How much he durst he knew by what he dar'd,
The less he had to lose, the less he car'd
To menage loathsom Life when Love was the Reward.

   This ponder'd well, and fix'd on his Intent,   485

In depth of Night he for the Pris'ner sent;
In secret sent, the publick View to shun,
Then with a sober Smile he thus begun.
The Pow'rs above who bounteously bestow
Their Gifts and Graces on Mankind below,   490
Yet prove our Merit first, nor blindly give
To such as are not worthy to receive:
For Valour and for Virtue they provide
Their due Reward, but first they must be try'd:
These fruitful Seeds within your Mind they sow'd;   495
'Twas yours t' improve the Talent they bestow'd:
They gave you to be born of noble Kind,
They gave you Love to lighten up your Mind,
And purge the grosser Parts; they gave you Care
To please, and Courage to deserve the Fair.   500

Thus far they try'd you, and by Proof they found
The Grain intrusted in a grateful Ground:
But still the great Experiment remain'd,
They suffer'd you to lose the Prize you gain'd;
That you might learn the Gift was theirs alone: 505
And when restor'd, to them the Blessing own.
Restor'd it soon will be; the Means prepar'd,
The Difficulty smooth'd, the Danger shar'd:
Be but your self, the Care to me resign,
Then *Iphigene* is yours, *Cassandra* mine.   510
Your Rival *Pasimond* pursues your Life,
Impatient to revenge his ravish'd Wife,
But yet not his; to Morrow is behind,
And Love our Fortunes in one Band has join'd:
Two Brothers are our Foes; *Ormisda* mine,   515
As much declar'd, as *Pasimond* is thine:
To Morrow must their common Vows be ty'd;
With Love to Friend and Fortune for our Guide,
Let both resolve to die, or each redeem a Bride.

Right I have none, nor hast thou much to plead;   520
'Tis Force when done must justify the Deed:
Our Task perform'd we next prepare for Flight;
And let the Losers talk in vain of Right:
We with the Fair will sail before the Wind,
If they are griev'd, I leave the Laws behind.   525

Speak thy Resolves; if now thy Courage droop,
Despair in Prison, and abandon Hope;
But if thou dar'st in Arms thy Love regain,
(For Liberty without thy Love were vain:)
Then second my Design to seize the Prey,   530
Or lead to second Rape, for well thou know'st the way.

    Said *Cymon* overjoy'd, do Thou propose
The Means to Fight, and only shew the Foes;
For from the first, when Love had fir'd my Mind,
Resolv'd I left the Care of Life behind.   535

    To this the bold *Lysymachus* reply'd,
Let Heav'n be neuter, and the Sword decide:
The Spousals are prepar'd, already play
The Minstrels, and provoke the tardy Day:
By this the Brides are wak'd, their Grooms are dress'd; } 540
All *Rhodes* is summon'd to the Nuptial Feast,   }
All but my self the sole unbidden Guest.   }
Unbidden though I am, I will be there,
And, join'd by thee, intend to joy the Fair.

    Now hear the rest; when Day resigns the Light,   545
And chearful Torches guild the jolly Night;
Be ready at my Call, my chosen few
With Arms administer'd shall aid thy Crew.
Then entring unexpected will we seize
Our destin'd Prey, from Men dissolv'd in ease;   550
By Wine disabled, unprepar'd for Fight;
And hast'ning to the Seas suborn our Flight:
The Seas are ours, for I command the Fort,
A Ship well man'd, expects us in the Port:
If they, or if their Friends the Prize contest,   555
Death shall attend the Man who dares resist.

    It pleas'd! The Pris'ner to his Hold retir'd,   }
His Troop with equal Emulation fir'd,   }
All fix'd to Fight, and all their wonted Work requir'd. }

    The Sun arose; the Streets were throng'd around, 560
The Palace open'd, and the Posts were crown'd:
The double Bridegroom at the Door attends
Th' expected Spouse, and entertains the Friends:
They meet, they lead to Church; the Priests invoke
The Pow'rs, and feed the Flames with fragrant Smoke: 565

This done they Feast, and at the close of Night
By kindled Torches vary their Delight,
These lead the lively Dance, and those the brimming Bowls invite.
   Now at th' appointed Place and Hour assign'd,
With Souls resolv'd the Ravishers were join'd: 570
Three Bands are form'd: The first is sent before
To favour the Retreat, and guard the Shore:
The second at the Palace-gate is plac'd,
And up the lofty Stairs ascend the last:
A peaceful Troop they seem with shining Vests,   575
But Coats of Male beneath secure their Breasts.
   Dauntless they enter, *Cymon* at their Head,
And find the Feast renew'd, the Table spread:
Sweet Voices mix'd with instrument ' Sounds
Ascend the vaulted Roof, the vaulted Roof rebounds.   580
When like the Harpies rushing through the Hall
The suddain Troop appears, the Tables fall,
Their smoaking Load is on the Pavement thrown;
Each Ravisher prepares to seize his own:
The Brides invaded with a rude Embrace   585
Shreek out for Aid, Confusion fills the Place:
Quick to redeem the Prey their plighted Lords
Advance, the Palace gleams with shining Swords.
   But late is all Defence, and Succour vain;
The Rape is made, the Ravishers remain: 590
Two sturdy Slaves were only sent before
To bear the purchas'd Prize in Safety to the Shore.
The Troop retires, the Lovers close the rear,
With forward Faces not confessing Fear:
Backward they move, but scorn their Pace to mend,   595
Then seek the Stairs, and with slow hast descend.
   Fierce *Pasimond* their passage to prevent,
Thrust full on *Cymon*'s Back in his descent,
The Blade return'd unbath'd, and to the Handle bent:
Stout *Cymon* soon remounts, and cleft in two   600
His Rival's Head with one descending Blow:
And as the next in rank *Ormisda* stood,
He turn'd the Point: The Sword inur'd to Blood,
Bor'd his unguarded Breast, which pour'd a purple Flood.

With vow'd Revenge the gath'ring Crowd pursues,   605
The Ravishers turn Head, the Fight renews;
The Hall is heap'd with Corps; the sprinkled Gore
Besmears the Walls, and floats the Marble Floor.
Dispers'd at length the drunken Squadron flies,
The Victors to their Vessel bear the Prize;   610
And hear behind loud Groans, and lamentable Cries.

   The Crew with merry Shouts their Anchors weigh
Then ply their Oars, and brush the buxom Sea,
While Troops of gather'd *Rhodians* croud the Key.
What should the People do, when left alone?   615
The Governor, and Government are gone.
The publick Wealth to Foreign Parts convey'd;
Some Troops disbanded, and the rest unpaid.
Rhodes is the Soveraign of the Sea no more;
Their Ships unrigg'd, and spent their Naval Store;   620
They neither could defend, nor can pursue,
But grind their Teeth, and cast a helpless view:
In vain with Darts a distant War they try,
Short, and more short the missive Weapons fly.
Mean while the Ravishers their Crimes enjoy,   625
And flying Sails, and sweeping Oars employ;
The Cliffs of *Rhodes* in little space are lost,
Jove's Isle they seek; nor *Jove* denies his Coast.

   In safety landed on the *Candian* Shore,
With generous Wines their Spirits they restore;   630
There *Cymon* with his *Rhodian* Friend resides,
Both Court, and Wed at once the willing Brides.
A War ensues, the *Cretans* own their Cause,
Stiff to defend their hospitable Laws:
Both Parties lose by turns; and neither wins,   635
'Till Peace propounded by a Truce begins.
The Kindred of the Slain forgive the Deed,
But a short Exile must for Show precede;
The Term expir'd, from *Candia* they remove;
And happy each at Home, enjoys his Love.   640

   Cymon and Iphigenia. 622 grind] grin'd F

PROLOGUE, EPILOGUE, SONG and SECULAR MASQUE from *THE PILGRIM*

PROLOGUE

How wretched is the Fate of those who write!
Brought muzled to the Stage, for fear they bite.
Where, like *Tom Dove*, they stand the Common Foe;
Lugg'd by the *Critique*, Baited by the *Beau*.
Yet worse, their Brother *Poets* Damn the Play,   5
And Roar the loudest, tho' they never Pay.
The Fops are proud of Scandal, for they cry,
At every lewd, low Character,—That's I.
He who writes Letters to himself, wou'd Swear
The World forgot him, if he was not there.   10
What shou'd a Poet do? 'Tis hard for One
To pleasure all the Fools that wou'd be shown: ⎫
And yet not Two in Ten will pass the Town.   ⎬
Most Coxcombs are not of the Laughing kind;   ⎭
More goes to make a Fop, than Fops can find.   15
   Quack *Maurus*, tho' he never took Degrees
In either of our Universities;
Yet to be shown by some kind Wit he looks,
Because he plai'd the fool and writ Three Books.
But if he wou'd be worth a Poet's Pen,   20
He must be more a Fool, and write again:
For all the former Fustian stuff he wrote,
Was Dead-born Doggrel, or is quite forgot;
His Man of *Uz*, stript of his *Hebrew* Robe,
Is just the Proverb, and *As poor as* Job.   25

Prologue, &c. Text from The Pilgrim, A Comedy: . . . Likewise A Prologue, Epilogue, Dialogue and Masque, Written by the late Great Poet Mr. Dryden, just before his Death, being the last of his Works, *1700, collated with* The Comedies, Tragedies, and Operas . . . with a Secular Masque, *1701*

One wou'd have thought he cou'd no lower Jog;
But *Arthur* was a Level, *Job*'s a Bog.
There, tho' he crept, yet still he kept in sight;
But here, he flounders in, and sinks down right.
Had he prepar'd us, and been dull by Rule,   30
Tobit had first been turn'd to Ridicule:
But our bold *Britton*, without Fear or Awe,
O're-leaps at once, the whole *Apocrypha*;
Invades the *Psalms* with Rhymes, and leaves no room
For any Vandal *Hopkins* yet to come.   35
    But what if, after all, this Godly Geer,
Is not so Senceless as it wou'd appear?
Our Mountebank has laid a deeper Train,
His Cant, like *Merry Andrew*'s Noble Vein,
Cat-Call's the Sects, to draw 'em in for gain.   40
At leisure Hours, in Epique Song he deals,
Writes to the rumbling of his Coaches Wheels,
Prescribes in hast, and seldom kills by Rule,
But rides Triumphant between Stool and Stool.
    Well, let him go; 'tis yet too early day,   45
To get himself a Place in Farce or Play.
We know not by what Name we should Arraign him,
For no one Category can contain him;
A Pedant, Canting Preacher, and a Quack,
Are Load enough to break one Asses Back: 50
At last, grown wanton, he presum'd to write,
Traduc'd Two Kings, their kindness to requite;
One made the Doctor, and one dubb'd the Knight.

EPILOGUE

PERHAPS the Parson stretch'd a point too far,
When with our *Theatres* he wag'd a War.
He tells you, That this very Moral Age
Receiv'd the first Infection from the Stage.

Prologue. 26 lower *1701*: longer *1700*   29 flounders *1701*: founders *1700*   40 for gain *1701*: again *1700*

But sure, a banish't Court, with Lewdness fraught,   5
The Seeds of open Vice returning brought.
Thus Lodg'd, (as Vice by great Example thrives)
It first debauch'd the Daughters and the Wives.
London, a fruitful Soil, yet never bore
So plentiful a Crop of Horns before.   10
The *Poets*, who must live by Courts or starve,
Were proud, so good a Government to serve;
And mixing with Buffoons and Pimps profain,
Tainted the Stage, for some small Snip of Gain.
For they, like *Harlots* under *Bawds* profest,   15
Took all th' ungodly pains, and got the least.
Thus did the thriving Malady prevail,
The Court, it's Head, the *Poets* but the Tail.
The Sin was of our Native growth, 'tis true;
The Scandall of the Sin was wholly new.   20
Misses there were, but modestly conceal'd;
White-hall the naked *Venus* first reveal'd.
Who standing, as at *Cyprus*, in her Shrine,
The Strumpet was ador'd with Rites Divine.
E're this, if Saints had any Secret Motion,   25
'Twas Chamber Practice all, and Close Devotion.
I pass the Peccadillo's of their time;
Nothing but open Lewdness was a Crime.
A *Monarch*'s Blood was venial to the Nation,
Compar'd with one foul Act of Fornication.   30
Now, they wou'd Silence us, and shut the Door
That let in all the barefac'd Vice before.
As for reforming us, which some pretend,
That work in *England* is without an end;
Well we may change, but we shall never mend. } 35
Yet, if you can but bear the present Stage,
We hope much better of the coming Age.
What wou'd you say, if we shou'd first begin
To Stop the Trade of Love, behind the Scene:
Where *Actresses* make bold with maried Men? } 40
For while abroad so prodigal the *Dolt* is,
Poor Spouse at home as ragged as a Colt is.
In short, we'll grow as Moral as we can,
Save here and there a Woman or a Man:

But neither you, nor we, with all our pains,⎫ 45
Can make clean work; there will be some Remains,⎬
While you have still your *Oats*, and we our *Hains*.⎭

SONG of a *Scholar* and his *Mistress*,
who being Cross'd by their Friends,
fell Mad for one another;
and now first meet in *Bedlam*

Musick within.

The Lovers enter at Opposite Doors, each held by a Keeper.

Phillis.   LOOK, look, I see—I see my Love appear:
     'Tis he—'Tis he alone;
     For, like him, there is none:
     'Tis the dear, dear Man, 'tis thee, Dear.

Amyntas.   Hark! the Winds War;   5
     The foamy Waves roar;
     I see a Ship afar,
     Tossing and Tossing, and making to the Shoar:
       But what's that I View,
       So Radiant of Hue,   10
     St. *Hermo*, St. *Hermo*, that sits upon the Sails?
       Ah! No, no, no.
     St. *Hermo*, Never, never shone so bright;
     'Tis *Phillis*, only *Phillis*, can shoot so fair a Light:
     'Tis *Phillis*, 'tis *Phillis*, that saves the Ship alone,   15
     For all the Winds are hush'd, and the Storm is over-blown.

Phillis.   Let me go, let me run, let me fly to his Arms.

Amyntas.   If all the Fates combine,
     And all the Furies join,
     I'll force my way to *Phillis*, and break through the Charms. 20

Here they break from their Keepers; run to each other, and embrace.

Phillis.   Shall I Marry the Man I love?
     And shall I conclude my Pains?
     Now blest be the Powers above,

           I feel the Blood bound in my Veins;

           With a lively Leap it began to move,   25

             And the Vapours leave my Brains.

Amyntas.   Body join'd to Body, and Heart join'd to Heart,

             To make sure of the Cure;

           Go call the Man in Black, to mumble o're his part.

Phillis.   But suppose he should stay—   30

Amyntas.   At worst if he delay;

            'Tis a Work must be done;

           We'll borrow but a Day,

             And the better the sooner begun.

                 CHORUS of Both.

       At worst if he delay, &c.

           They run out together hand in hand.

THE SECULAR MASQUE

               Enter Janus.

Janus.   CHRONOS, *Chronos,* mend thy Pace,

           An hundred times the rowling Sun

           Around the Radiant Belt has run

           In his revolving Race.

           Behold, behold, the Goal in sight,   5

           Spread thy Fans, and wing thy flight.

Enter Chronos, *with a Scythe in his hand, and a great Globe on his Back, which*
                he sets down at his entrance.

Chronos.   Weary, weary of my weight,

           Let me, let me drop my Freight,

             And leave the World behind.

           I could not bear   10

           Another Year

           The Load of Human-Kind.

               Enter Momus *Laughing.*

Momus.   Ha! ha! ha! Ha! ha! ha! well hast thou done,

            To lay down thy Pack,

             And lighten thy Back,   15

           The World was a Fool, e'er since it begun,

     And since neither *Janus*, nor *Chronos*, nor I,
      Can hinder the Crimes,
      Or mend the Bad Times,
     'Tis better to Laugh than to Cry.   20
Cho. of all 3. *'Tis better to Laugh than to Cry.*
Janus.   Since *Momus* comes to laugh below,
      Old Time begin the Show,
     That he may see, in every Scene,
     What Changes in this Age have been,   25
Chronos. Then Goddess of the Silver Bow begin.

     Horns, or Hunting-Musique within.

      Enter Diana.

Diana.   With Horns and with Hounds I waken the Day,
     And hye to my Woodland walks away;
     I tuck up my Robe, and am buskin'd soon,
     And tye to my Forehead a wexing Moon.   30
     I course the fleet Stagg, unkennel the Fox,
     And chase the wild Goats or'e summets of Rocks,
     With shouting and hooting we pierce thro' the Sky;
     And Eccho turns Hunter, and doubles the Cry.
Cho. of all. *With shouting and hooting, we pierce through the Skie,* 35
     And Eccho turns Hunter, and doubles the Cry.
Janus.   Then our Age was in it's Prime,
Chronos. Free from Rage.
Diana.   ————————And free from Crime.
Momus. A very Merry, Dancing, Drinking,
     Laughing, Quaffing, and unthinking Time. 40
Cho. of all. *Then our Age was in it's Prime,*
     Free from Rage, and free from Crime,
     A very Merry, Dancing, Drinking,
     Laughing, Quaffing, and unthinking Time.

     Dance of Diana's *Attendants.*

      Enter Mars.

Mars.   Inspire the Vocal Brass, Inspire;   45
     The World is past its Infant Age:
      Arms and Honour,
      Arms and Honour,

Set the Martial Mind on Fire,
And kindle Manly Rage.   50
Mars has lookt the Sky to Red;
And Peace, the Lazy Good, is fled.
Plenty, Peace, and Pleasure fly;
  The Sprightly Green
In *Woodland*-Walks, no more is seen;   55
The Sprightly Green, has drunk the *Tyrian* Dye.

Cho. of all. *Plenty, Peace, &c.*
Mars. Sound the Trumpet, Beat the Drum,
Through all the World around;
Sound a Reveille, Sound, Sound,   60
  The Warrior God is come.

Cho. of all. *Sound the Trumpet, &c.*
Momus. Thy Sword within the Scabbard keep,
  And let Mankind agree;
Better the World were fast asleep,   65
  Than kept awake by Thee.
The Fools are only thinner,
  With all our Cost and Care;
But neither side a winner,
  For Things are as they were.   70

Cho. of all. *The Fools are only, &c.*

Enter Venus.

Venus. Calms appear, when Storms are past;
Love will have his Hour at last:
Nature is my kindly Care;
Mars destroys, and I repair;   75
Take me, take me, while you may,
Venus comes not ev'ry Day.

Cho. of all. *Take her, take her, &c.*
Chronos. The World was then so light,
I scarcely felt the Weight;   80
Joy rul'd the Day, and Love the Night.
But since the Queen of Pleasure left the Ground,
  I faint, I lag,
  And feebly drag
The pond'rous Orb around.   85

Momus. All, all, of a piece throughout;

Pointing ⎫ to *Diana.* ⎭	Thy Chase had a Beast in View;
to *Mars.*	Thy Wars brought nothing about;
to *Venus.*	Thy Lovers were all untrue.
Janus.	'Tis well an Old Age is out,
Chro[nos].	And time to begin a New.
Cho. of all.	*All, all, of a piece throughout;*

90

Thy Chase had a Beast in View;
Thy Wars brought nothing about;
Thy Lovers were all untrue.

95

'Tis well an Old Age is out,
And time to begin a New.

Dance of Huntsmen, Nymphs, Warriours and Lovers.

The Fair Stranger

HAPPY and free, securely blest,
No Beauty cou'd disturb my Rest;
My Amorous Heart was in Despair
To find a new Victorious Fair.

'Till you descending on our Plains,   5
With Forrain Force renew my Chains.
Where now you rule without Controul,
The mighty Soveraign of my Soul.

Your Smiles have more of Conquering Charms,
Than all your Native Countries Arms;   10
Their Troops we can expel with Ease
Who vanquish only when we please.

But in your Eyes, oh! there's the spell;
Who can see them, and not Rebell?
You make us Captives by your stay,   15
Yet kill us if you go away.

The Fair Stranger. Text from |A New Collection of Poems on Several Occasions,
1701, collated with Tixall Poetry, *1813* (TP).
  Heading in TP Witty Mr. Henningam's Song   3 was in Despair] no conquering faire TP   4 To . . . Fair.] Had power to wound with new despaire, TP
6 renew] renew'd TP   9 Smiles] looks TP   11 Their] Your TP   12 Who]
They TP   when] while TP   13–16 TP *has*

> But all the force that in us lies,
> Yeilds no defence against your eyes.
> They make us languish whilst in sight,
> But absent, we must perish quite.

[*Lines on* Tonson]

[Now the Assembly to adjourn prepar'd,
When *Bibliopolo* from behind appear'd,
As well describ'd by th' old Satyrick Bard:]
With leering Looks, Bullfac'd, and Freckled fair,
With two left Legs, and Judas-colour'd Hair,
With Frowzy Pores, that taint the ambient Air.

Lines on Tonson. Text from Faction Display'd. A Poem, 1704. *The version in Powys's letter (see Commentary) runs:*

With leering look, bull faced and freckled fair,
With frowsy pores poisoning the ambient air,
With two left leggs and Judas coloured hair.

POEMS FROM
POETICAL MISCELLANIES:
THE FIFTH PART
(1704)

ON THE DEATH OF *AMYNTAS:*
A Pastoral ELEGY

'Twas on a Joyless and a Gloomy Morn,
Wet was the Grass, and hung with Pearls the Thorn;
When *Damon*, who design'd to pass the Day
With Hounds and Horns, and chase the flying Prey,
Rose early from his Bed; but soon he found   5
The Welkin pitch'd with sullen Clouds around,
An Eastern Wind, and Dew upon the Ground.
Thus while he stood, and sighing did survey
The Fields, and curs'd th' ill Omens of the Day,
He saw *Menalcas* come with heavy pace;   10
Wet were his Eyes, and chearless was his Face:
He wrung his Hands, distracted with his Care,

Poems. Text from the first edition, 1704

And sent his Voice before him from afar.
Return, he cry'd, return unhappy Swain,
The spungy Clouds are fill'd with gath'ring Rain;   15
The Promise of the Day not only cross'd,
But ev'n the Spring, the Spring it self is lost.
Amyntas,—Oh! he cou'd not speak the rest,
Nor needed, for presaging *Damon* guess'd.
Equal with Heav'n young *Damon* lov'd the Boy;   20
The boast of Nature, both his Parents Joy.
His graceful Form revolving in his Mind;
So great a Genius, and a Soul so kind,
Gave sad assurance that his Fears were true;
Too well the Envy of the Gods he knew: 25
For when their Gifts too lavishly are plac'd,
Soon they repent, and will not make them last.
For, sure, it was too bountiful a Dole,
The Mother's Features, and the Father's Soul.
Then thus he cry'd, The Morn bespoke the News,   30
The Morning did her chearful Light diffuse;
But see how suddenly she chang'd her Face,
And brought on Clouds and Rains, the Day's disgrace; }
Just such, *Amyntas*, was thy promis'd Race!
What Charms adorn'd thy Youth where Nature smil'd,   35
And more than Man was giv'n us in a Child.
His Infancy was ripe: a Soul sublime
In Years so tender that prevented time:
Heav'n gave him all at once; then snatch'd away,
E're Mortals all his Beauties cou'd survey,   } 40
Just like the Flow'r that buds and withers in a day. }

MENALCAS

The Mother Lovely, tho' with Grief opprest,
Reclin'd his dying Head upon her Breast.
The mournful Family stood all around;
One Groan was heard, one Universal Sound: } 45
All were in Floods of Tears and endless Sorrow drown'd. }
So dire a Sadness sate on ev'ry Look,
Ev'n Death repented he had giv'n the Stroke.

On the Death of Amyntas. 40 survey,] survey. *1704*

He griev'd his fatal Work had been ordain'd,
But promis'd length of Life to those who yet remain'd.   50
The Mother's and her Eldest Daughter's Grace,
It seems had brib'd him to prolong their space:
The Father bore it with undaunted Soul,
Like one who durst his Destiny controul:
Yet with becoming Grief he bore his part,
Resign'd his Son, but not resign'd his Heart.
Patient as *Job*; and may he live to see,
Like him, a new increasing Family:

DAMON

Such is my Wish, and such my Prophesie.
For yet, my Friend, the Beauteous Mold remains,   60
Long may she exercise her fruitful Pains:
But, ah! with better hap, and bring a Race
More lasting, and endu'd with equal Grace:
Equal she may, but farther none can go;
For he was all that was exact below.   65

MENALCAS

Damon, behold, yon breaking Purple Cloud;
Hear'st thou not Hymns and Songs Divinely loud?
There mounts *Amyntas*; the young Cherubs play
About their Godlike Mate, and Sing him on his way.
He cleaves the liquid Air, behold he Flies,   70
And every Moment gains upon the Skies;
The new come Guest admires th' Ætherial State,
The *Saphyr* Portal, and the *Golden* Gate;
And now admitted in the shining Throng,
He shows the Passport which he brought along;   75
His Passport is his Innocence and Grace,
Well known to all the Natives of the Place.
Now Sing yee joyful Angels, and admire
Your Brother's Voice that comes to mend your Quire:
Sing you, while endless Tears our Eyes bestow;   80
For like *Amyntas* none is left below.

ON THE DEATH of A Very Young
Gentleman

H E who cou'd view the Book of Destiny,
And read whatever there was writ of thee,
O *Charming Youth*, in the first op'ning Page,
So many Graces in so green an Age,
Such Wit, such Modesty, such strength of Mind,   5
A Soul at once so manly, and so kind:
Wou'd wonder, when he turn'd the Volume o're,
And after some few Leaves shou'd find no more.
Nought but a blank remain, a dead void space,
A step of Life that promis'd such a Race: 10
We must not, dare not think that Heav'n began
A Child, and cou'd not finish him a Man:
Reflecting what a mighty Store was laid
Of rich Materials, and a Model made:
The Cost already furnish'd; so bestow'd,   15
As more was never to one Soul allow'd;
Yet after this profusion spent in vain,
Nothing but mould'ring Ashes to remain.
I guess not, lest I split upon the Shelf,
Yet durst I guess Heav'n kept it for himself;   20
And giving us the use did soon recal,
E're we cou'd spare the mighty Principal.
    Thus then he disappear'd, was rarify'd,
For 'tis improper Speech to say he dy'd:
He was exhal'd: His great Creator drew   25
His Spirit, as the Sun the Morning Dew.
'Tis Sin produces Death; and he had none
But the Taint *Adam* left on ev'ry Son.
He added not, he was so pure, so good,
'Twas but th' Original forfeit of his Blood: 30
And that so little, that the River ran
More clear than the corrupted Fount began.
Nothing remain'd of the first muddy Clay,
The length of Course had wash'd it in the way.
So deep, and yet so clear, we might behold   35

The Gravel bottom, and that bottom Gold.
   As such we lov'd, admir'd, almost ador'd,
Gave all the Tribute Mortals cou'd afford.
Perhaps we gave so much, the Pow'rs above
Grew angry at our superstitious Love: 40
For when we more than Human Homage pay,
The charming Cause is justly snatch'd away.

   Thus was the Crime not his, but ours alone,
And yet we murmur that he went so soon;
Though Miracles are short and rarely shown.   45

   Hear then, yee mournful Parents, and divide
That Love in many which in one was ty'd.
That individual Blessing is no more,
But multiply'd in your remaining Store.
The Flame's dispers'd, but does not all expire,   50
The Sparkles blaze, though not the Globe of Fire.
Love him by Parts, in all your num'rous Race,
And from those Parts form one collected Grace;
Then, when you have refin'd to that degree,
Imagine all in one, and think that one is He.   55

THE LADY's SONG

I

A QUIRE of bright Beauties in Spring did appear,
   To chuse a *May*-Lady to govern the Year:
All the Nymphs were in White, and the Shepherds in Green,
The Garland was giv'n, and *Phillis* was Queen:
But *Phillis* refus'd it, and sighing did say,   5
I'll not wear a Garland while *Pan* is away.

II

While *Pan*, and fair *Syrinx*, are fled from our Shore,
The Graces are banish'd, and Love is no more:
The soft God of Pleasure that warm'd our Desires,
Has broken his Bow, and extinguish'd his Fires;   10
And vows that himself, and his Mother, will mourn,
'Till *Pan* and fair *Syrinx* in Triumph return.

III

Forbear your Addresses, and Court us no more,
For we will perform what the Deity swore:
But if you dare think of deserving our Charms,   15
Away with your Sheephooks, and take to your Arms;
Then Lawrels and Myrtles your Brows shall adorn,
When *Pan*, and his Son, and fair *Syrinx*, return.

Upon Young Mr. *Rogers* of
GLOCESTERSHIRE

OF gentle Blood, his Parents only Treasure,
Their lasting Sorrow, and their vanish'd Pleasure,
Adorn'd with Features, Virtues, Wit and Grace,
A large Provision for so short a Race;
More mod'rate Gifts might have prolong'd his Date,   5
Too early fitted for a better State;
But, knowing Heav'n his Home, to shun Delay,
He leap'd o'er Age, and took the shortest Way.

A SONG

I

FAIR, sweet and young, receive a Prize
Reserv'd for your Victorious Eyes:
From Crowds, whom at your Feet you see,
O pity, and distinguish me;
As I from thousand Beauties more   5
Distinguish you, and only you adore.

II

Your Face for Conquest was design'd,
Your ev'ry Motion charms my Mind;
Angels, when you your Silence break,
Forget their Hymns to hear you speak;   10
But when at once they hear and view,
Are loath to mount, and long to stay with you.

III

No Graces can your Form improve,
But all are lost unless you love;
While that sweet Passion you disdain,   15
Your Veil and Beauty are in vain.
In pity then prevent my Fate,
For after dying all Reprives too late.

SONG

Hɪɢʜ State and Honours to others impart,
　　But give me your Heart:
That Treasure, that Treasure alone
　　I beg for my own.
So gentle a Love, so fervent a Fire   5
　　My Soul does inspire.
That Treasure, that Treasure alone
　　I beg for my own.

Your Love let me crave,
　　Give me in Possessing   10
　　So matchless a Blessing,
That Empire is all I wou'd have.

　　Love's my Petition,
　　All my Ambition;
　　If e'er you discover   15
　　So faithful a Lover,
　　So real a Flame,
　　I'll die, I'll die,
　　So give up my Game.

UPON THE DEATH OF THE VISCOUNT DUNDEE

Epitaphium in Vice-Comitem Dundee

ULTIME Scotorum, potuit, quo sospite Solo,
Libertas patriæ salva fuisse tuæ.
Te moriente novos accepit Scotia Cives,
Accepitq; novos te moriente Deos:
Illa nequit superesse tibi, tu non potes illi,   5
Ergo Calidoniæ nomen inane vale.
Tuq; vale nostræ Gentis fortissime Ductor,
Optime Scotorum, atq; ultime Grahme vale.

English'd by Mr. Dryden

O Last and best of *Scots*! who didst maintain
Thy Country's Freedom from a Foreign Reign;
New People fill the Land now thou art gone,
New Gods the Temples, and new Kings the Throne.
Scotland and thou did each in other live,   5
Thou wouldst not her, nor could she thee survive;
Farewel! who living didst support the State,
And couldst not fall but with thy Country's Fate.

Upon the Death, &c. Text from Poems on Affairs of State . . . III, *1704, collated with
the version in* Poetical Miscellanies: The Fifth Part, *1704. The* Epitaphium *is not
printed in* Poet. Misc.   5 nequit superesse tibi] tibi superesse negat *Scott's version*
8 Optime] Ultime *Scott's version*   O Last and best, &c.   5 thou] Thee *Poet.
Misc.*   6 Thou wouldst not] Nor wou'dst thou *Poet. Misc.*   7 Farewel!
who living didst] Farewel, who dying did *Poet. Misc.*

EPITAPH *on the Monument of*
the Marquis of Winchester

HE who in impious Times untainted stood,
  And midst Rebellion durst be just and good;
Whose Arms asserted, and whose Sufferings more
Confirm'd the Cause for which he fought before,
Rests here, rewarded by an Heavenly Prince,   5
For what his Earthly could not recompence.
Pray (Reader) that such Times no more appear,
Or, if they happen, learn true Honour here.

  Ark of thy Age's Faith and Loyalty,
Which (to preserve them) Heav'n confin'd in thee,   10
Few Subjects could a King like thine deserve,
And fewer such a King so well cou'd serve.
Blest King, blest Subject, whose exalted State
By Sufferings rose, and gave the Law to Fate.
Such Souls are rare; but mighty Patterns given   15
To Earth, were meant for Ornaments to Heaven.

Epitaph on Mrs. Margaret Paston
of Barningham *in* Norfolk

SO fair, so young, so innocent, so sweet;
  So ripe a Judgment, and so rare a Wit,
Require at least an Age, in One to meet.
In her they met; but long they cou'd not stay,
'Twas Gold too fine to fix without Allay: 5
Heav'ns Image was in her so well exprest,
Her very Sight upbraided all the rest.
Too justly ravish'd from an Age like this;
Now *she* is gone, the World is of a Piece.

Epitaph. Text from 'Lintott's Miscellany', Miscellaneous Poems and Translations.
By Several Hands, *1712, Berkshire   Epitaph.* Text from 'Lintott's Miscellany', *1712*

[*Lines to Mrs* Creed]

So much religion in *your* name doth dwell,
Your soul must needs with piety excell.
Thus names, like   pictures drawn of old,
Their owners' nature and their story told.—
Your name but half expresses; for in you   5
Belief and practice do together go.
My prayers shall be, while this short life endures,
These may go hand in hand, with you and yours;
Till faith hereafter is in vision drown'd,
And practice is with endless glory crown'd.   10

[*Epitaph on* Erasmus Lawton]

STAY Stranger Stay and drop one Tear
She allways weeps that layd him Here
And will do, till her race is Run
His Father's fifth, her only Son.

Lines to Mrs. Creed. Text from Malone, The Prose Works of John Dryden, *1800 Epitaph.*
Text from the mural tablet in the church of Great Catworth, Huntingdonshire

ON THE MARRIAGE OF
THE FAIR AND VERTUOUS LADY,
MRS ANASTASIA STAFFORD,
WITH THAT TRULY WORTHY AND
PIOUS GENT.
GEORGE HOLMAN, ESQ.
A PINDARIQUE ODE

I

WHEN nature, in our northern hemisphere,
   Had shortned day-light, and deform'd the year;
      When the departing sun
      Was to our adverse tropique run;
   And fair St Lucy, with the borrow'd light,   5
   Of moon and stars, had lengthen'd night:
What more then summer's day slipt in by chance,
      To beautify the calendar?
What made a spring, in midst of winter to advance,
And the cold seasons leap into a youthfull dance,   10
      To rouse the drooping year?
   Was this by miracle, or did they rise
   By the bright beams of Anastasia's eyes?
      To light our frozen clime,
   And, happily for us, mistook their time?   15
'Twas so, and 'twas imported in her name;
From her, their glorious resurrection came,
   And she renewed their perisht flame.
   The God of nature did the same:
His birth the depth of winter did adorn,   20
And she, to marriage then, her second birth was born.
   Her pious family, in every state,
   Their great Redeemer well can imitate.
   They have a right in heaven, an early place;
   The beauteous bride is of a martyr's race: 25

On the Marriage, &c. Text from Tixall Poetry; with Notes and Illustrations by
Arthur Clifford, Esq., *1813*

And he above, with joy looks down,
I see, I see him blaze with his immortall crown.
He, on her nuptials, does his beams dispense,
Blessing the day with better influence;
He looks from heaven with joy, and gives her joy from thence.   30

II

Now, let the reasonable beast, call'd man;
Let those, who never truly scan
The effects of sacred Providence,
But measure all by the grosse rules of sence;
Let those look up and steer their sight,   35
By the great Stafford's light.
The God that suffered him to suffer here,
Rewards his race, and blesses them below,
Their father's innocence and truth to show;
To show he holds the blood of martyrs dear: 40
He crowned the father with a deathless diadem;
And all the days from him he took,
He numbred out in his eternal book:
And said, let these be safely kept for them,
The long descendants of that hallow'd stem.   45
To drye the mournfull widow's tears,
Let all those dayes be turn'd to years,
And all those years be whiten'd too:
Still some new blessing let 'em bring,
To those who from my martyr spring;   50
Still let them bloom, and still bestow
Some new content upon his race below.
Let their first revolution
Bestow a bride upon his darling son,
And crown those nuptials with a swift increase,   55
Such as the emptied ark did blesse:
Then, as the storms are more allay'd,
And waves decay'd,
Send out the beauteous blooming maid:
And let that virgin dove bring to her house again,   60
An olive branch of peace, in triumph o'er the main.
For whom, ye heavens! have ye reserv'd this joy?
Let us behold the man you chose;

How well you can your cares employ,
And to what armes your maid dispose: 65
Your maid, whom you have chang'd, but cannot lose:
Chang'd as the morn into the day,
As virgin snow that melts away,
And, by its kindly moisture, makes new flowers to grow.
See then, a bridegroom worthy such a bride!   70
Never was happy pair so fitly tied;
Never were virtues more allied;
United in a most auspicious hour—
A martyr's daughter weds a confessor!
When innocence and truth became a crime,   75
By voluntary banishment,
He left our sacrilegious clime,
And to a forrain country went;
Or rather, there, by Providence was sent:
For Providence designed him to reside,   80
Where he, from his abundant stock,
Might nourish God's afflicted flock,
And, as his steward, for their wants provide.
A troop of exiles on his bounty fed,
They sought, and found with him their daily bread;   85
As the large troop increast, the larger table spread.
The cruse ne're emptied, nor the store
Decreas'd the more;
For God supplied him still to give, who gave in God's own stead.
Thus, when the raging dearth   90
Afflicted all the Egyptian earth;
When scanty Nile no more his bounty dealt,
And Jacob, even in Canaan, famine felt;
God sent a Joseph out before;
His father and his brethren to restore: 95
Their sacks were filled with corn, with generous wine
Their soules refresht, their ebbing store,
Still when they came, supply'd with more,
And doubl'd was their corn:
Joseph himself by giving, greater grew,   100
And from his loins a double tribe increast the chosen crew.

INDEX OF POEMS

★ Plays of which Dryden is author or part author.

* Plays of which Dryden is author or part author.

   ★ Plays of which Dryden is author or part author.

INDEX OF FIRST LINES

PRINTED IN GREAT BRITAIN AT THE UNIVERSITY PRESS, OXFORD
BY VIVIAN RIDLER, PRINTER TO THE UNIVERSITY